Adobe® Creative Suite
Design Premium All-in
Desk Reference For Dummies

Common Menu Options

Option	How It's Used
New	Creates a new document in the native file format.
Open	Opens a dialog box where you can choose a (supported) file on your hard drive or a disk to open.
Close	Closes the current document; if you have unsaved changes, you're prompted to save those changes first.
Save	Saves the changes you've made to the current document.
Save As	Saves a new copy of the current document.
Place or Import	Imports a file, such as an image or sound file, into the current document.
Export	Exports the current data to a specified file format. You can sometimes select several different kinds of file formats to save the current data in.
Copy	Copies the currently selected data onto the computer's Clipboard.
Paste	Pastes the data from the Clipboard into the current document.
Undo	Undoes the most recent thing you did in the program.
Redo	Redoes the steps that you applied the Undo command to.
Zoom In	Magnifies the document so that you can view and edit the contents closely.
Zoom Out	Scales the view smaller so that you can see more of the document at once.
Help	Opens the help documentation for the current program.

Common Keyboard Shortcuts

Command	Windows Shortcut	Mac Shortcut
New	Ctrl+N	⌘+N
Open	Ctrl+O	⌘+O
Save	Ctrl+S	⌘+S
Undo	Ctrl+Z	⌘+Z
Redo	Shift+Ctrl+Z	Shift+⌘+Z
Copy	Ctrl+C	⌘+C
Paste	Ctrl+V	⌘+V
Print	Ctrl+P	⌘+P
Preferences (General)	Ctrl+K	⌘+K
Zoom In	Ctrl++ (plus sign)	⌘++ (plus sign)
Zoom Out	Ctrl+ − (minus sign)	⌘+ − (minus sign)
Help	F1 or sometimes Ctrl+?	F1 or sometimes ⌘+?

For Dummies: Bestselling Book Series for Beginners

Wiley, the Wiley Publishing logo, For Dummies, the Dummies Man logo, the For Dummies Bestselling Book Series logo and all related trade dress are trademarks or registered trademarks of John Wiley & Sons, Inc. and/or its affiliates. All other trademarks are property of their respective owners.

Adobe® Creative Suite 3 Design Premium All-in-One Desk Reference For Dummies®

Cheat Sheet

Common Panels

Note that panels are referenced as palettes in Photoshop.

- ✔ **Color:** Use the Color panel to select or mix colors for use in the current document. Choose different color modes, such as RGB and CMYK, from the panel menu (the arrow in upper-right corner).

- ✔ **Info:** The Info panel shows you information about the document itself or a particular selection you've made. The Info panel includes information on size, positioning, and rotation of selected objects. You can't enter data into the Info panel. It only displays information instead of accepting it, so you need to use the Transform panel to make modifications.

- ✔ **Swatches:** You can use the Swatches panel to create a library of color selections, which you can save and import into other documents or other programs. You can store colors and gradients that you use repeatedly in the Swatches panel.

- ✔ **Tools:** The Tools panel (commonly called the toolbox) is not available in all the Creative Suite programs, but it's a very important panel in the programs it does exist in. A program's toolbox contains the tools used in that program.

- ✔ **Layers:** The Layers panel is used to display and select layers. The Layers panel also enables you to change layer order and helps you select items on a particular layer.

- ✔ **Align:** The Align panel enables you to align selected objects to each other or align them in relation to the document itself. This palette makes it easy to do precise alignment with multiple objects.

- ✔ **Stroke:** The Stroke panel allows you to select strokes and change stroke attributes, such as the color, width/weight, style, and caps (ends). The program you're using determines what attributes you can change.

- ✔ **Transform:** The Transform panel is used to display and change the shear (skew), rotation, position, and size of a selected object in the document. You can enter new values for each of these transformations.

- ✔ **Character:** The Character panel is used to select fonts, font size, character spacing, and other settings related to using type in your documents.

Common Tools

Tool	What It Does
Selection	Selects elements in the document.
Marquee	Selects elements in a document using a rectangular or oval shape.
Lasso	Makes freehand selections in a document.
Magic Wand	Selects similar adjoining colors in a document.
Pencil	Makes freehand solid marks (with a hard edge) in the document.
Pen	Creates vector paths in a document.
Brush	Creates painterly brush marks in the document; brushes vary in size, shape, and pattern.
Text	Adds text to the document.
Shape	Creates various shapes in the document.
Scale	Increases or decreases the scale (size) of an element in the document.
Hand	Moves the contents of the document for viewing purposes.
Zoom	Changes the magnification of the document.

For Dummies: Bestselling Book Series for Beginners

Adobe®
Creative Suite® 3
Design Premium
ALL-IN-ONE DESK REFERENCE
FOR
DUMMIES®

by Jennifer Smith and
Christopher Smith

1807 WILEY 2007
BICENTENNIAL

Wiley Publishing, Inc.

Adobe® Creative Suite® 3 Design Premium All-in-One Desk Reference For Dummies®

Published by
Wiley Publishing, Inc.
111 River Street
Hoboken, NJ 07030-5774
www.wiley.com

Copyright © 2007 by Wiley Publishing, Inc., Indianapolis, Indiana

Published by Wiley Publishing, Inc., Indianapolis, Indiana

Published simultaneously in Canada

WILEY

About the Authors

Jennifer Smith is the co-founder and Vice President of Aquent Graphics Institute (AGI). She has authored numerous books on Adobe's software productsm including development of many of the Adobe Classroom in a Book titles. She regularly speaks at conferences and seminars, including the CRE8 Conference. Jennifer has worked in all aspects of graphic design and production, including as an art director of an advertising agency. Jennifer combines her practical experience and technical expertise as an educator. She has developed training programs for Adobe Systems and for all types of designers involved in creating print, Web, interactive, along with fashion and apparel. Her teaching and writing style shows the clear direction of a practiced designer with in-depth knowledge of the Adobe Creative Suite applications. When she's not speaking or teaching, she can be found in suburban Boston, Massachusetts with her husband and children.. You can learn about Jennifer's seminar and conference appearances at agitraining.com

Christopher Smith is co-founder and President of Aquent Graphics Institute (AGI), the training and professional development division of Aquent that serves creative and marketing organizations. An Adobe Certified Expert for multiple Adobe products, he has worked as part of the Adobe Creative Team to develop many of the Adobe Classroom in a Book series and has authored numerous books on both InDesign and Acrobat. Christopher manages content for the CRE8 Conference for creative professionals and also the Adobe Acrobat & PDF Conference. He has also served as an elected member of the School Board in his hometown in suburban Boston, Massachusetts, where he lives with his wife and children.

Fred Gerantabee is a New York-based interactive designer, developer, and educator with more than a decade of Web publishing experience. He has earned an Emmy Award for his work with Disney/ABC's Enhanced TV division, creating synchronous, FLASH-based applications and interactive games for major television events such as the 2004 Presidential Elections, the 76th and 77th Academy Awards, and Extreme Makeover: Home Edition. His experience spans production, design, and development, including motion graphics, CD-ROMs, scripting, and managing database-driven web sites. Fred is an Adobe Certified Expert for Flash, Dreamweaver, and Flash Lite. He serves as an instructor and author with Aquent Graphics Institute, and the (sometimes) principal of Groove York City Inc., a multimedia firm that spans digital design and audio production.

Dedication

Jennifer and Christopher Smith: To our parents, Ed and Nancy Smith, along with Mary Kelly. In loving memory of Jennifer's father, Joseph Kelly, the best teacher of all. Also to our perfect children, Kelly, Alex, Grant, Elizabeth, and Edward.

Fred Gerantabee: Love and thanks to my wonderful wife Samantha for all her support and love and my mom Francine for her never-ending support and encouragement. Big hugs to all my friends and family for good times and good vibes. Dedicated to the memory of my loving grandmother, Yolande Gray, and my father, Michael Nas Gueran, the greatest designer I've ever known. You are both missed each and every day.

Authors' Acknowledgments

Thanks to all our friends and colleagues at Adobe Systems for their support, encouragement, and faith in all our work, especially surrounding the Creative Suite 3 launch: Jane, Joe, Ron, Dave, Donna, Ali, Noha, Lynn, Adam, Jeffrey, Lori, Richard, and the many product team members who responded to our questions throughout the writing process.

A special thank you also to Fred Gerantabee, the master of all things Flash. Thanks for your significant contributions to this book.

Thank you also to Yvette Grimes for assistance in updating information.

To the highly professional instructional staff at Aquent Graphics Institute (AGI), we appreciate your great insight into the best ways to help others learn creative software applications.

Thanks to all at Wiley Publishing. This book involves a lot of detail and information and it was up to acquisitions editor, Melody Lane and her "tough love" to make sure that it got to the state it is now. Thanks to Kelly Ewing and technical editor Cathy Auclair for the great insight.

Grant, Elizabeth, and Edward — thanks for putting up with our long hours in front of the keyboard night after night.

Thanks to all of Kelly's friends for permission to use their photos.

Publisher's Acknowledgments

We're proud of this book; please send us your comments through our online registration form located at www.dummies.com/register/.

Some of the people who helped bring this book to market include the following:

Acquisitions, Editorial, and Media Development

Project Editor: Kelly Ewing

(Previous Edition: Colleen Totz)

Sr. Acquisitions Editor: Melody Layne

Technical Editor: Cathy Auclair

Editorial Manager: Jodi Jensen

Media Development and Quality Assurance: Angela Denny, Kate Jenkins, Steven Kudirka, Kit Malone

Media Development Coordinator: Jenny Swisher

Media Project Supervisor: Laura Moss-Hollister

Editorial Assistant: Amanda Foxworth

Sr. Editorial Assistant: Cherie Case

Cartoons: Rich Tennant (www.the5thwave.com)

Composition Services

Project Coordinator: Patrick Redmond

Layout and Graphics: Claudia Bell, Shawn Frazier, Denny Hager, Joyce Haughey, Stephanie D. Jumper, Barabara Moore, Heather Ryan, Ronald Terry, Julie Trippetti,

Proofreaders: Aptara, John Greenough

Indexer: Aptara

Anniversary Logo Design: Richard Pacifico

Publishing and Editorial for Technology Dummies

Richard Swadley, Vice President and Executive Group Publisher

Andy Cummings, Vice President and Publisher

Mary Bednarek, Executive Acquisitions Director

Mary C. Corder, Editorial Director

Publishing for Consumer Dummies

Diane Graves Steele, Vice President and Publisher

Joyce Pepple, Acquisitions Director

Composition Services

Gerry Fahey, Vice President of Production Services

Debbie Stailey, Director of Composition Services

Contents at a Glance

Table of Contents

Introduction

*A*dobe software has always been highly respected for creative design and development. Adobe creates programs that allow you to produce amazing designs and creations with ease. The Adobe Creative Suite 3 Design Premium is the company's latest release of sophisticated and professional-level software that bundles many separate programs together as a suite. Each program in the suite works individually, or you can integrate the programs together by using Version Cue, Adobe's work management software that helps keep track of revisions and edits, and Adobe Bridge, an independent program that helps you control file management, with thumbnails, metadata, and other organizational tools.

You can use the Adobe Creative Suite 3 Design Premium programs to create a wide range of products, from illustrations, page layouts, and professional documents, to Web sites and photographic manipulations. Integrating the Creative Suite 3 programs extends your possibilities as a designer. Don't worry about the programs being too difficult to figure out — just come up with your ideas and start creating!

About This Book

The *Adobe Creative Suite 3 Design Premium All-in-One Desk Reference For Dummies* is written in a thorough and fun way to show you the basics on how to use each of the programs included in the suite. You find out how to use each program individually and also how to work with the programs together, letting you extend your projects even further. You find out just how easy it is to use the programs through simple steps so that you can discover the power of the Adobe software. You'll be up and running in no time!

Here are some things you can do with this book:

+ Create page layouts using text, drawings, and images in InDesign.

+ Make illustrations using drawing tools with Illustrator.

+ Manipulate photographs using filters and drawing or color correction tools with Photoshop.

+ Create PDF documents using Adobe Acrobat or other programs.

+ Create Web pages and put them online with Dreamweaver.

+ Create animations and videos using Flash.

You discover the basics of how to create all these different kinds of things throughout the chapters in this book in fun, hands-on examples and clear explanations, getting you up to speed quickly!

Foolish Assumptions

You don't need to know much before picking up this book and getting started with the Design Premium Suite. All you have to know is how to use a computer in a very basic way. If you can turn on the computer and use a mouse, you're ready for this book. A bit of knowledge about basic computer operations and using software helps, but it isn't necessary. We show you how to open, save, create, and manipulate files using the Creative Suite 3 programs so that you can start working with the programs quickly. The most important ingredient to have is your imagination and creativity — we show you how to get started with the rest.

Conventions Used in This Book

Adobe Creative Suite 3 Design Premium is available for both Windows and the Macintosh. We cover both platforms in this book. Where the keys you need to press or the menu choice you need to make differs between Windows and the Mac, we let you know by including instructions for both platforms. For example:

✦ Press the Alt (Windows) or Option (Mac) key.

✦ Choose Edit➪Preferences➪General (Windows) or InDesign➪ Preferences➪General (Mac).

The programs in Design Premium Suite often require you to press and hold down a key (or keys) on the keyboard and then click or drag with the mouse. For brevity's sake, we shorten this action by naming the key you need to hold down and adding click or drag, as follows:

✦ Shift+click to select multiple files.

✦ Move the object by Ctrl+dragging (Windows) or ⌘+dragging (Mac).

The formatting conventions used in this book are listed here:

✦ **Bold:** We use bold to indicate when you should type something or to highlight an action in a step list. For example, the action required to open a dialog box would appear in bold in a step list.

✦ `Code font`: We use this computerese font to show you Web addresses (URLs), e-mail addresses, or bits of HTML code. For example, you'd type

a URL into a browser window to access a Web page, such as www.
google.com.

✦ *Italics:* We use italics to highlight a new term, which we then define. For
example, filters may be a new term to you. The word itself is italicized
and is followed by a definition to explain what the word means.

What You Don't Have to Read

This book is such a large text, you may wonder whether you have to read it
from cover to cover. You don't have to read every page of this book to discover how to use the programs in the Design Premium Suite. Luckily, you
can choose the bits and pieces that mean the most to you and will help you
finish a project you may be working on. Perhaps you're interested in creating
a technical drawing and putting it online. You can choose to read a couple
chapters in Book III on Illustrator and then skip ahead to Book VI on Dreamweaver and just read the relevant chapters or sections on each subject.
Later, you may want to place some associated PDF documents online, so
then you can read a few chapters in Book V on Acrobat or Book II on exporting InDesign documents. Find out how to create animations for Web and
video in Book VII covering Flash.

You don't have to read everything on each page, either. You can treat many
of the icons in this book as bonus material. Icons supplement the material in
each chapter with additional information that may interest or help you with
your work. The Technical Stuff icons are great if you want to find out a bit
more about technical aspects of using the program or your computer, but
don't feel that you need to read these icons if technicalities don't interest you.

How This Book Is Organized

The *Adobe Creative Suite 3 Design Premium All-in-One Desk Reference For
Dummies* is split into seven quick-reference guides or minibooks. You don't
have to read these minibooks sequentially, and you don't even have to read
all the sections in any particular chapter. You can use the Table of Contents
and the index to find the information you need and quickly get your answer.
In this section, we briefly describe what you find in each minibook.

Book I: Adobe Creative Suite 3 Basics

Book I shows you how to use the features in Design Premium programs that
are similar across all the programs described in this book. You discover the
menus, palettes, and tools that are similar or work the same way in most of
the Creative Suite 3's programs. You also find out how to import, export, and
use common commands in each program. If you're wondering about what

shortcuts and common tools you can use in the programs to speed up your workflow, then this part has tips and tricks you'll find quite useful. The similarities in all the programs are helpful because they make using the programs that much easier.

Book II: InDesign CS3

Book II describes how to use InDesign CS3 to create simple page layouts using text, images, and drawings. Hands-on steps show you how to use the drawing tools in InDesign to create illustrations and also use other menus and tools to add text and pictures. Importing stories and illustrations into InDesign is an important part of the process, so you find out how this task is done effectively as well. Book II shows you how easy it is to create effective page layouts using this powerful and professional design program.

Book III: Illustrator CS3

Book III starts with the fundamentals of Adobe Illustrator CS3 to help you create useful and interesting illustrations. Check out this minibook to discover how to take advantage of features that have been around for many versions of Illustrator, such as the Pen tool, as well as new and exciting features, such as vector tracing. See how to take advantage of the Appearance palette and save time by creating graphics styles, templates, and symbols. Pick up hard-to-find keyboard shortcuts that can help reduce the time spent mousing around for menu items and tools.

Book IV: Photoshop CS3

Book IV on Photoshop CS3 is aimed to help you achieve good imagery, starting with basics that even advanced users may have missed along the way. In this minibook, you find out how to color correct images like a pro and use tools to keep images at the right resolution and size, no matter whether the image is intended for print or the Web.

This minibook also shows you how to integrate new features in Photoshop, such as the new Quick Selection tool, Refine Edge feature, and Smart Filters, into your workflow. By the time you're finished with this minibook, you'll feel like you can perform magic on just about any image.

Book V: Acrobat 8.0

Adobe Acrobat 8.0 is a powerful viewing and editing program that allows you to share documents with colleagues, clients, and production personnel, such as printers and Web page designers. Book V shows you how you can save time and money previously spent on couriers and overnight shipping by taking advantage of annotation capabilities. Discover features that even advanced users may have missed along the way and see how you can feel comfortable about using PDF as a file format of choice.

Book VI: Dreamweaver CS3

Book VI shows you how creating a Web site in Dreamweaver CS3 can be easy and fun. Take advantage of the tools and features in Dreamweaver to make and maintain a very clean and usable site. Discover how to take advantage of improved CSS (Cascading Style Sheets) capabilities, as well as exciting rollover and action features that add interactivity to your site. In the past, these functions required lots of hand-coding and tape on the glasses, but now you can be a designer and create interactivity easily in Dreamweaver, no hand-coding or pocket protectors required.

Book VII: Flash CS3

Find out how to create interactive animations for the web and video. Start with the basics, such as creating simple animations with tweening, all the way up to animations that allow for user interaction. This timeline-based program may be different than anything that you've ever worked with, but it's sure to be an exciting program to discover.

Icons Used in This Book

What's a *For Dummies* book without icons pointing you in the direction of really great information that's sure to help you along your way? In this section, we briefly describe each icon we use in this book.

The Tip icon points out helpful information that is likely to make your job easier.

This icon marks a generally interesting and useful fact — something that you may want to remember for later use.

The Warning icon highlights lurking danger. With this icon, we're telling you to pay attention and proceed with caution.

When you see this icon, you know that there's techie stuff nearby. If you're not feeling very technical, you can skip this info.

You can use the Adobe Creative Suite 3 programs together in many different and helpful ways to make your workflow more efficient. Throughout this book, we explain just how you can implement integration wherever it's pertinent to the discussion at hand. We highlight these tidbits with the Integration icon — you won't want to miss this information.

Where to Go from Here

The *Adobe Creative Suite 3 Design Premium All-in-One Desk Reference For Dummies* is designed so that you can read a chapter or section out of order, depending on what subjects you're most interested in. Where you go from here is entirely up to you!

Book I is a great place to start reading if you have never used Adobe products or if you're new to design-based software. Discovering the common terminology, menus, and palettes can be very helpful for the later chapters that use the terms and commands regularly! If you really want to start with drawings and illustrations, then go to Book III on Illustrator.

Book I

Adobe Creative Suite 3 Basics

The 5th Wave   By Rich Tennant

"Hey – let's put scanned photos of ourselves through a ripple filter and see if we can make ourselves look weird."

Contents at a Glance

Chapter 1: Introducing Adobe Creative Suite 3

In This Chapter

✔ Looking over InDesign CS3

✔ Drawing with Illustrator

✔ Introducing Photoshop

✔ Getting started with Acrobat

✔ Creating Dreamweaver

✔ Moving into Flash

✔ Putting Adobe Bridge into your workflow

✔ Integrating the programs in Adobe Creative Suite 3

*W*ith this Creative Suite release, you not only get the tools you need to be creative for print and Web, but you also get Adobe Flash to make Web sites more engaging than ever.

The diverse software in Adobe Creative Suite 3 enables you to create everything from an interactive e-commerce Web site to a printed book. Each piece of software in the Adobe Creative Suite works on its own as a robust tool. Combine all the applications, including Adobe Bridge, and you have a dynamic workflow that just can't be matched.

In Book I, you discover the many features that are consistent among the applications. You find consistencies in color, file formats, and text editing, as well as general preferences for rulers and guides throughout all the applications in the Creative Suite 3. Book I also shows you where to find the new features and how to save time by taking advantage of them.

Introducing InDesign CS3

InDesign is a diverse and feature-rich page layout program. Using InDesign, you can create beautifully laid-out page designs. You can also execute complete control over your images, as well as export to interactive documents such as Acrobat PDF. InDesign allows you to accomplish the following:

✦ Use images, text, and even rich media to create unique layouts and designs.

✦ Import native files from Photoshop and Illustrator to help build rich layouts in InDesign that take advantage of transparency and blending modes.

✦ Export your work as an entire book, including chapters, sections, automatic numbered pages, and more.

✦ Create interactive PDF documents.

✦ Create drawings using the basic drawing tools included in the software.

InDesign caters to the layout professional, but it's easy enough for even beginners to use. You can import text from (Microsoft Word, Notepad, or Adobe InCopy, for example) as well as tables (say, from Microsoft Excel) into your documents alongside existing artwork and images to create a layout. In a nutshell, importing, arranging, and exporting work is a common process when working with InDesign. Throughout this entire process, you have a large amount of control over your work, whether you're working on a simple one-page brochure or an entire book of 800+ pages.

For those of you already using InDesign, the following sections cover some new features you discover in Book II.

✦ **Customize the control panel:** Pick your widgets and show only the widgets you want to use. Access the control panel's customization features by choosing Customize from the panels menu.

✦ **Multiple Place:** Seems like a rather simple improvement, but imagine the time you can save by placing multiple assets all in one place command. Simply choose File⇨Place and Ctrl+click (Windows) or ⌘+click the assets you want to place. Then choose Open.

Also, check out the thumbnail that appears in your cursor when you're placing an image or text file.

✦ **Move those pages:** Though you could move pages from one document to another in the past, you now have control over where the page is placed and in which document. Simply look for the Moving Pages dialog box to appear and enter where in the document the page should be placed. You can even choose which open document you want to move your page to.

✦ **InDesign CS3 sets your table:** Can all InDesign table users say *finally?* InDesign CS3 now allows you to create, edit, and apply table and cell formatting styles. Check out the new Table Styles and Cell Styles panel next time you're in InDesign 3.

+ **Relink my links:** Can you hear the sigh of relief? Now you can relink all missing links quickly with a check box called Relink All Instances in the Links palette.

+ **Organize your text styles:** Access your saved character and paragraph styles quickly by creating folders right in the Character and Paragraph Styles palettes.

+ **Drag and drop unformatted text:** Wow! You have to love this one. In InDesign CS3, you can now hold down the Shift key while dragging unformatted text to force it to change to the formatting of the destination. To enable drag and drop, choose Edit⇨Preferences⇨Type (Windows) or InDesign⇨Preferences⇨Type, and select Enable In Layout View.

+ **Frames that fit:** Now you can just double-click a frame handle to make the frame automatically fit your content. Also keep in mind that Frames in InDesign CS3 now allow you to control not only the crop amount but alignment inside of a frame. This feature is great if you want a consistent amount of white space on the inside of a frame before an image begins.

There are so many improvements to be noted here that we could go on forever. Just note these two little additional interesting improvements:

+ Spell check starts as soon as you choose Edit⇨Spelling⇨Check Spelling.

+ Many little dialog choices are remembered for you — for example, the last Export format you selected will be remembered.

Using Illustrator CS3

Adobe Illustrator is the industry's leading vector-based graphics software. Aimed at everyone from graphics professionals to Web users, Illustrator allows you to design layouts, logos for print, or vector-based images that can be imported into other programs, such as Photoshop, InDesign, or even Flash. Adobe also enables you to easily and quickly create files by saving Illustrator documents as templates (so that you can efficiently reuse designs) and using a predefined library and document size.

Illustrator also integrates with the other products in the Adobe Creative Suite by allowing you to create PDF documents easily within Illustrator. In addition, you can use Illustrator files in Photoshop, InDesign, and Adobe's special effects program, After Effects. Illustrator, allows you to beef up your rich interactive documents by introducing Flash features that give you the tools you need to build exciting interactive designs in Flash.

Here are some of the things you can create and do in Illustrator:

✦ Create technical drawings (floor plans, architectural sketches, and so on), logos, illustrations, posters, packaging, and Web graphics.

✦ Add effects, such as drop shadows and Gaussian blurs to vector images.

✦ Enhance artwork by creating your own custom brushes.

✦ Align text along a path so that it bends in an interesting way.

✦ Lay out text into multicolumn brochures — text automatically flows from one column to the next.

✦ Create charts and graphs using graphing tools.

✦ Create gradients that can be imported and edited in other programs, such as InDesign.

✦ Create documents quickly and easily using the existing templates and included stock graphics in Illustrator.

✦ Save a drawing in almost any graphic format, including Adobe's PDF, PSD, EPS, TIFF, GIF, JPEG, and SVG formats.

✦ Save your Illustrator files for the Web by using the Save For Web & Devices dialog box, which allows you to output HTML, GIF, and JPEG.

✦ Save Illustrator files as secure PDF files with 128-bit encryption.

✦ Export assets as symbols to Flash.

Think you know all there is to know about Adobe Illustrator? Here are tools and features that you can discover when reading Book III.

✦ **Vector Eraser:** How great is this new eraser tool? You can now use the interactive eraser tool to erase any vector content. What is even better is that this tool is selection aware, meaning that it doesn't erase anything outside the selected area.

✦ **Improved anchor controls:** Create an active path and note the additional controls in the Control palette. Activate and deactivate multiple anchor points and even delete multiple anchor points without breaking the path.

✦ **It's a flash to go to Flash:** Adobe Illustrator is the natural partner application to create vector graphics for Flash animations, and with this version, the integration is even better. Now in Illustrator CS3, you can preserve much more Symbol information along with Dynamic and Input text.

Use Symbols in Illustrator just like Symbols in Flash. Double-click an Adobe Illustrator Symbol to edit its definition. You can also define text as being Flash Dynamic or Input text so that it's properly exported.

The best integration feature is that you can now copy and paste from Illustrator right into Flash!

✦ **New document Profiles:** Pick whether you're creating a print, Web, or multimedia file in the File⇨New dialog box, and Illustrator automatically selects the correct Raster Settings and Color Profile, to name a few. You can override these settings, but it's nice to be set on the right track right from the beginning.

✦ **Know what you have to work with:** Want to know exactly how much space you have to work in when creating mobile or even film content? Take advantage of the new improved Crop Area tool. This tool is an interactive tool that allows you to drag out a crop area. You can use the control panel to edit this crop area. You can also select many preset crop values from the Preset drop-down menu in the Control Palette. Add rulers and reference points to help you improve your design as well.

There are many new features for you to investigate, many of them integrated in the chapters in Book III. Read Book III to see how to illustrate and create interesting designs using the wide range of drawing tools and controls available in Illustrator CS3.

Getting Started with Photoshop CS3

Photoshop is the industry-standard software for Web designers, video professionals, and photographers who need to manipulate bitmap images. Photoshop allows you to manage and edit images by correcting color, editing photos by hand, and even combining several photos together to create interesting and unique effects. Alternatively, you can use Photoshop as a painting program, where you can artistically create images and graphics. Photoshop even includes a file browser that lets you easily manage your images by assigning keywords or allowing you to search the images based on metadata.

Photoshop allows you to create complex text layouts by placing text along a path or within shapes. You can edit the text after it's been placed along a path; you can even edit the text in other programs, such as Illustrator CS3. Join text and images together into unique designs or page layouts.

Sharing images from Photoshop is very easy to do. You can share multiple images in a PDF file, create an attractive photo gallery for the Web with a few clicks of the mouse, or upload images to an online photo service. You can preview multiple filters (effects) at once without having to apply each filter separately. Photoshop CS3 also supports various artistic brush styles, such as wet and dry brush type effects and charcoal and pastel effects. Photoshop also has some great features for scanning. You can scan multiple images at once, and Photoshop is able to straighten each photo and save it as an individual file.

It's hard to believe that Photoshop can be improved upon, but Adobe has done it again in Adobe Photoshop CS3. Find these new features and many more in Book IV.

✦ **New savvier workspace:** Saving your workspace is great, but now in Photoshop CS3, you can collapse those palettes to tabs. Keep those palettes handy, but organize your space with this handy new feature.

✦ **Convert To Timeline:** Yes, you see it correctly . . . a timeline in Adobe Photoshop. You can use the Animation palette the same way as in previous versions, but now you can convert the Animation palette to a Timeline palette. Using the Timeline, you can blend, or *tween,* one layer attribute, such as position, opacity, and style, to another. You can now even tween global lighting.

✦ **Improved Curve Controls:** The improvement in the Curves palette is great for everyone who likes the visual sliders in the Levels palette, but wants more advanced capabilities. The Curves palette now includes a grayed-out histogram, built right in, as well as sliders for clipping the tone curve.

✦ **New Quick Select tool and the New Refine Edge dialog box:** The Quick Select tool allows you to quickly make a selection without precisely tracing the edges of the area. While you drag the mouse, you see a live preview of the selection. More processing is done when you release the mouse to improve the edge of the selection. Use the Refine Edge dialog box to improve the quality of the selection edges. It also lets you visualize the selection in different ways to further improve the usability of the controls. The Refine Edges dialog box is available in the Quick Select toolbar or by choosing Select⇨Refine Edge with an active selection.

✦ **Copying made easy for those creating html slices:** The command Edit⇨ Copy, Ctrl+C (Windows), or ⌘+C (Mac) is now enabled when slices are selected in the document and when no active selection exists. Copying slices copies all layers in the selected slices, which allows you to copy and then paste sliced sections of images right into Dreamweaver and GoLive! The Clipboard also contains information about the path and filename of the parent document, which Dreamweaver uses.

✦ **Even better Camera Raw:** Camera Raw 4.0 is included as part of Photoshop CS3. If you haven't taken advantage of this plug-in, you'll really want to try it! Many digital cameras have a raw format selection in the settings; take some shots and simply choose File⇨Open or File⇨ Browse to launch Adobe Bridge and then select your raw image. The new and improved Camera Raw dialog box appears automatically. In this version, the Fill Light feature has been added, as well as the ability to edit JPEGs and TIFFS in Camera Raw.

✦ **Video Cloning:** Could the Clone Stamp tool get any better? Yes, with the help of the new Clone Source palette (choose Window⇨Clone Source). This new palette, available in Photoshop CS3 Extended, adds controls for setting multiple clone sources, as well as scaling and rotating each clone source. A clone source can be a specific layer or frame in the current document, or a frame or layer from an entirely separate document. Note that the clone stamp and healing brush continue to work as they did in CS2. The Clone Source palette is not required.

✦ **Open as Smart Object:** Smart is right! This is one of those features that makes you say, "Cool." Open any image as a Smart Object (File⇨Open As Smart Object), scale it, run some filters on it, and then double-click the Smart Object layer automatically created in the Layer's palette. The original opens, intact. Make some dramatic changes to your original and return to the file you opened as a Smart Object. Voilá! The images are linked. Smart objects were added in CS2, but this new open capability is especially helpful when you want to open Camera Raw images as a Smart Object.

✦ **3D files in Photoshop Extended:** Photoshop's 3D file support allows you to open and work with 3D files created by programs like Acrobat 3D, 3D Studio, and Maya. Supported 3D file formats include .U3D, .3DS, and Sony Collada.

Photoshop places 3D models on a separate 3D layer in your image. On the 3D layer, you can move or scale a 3D model, change the lighting, or change render modes — for example, from solid to wireframe mode.

You can add multiple 3D layers to an image, combine a 3D layer with 2D layers to create a backdrop for your 3D content, or convert a 3D layer into a 2D layer or a Smart Object.

There is much more to see in Photoshop CS3. Book IV shows you the diverse capabilities of Photoshop. From drawing and painting to image color correction, Photoshop has many uses for print and Web design alike.

Working with Acrobat 8.0

Acrobat 8.0 Professional is aimed at both business and creative professionals, and provides an incredibly useful way of sharing, security, and reviewing the documents you create in your Design Premium Suite applications.

Portable Document Format (PDF) is the file format used by Adobe Acrobat. It's used primarily as an independent method for sharing files. This format allows users who create files on either Macintosh or PC systems to share files with each other, and with users of handheld devices or Unix computers. PDF files generally start out as other documents — whether from a word processor or a sophisticated page layout and design program.

While PDF files can be read on many different computer systems using the free Adobe Reader, users with the Professional or Standard version of Adobe Acrobat can do much more with PDF files. With your version of Acrobat, you can create PDF documents, add security to them, use review and commenting tools, edit the documents, and build PDF forms.

Use Acrobat, to perform some of the following tasks:

+ **Create interactive forms that can be filled out online.**

+ **Allow users to embed comments within the PDF files to provide feedback. Comments can then be compiled from multiple reviewers and viewed in a single summary.**

+ **Create PDF files that can include MP3 audio, video, SWF, and even 3D files.**

+ **Combine multiple files into a single PDF and include headers and footers, as well as watermarks.**

+ **Create secure documents with encryption.**

+ **Take advantage of a new, intuitive user interface:** You can now complete tasks more quickly with a streamlined user interface, new customizable toolbars, and a Getting Started page to visually direct you to commonly used features. In other words, you get an interface more in line with what you may see in the rest of the Creative Suite products.

+ **Combine multiple files into a PDF package:** You can combine multiple files into a searchable, sortable PDF package that maintains the individual security settings and digital signatures of each included PDF document.

+ **Auto-recognize form fields:** You can automatically locate form fields in static PDF documents and convert them to interactive fields that can be filled electronically by anyone using Adobe Reader software (Windows only).

+ **Manage shared reviews:** You can easily conduct shared reviews — without IT assistance — that allow review participants to see one another's comments and track the status of the review. Shared reviews are possible through Acrobat Connect, formerly Breeze.

+ **Enable advanced features in Adobe Reader:** In Acrobat 8.0, you can enable anyone using free Adobe Reader software to participate in document reviews, fill and save electronic forms offline, and digitally sign documents.

+ **Don't show them that!** Worried about exposure? Permanently remove metadata, hidden layers, and other concealed information and use redaction tools to permanently delete sensitive text, illustrations, or other content.

✦ **Save your PDF to Microsoft Word:** This feature is a treasure! You can now take advantage of improved functionality for saving Adobe PDF files as Microsoft Word documents, retaining the layout, fonts, formatting, and tables.

✦ **Enjoy improved performance and support for AutoCAD:** Those of you using AutoCad can now more rapidly convert AutoCAD drawing files into compact, accurate PDF documents, without the need for the native desktop application.

Want to discover other great Acrobat improvements? Read Book V to find out all about Acrobat and PDF creation.

Introducing Dreamweaver CS3

Dreamweaver CS3 is used to create professional Web sites quickly and efficiently, without the need to know or understand HTML (HyperText Markup Language). You can work with a visual authoring workspace (commonly known as a *Design view*), or you can work in an environment where you work with the code. Dreamweaver enables you to set up entire Web sites of multiple pages on your hard drive, test them, and then upload them to a Web server. With the new integration capabilities, you can now create pages easily that contain imagery from Adobe Illustrator, Photoshop, and Flash.

Dreamweaver also has built-in support for CSS (Cascading Style Sheets). CSS is a language that allows you to format your Web pages and control text attributes, such as color, size, and style of text. CSS gives you control over the layout of the elements on your Web.

✦ **Improved integration with Photoshop:** You can now copy and paste information from a layered Photoshop CS3 document directly into Dreamweaver CS3. Dreamweaver CS3 offers you options for creating the best image to be used on a Web page. After the image is placed on your Web page you can click on the Edit button, and the original layered PSD document opens in Photoshop CS3, allowing you to make edits that are automatically saved back to the image on the page.

✦ **Ajax** (*Asynchronous JavaScript and XML*): Sounds like a very big word, but you don't have to have lots of tape on your glasses to take advantage of this Web development technique for creating interactive Web applications. Using the Ajax is meant to increase the Web page's interactivity, speed, and usability because it allows for the exchange of small amounts of data with the server behind the scenes, so that the entire Web page doesn't have to be reloaded each time the user requests a change.

✦ **Spry framework for Ajax:** The Spry framework for Ajax lets you create interactive Web pages without writing JavaScript or XML code. Spry includes a collection of widgets that helps you easily add things such as drop-down menus, tables, and tabbed interfaces. For example, you can create a photo gallery in which a person can click a smaller image and have a larger image of the same photo appear.

✦ **Improved CSS capabilities:** Yes, if you're involved in any way, shape, or form with creating pages, you probably realize that using CSS (Cascading Styles Sheets) is the way to go. They give you the control and power you need to create well-designed compact and user-friendly pages. Dreamweaver CS3 helps you with that by offering starter pages created with CSS and CSS hinting built into the code view that explain the layout to help you to customize the template.

✦ **Browser compatibility check (BCC) enhancements:** Sure, many Web editors inform you somehow that you may be using incompatible elements on your page, but Dreamweaver takes that one step further by checking cross-platform browsers, no matter what computer you are using. The report also explains the problem and gives you a link to a Web site where you can discover how to fix it.

Go to Book VI to find out how to use Dreamweaver CS3 to create exciting Web sites that include text, images, and multimedia.

Moving into Flash

Now part of the Adobe Creative Suite, Flash combines stunning motion graphics, visual effects, and interactivity that have made it the industry standard for creating Web sites, CD-ROM presentations, and interactive learning tools.

Create graphics and type in Flash with its comprehensive set of drawing tools and then put them in motion with timeline-based animation, movie clips, and interactive buttons. Add photos, sound, and video for an even richer experience or use Flash's built-in scripting language, ActionScript, to create complex interactive environments that stand out.

The most recent versions of Flash have continued to revolutionize the way Web sites, presentations, and rich Internet applications are built. With improved drawing tools, advanced video features, effects filters, and further improvements on ActionScript, Flash's powerful built-in scripting language, Flash 9 promises to continue its place as the "king of all media."

With the recent addition of Flash to the Adobe product line, creative professionals can look forward to further integration and exchange with industry-standard tools, such as Illustrator and Photoshop.

Current and new users alike will find some welcome (and long awaited) new features in Flash CS 3. Here's a few of the most notable:

✦ **Pen tool:** Pen tool users, rejoice! The new Pen tool now behaves much more like its distant, older cousins in Illustrator and Photoshop. With improved handling and the addition of the Add, Subtract, and Convert anchor point tools, the new Pen tool is a big deal for all users, particularly those who want the ability to create accurate, complex illustrations.

✦ **Shiny new interface:** Flash's new interface retains many of its familiar features, but has borrowed some of the look, feel, and functionality of its cousins, Photoshop and Illustrator.

✦ **Video:** While Flash has supported video for several versions now, the new Flash video encoder is easier and more intuitive to use. The ability to export QuickTime video has been greatly improved and enhanced.

✦ **Illustrator Import:** For those of you who love to work in Adobe Illustrator, you now have more options than ever to import artwork into Flash 9/CS3, including the ability to distribute Illustrator layers into Flash as keyframes and individual or composite layers. The resulting quality has also improved dramatically, making sure that what you see in Illustrator is exactly what you get in Flash.

✦ **ActionScript 3:** Flash's powerful scripting language gets an overhaul that promises better performance and debugging features in conjunction with Flash Player 9. Now fully compliant on the international ECMAScript standard, ActionScript has moved several steps closer to being an *OOP* (**O**bject **O**riented **P**rogramming) language. What does this change mean to you? It means that you can do a whole lot more with ActionScript, including fancy visual effects to complex tasks, such as connecting to databases.

Bridging the Gap

Adobe Bridge is really an incredible application, especially with this release as the processing speed is greatly improved and new features are available.

Bridge CS3 is a separate application that you can accessed through the Creative Suite applications. It allows you to quickly access and manage multiple documents, such as images, text files, and Adobe Stock photos, which you can use in all the CS3 applications. Bridge CS3 also has a home area where users can get updates and tip and tricks about all programs in the Creative Suite.

Integrating Software and Version Cue

With so many great pieces of software in a single package, it's only natural that you'll want to start using the programs together to build exciting projects. You may want to design a book using InDesign and then create a Web site for that content in Dreamweaver. Similarly, you may want to take a complex PDF file and make it into something that everyone can view online. Or you might create a symbol or Flash text in Illustrator and complete the animation in Flash. All the tools in the Adobe Creative Suite are built to work together, and achieving these tasks suddenly becomes much easier to do.

Integrating software is typically advantageous to anyone. Integration allows you to streamline the workflow among programs and sometimes team members. Tools exist that allow you to drop native images into Dreamweaver, InDesign Illustrator, and Flash. Using Adobe Bridge, you can view your files and investigate specifics about the file, such as color mode and file size, before selecting them for placement.

Chapter 2: Using Common Menus and Commands

In This Chapter

✔ Discovering the CS3 common menus

✔ Addressing CS3 alerts

✔ Speeding up your workflow with shortcuts

*W*hen you work with Adobe Creative Suite 3 Design Premium, you may notice that many menus, commands, and options are similar among its various programs. Discovering how to use menus and dialog boxes is essential to using the programs in CS3.

You may already be familiar with using dialog boxes and menus from other software packages. The way you use these elements is pretty much the same for any program. Some specific keyboard shortcuts are the same across programs, even ones made by different software companies. This consistency makes finding out how to use the commands and options very easy. This chapter provides an overview of some of the common menus, dialog boxes, options, commands, and preferences that exist in most or all of the programs in Adobe CS 3 Design Premium.

Discovering Common Menus

When you work with programs in Adobe CS3 Design Premium, you probably notice that many of the menus in the main menu bar are the same. And then you probably see that these menus often contain many of the same commands across each program. These menus are somewhat similar to other graphics programs you may have used. Similar functionality makes finding certain commands easy, even when you're completely new to the software you're using.

Menus contain options and commands that control particular parts or functions of each program. You may have the option of opening a dialog box, which is used to input settings or preferences or to add something to a document. A menu may also contain commands that perform a particular action. For example, you may save the file as a result of selecting a particular command in a menu. Menus that commonly appear in the CS3 programs are:

✦ **File:** Contains many commands that control the overall document, such as creating, opening, saving, printing, and setting general properties for the document. The File menu may also include options for importing or exporting data into or from the current document.

✦ **Edit:** Contains options and commands for editing the current document. Commands include copying, pasting, and selecting and options for opening preferences and setting dialog boxes that are used to control parts of the document. Spell-checking and transforming objects are also common parts of the Edit menu.

✦ **View:** Contains options for changing the level of magnification of the document. The View menu also sometimes includes options for viewing the workspace in different ways, showing rules, grids, or guides, and turning on and off snapping.

✦ **Window:** Contains options that are primarily used to open or close whatever palettes are available in the program. You can also choose how to view the workspace and save a favorite arrangement of the workspace.

✦ **Help:** Contains the option to open the Help documentation that's included with the program. This menu may also include information about updating the software, registration, and tutorials.

Adobe Design Premium on the Mac also has an additional menu that bears the name of the program itself. This menu includes options for showing or hiding the program on the screen, opening preferences, and opening documents that provide information about the software.

Figure 2-1 shows a menu in Photoshop that contains many common options to control the program.

Figure 2-1: Menus in Photoshop allow you to choose and control different options.

Notice that more menus are available in the programs than are in the previous list. Each program has additional program-specific menus that are determined by the specific needs of whatever software you're using. For example, Photoshop has an Image menu that enables you to resize the image or document, rotate the canvas, and duplicate the image, among other functions. InDesign has a Layout menu that allows you to navigate throughout the document, edit page numbering, and access controls for creating and editing the document's table of contents. What additional menus exist in each program is determined by what the software is designed to do; we discuss these menus where appropriate throughout the book.

Using Dialog Boxes

A *dialog box* is a small window that contains a combination of options formatted as drop-down lists, panes, lists, text fields, option buttons, check boxes, and buttons that enable you to make settings and enter information or data as necessary. The dialog boxes enable you to control the software or your document in various ways. For example, when you open a new file, you typically use the Open dialog box to select a file to open. When you save a file, you use a Save As dialog box to select a location to save the file in, name it, and execute the Save command.

Some dialog boxes also include tabs. These dialog boxes may need to contain many settings of different types that are organized into several sections using tabs. Dialog boxes typically have a button that executes the particular command, and one that cancels and closes the dialog box without doing anything. Figure 2-2 shows a common dialog box.

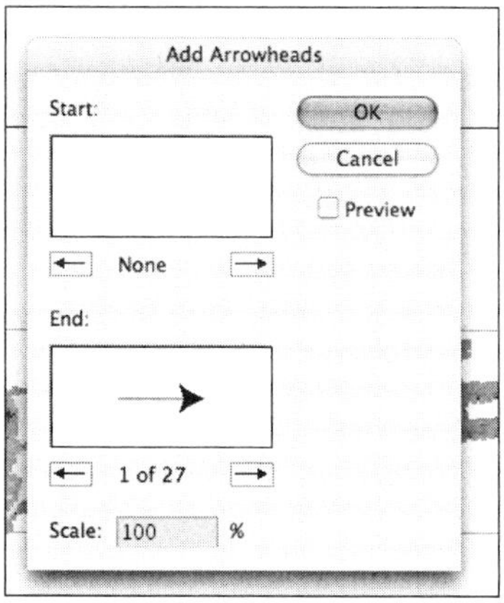

Figure 2-2:
An example
of a dialog
box for
creating
arrowheads
in Illustrator
CS3.

A dialog box in Windows is a lot like a dialog box you find on the Mac. They perform similar functions and include the same elements to enter or select information. For example, some of the functions dialog boxes perform include the following:

✦ Save a new version of a file.

✦ Set up your printing options or page setup.

✦ Set up the preferences for the software you're using.

✦ Check spelling of text in a document.

✦ Open a new document.

When you have a dialog box open in the program you're using, the window pops up on the screen. Before you can begin working with the program again, you have to close the dialog box. You can close the dialog box either by making your choices and clicking a button (such as Save or OK) when you're finished, or clicking the Cancel button to close the dialog box without making any changes. You can't use the program you're working with until the dialog box is closed.

Encountering Alerts

Alerts are common on any operating system and in most programs. *Alerts* are similar to dialog boxes in that they're small windows that contain information. However, alerts are different from dialog boxes because you can't edit the information in an alert. Alerts are designed to simply tell you something and give you one or more options made by clicking a button. For example, you may encounter an alert that indicates you can't select a particular option. Usually you see an OK button to click to acknowledge and close the alert. You may have other buttons on the alert that will cancel what you were doing or a button that opens a dialog box. Figure 2-3 shows a typical alert.

Figure 2-3:
An alert in
InDesign
CS3.

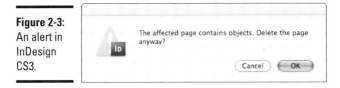

Alerts are also sometimes used to confirm actions before executing them. Sometimes these alert windows also offer the option (typically in the form of a check box) of not showing the alert or warning again. You may want to select this option if you repeatedly perform an action that shows the warning and you don't need to see the warning each and every time.

Using Common Menu Options

Various menu options are typically available in each of the CS3 programs. However, within each of these menus, several other options are available. Some of the options open dialog boxes, and those options are typically indicated by an ellipsis that follows the menu option, as shown in Figure 2-4.

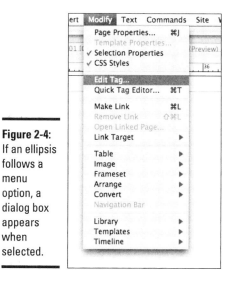

Figure 2-4:
If an ellipsis follows a menu option, a dialog box appears when selected.

The following menu options are found in several of the CS3 programs, and these commands either perform similar (or the same) functions, or they open similar dialog boxes:

✦ **New:** Creates a brand new document in the native file format. For example, in InDesign a new INDD file is created by choosing File↪New↪Document. You can sometimes choose what type of new file you want to create.

✦ **Open:** Opens a dialog box where you can choose a (supported) file on your hard drive or a disk to open.

+ **Close:** Closes the current document. If you have unsaved changes, you're prompted to save those changes first.

+ **Save:** Saves the changes you have made to the current document.

+ **Save As:** Saves a new copy of the current document.

+ **Import:** Imports a file into the current document, such as an image or sound file.

+ **Export:** Exports the current data to a specified file format. You can sometimes select several different kinds of file formats to save the current data in.

+ **Copy:** Copies the currently selected data onto the computer's Clipboard.

+ **Paste:** Pastes the data from the Clipboard into the current document.

+ **Undo:** Undoes the most recent thing you did in the program. For example, if you just created a rectangle, the rectangle is removed from the document.

+ **Redo:** Redoes the steps that you applied the Undo command to. For example, if you removed that rectangle you created, the Redo command adds it back to the document.

+ **Zoom In:** Magnifies the document so that you can view and edit the contents closely.

+ **Zoom Out:** Scales the view smaller so that you can see more of the document at once.

+ **Help:** Opens the help documentation for the current program.

About Contextual Menus

Contextual menus are available in all kinds of programs; they're an incredibly useful, quick way to make selections or issue commands. Contextual menus include some of the most useful commands you may find yourself choosing over and over again.

A *contextual menu* is similar to the menus that we describe in the previous sections; however, it's context-sensitive and opens when you right-click (Windows) or ⌘+click (Mac) something in the program. *Contextual* means that what options appear in the menu depends on what object or item you right-click (Windows) or ⌘ +click (Mac). For example, if you open a contextual menu when the cursor is over an image, commands involving the image are listed in the menu. However, if you right-click (Windows) or ⌘ +click (Mac) the document's background, you typically see options that affect the entire document instead of just a particular element within it. This means that you can select common commands specifically for the item that you've selected. Figure 2-5 shows a contextual menu that appears when you right-click (Windows) or ⌘ +click (Mac) an object in InDesign.

Figure 2-5:
Open a contextual menu in Windows by right-clicking an image or object.

Keep in mind that the tool you select in the toolbox may affect which contextual menus you can access in a document. You may have to select the Selection tool first to access some menus. If you want to access a contextual menu for a particular item in the document, make sure that the object is selected first before you right-click (Windows) or Ctrl+click (Mac).

If you're using a Mac, you can right-click to open a contextual menu if you have a two-button mouse hooked up to your Mac. Otherwise, you'd Ctrl+ click to open a contextual menu.

Using Common Shortcuts

Shortcuts are key combinations that enable you to quickly and efficiently execute commands, such as saving, opening, or copying and pasting objects. Many of these shortcuts are listed in the menus discussed in the previous sections. If the menu option has a key combination listed next to it, you can press that key combination to access the command instead of using the menu to select it. Figure 2-6 shows associated shortcuts with a menu item.

For example, if you open the File menu, next to the Save option is Ctrl+S (Windows) or ⌘+S (Mac). Instead of choosing File⇨Save, you can press the shortcut keys to save your file. This is a very quick way to execute a particular command.

File	
New...	Ctrl+N
Open...	Ctrl+O
Browse...	Alt+Ctrl+O
Open As...	Alt+Shift+Ctrl+O
Open Recent	▶
Edit in ImageReady	Shift+Ctrl+M
Close	Ctrl+W
Close All	Alt+Ctrl+W
Close and Go To Bridge...	Shift+Ctrl+W
Save	Ctrl+S
Save As...	Shift+Ctrl+S
Save for Web...	Alt+Shift+Ctrl+S
Revert	F12

Figure 2-6:
Shortcuts
are shown
next to their
associated
commands.

Some of the most common shortcuts in the Adobe Creative Suite 3 Design Premium programs are listed in Table 2-1.

Table 2-1	Common Keyboard Shortcuts	
Command	*Windows Shortcut*	*Mac Shortcut*
New	Ctrl+N	⌘+N
Open	Ctrl+O	⌘+O
Save	Ctrl+S	⌘+S
Undo	Ctrl+Z	⌘+Z
Redo	Shift+Ctrl+Z	Shift+⌘+Z
Copy	Ctrl+C	⌘+C
Paste	Ctrl+V	⌘+V
Print	Ctrl+P	⌘+P
Preferences (General)	Ctrl+K	⌘+K
Help	F1 or sometimes Ctrl+?	F1 or sometimes ⌘+?

Many additional shortcuts are available in each program in the CS3 programs, and not all of them are listed in the menus. You can find these shortcuts throughout the documentation provided with each program. Memorizing the shortcuts can take some time, but the time you save in the long run is worth it.

Changing Your Preferences

Setting your preferences is important when you're working with new software. Understanding what the preferences can do for you gives you a good idea about what the software does as well. All the programs in the Design

Premium Suite have different preferences; however, the way that the Preferences dialog box works in each program is the same.

The Preferences dialog box for each program can be opened by choosing Edit⇨Preferences (Windows) or Program Name⇨Preferences⇨General (Mac). The Preferences dialog box opens, as shown in Figure 2-7.

The Preferences dialog box contains a great number of settings you can control by entering values into text fields, using drop-down lists, buttons, check boxes, sliders, and other similar controls. Preferences can be quite detailed. However, you don't have to know what each preference does or even change any of them. Most dialog boxes containing preferences are quite detailed in outlining what the preferences control and are therefore intuitive to use. Adobe also sometimes includes a Description area near the bottom of the dialog box. When you mouse over a particular control, a description of that control appears in the Description area.

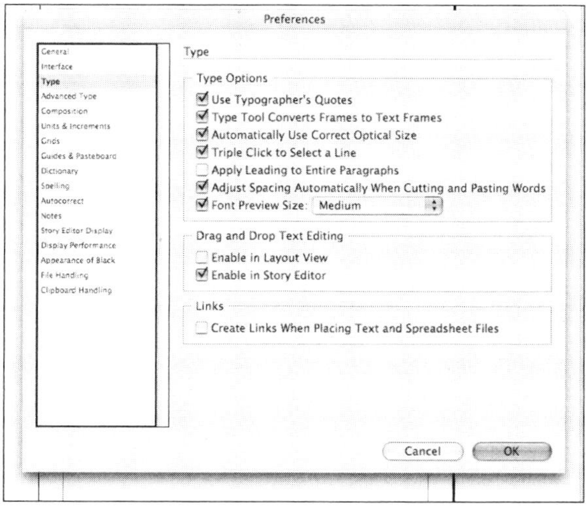

Figure 2-7:
Click an item in the list on the left side of the InDesign preferences dialog box to navigate from one topic to the next.

In some Preferences dialog boxes, the left side of the dialog box has a list box containing the different categories of preferences that you can change. When you're finished changing the settings in that topic, select a new topic from the list and change the settings for another topic.

In some programs, not all the settings you can modify are in the Preferences dialog box. For example, in Illustrator, you can change your color settings by choosing Edit⇨Color Settings to open the Color Settings dialog box, as shown in Figure 2-8. What is very useful about this dialog box is that when you mouse over particular drop-down lists or buttons, a description of that control appears at the bottom of the dialog box.

By launching Adobe Bridge and choosing Edit⇨Creative Suite Color Settings, you can change the color settings preferences across all of the Design Premium programs at once.

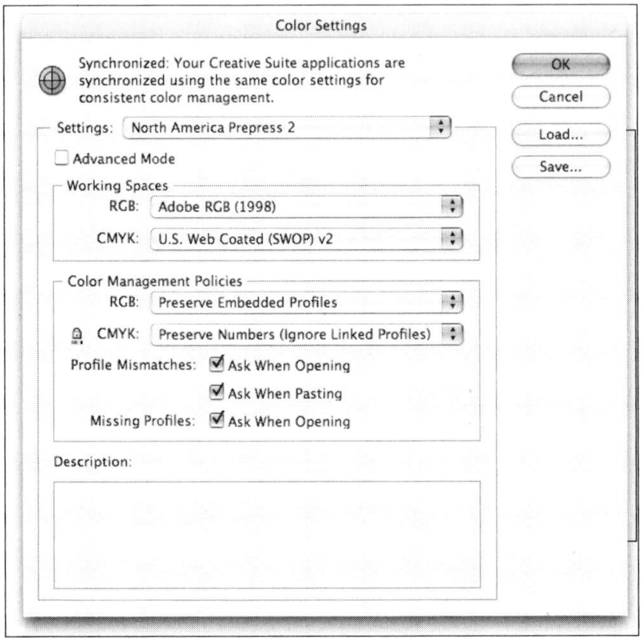

Figure 2-8:
The Color Settings dialog box.

In many CS3 programs, you have an option for setting up the main preferences for the overall document, such as setting up the page dimensions, number of pages in the document, or the orientation (landscape or portrait) of the pages. In Dreamweaver and Photoshop, these kinds of options are available by choosing File⇨Page Setup; in InDesign, Acrobat, and Illustrator, you choose File⇨Document Setup. Figure 2-9 shows a Document Setup dialog box.

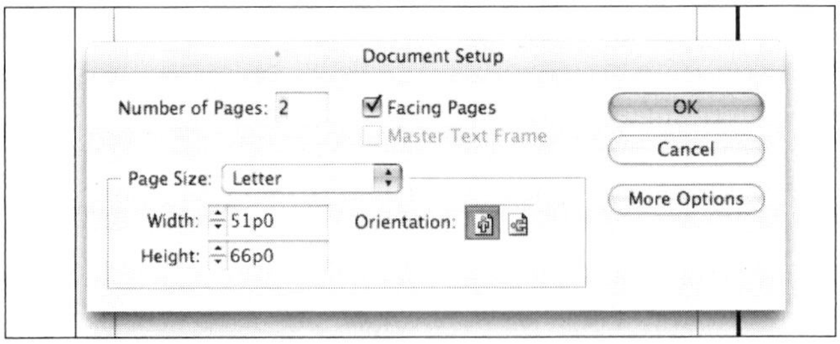

Figure 2-9:
The InDesign Document Setup dialog box.

Chapter 3: Exploring Common Panels

In This Chapter

✓ Manipulating panels and panels in the workspace

✓ Discovering different kinds of panels

✓ Getting to know the common panels in Adobe Creative Suite 3

*P*anels and palettes are an integral part of working with most of the programs in Adobe Creative Suite 3 because they contain many of the controls and tools that you use when you're creating or editing a document.

All the applications in Adobe Creative Suite 3 use panels except for Photoshop, where they're referred to as palettes. In this chapter, all references are for panels, unless there is a direct reference to Photoshop.

The basic functionality of panels is quite similar across the programs in the Adobe Creative Suite, and the purpose of all panels is the same. Panels offer you a great deal of flexibility in how you organize the workspace and what parts of it you use. What you use each program for and the level of expertise you have may affect what panels you have open at a given moment. This chapter gives you an overview of how to work with the panels you find in Adobe Creative Suite 3.

Synchronized Workspace

One thing that you immediately notice when opening the applications in the Creative Suite is the new synchronized workspace. All the applications look very similar and have the same set of features to help you organize your workspace.

The tools in InDesign, Illustrator, and Photoshop now appear as a space-saving, single-column toolbar, and panels are arranged in convenient, self-adjusting docks that can be widened to full size, narrowed to icons, or collapsed to icons.

Here are some pointers to help you navigate the new workspace.

✦ Expand your tools to two columns by clicking the right-facing double arrows in the gray bar on top of the tools.

✦ Collapse the tools to a single column by clicking the left-facing double arrows in the gray bar on top of the tools.

✦ To expand a docked panel, simply click the icon in the docking area. The panel that you selected expands, but will put itself away when you select a different panel.

If you're having difficulty identifying the panel, you can choose the panel you want from the Window menu.

✦ Expand all the docked panels by clicking the left-facing double-arrow icon at the top of the docking area; put them away by clicking the right-facing double-arrow icon in the gray bar above the panels (see Figure 3-1).

✦ To undock a panel, simply click the tab (where the panel name is located) and drag it out of the docking area. You can re-dock the panel by dragging the panel back into the docking area.

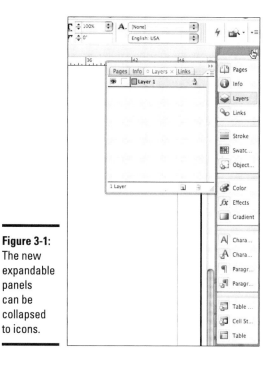

Figure 3-1:
The new expandable panels can be collapsed to icons.

Using Panels in the Workspace

Panels are small windows in a program that contain controls such as sliders, menus, buttons, and text fields that you can use to change the settings or attributes of a selection or of the entire document. Panels may also include information about a section or about the document itself. You can use this information or change the settings in a panel to modify the selected object or the document you're working on.

Whether you're working on a Windows machine or on a Mac, panels are very similar in the way they look and work. Here are the basics of working with panels:

✦ **Opening:** Open a panel in one of the Creative Suite programs by using the Window menu; choose Window and then select the name of a panel. For example, to open the Swatches panel (which is similar in many programs in the suite), you choose Window⇨Swatches.

✦ **Closing:** If you need to open or close a panel's tab or panel altogether, just choose Window⇨Name *of Panel's tab.* Sometimes a panel contains a close button (an X button in Windows or the red button on a Mac), which you can click to close the panel.

✦ **Organizing the workspace:** All the programs in the Creative suite now offer options for workspaces organization. You can return to the default workspace, which puts panels back in their original location, by choosing Window⇨Workspace⇨Default. You can also open the frequently used palettes, position them where you want, and save a customized workspace by choosing Window⇨Workspace⇨Save Workspace. Name the Workspace and click OK; the workspace is now a menu item that you can select from the workspace menu.

You can also choose from a wide range of included presets, designed for a variety of specialized tasks.

✦ **Accessing the panel menu:** Panels have a menu called the panel menu, shown in Figure 3-3. The panel menu opens when you click the arrow in the upper-right corner of the panel. The panel menu contains a bunch of options that you can select that relate to the tab that is currently selected when you click the panel menu. When you select one of the options in the menu, it may execute an action or open a dialog box. Sometimes a panel menu has very few options, but particular panels may have a whole bunch of related functionality and therefore many options in the panel menu.

✦ **Minimizing/maximizing:** All you need to do to minimize a selected panel is to click the minimize button in the title bar of the panel (if it's available). If the panel is undocked, you can also double-click the tab itself (of an undocked panel) in the panel. This will either partially or fully minimize the panel. If it only partially minimizes, double-clicking the tab again will fully minimize the panel. Double-clicking the active tab when it's minimized maximizes the panel again.

Panels that partially minimize give you the opportunity to work with panels that have differing amounts of information. This simplifies the workspace while maximizing your screen real estate.

Most panels contain tabs, which help organize information and controls in a program into groupings. Panel tabs contain a particular kind of information about a part of the program; a single panel may contain several tabs. The name on the tab usually gives you a hint about the type of function it controls or displays information about, and it is located at the top of the panel, as shown in Figure 3-2.

Figure 3-2:
The name of the panel is in the tab; inactive tabs are dimmed.

Moving panels

You can move panels all around the workplace, and you can add or remove single tabs from a panel. Each panel snaps to other panels, which makes it easier to arrange panels alongside each other. Panels can overlap each other as well. To snap panels to each other, drag the panel to a new location on-screen, as shown in Figure 3-3; you see the top bar of the panel become shaded indicating that it is becoming part of another palette's group.

Grouping similar tabs by moving them into a single grouped panel is a good idea — it makes accessing the different functions in your document a lot easier because you have less searching to do to find related functions for a task if similar panels are grouped together.

You can hide all panels by pressing the Tab key. Press the Tab key again to reveal all the panels you have hidden.

Figure 3-3:
To move a
panel, just
drag it to
a new
location
using the
tab at
the top.

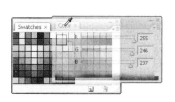

Looking at common panels

Many panels are similar across programs in the Creative Suite. Although each panel does not have exactly the same contents in each of the programs it is included in, many are extremely similar in what each contains. You use these panels in very similar ways, no matter what program or operating system you're using.

Acrobat does not contain numerous panels like the other programs in the Creative Suite. Instead, Acrobat relies mainly (but not entirely) on a system of menus and toolbars filled with buttons and drop-down lists. In Acrobat, you can open dialog boxes that contain a bunch of settings that you can enter for your documents.

The following panels aren't available in *all* the programs in the Creative Suite. However, you find them in most of the programs:

✦ **Color:** The Color panel is used to select or mix colors to use in the document you're currently working on. You can use different color modes and several ways of mixing or choosing colors in the Colors panel.

✦ **Info:** The Info panel shows you information about the document itself or a particular selection you have made. The Info panel includes information on size, positioning, and rotation of selected objects. You can't enter data into the Info panel. It only displays information instead of accepting it, so you would have to use the Transform panel to make these modifications if necessary.

✦ **Swatches:** The Swatches panel can be used to create a library of swatches, which can be saved and imported into other documents or other programs. You can store colors and gradients that you use repeatedly in the Swatches panel.

✦ **Tools:** The Tools panel (commonly called the toolbox) is not available in all the Creative Suite programs, but it's a very important panel in the programs it does exist in. The toolbox is used to select tools such as the Pencil, Brush, or Pen tool that you use to create objects in a document.

✦ **Layers:** The Layers panel is used to display and select layers. The Layers panel also enables you to change layer order and helps you select items on a particular layer.

✦ **Align:** The Align panel enables you to align selected objects to each other or align them in relation to the document itself. This enables you to arrange objects in a precise way.

✦ **Stroke:** The Stroke panel allows you to select strokes and change the attributes of those strokes, such as the color, width/weight, style, and cap. The program you're using determines what attributes you can change.

✦ **Transform:** The Transform panel is used to display and change the shear (skew), rotation, position, and size of a selected object in the document. You can enter new values for each of these transformations.

✦ **Character:** The Character panel is used to select fonts, font size, character spacing, and other settings related to using type in your documents.

Chapter 4: Using Common Plug-Ins

In This Chapter

✔ Discovering the real purpose of filters and plug-ins

✔ Using common plug-ins and filters in Adobe Creative Suite 3

*M*any Creative Suite applications enable you to use plug-ins, filters, or extensions to change parts of the document. Even if you haven't used Photoshop, you're probably already familiar with some of the popular Photoshop filters, such as filters for adding special kinds of blurs, patterns, and color effects to images.

Filters, plug-ins, and extensions are all pieces of software that you install or save on your computer that work as "add-ons" to existing programs. For example, a plug-in may enable you to integrate with a different program, or it may help add functionality to the program (such as the ability to create 3D text). Plug-ins may allow you to change the appearance of an object in your software, or add a 3D effect to a video file. This chapter shows you common plug-ins, extensions, and filters and how to use them in the Creative Suite.

Looking at Common Plug-Ins and Filters

Plug-ins are sometimes used for similar tasks in several programs. Plug-ins are designed to enable a program to do extra things that it wouldn't otherwise be able to do. Or, if you're capable of replicating the task that the plug-in does, there is another advantage: Plug-ins and filters dramatically speed up the creative process. At the mere click of a button, you can add an amazing effect to your project that may have taken many hours to accomplish without the plug-in.

Additional filters and plug-ins for the programs are available or linked from the Adobe Web site. It's also very easy to find plug-ins on the Web for download as well. A search yields many results for these packages. A good place to start is at the Adobe Studio Exchange, located at `http://share.studio.adobe.com`. This site includes a wealth of tools that you can download and install for the Creative Suite.

Installing plug-ins

Plug-ins can be installed in a few different ways. Sometimes they're installed using an executable file: You double-click the file on your hard drive, and it automatically installs the software. This is a lot like installing any other program on your computer, such as the programs in the Creative Suite itself. Sometimes you're given individual files that need to be placed in a folder first. In this case, you need to find the Plug-Ins folder on your computer in the install directory of the program the plug-in or filter is for. For example, if your plug-in was for InDesign on Windows, you would need to find this directory: `C:\Program Files\Adobe\InDesign CS3\Plug-Ins`. You would then copy and paste or move the plug-in file you downloaded into this directory on your hard drive.

If your plug-in was for Photoshop on the Mac, you would need to find this folder on your hard drive: `Applications\Adobe Photoshop CS3\Plug-Ins`. You would then copy and paste or move the plug-in file into this folder.

If it's not clear how to install a plug-in, then locate instructions for the software that explain how to install it on your computer. You can find instructions on the manufacturer's Web site, or instructions may be bundled with the plug-in file itself.

Filters for Photoshop are probably the most common kind of add-on you will find online. Many filters do cost money; however, some filters are offered for free.

Plugging in to InDesign

InDesign offers many filters for importing and exporting text. Plug-ins are available that enable you to work with PageMaker and for helping to import and paste in other content. Many plug-ins for InDesign are designed to help you with the following functions:

+ Lay out spreads correctly for a printer.

+ Create complicated indexes and tables of contents.

+ Create cross-references within your documents.

+ Create page previews and thumbnails of your documents.

Other filters created for InDesign can help you import certain content, such as text. A lot of the time, you will find that text formatting is lost when you import content into InDesign. Filters can help you retain this original formatting when you're importing text. These plug-ins and filters are just a small sample of what is available for InDesign. In all likelihood, many more plug-ins will be created for the software.

Adding on to Photoshop

Photoshop has a lot of plug-ins and filters already included with the program when you install it that give more functionality to the program. Not only can you find additional filters, but you can also find plug-ins to add new features that can inevitably add some interesting effects to your documents. You can also find a plug-in that installs a great number of filters into Photoshop. The kinds of filters and plug-ins you can find for Photoshop create the following effects:

✦ Remove blemishes and scratches from photos using special tools.

✦ Create 3D text, objects, and effects using several different plug-ins. Effects include drop shadows, bevels, and embosses that go beyond what is already available in Photoshop.

✦ Use special masking tools to create amazing effects.

✦ Liquify an image, colorize an image, and other great image modification effects.

✦ Use one of thousands of special effects made by many companies to enhance, modify, and add to your images.

✦ Add a frame from a library to place around your favorite images.

These are only some of the many Photoshop plug-ins (which are commonly a set of many filters bundled together) available.

Many plug-ins have custom interfaces that you can use to make your settings. These interfaces include sliders, text fields, and buttons, and usually a thumbnail preview of how the filter is affecting the image. These interfaces vary greatly in style and features, but they're usually fairly intuitive and easy to use.

Using Illustrator plug-ins

You can find many tools to extend the capabilities of Illustrator. Plug-ins are available that enable you to take 3D illustration farther than the standard 3D features allow. You can create forms from your drawings and also take your 3D files and turn them into line drawings. Other plug-ins, ranging from simple to very complex, allow you to

✦ Create multipage documents.

✦ Organize your font sets.

✦ Add common symbols (such as road signage) to use in your documents. The symbols are organized into libraries that you can use right in the Illustrator workspace.

+ Import CAD files into a document.

+ Create interactive documents.

+ Handle patterns geared at creating textures and backgrounds.

You can enhance Illustrator's capabilities after you download and install a few plug-ins. Simple projects become much more interesting or complex by merely entering a value and clicking a button.

Some fun things to download and install into Illustrator are custom brushes. This means that you can have a wider array of brushes available to work with when you create drawings and illustrations. Styles can also be installed into Illustrator and usually obtained for free. You can also download and install custom brushes for Photoshop.

Adding on capabilities to Acrobat

Acrobat has several plug-ins available that help speed up and diversify your project workflow. Some plug-ins available for Acrobat are designed to help you

+ Add stamps and watermarks to the documents.

+ Add features such as page numbering and watermarks.

+ Streamline productivity by offering solutions for batch processing.

+ Convert file formats to diversify what kinds of documents you can create from Acrobat.

+ Secure your PDF files with forms of encryption.

+ Work with and fix the PDF in prepress quickly and efficiently.

Many of the plug-ins available for Acrobat enable you to batch process the pages in a document. This means that all the pages are processed at one time. Many plug-ins for Acrobat help save you a lot of time when you're creating PDF files. Plug-ins are usually designed to be very easy to use and can thus save you from having to perform a tedious and repetitive task.

Plug-ins for Acrobat are available from the Adobe Web site, as well as numerous third-party Web sites.

Extending Dreamweaver

Dreamweaver offers you a quick and easy way to make Web pages, but you can add more tools to Dreamweaver to diversify what the program can do.

These extensions (essentially, plug-ins) also speed up the process of creating Web sites. Some of the available plug-ins are described in the following list. Plug-ins available for Dreamweaver can

✦ Add e-commerce modules to a Web site automatically using Dreamweaver.

✦ Create professional DHTML and CSS-based vertical and horizontal menus.

✦ Add a Calendar popup.

✦ Add PayPal to your Web site.

Dreamweaver also allows you to use Behaviors in the program. *Behaviors* are premade JavaScript scripts that can be added to your Web sites for additional interactivity or interest. You can also use premade templates for your sites, many of which are available at http://share.studio.adobe.com.

You can customize templates in Dreamweaver so that they're original and unique when you put the pages online. Behaviors and templates (as well as tutorials and more plug-ins) are available from the Adobe Studio Exchange. Go to http://share.studio.adobe.com to check out what's available for you to download.

Using Filters

You can install plug-ins or filters into your Creative Suite programs. A filter can enhance an existing photo in a very exciting way. After you've installed a plug-in into Photoshop or Illustrator that includes a bunch of additional filters, you will want to check out what it can do to your photos. An example of this follows.

Install some filters for Photoshop (or Illustrator). After you've completed the installation and restarted your computer, if necessary, open Photoshop and locate the Filter menu option (the new filters are available in this menu). To use a filter, follow these steps:

1. **Choose an interesting photo that you want to apply an effect to and open the file in Photoshop.**

Choose a photo that has many colors or a lot of contrast to work with.

2. **Choose a filter from the Filter menu.**

Select a filter that you have installed from the Filter menu. If you haven't installed any plug-ins or filters, you can choose one that is already included in Photoshop, such as Filter➪Blur➪Motion Blur.

3. Modify the filter's settings, if necessary, and click the OK button to apply the effect.

Sometimes, you have a thumbnail preview to assess how the filter changes the image. For some filters and plug-ins, you even use a custom interface to manipulate the document. You can then change the settings accordingly until you're happy with the modifications that will be applied.

4. Look at the image after you have chosen and applied the filter.

Your image is updated immediately. If you're unhappy with the results, you can either undo your changes by choosing Edit⇨Undo, or you can apply the filter again.

Filters add a great deal of interest and variety to a document. However, you can easily go overboard when using filters and plug-ins. You can use filters in many different ways in the Design Premium Suite — and some of these ways you use filters (and the filters themselves) are considered better than others. Going into filter overload is easy, particularly when you first start using filters. This is okay when you're experimenting with filters; just make sure that you don't use too many filters on one part of an image when you're creating a final project. For example, if you bevel and emboss a particular letter in a few different ways, that character can become illegible. Similarly, adding a huge drop shadow can distract the eye from other parts of the text.

The trick is knowing what you intend to accomplish with your document before you actually go about creating it. If you set out to create your project with a particular design in mind, you can sometimes achieve better results. Try drawing out your ideas on paper first, writing down some notes about what you want to achieve, and thinking about the plug-ins you want to use to achieve it. Use one filter at a time and make sure that you like the results before moving on to the next. The alternative is to continue adding filter upon filter to achieve a particular result when you aren't quite sure what you're after or how to get there. You can end up with a picture with too many filters applied and an unpleasant result. With a clear idea of what you want out of a picture, and what filters you need to achieve that effect, you'll use filters in a much more successful way.

Chapter 5: Importing and Exporting

In This Chapter

✓ Integrating Adobe Bridge into your workflow

✓ Importing content

✓ Moving files from one CS3 application to another

✓ Exporting content out of your documents

✓ Exporting content from the CS3 programs

*I*mporting and exporting content is an important task for much of the creative process you experience while using programs in the Creative Suite. You commonly find yourself importing content to work within your documents. You may want to import text composed by a designated writer into an InDesign document so that you can include the content in a page layout. Or you may want to import a 3D design into an Illustrator document so that you can use the image in a design. Importing is necessary in all kinds of circumstances during a typical workflow.

Exporting content from each program is sometimes necessary when you want to save the document as a different file format. You may want to do this for compatibility reasons: Your audiences, or those you're working with, need a different file format in order to open your work; or you may need to export to a different file format in order to import the work into a different program.

Discovering the Adobe Bridge Application

With this version, Adobe has dramatically enhanced the Adobe Bridge application. With the Creative Suite, you not only get the integration of the Version Que workflow management system, but you get the Bridge application to help you organize and manage your assets, such as pictures, text, and even movie files. It acts like a hub for the Creative Suite. For example, by choosing to open files using the Bridge interface, you can browse directories quickly and see previews of your files, as shown in Figure 5-1. You can even use the new filter panel to help you find files, and view metadata to your file, including important information such as keywords.

Compact mode

Delete

Rotate 90° clockwise

Go backward

Rotate 90° counterclockwise

Go forward

Go up

Create new folder

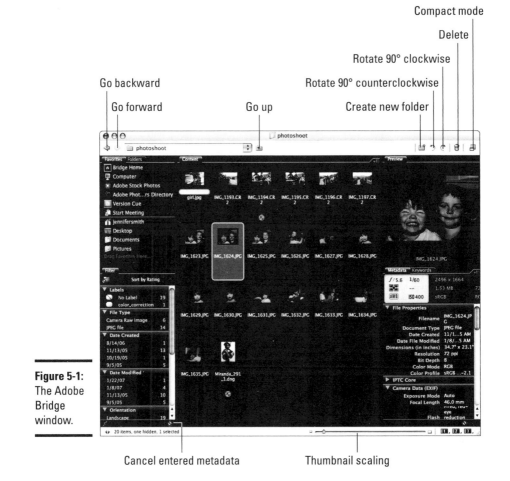

Figure 5-1:
The Adobe
Bridge
window.

Cancel entered metadata

Thumbnail scaling

Not only does the Bridge make a great deal of information accessible, you
can use the Bridge as a central resource for all your Help needs. Adobe even
provides reasonably priced stock photos that you can access, search, and
even pay for right in the Bridge software.

Accessing the Bridge software

First, it's helpful to know where to locate the Adobe Bridge application. It
should already be in your system if you went through a standard installation
of the entire Creative Suite. Otherwise, you'll have to go back and choose to
install the Bridge software using your installation CDs. After you install the
Bridge software, you can open it in the following two ways:

✦ Access the Bridge software using the directory system of your computer. Choose C:\Programs\Adobe\Adobe Bridge\Bridge (Windows) or (Mac) Hard Drive\Applications\Adobe Bridge\Bridge.

✦ Select the Go To Bridge button in the upper-right of the Options palette (Photoshop), or control panel (Illustrator and InDesign), as shown in Figure 5-2. If you don't see the Go To Bridge icon, like in Dreamweaver, you can choose File⇨Browse In Bridge.

Go To Bridge button

Figure 5-2:
Access
the Bridge
application
using the Go
To Bridge
button.

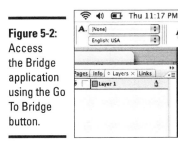

Navigating the Bridge

To navigate the Bridge, simply use the Folders panel in the upper-left to choose the folder you want to view. Watch in amazement as previews are created and automatically replace the standard file format icon.

The Bridge may take a fair amount of time to build the preview the first time you use it, so be patient. You can choose Tools⇨Cache⇨Build Cache to save this data, or Purge to free up file space.

Select an individual file by clicking it once (twice will open it), or select multiple files by pressing Ctrl and clicking the mouse (Windows) or pressing ⌘ and clicking the mouse (Mac OS).

With one or more files selected, you can do the following:

✦ Relocate the file(s) to another location by dragging them to a folder in the Folders panel in the upper-left corner. Use the Bridge as a Central filing system. Using the commands in the File menu, you can create new folders and delete or move files or groups of files.

✦ Read Metadata in Metadata panel in the lower-right corner. This includes information such as Camera, Flash, F-stop, and more, as shown in Figure 5-3.

✦ Enter your own Metadata for any item listed with a pencil icon to the right.

✦ Use the Keywords panel, shown in Figure 5-4, to enter your own keywords to help you find your images later.

✦ Choose Edit⇨Find or the Filter panel to locate your files within the Bridge by using criteria such as Keywords, Description, Date Created, and more.

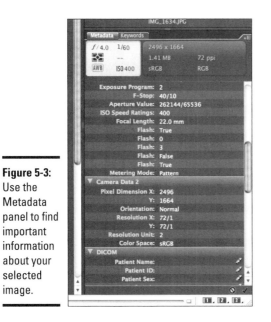

Figure 5-3: Use the Metadata panel to find important information about your selected image.

✦ Create image stacks. You can select many files in Bridge by holding down the Ctrl key (Windows) or ⌘ key (Mac) and clicking on multiple files. You can then Choose Stacks⇨Group As Stack, or use the keyboard shortcut Ctrl+G (Windows) or ⌘+G (Mac OS). This stacks the images into one compact thumbnail. The number of images in the stack is shown in the upper-left of the image stack. To re-open the stack, just click the stack number; close it again by reclicking the stack number. If you decide you don't want the stack any more, you can choose Stacks⇨ Ungroup From Stack, or use the keyboard shortcut Ctrl+Shift+G (Windows) or ⌘+Shift+G (Mac OS).

✦ Check under the Tools menu for application specific tools, such as Contact Sheet II, and PDF Presentation.

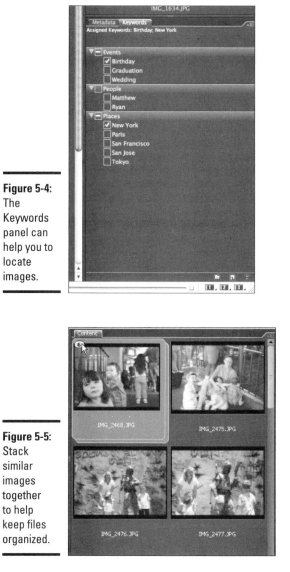

Figure 5-4:
The
Keywords
panel can
help you to
locate
images.

Figure 5-5:
Stack
similar
images
together
to help
keep files
organized.

Managing color

What a time-saver and production boost! The Color Settings that you use to have to set in each individual application can be set across the board in all Creative Suite applications. Create consistent color choices in all the Creative applications using the synchronized color management controls that Adobe Bridge offers.

Choose Edit➪Creative Suite Color Settings to choose a color management setting that will remain consistent through all your Creative Suite applications, as shown in Figure 5-6. Read more about what these settings mean in Book IV, Chapter 7.

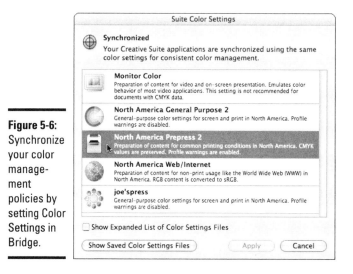

Figure 5-6:
Synchronize your color management policies by setting Color Settings in Bridge.

Importing Files into a Document

Importing files is a similar process, no matter what program you're working with. Importing content is more important in some programs than others. A program like InDesign relies on importing content into a document that is then incorporated into a page layout. However, in programs like Photoshop, importing content is much less important because you'll frequently start out with editing an image you *open* in Photoshop. In this section, we take a look at importing content into each program.

Placing content in InDesign

Placing content in InDesign is a familiar task when you're creating a new layout. You need to import images and text for many of your layouts. When you choose File➪Place, you can then select text or image files from your hard drive or network. You can also choose sound and video files that you can use when you're creating PDF documents for electronic distribution. After you choose a file to import, a new cursor icon appears, with a thumbnail preview of your image, when you place it over the page or pasteboard. To place the imported content, click the page where you want the upper-left corner to be placed.

When you import different kinds of images, you're presented with the Place dialog box, which allows you to select a variety of options for importing the selected content. However, to access additional settings you must select the Show Import Options check box in the Place dialog box. In Figure 5-7 you see the additional options that appear when an image is placed.

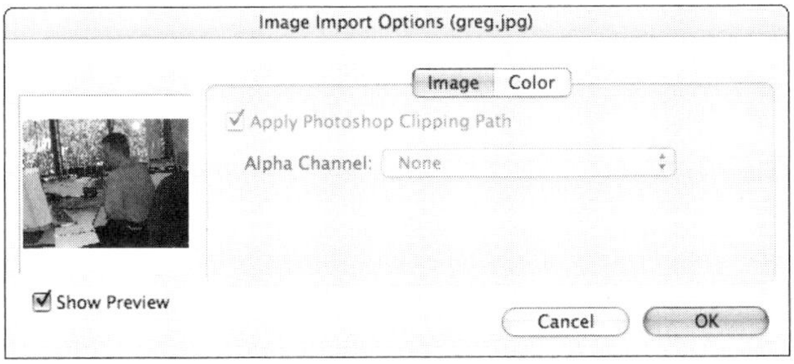

Figure 5-7:
When
importing
text and
graphics,
you can see
additional
options
using Import
Options.

Image Import Options (greg.jpg)

Image Color

☑ Apply Photoshop Clipping Path

Alpha Channel: None

☑ Show Preview

Cancel   OK

Select a file and click the Open button. Another dialog box opens with options specific to the type of file you're importing. For example, if you're importing a bitmap image (say, a JPEG), you can choose how you want the bitmap to appear, whether it contains a background or color management information, and other such options.

When you import text information, you may lose some text formatting that was made in the original file. Anything that InDesign doesn't understand won't be imported into the document. Column information, as well as margins, are also typically not retained when you import text. However, some plug-ins are available that help remedy the situation to some extent.

You can use the Go To Bridge button in the upper-right corner of the InDesign control palette to open Adobe Bridge. Then, simply drag and drop the images you want to use right from Bridge.

Adding content to a Photoshop file

In Photoshop, you can choose to open an image to work with or you can import content into a document that is already open. Choose File➪Place to import PDF, AI, EPS, or PDP files. These files import onto a new layer in the document, and you can then use tools to manipulate the imported content, as shown in Figure 5-8.

Figure 5-8:
Imported
content is
placed on a
new layer;
in this
example, the
Illustrator file
has been
placed and
converted to
a Smart
Object.

As a default, your placed Illustrator files in Photoshop maintain a connection back to a copy of the original file. This is the Smart Object feature that you can read about in Book IV. Double-click the placed artwork layer to open and edit the copy. After the file has been saved, the changes are immediately reflected back in Photoshop! Note that your original file is not changed; Photoshop actually builds a copy of your original file right into the PSD file.

You can import photos from a camera or a scanner into Photoshop. In Windows, you can use Windows Image Acquisition (WIA) to import an image from either a digital photo or a scanner. To do so, you choose File➪Import➪ WIA Support. If you're importing content from a scanner, you may have an additional menu option. The menu option name may vary, but you can access it from the File➪Import submenu.

Want to import images from your digital camera right into Adobe Bridge? Try the new Get Photos from Camera feature under the file menu.

Placing files into Illustrator

Illustrator allows you to place images and other forms of data in a new document. You can import Photoshop, PDF, image, and vector files by choosing File➪Place. The Place dialog box appears, allowing you to choose a file to import. Click Place (Windows) or Place (Mac) to import the file. An Import dialog box may appear at this point, depending on the type of file you're importing. This dialog box offers you several options for choosing a way to import the content into Illustrator. You can sometimes choose between flattening layers or retaining layers when you import a document containing layers.

EPS is a commonly used file format for saving vector drawings (although it can be used for other file types as well). Because this file format is used in many programs, you may find other people giving you these files to work with. To import an EPS document, you also choose File⇨Place; after you import an EPS document into Illustrator, the file is converted to Illustrator objects.

You can also import text files into Illustrator. Microsoft Word, TXT, RTF, and Unicode, among other text documents, are all supported by Illustrator and you can import them by choosing File⇨Place. When you import the text file, you're prompted to choose the character set used for the text.

Not only can you use the Place command for importing files, but you can copy and paste from other programs. You can select part of an image in Photoshop and copy it onto the Clipboard by pressing Ctrl+C (Windows) or ⌘+C (Mac), and then pasting it into the Illustrator document. ***Remember:*** You should try to use the Place command whenever possible to avoid losing quality in the content you're importing. Also, transparency isn't supported from one application to another when you copy and paste, but it is when Place is used.

When you have particular plug-ins installed, you can import additional file types, such as CAD files.

Adding to Acrobat

Adobe Acrobat is primarily a tool for sharing completed documents — you will do most of your document construction and editing in other programs, such as InDesign or Illustrator. However, you can import several kinds of data into PDF documents, and there are some creative things that you can also place into PDF files as well:

✦ **Comments:** Probably the most useful and common items to import into an Adobe PDF file are comments made using the review and markup tools provided by Adobe Acrobat. By importing comments into a PDF file, you can consolidate suggestions and input from several reviewers (those editing a document) into a single document. This feature helps the reviewing process when many people are working on a single document. To import someone's comments into a PDF, choose Comments⇨ Import Comments. If you're reviewing a document, you can also export only the comments rather than send the document owner the entire PDF file.

✦ **Form data:** You can import form data into a PDF document by choosing Forms⇨Manage Form Data⇨Import Data The data that you import can be generated by exporting the form data from another PDF form, or it can come from a delimited text file. This allows you to share form data between forms or from a database.

✦ **Trusted identities:** If you share digitally signed files or secured files with other Acrobat users, you can import the public version of their signature file into your list of trusted users with whom you share files. To import the identity of a user, choose Advanced⇨Manage Trusted Identities and then click the Add Contacts button in the Manage Trusted Identities dialog box that appears.

✦ **Multimedia files:** If you've ever had the urge to add a movie or sound file into your PDF documents, you're in luck. By using the Sound tool or Movie tool, you can identify the location on the page where you want the file to appear, and then choose whether to embed the multimedia file (compatible with Acrobat 6 or later) or create a link to the file (compatible with Acrobat 5 and earlier).

✦ **Buttons:** Creating buttons to turn pages, print a document, or go to a Web site makes your PDF files easier to use. Adding custom button images, such as pictures of arrows or a printer icon, makes your document unique. Use the button tool to create the location of the button and then select the graphic file that will be used as the image on the button. The image file that you use must first be converted to a PDF graphic.

✦ **Preflight information:** If you're creating a PDF file that will be sent to a commercial printer for reproduction, you may want to preflight the book to check that it meets the specifications and needs of the printer. If your printer has supplied a preflight profile for Acrobat, you can import the profile to ensure that Acrobat checks for the things your printer has requested, such as certain font types or color specifications. Import a preflight profile by choosing Advanced⇨Print Production⇨Preflight and in the Preflight window that opens choose Options⇨Import Preflight Profile.

Importing into Dreamweaver

In Dreamweaver, you can import several different kinds of files into a site you're creating:

✦ Use the Insert menu item to insert images and other media, such as Flash, FlashPaper and Flash Video.

✦ Import XML files and XHTML Exports from InDesign.

✦ You can cut and paste a layered file in Photoshop; simply choose Edit⇨ Copy Merged and paste it right into Dreamweaver. An Image Preview window appears (see Figure 5-9), allowing you to optimize the image for the Web. Choose your settings and click OK. (You can read about the best settings for Web imagery in the Book IV.)

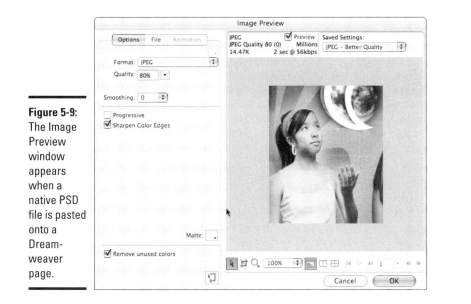

Figure 5-9:
The Image
Preview
window
appears
when a
native PSD
file is pasted
onto a
Dream-
weaver
page.

Exporting Your Documents

Exporting content from your Adobe Creative Suite documents is important if you're working with importing the content into another program, placing the document where it's publicly available and where it needs to be interpreted on other computers. Similarly, you may be working with a team of individuals who need your document to be readable on their machines when it's imported into other programs. Exporting your document as a different file format helps solve these issues, and the Adobe Creative Suite offers you the flexibility of allowing you to export your document as many different file formats.

Other programs sometimes accept native Adobe documents as files that you can import. For example, Adobe Flash CS3 can import Illustrator AI files, Photoshop PSD files, and PDF documents.

Exporting from InDesign

InDesign enables you to export your pages or book as several file types. Most notably, you can export your layouts as a PDF document, which anyone who has the free Adobe Reader installed can view. InDesign can also export to other image and vector formats, such as EPS and JPEG. An InDesign document can also export to SVG and XML, which is useful when you export something for the Web. InDesign has the very handy feature to package up your work for Dreamweaver. By choosing File⇨Cross-media

Export➪XHTML/For Dreamweaver, you can export a project you're working on and have it ready for page creation in Dreamweaver (see Figure 5-10).

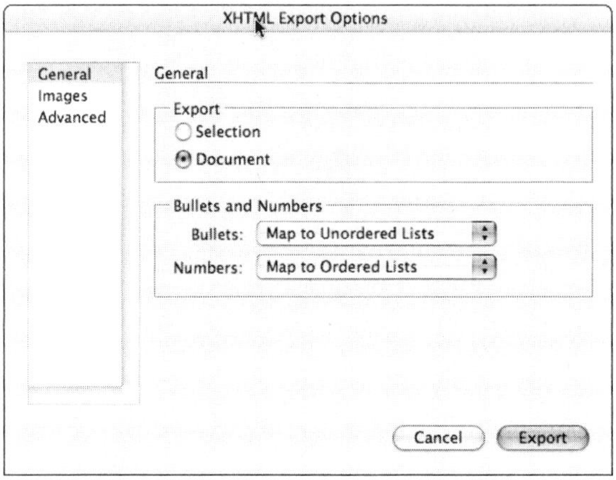

Figure 5-10:
The Export
XHTML
Options
dialog box
in InDesign.

Exporting content from Photoshop

Photoshop can export paths in a document to Illustrator (an AI file). This means that your work in Photoshop is easy to manipulate after you open it using Illustrator.

You have another option, though: You can export your Photoshop file using the new Zoomify feature. This great feature can export a large file to a smaller, more compact SWF file. This file can be easily sent via e-mail and opened using the free Flash Player that most everyone already has installed.

To use Zoomify, do the following:

1. **Choose File➪Export➪Zoomify.**

2. **Click Folder in the Output Location section of the Zoomify dialog box and choose a folder location to save your SWF file to.**

3. **Choose the quality and size and click OK.**

The Zoomify Preview window appears (see Figure 5-11). Use this window to zoom in to see detail.

You can then retrieve the files that were created in your destination folder and post them online, or attach them to an e-mail message.

Figure 5-11:
The image
before it
rebuilds
after a zoom
in, and the
image after
it rebuilds.

Exporting Illustrator files

Illustrator supports exporting to many different file formats. You can export files in a long list of image formats. Choose File⇨Export, and the Export dialog box opens. Click the Save As Type (Windows) or Format (Mac) drop-down list to view the exportable file formats.

After you choose a file type to export to, a second dialog box may appear, allowing you to enter a bunch of settings for the exported file.

Try choosing the Flash SWF file format when you export a file. A second dialog box opens that includes many settings, such as options to generate an HTML page, save each layer as a separate SWF document, and preserve editability (when possible). The options that are available when you export a document depend on the type of file format to which you're exporting.

Exporting Acrobat content

Acrobat allows you to export certain parts of a PDF document that you're working on. For example, you may be using *form data* — the data that is filled into a form made of text fields and so on — in one of your files. You can export this data from Acrobat and then send it online, which is great because PDF documents tend to be rather large for the Web. Therefore, only a small amount of formatted data is sent online rather than a huge PDF file.

You can also export parts of an Acrobat document to use in other programs. You can export comments in a PDF to a Microsoft Word file that was used to create PDF by choosing Comments➪Export Comments➪To Word. You can also export comments to an AutoCAD file (assuming that it was used to create the PDF). In both cases, you need the original document that was used to generate the PDF file in order to successfully import the comments.

Similarly, you can export all comments from a PDF file by choosing Comments➪ Export Comments➪To File and then import them into another version of the same document. You can use this option to consolidate comments from multiple reviewers, or overlay comments from a draft with a final version to confirm that all edits were completed.

Exporting Dreamweaver content

In Dreamweaver, you can export your sites so that they're prepared for publishing and ready to be placed on a live Web site. The site you're working on in Dreamweaver is exported onto your hard drive before you put it somewhere on a server. The HTML styles used in a site you're working on can be exported and saved as an XML document, which in turn can be reused if necessary. These files can then be imported into another Dreamweaver project you're working on.

Chapter 6: Handling Graphics, Paths, Text, and Fonts

In This Chapter

✔ Livening up your documents with graphics

✔ Getting control of paths and strokes

✔ Getting the scoop on text and font fundamentals

✔ Creating a layout

Graphics, paths, text, and fonts are all integral parts of creating documents with the Adobe Creative Suite 3 Design Premium. You must know how to handle each element in your documents and how to work with these elements together. Discovering the different ways you can work with images, text, and drawing is the fun part!

Whether you're designing Web sites or creating a brochure's layout, you can use these elements on their own or together, and it's likely you'll find out something new each time you work with them. A layout can include text, images, and drawings, but sometimes it will include more. If you're creating documents for the Web or you're creating PDF files with multimedia elements, you may be working with sound, animation, and video alongside text, images, and illustrations.

Using Graphics in Your Documents

Graphics are made up of many things. A *graphic* can be an image, a drawing, or a vector graphic. You can create graphics manually by making marks on a page, or you can create them electronically using software, such as the programs we're discussing in this book. Graphics can be displayed in many formats, such as on a computer screen, projected onto a wall, or printed in a magazine or book.

Computer graphics come in many forms, grouped by the way they're created electronically. Bitmap and vector graphics are formed in different ways to achieve the end result that you use in your documents.

Working with bitmap images

Bitmap images are pictures that are made up of many tiny squares, or *bits,* on an invisible grid. When these dots are next to each other, the picture is formed, depending on where and how the colors are arranged on the grid. The dots are also called *pixels,* and if you zoom in far enough, you can even see the blocky pixels that make up the image, as shown in Figure 6-1. At 400-percent zoom, notice how the image in Figure 6-1 is made of large squares, and it's hard to make out what the photograph is of anymore. However, when you just look at most bitmap images at actual size, you don't even see any of the dots making up the picture.

Bitmaps are a great way to display photographs and apply effects to text. When you paint or create detailed graphics, you frequently use bitmaps. However, you should remember that you can lose some quality if you *scale* (change the size of) the image. Resizing the small pixels causes the image to lose definition and quality. Most problems occur when an image is enlarged. Common kinds of bitmap files are JPEG, GIF, TIFF, BMP, and PICT. You can read more about bitmapped images in Book IV.

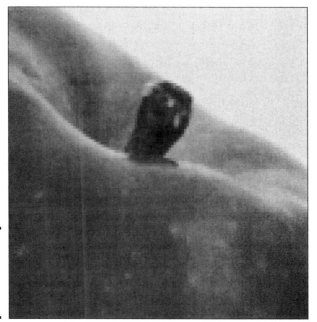

Figure 6-1:
A bitmap
image is
created
from pixels.

The term *raster image* refers to these bitmap images as well. A *raster* is the grid on which all those pixels are placed over the area of the graphic itself. *Rasterizing* an image means that you take a vector image (described in the following section) and change it into a bitmap (or raster) image.

Discovering vector graphics

A *vector image* (or graphic or drawing) is very different from a bitmap image. A vector image is created by a series of mathematical calculations or code that describes how the image should be formed. These calculations tell the computer how the lines should display and render on the page.

Vector images are usually (but not always) a smaller file size than bitmap graphics. This is because the information that's required to make the calculations that create the vector image is usually smaller in file size than the information that makes up each pixel of a bitmap. Compression can lessen a bitmap's file size, but bitmaps are usually larger and slower to display than vectors.

For this reason, and also because vectors are great when it comes to scaling an image, as shown in Figure 6-2, these graphics are well suited for the Web.

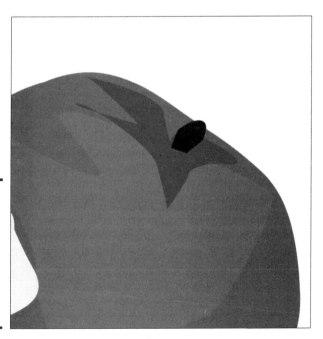

Figure 6-2: A vector image is mathe-matically created, so it's smooth at any zoom level.

Scaling is easy to do when you're using vectors because the program needs to modify the calculations only slightly to make the image larger or smaller. This means the file size won't change, and the scaling is very quick to accomplish. You can scale the image on a Web page to fill the browser window, whatever size it is, or make the image huge for a large banner you're printing. The quality won't degrade, and the file size remains the same.

Vectors aren't always perfect for the Web though. A bitmap is frequently the best way to display a photograph because if you change a bitmap image into a vector drawing (which is possible through the use of tools), you lose too much of the photograph's detail for many purposes. Also, certain effects, such as drop shadows, are best displayed as a bitmap image.

Working with Paths and Strokes

Paths are the vector lines and outlines that you create in a document. You can use paths to outline an image, separate areas of text, or be part of an illustration you create. You typically make paths with a Line tool or Pen tool, or the shape tools. You can use these tools to create paths of different shapes and sizes. You also can use tools to modify the color and size of *strokes* (the actual line that makes up a path).

You can use paths to create clipping paths and paths for text. *Clipping paths* are used to mask (or *hide*) elements on a page. You define that mask using paths to create a shape for that area you need to hide. Clipping paths can even be saved in a file and imported into a different design pattern. A common workflow is to create an image in Photoshop CS3 with a clipping path and import that image into InDesign. InDesign can interpret the clipping path, meaning that you could remove the area you want to mask automatically.

When you want to create text that flows along a path, you begin by creating a new path and then use the Type On A Path tool to type text directly onto that path. For example, in Illustrator, you'd create a path using the Pen tool and then select the Type On A Path tool in the toolbox. If you click the tool on the path you created, you can type new text along that path.

A *stroke* is the color, width, and style of the line that makes up the path you create. You might draw a line with the Pen tool, and the line making up that path is the stroke. However, that path can also have no stroke (represented as a diagonal line in the tools palette), which means you won't see the path itself. However, you may see a color or pattern filling that stroke (the *fill*), as shown in Figure 6-3.

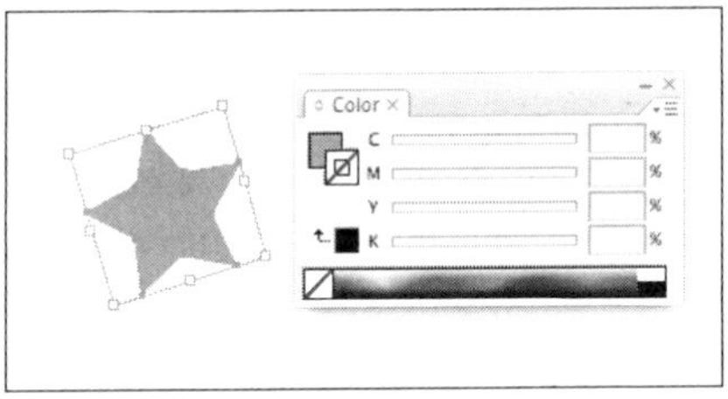

Figure 6-3:
This path
has a fill but
no stroke
applied to it.

You can change the color, width, style (or *type*), and shape of a stroke using controls and tools in the toolbox and the Stroke palette in Illustrator and InDesign. This means that you can create dashed or solid strokes of different patterns that are wide or narrow. Some of these kinds of strokes are shown in Figure 6-4.

Figure 6-4:
Paths that
have
different
kinds of
strokes can
help you add
a creative
flair to your
InDesign
and
Illustrator
document.

Adding Text

You may add text to your projects for different reasons. Text is frequently used to educate and inform people who read it, and this kind of document is a lot different from those that use text for artistic purposes only. For example, if you're creating an article, you may place the text in columns on the page with a large title at the top. Other times, you may use text as a creative element, or even as an object instead of a letter. Alternatively, you may be laying out a Web page and use the text for both a creative element in an animation, as well as the content on pages that make up the Web site.

You can add text to a document by using the Text tool or by importing the text from another source, such as Microsoft Word. You can create a single line of text in a text field, or large blocks of text with or without columns. Text fields can be rotated and resized, and you can change the color, font face, orientation, and character size of the text.

Text can also be placed on a path, as we mention briefly in the previous section, "Working with Paths and Strokes." This allows you to add text to your documents in a different way, because you can draw a path and have the text follow it. Paths are particularly useful for headings on a page, footers, and artistic works that use text as one of the elements.

Using fonts

A *font* refers to the typeface of a set of characters. You can set the font to be a number of sizes, such as a miniscule size of 2 or a gargantuan size of 200. Fonts are given names, such as *Times New Roman* or *Comic Sans,* which you choose from when you add text to your document.

You may also hear about *glyphs,* which refers to an actual character itself. For example, S is a glyph, which is different from the T glyph. A set of glyphs makes up a font. You can view glyphs in the Glyph palette in Illustrator (choose Window⇨Type⇨Glyphs), which is especially useful when you're using fonts like Wingdings that are exclusively made of pictures instead of the usual letters and numbers that make up your keyboard.

What fonts you use can make a huge difference to the look, feel, and style of your designs or documents. Whether you're working on a layout for a magazine article or creating a digital piece for an art gallery, the kinds of fonts you use determine a lot about the feel of the work.

Two major groupings for fonts exist, which are illustrated in Figure 6-5:

✦ **Serif:** Characters have a small line that intersects the end of each line in a character, such as the little feet at the bottom of the *r* on the left side of Figure 6-5.

✦ **Sans-serif:** Characters don't have the small intersecting lines at the end of a line in a character.

What kind of fonts you use (serif or sans-serif) can help with the feel for a piece. Sometimes sans-serif fonts feel more modern, while serif sometimes looks more historical, formal, or literary in nature. This, of course, is all a matter of opinion and what you're used to seeing. Take a moment to look around the Web and your house at how text is used in your books, magazines, advertisements, and even the newspaper. How text is commonly used greatly affects how other people view your work and find the overall *feel* of the presentation. Finding a proper fit, and an appropriate font, is sometimes a challenging design task, but it can also be a lot of fun.

Figure 6-5:
Spot the difference! A serif font is on the left, and sans-serif is on the right.

Discovering types of fonts

Although you can find a gadzillion fonts for free on the Internet, you should be concerned about the quality of your finished product. Typically, those in the professional graphics industry will use Postscript fonts, and preferably OpenType fonts, which are more reliable when printing, as compared to TrueType fonts, which may reflow when outputting to different resolutions.

TrueType

Like other digital typefaces, the TrueType font file contains information such as outlines, hinting instructions, and character mappings (which characters are included in the font). Available for both the Mac and Windows formats, there are slight differences in the TrueType fonts designed for each OS; therefore, Mac and Windows users can't share TrueType fonts.

Postscript (Type 1)

Postscript is a scaleable font system that is compatible with Postscript printers. It allows users to see fonts on the screen the same way they would be printed. Type 1 font files consist of two files — a screen font with bitmap information for on-screen display, and a file with outline information for printing the font. For high-end printing, both of the Type 1 font files must be included with the application file. Due to differences in their structure, Mac and Windows PostScript Type 1 fonts are not cross-platform compatible.

OpenType

OpenType is font technology that was created in a joint effort between Adobe and Microsoft and is an extension of the TrueType font format that can also contain PostScript data. OpenType fonts are cross-platform — the same font file works under both Macintosh and Windows operating systems. This digital type format offers extended character sets and more advanced typographic controls. Like TrueType, a single file contains all the outline, metric, and bitmap data for an OpenType font. Although any program that supports TrueType fonts can use OpenType fonts, not all non-Adobe programs can access the full features of the OpenType font format at this time.

You can find the symbols in the Font menus of many of the CS 3 programs representing the type of font.

Using text and fonts on the Web

Using text and fonts on the Web is a difficult task at times. When you use fonts in a Web page, system fonts are used to display text. You will usually specify a font or group of fonts to use on each page, and the fonts that are installed on the visitor's computer are used to display the text. The problem arises if you use (or want to use) fonts that aren't installed on the visitor's computer. If you choose to use the Papyrus font and the visitor doesn't have that font, then a different one is substituted, and the page looks completely different as a result.

When you're using Dreamweaver to create Web pages or entire sites, you can set up a set of fonts that you want to use on each page. These fonts are similar in how they look, and if one of the fonts isn't available, then the next font is used instead. Among the fonts in the set, at least one of them should be installed on the visitor's computer. This ensures that even if your pages don't look exactly like you planned, they will look very similar to your original layout.

You can use Photoshop and Illustrator to create an image using any font installed on your computer and then save that image for the Web (File↔Save for Web & Devices). Then you can place that image in your Web page using Dreamweaver. This option is best used for small amounts of text — say, for buttons in a navigation bar, headings to separate areas of text, or a customized banner at the top of your Web page.

The Fundamentals of Page Layout

Page layout incorporates the many elements that we discuss in previous sections of this chapter, mainly text and images (and sometimes other forms of multimedia), to create a design on a page. When you're creating a page design, you must think about how people view a layout, such as how the eye moves across the page to take in the flow of information. Also consider how the elements are arranged and how much empty space is around them.

Two main kinds of page layout are discussed in this book: layout intended for print, and layout intended for the Web. Both of these formats require you to work with many of the same elements. You'll most likely create your content using the same programs.

Image manipulation for the Web is frequently done using Photoshop. Photoshop is also the standard program for manipulating and correcting images intended for print. You can even design a page for print, but also put it online by using InDesign's Export XHTML /Dreamweaver.

However, you have to make certain considerations when you put something online. Navigation, usability, file size, dimensions, and computer capabilities are considerations for the Web that aren't a concern when you're working for print. However, resolution, colors, and cropping (to name a few) are considerations of someone designing a piece for print, which aren't concerns for the Web.

Layout for print

When you design a page layout for print, you have to take into account the size and type of paper that will be used. Sometimes, you'll create letterhead with certain elements on the page remaining the same, while other elements (the main content) differ from page to page. You can also create page layouts that serve as templates for a book and use particular elements repeatedly in varying ways throughout the pages (such as bullets or sidebars). Page size, font size, and image resolution are all important considerations in print.

On-screen image resolution is measured in pixels per inch (ppi), which refers to the number of pixels that are within one inch on-screen. The printed resolution of an image is measured in dots per inch (dpi) — a dot of ink is printed for each pixel. A higher dpi means that the image is clearer with finer detail, which is very important for print. ***Remember:*** Printed images almost always use a higher resolution than on-screen images, so you may find that an image that is 4 x 4 inches on-screen (at 72 ppi) prints out at less than 1 x 1 inch (at 300 dpi). Read more about resolution in Book IV.

Templates are available for page layouts that take into consideration common dimensions of paper and help you lay out your content into a defined area. Many different kinds of templates are available online, and you can download them sometimes for free, but others are available for a small or modest fee depending on the template. For example, if you're creating a brochure, you may have to think about where the page will be folded, and how to orient your images and text so that they're facing the correct way when the brochure is read.

A few things to think about when you're laying out a page include the following:

✦ You should try to use a grid and snapping-to-align elements whenever possible. If certain elements on your page aren't aligned, there should be a good reason for this.

✦ The eye will travel in the direction of the elements on the page. For example, if you have a picture of a person facing away from the center of a spread, the eye will travel in that direction. Make sure that the eye travels to the important elements on the page.

✦ Try dividing your pages into thirds, which is called the *rule of thirds*. Parts of your layout should fall into these three areas.

Web page layout

Layout for the Web is quite different from layout for a document that you intend to print. However, many of the same issues arise in both print and Web layout, such as keeping your text legible and flowing across the page (or screen) in an intelligent way. In Web layouts, navigation and usability open up a few doors for things you should consider when planning a Web page:

✦ **Usability:** A usable site is accessible to most, if not all, of your visitors. This means that visitors can access your content easily because the text is legible, the file formats work on their computers, and they can find content on your site. Also, if the visitor has a challenge, such as a sight or reading disability, he or she can use software on the computer so that the site is read or described aloud.

✦ **Size:** File size should always be kept to a minimum, which may mean changing your layout to accommodate for this. If many of the parts of your design require large images, you may need to change the design completely to reduce your file size. Also, you need to design the page with monitors in mind. If a visitor has his or her monitor set to a resolution of 800 x 600, then your site will scroll horizontally if it's designed any larger than 780 pixels wide. Most Web surfers dislike scrolling horizontally, so the dimensions of the visitor's display should be considered when designing sites.

✦ **Navigation:** Users have to navigate between pages on your site. To do so, you need to create links to those pages by using buttons, text links, menus, and so on. Making that navigation easy to find and use takes some forethought and planning. Be sure that navigation is a big part of your plans when designing the layout of your site.

Not only do you have to think about usability and navigation, but you have to account for the different kinds of computers accessing the page, and how people from all over the world may be trying to access your page. If you need your page to be universal, you may need to translate it into different languages and use different character sets. (This is true of print as well, if you're designing a page that requires a special character set other than the ones you regularly use.)

Because you may be using multimedia elements alongside text (such as images, video, animation, and so on), you're constrained to the dimensions and color limitations of a computer monitor and have to think about both file size and scrolling.

There are many differences between preparing a layout for the Web and for print; however, you will find that you use many of the same tools for both (although you save or export your files in a different way), and a great deal of information crosses over between the two mediums.

Chapter 7: Using Color

In This Chapter

✔ Discovering color modes

✔ Finding out about swatches

✔ Using color for print

✔ Using color on the Web

*U*sing color in your documents is probably one of the most important considerations you can make in your projects. The colors you use, the mode that you use them in, and even the way you select colors make a difference in the way you create a document and the final output of that document. Even though you can create a document that looks the same on a monitor in different color modes, how that file prints onto paper is a different matter. Color is a very broad subject, and in this chapter, you find out the basics of how color affects the projects you work on.

Figuring out what kinds of colors you're using is important, and this decision is greatly determined by what kind of output you've planned for the document. Different color modes are appropriate for work for the Web and work that you're having professionally printed. Monitors and printers have different modes for color, which means that you need to work with your files in different color modes (although you can change the mode after you start working on a file, if necessary). You may also find yourself in situations where very particular colors are required in your work. You may be working with specific colors that a company needs to match its logo, or creating an image that replicates how a building should be painted with specific colors of paint. You may need to use particular Pantone colors or color mixes, if not for the printing process, for the purpose of matching a client's needs.

In this chapter, we introduce you to the different color modes and how to use them. You discover new terminology and how to find, mix, and add colors to your documents in the Creative Suite.

Looking at Color Modes and Channels

Several different color modes are available for use in the Creative Suite applications. When you start a new document in Photoshop and Illustrator, you can choose the color mode you want to work in. In fact the new version of Illustrator helps you by automatically assigning a color mode based upon your output profile. The choice you make affects the colors in the Swatches panel, as well as some other panels, such as Brushes and Symbols. You can change your color mode later by choosing File⇨Document Color Mode. If you're working with print, generally you use CMYK mode. If you're working on files that are to be displayed on a monitor, then RGB is the choice.

Photoshop still refers to the Swatches and Color as palettes, whereas the other applications in the suite are called panels.

Using RGB

RGB (Red, Green, Blue) is the color mode used for on-screen presentation, such as an image displayed on the Web or a broadcast design for TV. Each of the colors displayed on-screen has a certain level (between 0 and 100 percent) of red, green, and blue to create the color. In a color mixer, you can either use sliders to set the level in values, as shown in Figure 7-1, or you can enter a percentage into a text field (such as in CMYK color mode).

Figure 7-1:
Mixing colors in RGB mode.

Note the Cube displays an icon on the color panel if a color you have created isn't within the color range for two models, Web colors and CMYK.

✦ Click the Web Cube icon to convert the selected color to the closest Web-safe color.

✦ Click the CMYK warning exclamation point to convert to a color that is suitable for the CMYK gamut. Color is discussed in the Book IV, including more details about how you can adjust the Color Settings dialog box.

When you create a Web page, the color is represented as a hexadecimal number. A *hexadecimal number* starts with a pound sign (#) followed by three pairs of letters and numbers (A–F and 0–9) — the first pair for red, the second pair for green, and the last pair for blue. The lowest value (the least amount of the color) in a hexadecimal number is 0 (zero), and the highest value (the greatest amount of the color) is F. For example, #000000 is black, #FFFFFF is white, #FF0000 is red, and #CCCCCC is a light gray. To see what a particular hexadecimal color looks like, go to Webmonkey at www. webmonkey.com/webmonkey/reference/color_codes.

Working with CMYK

The RGB (Red, Green, Blue) color mode is the color standard for monitors and the Web, and CMYK — Cyan, Magenta, Yellow, and Key (or Black) — is the standard color mode for print media, particularly in commercial printing such as that done by a service provider.

The CMYK color scheme is based on pigment (a substance used as coloring) color separation, and it describes how light reflects off pigments. When you work with this color mode, you create black by adding the maximum values of cyan, magenta, and yellow all at once. You can create different levels of gray by combining equal, but not maximum, amounts of cyan, magenta, and yellow. White is simply the absence of all color. Many color printers you find today work using the CMYK color model and can simulate almost any color by printing two colors very close to each other; however, some at-home desktop printer models made by Epson, Hewlett-Packard (HP), and Canon use their own color systems to print your work.

Saving in grayscale

You've seen a lot of grayscale so far because that is how the pictures were printed in this book. *Grayscale* refers to when color images are displayed or printed in black and white. Grayscale refers to the different shades of gray that can be used when printing using only black ink on a white page. Halftone patterns are used to help simulate different color values. This is accomplished by adding dots to simulate shadows and gradients between colors. *Halftone patterns* are created when an image uses dots of varying diameter, or it uses many small dots in the same area to simulate different shades of gray.

Looking at color channels

When you work with an image in Photoshop, the image has at least one (but typically more) color channels. A *color channel* stores information about a particular color in a selected image. For example, an RGB image has three color channels: one that handles the reds (R), one for handling green information (G), and the last for information about the blues (B).

In addition to each of the color channels, you can have an *alpha channel.* The alpha channel holds the transparency information about a particular image. If you're working with a file format that supports transparency, you can add and use the alpha channel to save alpha information.

In Photoshop, you can access the channels in your image by choosing Windows➪Channels. When the Channels palette opens, you can toggle visibility of each icon by clicking the eye icon next to each channel (see Figure 7-2).

Figure 7-2:
This RGB file is created from a Red, Green, and Blue channel.

Choosing Colors

When you create a document, you may have to consider what colors you use, or you may have the freedom to use an unlimited number of colors. If you print your documents, you can choose a specific set of colors to use. You may be restricted to only the two colors in a company logo, or you may have to print in grayscale. So finding the colors you need to use in each program is important, and then figuring out how to access those colors repeatedly in a document saves you a great deal of time.

Using swatches

Swatches are a good way to choose a color, particularly when you intend to print the document. The Swatches panel in the Creative Suite programs, shown in Figure 7-3, contains colors and sometimes gradients. You can create libraries of swatches that contain colors that you can use repeatedly across several documents.

Figure 7-3:
The Swatches panels are similar in most suite applications; this is the Photoshop Swatches palette.

Click to open the
panel or palette menu

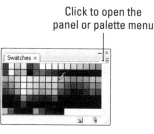

You can choose libraries of swatches from the panel or palette menu, or you can load and save swatch libraries. You can customize a swatch library by adding or deleting colors.

When printing your work professionally, it's advisable to work with *named colors* so that the service provider (commercial printer) knows exactly what inks to use when it outputs your work. An example of a named color is *Pantone 2747 M*. The best way to work with named colors is by using swatches to choose your colors. When you mix your own colors, you can end up working with unnamed colors. When a printing press looks at your documents, it's sometimes too difficult to determine exactly what color you want to print when the color is unnamed.

Mixing colors

A color mixer is found in the Color panel, and it helps you choose colors. You can use the Eyedropper tool to choose a color, or you can enter values for each hue or percentages if you prefer that instead. You can use one of several different color modes in the programs that you use, which offers you a lot of flexibility for all of your projects.

Follow these steps to choose a color in a specified color mode:

1. **In a program that has a Color panel, choose Window⊏⊐Color to open the Color panel (if it's not already open).**

The Color panel is available in Photoshop, Illustrator, and InDesign.

2. **Click the Color panel menu to choose a new color mode.**

Open this menu by clicking the arrow button in the upper-right corner of the Color panel.

3. **Choose the RGB color mode from the panel menu that opens.**

The panel switches to RGB color mode.

4. **In the Color panel, click either the Fill box (solid square) or Stroke box (hollow square) to choose what color you want to change.**

If you click the Fill box, you can modify the color of a *fill* (the color inside a shape). If you click the Stroke box, then you can modify the color of a *stroke* (the outline of a shape or a line).

5. **Use the sliders in the Color panel to change the color values.**

You can also change the percentage values to the right of each slider.

6. **After you've chosen a color that you're happy with, return to your document and create a new shape that uses that color.**

For instructions on how to create shapes in InDesign, see Book II.

Hold down the Shift key when adjusting any one-color slider, and the other color sliders adjust proportionally to provide you with various tints from your original.

Using Color on the Web

In the past, you had to be very conscious of what colors you used on the Web. Some computer monitors were limited in the number of colors they could display. Nowadays, color monitors are much more advanced and can handle a full range of colors, so images on the Web are much more likely to be properly displayed.

It doesn't have to do with color, but Macintosh and Windows computers usually display your work differently because of gamma differences on these machines. Generally speaking, colors on a Mac appear lighter, and colors on a PC look darker. You can account for this difference by making a Mac version of your site, videos, and so on look darker so that both are the same (or you can make the Windows version lighter), but these changes aren't usually necessary.

Even though most computers can handle a full range of colors, you may have to consider color limitations. If you're designing a site specifically targeted at old computers or a certain user base, you may have to limit your colors to the 256 Web-safe colors, which means that any other colors used are approximated, which can look poor. If it's likely that your site will be viewed by users with older computers, consider the following:

✦ Use a Web-safe panel of 216 colors to design your Web sites so that you specifically design with those older displays in mind and know what the pages will look like. This number is 216 instead of 256 because the lower number is compatible with both Mac and Windows computers. This panel is usually called the *Web-safe panel* or *Web-safe RGB,* and you can access it from the Swatches panel menu in Photoshop and Illustrator.

✦ Avoid using gradients whenever possible because they use a wide range of colors (many unsupported in a limited Web panel).

✦ If a color is approximated because it can't be handled by someone's computer, that color is *dithered* — the computer tries to use two or more colors to achieve the color you specified, causing a typically displeasing granular appearance. So a limited number of colors can have a negative affect on an image; notice the granular appearance on what should be the shadow of an apple in Figure 7-4.

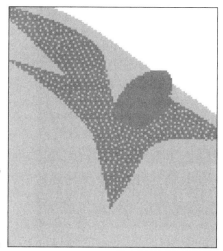

Figure 7-4:
The shadow of the apple is dithered.

If you keep the preceding elements in mind, you should be ready to start designing for the Web! Remember also that you don't have to worry about using the Web-safe panel if you're designing primarily for modern computers.

Chapter 8: Printing Documents

In This Chapter

✔ Understanding color and black-and-white printing

✔ Choosing a printer

✔ Outputting your work

*Y*ou can print documents in many ways with the Adobe Creative Suite 3. Similarly, you can print many different kinds of documents. You can create anything from a CD-ROM sticker to a 300-page book to a T-shirt iron-on transfer using the programs you find in the Creative Suite. But whatever you're working on, it's a good idea to know the options that are available for printing your work. Knowing the kinds of printers you can work with, what to buy (and from where) in order to use them, and how to save your work help improve the quality of the print job when you've finished your work.

Choosing Printers

When it comes to printers, you encounter hundreds of options at a great variety of prices. Printers can differ greatly when it comes to quality, cost of maintenance, and the speed at which the printer is able to print. Some inkjet printers excel at printing full-color photos but aren't great at printing text; a low-end or medium-end laser printer may print black-and-white documents at good speed and quality, but you can't print in color.

Using consumer printers

Currently, the most common type of consumer (home) printer is an inkjet printer. *Inkjet printers* work by spraying ink stored in cartridges onto a sheet of paper as it passes through the printer. This type of printer is common in households because it's the least expensive type of color printer. It's also versatile. You can walk into virtually any computer store and buy a color inkjet printer (which can print resumes, photos, and brochures) for a low price.

The one drawback of inkjets is that they can be expensive to maintain in the long run. Depending on how much you print, you may need to replace the black or color cartridges pretty often, which can get costly and quickly exceed the cost of the printer itself.

Looking at professional printers

Professional printers typically have a more rounded feature set compared to consumer printers. Professional printers can either be inkjet or laser printers and can even perform multiple functions within the office. Not surprisingly, printers that have several roles within the office are often referred to as *multifunction* or *all-in-one* printers and typically also include scanning, photocopying, or faxing capabilities in addition to printing. These all-in-one units are great for small offices and home offices because they save the consumer some money while providing access to a variety of useful tools.

Laser printers have several benefits: They typically produce a higher quality printout and print pages faster than inkjet printers, as well as produce a clean, professional-looking document. You can also print more pages per ink cartridge, saving you money in consumables.

Buying a Printer

Some common features to look for when purchasing a printer (either consumer or professional) are

+ **Speed:** Printers are rated in *pages per minute* (PPM). Low-end inkjet printers typically print about 12 or fewer PPM when printing black-and-white pages. When printing color documents, the number of pages printed per minute will be less.

+ **Color:** Almost all inkjet printers can print in color, but most laser printers print only in black and white. Color printers can be expensive to maintain because most inkjet printers have one cartridge for black ink and a second cartridge for colored inks. When one color runs out, you're forced to replace the entire cartridge, or all the colors won't look right when you print the document. Color laser printers are available, although they're usually very expensive.

+ **Resolution:** Similar to monitors, a printer's quality can be rated in resolution. Higher resolution means images and text will appear crisper. Low-end or older inkjet printers may print only a maximum of 600 dpi (dots per inch), which is more than fine for text but may be low if you want to print high-quality photographs.

+ **Connectivity:** You can connect a printer to your computer in three ways. Older printers typically connect to your system using a parallel (36-pin) port, whereas newer printers often offer both parallel and USB connections. The third way of connecting to a printer is by connecting a printer to your network, although this option is usually seen only on professional printers.

✦ **Duplexing:** Another feature to consider is duplexing. *Duplexing* refers to the ability to print on both sides of a sheet of paper without you manually flipping the piece of paper and placing it back in the paper tray.

Printing Your Work

When it comes to printing, countless options and settings can affect the final result of your document. Whether you're printing banners, business cards, T-shirt iron-on transfers, or lost cat posters, you must be aware of several things, such as paper quality, printer quality, and ink usage. You also have to decide whether to print the documents yourself at home or take them to a professional printing business to get the work done.

While RGB (Red, Green, Blue) is the color standard for the Web, CMYK — Cyan, Magenta, Yellow, and Key (or Black) — is the standard in print. For information about using the RGB and CMYK color modes in the Creative Suite, see Chapter 7 of this minibook.

Choosing where and how to print

You can choose from several options when it comes to printing your files. You can take your digital files to a *printing service provider,* which is an establishment that prints electronic documents (such as FedEx Kinko's), or even print the files yourself at home on your inkjet or laser printer. Each option has several advantages and disadvantages. Depending on how many copies and the number of colors, having your files printed professionally can be cost prohibitive. Having your files printed by a professional print house, however, almost always means the print quality will be much better than if the document was printed on a low-end inkjet printer.

Naturally, if you're only printing flyers to distribute around the neighborhood, you may not need high-quality output, and a home inkjet or laser printer would be more than adequate. However, it may be cheaper to print documents professionally than it is to print documents at home if you're going to go through large amounts of black ink or perhaps one or two cartridges of toner.

If you're using an inkjet printer, often you can get an average of 400 to 600 pages of black text before you need to replace a cartridge; a laser printer prints around 2,500 to 4,000 pages before you need to purchase new toner. Simply using a laser printer can save hundreds of dollars a year, depending on the number of pages you need to print and whether you need to print in color. If you need to print in color, many color laser printers are available (although they can be expensive). Entry-level color laser printers can cost around $500; some high-end color laser printers can cost more than $10,000. In comparison, black-and-white laser printers can cost as little as about $100. So unless you plan on doing lots of printing, outsourcing your printing to a service provider may be the best solution.

The kind of printer you use (such as a commercial or PostScript printer, or a low-cost household inkjet) makes a great difference in the quality of output. Some of your illustrations or layouts will look a lot better when printed commercially depending on what's in your document. You can find more information on PostScript features in Books II and III.

Looking at paper

Before printing your documents, you need to consider the type of paper that is best for the job. If you're printing on glossy paper, you need to make sure that the paper works with your printer type. Although most glossy paper works fine in inkjet or laser printers, some brands or types of paper may not.

Always double-check paper when purchasing it to make sure that it won't damage your printer. The kinds of printers supported by the type of paper will be listed on the paper's packaging.

One benefit to using glossy paper is that it has a finish similar to photo paper finish, which can make your printouts appear to have a higher quality.

Using a good paper can result in photos that have richer colors and show more detail. When purchasing printer paper, here are some important characteristics to look out for:

+ **Brightness:** *Brightness,* not surprisingly, refers to how bright the paper is. Higher numbers mean the paper looks brighter and cleaner.

+ **Weight:** *Weight* refers to how heavy the paper is. Higher weights mean a thicker, more durable piece of paper.

+ **Opacity:** *Opacity* refers to how translucent, or transparent, the paper is. If the paper is too thin, then too much light can pass through it; also, it may be possible to see the ink through the other side of the page (which can be a problem if you want to print on both sides of the sheet). Opacity relates to weight, in that a heavier sheet of paper would be thicker and allow less light to pass through it.

+ **Texture:** Texture can provide dramatic differences between inkjet and laser printers. Inkjet printers spray ink onto a page, so having a slightly textured surface to print on can be beneficial because the texture allows ink to dry somewhat faster and bleed a little less, making the finished product look a little sharper. When using a laser printer, the opposite is true. Having a smooth, flat surface for the toner to transfer onto produces better results.

Remember that you may not always print on 8.5-x-11-inch paper (also referred to as Letter or A4). Many printers also allow you to print onto envelopes, labels, stickers, business cards, and even iron-on transfers. You can use iron-on transfers to create your own T-shirts with your company logo or shirts with your face on the front. Some newer printers even allow you to print directly onto the surface of a CD-ROM. You can even purchase small printers that were designed solely to print standard-sized photographs.

Another important note is the difference in paper sizes globally. While the United States and Canada use inches to measure paper, the rest of the globe uses a metric system based on an ISO standard. The North American Letter format may be replaced by the ISO A4 format. The other differences between the U.S. and Canadian systems from the ISO is that the ISO paper sizes always follow a set ratio, while the U.S. and Canadian systems uses two different aspect ratios.

Saving files for a service provider

When working with a professional print service provider, you need to check to make sure which file formats it'll accept. Almost all print service providers will accept files created using an Adobe program (Illustrator, Photoshop, InDesign, Acrobat, and so on), as well as files created using QuarkXPress, CorelDRAW, or other professional-level programs. You'll also need to confirm what version and operating system the service provider will accept, because it may be necessary to save your files so that they're compatible with whichever version of software the service provider uses.

You may have to export your work as a different file format, such as PDF, if your service provider doesn't accept InDesign files. To export to PDF in InDesign, choose File⇨Export and select PDF from the Save As Type (Windows) or Format (Mac) drop-down list. When you click the Save button, the Export PDF dialog box appears, as shown in Figure 8-1. Read specifics about the settings in Book V.

If you've linked your graphics within your files instead of embedding them, you'll also want to use an uncompressed file format, such as EPS or TIFF. Using an uncompressed file format ensures that you aren't losing quality each time the image file is saved, which would happen if you used JPEG images.

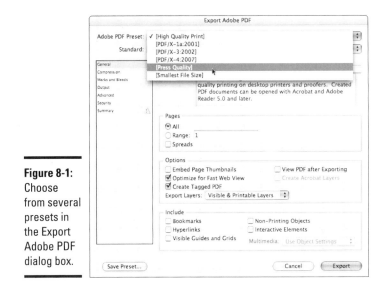

Figure 8-1:
Choose
from several
presets in
the Export
Adobe PDF
dialog box.

Printing at home

When you're ready to print your documents, you can access the Print dialog box and then specify a number of settings depending on what kind of printer you have installed. For this example, we assume that you have Acrobat Distiller (from Adobe Acrobat) installed on your system, as it installs with the default install of the suite.

Though you can simply save a Photoshop PDF from the regular Save menu, we take you through the steps of creating a PDF file from Photoshop's Print dialog box. Using the Print dialog box, you can take advantage of additional options that aren't available in the Save menu, such as the ability to preview your printed document, scale your image and apply color settings.

To print a file as a PDF from Photoshop CS3, follow these steps:

1. **Choose File⇨Print.**

In this case, we're using Photoshop CS3 on the Macintosh. The Print dialog box opens, as shown in Figure 8-2.

The Print dialog box differs, depending on which program you're using. In this window, Photoshop allows you to change the scale of the image by entering a value in the scale text box, or selecting and dragging a handle on the preview image in the upper-left corner.

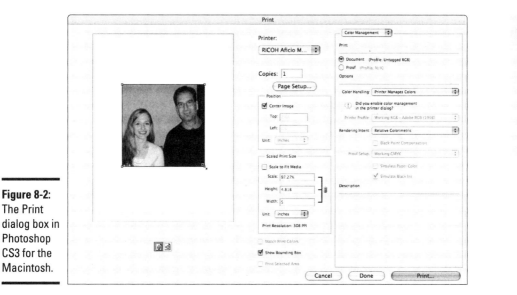

Figure 8-2:
The Print
dialog box in
Photoshop
CS3 for the
Macintosh.

2. Click on the Printer drop-down menu and choose Acrobat PDF 8.0.

If you want to choose the settings for an installed printer, you can also select it here.

3. If necessary, scale the image to fit the paper and then click the Print button.

A second Print dialog box appears.

4. From the Printer drop-down list, choose Adobe PDF 8.0.

Leave the Preset set to Standard.

5. Click Copies And Pages and select PDF Options from the drop-down list.

The Adobe PDF Settings appear.

6. Click the Adobe PDF Settings drop-down list and select the quality of PDF that you want to create.

In Figure 8-3, High Quality Print was selected.

7. If you want to see your PDF file right after it's created, choose Acrobat from the After PDF Creation drop-down list and click Print.

The Save To File dialog box appears.

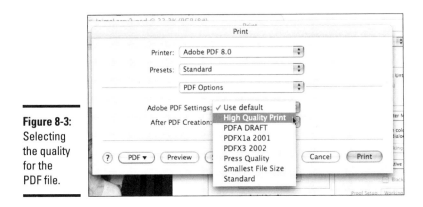

Figure 8-3:
Selecting
the quality
for the
PDF file.

8. **Choose a name for the PDF, navigate to the location that you want to save the file to, and click Save.**

   The document is saved as a PDF file.

Because most printers have custom interfaces for defining settings, you may need to consult your printer's documentation for detailed information on using the printer's features.

Book II

InDesign CS3

The 5th Wave   By Rich Tennant

"Well, there's your drawing scanned into your book report. I just can't figure out what that grey fuzzy thing is along the edge."

Contents at a Glance

Chapter 1: What's New in InDesign CS3

In This Chapter

✓ Creating object effects

✓ Controlling finer transparency controls

✓ Using table and cell styles

✓ Using improved long document support

✓ Taking advantage of the customizable user interface

✓ Placing InDesign documents

*I*nDesign CS3 is packed with great features that new and old users will be excited about. These new features are sure to save lots of time and even keep you from jumping in to Adobe Illustrator and Photoshop for interesting effects. In this chapter, you discover these features and check out references to chapters within this minibook that you can go to for more details.

Incredible New Object Effects

You can now apply a variety of Photoshop effects directly to objects in your InDesign document. Not only is it great that you can apply inner shadows, bevels, outer and inner glows, and more in InDesign, but the effects are applied in a way that is nondestructive to the original object. This means that you can undo the effects at anytime, giving you the opportunity to experiment and be more creative.

Notice in Figure 1-1 that the text is selected, and various options are selected in the Effects palette.

You probably want to experiment with this feature immediately. Select an object in InDesign and choose Object⇨Effects⇨Transparency (or any feature — they all open the Effects dialog box.) Check the boxes to the left of the Effects to activate them and click the Effects name to see its options appear on the right. Read Chapter 6 of this minibook for more details on how to take advantage of the new Effects feature and how to save combinations of effects as object styles.

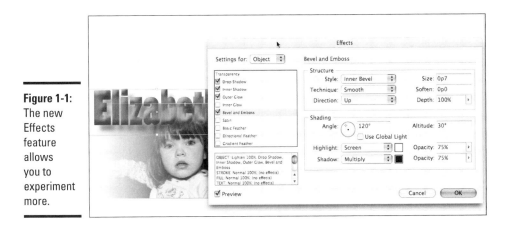

Figure 1-1:
The new
Effects
feature
allows
you to
experiment
more.

Advanced Transparency Control

Now in InDesign CS3, you have the ability to apply transparency settings independently to an object's fill, stroke, and content. Apply blends, opacity, and creative effects to achieve incredible visual looks. Using the Effects panel (choose Window➪Effects), you can select an object's fill or stroke and adjust the opacity, as well as apply effects independently to each. You can read more about using Transparency in Chapter 7 of this minibook.

Place Multiple Objects at Once

You can import multiple files in a single step using the Place dialog box or by dragging multiple files to InDesign from the desktop or Adobe Bridge CS3. But wait! You can now see thumbnail previews and cycle through the files loaded in the Place cursor. Read more about placing images in Chapter 4 of this minibook.

Expanded Quick Apply

Many seasoned InDesign users didn't know Quick Apply existed in previous versions, but you can't miss it now.

Using the Quick Apply button in the Control panel or pressing Ctrl+ Return (Windows) or ⌘+Return (Mac OS), you can instantly format your selection with styles and even access menu commands, all while keeping your hands on the keyboard. Type a few letters into the Quick Apply panel, and any available command, text variable, script, or style appears in a list that you can navigate. You can read more about applying styles in Chapter 8 of this minibook.

Faster and Better Fitting Controls

Make your InDesign templates more efficient by setting the default fit behavior of frames. In Adobe InDesign CS3, you can set the fit options of a frame (such as fit method, alignment, and cropping) by choosing Object⇨Fitting⇨ Frame Fitting Options, even when the frame is empty. As soon as you place content such as an image into a frame, it fits perfectly. In addition, you can instantly fit a graphics frame or text frame to the size of its content by double-clicking a frame handle.

Improved Pages Panel

You can easily navigate a document and arrange pages with thumbnail previews, in the Pages panel. Quickly get to the page you need by using a mouse scroll wheel or a grabber hand that automatically appears in the panel. A context menu gives you fast access to menu commands, and when dragging pages to a new location, the Pages panel automatically scrolls to pages that are out of view.

Table and Cell Styles

This feature is long overdue. Creating tables in InDesign has always been a breeze, but saving the styles required a good memory or the purchase of a third-party plug-in. No more; you can now format tables quickly and consistently with styles for both tables and cells. You simply create a style, store it in the Table Styles panel, and instantly apply it to any table, including spreadsheets from Excel or Word (see Figure 1-2). You can even apply a cell style to a selected region of cells.

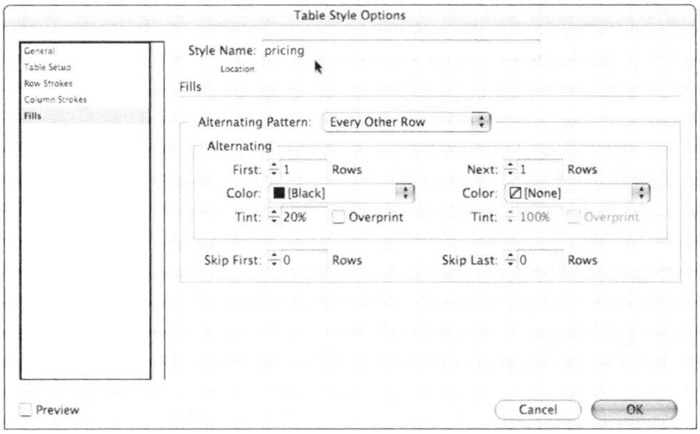

Figure 1-2:
Save table
styles in
InDesign
CS3.

Standardized and Customizable Interface

In Adobe InDesign CS3, you can adapt the user interface to fit your needs by taking advantage of the new flexible and space-saving panels. You can dock panels as icons and keep them accessible. You can then quickly expand and collapse panels so that you see them only when you need them. You also can customize your menus by choosing Edit➪Menus. Using this feature you can turn menu items visibility on or off and even color-code the menu items that you want to recognize quickly.

Save all your interface changes as workspaces so that you can apply them at any time.

Placed InDesign documents

Those creating advertising sections of newspapers will love this feature, as will pretty much any user. In InDesign CS3, you can now place an InDesign document inside another. You can reuse InDesign layouts in new projects for improved design consistency and streamlined workflow. If another user, or even you, updates the placed InDesign file, the Links panel notes that the file has been updated, just like linked images.

Chapter 2: Introducing InDesign CS3

*I*nDesign is one of the most sophisticated page layout programs available on the market. Not only can you create professional-looking documents, such as newsletters, books, and magazines, but you can integrate your documents with other Adobe applications. For example, you can create a document that includes hyperlinks and video and export it to PDF, or you can export XML (Extensible Markup Language) from InDesign and import the XML into Dreamweaver to create Web pages. Now in InDesign CS3, you can even import an InDesign document into an InDesign document!

As powerful of an application InDesign is, you'd think it would be difficult to use, but it really is not. This minibook shows you how to use InDesign to make creative page layouts. In this chapter, you discover the InDesign interface and start your first publication.

Getting Started with InDesign CS3

InDesign creates multiple page layouts that include type, graphics (such as fills and strokes), and images. The InDesign document you see in Figure 2-1 includes elements from Adobe Illustrator (logos), and Photoshop (images). If this file were to be exported as a PDF, it could include video and even Flash files.

In this section, you get familiar with creating and opening documents in InDesign. Through the rest of the chapters in this minibook, you discover how to add various elements to your pages.

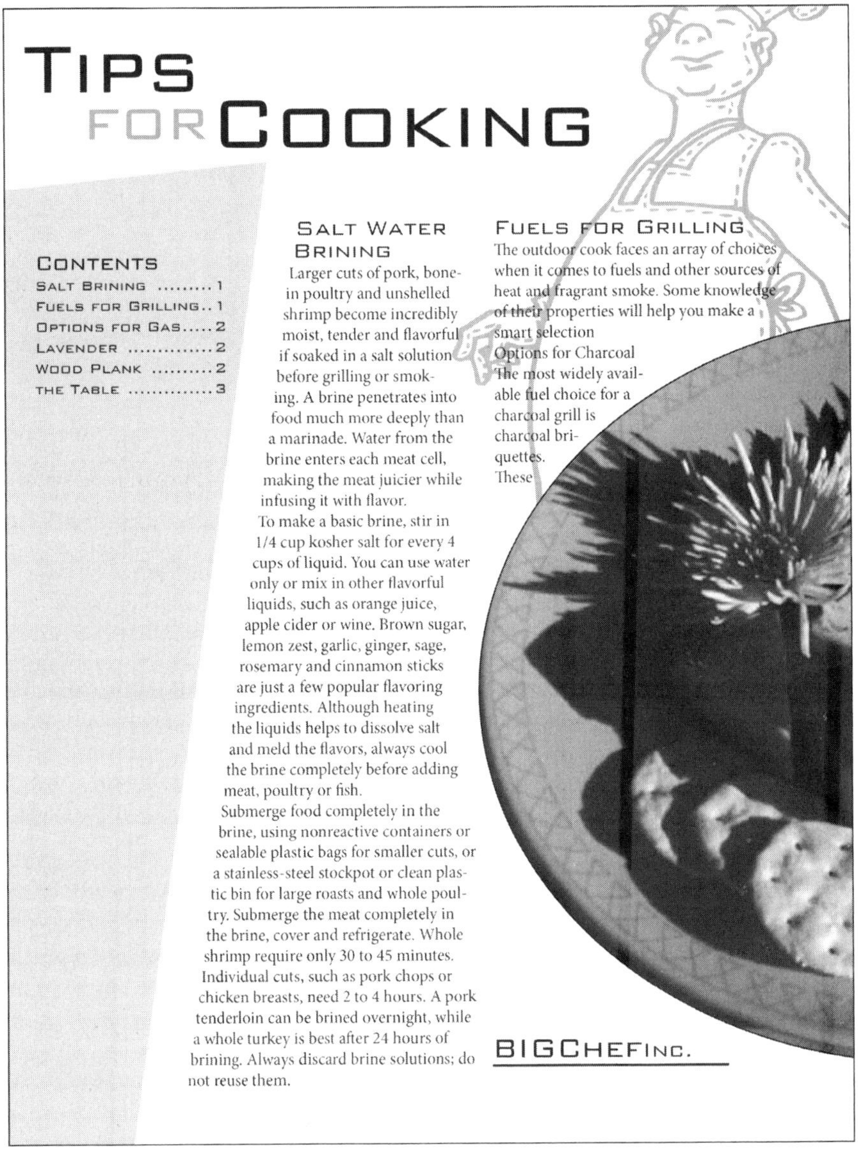

TIPS
FOR COOKING

CONTENTS

SALT WATER BRINING

Larger cuts of pork, bone-in poultry and unshelled shrimp become incredibly moist, tender and flavorful if soaked in a salt solution before grilling or smoking. A brine penetrates into food much more deeply than a marinade. Water from the brine enters each meat cell, making the meat juicier while infusing it with flavor.

To make a basic brine, stir in 1/4 cup kosher salt for every 4 cups of liquid. You can use water only or mix in other flavorful liquids, such as orange juice, apple cider or wine. Brown sugar, lemon zest, garlic, ginger, sage, rosemary and cinnamon sticks are just a few popular flavoring ingredients. Although heating the liquids helps to dissolve salt and meld the flavors, always cool the brine completely before adding meat, poultry or fish.

Submerge food completely in the brine, using nonreactive containers or sealable plastic bags for smaller cuts, or a stainless-steel stockpot or clean plastic bin for large roasts and whole poultry. Submerge the meat completely in the brine, cover and refrigerate. Whole shrimp require only 30 to 45 minutes. Individual cuts, such as pork chops or chicken breasts, need 2 to 4 hours. A pork tenderloin can be brined overnight, while a whole turkey is best after 24 hours of brining. Always discard brine solutions; do not reuse them.

FUELS FOR GRILLING

The outdoor cook faces an array of choices when it comes to fuels and other sources of heat and fragrant smoke. Some knowledge of their properties will help you make a smart selection
Options for Charcoal
The most widely available fuel choice for a charcoal grill is charcoal briquettes. These

BIGCHEFINC.

Figure 2-1: A sample page layout from InDesign.

Creating a new publication

After you launch InDesign, you can create a new InDesign document (also referred to as a *publication*). Just follow these steps to create a new publication:

1. **Choose File⇨New⇨Document.**

The New Document dialog box opens.

2. **Enter a value for the number of pages for the document in the Number Of Pages text field.**

This value can be between 1 and 9999. If you want a text frame on the master page, select the Master Text Frame check box.

You can discover more about text frames in Chapter 4 of this minibook.

3. **Select the Facing Pages check box if you want the pages arranged as spreads.**

With this option checked, the pages in your document are arranged in pairs, so you have *spreads,* which are facing or adjacent pages in a layout. For example, you'd select this option if you're creating a publication that will be arranged like a book. If you deselect this option, pages are arranged individually.

4. **Choose a page size for the document from the Page Size drop-down list.**

The page size should be set to the size of paper you intend to print on or display the content at. The Width and Height values below this drop-down list change, depending on the size you choose.

5. **Choose Portrait (vertical) or Landscape (horizontal) orientation for the orientation of the pages throughout the document.**

Click the button on the left for Portrait or the button on the right for Landscape. A portrait layout is narrow and tall, while a landscape layout is short and wide.

6. **Choose a number for the columns on the page.**

This step sets guides for columns where you plan to input text. You can also enter a value in the Gutter field (the *gutter* is the space in between each of the columns). For more information about using columns in page layout, see Chapter 5 of this minibook.

7. **Choose values for the page margins.**

Notice the Make All Settings The Same button in the middle of the four text fields where you enter the margin values. Click this button to set all margins to the same value.

Book II
Chapter 2

Introducing
InDesign CS3

If you see Top, Bottom, Inside, and Outside, you're specifying margins for a page layout that has facing pages. (The Facing Pages check box is selected in the dialog box.) If you see Top, Bottom, Left, and Right, you're creating a page layout without facing pages. The inside margins refer to the margins at the middle of the spread, and the outside margins refer to the outer left and right margins. You can set the Inside setting to accommodate the binding of a book.

If you're going to use the same settings over and over, saving those settings as a preset is a good idea. Click the Save Preset button in the New Document dialog box after making your settings (before you click OK). Enter a name for the preset and then click OK. After you save your settings, you can select the settings from the Document Preset drop-down list (at the top of Figure 2-2) whenever you create a new document.

8. **When you're finished, click OK.**

After you click OK in the New Document dialog box, the new document is created with the settings you just specified.

We discuss margins, columns, orientation, and page size in further detail in Chapter 5 of this minibook.

Opening an existing publication

You may have InDesign files on your hard drive that you created or have saved from another source. To open existing InDesign documents (`*.indd`), follow these steps:

1. **Choose File➪Open.**

   The Open dialog box appears.

2. **Browse through your hard drive and select a file to open.**

   Select a file by clicking the document's title. To select more than one document, press Ctrl (⌘ on the Mac) while you click the filename.

3. **Click the Open button to open the file.**

   The file opens in the workspace.

Looking at the document setup

If you need to change the size of your pages or the number of pages in a document that is already open in the workspace, you can make those changes in the Document Setup dialog box. To access and modify settings in the Document Setup dialog box, follow these steps:

1. **Choose File⇨Document Setup.**

The Document Setup dialog box opens.

2. **Change the value in the Number Of Pages text field if you need the number of pages in your document to be greater or less than the current value.**

The number of pages in your document updates after you close this dialog box. You can also change this number later by using Layout⇨ Pages⇨Insert Pages or by using the Pages panel.

3. **Change the size of the page by selecting a new option from the Page Size drop-down list or manually enter values into the Width and Height text fields.**

You can also click the up and down arrows in the Width and Height text fields to choose a new value.

4. **Change the page orientation by clicking the Portrait or the Landscape button.**

The page orientation updates in the workspace after you exit this dialog box.

5. **Click OK when you're finished changing your document setup.**

The modifications are applied to the currently open document.

A Tour of the Workspace

Just like the other applications in the CS3 Suite, InDesign has a new standardized layout. Using panels that can be docked and a single row toolbar, you can keep much more space open in your work area.

The InDesign workspace, or user interface, is designed to be intuitive and efficient. You will use several panels over and over again, so it's a good idea to keep them accessible. Many of these panels are already docked off to the right in the default user workspace. Figure 2-2 shows how the InDesign workspace layout looks on a Macintosh. The Windows workspace is slightly different from the Macintosh version. You'll notice a difference in the main menu bar.

Here are the elements that create the InDesign workspace:

✦ **Page:** The main area of the InDesign workspace is called a page. A *page* is the area that is printed or exported when you're finished making a layout.

New single row toolbar   Menu bar   Panel Docking area

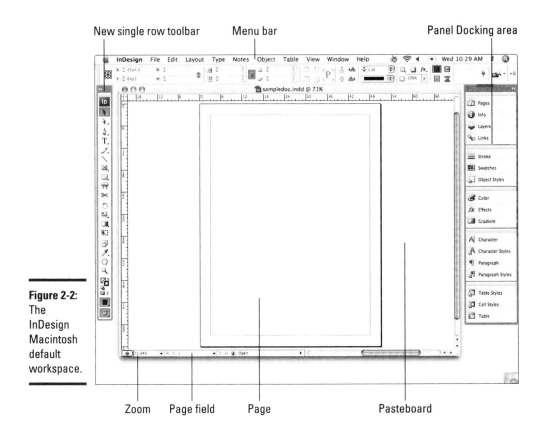

Figure 2-2:
The
InDesign
Macintosh
default
workspace.

Zoom   Page field   Page   Pasteboard

✦ **Master page:** You can define how certain text elements and graphics appear in an entire document (or just portions of it) by using a master page. A *master page* is a lot like a template for your document because you can reuse elements throughout the pages. For example, if you have an element you want on each page (such as page numbering), you can create it on the master page. If you need to change an element on the master page, you can change it at any time, and your changes are reflected on every page that the master page is applied to.

✦ **Spread:** A spread is referring to a set of two (or more) facing pages. You usually see spreads like these in magazines when you open them up and a design spreads across both pages.

✦ **Pasteboard:** The area around the page (and actually includes the page or spread as well) is called the pasteboard. You can use the pasteboard to store content until you're ready to lay it out on the page or spread you're working on. Pasteboards aren't shared between pages or spreads. For example, if you have certain elements placed on a pasteboard for pages 4 and 5, you can't access these elements when you're working on pages 8 and 9.

Tools

The toolbar (also called the Tools panel) is where you find tools to edit, manipulate, or select elements in your document. Simply use your cursor and click a tool to select it. See Figure 2-3 for the default toolbar layout.

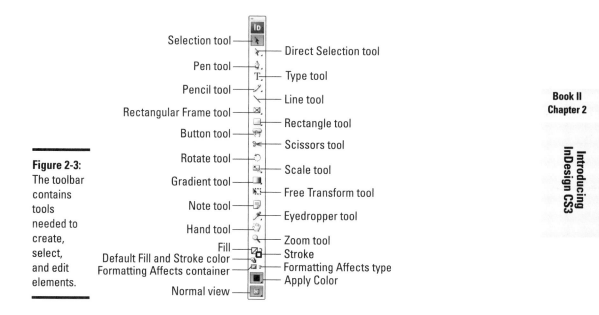

Figure 2-3: The toolbar contains tools needed to create, select, and edit elements.

Selection tool — Direct Selection tool
Pen tool — Type tool
Pencil tool — Line tool
Rectangular Frame tool — Rectangle tool
Button tool — Scissors tool
Rotate tool — Scale tool
Gradient tool — Free Transform tool
Note tool — Eyedropper tool
Hand tool — Zoom tool
Fill — Stroke
Default Fill and Stroke color
Formatting Affects container — Formatting Affects type
— Apply Color
Normal view

Book II Chapter 2

Introducing InDesign CS3

If you decide that a single row toolbar is just not for you, go back to the previous versions toolbar by clicking the gray bar at the top of the toolbar. If you want to relocate the toolbar, click the silver bar directly above the ID logo and drag to a new location.

You can find out more about these tools and how to use them in the related chapters of this minibook. For example, we discuss the drawing tools in Chapter 3 of this minibook.

Using the tools in the toolbar, you can

✦ **Create:** Create stunning new content on a page using drawing, frame, and text tools.

✦ **Select:** Select existing content on a page to move or edit.

✦ **View:** Move (pan) and magnify the page or spread.

✦ **Edit:** Edit existing objects, such as shapes, lines, and text. Use the Selection tool to select existing objects so that you can change them.

When a tool has a small arrow next to the button's icon, it means more tools are hiding behind it. When you click the tool and hold the mouse button down, a menu opens that shows you other available tools. Just move the mouse down this menu and release the button when the tool you want is highlighted.

Menus

The menus in the main menu bar are used to access some of the main commands and control the user interface of InDesign. They also allow you to open and close panels used to edit and make settings for the publication.

InDesign menu commands, such as New, Open, and Save, are similar to most other applications you're probably familiar with. The InDesign menus also include commands that are especially used for page layout, such as Insert With Placeholder Text. For more information on using menus, see Book I, Chapter 2. Remember to refer to the common commands and shortcuts that are also detailed in that chapter.

The InDesign main menu has the following options:

✦ **File:** This menu includes some of the basic commands to create, open, and save documents. It also includes the Place command to import new content and many options to control document settings, exporting documents, and printing.

✦ **Edit:** You can access many commands for editing and controlling selection in this menu — such as copying and keyboard shortcuts. The Dictionary and spell check are found in this menu, too.

✦ **Layout:** This menu allows you to create guides. These options help you lay elements on the page accurately and aligned. The menu also allows you to navigate through the document's pages and spreads.

✦ **Type:** This menu allows you to select fonts and control characters in the layout. You can access the many settings related to text in this menu, which opens up the associated panel where you make the changes.

✦ **Notes:** Collaborate with others better than ever before with the new Notes menu. Create, edit, and delete notes to others who are reviewing the InDesign document by using this menu.

✦ **Object:** You can modify the look and placement of objects on the page using this menu. What options are available in this menu depend on what you have selected in the workspace, such as a text field or an image.

✦ **Table:** This menu enables you to create, set up, modify, and control tables on the page.

✦ **View:** You can modify the view of the page from this menu, including zooming in and out, as well as work with guides, rulers, or grids to help you lay out elements.

✦ **Window:** Use this menu to open and close panels or switch between open documents.

✦ **Help:** This menu is where you can access the Help documents for InDesign and configure any plug-ins you have installed.

Panels

In the default layout, you see a large area for the document, typically referred to as the page. To the right of the page are several *panels* that snap (are *docked*) to the edge of the workspace. Panels are used to control the publication and edit elements on your pages. *Docked* panels are panels attached to the edge of the user interface. Panels can be maximized and minimized away from the main work area, moved around, or closed altogether.

To expand a panel, you can simply click the panel name, and it automatically expands. The magic of this new and improved panel system is that the panels you expand are automatically collapsed again when a different panel is selected.

If you'd rather work with all panels expanded, simply click the left-facing double-arrows in the gray bar above the panels. You can collapse all the panels again by clicking the right facing double-arrows in the gray bar above the expanded panels.

Even though some of the InDesign panels perform different functions, similar panels are grouped together depending on what they're used for. You can change the groupings by clicking and dragging a panel's tab into another grouping.

Some panels work intelligently when you're manipulating content on an InDesign page. If you work with a particular element, for example, the associated panel is activated. Throughout the later chapters of this minibook, you discover these specific panels as you create layouts. For now, we briefly show you two of the general InDesign panels: the Control panel and the Pages panel.

Control panel

The Control panel is used to edit just about any element in InDesign, as shown for the Type tool in Figure 2-4. This panel is *context sensitive,* so it changes depending on what you've selected on a page. For example, if you have text selected on the page, it displays options allowing you to edit the text. If you have a shape selected, then it displays options allowing you to modify the shape.

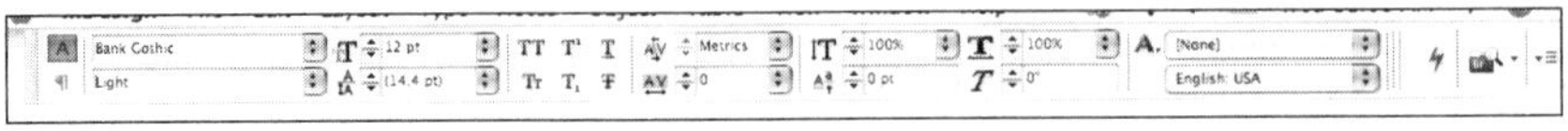

Figure 2-4:
The control panel as it appears when the Text tool is active.

The Control panel also has a toggle that enables you to toggle the current relevant panel between open and closed; Figure 2-5 shows the Control panel when a stroke is selected, the panel menu allows you to select specific stroke options.

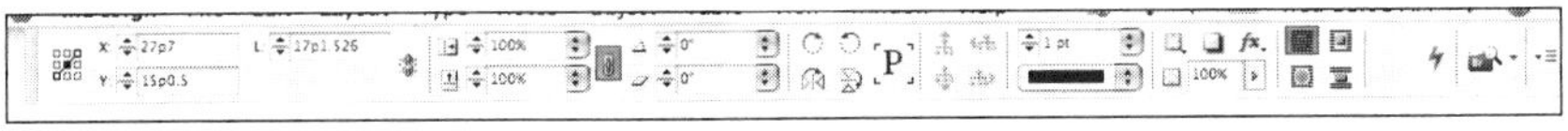

Figure 2-5:
The control panel as it appears when a stroke is active.

Pages panel

You can control pages by using the Pages panel, shown in Figure 2-6. This panel allows you to arrange, add, and delete pages in your document. You can also navigate between pages using this panel, which we discuss further in Chapter 5 of this minibook.

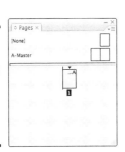

Figure 2-6:
Use the Pages panel to add, delete, and move pages.

You can hide all the panels that are open (including the control panel) by pressing the Tab key; press Tab for them to return to view. In InDesign CS3, you can leave the tools and palettes hidden and access them when you want by moving your cursor to the left or right side of the work area. Pause when you see a tinted vertical gray bar appear, and the tools or panels (depending upon which side of the workspace you are in) reappear! By the way, they go away again after you leave the area.

Page controls

You can also control which spread you see and the magnification of the pages by using a drop-down list at the bottom of the interface. Refer to Figure 2-4 to see where to access the page controls (the lower-left corner: Zoom and Page fields).

Book II
Chapter 2

You can navigate through the document's pages by using the left and right arrow buttons on either side of the page number. You can manually enter a value into the magnification text field and press Enter, or choose a preset value from the drop-down list.

Contextual menus

Contextual menus (or context menus) are menus that pop up when you right-click (Windows) or Ctrl-click (Mac) the mouse. Contextual menus change depending on what you click. If you don't have any elements selected, the contextual menu opens for the overall InDesign document, allowing you to select options such as Zoom, Paste, Rulers, and Guides. If you have an element selected, your options include transforming, modifying, or editing the object.

Contextual menus are context sensitive (hence the name!). Remember to select an element on the page before you right-click to open the contextual menu. If you don't select the object first, the menu is for the document instead of for the object.

You can find out more about editing and transforming elements in Chapters 3 and 4 of this minibook.

Setting Up the Workspace

Workspace settings are important to know about because they help you create quality page layouts. Overall document settings enable you to show grids or use guides that help you align elements on the page. Grids and guidelines are pretty much the same thing, except that grids are designed to repeat across the page and be a specified distance apart. Neither guides nor grids print when you print your document.

Introducing
InDesign CS3

Showing and hiding grids and guides

Use grids when you need to align elements to the overall document. Elements in your layout can snap to a grid, which can help you align several elements or accurately space objects apart from each other. Guides can be placed anywhere on the page (and pasteboard) and are used to accurately position objects in your layout. Guides are different from grids, which can't be freely placed just anywhere on the page. Objects can snap to guides just like they can snap to a grid.

The *document grid* is used for aligning elements on the page, and the *baseline grid* is used for aligning columns of text. To show the document grid, choose View⇨Grids & Guides⇨Show Document Grid; to show the baseline grid, choose View⇨Grids & Guides⇨Show Baseline Grid. You can immediately see the difference between these two kinds of grids. After you're done viewing grids, you can remove the grids by choosing View⇨Grids & Guides⇨Hide Document Grid or View⇨Grids & Guides⇨Hide Baseline Grid.

Figure 2-7 shows what grids look like on a page.

To snap objects to a guide or the document grid, you must have snapping enabled. To enable snapping, choose View⇨Grids & Guides⇨Snap to Guides or View⇨Grids & Guides⇨Snap to Document Grid.

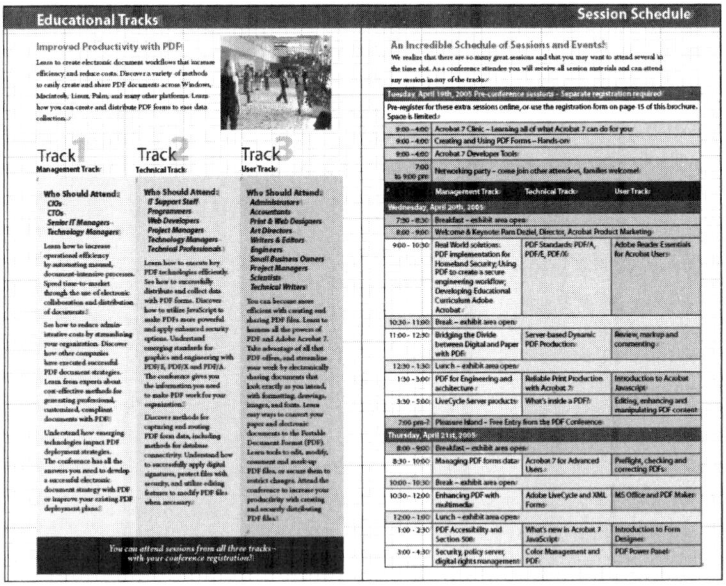

Figure 2-7:
A layout with the grids visible.

To create a guide and show or hide guides, follow these steps:

1. **Make sure that rulers are visible by choosing View⇨Show Rulers.**

Rulers appear in the workspace. If you already have rulers visible, the option View⇨Hide Rulers is in the View menu. Do not hide the rulers.

2. **Move the cursor to a horizontal or vertical ruler.**

Make sure that your cursor is over a ruler.

3. **Click the ruler and drag the mouse toward the page.**

A *ruler guide* shows on the page as a line.

4. **Release the mouse where you want the guide.**

You have just created a ruler guide!

5. **To hide the guide, choose View⇨Grids & Guides⇨Hide Guides.**

This step hides the guide you created, but it doesn't delete it. You can make the guide reappear easily in the next step.

6. **To see the guide again, choose View⇨Grids & Guides⇨Show Guides.**

The guide you created is shown on the page again.

You can find out more about the different kinds of guides and how to use them in page layout in Chapter 5 of this minibook.

You can control the color of the guides and grid in your preferences. Access the preferences by choosing Edit⇨Preferences⇨Grids (Windows) or InDesign⇨ Preferences⇨Grids (Mac OS). When the Preferences dialog box opens, you can change the color and spacing of the lines. Click Guides & Pasteboards in the list on the left to change the color settings for guides.

Snapping to a grid or guide

You can have elements on the page snap to a grid or a guide. Grid or guide snapping is very useful so that you don't have to try to eyeball the alignment of several elements to one another, because they're precisely aligned to a grid or guide. In fact, grids and guides are fairly useless unless you have elements snap to them! To make sure that this setting is enabled, choose View⇨ Grids & Guides⇨Snap To Document Grid or View⇨Grids & Guides⇨Snap To Guides.

You can view a print preview of your document by clicking the Preview Mode button at the very bottom of the toolbar. When you click this button, all the object bounding boxes, guides, and the grid disappear.

Saving a custom workspace

You can rearrange panels in InDesign in a particular order, layout, and quantity. You may never use particular panels that are open by default, or you may always use ones that are closed by default. Often times, you create a workspace that is just right for you, and you don't want to lose it after you shut down InDesign or your computer. Luckily, you can save your workspace so that when you return to InDesign, you can use the same workspace again.

To save a custom workspace, follow these steps:

1. **Have the InDesign workspace configured in the way you want to save it.**

   This workspace will be saved as a custom workspace.

2. **Choose Window⇨Workspace⇨Save Workspace.**

   The Save Workspace dialog box opens.

3. **Type a new name for the workspace into the Name text field.**

   When you finish, this name is displayed in the workspaces menu.

4. **Click the OK button.**

   The custom workspace is saved.

To access your workspace, choose Window⇨Workspace⇨Your Workspace (where *Your Workspace* is the name you gave the workspace in Step 3).

You can delete the workspace if you no longer want it saved. Simply choose Window⇨Workspace⇨Delete Workspace.

Working with Publications

After you're comfortable getting around the InDesign workspace, you're ready to begin working with a new document. After you have started working on a document, it's important to find out how to import content from other programs and to save that document on your hard drive. A lot of the content you work with in InDesign is imported from other programs. Then the content is organized, modified, and integrated into a layout using InDesign. To begin, we show you the steps needed to import content and save new files.

We show you how to open new and existing documents earlier in the chapter; refer to the sections, "Creating a new publication" and "Opening an existing publication."

You may also be working with templates. *Templates* are layouts that you reuse by applying them to a document that requires a particular pre-designed format. For example, a company may use a template for its official letterhead because every new letter requires the same page format and design. InDesign templates use the .indt file extension.

Importing new content

You can use many different kinds of content in an InDesign document because you can import many supported file types. InDesign enables you to import text, formatted tables, and graphics that help you create an effective layout. This ability makes integration with many different programs easy.

Follow these steps to import an image file into InDesign. (In this example, we import a bitmap graphic file.)

1. **Choose File↪New↪Document.**

The New Document dialog box appears.

2. **Review the settings and click the OK button.**

A new document opens. Feel free to alter the settings before clicking the OK button, if necessary. You may want to change the Number Of Pages setting or change the orientation of the pages, but it's not necessary to do so.

3. **Choose Edit↪Place.**

The Place dialog box opens, enabling you to browse the contents of your hard drive for supported files. If you select the Show Import Options check box, another dialog box opens before the file imports. Leave this option deselected for now.

4. **Click the file you want to import and then click the Open button.**

Certain files, such as bitmap photo and graphic files and PDFs, show a thumbnail preview at the bottom of the dialog box.

When you click the Open button, the Place dialog box closes, and your cursor becomes an upside-down L.

5. **Click the page where you want the upper-left corner of the imported file (in this case, an image) to appear.**

The image is placed on the page.

In Designs CS3, you can Ctrl+click (windows) or ⌘+click (Mac OS) to place multiple files. After you select the images and click OK, each click places an image on the page. You even see a thumbnail of the image before it's placed and can scroll through the loaded images using the arrow keys.

For general information on importing and exporting in the Adobe Creative Suite, check out Book I, Chapter 5. For more information on importing different kinds of file formats, such as text, images, and PDFs, refer to Chapters 4 and 5 in this minibook.

You can also import different kinds of file formats, such as text and Excel tables.

Viewing content

You can view elements in several different ways on your document's pages. Sometimes you need to see your drawings and images close up so that you can make precise edits, or you need to move the page around to see something that may extend past the workspace. InDesign offers the following ways to navigate your documents:

+ **Scroll bars:** You can use the scroll bars to move the pages around. The scroll bars are located below and to the right of the pasteboard. Click a scroll bar handle and drag it left and right or up and down.

+ **Zoom:** Zoom in or out from the document to increase or decrease the display of your document. Select the Zoom tool (the magnifying glass icon) from the toolbar and click anywhere on the page to zoom in. Press Alt (Windows) or Option (Mac) and click to zoom out.

+ **Hand tool:** Use the Hand tool to move the page around. This tool is perhaps the best and quickest way to move your pages around and navigate the document. Select the Hand tool by pressing the Spacebar and then click and drag to move around the pasteboard.

Saving your publication

Even the best computers and applications fail from time to time, so you don't want to lose your hard work unnecessarily. Saving your publication often is important so that you don't lose any work if your computer or software crashes, or the power goes out.

To save a file, choose File⇨Save or press Ctrl+S (Windows) or ⌘+S (Mac).

Some people save different versions of their files. You may want to do this in case you want to revert back to an earlier version of the file. For example, you may decide to make a radical change to your page layout, but you want to keep an earlier version in case the radical change just doesn't work out.

Remember to choose File⇨Save before proceeding if you want the current document to save the revisions you've made since you last saved the file. All new additions to the document will be made in the new version of the file.

To save a new version of the current document and then continue working on the new document, follow these steps:

1. **Choose File⇨Save As.**

The Save As dialog box opens.

2. **Choose the directory you want to save the file in.**

3. **In the File Name text field, enter a new name for the document.**

This step saves a new version of the file. Consider a naming scheme at this point. If your file is called myLayout.indd, you might call it myLayout02.indd to signify the second version of the file. Future files can then increase the number for each new version.

4. **Click the Save button when you're finished.**

This step saves the document in the chosen directory with a new name.

The File⇨Save As command is also used for other means. You may want to save your design as a template. After you create the template, choose File⇨Save As and then choose InDesign CS3 template from the Save As Type (Windows) or Format (Mac) drop-down list.

You can also choose File⇨Save a Copy. This command saves a copy of the current state of the document you're working on with a new name, but you then continue working on the original document. Both commands are very useful for saving incremental versions of a project that you're working on.

To find out more about working with files, go to Chapter 8 of this minibook.

**Book II
Chapter 2**

Introducing
InDesign CS3

Chapter 3: Drawing in InDesign

In This Chapter

- ✔ Discovering the drawing tools
- ✔ Drawing and editing shapes and paths
- ✔ Introducing corner effects
- ✔ Working with fills and layers

*M*any of the tools that you find in the InDesign toolbar are used for drawing lines and shapes on a page. This means you have several different ways of creating interesting drawings for your publications. You can create anything from basic shapes to intricate drawings inside InDesign, instead of having to use a drawing program like Illustrator. Even though InDesign doesn't replace Illustrator (see Book III), which has many more versatile drawing tools and options for creating intricate drawings, InDesign is adequate for simple drawing tasks. In this chapter, you discover how to use the most popular InDesign drawing tools and also how to add colorful fills to your illustrations.

Getting Started with Drawing

When you're creating a document, you may want drawn shapes and paths to be a part of the layout. For example, you may want to have a star shape for a yearbook page about a talent show or run text along a path. Whatever it is you need to do, you can draw shapes and paths to get the job done.

Paths and shapes

Paths can take a few different formats. They can either be open or closed, with or without a stroke:

- ✦ **Path:** The outline of a shape or object. Paths can be closed and have no gaps, or they can be open like a line on the page. You can draw freeform paths, such as squiggles on a page, freely by hand.

- ✦ **Stroke:** A line style and thickness that you apply to a path. A stroke can look like a line or like an outline of a shape.

Figure 3-1 shows the different kinds of paths and strokes that you can create.

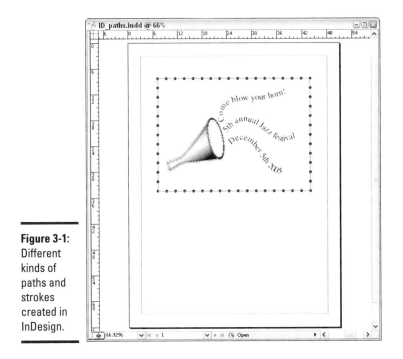

Figure 3-1:
Different
kinds of
paths and
strokes
created in
InDesign.

Paths contain points where the direction of the path can change. (You can find out more about points in the following section, "Points and segments.") You can make paths by using freeform drawing tools, such as the Pen or Pencil tools, or by using the basic shape tools, such as the Ellipse, Rectangle, Polygon, or Line tools.

The shape tools create paths in a predefined way so that you can make basic geometric shapes, such as a star or ellipse. All you need to do is select the shape tool, drag the cursor on the page, and the shape is automatically drawn. Creating shapes this way is a lot easier than trying to manually create them using the Pen or Pencil tool! See Figure 3-2 for shapes drawn using the shape tools found in the toolbar.

You can change shapes into freeform paths, like those drawn using the Pencil or Pen tools. Similarly, you can make freeform paths into basic shapes. Therefore, you don't need to worry about which tool you initially choose.

We created the stars and starburst shown in Figure 3-2 by double-clicking the Polygon tool and changing the options. Read more about the Polygon tool in the "Drawing Shapes" section of this chapter.

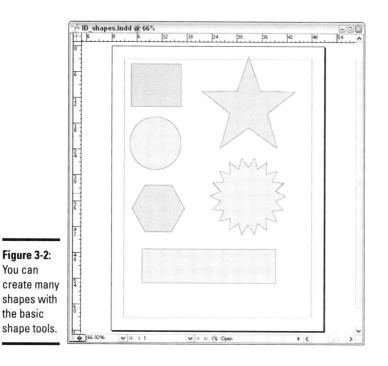

Figure 3-2:
You can
create many
shapes with
the basic
shape tools.

Points and segments

Paths are made up of points and segments:

✦ **Point:** Where the path changes somehow, such as changing direction.
There can be many points along a path that are joined with segments.
Points are sometimes called *anchor points*. You can create two kinds of
points:

- **Corner points:** These points have a straight line between them.
Shapes like squares or stars have corner points.

- **Curve points:** These points are along a curved path. Circles or
snaking paths have lots of curve points.

✦ **Segment:** A line or curve connecting two points — kind of like connect
the dots!

Figure 3-3 shows corner points and curve points joined together by
segments.

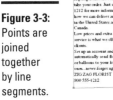

Figure 3-3:
Points are
joined
together
by line
segments.

Getting to Know the Tools of the Trade

This section introduces you to tools that you'll probably use the most when creating drawings in your publications. When you draw with these tools, you're using strokes and fills to make designs. This section shows you what these common tools can do to help you create basic or complex illustrations in InDesign.

The Pencil tool

The Pencil tool is used to draw simple or complex shapes on a page. Because the pencil is a freeform tool, you can freely drag the Pencil tool all over the page and create lines or shapes, instead of having them automatically made for you like when you use basic shape tools. The pencil is a very intuitive and easy tool to use. You find out how to use the pencil tool in the section "Drawing Freeform Paths," later in this chapter.

The Pen tool

The Pen tool is used to create complex shapes on the page. The Pen tool works together with other tools, such as the Add, Remove, and Convert Point tools. The pen works by adding and editing points along a path, thereby manipulating the segments that join them.

Drawing with the Pen tool isn't easy at first. In fact, it takes many people a considerable amount of time to use this tool well. Don't get frustrated if you don't get used to it right away — the Pen tool can take some practice in order to get it to do what you want it to. You find out how to use the Pen tool in the "Drawing Freeform Paths" section, later in this chapter.

Basic shapes and frame shapes

Basic shapes are preformed shapes that you can add to a document by using tools in the toolbar. The basic shape tools include the Line, Rectangle, Ellipse, and Polygon tools.

You can also draw these shapes and turn them into *frames* (containers that hold content in your document) if you want. You can use a frame as a text frame or as a graphic frame that is used to hold pictures and text. Draw a basic shape and then convert the shape to a graphic or text frame by choosing Object⇨Content⇨Text or Object⇨Content⇨Graphic. We discuss graphic and text frames in more detail in Chapters 3 and 4 of this minibook.

The Frame and Shape tools look the same and can even act the same. Both can hold text and images, but look out! By default, shapes created with the Frame tool have a 1-pt black stroke around them. Many folks don't see this on the screen but later discover that they have strokes around their text boxes when they print. Stick with the shape tools, and you'll be fine.

Drawing Shapes

InDesign allows you to create basic shapes in your document. You can easily create a basic shape by following these steps:

1. **Create a new document by choosing File⇨New.**

2. **When the New Document dialog box appears, click the OK button.**

A new document opens.

3. **Select the Rectangle tool in the toolbar.**

4. **Click anywhere in the page and drag the mouse diagonally.**

When the rectangle is the desired dimension, release the mouse button. You've created a rectangle.

That's all you need to do to create a basic shape. You can also use these steps with the other basic shape tools (the Line, Ellipse, and Polygon tools) to create other basic shapes. To access the other basic shapes from the toolbar, follow these steps:

1. **Click the Rectangle tool and hold down the mouse button.**

A menu with all the basic shapes opens.

2. **Release the mouse button.**

The menu remains open, and you can mouse over the menu items. The menu items become highlighted when the mouse pointer is over each item.

3. **Select a basic shape tool by clicking a highlighted menu item.**

The new basic shape tool is now active. Follow the preceding set of steps to create basic shapes using any of these tools.

To draw a square shape, use the Rectangle tool and press the Shift key while you drag the mouse on the page. The sides of the shape are all drawn at the same length, so you get a perfect square. You can also use the Shift key with the Ellipse tool if you want a perfect circle — just hold down Shift while you're using the Ellipse tool. Make sure that you release your mouse before the Shift key for this constrain shape trick to work!

Creating a shape with exact dimensions

Dragging on the page to create a shape is easy, but making a shape with precise dimensions using this method requires a few more steps. If you want to make a shape that's a specific size, follow these steps:

1. **Select the Rectangle tool or the Ellipse tool.**

The tool is highlighted in the toolbar.

2. **Click anywhere on the page, but don't drag the cursor.**

This point becomes the upper-right corner of your Rectangle or Ellipse *bounding box* (the rectangle that defines the object's vertical and horizontal dimensions). After you click to place your corner, the Rectangle or Ellipse dialog box appears.

3. **In the Width and Height text fields, enter the dimensions you want the shape to be created at.**

4. **Click OK.**

The shape is created on the page, with the upper-right corner at the place where you initially clicked on the page.

Using the Polygon tool

A polygon is a shape that has many sides. For example, a square is a polygon with four sides, but the Polygon tool enables you to choose the number of sides you want for the polygon you create. When you're using the Polygon tool, you may not want to create a shape with the default number of sides. You can change these settings before you start drawing the shape.

To customize the shape of a polygon, follow these steps:

1. **Select the Polygon tool in the toolbar by selecting the Rectangle tool and holding down the mouse button until the menu pops up.**

2. **Double-click the Polygon tool in the toolbar.**

The Polygon dialog box opens.

3. **In the Number Of Sides text field, enter the number of sides you want the new polygon to have.**

4. **If you want to create a star instead of a polygon, enter a number in the Star Inset text field for the percentage of the star inset you want the new shape to have.**

A higher percentage means the sides will be inset further toward the center of the polygon, creating a star. If you want a regular polygon and not a star, enter 0 in the Star Inset text field. If you want a star, enter 50%, a starburst with about 25%.

5. **Click OK.**

6. **Move your cursor to the page and click and drag to create a new polygon or star.**

Your new polygon or star appears on the page.

Figure 3-4 shows what a few different polygons and stars with different settings look like.

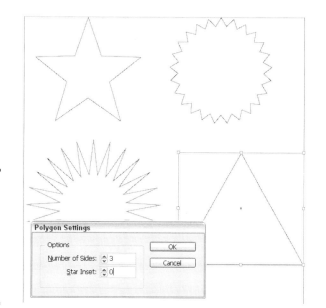

Figure 3-4:
Change the star inset percentage to create different kinds of shapes.

Editing Basic Shapes

You can edit basic shapes using several panels in InDesign. This means you can create original shapes and craft exactly the kind of design you require in your page layout. You aren't stuck with the predetermined shapes, such as a square or oval: You can make these forms take on much more complicated or original shapes.

You can edit basic shapes in InDesign in only a few ways. You can edit shapes and manipulate their appearance in other ways. We cover some of these ways, such as editing fills, in the section "Using Fills."

Changing the size using the Transform panel

You can change the size of a shape by using the Transform panel. Here's how:

1. **With the Selection tool (the tool that's used to select objects), select the shape that you want to resize.**

When the shape is selected, a bounding box appears around it. You can see a selected shape in Figure 3-5.

Bounding box

Selected object

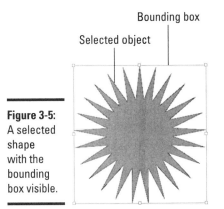

Figure 3-5:
A selected shape with the bounding box visible.

2. **Open the Transform panel by choosing Window⇨Object And Layout⇨ Transform.**

3. **In the Transform panel that appears, enter different number values in the W and H fields to change the size of the shape.**

The shape changes size on the page automatically to the new size dimensions that you specify in the Transform panel.

Changing the stroke of a shape

You can change the stroke of shapes you've created. The stroke is the out-line that appears around the edge of the shape. The stroke can range from no stroke to a very thick stroke, and it's measured in point sizes. Even if a shape has a stroke set to 0 points, it still has a stroke! You just can't see the stroke.

Follow these steps to edit the stroke of your shapes:

1. **Select a shape on the page.**

A bounding box appears around the selected shape.

2. **Select a new width for the Stroke using the stroke weight drop-down list on the control panel.**

As soon as a value is selected, the stroke automatically changes on the page. This number is measured in points. You use some of the other options in the following exercise.

You can click in the Stroke text field and manually enter a numerical value for the Stroke width. The higher the number you enter, the thicker the stroke. You can also change the style of the stroke with the Stroke panel by following these steps:

**Book II
Chapter 3**

1. **With a basic shape selected, select the stroke type from the drop-down list on the control panel and select a new line.**

As soon as a value is selected, the stroke automatically changes.

2. **Choose a new line weight from the Weight drop-down list.**

We chose 10 points. The shape automatically updates on the page.

Want to create custom dashes? See more options by choosing Window⇨ Stroke panel. Select a dashed stroke and notice at the bottom of the Stroke panel that you can define the dash and gap size. Enter one value for an even dash, or several numbers for custom dashes for maps diagrams, fold marks, and more!

Add special ends to the lines using the Start and End drop-down lists. For example, you can add an arrowhead or large circle to the beginning or end of the stroke. The Cap and Join buttons allow you to choose the shape of the line ends, and how they join with other paths when you're working with complex paths or shapes. For more information on creating and editing lines and strokes, see Book I, Chapter 6.

Changing the shear value

You can change the shear of a shape by using the Transform panel. Skew and *shear* are the same thing — it means that the shape is slanted, so you create the appearance of some form of perspective for the skewed or sheared element. This transformation is useful if you want to create the illusion of depth on the page.

Follow these simple steps to skew a shape:

1. **With a basic shape selected, choose Window⇨Object and Layout⇨ Transform.**

2. **Select a value from the Shear drop-down list in the lower-right corner of the Transform panel.**

   After selecting a new value, the shape skews (or shears), depending on what value you select. Manually entering a numerical value into this field also skews the shape.

Rotating a shape

You can change the rotation of a shape by using the Transform panel. The process of rotating a shape is very similar to how you skew a shape (see the preceding section):

1. **With a basic shape selected, choose Window⇨Object And Layout⇨ Transform.**

   The Transform panel opens.

2. **Select a value from the Rotation drop-down list.**

   After selecting a new value, the shape automatically rotates, based on the rotation angle you specified. You can also manually enter a value into the text field.

Drawing Freeform Paths

You can use different tools to draw paths. For example, you can use the Pencil tool to draw freeform paths. These kinds of paths typically look like lines, and you can use the Pencil and Pen tools to create simple or complex paths.

Using the Pencil tool

The Pencil tool is perhaps the easiest tool to use when drawing freeform paths (see Figure 3-6). Follow these steps to get started:

1. **Create a new document by choosing File⇨New and clicking OK in the New Document dialog box that appears.**

2. **Select the Pencil tool in the toolbar.**

3. **Drag the cursor around the page.**

   You have created a new path by using the Pencil tool.

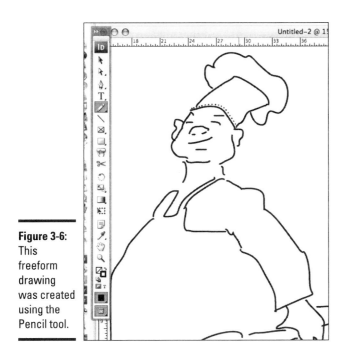

Figure 3-6:
This freeform drawing was created using the Pencil tool.

Using the Pen tool

Using the Pen tool is different from using the Pencil tool. When you start out, the Pen tool may seem a bit complicated — but after you get the hang of it, using the Pen tool isn't too hard after all. The Pen tool uses points to create a particular path. You can edit these points in order to change the segments between them. Getting control of these points can take a bit of practice.

To create points and segments on a page, follow these steps:

1. **Close any existing documents and create a new document by choosing File⇨New Document.**

2. **Click OK in the New Document dialog box that appears.**

   A new document opens using the default settings.

3. **Select the Pen tool in the toolbar.**

4. **Click anywhere on the page and then click a second location.**

   You've created a new path with two points and one segment joining them.

5. **Ctrl-click (Windows) or ⌘-click (Mac) on an empty part of the Page to deselect the current path.**

After you deselect the path, you can create a new path or add new points to the path you just created.

6. Add a new point to a selected segment by hovering over the line and clicking.

A small + icon appears next to the Pen tool's cursor. You can also do the same thing by selecting the Add Anchor Point tool (located in the menu that flies out when you click and hold the Pen icon in the toolbar).

7. Repeat Step 6, but this time click a new location on a line segment and drag away from the line.

This creates a curved path. The segments change and curve depending on where the points are located along the path. The point you created is called a curve point.

Editing Freeform Paths

Even the best artists sometimes need to make changes or delete parts of their work. If you've made mistakes or change your mind about a drawing, follow the steps in this section to make your changes.

In order to change a path segment, you need to select a point with the Direct Selection tool (upper-right of the toolbar). When a point is selected, it appears solid; unselected points appear hollow.

All you need to do to select a point is use your cursor to click the point itself. Then you can use the handles that appear when the point is selected to modify the segments as follows:

1. Select the Direct Selection tool from the toolbar and then click a point.

The selected point appears solid and, if a curve, may have handles extending from it.

2. Select a handle end and drag the handle left or right.

The path changes, depending on how you drag the handles.

A curved point and a corner point edit differently when you select and drag them. Curve points have handles that extend from the point, but corner points don't. However, you can edit a corner point without needing handles by dragging it in any direction.

To understand how the Convert Point tool works the best, you should have a path that contains both straight and curved segments. Follow these steps to change a corner point into a curved point and vice versa:

1. Select the Convert Direction Point tool.

This tool resides in a menu under the Pen tool in the toolbar. Hold the mouse button down over the Pen tool icon until a menu appears; select the Convert Direction Point tool from the menu.

2. Click a curved point with the Convert Direction Point tool.

The point you click changes into a corner point, which changes the path's appearance.

3. Click and drag a corner point with the Convert Direction Point tool.

The point is modified as a curved point. This changes the appearance of the path again.

This tool is handy when you need to alter the way your path changes direction. If you need to manipulate a point in a different way, you may need to change its type by using the Convert Direction Point tool.

Making Corner Effects

You can use corner effects on basic shapes to customize the shape's look. Corner effects are great for adding an interesting look to borders. You can be very creative with some of the shapes you apply effects to or by applying more than one effect to a single shape. Here's how to create a corner effect on a rectangle:

1. Select the Rectangle tool and create a new rectangle anywhere on the page.

Hold the Shift key when using the Rectangle tool if you want to create a square.

2. With the Selection tool, select the shape and then choose Object⇨ Corner Options.

The Corner Options dialog box opens.

3. Choose an effect from the Effects drop-down list and enter a value into the Size text field.

4. Click OK.

The corner effect is applied to the shape.

Using Fills

A fill is located inside a path. You can fill your paths and shapes with several different kinds of colors, transparent colors, or even gradients. Fills can help you achieve artistic effects and illusions of depth or add interest to a page design.

You may have already created a fill. The toolbar contains two swatches: one for the stroke (a hollow square) and one for fill (a solid box). (Refer to Figure Chapter 2 of this minibook to locate the Fill and Stroke boxes.) If the Fill box contains a color, your shape will have a fill when it's created. If the Fill box has a red line through it, the shape is created without a fill.

Creating basic fills

You can create a basic fill in several different ways. One of the most common ways is to specify a color in the Fill swatch before you create a new shape. To create a shape with a fill, follow these steps:

1. **Make sure the Fill box is selected so that you aren't adding color to the stroke instead.**

2. **Open the Color panel by choosing Window⇨Color.**

3. **Select a color in the Color panel.**

You can enter values into the CMYK fields manually or by using the sliders. Alternatively, you can use the Eyedropper tool to select a color from the color ramp at the bottom of the Color panel. For more information on color modes (such as CMYK and RGB color modes), refer to Book I, Chapter 7.

Use the Color panel menu to select different color modes if CMYK isn't already selected. Click and hold the arrow button and select CMYK from the Color panel menu.

The Fill box in the toolbar is updated with the new color you have selected in the Color panel.

4. **Create a new shape on the page.**

Select a shape tool and drag on the page to create a shape. The shape is filled with the fill color you chose.

As in the other Creative Suite 3 applications, you can create tints of a color built with CMYK by holding down the Shift key while dragging any color's slider. All color sliders will then move proportionally.

You can also choose to use color swatches to select a fill color by using the Swatches panel (choose Window⇨Swatches to open the Swatches panel).

Create a new color swatch (of your present color) by clicking the New Swatch button at the bottom of the panel. Double-click the new swatch to add new color properties by using sliders to set CMYK color values or by entering numbers into each text field.

Perhaps you already have a shape without a fill, and you want to add a fill to it. Select the shape and with the Fill box in the toolbar selected, select a color from the Color or Swatches panel. A new fill color is applied to the shape.

You can drag and drop a swatch color to fill a shape on a page, even if that shape isn't selected. Open the Swatches panel by choosing Window➪ Swatches and then drag the color swatch over to the shape. Release the mouse button, and the fill color is automatically applied to the shape.

Making transparent fills

Fills that are partially transparent can create some very interesting effects for the layout of your document. You can set transparency to more than one element on the page and layer those elements to create the illusion of depth and stacking.

Follow these steps to apply transparency to an element on the page:

1. **With the Selection tool, select a shape on the page.**

A bounding box appears around the selected shape.

2. **Open the Effects panel by choosing Window➪Effects.**

3. **Use the Opacity slider to change how transparent the shape appears.**

Click the arrow to open the slider, or click in the text field to manually enter a value using the keyboard. The effect is immediately applied to the selected shape.

4. **Select Stroke or fill in the Effects panel to apply a separate opacity to each.**

Looking at gradients

A *gradient* is the color transition from one color (or no color) to a different color. It can have two or more colors in the transition.

Gradients can add interesting effects to shapes, including 3D effects. Sometimes you can use a gradient to achieve glowing effects or the effect of light hitting a surface. The two kinds of gradients available in InDesign are radial and linear, as shown in Figure 3-7:

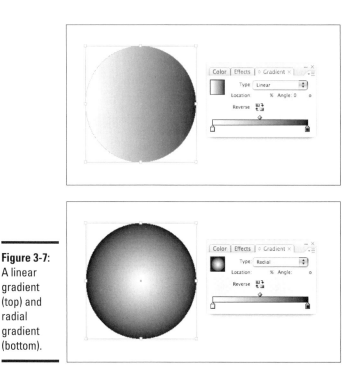

Figure 3-7:
A linear
gradient
(top) and
radial
gradient
(bottom).

✦ **Radial:** A transition of colors in a circular fashion from a center point radiating outwards.

✦ **Linear:** A transition of colors along a straight path.

You can apply a gradient to a stroke a fill or even text. To apply a gradient to a stroke, simply select the stroke instead of the fill. Even though you can apply a gradient to the stroke of live text, you'll create a printing nightmare . . . use these features sparingly!

Here's how to add a gradient fill to a shape:

1. **Using the Selection tool, select the object that you want to apply a gradient to and then choose Window⇨Swatches.**

The Swatches panel opens.

2. **Choose New Gradient Swatch from the Swatches panel menu.**

The New Gradient Swatch dialog box opens (see Figure 3-8).

3. **Type a new name for the swatch into the Swatch Name field.**

Sometimes giving the swatch a descriptive name, such as what the swatch is being used for, is helpful.

```
                    New Gradient Swatch
    Swatch Name: New Gradient Swatch              ⬭ OK ⬭
           Type: Radial            ⬍              ( Cancel )
      Stop Color:                  ⬍              (  Add   )
    ┌──────────┐
    │          │   Cyan    ─────────────○──  %
    │          │  Magenta  ─────────────○──  %
    │          │   Yellow  ─────────────○──  %
    └──────────┘   Black   ─────────────○──  %

    Gradient Ramp  ▭━━━━━━━◇━━━━━━━━▮
                    △
                    Location:       %
```

Figure 3-8:
The New
Gradient
Swatch
dialog box.

4. **Choose Linear or Radial from the Type drop-down list.**

   This option determines the type of gradient the swatch will create each time you use it. We chose Radial from the drop-down list.

5. **Manipulate the gradient stops below the Gradient Ramp to position each color in the gradient.**

   Gradient stops are the color chips located below the Gradient Ramp. You can move the diamond shape above the Gradient Ramp to determine the center point of the gradient. You can select each gradient stop to change the color and move them around to edit the gradient. When the gradient stops are selected, you can change the color values in the Stop Color area by using sliders or by entering values in each CMYK text field.

   You can add a new color to the gradient by clicking the area between the gradient stops. Then you can edit the new stop just like the others. To remove the gradient stop, drag the stop away from the Gradient Ramp.

6. **Click OK when you're finished.**

   The gradient swatch is created and applied to the selected object.

To edit a gradient, double-click the gradient's swatch. This step opens the Gradient Options dialog box, which allows you to modify the settings made in the New Gradient Swatch dialog box.

Removing fills

Removing fills is even easier than creating them:

1. **Select the shape using the Selection tool.**

   A bounding box appears around the shape.

2. **Click the Fill box in the toolbar.**

3. **Click the Apply None button located below the Fill box.**

   This button is white with a red line through it. The fill is removed from the selected shape, and the Fill box is changed to no fill. You will also see the None fill on the Swatches and Color panels.

   If you're using a single row toolbar, you won't see the Apply None button unless you click and hold down on the Apply Gradient (or Color) button because the button is hidden beneath it.

Adding Layers

Layers are like transparent sheets that are stacked on top of one another. If you add layers to your drawings, you can create the appearance that graphics are stacked on top of one another. The Layers panel allows you to create new layers, delete layers you don't need, or even rearrange them to change the stacking order. Here's how you work with layers in InDesign:

1. **Open the Layers panel by choosing Window⇨Layers.**

   This panel allows you to create, delete, and arrange layers.

2. **Draw a shape on the page using a shape tool.**

   Create the shape anywhere on the page. Create it large enough so that you can easily stack another shape on top of part of it.

3. **Create a new layer by clicking the Create New Layer button in the Layers panel.**

   A new layer is stacked on top of the currently selected layer and becomes the active layer.

   Double-click a layer to give it an appropriate name, or even better yet, hold down the Alt (Windows) or Option (Mac OS) key and click the New Layer button to bring up the Layer options dialog box before the layer is created.

   Make sure that the layer you want to create content on is selected before you start modifying the layer. You can tell what layer is selected because the selected layer is always highlighted in the Layers panel. You can easily accidentally add content to the incorrect layer if you don't check this panel frequently. (If you add an item to the wrong layer, you can always cut and paste items to the correct layer.)

4. **Make sure a shape tool is still selected and then create a shape on the new layer by dragging the cursor so that part of the new shape covers the shape you created in Step 2.**

   The new shape is stacked on top of the shape you created earlier.

Chapter 4: Working with Text and Text Frames

In This Chapter

✔ Understanding text and frames in a publication

✔ Adding and importing text

✔ Exploring text frame options

✔ Modifying text frames

✔ Changing paragraph settings

✔ Editing with text editors and spell checking

✔ Working with tables

✔ Creating and editing text on a path

*M*ost of your publications will contain text, so knowing how to use and modify text are very important in InDesign. Text is made up of characters, and the characters are styled in a particular font. (If you're wondering about fonts, check out Book I, Chapter 6, where we explain more about fonts and font faces.)

This chapter explains how InDesign uses text in publications and gets you started editing and manipulating text in *text frames* — containers on the page that hold text content. The most important things you can take away from this chapter are how to add text to your publication and then change the text so that it looks how you want it to look when laid out on the page. In Chapter 5 of this minibook, you find out how to create effective layouts that contain both text and graphics so that your audience will be encouraged to read everything you have to say!

Understanding Text, Font, and Frames

Text is usually integral to a publication because it contains specific information you want or need to convey to an audience. Understanding some of the terminology that appears in the following pages is important: *Text* and *font* refer to similar things, although they're quite different from each other in the specifics:

✦ **Text:** The letters, words, sentences, and/or paragraphs making up content within the text frames in your publication.

✦ **Font:** The particular design forming a set of characters used for text. You can find thousands of styles of fonts to choose from and install on your computer for your use.

Frames are like containers that are used to hold content. You can use the following two kinds of frames together in a publication:

✦ **Text frame:** Contains text in a publication. You can link text frames so that text flows from one text frame to another, and you can have text wrap around graphic frames.

✦ **Graphic frame:** A graphic frame holds an image that you place into your publication.

The nice thing about shapes and frames is that they automatically change to adapt to the content that is placed in them! You can use both the Frame and Shape tools for text and graphics.

Creating and Using Text Frames

Text frames contain any text that you add to a publication. You can create a new text frame in many different ways. InDesign also allows you to add text to creative shapes that you draw, thereby changing them into text frames. Creating and using text frames in your publication is important because you'll typically use a lot of text. Throughout this section, we show you how to create text frames in different but important ways using three different tools. (If you need a refresher on the InDesign tools, check out Chapter 2 of this minibook.)

Text frames are sometimes automatically created when you import text into a publication. You find out how to do this in the "Importing text" section, later in this chapter.

Creating text frames with the Type tool

You can use the Type tool to create a text frame. If you take the Type tool and click the page, nothing happens unless you've first created a frame to put text in. Here's how to create a text frame using the Type tool:

1. **Select the Type tool in the toolbox and place it over the page.**

The Type tool cursor appears, as shown in Figure 4-1. The cursor is an I-bar. Move the cursor to where you want the upper-left corner of your text frame to be.

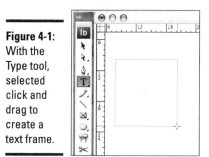

Figure 4-1:
With the
Type tool,
selected
click and
drag to
create a
text frame.

2. **Drag diagonally to create a text frame.**

When you click, the mouse has a cross-like appearance. When you drag, an outline of the text frame appears, giving you a reference to its dimensions (refer to Figure 4-1).

3. **Release the mouse button when the frame is the correct size.**

The text frame is created, and an insertion point is placed in the upper-left corner of the frame. You can start typing on the keyboard to enter text or import text from another source. (We cover this process in the later section appropriately named "Importing text.")

Creating text frames with the Frame tool

You can use the Frame tool to create frames that are rectangular, oval, or polygonal. Then, after you've placed the frame on the page, you can turn it into a text frame or back into a graphic frame. To create a new text frame with the Frame tool, follow these steps:

1. **Choose the Frame tool from the toolbox and drag diagonally to create a new frame.**

A new frame is created on the page.

2. **Select the Type tool and click inside of the frame.**

The X across the frame disappears, and the frame is now a text frame instead of a graphic frame.

An insertion point appears in the upper-left corner of the text frame. If you start typing, the frame fills with text.

3. **Choose the Selection tool and use it to move the text frame.**

You can move the text frame to a new location if you click within the frame using the Selection tool and drag it to a new location. An outline of the frame moves with the cursor, as shown in Figure 4-2, so that you can see where the text frame is placed when you release the mouse button.

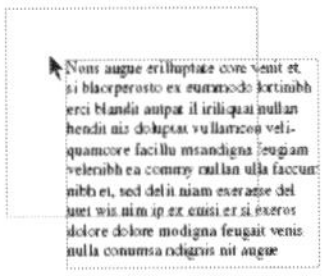

Figure 4-2:
An outline
of the text
frame shows
where you're
moving the
frame.

Creating text frames from a shape

If you have an interesting shape that you've created with the drawing tools that we discuss in Chapter 3 of this minibook, you can easily change that shape into a text frame. You can then add text within the shape. Just follow these steps:

1. **With the Pen, Pencil, or a shape tool, create a shape with a stroke color and no fill.**

   A shape is created on the page that doesn't have a solid color for the fill. We used the Pencil tool to create a freeform shape for this example.

2. **Select the Type tool from the toolbox.**

   The Type tool becomes active.

3. **Click within the shape you created in Step 1 and enter some text.**

   This changes the shape into a text frame that you can enter text into. Notice how the text is confined within the shape as you type.

Adding Text to Your Publication

In the previous section's step lists, we show you how to add text simply by clicking in the text frame and typing new content. You can add text to your publications in other ways, which is particularly useful when you use other applications to edit documents containing text.

Importing text

In the previous section, we show you how to enter text directly into a text frame in InDesign. You can also import text that you have created and/or edited using other software, such as Microsoft Word, Microsoft Excel, or Adobe InCopy (used for word processing). Importing externally edited text is a typical workflow when creating a publication, as dedicated text editing software is frequently used to edit manuscripts before they go to layout.

To import text into InDesign, follow these steps:

1. Choose File⇨Place.

The Place dialog box opens. Choose an importable file (such as a Word document, InCopy story, or a plain text file) by browsing through your hard drive.

2. Select a document to import and click the Open button.

The Place Text icon, the cursor arrow, and a thumbnail of your text appear. Move the cursor around the page to where you want the upper-left corner of the text frame to be created when the document is imported.

3. Click to place the imported text.

This step creates a text frame and imports the story into InDesign.

If you select a text frame *before* importing text, the text is automatically placed inside the text frame — so, in this case, you wouldn't have to use the cursor to place the text. You can move the text frame anywhere on the page after the text is added, or resize the frame, if necessary.

Controlling text flow

Control the flow of the text by using these simple modifier keys while placing text:

✦ Choose File⇨Place, select the text you want to import, and click OK. Hold down the Shift key when clicking to place the text. The text is imported and automatically flows from column to column or page to page until it runs out. InDesign even creates the pages for you if you don't have enough ready.

✦ Choose File⇨Place, select the text you want to import, and click OK. Hold down the Alt (Windows) or Option (Mac OS) key. Then click and drag a text area. (Don't let go of that Alt or Option key!) You can continue clicking and dragging additional text frames, and your text will flow from one text frame to another until you run out of copy!

If you check Show Import Options in the Place window, a second window appears in which you can choose to remove styles and formatting from text and tables. This will then bring in clean, unformatted text for you to control.

Adding placeholder text

Suppose that you're creating a publication, but the text you need to import into the publication isn't ready to import into InDesign. (Perhaps it's still being created or edited). Instead of waiting for the final text, you can use placeholder text and continue to create your publication's layout. *Placeholder text* is commonly used to temporarily fill a document with text. The text looks a lot like normal blocks of text, which is more natural than trying to paste the same few words over and over to fill up a text frame. However, placeholder text is actually not in any particular language at all because it's just being used as filler.

InDesign has the ability to add placeholder text into a text frame automatically. Here's how you do it:

1. **Create a frame on the page by selecting the Type tool and dragging diagonally to create a text frame.**

A text frame is created on the page with an insertion point active. If you create a frame using the Frame tool, remember to click the frame using the Type tool or choose Object⇨Content⇨Text to convert it into a text frame before moving on to Step 2.

2. **Choose Type⇨Fill With Placeholder Text.**

The text frame is automatically filled with characters and words, similar to Figure 4-3.

Figure 4-3:
The text frame filled with placeholder text.

Copying and pasting text

Another way to move text from one application into your publication is by copying and pasting the text directly into InDesign. If you select and copy text in another program, you can paste it directly into InDesign from your computer's Clipboard. Here's how:

1. **Highlight the text that you want to use in your publication and press Ctrl+C (Windows) or ⌘+C (Mac) to copy the text.**

   When you copy the text, it sits on the Clipboard until it's replaced with something new. This means that you can transfer this information into InDesign.

2. **Open InDesign and press Ctrl+V (Windows) or ⌘+V (Mac) to create a new text frame and paste the text into it.**

   A new text frame appears centered on the page with your selected text inside it.

 You can also click in a text frame and press Ctrl+V (Windows) or ⌘+V (Mac) to paste text from the Clipboard directly into an existing frame. You can do the same thing with an image, as well.

All you need to do is double-click a text frame if you want to access, edit, type, or paste some text into it.

Looking at Text Frame Options

In the previous sections of this chapter, we show you how to create text frames and enter text into them. In this section, we show you how to organize text frames in your publication and achieve results you need. Controlling text frames so that they do what you need them to do is a matter of knowing how they work after you have text in them.

You're given a lot of control over the text in your publication. Changing text frame options allows you to change the way text is placed inside a frame. Changing these kinds of settings is sometimes important when you're working with particular kinds of fonts. (To read more about fonts, check out Book I, Chapter 6, where we discuss graphics, strokes, text, and fonts.)

The text frame contextual menu contains many options for the text frame. This menu allows you to perform basic commands, such as copy and paste, fill the text frame with placeholder text, make transformations, add or modify strokes, and change the kind of frame it is. Access the text frame's contextual menu by right-clicking (Windows) or Ctrl+clicking (Mac) a text frame. You can also find most of these options in the Type and Object menus, as well.

Changing text frame options

To change text frame options that control the look of the text within the frame, follow these steps:

1. **Create a rectangular text frame on the page, select the frame, and choose Object⇨Text Frame Options.**

   You can also press Ctrl+B (Windows) or ⌘+B (Mac) or use the text frame's contextual menu to open the Text Frame Options dialog box.

   You can tell that a text frame is selected when it has handles around its bounding box.

   The Text Frame Options dialog box appears, showing you the current settings for the selected text frame.

2. **Select the Preview check box to automatically view updates.**

   Now any changes you make in the dialog box are instantly updated on the page. This means you can make your changes and see how they will look before you apply them.

3. **In the Inset Spacing area of the dialog box, change the Top, Bottom, Left, and Right values.**

   These values are used to inset text from the edges of the text frame. The text is pushed inside the frame edge by the value you set.

   You can also indent your text, which we discuss in the section, "Indenting your text," later in this chapter. You can choose how to align the text vertically (Top, Center, Bottom, or Justify) using this dialog box. You can align the text to the top or bottom of the text frame, center it vertically in the frame, or evenly space the lines in the frame from top to bottom (Justify).

4. **When you're finished making changes in this dialog box, click OK.**

   The changes you made are applied to the text frame.

Using and modifying columns

You can specify that the document contain a certain number of columns on the page when you create a new publication. Using columns allows you to snap new text frames to the columns so that they are properly spaced on the page. You can even modify the amount of the *gutter,* which is the spacing between the columns.

You can also create columns within a single text frame by using the Text Frame Options dialog box. You can add up to 40 columns in a single text frame. If you already have text in a frame, it's automatically divided amongst the columns you add. The following steps show you how to add columns to a text frame on a page:

1. **Create a rectangular text frame on the page.**

Use the Text or Frame tool to create the text frame. You can create columns in text frames that are rectangular, oval, or even freehand shapes drawn on the page.

2. **Select the text frame and enter some text.**

You can type some text, paste text copied from another document, or add placeholder text by choosing Type⇨Fill With Placeholder Text.

3. **With the text frame still selected, choose Object⇨Text Frame Options.**

The Text Frame Options dialog box opens. Be sure to select the Preview check box in the dialog box, which enables you to immediately view the changes your settings make to the frame on the page.

4. **In the Columns section, change the value in the Number text field.**

In this example, we entered 2 in the Number text field. The selected text frame divides the text in the frame into two columns.

5. **Change the width of the columns by entering a new value in the Width text field.**

The width of the columns is automatically set, depending on the width of the text frame you created. We entered 10 (picas) in the Width text field for this example. The text frame changes size depending on the width you set in this column. When you click in a different text field in the dialog box, the text frame updates on the page to reflect the new value setting.

6. **Change the value in the Gutter text field.**

The gutter value controls how large the space is in between columns. If the gutter is too wide, change the value in the Gutter text field to a lower number. We entered 0p5 in the Gutter text field for this example to change the gutter to half a point in width.

7. **When you're finished, click OK to apply the changes.**

The changes are applied to the text frame you modified.

After you create the columns in the text frame, you can resize the frame by using the handles on its bounding box, which is detailed in the upcoming section, "Resizing and moving the text frame." The columns resize as necessary to divide the text frame into the number of columns you specified in the Text Frame Options dialog box. If you select the Fixed Column Width check box in the Text Frame Options dialog box, your text frames will always be the width you specify, no matter how you resize the text frame. When resizing the text frame, the frame snaps to the designated fixed width.

Book II
Chapter 4

Working with Text and Text Frames

Modifying and Connecting Text Frames on a Page

Making modifications to text frames and then connecting them to other text frames in a publication so that the story can continue on a separate page is vital in most publications. You will typically be working with stories of many paragraphs that need to continue on different pages in the document.

When you have a text frame on the page, you need to be able to change the size, position, and linking of the frame. You need to link the frame to other frames on the page so that the text can flow between them. This is important if you're creating a layout that contains a lot of text.

If you paste more text content than is visible in the text frame, the text still exists beyond the boundaries of the text frame — so if you have a text frame that is 20 lines tall, but you paste 50 lines of text in, the last 30 lines are cropped off. You need to resize the text frame or have the text flow to another frame in order to see the rest of the text you pasted. You can tell that the frame has more content when you see a small plus sign (+) in a special handle on the text frame's bounding box.

Resizing and moving the text frame

When creating most layouts, you regularly resize text frames and move them around the document while you figure out how you want the page layout to look. You can resize and move a text frame by following these steps:

1. **Use the Selection tool to select a text frame on the page.**

A bounding box with handles appears on the page. If the text frame has more text than it can show at the current size, a small handle with a red box appears on the bounding box. Therefore, you can't use this handle to resize the text frame.

2. **Drag one of the handles to resize the text frame.**

The frame automatically updates on the page as you drag the handles, as shown in Figure 4-4. Change the width or height by dragging the handles at the center of each side of the frame, or change the height and the width at the same time by dragging a corner handle.

Shift+drag a corner handle to scale the text frame proportionally.

3. **When you're finished resizing the text frame, click the middle of a selected frame and move it around the page.**

If you click within the frame once and drag it, you move the frame around the page. An outline of the frame follows your cursor and represents where the frame is placed if you release the mouse button. Simply release the frame when you're finished moving it.

If you're using guides or grids on the page, the text frame snaps to them. Also, if you opened a document with columns, the text frame snaps to the columns when you drag the frame close to the column guidelines. You can find out about guides, grids, and snapping in Chapter 5 of this minibook.

Figure 4-4:
Resize a text frame by dragging the handles of the bounding box.

You can also use the Transform panel in order to change the location and dimensions of a text frame. If the Transform panel isn't already open, choose Window⇨Object And Layout⇨Transform to open the panel. Then follow these steps:

1. **Change the values in the X and Y text fields.**

Enter 1 in both the X and Y text fields to move the text frame to the upper-left corner of the page.

The X and Y coordinates (location) of the text frame update to 1,1. A small square can be seen in the middle of the text frame. This square is the reference point of the text frame, meaning that the X and Y coordinates you set match the position of this point of the text frame.

 Change the reference point by clicking any point in the reference point indicator in the upper-left of the control panel.

2. **Change the values in the W and H text fields.**

For this example, we entered 35 (picas) in the W and H text fields. The text frame's width and height changes to the dimensions you specify. Using the Transform panel to change the width and height is ideal if you need to set an exact measurement for the frame.

 Not only can you resize and move text frames, you can also change their shape. Select a text frame and choose the Direct Selection tool from the toolbox. You can then select the corners on the text frame and move them to reshape the text frame.

Threading text frames

Understanding how to thread text frames together is very important if you plan to build page layouts with a lot of text. *Threading* is when text frames are arranged so that the text in one frame continues on in a second text frame. Threading is useful for most layouts because you won't always be able to include all your text in a single frame.

First, you should take a look at some of the terminology because Adobe has some special names it likes to use for text frames that are linked together. Figure 4-5 shows some of the icons that we refer to in the following list:

✦ **Flowing:** When text starts in one frame and continues in a second frame.

✦ **Threading:** When two text frames have text flowing from the first to the second frame, the text frames are considered to be threaded.

✦ **Story:** The group of sentences and paragraphs you have in a threaded text frame or frames.

✦ **In port:** An icon on the upper-left side of a text frame's bounding box that allows you to tell whether a frame is the first frame in a story or has text flowing in from another frame. An in port icon has a story flowing into it if it contains a small arrow; otherwise, the in port icon is empty.

✦ **Out port:** An icon on the lower-right side of the text frame's bounding box that allows you to tell whether a frame has text flowing out of it. The out port icon contains a small arrow if the frame is threaded to another frame; an empty out port icon signifies the frame is not connected to another text frame.

If a text frame isn't connected to another frame and has *overset text* (more text than can be displayed in a text frame), the out port shows a small red + icon.

Find a block of text that you want to thread (if you use a block of text that has formed sentences, as opposed to placeholder text, the process of connecting text and threading it through multiple frames is better illustrated) and then follow these steps:

1. **Copy some text onto the Clipboard, such as text from the InDesign help files, a page loaded in a Web browser window, or a document you have in Word, Notepad, or SimpleText.**

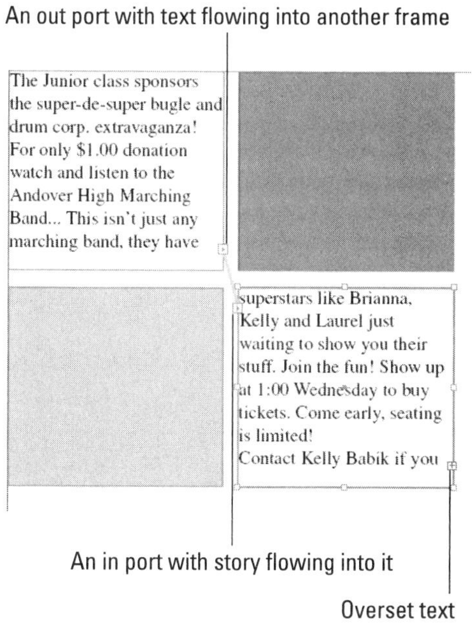

An out port with text flowing into another frame

Figure 4-5:
The in port
and out port
depict
threaded
text frames.
A special
icon shows if
text extends
past the text
frame and is
not threaded
to another
frame.

The Junior class sponsors
the super-de-super bugle and
drum corp. extravaganza!
For only $1.00 donation
watch and listen to the
Andover High Marching
Band... This isn't just any
marching band, they have

superstars like Brianna,
Kelly and Laurel just
waiting to show you their
stuff. Join the fun! Show up
at 1:00 Wednesday to buy
tickets. Come early, seating
is limited!
Contact Kelly Babik if you

An in port with story flowing into it

Overset text

It doesn't matter what kind of content you're pasting in. You only need to make sure the text is a few paragraphs long so that you have enough text to flow between frames.

In Figure 4-10, you can see the text thread represented with a line connecting one text frame to another. InDesign shows you text threads if you choose View⇨Show Text Threads.

2. **Use the Type tool to create two text frames on a page.**

The text frames can be above or beside one another, similar to the layout in Figure 4-11.

3. **Using the Text tool, click in the first text frame, which should be above or to the left of the second text frame.**

A blinking insertion point appears in the first text frame, allowing you to enter or paste text into the frame.

4. **Press Ctrl+V (Windows) or ⌘+V (Mac) to paste the text into the text frame.**

The text you've copied on the Clipboard enters into the frame. If you've pasted enough text, you should see the overset text icon (a red +) on the lower-right side of the text frame, as shown in Figure 4-6. If you don't see the overset text icon, use the Paste command a second time so that more text is entered into the frame.

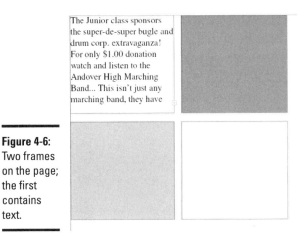

The Junior class sponsors the super-de-super bugle and drum corp. extravaganza! For only $1.00 donation watch and listen to the Andover High Marching Band... This isn't just any marching band, they have

Figure 4-6:
Two frames on the page; the first contains text.

5. **Click the overset text icon.**

The cursor changes into the loaded text icon. This icon means you can select or create another text frame to thread the story.

6. **Move the cursor over the second text frame and click.**

The cursor changes into the thread text icon when it's poised over the second text frame. When you click the second text frame, the two frames are threaded because the text continues in the second frame.

You can continue creating more frames and threading them. You can thread them on the same page or on subsequent pages in the document.

You can *unthread* text as well, which means you're breaking the link between two text frames. You can rearrange which frames are used to thread text, such as changing what page the story continues on when it's threaded to a second text frame. Break the connection by double-clicking the in port or the out port icon of the text frame that you want to unthread. The frame is then unthreaded (but no text is deleted).

If you don't have multiple pages in your document, choose File➪Document Setup. Change the value in the Number Of Pages text field to 2 or greater and click OK when you're finished. Now you can click through the pages using the Page Field control at the bottom of the workspace.

Adding a page jump number

If you have multiple pages, you can add a *page jump number* (text that notifies a reader where the story continues if it jumps to a text frame on another page) to an existing file. Before you start, make sure that a story threads between text frames on two different pages and then follow these steps:

1. **Create a new text frame on the first page and type continued on page.**

2. **Use the Selection tool to select the text frame you just created.**

3. **Move the text frame so that it slightly overlaps the text frame containing the story.**

   You need to allow InDesign to know what text frame it's tracking the story from or to. You need to overlap the two text frames (and keep them overlapped), as shown in Figure 4-7, so that InDesign knows to associate these text frames (the continued notice text frame and the story text frame) with each other.

Figure 4-7:
Slightly overlap the two text frames so that the story can be tracked properly.

You can then group these two text frames, which means that they'll move together. Choose Object⇨Group with both text frames selected. (Shift+click with the Selection tool to select both text frames.)

4. **Double-click the new text frame (which contains the text "continued on page") to place the insertion point where you want the page number to be inserted.**

   The page number will be inserted where you have the insertion point, so make sure that a space appears after the preceding character.

5. **Choose Type⇨Insert Special Character⇨Markers⇨Next Page Number.**

   A number is added into the text frame. This number is sensitive to where the next threaded text frame is, so if you move the second text frame, the page number automatically updates.

You can do the same thing for adding where a story is continued *from*. Repeat these steps, except when you get to Step 4, choose Type⇨Insert Special Character⇨Markers⇨Previous Page Number.

Understanding Paragraph Settings

You can change the settings for an entire text frame or a single paragraph in a text frame in several ways. You can use the Paragraph panel to make adjustments to a single paragraph or an entire text frame's indentation, justification, and alignment. Open the Paragraph panel by choosing Window⇨ Type & Tables⇨Paragraph.

If you want the changes in the Paragraph panel to span across all the text frames you create, don't select any paragraph or text frame before making the changes; instead, select the entire text frame or frames on the page first. Then the selections you make in the Paragraph panel will affect all the paragraphs in the selected text frame(s) instead of just one paragraph. If you want the selections you make in the Paragraph panel to affect just one paragraph within a text frame, select that paragraph first and then make your changes.

Indenting your text

You can indent a paragraph in a story using the Paragraph panel. Indentation moves the paragraph away from the edges of the text frame's bounding box. Here's how you modify indentation:

1. **Create a text frame on the page and fill it with text.**

   You can fill the text frame by typing text, copying and pasting text, or by inserting placeholder text by choosing Text⇨Fill with Placeholder Text.

2. **Make sure that the insertion point is blinking in the text frame in the paragraph you want to change or use the Selection tool to select the text frame.**

3. **Open the Paragraph panel by choosing Window⇨Type & Tables⇨ Paragraph.**

   The Paragraph panel opens, showing the text frame's current settings. See Figure 4-8 to find out the name of each setting control.

4. **Change the value in the Left Indent text field and press Enter.**

5. **Change the value in the First Line Left Indent text field and press Enter.**

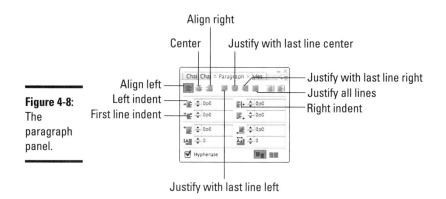

Figure 4-8:
The paragraph panel.

Align right
Center
Justify with last line center
Align left
Left indent
First line indent
Justify with last line right
Justify all lines
Right indent
Justify with last line left

If you want to change all the paragraphs in a story, then click the insertion point in a paragraph and choose Edit➪Select All before changing your settings.

Text alignment and justification

You can use the alignment and justification buttons in the Paragraph panel to format your text frames. *Align* helps you left, center, or right align the text with the edges of the text frames. *Justification* allows you to space the text in relation to the edges of the text frame. It also allows you to justify the final line of text in the paragraph. (Refer to Figure 4-14 to see the align and justify buttons in the Paragraph panel.) To align and/or justify a block of text, click one of the align and justify buttons.

Saving a paragraph style

Ever go through all the work of finding just the right indent, font, or spacing that you want in your copy just to find that you have to apply those attributes a hundred times to complete your project? How about when you decide that the indent is too much? Wouldn't it be nice to change one indent textbox and have it update all other occurrences? You can do this by using Paragraph styles in InDesign.

To create a paragraph style, follow these steps:

1. **Create a text frame, add text, and apply a first-line indent, any size of indent that you want to use.**

Select some of the text. It doesn't even have to be all of it.

2. **Choose Window➪Type & Tables➪Paragraph Styles.**

The Paragraph Styles panel opens.

3. **From the Paragraph Styles panel's menu, choose New Paragraph Style.**

   The New Paragraph Style dialog box opens. Note that every attribute, font, size, indent, and so on is already recorded in this unnamed style. You don't have to do anything at this point but name the style.

4. **Change the name from Paragraph Style 1 to something more appropriate, such as BodyCopy, and click OK.**

   Your style has been created! After you click OK, the dialog box closes, and the new style is added to the Paragraph Styles panel list. You can modify the settings by double-clicking the style name in the Paragraph Styles panel. You can apply the style to other text frames by selecting the frame and clicking the style in the Paragraph Styles panel.

If you want to change an existing style, the New Paragraph Style dialog box has several different areas in a large list on the left side. Select an item in the list to view and change the associated paragraph properties on the right side of the dialog box to update all usages of that paragraph style.

You can import paragraph styles from other documents or from a file on your hard drive. This is particularly useful when you need to use a particular set of styles for a template. To import paragraph styles, choose Load Paragraph Styles from the Paragraph Styles panel menu. A dialog box prompts you to browse your hard drive for a file. Select the file to load and click OK.

Editing Stories

Your publications will likely have a lot of text in them, and some of that text may need to be edited. InDesign has a built-in story editor for editing text. This feature can be useful when it's inconvenient or impossible to open another text editor to make changes.

InDesign solidly integrates with another Adobe product called InCopy, which is a text editor that is similar to Microsoft Word, but has integration capabilities with InDesign for streamlined page layout.

Using the story editor

The InDesign story editor allows you to view the story outside tiny columns and format the text as necessary. To open the story editor to edit a piece of text, follow these steps:

1. **Find a piece of text that you want to edit and select the text frame with the Selection tool.**

A bounding box with handles appears around the text frame.

2. **Choose Edit➪Edit In Story Editor.**

   The story editor opens in a new window right in the InDesign workspace.

3. **Edit the story in the window as necessary, and click the close button when you're finished.**

   Your story appears in one block of text. Any paragraph styles that you apply to the text in the story editor are noted in an Information pane at the left side of the workspace.

Checking for correct spelling

Typos and spelling errors are very easy to make. Therefore, it's important to check for correct spelling in a document before you print it or export it to a PDF. Here's how to check for spelling in InDesign:

1. **Choose Edit➪Spelling➪Check Spelling.**

2. **In the Check Spelling dialog box that appears, choose a selection to search from the Search drop-down list and then click the Start button.**

   The spell check automatically starts searching through the story or document.

3. **Either click the Skip button to ignore a misspelled word or select a suggested spelling correction from the list in the Suggested Corrections pane and click the Change button. Choose Ignore All to ignore any more instances of that word.**

   The spelling is corrected right in the text frame and moves on to the next spelling error.

4. **To stop the spell check, click the Done button; otherwise, click OK when InDesign gives you an alert that the spell check is done.**

Using dictionaries

New in this version, you can easily add words such as proper nouns to your dictionary by clicking the Add button.

You can create a user dictionary, or you can add user dictionaries from previous InDesign versions, from files that others have sent you, or from a server. The dictionary you add is used for all your InDesign documents.

Follow these steps to create your own custom dictionary:

1. **Choose Edit➪Preferences➪Dictionary (Windows) or InDesign➪ Preferences➪Dictionary (Mac OS).**

The Preferences dialog box appears with the Dictionary section visible.

2. **From the Language drop-down menu, choose the language of your dictionary.**

3. **Click the New User Dictionary button below the Language menu.**

4. **Specify the name and location of the user dictionary and then click OK.**

If you want to see when there is a spelling error, without having to access the Check Spelling dialog box, choose Edit⇨Spelling⇨Dynamic Spelling. Unknown words are then highlighted. To correct the spelling, right-click (Windows) or ⌘+click (Mac OS) and select the correct spelling from the contextual menu or add the word to your dictionary.

Using Tables

A table is made of columns and rows, which divides a table into cells. You see tables every day on the television, in books and magazines, and all over the Web. In fact, a calendar is a table: All the days in a month are shown down a column, every week is a row, and each day is a cell. You can use tables for many different things, such as listing products, employees, or events.

The following list describes the components of a table and how you can modify them in InDesign:

✦ **Rows:** Rows extend horizontally across the table. You can modify the height of a row.

✦ **Columns:** Columns are vertical in a table. You can modify the width of a column.

✦ **Cells:** Each cell is a text frame. You can enter information into this frame and format it like any other text frame in InDesign.

Creating tables

The easiest way to create a table is to have data ready to go. (Mind you, this is not the only way.) But flowing in existing data is the most dynamic way of seeing what InDesign can do with tables.

1. **Create a text area and insert tabbed copy into it.**

   The example used is dates for an event:

Summer Events

June   July   August

1   2   3

4   5   6

Notice that the text was simply keyed in with the tab key pressed between each new entry. The text doesn't even need to be lined up.

2. **Select the text and choose Table⇨Convert Text To Table.**

The Convert Text To Table Options window appears. You can select columns here or let the tabs in your text determine columns. You can find out more about Table styles in the "Creating table styles" section of this chapter.

3. **Click OK to accept the default settings.**

4. **To stretch the table in or out, hold down the Shift key and grab the outside right border.**

The cells proportionally accommodate the new table size.

5. **Merge the top three cells by clicking and dragging across the entire top row and then choose Table⇨Merge Cells.**

To create a new table without existing text, follow these steps:

1. **Create a new text frame using the Type tool.**

The insertion point should be blinking in the new text frame you create. If it isn't, or if you created a new frame another way, double-click the text frame so that the insertion point (I-bar) is active. You can't create a table unless the insertion point is active in the text frame.

2. **Choose Table⇨Insert Table.**

3. **In the Insert Table dialog box that opens, enter the number of rows and columns you want to add to the table in the Rows and Columns text fields and then click OK.**

In this example, 6 rows and 3 columns were entered.

Editing table settings

You can control many settings for tables. InDesign allows you to change the text, fill, and stroke properties for each cell or the table itself. Because of this flexibility, you can create fully customized tables to display your information in an intuitive and creative way. In this section, we show you some of the basic options you have for editing your tables.

To get started editing the table settings, follow these steps:

1. **Select the table you want to make changes to by clicking in one of the cells.**

2. **Choose Table➪Table Options➪Table Setup.**

   The Table Options dialog box opens with the Table Setup tab selected. The dialog box contains several tabs that contain settings you can change for different parts of the table.

   The Table Setup tab allows you to edit the columns and rows, border, and spacing, as well as how column or row strokes are rendered in relation to each other. For example, we changed the number of rows and columns and changed the table border weight to a 3-pt stroke.

3. **Select the Preview check box at the bottom of the dialog box.**

   The Preview is activated so that you can view the changes you made on the page while you're using the dialog box.

4. **Click the Row Strokes tab and change the options.**

   For this example, we selected Every Second Row from the Alternating Pattern drop-down list, changed the Table Border Weight to 2, and changed the Color property for the first row to C=15 M=100 Y=100 K=0 (This is the CMYK equivalent of red.).

   This step causes every second row to have a red, 2-pt stroke. You can also click the Column Strokes tab if you want to change the properties for column strokes. The two tabs work the same way.

5. **Click the Fills tab and change the options.**

   For this example, we chose Every Other Column from the Alternating Pattern drop-down list, changed the Color property to the same CMYK equivalent of red, and left the Tint at the default of 20%. This step changes the first row to a red tint.

6. **Click OK.**

   The changes you made in the Table Options dialog box are applied to the table.

7. **Click in one of the table cells so that the insertion point is blinking.**

   The table cell is selected.

8. **Find an image that you can copy onto the Clipboard. Press Ctrl+C (Windows) or ⌘+C (Mac) to copy the image.**

9. **Return to InDesign and paste the image into the table cell by pressing Ctrl+V (Windows) or ⌘ +V (Mac).**

The image appears in the table cell, and the height and/or width of the cell changes based on the dimensions of the image. Make sure that the insertion point is active in the cell if you have problems pasting the image.

Not only can you change the table itself, but you can customize the cells within the table as well. Choose Table⇨Cell Options⇨Text to open the Cell Options dialog box. You can also make changes to each cell by using the Paragraph panel. Similarly, you can change the number of rows, columns, and their widths and heights using the Tables panel. Open the Tables panel by choosing Window⇨Type and Tables⇨Table.

InDesign allows you to import tables from other programs, such as Microsoft Excel. If you have a spreadsheet you want to import, use the File⇨Place command. The spreadsheet is imported into InDesign as a table that you can further edit as necessary.

Creating table styles

If you've spent the time customizing strokes, fills, and spacing for your table, you certainly will want to save it as a style. Creating a table style allows you to re-use your table setup for future tables.

1. **Make a table look the way you want.**

The easiest way to create a table style is to go through the table setup and make a table look the way you want it at completion.

2. **Select the table.**

Click and drag to select it with the text tool.

3. **Choose Window⇨Type and Tables⇨Table Styles.**

The Table Styles panel appears.

4. **Hold down the Alt (Windows) or Option (Mac OS) key and click the Create New Style button at the bottom of the Table Styles panel.**

The New Table Style dialog box appears.

5. **Name the style and click OK.**

Your table attributes have been saved as a style.

If you want to edit table style attributes, you can simply double-click on the named style in the Table Styles panel. (Make sure nothing is selected.)

Looking at Text on a Path

You can create some interesting effects using text on a path. Using the Type On A Path tool, you can have text curve along a line or shape. This feature is particularly useful when you want to create interesting titling effects on a page.

To create text on a path, follow these steps:

1. **Use the Pen tool to create a path on the page.**

   Create at least one curve on the path after you create it. Feeling uncomfortable using the Pen tool? In Chapter 3 of this minibook, we show you how to wield it with confidence.

2. **Click and hold the Type tool to select the Type On A Path tool.**

3. **Move the cursor near the path you created.**

   When you move the cursor near a path, a + symbol appears next to the cursor. This cursor means you can click and start typing on the path.

4. **Click when you see the + icon and type some text onto the path.**

   An insertion point appears at the beginning of the path after you click, and you can then add text along the path. You select type on a path as you would normally select other text: by dragging over the text to highlight it.

To change properties for type on a path, you can use the Type On A Path Options dialog box, which you access by choosing Type⇨Type On A Path⇨ Options. The Type On A Path Options dialog box allows you to use effects to modify how each character is placed on the path. You can also flip the text, change character spacing, and change how the characters align to the path in the Align drop-down list, or to the stroke of the path in the To Path drop-down list. Play with the settings to see how they affect your type. Click OK to apply your changes; to undo anything you don't like, press Ctrl+Z or ⌘+Z.

Chapter 5: Understanding Page Layout

In This Chapter

↙ **Working with image files**

↙ **Selecting images on the page**

↙ **Knowing page layout settings**

↙ **Using text and graphics in your layouts**

↙ **Working with pages**

↙ **Using master pages and spreads**

This chapter shows you how to put graphics and text together so that you can start creating page layouts. Interesting and creative page layouts help draw interest to the pictures and words contained within the publication. An interesting layout motivates more of the audience to read the text you place on a page.

Importing Images

You can add several kinds of image files to an InDesign document: Some of the most common kinds are JPEG, TIF, GIF, and PSD. Images are imported into graphic frames, which are instantly created when you add the image to the page.

InDesign allows you to make specific settings, such as those for quality, linkage, and color management, when importing an image. You can make additional settings when you import an image using the Image Import Options dialog box. In the "Accessing image import options" section, you see how to change various import options, but for now, to import an image into InDesign (without changing the import settings), follow these steps:

1. **Make sure that nothing on the page is selected.**

If an object on the page is selected, click an empty area so that the element is deselected before you proceed.

2. **Choose File⇨Place.**

The Place dialog box opens, where you can browse through your hard drive for image files to import. This dialog box allows you to import various kinds of files into InDesign, not just images.

3. **Select the image that you want to import and click Open.**

The Place dialog box closes, and your cursor displays a thumbnail of the image you selected.

Now in CS3, you can import multiple images at one time. Simply hold down the Ctrl key (Windows) and select multiple files in the Place dialog box, or use the ⌘ key (Macintosh) and click on multiple files.

4. **Move the cursor to where you want the upper-left corner of the image to be placed on the page and then click the mouse.**

The image is imported and placed into the publication as a graphic frame. You can now resize, move, and modify the image.

Don't worry if the image imports and is too large for the layout or needs to be cropped — for more information about selecting graphic frames and modifying them, check out Chapter 6 of this minibook. To find out about importing and working with text and stories, refer to Chapter 4 of this minibook.

It's sometimes easier to create a graphic frame and then add an image to it. Now in CS3, you can set fitting properties before you import an image. To set fitting in a blank frame, choose Object⇨Fitting⇨Frame Fitting Options.

Accessing image import options

To open the Image Import Options dialog box, follow these steps:

1. **Choose File⇨Place.**

The Place dialog box opens.

2. **Select the Show Import Options check box.**

3. **Select an image to import and click Open (Windows) or Choose (Mac).**

The Image Import Options dialog box opens.

Importing PDFs

When you import PDF files, you can preview and crop the pages by using the Place PDF dialog box (choose File⇨Place). You can import only one page at a time, so you'll need to use the Forward and Back buttons under the preview to select a page to place in the publication. Also, you can't import any video, sound, or buttons, and you can't edit the PDF after it's imported into InDesign.

The Place PDF dialog box offers the following options:

✦ **Crop:** You can crop the page you're importing using this drop-down list. Some options are unavailable because they depend on what is in the PDF you're importing. The hatched outline in the preview shows you the crop marks.

✦ **Transparent Background:** If you select this check box, the PDF background is made transparent so that elements on the InDesign page show through. The PDF background is imported as solid white if this option isn't selected.

Linking and Embedding Images

You can either have your images linked to a publication or embedded within it. Instead of importing images or files directly into InDesign and embedding them, you can link the content to the file instead. Here's the difference between linking and embedding:

✦ **Linking:** The image that appears in the InDesign document is basically a preview of the actual image file stored on your hard drive. If the file you linked to your InDesign document is changed (the name and location must remain the same), the link breaks, and the image no longer appears in your layout.

✦ **Embedding:** The image is copied into and saved within the publication itself. It doesn't matter where the file you imported is or if you alter that file because an embedded image is stored within the InDesign document itself.

When you print or export the publication you're working on, the information is added to the document from linked files (if you have any). This means you have to be careful to keep all your linked files together with the InDesign document, particularly if you send or save it to a different location. You can update the links for an image by selecting it in the Links panel and choosing Relink from the Links panel menu. You're prompted to find that file on your hard drive so that the file can be linked to the new location.

If you choose to use embedded images instead of linked images, be aware that your publication's file size increases because of the extra data that is being stored within it.

Images 48K or smaller are automatically embedded within the publication. If an imported image is larger than that, the file is linked. To find out what files are embedded or linked, you need to look at the Links panel. Open the panel by choosing Window⇨Links and see whether you have any linked or embedded images listed in the panel.

You can choose to embed a file using the Links panel menu. Click the triangle in the upper-right corner to access the menu and select Embed File if you want a linked file to be embedded within the document. Alternatively, choose Unembed from the Link panel menu to link a file instead of having it embedded in the document.

Setting Image Quality and Display

You can set different quality settings for how your images import and display in the workspace. These settings may help speed up your work (set at a lower quality) or give you a better idea of the finished print project (set at a higher quality). These settings are only applicable to how you see the images while using InDesign: They have no bearing over the final printed or exported product.

To change image display quality, choose Edit⇨Preferences⇨Display Performance (Windows) or InDesign CS⇨Preferences⇨Display Performance (Mac). You can then select one of the following settings from the Default View drop-down list:

✦ **Fast Display:** In order to optimize performance, the entire image or graphic is grayed out.

✦ **Typical Display (Default):** This setting tends to make bitmaps look a little blocky, particularly if you zoom in. The speed of zooming in and out is increased if you select this option. InDesign uses a preview that it's created (or was already imported with the file) to display the image on the screen.

✦ **High Quality Display:** The original image is used to display on-screen. This allows you to preview a very accurate depiction of what the final layout will look like, but you may find that InDesign runs slowly when you use the High Quality option.

Notice the difference between these settings in Figure 5-1.

Figure 5-1: From left to right: Fast Display, Typical Display, and High Quality Display.

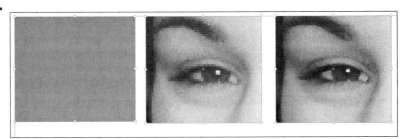

To change the display for individual images, select the graphic frame and choose View➪Display Performance. Then choose one of the three options from the submenu.

Selecting Images

After you import an image into your document, you can select images in several different ways using the Selection or Direct Selection tools. This is useful when you want to select and edit just the graphic frame, or just the image inside of it.

To select and then edit an image on the page, follow these steps:

1. **Place an image on a page by importing it or pasting it into InDesign.**

   The image is placed within a graphic frame.

2. **Using the Selection tool, drag one of the corner handles on the graphic frame.**

   The graphic frame is resized, but not the image. The image appears to be cropped because you resized the graphic frame — but the image remains the same size within the frame, as shown in the center of Figure 5-2.

3. **Choose Edit➪Undo or press Ctrl+Z (Windows) or ⌘+Z (Mac) to undo the changes to the image.**

   The image returns to its original appearance on the page.

4. **Using the Direct Selection tool, click the picture and then drag one of the corner handles.**

   The image inside the graphic frame resizes, but the graphic frame remains the same size.

5. **Click within the image and drag to move the image within the graphic frame-bounding box.**

   A hand appears when you move the cursor over the graphic; when you move the image just past the edge of the graphic frame boundaries, that part of the image isn't visible anymore, as shown on the right of Figure 5-2.

When repositioning a graphic within a frame, click and hold. When you do so, the entire image appears (screened outside the frame area), as shown in the image on the right in Figure 5-6. Seeing the dimmed image allows you to crop more effectively.

Figure 5-2:
The original image in a graphic frame (left); inside a frame that has been resized (center); in the process of being repositioned in the frame (right).

You can set the frame or image to resize by choosing Object⇨Fitting and selecting the option that you want. You can even set this fitting before you place an image, which is especially helpful when creating templates. Resize before an image is placed by choosing Object⇨Fitting⇨Frame Fitting Options.

Manipulating Text and Graphics in Layout

InDesign offers many tools that help you work with text and graphics together in a layout. From the tools in the toolbox to commands to panel options, InDesign offers you an immense amount of control over how you can manipulate graphics and text in a spread.

Page orientation and size

When you open a new document, you can set the page orientation and size. If you ever need to change your settings after you've created a document, choose File⇨Document Setup and change the following options. (These settings affect all pages in your document.)

+ **Page Orientation:** Select either Landscape or Portrait. One of the first things you decide upon when you create a new document is how your pages will be oriented. A landscape page is wider than it is tall; a portrait orientation is taller than it is wide.

+ **Page Size:** Choose from many standardized preset sizes, such as Letter, Legal, and Tabloid. Alternatively, you can set a custom page size for the document. Make sure that you properly set the page size so that it fits the kind of paper you need to print on.

Margins and columns

Margins, columns, and gutters help divide a page for layout and confine its dimensions:

✦ **Margin:** The area between the edge of the page and the main printed area. Together, the four margins (top, bottom, left, and right) look like a rectangle around the page's perimeter. Margins don't print when you print or export the publication.

✦ **Column:** Columns divide a page into sections used for laying out text and graphics on a page. A page has at least one column when you start, which is between the margins. You can add additional column guides to this, which are represented by a pair of lines separated by a *gutter* area. Column guides aren't printed when you print or export the publication.

✦ **Gutter:** The space between two columns on the page. A gutter prevents columns from running together. You can define the gutter's width in your settings; see Chapter 4 of this minibook for more information.

You can set margins and columns when you create a new document, which we discuss in Chapter 2 of this minibook. However, you can also modify margins and columns after the document has been created and specify different values for each page. You can modify the gutter, which is the width of the space between each column.

You can change margins and columns by setting new values in the Margins And Columns dialog box. Choose Layout➪Margins And Columns and then modify each individual page.

Margins and columns are useful for placing and aligning elements on a page. These guides can have objects snap to them, enabling you to accurately align multiple objects on a page.

Using guides and snapping

Using guides when you're creating your page layouts is a good idea because guides help you more precisely align elements on a page and position objects in the layout. Aligning objects by eyeballing them is difficult because you often can't tell if an object is out of alignment by a small amount unless you're zoomed in to a large percentage.

Make sure that snapping is enabled by choosing View➪Grids And Guides➪ Snap To Guides. *Snapping* makes guides and grids useful. When you drag the object close to the grid, the object attaches to the guideline like it's a magnet. Getting an object aligned to a guide isn't easy or even possible to do by eyeballing it, so snapping is essential when using guides.

Because guides are very useful in creating a layout, check out the following kinds available in InDesign (refer to Figure 5-3):

✦ **Column guides:** These guides are set when you open a new document in InDesign. Column guides evenly distribute the page into columns and can be used to align text frames in a document. They don't always have to be equally spaced the way they are originally placed on a page. You can drag columns to a new location manually. Simply click a column guide directly on a line and drag the line to a new location. The cursor changes to a double-ended arrow while you drag the column guide to a new location.

✦ **Margin guides:** Margin guides are the guidelines discussed in the previous section that define the area between the edge of the page and the main printable area.

✦ **Ruler guides:** Ruler guides are ones you manually define; they can be used to align graphics, measure an object, or specify the location of a particular asset you want to lay out. See Chapter 2 of this minibook for details about adding ruler guides to the workspace.

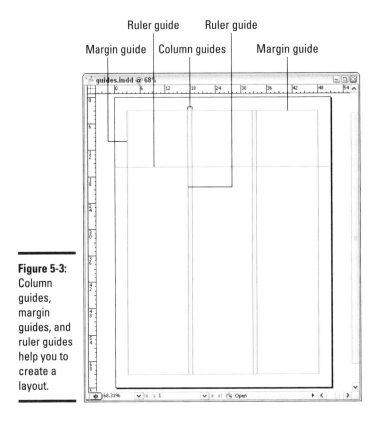

Figure 5-3:
Column guides, margin guides, and ruler guides help you to create a layout.

To find out how to show and hide grids and guides, refer to Chapter 2 of this minibook.

Locking objects and guides

You can lock elements, such as objects and guides, in place. This feature is particularly useful after you've carefully aligned elements on a page. Locking objects or guides prevents you from accidentally moving them from that position.

To lock an element, follow these steps:

1. **Use a drawing tool to create an object on a page and then select it using the Selection tool.**

A bounding box with handles appears when the object is selected.

2. **Choose Object⇨Lock Position.**

The object is locked in position. Now when you try to use the Selection or Direct Selection tools to move the object, it doesn't move from its current position.

To lock guides in place, follow these steps:

1. **Drag a couple ruler guides onto the page by clicking within a ruler and dragging toward the page.**

A line appears on the page. (If rulers aren't visible around the pasteboard, choose View⇨Rulers.)

2. **Drag a ruler guide to a new location if needed; when you're happy with the ruler guides' placement, choose View⇨Grids And Guides⇨ Lock Guides.**

All guides in the workspace are locked. If you try selecting a guide and moving it, the guide remains in its present position. If you have any column guides on the page, they are locked as well.

Use layers in your publications for organization. Layers are a lot like transparencies that lay on top of each other, so they can be used for stacking elements on a page. For example, you may want to stack graphics or arrange similar items (such as images or text) onto the same layer. Each layer has its own color of bounding box, which helps you tell which item is on which corresponding layer. For more information on layers in general, refer to Book III, Chapter 8.

Merging Text and Graphics

When you have text and graphics together on a page, they should flow and work with each other in order to create an aesthetic layout. Luckily, you can work with text wrap to achieve a visual flow between text and graphics. In this section, you discover how to wrap text around images and graphics in your publications.

Wrapping objects with text

Images can have text wrapped around them, as shown in Figure 5-4. Wrapping is a typical feature of page layout in print and on the Web. You can choose different text wrap options by using the Text Wrap panel, which you open by choosing Window⇨Text Wrap. Use the five buttons at the top of the panel to set what kind of text wrapping you want to use for the selected object. Below the buttons are text fields where you can enter offset values for the text wrap. The fields are grayed out if the option isn't available.

The drop-down list at the bottom of the Text Wrap panel is used to choose from various contour options. Choose from the following options to wrap text around an object's shape:

✦ **No Text Wrap:** Click this button to use the default setting or to remove any text wrapping from the selected object.

✦ **Wrap Around Bounding Box:** Click this button to wrap text around all sides of the bounding box of the object.

Offset: Enter an amount to offset the text from wrapping around the object.

✦ **Wrap Around Object Shape:** Click this button to wrap text around the edges of an object.

Contour Options: Select a contour from this drop-down list, which tells InDesign how the edges of the image are determined. You can choose from various vector paths or the edges to be detected around an object or image with transparency.

Top Offset: Enter a value for the top offset modifier to offset the text wrapping around the object.

✦ **Jump Object:** Click this button to have the text wrapping around the image jump from above the image to below it, with no text wrapping to the left or right of the object in the column.

✦ **Jump To Next Column:** Click this button to cause text to end above the image and then jump to the next column. No text is wrapped to the left or right of the image.

Offset: Enter offset values for text wrapping on all sides of the object.

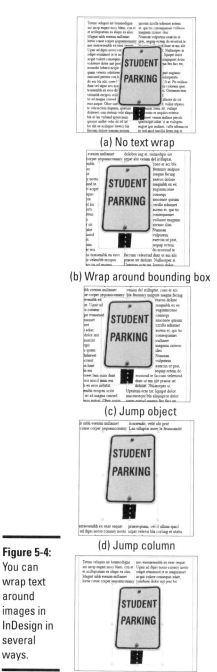

(a) No text wrap

(b) Wrap around bounding box

(c) Jump object

(d) Jump column

(e) Jump to next column

Figure 5-4:
You can wrap text around images in InDesign in several ways.

To add text wrapping to an object (a drawing or image:

1. **Create a text frame on the page.**

   Add text to the text frame by typing, pasting text from elsewhere, or filling it with placeholder text. This text will wrap around the image, so make sure that the text frame is slightly larger than the graphic frame you'll use.

2. **Using the Selection tool, select a graphic frame on the page and move it over the text frame.**

   Bounding box handles appear around the edges of the image or graphic.

3. **Open the Text Wrap panel by choosing Window⇨Text Wrap.**

   The Text Wrap panel opens.

4. **With the graphic frame still selected, click the Wrap Around Object Shape button.**

   The text wraps around the image instead of hiding behind it.

5. **If you're working with an image that has a transparent background, choose Detect Edges Or Alpha Channel from the Contour Options drop-down list.**

   The text wraps around the edges of the image, as shown in the third example in Figure 5-9.

Modifying a text wrap

If you've applied a text wrap around an object (as we show you how to do in the preceding section), you can then modify that text wrap. If you have an image with a transparent background around which you've wrapped text, InDesign created a path around the edge of the image; if you have a shape you created with the drawing tools, InDesign automatically uses those paths to wrap text around.

Before proceeding with the following steps, be sure that the object uses the Wrap Around Object Shape text wrap. (If not, open the Text Wrap panel and click the Wrap Around Object Shape button to apply the text wrapping.) Remember to choose Detect Edges if you're using an image with a transparent background.

To modify the path around an image with text wrapping by using the Direct Selection tool, follow these steps:

1. **Select the object using the Direct Selection tool.**

   The image is selected, and you can see the path around the object.

2. **Drag one of the anchor points on the path using the Direct Selection tool.**

   The path is modified according to how you move the point. (For more about manipulating paths, take a look at Chapter 3 of this minibook.) The text wrapping immediately changes, based on the modifications you make to the path around the object.

3. **Select the Delete Anchor Point tool from the toolbox and delete one of the anchor points.**

   The path changes again, and the text wrapping modifies around the object accordingly.

You can also use the Offset values in the Text Wrap panel to determine the distance between the wrapping text and the edge of the object. Just increase the point values to move the text farther away from the object's edge.

Working with Pages and the Pages Panel

Pages are the central part of any publication. The page is where the visible part of your publication is actually created. Navigating and controlling pages is a large part of what you do in InDesign. The Pages panel allows you to select, move, and navigate through pages in a publication. When you use default settings, pages are created as *facing pages,* which means they're laid out as two-page spreads. Otherwise, pages are laid out individually. This is reflected, and can also be changed, in the Pages panel.

The Pages panel, which you open by choosing Window⇨Pages, also allows you to add new pages to the document, duplicate pages, or delete a page. The Pages panel, shown in Figure 5-5, contains two main areas: the master pages section (upper section) and the section containing the document's pages (lower section).

To discover more about master pages and how they differ from regular pages in your document, refer to "Using Master Spreads in Page Layout" later in this chapter.

Selecting and moving pages

Use the Pages panel to select a page or spread in your publication. Select a page by clicking the page. If you Ctrl+click (Windows) or ⌘+click (Mac) pages, you can select more than one page at a time. The Pages panel also allows you to move pages to a new position in the document. Select a page in the document pages area of the panel and then drag it where you want to move the page. A small line and changed cursor indicate where the page will be moved. You can move a page in between two pages in a spread; a hollow line indicates where you're moving the page. If you move a page after a spread, a solid line appears. Release the mouse button to move the page to the new location.

Documents pages

Master pages

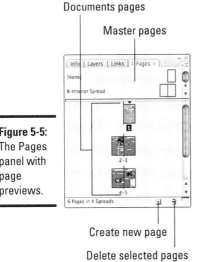

Figure 5-5:
The Pages panel with page previews.

Create new page

Delete selected pages

Adding and deleting pages

You can also add new pages to the publication by using the Pages panel. To add a new page, follow these steps:

1. **Open the Pages panel by choosing Window⇨Pages.**

The Pages panel opens.

2. **Click the Create New Page button.**

A new page is added to the document.

3. **Select one of the pages in the Pages panel.**

The selected page is highlighted in the Pages panel.

4. **Click the Create New Page button again.**

A new page is added following the selected page.

To delete a page, select the page in the Pages panel and click the Delete Selected Pages button. The selected page is removed from the document.

Numbering your pages

When you're working with longer documents, adding page numbers before you print or export the publication is a good idea. You don't have to add them manually: InDesign has a special tool that allows you to number pages automatically. This tool is particularly useful when you move pages around the document. You don't have to keep track of updating the numbering when you make these kinds of edits.

To number pages, follow these steps:

1. **Create a text frame on the page where you want the page number to be added.**

2. **Double-click the text frame so that the insertion point is blinking in the frame.**

3. **Choose Type⇨Insert Special Character⇨Markers⇨Current Page Number.**

    The current page number appears in the text frame you selected. If you added the page number to a master page, then the master pages' letter appears in the field instead.

If you want page numbers to appear on all pages in the document, you need to add the text frame to a master page. Remember that page numbers are added only to the pages in your document associated with that master page. If you add the page number on a regular page in the document, it adds the page number only to that single page.

To modify automatic numbering settings, choose Layout⇨Numbering And Section Options. You can choose to have numbering start from a specific number or use a different style, such as Roman numerals.

Using Master Spreads in Page Layout

Master pages are a lot like templates that you use to format your page layouts. The settings, such as margins and columns, are applied to each layout that the master page is applied to. If you put a page number on a master page, then it also appears on each page that uses the layout. You can have more than one master page in a single publication, and you can choose which pages use a particular master page.

A master page or spread typically contains parts of a layout that are applied to many pages. It has elements that are used on many pages, such as page numbering, text frames to enter text into, background images, or a heading that's used on every page. You can't edit the items you have on a master page on the pages assigned to it — you can edit those items on the master page only.

Master pages are lettered. The first master page is called the A-Master by default. If you create a second master page, it's then called the B-Master by default. When you create a new publication, the A-Master is applied to all the pages you initially open in the document. You can add pages at the end that don't have a master applied to them.

Creating master pages and applying them to your publication enables you to create a reusable format for your publication, which can dramatically speed up your workflow when you put together documents using InDesign.

Creating a master spread

You may need more than one master page or master spread for your document. You may have another series of pages that need a unique format. In this situation, you'd need to create a second master page. You can create a master page or a master spread from any other page in the publication, or you can create a new one using the Pages panel.

To create a master page using a page in the publication, do one of the following:

✦ Choose New Master from the Page panel's menu and then click OK. A blank master page is created.

✦ Drag a page from the pages section of the panel into the master page section of the Pages panel. The document page turns into a master page.

If the page you're trying to drag into the master pages section is part of a spread, you need to select *both pages in the spread* before you drag it into the master pages section. You can drag individual pages into the master page section only if they're *not* part of a spread.

Applying, removing, and deleting master pages

After you create a master page, you can apply it to a page. You can also remove a page from a master page layout as well as delete a master page altogether:

✦ **To add master page formatting to a page or spread in a publication:** In the Pages panel, drag the master page you want to use from the master page section on top of the page you want to format in the document pages section. When you drag the master page on top of the page, it will have a thick outline around it. Release the mouse button when you see this outline, and the formatting is applied to the page.

✦ **To remove any master page applied to a document page:** In the Pages panel, drag the None page from the master area in the Pages panel onto that document page. You may need to use the scroll bar in the master pages area of the Pages panel to find the None page.

✦ **To delete a master page:** In the Pages panel, select the unwanted master page and then choose Delete Master Spread from the panel menu.

This action *permanently* deletes the master page — you can't get it back — so think carefully before deleting a master page.

Chapter 6: Clipping Paths, Transforming Objects, and Alignment

In This Chapter

✓ Transforming objects with the Transform panel and the Free Transform tool

✓ Rotating and scaling objects

✓ Shearing and reflecting objects

✓ Adding a clipping path

✓ Aligning objects in a layout

*I*n this chapter, you discover several different ways to manipulate and arrange objects on a page. You find out how to use the Transform panel and other tools in the toolbox to transform objects on page layouts. You can make the same transformation in many different ways in InDesign, so for each way you can transform an object, we show you a couple of different ways to get the same job done.

Aligning and/or distributing objects and images helps you organize elements logically on a page. In this chapter, you find out how to align objects using the Align panel. In Chapter 5 of this minibook, we touch on clipping paths. This chapter provides more information about clipping paths. We show you how to create a new path to use as a clipping path for an image in your document.

Working with Transformations

Chapter 3 of this minibook shows you how to transform graphic objects by skewing them. You can manipulate objects in InDesign in many other ways. You can transform an object by using the Object⇨Transform menu, the Transform panel, or the Free Transform tool.

Looking at the Transform panel

The Transform panel (shown in Figure 6-1) is extremely useful for changing the way an image or graphic looks and also for changing the scale, rotation, or skew of the selected object. You can choose from a range of values for some of these modifiers or manually set your own by typing them.

The Transform panel offers the following information and functionality:

✦ **Reference point:** Indicates which handle is the reference for any transformations you make. For example, if you reset the X and Y coordinates, the reference point is set to this position.

✦ **Position:** Change these values to reset the X and Y coordinate position of the selected object.

Reference point indicator

Figure 6-1:
The Transform panel makes it easy to resize, rotate, and reposition the selected objects.

Palette menu

Rotating angle
Shear X angle

Scale Y

Scale X

Constrain proportions

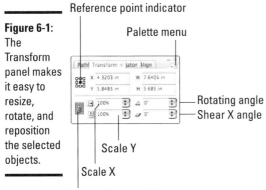

✦ **Size:** The W and H text fields are used to change the current dimensions of the object.

✦ **Scale:** Enter or choose a percentage from the Scale X Percentage and Scale Y Percentage drop-down lists to scale (resize) the object on either of these axes.

✦ **Constraining proportions:** Click the Constrain Proportions button to maintain the current proportions of the object that's being scaled.

✦ **Shearing:** Enter or choose a negative or positive number to modify the shearing angle (skew) of the selected object.

✦ **Rotation angle:** Set a negative value to rotate the object clockwise; a positive value rotates the object counterclockwise.

When you're scaling, shearing, or rotating an object in your layout, it transforms based on the reference point in the Transform panel. For example, when you rotate an object, InDesign considers the reference point to be the center point of the rotation.

Click a new reference point square in the Transform panel to change the reference point of the graphic to the equivalent bounding box handle of the currently selected object.

You can access dialog boxes for each kind of transformation by choosing Object⇨Transform. These dialog boxes have very similar functionality to the Transform panel, although they offer additional options, such as only affecting the path or frame and not modifying the content within.

Using the Free Transform tool

The Free Transform tool is a multipurpose tool that allows you to transform objects in different ways. Using the Free Transform tool, you can move, rotate, shear, reflect, and scale objects.

The different functions of the Free Transform Tool are represented in InDesign by different cursors, as shown in Figure 6-2.

Figure 6-2:
Different cursors indicate options for using the Transform tool.

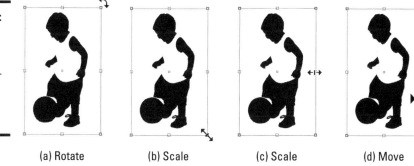

(a) Rotate   (b) Scale   (c) Scale   (d) Move

To move an object using the Free Transform tool, follow these steps:

1. Use the Selection tool to select an object on the page.

You can use an object that is already on the page or create a new shape using the drawing tools. When the object is selected, you'll see handles around the edges.

**Book II
Chapter 6**

Clipping Paths, Transforming Objects, and Alignment

2. **Select the Free Transform tool from the toolbox.**

The cursor changes to the Free Transform tool.

3. **Move the cursor over the middle of the selected object.**

The cursor changes its appearance to indicate that you can drag to move the object (refer to Figure 6-2). If you move the cursor outside the edges of the object, the cursor changes when the other tools, such as rotate, scale, and shear, become active.

4. **Drag the object to a different location.**

The object is moved to a new location on the page.

Rotating objects

You can rotate an object using the Free Transform tool or the Transform panel. Using the panel allows you to enter a specific degree that you want the object to rotate. The Free Transform tool lets you visually manipulate the object on the page.

To rotate an image using the Free Transform tool, follow these steps:

1. **Select an object on the page using the Selection tool.**

Handles appear around the edges of the object. You can rotate any object on the page.

2. **Select the Free Transform tool in the toolbox and move it near the handle of an object outside of the bounding box.**

The cursor changes when you move it close to the handle of an object. For rotation, you must keep the cursor just outside of the object.

3. **When the cursor changes to the rotate cursor, drag to rotate the object.**

Drag the cursor until the object is rotated the correct amount.

Alternatively, you can use the Rotate tool to spin an object by following these steps:

1. **With the object selected, select the Rotate tool in the toolbox and move the cursor near the object.**

The cursor looks similar to a cross hair.

2. **Click the cursor anywhere on the page near the object.**

The point the object rotates around is set on the page.

3. Drag the cursor outside of the object.

The object rotates around the reference point you set on the page. Hold the Shift key if you want to rotate in 45-degree increments.

You can also rotate objects using the Transform panel. Here's how:

1. Select an object on the page using the Selection tool.

The bounding box with handles appears around the selected object.

2. If the Transform panel isn't open, press F9 to open it.

The Transform panel appears.

3. Select a value from the Rotation angle drop-down list or click the text field and enter a percentage.

The object rotates to the degree that you set in the Transform panel, as shown in Figure 6-3. Negative angles (in degrees) rotate the image clockwise, and positive angles (in degrees) rotate the image counterclockwise.

Figure 6-3: Rotating an object by using the Transform palette.

Scaling objects

You can scale objects by using the Transform panel (refer to Figure 6-1), the Scale tool, or the Free Transform tool. The Transform panel allows you to set exact width and height dimensions that you want to scale the object to, just like you can set exact percentages for rotating.

To scale an object by using the Free Transform tool or the Scale tool, follow these steps:

1. Select an object on the page.

A bounding box appears around the object.

2. Select the Free Transform tool or the Scale tool from the toolbox.

3. Move the cursor directly over a corner handle.

The cursor changes into a double-ended arrow, as shown in Figure 6-4.

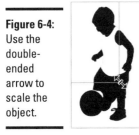

Figure 6-4:
Use the double-ended arrow to scale the object.

4. Drag outward to increase the size of the object; drag inward to decrease the size of the object.

If you want to scale the image proportionally, hold down the Shift key while you drag.

5. Release the mouse button when the object is scaled to the correct size.

To resize an object using the Transform panel, just select the object and enter new values into the W and H text fields in the panel. The object then resizes to those exact dimensions.

Shearing objects

Shearing an object means that you're skewing it horizontally, slanting it to the left or right. A sheared object may appear to have perspective or depth because of this modification. You use the Shear tool to create a shearing effect, as shown in Figure 6-5.

Figure 6-5:
The original image is on the left, and the sheared image is on the right.

Follow these steps to shear an object:

1. **Select an object on the page.**

The bounding box appears around the object that is selected.

2. **Choose the Shear tool in the toolbox.**

The cursor changes so it looks similar to a cross hair.

3. **Click anywhere above or below the object and drag.**

The selected object shears depending on the direction that you drag. Press the Shift key as you drag to shear an object in 45-degree increments.

**Book II
Chapter 6**

**Clipping Paths,
Transforming Objects,
and Alignment**

To shear objects using the Free Transform tool, begin dragging a handle and then hold down Ctrl+Alt (Windows) or ⌘+Option (Mac) while dragging.

You can also enter an exact value into the Transform panel to shear an object. Select the object and then enter a positive or negative value into the panel representing the amount of slant you want to apply to the object.

You can apply shear by choosing Object⇔Transform⇔Shear to display the Shear dialog box.

Reflecting objects

You can reflect objects to create mirror images by using the Transform panel menu. The menu provides several additional options for manipulating objects.

Follow these steps to reflect an object:

1. **Select an object on the page and then open the Transform panel by pressing F9.**

The object's bounding box and handles appear. The Transform panel shows the current values of the selected object.

2. **Click the panel menu in the Transform panel.**

The menu opens, revealing many options available for manipulating the object.

3. **Select Flip Horizontal from the Transform panel menu.**

The object on the page flips on its horizontal axis. You can repeat this step with other reflection options in the menu, such as Flip Vertical.

You can also reflect objects with the Free Transform tool by dragging a corner handle past the opposite end of the object. The object reflects on its axis.

Understanding Clipping Paths

Clipping paths allow you to create a path that crops out a part of an image based upon the path, such as removing the background area of an image. This shape can be one that you create using InDesign, or you can import an image that already has a clipping path. InDesign can also use an existing alpha or mask layer, such as one created using Photoshop or Fireworks, and treat it like a clipping path. Clipping paths are useful when you want to block out areas of an image and have text wrap around the leftover image.

You can create a clipping path right in InDesign using a drawing tool, such as the Pen tool. You use the tool to create a shape and then paste an image into this shape on the page. Here's how:

1. Choose File⇨Place and browse to locate an image.

2. Using the Pen tool, create a path right on top of the image.

The path should be created so that it can contain the image.

3. Using the Selection tool, click to select the image and then choose File⇨Cut.

4. Select the shape you created in Step 1 and choose Edit⇨Paste Into.

The image is pasted into the selected shape that you drew with the Pen tool.

Arranging Objects on the Page

In other chapters of this minibook, we show you how to arrange objects on the page. However, you can arrange text or objects in a few other ways. This section covers the additional ways you can arrange objects, which gives you more control over the placement of elements in your document.

Aligning objects

You can align objects on a page using the Align panel (choose Window⇨ Object And Layout⇨Align). This panel gives you control over how elements align to one another or to the overall page. The Align panel has many buttons to control selected objects. Mouse over a button to see its ToolTip describing how that button aligns elements.

If you're not sure what each button does after reading the associated ToolTip, then look at the icon on the button. It's sometimes helpful in depicting what the Align button does to the selected objects.

Here's how you align elements on the page:

1. **Select several objects on the page using the Selection tool.**

   Hold the Shift key while clicking each object to select several objects.

   Each of the objects is selected as you click them on the page. If you don't have a few objects on a page, then quickly create a couple of new objects by using the drawing tools.

2. **Choose Window⇨Object And Layout⇨Align.**

   The Align panel opens.

3. **Select the kind of alignment you want to apply to the selected objects.**

   Try clicking the Align Vertical Centers button. Each of your selected objects aligns to the vertical center point on the page.

Distributing objects

In the preceding step list, we show you how to align a few objects on a page, which is easy enough. However, what if the objects that you're aligning aren't distributed evenly? Maybe their centers are lined up, but there's a large gap between two of the images and a narrow gap between the other ones. In that case, you need to *distribute* objects as well as align them. You distribute objects on the page to space them relative to the page or each other in different ways. Here's how:

1. **Select objects on a page that are neither aligned nor evenly distributed by using the Selection tool while holding the Shift key.**

   The objects are selected as you click each one. All the objects you select will be aligned to each other on the page.

2. **If the Align panel is not open, choose Window⇨Object And Layout⇨ Align.**

   The Align panel opens.

3. **Click the Distribute Horizontal Centers button (where the hand cursor is pointing in Figure 6-11) and then click the Align Vertical Centers button directly above it on the Align panel.**

The selected objects are distributed evenly and aligned horizontally on the page.

Book II
Chapter 6

Clipping Paths, Transforming Objects, and Alignment

·

Chapter 7: Understanding Color and Printing

In This Chapter

✔ Using color in page layout

✔ Looking at color controls and models

✔ Discovering swatches and swatch libraries

✔ Understanding bleeding and trapping

✔ Looking at printing and preferences

Color is an important and complicated subject, especially in page layout; however, you probably already understand many of the concepts because the media bombards you with advertisements all the time. If you think about the advertisements you remember the most, you get an idea of the kinds of things that are successful in catching someone's attention. These ads often rely on color to relay an effective message. The success of printed ads greatly relies on *how* color is used in the layout. Color greatly enhances the message being relayed to readers. In this chapter, you find out some of the fundamental aspects of working with color and the basics on how to prepare a document for printing.

For more information on general subjects about color, refer to Book I, Chapter 7, which covers subjects such as color modes, inks, printers, and basic color correction across the programs in the Adobe Creative Suite.

Selecting Color with Color Controls

You have several different color modes and options when working in InDesign. Because color in print media can be quite a science, it's important to have a lot of control over how your documents print on the page. In Chapter 3 of this minibook, we show you how to add color to drawings with the Color panel. In this section, we cover using the Color panel to choose colors and apply them to the elements on your page.

Swatches are used in many of the other chapters in this minibook. It's a good idea to use swatches whenever possible because swatches use named colors that a service provider can match exactly. Swatches can be exactly the same in appearance as any color you choose that's unnamed, but a swatch establishes a link between the color on the page and the name of a color, such as a Pantone color number. You discover more about these kinds of color in the later section, "Using Color Swatches and Libraries."

You can use color controls for choosing colors for selections in the document:

✦ **Stroke color:** The Stroke color control allows you to choose colors for strokes and paths in InDesign. A hollow box represents the Stroke color control.

✦ **Fill color:** The Fill color control allows you to choose colors for filling shapes. A solid square box represents the Fill color control.

   You can toggle between the Fill and Stroke color controls by clicking them. Alternatively, you can press X on the keyboard to toggle between selected controls.

✦ **Text color:** When you're working with text, a different color control becomes active. The Text color control is visible and displays the currently selected text color. Text can have both the stroke and fill colored.

To apply colors to selections, you can click the Apply color button below the color controls in the toolbox. Alternatively, you can select and click a color swatch.

The default colors in InDesign are a black stroke and no color for the fill. Go back to the default colors at any time by pressing D. This shortcut works while on any tool except the Type tool.

Understanding Color Models

You can use any of three kinds of color models in InDesign: CMYK, RGB, and LAB colors. A *color model* is a system used for representing each color as a set of numbers or letters (or both). The best color model to use depends on how you plan to print or display your document:

✦ If you're creating a PDF that will be distributed electronically and probably won't be printed, use the RGB color model. RGB is how colors are displayed on a computer monitor.

✦ You must use the CMYK color model if you're working with *process color:* Instead of having inks that match specified colors, four ink colors are layered to simulate a particular color. Note that the colors on the monitor may differ from what is actually printed. Sample swatch books and numbers can help you determine what colors you need to use in your document to match what will be printed in the end.

✦ If you know that the document needs to be printed by professionals who determine what each color is before it's printed, it doesn't matter whether you use RGB, Pantone, or LAB colors. You have to make sure that you use named colors (predetermined swatches are a good idea) so that the service provider knows which color should be printed. In this case, you're using *spot colors,* which are mixed inks that match the colors you specify in InDesign.

For more information on color models and inks, check out Book I, Chapter 7. This chapter explains how colors are determined in the different color modes.

Book II
Chapter 7

Understanding
Color and Printing

Using Color Swatches and Libraries

The Swatches panel and swatch libraries help you choose colors. Swatch libraries help you use colors for specific publishing purposes. The colors you use in a document can vary greatly depending on what you're creating the document for. For example, one publication you make with InDesign may be for a catalog that only has two colors; another may be for the Web, where you have many colors available to you.

The Swatches panel

You can create, apply, and edit colors using the Swatches panel. In addition to solid colors, this panel also allows you to create and edit tints and gradients and then apply them to objects on a page. Choose Window➪Swatches to open or expand the Swatches panel.

To create a new color swatch to use in your document, follow these steps:

1. **Click the arrow in the upper-right corner to open the Swatches panel menu; choose New Color Swatch.**

The New Color Swatch dialog box opens.

2. **Type a new name for the color swatch or leave the color named by color values.**

(The colors in the Swatches panel appear this way as a default.)

This name is displayed next to the color swatch when it's entered into the panel.

3. **Choose the color type from the Color Type drop-down list.**

   Are you using a spot color (Pantone, for example) or CMYK (color created from a combination of cyan, magenta, yellow, black)?

4. **Choose the color mode.**

   Using the Color Mode drop-down list, select a color mode. For this example, we use CMYK. Many of the other choices that you see are prebuilt color libraries for various systems.

5. **Create the color using the color sliders.**

   Note that if you start with Black, you have to adjust that slider to the left to see the other colors.

6. **Click OK or Add.**

   Click Add if you want to continue adding colors to your Swatches panel or click OK if this color is the only one you're adding. The color(s) are added to the Swatches panel.

You can make changes to the swatch by selecting the swatch in the Swatches panel and then choosing Swatch Options from the panel menu.

Swatch libraries

Swatch libraries, also known as color libraries, are standardized sets of named colors that help you because they're the most commonly and frequently used sets of color swatches. This means that you can avoid trying to mix your own colors, which can be a difficult or tedious process to get right. For example, InDesign includes a swatch library for Pantone spot colors, and a different library for Pantone process colors. These libraries are very useful if you're working with either color set. (Refer to the earlier section, "Understanding Color Models," where we explain the difference between spot and process colors.)

To choose a swatch from a swatch library, follow these steps:

1. **Choose New Color Swatch from the Swatches panel menu.**

   The New Color Swatch dialog box opens.

2. **Select the color type you want to work with from the Color Type drop-down list.**

   Choose from Process or Spot Color types.

3. **Select a color library from the Color Mode drop-down list.**

The drop-down list contains a list of color swatch libraries to choose from, such as Pantone Process Coated or TRUMATCH. After choosing a swatch set, the library opens and appears in the dialog box. For this example, we chose the standard Pantone solid coated. If you're looking for the standard numbered Pantone colors, this set is the easiest to choose from. The Pantone solid-coated library of swatches loads.

4. Pick a swatch from the library.

Type a Pantone number, if you have one, in the Pantone text box. Most companies have set Pantone colors that they use for consistency. You can also scroll and click a swatch in the library's list of colors, as shown in Figure 7-1.

Figure 7-1:
Choose a color from the swatch library to add it to the Swatches panel.

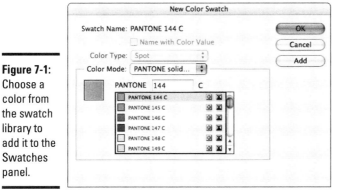

Picking Pantone colors this way is rarely accurate. Spending the money on the PANTONE(r) solid to process guide is a wise investment. Get more details about this guide at www.pantone.com.

5. Click the Add button.

This step adds the swatch to your list of color swatches in the Swatches panel. You can add as many color swatches as you like.

6. When you're finished adding swatches, click the Done button.

After you add a new color, the swatch is added to the list of swatches in the Swatches panel and is ready to use in your project. Look in the Swatches panel to see the newly added colors.

Printing Your Work

You can print your work from an InDesign document in many different ways, using many kinds of printers and processes. You can either use a printer at home or in your office, which are of varying levels of quality and design, or you can take your work into a professional establishment to print. Printing establishments (or service providers) also vary in the quality of production they can offer you.

This section looks at the different ways you can set up your document for printing, and the kinds of issues you may encounter during this process.

What is a bleed?

If you want an image or span of color to go right to the edge of a page, without any margins, you need to *bleed* off the edge of the document. Bleeding extends the print area slightly beyond the edge of the page into the area that will be cut as usual during the printing process. When you print your work, you can turn on crop and bleed marks to show where the page needs to be trimmed and to make sure that the image bleeds properly. We cover this topic in the last section of this chapter, "Doing it yourself: Printing at home or in the office."

About trapping

When you print documents, the printer is seldom absolutely perfect when creating a printed page with multiple inks. The *registration* (which determines the alignment of the separate colors when printed) will most surely be off. This discrepancy can potentially cause a gap between two colors on the page so that unprinted paper shows through between them. To solve this problem, you use *trapping*. Trapping overlaps elements on the page slightly so that you don't have that gap in between the elements. The basic principle of trapping is to spread the lighter of the colors into the other. See Figure 7-2 for an example.

Figure 7-2:
Text as it appears in InDesign (left). Text (right) as it appears when printed with trapping applied.

InDesign has built-in software for trapping. The settings you make are applied to the entire page. You choose settings in the Trap Presets panel. You can use the default settings, customize the trapping settings, or decide not to use trapping at all. To modify the default settings and then apply the customized settings, follow these steps:

1. **Choose Window➪Output➪Trap Presets.**

The Trap Presets panel opens. The Trapping presets in InDesign are document-wide, but you can assign individual trappings by using the Window➪Attributes panel to overprint strokes on selected art only.

2. **Double-click [Default] in the panel's list.**

The Modify Trap Preset Options dialog box opens, as shown in Figure 7-3. The default settings are perfectly adequate for many printing jobs.

3. **Change the trap preset options, if you know what is necessary, and then click OK to close the dialog box.**

If you don't know what to change, you should investigate the options for a better understanding of how they work. You can also get settings from your print provider.

4. **In the Trap Presets panel, choose New Preset from the panel menu.**

The New Trap Preset dialog box opens.

5. **Type an appropriate name for the new trap preset.**

You see this name in the list of trap presets in the Trap Presets panel when it's opened. You might create a name for a printer that has different settings than another.

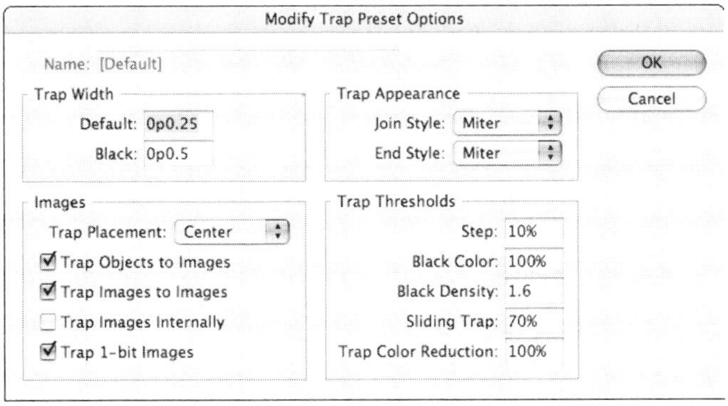

Figure 7-3:
The Modify
Trap Preset
Options
dialog box.

Modify Trap Preset Options

Name: [Default]

Trap Width
Default: 0p0.25
Black: 0p0.5

Trap Appearance
Join Style: Miter
End Style: Miter

OK
Cancel

Images
Trap Placement: Center
☑ Trap Objects to Images
☑ Trap Images to Images
☐ Trap Images Internally
☑ Trap 1-bit Images

Trap Thresholds
Step: 10%
Black Color: 100%
Black Density: 1.6
Sliding Trap: 70%
Trap Color Reduction: 100%

6. Review and make any changes to the new preset in the dialog box.

You can change the presets in the following ways:

- **Trap Width:** The Default value specifies the width of the trap for any ink that you use in the document, except for black. The value for black is entered into the Black text field.

- **Images:** These settings control how InDesign handles trapping between elements on the document page and any imported graphics on it. Use the Trap Placement drop-down list to define how images trap to objects on the page. When you have bitmap images next to each other, select the Trap Images To Images check box.

- **Trap Appearance:** These settings allow you to do some fine-tuning and change how the corner points appear in trapping. You can select how you want the corner points to appear with the Join Style drop-down list; you can select how you want end points to appear (over-lapped or separated) from the End Style drop-down list.

- **Trap Thresholds:** These settings allow you to control how InDesign traps the areas between two colors in your document. You can con-trol whether InDesign traps two objects of similar colors (for exam-ple, how different do these colors have to be before InDesign starts trapping).

7. Click OK to create the trap preset.

The New Trap Preset dialog box closes, and the customized preset is added to the panel.

To assign a trap preset to a number of pages (or all of them), click the arrow in the upper-right corner of the Trap Preset panel and choose Assign Trap Preset from the panel menu. The dialog box that opens allows you to choose a trapping style and assign it to all pages or a range of pages. Click the Assign button to assign the preset before clicking the Done button.

There are also other ways to apply trapping to your document manually. This process goes beyond the scope of this book, but is worthwhile to look into if you want to fully realize what trapping is all about. Refer to *InDesign CS2 Bible* (written by Galen Gruman and published by Wiley Publishing, Inc.) for more information on trapping.

Taking your files to a service provider

If you're taking your file to a professional print service (service provider), you may have to save the .indd document as a different format. Even though they should, not all service providers will have InDesign on hand.

There are two major groups of printers: PostScript and non-PostScript. PostScript printers take files written in the PostScript language and read the files to print them. PostScript files describe the contents of each page and how they should look when printed. Most printers you find in a home or office are not PostScript printers.

If you're giving the file to someone to print, you can pass on your work in a few different ways. You can give the person printing the document your original InDesign document. Of course, he (or the business) must have a copy of InDesign on hand to open the file. Or you can send a PostScript file or PDF file to print. Sometimes, you have to ask what the preferred file type for opening and printing the document is. You're probably best off sending the original InDesign file (if you can) or a PDF. When you create a PDF, your documents should print accurately.

The *Preflight* feature is used to check for quality in your document, and tell you information about the document you're printing (such as listing the fonts, print settings, and inks that you're using). Using Preflight can help you determine whether your InDesign document has unlinked images or missing fonts before printing your document. Choose File⇨Preflight to access the Preflight dialog box.

You can determine whether any elements associated with the file are missing and then package it into a single folder to take the document to a service provider. Here's how:

1. **Choose File⇨Preflight.**

The Preflight dialog box opens. The Summary screen is open to begin with, and it shows you all the current images and fonts found in the document. Essentially, the summary is based on an analysis of the document.

2. **Click Fonts in the list on the left side of the dialog box.**

Any fonts in your document are listed in this screen. Select fonts on this list and click the Find Font button to discover where they're located on your hard drive. These fonts are directly saved into the package folder when you're finished.

3. **Click Links And Images in the list on the left side of the dialog box.**

The Links And Images screen lists the images within your document. You have to find the image, update it, and repair links before packing the file. If any images aren't properly linked, your document is incomplete and will print with pictures missing. Also, make sure that if you're sending your work to a professional printer, you have properly converted your images to CMYK. For your desktop printer, RGB should be fine.

4. **When you're finished, click the Package button at the bottom of the dialog box.**

   Your document and all the associated files are saved into a folder. You're given the opportunity to name the folder and specify a location on the hard drive.

Doing it yourself: Printing at home or in the office

You have probably printed other kinds of documents in the past, and perhaps you've even played with the printer settings. These settings depend on what kind of printer you're using and associated printer drivers you have installed on your system. Whatever operating system you work with, and whatever printer you use, you have some settings that control the printer's output. This section deals only with the more basic and common kinds of printing that you may perform at home or in the office.

Choose File➪Print to open the Print dialog box. Many printing options are available in the list on the left side of the Print dialog box. Click an item, and the dialog box changes to display the settings you can change for the selected item.

The options you're most likely to use when printing InDesign documents are as follows:

+ **General:** Allows you to set the number of copies of the document you want to print and the range of pages to print. You can select the Reverse Order check box to print from the last to first page. Select an option from the Sequence drop-down list to print only even or odd pages instead of all pages. If you're working with spreads that need to be printed on a single page, select the Spreads check box.

+ **Setup:** This screen is where you can define the paper size, orientation (portrait or landscape), and scale. You can scale a page so that it's up to 1000 percent of its original size or as little as 1%. You can optionally constrain the scale of the width and height so that the page remains at the same ratio. The Page position drop-down list is useful when you're using paper that is larger than the document you have created. This option helps you to center the document on the larger paper.

+ **Marks And Bleed:** The settings on this screen allow you to turn on or off many of the printing marks in the document, such as crop, bleed, and registration marks. For example, you may want to show these marks if you have a bleed extending past the boundaries of the page and need to show where to crop each page. This screen also shows a preview of what the page looks like when printed. You can also select options to print page information (such as filename and date) on each page.

✦ **Output:** This area allows you to choose how you're going to print the pages — for example, as a separation or composite, with which inks (if you are using separations), with or without trapping, and so forth. InDesign can separate and print your documents as plates (which are used in commercial printing) from settings you specify here.

✦ **Graphics:** This screen controls how graphics and fonts in the document are printed. The Send Data drop-down list controls bitmap images and how much of the data from these images is sent to the printer. The All option sends all bitmap data, the Optimized Subsampling option sends as much image data as the printer can handle, the Proxy option prints lower-quality images mostly to preview them, and the None option prints placeholder boxes with an X through them.

✦ **Color Management:** In this area, you choose how you want color handled upon output. If you have profiles loaded in your system for your output devices, you can select them here.

✦ **Advanced:** Use this area to determine how you want images to be sent to the printer. If you don't have a clue about Open Prepress Interface (OPI), you can leave this setting at the default. Also known as image-swapping technology, *OPI* is the process that allows low-resolution images inserted into InDesign to be swapped with the high-resolution version for output.

Flattening needs to be addressed if you used a drop shadow, feathered an object in InDesign, or applied transparency to any of your objects, even if they were created in Photoshop or Illustrator.

Use the preset Medium Resolution for desktop printers and High Resolution for professional press output.

✦ **Summary:** This window doesn't allow for modifications, but provides you a good overview of all your print settings.

After you make your settings, click the Save Preset button if you want to save the changes you've made. If you think you may print other documents with these settings repeatedly, using the Save Preset feature can be a great timesaver.

After you click the Save Preset button, the Save Preset dialog box opens, where you can enter a new name to save the settings as. The next time you print a document, you can select the saved preset from the Print Preset drop-down list in the Print dialog box.

Click the Print button at the bottom of the Print dialog box when you're ready to print the document.

Chapter 8: Exporting Your Work

In This Chapter

✔ **Looking at file formats**

✔ **Exporting to different file formats**

*Y*ou can export publications into several different kinds of file formats from InDesign, just as you can import various kinds of file formats. In this chapter, we take a closer look at the different kinds of files you can create electronically with an InDesign document.

Understanding File Formats

What kind of file format you decide to export to depends on what you're going to use the file for. The first thing you want to do is figure out what you need your content to do. Does it need to be on a Web page, or do you need to send the file by e-mail? Do you need to import the content into a different program, such as Macromedia Flash or Adobe Illustrator? Do you need to take a particular kind of file somewhere else to print it out?

Exporting your files to a particular format is how you can take your content from InDesign and make it "portable" for integration or display purposes. You can choose from a range of formats, and you can control many settings to customize how the file is exported.

You can export a file in several different file formats from InDesign. You can export to image files (JPEG and EPS). You can also export to an InCopy story, XML files, SVG files, Adobe PDF format, and rich or plain text.

Different file formats are used for different purposes. Here are some of the things you can do with files exported from InDesign:

✦ **Image files:** Image files such as JPEG and EPS can be exported from InDesign and then imported into other software programs. You can export these images for use in print after being imported into a different graphics program, or you can use the images on the Web. It all depends on how you set up the document for export and the settings you use.

✦ **PDFs:** PDF (Portable Document Format) is a common format used extensively for distributing files, such as e-books, brochures, and so on. You may need to distribute the file to a wide audience or to a service provider for printing. Anyone who has installed the Adobe Reader (also known as Acrobat Reader) on his computer can view your document. PDF is also used for importing as an image or text into other programs, such as Macromedia Flash MX 2004.

✦ **InCopy stories:** InCopy is tightly integrated with InDesign and is used to create and edit text documents. Therefore, if you have InCopy, you can export to it when you want to extensively edit the text in your file. InCopy is used for word processing and is designed to integrate with InDesign for associated page layout. You can read more about this application at www.adobe.com/products/incopy.

✦ **SVG files:** You can export as SVG (Scalable Vector Graphics), which is a file format that combines XML and CSS to display your files. SVG is a vector-based format that is also used for displaying content online through use of an oversized plug-in called SVG Viewer. You can download it for Mac or Windows platforms from www.adobe.com/support/downloads/main.html (look under the "Readers" section).

✦ **Text files:** Text files are a simple way to export your content. If you need the text from your document only to incorporate or send elsewhere, you can export as plain (Text Only), tagged, or rich text. If you need to send your document to someone who doesn't have InDesign, then exporting as text may be a good option.

After determining which file format you want to export your file as, take a look at how to export these files and the different kinds of settings you can control when doing so. The rest of this chapter shows you how to export different file types from InDesign.

Exporting Publications

You can export publications from the Export dialog box. Access the Export dialog box by choosing File➪Export. From this main Export dialog box, you can choose the file format, a name for the file, and a location to save it in. After specifying a name, location, and a format to export to for the new file, click Save, and a new dialog box opens where you can make settings specific to the file format you picked. We discuss some of the most common file formats that you're likely to use for export in the following sections.

Exporting PDF documents

InDesign allows you to export a PDF file of your document or book. If you choose to export a PDF document, you have many options available to customize the document you're exporting. You can control the amount of compression for the document, the marks and bleeds you have in InDesign, and security settings. Here's how you export a PDF:

1. **Choose File⇨Export.**

The Export dialog box opens.

2. **Choose a location in which to save the files and enter a new filename.**

Browse to a location on your hard drive using the Save In drop-down list if you're using Windows and name the file in the File Name text field. Name the file in the Save As text field on the Mac and choose a location using the Where drop-down list.

3. **Select PDF from the Save As Type (Windows) or Format (Mac) drop-down list.**

4. **Click Save.**

The Export PDF dialog box appears with the General options screen open.

5. **Choose a Preset.**

These presets are very good and easy to use. If you're familiar with Adobe Acrobat and the Adobe Distiller functions, they're the same. For more detailed information about what each setting does, see Book V.

6. **Leave the Standard drop-down menu at None.**

Unless, of course, you know about PDF/X and know which form of it to select. The details of PDF/X are explained in Book V.

7. **Select a range of pages to export.**

You can choose to export all pages or a range of pages.

8. **Choose a compatibility setting for the PDF from the Compatibility drop-down list.**

Compatibility settings determine what kind of reader is required to view the document. Setting compatibility to Acrobat 5 (PDF 1.4) ensures a wide audience can view your PDF. Some PDF readers may not be able to interpret certain features in your document if you choose compatibility for a higher version.

9. **Choose whether to embed thumbnails, whether to optimize the document, and what kinds of elements to include in the file.**

Other settings allow you to include bookmarks, links, and other elements in the file. Unless you've added any of these elements, you don't need to worry about selecting these options. You may want to embed thumbnail previews, but an Acrobat user can create his own thumbnails when the file is open as well.

Click Security in the list on the left of the Export PDF dialog box to open the Security screen, where you can specify passwords to open the document. You can also choose a password that is required to print or modify the PDF file.

10. **Click the Export button to export the file.**

The file is saved to the location you specified in Step 2.

You can choose a preset to export your work from the Preset drop-down list on the General screen. These presets automatically change the export settings for your document. For example, you can select Screen from the Preset drop-down list if you're displaying your work online, or select Print if you plan for the PDF to be printed on home printers. Select Press if you intend to have the PDF professionally printed.

Exporting EPS files

From InDesign, you can export EPS files, which are useful for importing into other programs. EPS files are single-page graphics files, which means each exported InDesign page is saved as a separate EPS file. Here's how to export EPS files:

1. **Choose File➪Export.**

The Export dialog box opens.

2. **Select a location on your hard drive to save the EPS files, enter a new filename, and select EPS from the Save As Type (Windows) or Format (Mac) drop-down list; click Save.**

The Export EPS dialog box opens.

3. **Choose a page or range of pages to export.**

Select the All Pages option to export all pages or select the Ranges option and enter a range of pages. If you want spreads to export as one file, then select the Spreads check box.

If you're creating more than one EPS file (for example, exporting more than one page of your InDesign document), then the file is saved with the filename, an underscore, and then the page number. For example, page 7 of a file called cats.indd would be saved as cats_7.eps in the designated location.

No need to export an EPS to place an InDesign file into another InDesign file! If you're creating classified pages or any page that contains other InDesign pages, you can save yourself a few steps by simply choosing File⇨Place and selecting the InDesign file.

4. **From the Color drop-down list, select a color mode; from the Embed Fonts drop-down list, select how you want fonts to be embedded.**

    From the Color drop-down list, select Leave Unchanged to retain the color mode you're using for the InDesign document. You can also change the color mode to CMYK, Gray (grayscale), or RGB. For more information on color modes, flip to Chapter 7 of this minibook.

    From the Embed Fonts drop-down list, select Subset to embed only the characters that are used in the file. If you select Complete, all the fonts in the file are loaded when you print the file. Selecting None means that a reference to where the font is located is written into the file.

5. **Choose whether you want a preview to be generated for the file.**

    A preview (a small thumbnail image) is useful if an EPS file can't be displayed. For example, if you're browsing through a library of images, you'll see a small thumbnail image of the EPS file; so whether or not you use the image or can open it on your computer, you can see what the file looks like. From the Preview drop-down list, you can select TIFF to generate a preview; select None if you don't want a preview to be created.

6. **Click the Export button to export the files.**

    The files are saved to the location you designated in Step 2.

Exporting JPEG files

You can export JPEG files from an InDesign document. You can export a single object on the selected page, or you can export entire pages and spreads as a JPEG image. JPEG files allow you to effectively compress full color or black-and-white images.

To export a JPEG image, follow these steps:

1. **Select an object on a page or make sure that no object is selected if you want to export a page or spread.**

2. **Choose File⇨Export.**

    The Export dialog box opens.

3. **Type a filename, locate where you want to save the file on your hard drive, and select JPEG from the Save As Type (Windows) or Format (Mac) drop-down list; click Save.**

    The Export JPEG dialog box opens.

4. **If you want to export a page, select the Page option and enter the page number; if you want to export the currently selected object, make sure that the Selection option is selected.**

The selection option is available only if a selection was made in Step 1.

5. **Choose an image quality and format to export.**

The Image Quality drop-down list controls the amount of compression used when you export the JPEG. The Maximum option creates an image with the highest file size and best quality, while the Low option creates a smaller file of lesser quality because it includes less image information.

If you choose the Baseline format from the Format Method drop-down list, the entire image has to be downloaded before it displays in a Web browser. Select Progressive to show the image in a progressively complete display as it downloads in a Web browser.

6. **Click the Export button.**

The file exports and saves to the location that you specified in Step 3.

Exporting SVG files

You can export to SVG using the Export dialog box. You can export a spread, pages, or even a single element from a page of the InDesign document. Here's how you export an SVG file:

1. **Select an object on a page or make sure that no object is selected if you want to export a page or spread.**

2. **Choose File⇨Export.**

The Export dialog box opens.

3. **Choose a location to save the files, enter a new filename, and select SVG from the Save As Type (Windows) or Format (Mac) drop-down list; click Save.**

The SVG Options dialog box opens.

4. **Select a page, range of pages, spreads, or selection to export in the SGV Options dialog box.**

If you've selected an object, select the Export Selection check box. Alternatively, you can select the Range option and enter values for a range of pages to export. If you chose to export pages, each page (or spread) is exported as a separate SVG file.

5. **Choose to use glyphs or a character set in the Fonts section.**

If you don't plan to change text in the document, you can embed glyphs by selecting Only Glyphs Used from the Subsetting drop-down list.

A *glyph* is a single character. For example, N is a glyph, which is different from the P glyph, and a set of glyphs makes up a particular font. The Only Glyphs Used setting means that only the characters you use export in the document. Otherwise, you can choose to use a set of characters (such as Common English) to export, which means all the characters in the English or Roman characters are included for the fonts you use.

You can also choose not to embed characters at all and use system fonts on the user's system. This option means the user has to have the fonts you use installed on his system for the characters to display properly, or a default font is used as a replacement.

6. **Choose to embed or link to bitmap image files used in the Images section.**

If you select the Embed option, your bitmap images in the SVG file are larger when they export because the image is included within the file itself. If you select the Link option, then the SVG file is smaller, but you have to make sure to include the bitmap images with the SVG files when you upload or send your work. InDesign converts your images into JPEG files and saves them with the SVG file.

Use the Description area to discover more about each setting. Hover your cursor over a setting, and a description of the setting appears at the bottom of the dialog box.

7. **Click the Export button to export the file.**

The files are exported and saved to the location you designated in Step 3.

Exporting text files

You can export plain or rich text from an InDesign document, or as an InDesign tagged text format. These formats can be slightly different, depending on the text in your document.

To export text, follow these steps:

1. **Select the Text tool from the toolbox and select some text within a text frame in your document.**

You must have text selected in order to see text export options in the Export dialog box.

2. **Choose File➪Export.**

The Export dialog box opens.

3. **Enter a filename, select a location to save the file in, and select Text Only from the Save As Type (Windows) or Format (Mac) drop-down list; click Save.**

The Text Export Options dialog box opens.

4. Choose a platform and encoding for the export.

Select either Windows or Macintosh from the Platform drop-down list to set the PC or Mac operating system compatibility. Select an encoding method for the platform you choose from the Encoding drop-down list; you can choose either Default Platform or Unicode.

Unicode is a universal character-encoding standard that is compatible with major operating systems. *Encoding* refers to how characters are represented in a digital format, and it's essentially a set of rules that determines how the character set is represented by associating each character with a particular code sequence.

5. Click the Export button.

The file exports and saves to the location that you specified in Step 3.

Chapter 9: Integrating InDesign

In This Chapter

✔ **Integrating Version Cue**

✔ **Exporting to Acrobat**

✔ **Working with Photoshop files**

✔ **Using Illustrator files in InDesign**

✔ **Using InDesign and Dreamweaver**

The Adobe Creative Suite and InDesign offer you a multitude of options to integrate all the Creative Suite 3 applications. (When you *integrate* products, you work on a single project using more than one piece of software.

When software products are built as a suite, it typically is an advantage to the user. Software designers create ways that the user can integrate the products to work together and give the user more power to maintain a workflow, check errors, and help with consistency in a project. By making the Adobe Creative Suite 3 products work together, you can get some incredible results!

Using InDesign with Version Cue

Using Adobe Version Cue, you can keep a project organized and accessible from all the Creative Suite applications. Many users don't jump right in because they've never experienced the convenience project management software provides, but we guarantee that you'll love it.

Adobe Version Cue manages files you author in the following Adobe Creative Suite components: Photoshop, InDesign, Illustrator, Dreamweaver, Flash, and Acrobat 8. In Version Cue, you create projects, either new, blank projects that you save into, or new projects from existing work.

You and other users can then access the projects through the Creative Suite applications. Version Cue manages files stored in projects, which keep all the files related to an assignment together in one place. Version Cue can even keep track of non-Adobe files, such as spreadsheets and invoices. Because Version Cue works in each Creative Suite component, your design process isn't interrupted when you work on each file in a project.

You can use Version Cue to track changes to files as you work on them. You can even keep several versions of each file for future reference. By using Version Cue, multiple users can access files in a project, work on them, and "lock out" anyone else who may want to work on the file at the same time. Benefit to this one: No changes being overwritten accidentally by another person on your team!

The following list is a quick look at what you can do with Version Cue:

✦ Create a new project and organize all your files into that single project

✦ Make your projects secure, private, or shared

✦ Create and manage different versions of a file

✦ Insert comments that you can refer to later

✦ Browse projects with comments, thumbnails, and information on each file contained within the project

✦ Back up projects

✦ Set and remove permissions on the project files (if you're working with the more advanced features of Version Cue)

✦ Add users to a project, who can work on and edit files

✦ Share projects among several users

You must have Version Cue CS3 installed on your system before you can use these features. Version Cue is enabled in InDesign as a default. You can verify that Version Cue CS3 is installed by following these steps:

1. **Choose Edit⇨Preferences⇨File Handling (Windows) or InDesign⇨ Preferences⇨File Handling (Mac OS).**

The Preferences dialog box appears with the File Handling screen open.

2. **If the Enable Version Cue check box isn't selected, click it and then click OK.**

You must restart InDesign before your modifications take effect.

Setting up a Project file

The scope of this book doesn't allow for a lot of detail in project management, but it's helpful to know how to set up a project file and save to it. To set up a project folder, follow these steps:

1. **Launch Version Cue CS3 (Windows) in the control panel.**

If you're working on a Mac, choose Apple⇨System Preferences⇨Other⇨ Version Cue CS3.

You may not want the Version Cue server on your computer. You can install it on another computer that can act as your server.

2. **In the Adobe Version Cue CS3 dialog box, choose whether you want others to see the Version Cue server and how many users will be allowed and then click Start to start the server.**

You're directed to the browser interface of Version Cue.

3. **In the Initial Configuration window, create a password and define the server name, as shown in Figure 9-1.**

You can also set up the server visibility and set preferences as to how users can access your server.

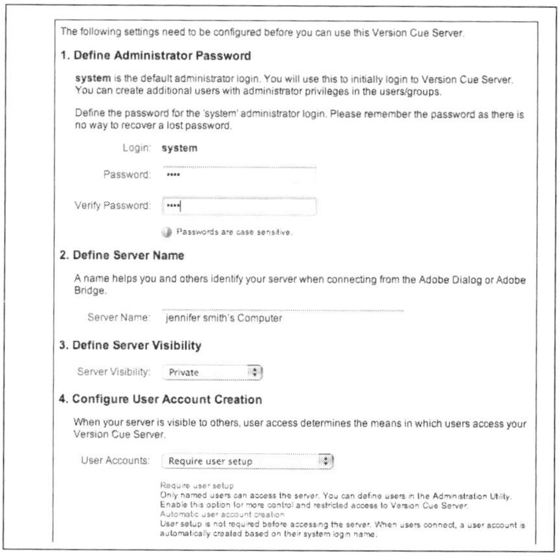

Book II
Chapter 9

Integrating InDesign

The following settings need to be configured before you can use this Version Cue Server.

1. Define Administrator Password

system is the default administrator login. You will use this to initially login to Version Cue Server. You can create additional users with administrator privileges in the users/groups.

Define the password for the 'system' administrator login. Please remember the password as there is no way to recover a lost password.

Login: **system**

Password: ••••

Verify Password: ••••

Passwords are case sensitive.

2. Define Server Name

A name helps you and others identify your server when connecting from the Adobe Dialog or Adobe Bridge.

Server Name: jennifer smith's Computer

3. Define Server Visibility

Server Visibility: Private

4. Configure User Account Creation

When your server is visible to others, user access determines the means in which users access your Version Cue Server.

User Accounts: Require user setup

Require user setup
Only named users can access the server. You can define users in the Administration Utility. Enable this option for more control and restricted access to Version Cue Server.
Automatic user account creation
User setup is not required before accessing the server. When users connect, a user account is automatically created based on their system login name.

Figure 9-1:
Configuring
Version Cue.

4. **Once you fill in the password and change other options, click the Save & Continue button.**

The Version Cue CS3 Server Administration window appears.

5. **Type your login and password.**

The Version Cue interface makes it easy to follow along to create a new project folder and assign users. Once you complete this process, you can start taking advantage of its benefits.

If you want more help with setting up a project using Version Cue, launch the Adobe Bridge application, which resides in the same folder as your other Adobe Creative Suite applications. Click Version Cue in the left column and choose Help⇨Version Cue Help.

6. **Click Create A Project.**

7. **Select Blank Project, create a name (perhaps *test project*), and enter it in the Project Name text box.**

8. **Check the box to Share This Project With Others.**

9. **Click the Create button.**

10. **When the New Project window appears, click OK.**

    A new project is created.

Adding a user to the project

To add a user to the project, simply follow these steps:

1. **Click the Users/Groups tab at the top of the Version Cue CS3 window.**

2. **Click the New button at the bottom of the Users window.**

   The New User dialog box appears.

3. **Create a username, login, and password.**

4. **Choose an admin access level of user for those logging in who you don't want to have administrative controls.**

   For yourself, you'd want to choose System Administrator from the Admin Access level drop-down list.

   Pick something easy to remember!

5. **Click the Save button and close the Version Cue CS3 interface window.**

Saving a file into a project

In InDesign, create a new document or open an existing one that you want to save in a project file. To save the file into a project, follow these steps:

1. **Choose File⇨Save As.**

2. **In the Save As window, click the Use Adobe Dialog button.**

   The Save dialog box appears.

3. **Click Version Cue from the panel on the left.**

Your user name is now listed.

4. **Double-click your user name.**

5. **Double-click the project and name and save your file.**

This is just a start. Once you save into a project, you can save various versions, set up other users to share that file (remember that they're locked out if you're using it), and help you keep entire projects organized . . . what fun!

Integrating InDesign with Acrobat

You can import, export, and create documents for creating PDF files using InDesign. You can further manipulate these files using Adobe Acrobat, or you can build in certain features using InDesign. In Chapter 8 of this minibook, you discovered more about exporting PDF files from InDesign. In this chapter, we look at some of the other ways that you can control PDF attributes right in InDesign.

InDesign is one of the best ways to design and create PDF documents. With InDesign, you can add features and interactivity to a PDF in the following ways:

✦ Add clickable elements, such as hyperlinks and bookmarks.

✦ Add buttons that perform actions.

✦ Add movies (such as Flash SWF files or QuickTime movies) and sound files.

Creating a hyperlink

You can add hyperlinks to link to another piece of text, a page, or a URL (a Web site address). To create a URL hyperlink in a PDF using InDesign, follow these steps:

1. **Open a new document that includes some text in a text frame.**

Choose a document that you want to add a hyperlink to.

2. **Open the Hyperlinks panel by choosing Window⇨Interactive⇨ Hyperlinks.**

The Hyperlinks panel opens. Notice that the panel's menu contains several options, and you can use buttons along the bottom of the panel to add new hyperlinks or delete links from the panel.

3. Use the Text tool to select some text.

Select the text that you want to make into a hyperlink.

4. Click the Create New Hyperlink button at the bottom of the Hyperlinks panel.

The New Hyperlink dialog box opens. Make sure that URL is selected in the Type drop-down list.

5. Type a URL in the URL text field, if necessary.

The type you enter is the Web page the URL links to. Make sure that it's a complete URL, such as `http://www.yourdomain.com`. This field also accepts `mailto:` actions if you want to create an e-mail link. Simply enter an e-mail address, such as `mailto:you@yourdomain.com`, in the URL text field.

6. Choose an appearance for the clickable text.

Under the Appearance section, you can choose to have a visible or invisible rectangle (whether you want a rectangle to appear around the link). Then you can choose the highlight, color, width, and style of your link.

7. Click OK when you're finished.

The dialog box closes. When you export your document as a PDF, this text will be clickable. Clicking the text opens a browser window to the Web page you entered in the URL text field. Make sure that the Hyperlinks check box is selected in the Export PDF dialog box when you create the PDF file.

You can also select a URL that exists in your text frame. To do so, select the URL and right-click (Windows) or Ctrl+click (Mac) the selected text. Choose Interactive➪New Hyperlink Destination, and the dialog box opens where you can edit the link. Click OK, and a hyperlink is created.

Adding a media file

In this section, we show you how to add some basic interactivity to a PDF file using InDesign by adding a movie file. You can add an SWF file or an MOV file, depending on what you have available. These media files won't play while you're using InDesign. However, the files will play if you export the document to PDF or XML. To view a movie in a PDF file, double-click the movie.

You can add the following movie files to a PDF: SWF, MOV, AVI, and MPEG. And you can add these audio files: AIF, AU, and WAV.

To add a media file to a PDF document using InDesign, follow these steps (remember that you need at least Acrobat Reader 6 to view the PDF and play the media file):

1. Choose File⇨Place.

The Place dialog box opens, where you can choose a media file to import. Choose an SWF, MOV, AVI, or MPEG to import.

You can import only SWF files created for the Flash 5 Player and earlier. You can't import files into InDesign created for Flash Player 6 or Flash Player 7.

2. Click within the document window to place the media file on the page.

**Book II
Chapter 9**

The Place cursor appears after you select a file to import into the document. Click where you want the upper-left corner to be situated on the page.

3. Export the PDF file by choosing File⇨Export and choosing Adobe PDF from the Save As Type (Windows) or Format (Mac) drop-down list and then click Save.

The Export PDF dialog box appears.

4. Choose Acrobat 6 or higher from the Compatibility drop-down menu and then make sure that the Interactive Elements check box is selected in the Export PDF dialog box.

5. In the Multimedia drop-down list, you can select the Embed option to include the movie in the PDF, increasing the file size, the Link option to create a link to the movie file in the PDF (you must have the file accessible to the PDF when you send it to someone or put it online), or the Use Object Settings option to use the settings already made in InDesign.

If you play the file in Acrobat Reader 6 or greater, the video plays when you double-click the frame.

Integrating InDesign with Photoshop

Many people create their designs in Photoshop (which we discuss thoroughly in Book IV) and then import the native PSD files from Photoshop 4 or greater right into InDesign. InDesign supports many of the features you can find in Photoshop, so you can have additional control over the designs after the image is imported into InDesign.

Here's a great feature that you'll be thrilled with: InDesign CS3 lets you import a layered Photoshop file, turn on and off the layers, or even choose a layer comp to be placed. Follow these steps:

1. **Have a layered Photoshop file ready to place.**

2. **In InDesign, choose File⇨Place.**

3. **Browse to the location of your layered image file and check Show Import Options.**

   A window similar to the one you see in Figure 9-2 appears.

4. **Click the Layers tab and turn off and on the visibility of the layers you want to change or select a saved layer comp from the Layer Comp drop-down list.**

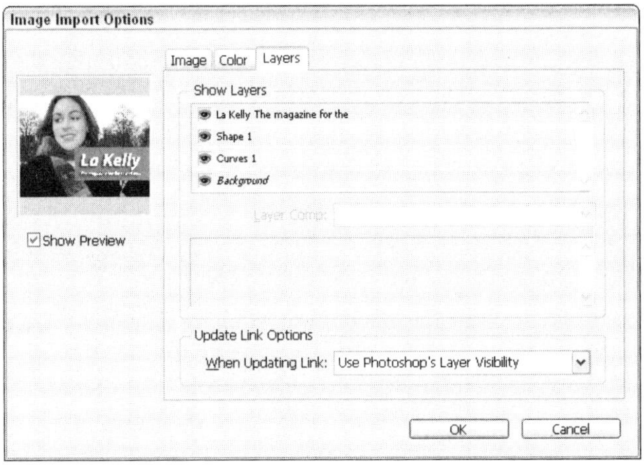

Figure 9-2: InDesign CS3 allows you to choose which layers you want to place.

Transparency support and clipping paths

Many Photoshop files use transparency. The transparency in the PSD files is imported and interpreted by InDesign. This feature is particularly useful when you have an established background or want to have an interesting text wrap around an image that you import from Photoshop. Basically, you can use the transparency as a *clipping path* in InDesign. Clipping paths are like hard-edged masks that hide parts of an image, such as a background that you don't want visible around a certain part of the image. (See Book IV, Chapter 4, for more about Photoshop clipping paths.)

You can use alpha channels, paths, and masks that you create in Photoshop in InDesign. InDesign recognizes these parts of the PSD, so you can use them when you're wrapping text around the image or when you want to create a clipping path. Alternatively, you can also use these parts to remove a background from the image. For example, if you have an image with one of these assets, you can use the Detect Edges feature in InDesign to detect the edges and wrap text around the image. (We explain text wrapping in Chapter 4 of this minibook.)

Photoshop spot colors in InDesign

If you're using spot colors in an image you import from Photoshop, those colors show up in the Swatches panel in InDesign. There is a chance that a color from your spot colors channel won't be recognized. If that's the case, the color is shown as gray instead. You can find more information on spot and process colors in Chapter 7 of this minibook.

You can use the swatches imported with the Photoshop file with other parts of your file. Simply use the swatches as you would any other swatch in InDesign. You can't delete these swatches unless you remove the Photoshop file that you imported into InDesign. For more information about using the Swatches panel in InDesign, see Chapter 7 of this minibook.

Integrating InDesign with Illustrator

Illustrator (which we discuss at great length in Book III) is a tremendous drawing program that enables you to create complex drawings. Therefore, it's a great tool to use for creating illustrations bound for InDesign page layouts. Luckily, you have several ways to control your Illustrator artwork directly in InDesign, which we discuss in this section. You can import Illustrator 5.5 files and greater into InDesign and maintain the editability of the objects from the AI (Illustrator) file within InDesign, which means that you can edit the objects further after they're imported. Also, any transparency in the AI file is preserved when you import it, meaning that you can wrap text around the drawings you create.

You can also copy and paste graphics from Illustrator to InDesign and then edit them directly in InDesign.

Integrating InDesign with InCopy

Adobe InCopy is text-editing software that enables writers to write and edit documents while layout is prepared separately. InCopy is similar to

Microsoft Word in that you can make notes and comments, track changes, and use other similar editing features.

You may not have InCopy installed (it isn't part of the Adobe Creative Suite), but there are several important ways that you can integrate this Adobe software with InDesign that you shouldn't overlook. If you're extensively editing stories, you may want to consider using InCopy for writing the text and importing and editing it further using InDesign.

Using InCopy together with InDesign enables you to use a particular workflow because you can tell whether a file needs to be updated, or if it's currently being edited, by a series of icons that appear on the page in InDesign. The following sections show some of the ways that you can directly manipulate InCopy stories using InDesign.

Importing InCopy stories

Here are the steps for importing stories from InCopy:

1. **In InCopy, create and save a text file.**

If you don't have a copy of InCopy, you can download a 30-day trial version from www.adobe.com.

2. **Return to InDesign, create a text frame, and keep it selected.**

3. **Choose File⇨Place.**

4. **Browse to locate your InCopy file.**

(InCopy files end with the file extension .incx.)

The InCopy story is placed into the text frame and in the Links panel, just like a graphic.

Updating InCopy stories

When a file is out of date, you need to update that story so that the most recent revisions are available to you for editing.

When you see the warning icon, you can follow these steps to update the InCopy story from InDesign:

1. **Choose the story listed in the Links panel.**

2. **Select the button Update Link in the bottom of the Links panel.**

The story updates, and the icon disappears. You can now work with the up-to-date version of the story in InDesign.

Integrating InDesign with Dreamweaver

Exporting an InDesign document for Dreamweaver allows you to take InDesign documents (or even complete books) and package them up for further editing in Dreamweaver CS3. This feature enables you to put InDesign documents on the Web and make them available to a wide audience.

To export a document for Dreamweaver, follow these steps:

1. **With an InDesign document open, choose File⇨Cross-media Export⇨ XHTML/Dreamweaver.**

   The Save As window appears.

2. **Find a location on your hard drive for the package and enter a name for your html file in the Save As text field.**

3. **Click the Save button.**

   The XHTML Export Options dialog box appears. In this dialog box, you can determine whether you're exporting only the selection (if you had something selected) or the entire document. You can also map how you want the bullets handled.

4. **Select Images in the left column to see options for saving optimized images.**

5. **Leave the Image Conversion set to automatic to let InDesign decide whether an image is best saved as a GIF or JPEG, or determine which format you would prefer all images to be saved in.**

6. **Select Advanced to determine how Cascading Styles Sheets are handled, if you want them, or if you want them to reference an external CSS style that it will link to.**

7. **Once you have completed the options, click the Export button.**

   You can now open, and further edit, the file in Dreamweaver.

Book III

Illustrator CS3

The 5th Wave   By Rich Tennant

"Are you using that 'clone' tool again?!"

Contents at a Glance

Chapter 1: What's New in Adobe Illustrator CS3?

In This Chapter

✔ Working in the new streamlined interface

✔ Going live with color

✔ Integrating Flash

✔ Drawing with new tools

✔ Easily erasing vector paths

✔ Getting to know the Isolation mode

✔ Using the new cropping tool

Yes, Adobe has done it again — an even better Adobe Illustrator, and you can discover the best new features in this chapter. This chapter breezes through the new features to open your eyes to exciting new work methods. Don't forget to look for references to where you can get more in-depth knowledge in other locations of this book.

Integrated Interface

As you may guess, Adobe Illustrator follows the other products in the suite with its similar interface, which makes it easy for you to set up efficient workspaces and keep just the tools you need handy.

The user experience is noticeably different right away. As you launch Adobe Illustrator CS3, a splash screen appears, asking whether you're opening an existing document or if you're creating a new print, Web, mobile device, video, CMYK, RGB, or template file. By selecting the appropriate selection, you'll have the correct tools and preferences set up from the beginning.

Just like many of the other CS3 applications, you now have a space-saving one-column toolbar that you can switch back to two by clicking on the gray bar at the top of the toolbar and a palette system that you can collapse to icons (see Figure 1-1).

Figure 1-1:
The space-saving interface in Adobe Illustrator CS3.

Live Color

Gain your color confidence! Live Color allows for complete color exploration in addition to timesaving features to apply color schemes to your Illustrator objects. If you've ever been frustrated by having to color objects individually, you're sure to appreciate the new, interactive way to create and apply color schemes.

Live Color includes the Color Guide panel (see Figure 1-2), which includes features that allow you to save color groups without affecting your artwork.

Use the Color Guide to find compelling colors and save them to color groups in your Swatches panel. You can create color schemes based on 23 classic color-harmony rules, such as Complementary, Analogous, Monochromatic, and Triad, or you can create custom harmony rules. Even if you've gone through art school, using Live Colors beats trying to figure out a color scheme on your own. (Read more about Live Color in Chapter 9 of this minibook.)

TECHNICAL STUFF

Vector graphics

Vector graphics are made up of lines and curves defined by mathematical objects called *vectors.* Because the paths (the lines and curves) are defined mathematically, you can move, resize, or change the color of vector objects without losing quality in the graphic.

Vector graphics are resolution-independent; that is, they can be scaled to any size and printed at any resolution without losing detail. On the other hand, bitmap graphics have a predetermined amount of pixels creating them, so you can't scale (resize) them easily — if you scale them smaller, you throw out pixels; if you scale them bigger, you end up with a blocky, jagged picture.

Many companies have their logos created as vectors to avoid problems with scaling: A vector graphic logo maintains its high-quality appearance at any size.

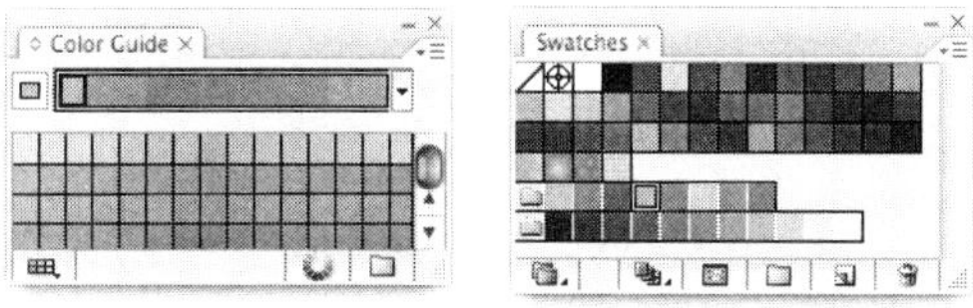

Figure 1-2:
The new Color Guide allows you to create color groups that you can then store in the Swatches panel.

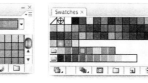

Flash Integration

Flash is vector, and Illustrator is *vector,* which means illustrations created in these applications are composed of mathematically created line and curve segments. Why can't they be better friends? Well, in this version, they're great buddies. Not only do you have the ability to do simple tasks like cut and paste from Adobe Illustrator directly into Flash files, but you also can transfer Illustrator layers and grouping structures along with all object names. (Read more about Flash integration with the CS3 products in Book 7 on Flash.)

Improved Drawing Controls

Illustrator drawing tools have long been the industry standard for power and versatility, but they've also always been a little unnatural and tedious to those who are new to using vector drawing tools. Now, in Adobe CS3, the drawing tools have been improved to allow you to work faster and get better results, starting with Point selection: Simply move your cursor over an anchor point (with the direct selection tool), and it's enlarged to help you see it better.

The control panel has gained additional tools to help you change curved corners to rounded curves, or back again. You can also connect and remove anchor points quickly with the improved path controls shown in Figure 1-3.

Figure 1-3:
New tools in the control panel help edit paths.

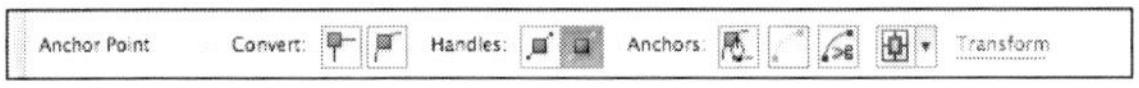

Read more about improved performance and how to use the drawing tools in Chapter 5 of this minibook.

Erase It Away

If you're an experienced Illustrator user, you'll really appreciate the new Eraser tool. It lets you erase as easily as you create, even reconnecting paths as you erase over shapes and paths. You can make the eraser larger or smaller by double-clicking the Eraser tool and changing the options in the Eraser Tool Options window, shown in Figure 1-4.

Figure 1-4:
The new Eraser tool makes it easy to take away shapes and paths, just where you want.

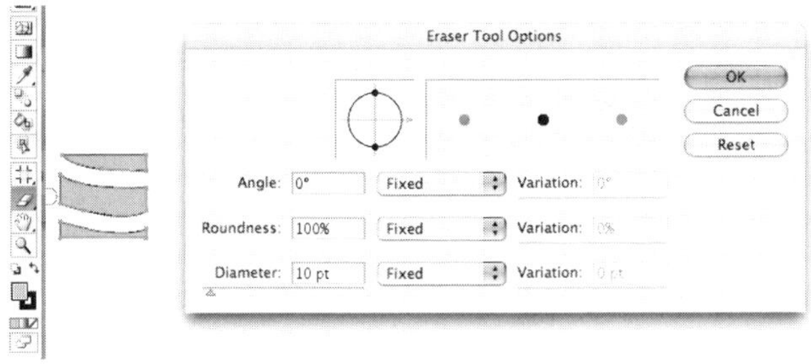

Isolation Mode

Those of you who build a little more than text art and the occasional logo will appreciate the new Isolation mode that allows you to take selected objects into a mode that protects other artwork. Isolation mode is truly essential if you work on complex artwork and spend a lot of time grouping, hiding, locking, and restacking layers to access objects for editing.

To use this new mode, just use the Selection tool to double-click any grouped set of objects. The rest of your artwork becomes inaccessible, as shown in Figure 1-5. This feature is truly a timesaver!

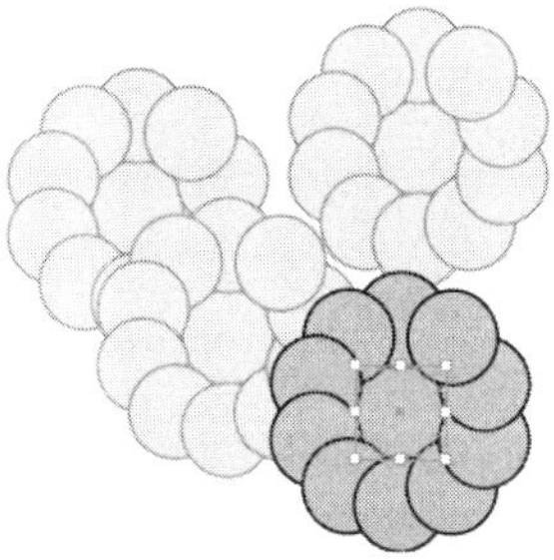

Figure 1-5:
Double-click a group using the Selection tool to enter the Isolation mode.

New Cropping Tool

Use the new cropping tool with a powerful option to get just what you need in your Illustrator document. When the new Crop Area tool is selected, options appear in the Control panel for measure as well as Presets that you can choose from. Want even more control? Double-click the Crop Area tool for additional options, shown in Figure 1-6.

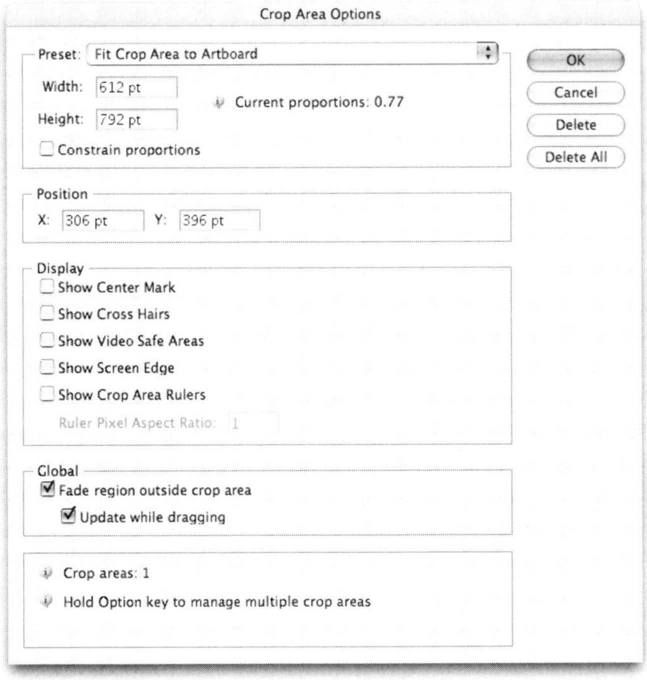

Crop Area Options

Preset: | Fit Crop Area to Artboard

Width: 612 pt
Height: 792 pt
Current proportions: 0.77

☐ Constrain proportions

OK
Cancel
Delete
Delete All

Position

X: 306 pt   Y: 396 pt

Display
☐ Show Center Mark
☐ Show Cross Hairs
☐ Show Video Safe Areas
☐ Show Screen Edge
☐ Show Crop Area Rulers
    Ruler Pixel Aspect Ratio: 1

Global
☑ Fade region outside crop area
    ☑ Update while dragging

ⓘ Crop areas: 1
ⓘ Hold Option key to manage multiple crop areas

Figure 1-6:
The Crop
Area tool
options.

Chapter 2: Discovering Illustrator CS3

Adobe Illustrator goes hand in hand with the other Adobe products but serves its own unique purpose. Adobe Illustrator creates single-page artwork, not lengthy documents with repeated headers, footers, and page numbers, such as documents created in InDesign, and not artwork created out of pixels, such as images edited or created in Photoshop. Illustrator is generally used to create logos, illustrations, maps, packages, labels, signage, Web art, and more.

Deciding When to Use Illustrator CS3

So how do you draw the line and decide when to create graphics in Illustrator rather than Photoshop? By using Illustrator, you gain the following benefits:

✦ Illustrator can save and export graphics into most file formats. By choosing to save or export, you can create a file that can be used in most other applications. For instance, Illustrator files can be saved as .svg, .bmp, .tiff, .pdf, .jpg, and even as a Flash .swf file, to name a few.

✦ Illustrator files are easily integrated into other Adobe applications. You can save Illustrator files in their native format and open or place them in other Adobe applications, such as InDesign, Photoshop, Dreamweaver, and Flash. You can also save Adobe Illustrator artwork in the .pdf format (Acrobat Portable Document Format). This format allows anyone using the free Acrobat Reader software to open and view the file, but editing capabilities are still maintained when the file is later opened in Illustrator.

✦ Illustrator is resolution-independent. Resolution of Illustrator vector artwork isn't determined until output. In other words, if you print to a 600-dpi (dots per inch) printer, the artwork is printed at 600 dpi; print to a 2,400-dpi printer, and the artwork will print at 2,400 dpi. Illustrator graphics are very different from the bitmap images you create or edit in Photoshop, where resolution is determined upon creation of the artwork.

✦ Illustrator has limitless scalability, which means that you can create vector artwork in Illustrator and scale it to the size of your thumb or the size of a barn, and it will still look good. See the "Vector graphics" sidebar in Chapter 1 of this minibook for more information.

Opening an Existing Document

To familiarize yourself with the basics of Illustrator and what the work area looks like, jump right in by opening an existing document in Illustrator. If you don't have an Illustrator file already created, you can open one of the sample files that is packaged with the Illustrator application. For example, you can open the file named Cheshire Cat.ai in the Sample Art folder. The path to the file is C:\Programs\Adobe\Adobe Illustrator CS3\Cool Extras\Sample Files\Sample Art (Windows) or Applications\Adobe Illustrator CS3\ Cool Extras\Sample Files\Sample Art\ (Mac).

When you launch Illustrator CS3 for the first time, a Welcome screen appears, giving you various options. Click the Open icon and then browse to locate a file to open. (Note that you can uncheck the Don't Show Again check box to not see the Welcome screen at launch.)

If your preferences have been changed from the original defaults, the Welcome screen may not appear. To open a file in that case, choose File↪ Open and select the file in the Open dialog box. The Open dialog box is used to open existing Adobe Illustrator files, or even files from other Adobe applications.

Use File⇨Open to open PDFs in Illustrator as well as many other file formats.

Creating a New Document

To create a new document in Illustrator, follow these steps:

1. **Choose File⇨New.**

The New Document dialog box appears, as shown in Figure 2-2. This dialog box enables you to determine the new document's profile, size, units of measurement, color mode, and page orientation.

2. **Enter a name for your new file in the Name text field.**

You can determine the name of the file now or when you save the document later.

3. **Choose a New Document Profile from a drop-down list.**

Selecting the correct profile sets up preferences, such as resolution and colors, correctly. Select the Advanced tab to see what changes are selected for each profile and change them if necessary.

4. **Set the size of the document page by choosing from the Size drop-down list or by typing measurements in the Width and Height text fields.**

The size can be set from several standard sizes available in the Size drop-down list, or you can enter your own measurements in the Width and Height text fields. Note that several Web sizes are listed first, followed by other typical paper sizes.

5. **Select the type of measurement that you're most comfortable with by choosing from the Units drop-down list.**

Note that your selection sets all measurement boxes and rulers to the increments you choose: points, picas, inches, millimeters, centimeters, or pixels.

6. **Pick the orientation for the artboard.**

The *artboard* is your canvas for creating your artwork in Illustrator. You can choose between Portrait (the short sides of the artboard at the top and bottom) and Landscape (the long sides of the artboard on the top and bottom).

7. **When you're finished making your selections, click OK.**

An Illustrator artboard appears.

Don't worry if document size and color mode need to be changed at a later point. You can change them by choosing File➪Document Setup and making changes in the Document Setup dialog box.

Taking a Look at the Document Window

To investigate the work area and really get familiar with Illustrator, open a new document and take a look around. In the Illustrator work area, you have a total of 227 inches in width and height to create your artwork in. That's great, but it also leaves enough space to lose objects, too! The following list explains the areas that you'll work with as you create artwork in Illustrator:

✦ **Imageable area:** The space inside the innermost dotted lines, which marks the printing area on the page. Many printers can't print all the way to the edges of the paper, so the imageable area is determined by the printer that you have selected in the Print dialog box. To turn off or on this dotted border, choose View➪Hide/Show Page Tiling.

You can move the imageable area around on your page by using the Page tool. See the nearby sidebar, "The Page tool," for more on this tool.

✦ **Edge of the page:** The page's edge is marked by the outermost set of dotted lines.

The Page tool

Use the Page tool to move the printable area of your page to a different location. For example, if you have a printer that can print only on paper that is 8.5 x 11 inches or less, but you have a page size of 11 x 17, you can use the Page tool (a hidden tool accessed by holding down the mouse button on the Hand tool) to indicate what part of the page you want to print. Follow these steps to use the Page tool:

1. **When adjusting page boundaries, choose View➪Fit in Window so that you can see all of your artwork.**

2. **Hold down on the Hand tool to select the hidden Page tool.**

The pointer becomes a dotted cross when you move it to the active window.

3. **Position the mouse over the artboard and click and drag the page to a new location.**

As you drag, the Page tool acts as if you were moving the page from its lower-left corner. Two gray rectangles are displayed. The outer rectangle represents the page size, and the inner rectangle represents the printable area of a page. You can move the page anywhere on the artboard; just remember that any part of a page that extends past the printable area boundary isn't printed.

✦ **Nonimageable area:** The space between the two sets of dotted lines representing the imageable area and the edge of the page. The nonimageable area is the margin of the page that can't be printed on.

✦ **Artboard:** The area bounded by solid lines that represents the entire region that can contain printable artwork. By default, the artboard is the same size as the page, but it can be enlarged or reduced. The U.S. default artboard is 8.5 x 11 inches, but it can be set as large as 227 x 227 inches. You can hide the artboard boundaries by choosing View⇨Hide Artboard.

✦ **Scratch area:** The area outside the artboard that extends to the edge of the 227-inch square window. The scratch area represents a space on which you can create, edit, and store elements of artwork before moving them onto the artboard. Objects placed onto the scratch area are visible on-screen, but they don't print. However, objects in the scratch area will appear if the document is saved and placed as an image in other applications.

Basically, the rules regarding the work area are simple: If you're printing directly from Adobe Illustrator, make sure that you choose the proper paper size and printer in the Print dialog box. Open the Print dialog box by choosing File⇨Print. If you're creating artwork for another application, such as for a document you're creating in InDesign, the boundaries have no effect on what appears in the Illustrator file. Everything in Illustrator's scratch area will appear in the other application.

Becoming Familiar with the Tools

As you begin using Adobe Illustrator, you'll find it helpful to be familiar with its tools. Tools are used to create, select, and manipulate objects in Illustrator. The tools should be visible as a default, but if not, you can access them by choosing Window⇨Tools.

Table 2-1 lists the tools that we show you how to use throughout this minibook. Hover the cursor over the tool in the toolbox to see the name of the tool appear in a ToolTip. In parentheses on the ToolTip (and noted in the second column of Table 2-1) is the keyboard command that you can use to access that tool. When you see a small triangle at the lower-right corner of the tool icon, you know that it contains additional hidden tools. Select the tool and hold the mouse button to see any hidden tools.

Table 2-1		Illustrator CS2 Tools	
Icon Covered	*Tool/Keyboard Command*	*What It Does*	*Chapter in This Minibook*
	Selection Tool (V)	Activates objects	3
	Direct Selection (A)	Activates individual points or paths	3
	Group Selection (A)	Selects grouped items	3
	Magic Wand (Y)	Selects based upon similarity	3
	Lasso (Q)	Selects Freehand	3
	Pen (P)	Creates paths	5
	Type (T)	Creates text	6
	Line Segment (/)	Draws line segments	5
	Shape Tool (M)	Creates shape objects	4
	Paint Brush (B)	Creates paths	5
	Pencil (N)	Creates paths	5
	Rotate (R)	Rotates objects	10
	Scale (S)	Enlarges or reduces objects	10
	Warp (Shift+R)	Warps objects	10

Icon Covered	Tool/Keyboard Command	What It Does	Chapter in This Minibook
	Free Transform (E)	Transforms objects	10
	Symbol Sprayer (Shift+S)	Applies Symbol instances	11
	Graph Tool (J)	Creates graphs	11
	Mesh (U)	Creates a gradient mesh	11
	Gradient (G)	Modifies gradients	11
	Eyedropper (I)	Copies and applies attributes	9
	Blend (W)	Creates transitional blends	11
	Live Paint Bucket (K)	Applies color to strokes and fills	9
	Live Paint Selection (Shift+L)	Selects Live Paint Areas Tool	8
	Slice Tool (Shift K)	Creates HTML slices	13
	Crop Area Tool (Shift+O)	Crops multiple areas	1
	Eraser Tool (Shift+E)	Erases vector paths	3
	Scissors (C)	Cuts paths	5
	Hand (H)	Navigates on the page	2
	Zoom (Z)	Increases and decreases the on-screen view	2

**Book III
Chapter 2**

**Discovering
Illustrator CS3**

Checking Out the Panels

The new standardized interface is a great boost for users as Illustrator's panel system is similar to all the other products in Adobe's Creative Suites. This consistency makes working and finding tools and features easier.

When you first open Illustrator, you'll notice the one-column toolbar and the panels that have been reduced to icons on the right. To select a panel, click the appropriate icon, and the Fill panel appears.

How do you know which icon brings up which panel? Good question. If you're hunting around for the appropriate panels, you can do one of three things.

✦ **Choose Window and select the named panel from a list.**

✦ **Position your mouse on the left side of the icons, when you see the double arrow icon, click and drag to the left.** The panel names appear.

✦ **Click the Expand dock gray bar at the top of the icons.** The panels expand so that you can see their contents and names. See Figure 2-1 to see the panels in iconic and expanded views.

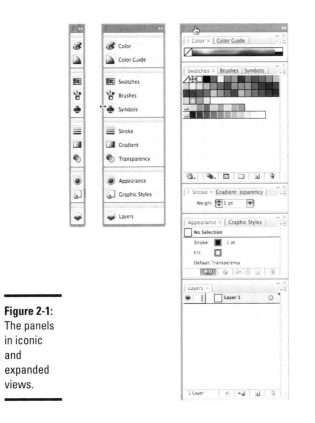

Figure 2-1:
The panels
in iconic
and
expanded
views.

The panels that you see as a default are docked together. To *dock* a palette means that, for organizational purposes, the panel is attached in the docking area.

You can arrange panels to make them more helpful for production. You may choose to have only certain panels visible while working. Here's the low-down on using Illustrator's panels:

✦ To see additional options for each panel, click the Show Options button on the upper-right side of the panel (see Figure 2-2.)

Figure 2-2:
Each panel has additional options available.

✦ To move a panel group, click and drag above the tabbed panel name.

✦ To rearrange or separate a panel from its group, drag the panel's tab. Dragging a tab outside the docking area creates a new separate panel window.

✦ To move a tab to another palette, drag the tab to that palette.

Look out for those panels — they can take over your screen! Some panels, but not all, can be resized. Panels that you can resize have an active lower-right corner (denoted by three small lines in the corner). To change the size of a panel, drag the lower-right corner of the panel (Windows) or drag the size box at the lower-right corner of the panel (Mac).

As you become more efficient, you may find it helpful to reduce the clutter on your screen by hiding all panels except those that are necessary for your work. Save your own panel configuration by choosing Window⇨Workspace⇨Save Workspace. Choose Window⇨Workspace⇨[Basic] to return to the default workspace.

Book III
Chapter 2

Discovering
Illustrator CS3

Changing Views

When you're working in Illustrator, precision is important, but you also want to see how the artwork really looks. Whether for the Web or print, Illustrator offers several ways in which to view your artwork:

✦ **Preview and Outline views:** By default, Illustrator shows the Preview view, where you see colors, stroke widths, images, and patterns as they should appear when printed or completed for on-screen presentation. Sometimes this view can become a nuisance, especially if you have two thick lines and you're trying to create a corner point by connecting them. At times like this, or whenever you want the strokes and fills reduced to the underlying structure, choose View➪Outline. You now see the outline of the illustration, as shown in Figure 2-3.

Figure 2-3:
Preview
mode (left)
and Outline
mode (right).

✦ **Pixel view:** If you don't want to be surprised when your artwork appears in your Web browser, use the Pixel view. This view, shown in Figure 2-4, maintains the vectors of your artwork, but gives you a view showing how the pixels will appear when the image is viewed on-screen, as if on the Web.

Figure 2-4:
See how
your
artwork
translates
into pixels
in the
Pixel view.

Pixel view is great for previewing what your text will look like on-screen — some fonts just don't look good as pixels, especially if the text is small. Using Pixel view, you can go through several different fonts until you find one that is more readable as pixels.

✦ **Overprint view:** For those of you in print production, the Overprint preview can be a real timesaver. Choose View➪Attributes to bring up the Attributes palette, which you can use to set the fill and stroke colors to overprint. This view creates additional colors when printing and aids printers when trapping abutting colors.

Trapping is the slight overprint of a lighter color into a darker color to correct for press *misregistration.* When several colors are printed on one piece, the likelihood that they'll be perfectly aligned is pretty slim! Setting a stroke to Overprint on the Window⊅Attributes palette is one solution. With overprint selected, the stroke is overprinted on the touching colors. This mixing of color produces an additional color, but is less obvious to the viewer than a white space created by misregistration. Select Overprint to see the result of overprinting in Overprint view in Figure 2-5.

Figure 2-5:
Overprint
view.

Navigating the Work Area with Zoom Controls

You can navigate the work area efficiently by using the Hand tool and the various zoom controls. You can change the magnification of the artboard in several ways, including using menu items, the Zoom tool, and keyboard commands. Choose the method you feel most comfortable with:

Book III
Chapter 2

Discovering
Illustrator CS3

✦ **Hand tool:** Scroll around the document window by using the scrollbars or the Hand tool. The Hand tool gives you the ability to scroll by dragging. You can imagine you're pushing a piece of paper around on your desk when you use the Hand tool.

Hold down the spacebar to temporarily access the Hand tool while any tool (except the Type tool) is selected. Holding down the spacebar while the Type tool is selected only gives you spaces!

✦ **View menu:** Using the View menu, you can easily select the magnification that you want from a choice of four: Zoom In, Zoom Out, Fit In Window (especially useful when you get lost in the scratch area), and Actual Size (gives you a 100-percent view of your artwork).

✦ **New Crop Area tool:** Using the new Crop Area tool you can define crop areas interactively for print or export. You can choose preset formats and define multiple crop areas.

✦ **The Zoom tool:** Using the Zoom tool, you can click the document window to zoom in; to zoom out, Alt+click (Windows) or Option+click (Mac). Double-click with the Zoom tool to quickly resize the document window to 100 percent. Control what is visible when using the Zoom tool by clicking and dragging over the area that you want zoomed into.

✦ **Keyboard shortcuts:** If you're not the type of person who likes to use keyboard shortcuts, you may change your mind about using them for magnification. They make sense and are easy to use and remember. Table 2-2 lists the most popular keyboard shortcuts to change magnification.

The shortcuts in Table 2-2 require a little coordination to use, but they give you more control in your zoom. While holding down the keys, drag from the upper-left to the bottom-right corner of the area you want to zoom to. A marquee appears while you're dragging; when you release the mouse button, the selected area zooms up to the size of your window! The Zoom Out command doesn't give you that much control; it simply zooms back out, much like the commands in Table 2-2.

Table 2-2	Magnification Keyboard Shortcuts	
Command	*Windows Shortcut*	*Mac Shortcut*
Actual Size	Ctrl+1	Replace+1
Fit in Window	Ctrl+0 (zero)	Replace +0 (zero)
Zoom In	Ctrl++ (plus)	Replace ++ (plus)
Zoom Out	Ctrl+– (minus)	Replace +– (minus)
Hand tool	Spacebar	Spacebar

Table 2-3	Zoom Keyboard Shortcuts	
Command	*Windows Shortcut*	*Mac Shortcut*
Zoom In to Selected Area	Ctrl+spacebar+drag	Replace +spacebar+drag
Zoom Out	Ctrl+Alt+spacebar	Replace+Option+spacebar

Chapter 3: Using the Selection Tools

In This Chapter

↳ **Anchor points, the bounding boxes, and selection tools**

↳ **Working with selections**

↳ **Grouping and ungrouping selections**

↳ **Constraining movement and cloning objects**

You've probably heard the old line, "You have to select it to affect it." This statement is so true. When you're ready to apply a change to an object in Illustrator, you must have that object selected, or Illustrator won't know what to do. You'll sit there clicking a color swatch over and over again, and nothing will happen. Although making selections may sound simple, it can become more difficult when working on complicated artwork.

Getting to Know the Selection Tools

Before delving into the world of selecting objects in Illustrator, you must know what the selection tools are. In this section, we take you through a quick tour of anchor points (integral to the world of selections), the bounding box, and, of course, the selection tools (yes, there are more than one).

Anchor points

To understand selections, you must first understand how Illustrator works with *anchor points*. Anchor points act like handles and can be individually selected and moved to other locations. Essentially, the anchor points are what you use to drag objects or parts of objects around the workspace. After you've placed anchor points on an object, you can then create strokes or paths from the anchor points.

You can select several anchor points at the same time (Figure 3-1) or only one (Figure 3-2). Selecting several anchor points at once enables you to move the entire object without changing the anchor points in relationship to one another. You can tell which anchor points are selected and active because they appear as solid boxes.

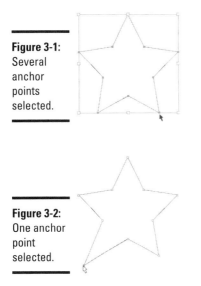

Figure 3-1:
Several
anchor
points
selected.

Figure 3-2:
One anchor
point
selected.

Bounding box

As a default, Illustrator shows a bounding box when an object is selected with the Selection tool (a bounding box is shown in Figure 3-1). This feature can be helpful if you understand its function, but confusing if you don't know how to use it.

By dragging on the handles, you can use the bounding box for quick transforms, such as scaling and rotating. To rotate, you pass the mouse cursor (without clicking) outside a handle until you see a rotate symbol, and then drag.

If the bounding box bothers you, you can turn off the feature by choosing View➪Hide Bounding Box.

Selection tools

Illustrator CS3 offers three main selection tools:

✦ **Selection tool:** Selects entire objects or groups. This tool activates all anchor points in an object or group at the same time, allowing you to move an object without changing its shape.

✦ **Direct Selection tool:** Selects individual points.

✦ **Group Selection tool:** Hidden in the Direct Selection tool in the toolbox, you use this tool to select items within a group. This tool adds grouped items as you click an object in the order in which objects were grouped. This selection tool will become more useful to you as you find out about grouping objects in Illustrator.

You can select an object with the Selection tool using one of three main methods:

✦ Click the object's path.

✦ Click an anchor point of the object.

✦ Drag a marquee around part or all of the object's path. (In the later section, "Using a marquee to select an object," we discuss using the marquee method.)

Use the Magic Wand selection tool to select objects with like values, such as fill and stroke colors, based upon a tolerance, and stroke weight. Change the options of this tool by double-clicking the Magic Wand tool.

Use the Lasso tool to click and drag around anchor points that you want to select.

Working with Selections

After you have an understanding about the basics of selections, you probably will be anxious to jump in and start with the selecting. So in this section, we introduce you to the basics: making a selection, working with anchor points and the marquee, making multiple selections, and, of course, saving your work.

Creating a selection

To work with selections, you need to actually have something on the page in Illustrator. Use the following techniques to make a selection:

1. **Create a new page in Adobe Illustrator (any size or profile is okay).**

Alternatively, you can open an existing illustration; see Chapter 2 of this minibook for instructions.

2. **If you're starting from a new page, create an object to work with.**

For example, select the Rectangle tool and click and drag from the top left to the lower right to create a shape.

Exact size doesn't matter, but make it large enough that you can see it. To start over, choose Edit⇨Undo, or press Ctrl+Z (Windows), or ⌘+Z (Mac).

As a default, all shapes start out having a black stroke and a white fill (see Figure 3-3). If yours is not black and white, press D, which changes the selected object to the default colors.

Figure 3-3:
Create a
rectangle to
practice
using the
Selection
tools.

3. **Using the Selection tool, click the object to make sure that it's active.**

Note that all anchor points are solid, indicating that all anchor points are active, as shown in Figure 3-4. As a default, you see many additional points that you can use to transform your selected object.

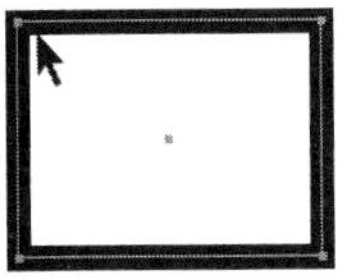

Figure 3-4:
All anchor
points
activate
with the
Selection
tool.

4. **Click and drag the rectangle to another location.**

All anchor points travel together.

5. **When completed, deactivate your selection.**

You can use one of these three methods:

- Choose Select⇨Deselect.
- Ctrl+click (Windows) or ⌘+click (Mac) anywhere on the page.
- Use the key command Ctrl+Shift+A (Windows) or ⌘ +Shift+A (Mac).

Selecting an anchor point

When you have a selection to work with (see the preceding numbered list), you can deselect all the active anchor points and then make just one anchor point active. Just follow these steps:

1. **Make sure that the object isn't selected by choosing Select⇨Deselect.**

2. **Select the Direct Selection tool (the white arrow) from the toolbox.**

3. **Click one anchor point.**

Only one anchor point (the one you clicked) is solid, and the others are hollow, as shown in Figure 3-5.

Figure 3-5:
Only the selected anchor point becomes active when selected with the Direct Selection tool.

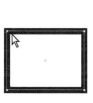

4. **Click and drag that solid anchor point using the Direct Selection tool.**

Only that one anchor point moves.

New in Illustrator CS3, an anchor point actually enlarges when you cross over it using the Direct Selection tool. This enlargement is a big break for those who typically have to squint to see where the anchor points are positioned.

Using a marquee to select an object

Sometimes it's easier to surround what you want selected by dragging the mouse to create a marquee. Follow these steps to select an object by creating a marquee:

1. **Choose the Selection tool.**

2. **Click outside the object (we use a rectangle in this example) and drag over a small part of it, as shown in Figure 3-6.**

The entire object becomes selected.

Figure 3-6:
Selecting an
entire object
with a
marquee
and the
Selection
tool.

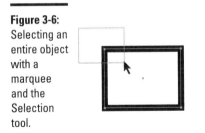

You can also select just one anchor point in an object by using the marquee
method:

1. **Make sure that the object isn't selected by choosing Select⇔Deselect
   and then choose the Direct Selection tool.**

2. **Click outside a corner of the object and drag over just the anchor
   point that you want to select.**

   Notice that only that anchor point is active, which can be a sight-saver
   when you're trying to select individual points (see Figure 3-7).

Figure 3-7:
Selecting
individual
anchor
points with
a marquee
and the
Direct
Selection
tool.

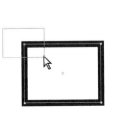

You can use this method to cross over just the two top points or side anchor
points to activate multiple anchor points as well.

Selecting multiple objects

If you have multiple items on your page, you can select them by using one of
the following methods:

✦ Select one object or anchor point and then hold down the Shift key and click another object or anchor point. Depending on which selection tool you're using, you'll either select all anchor points on an object (Selection tool) or additional anchor points only (Direct Select tool).

You can use the Shift key to deactivate an object as well. Shift+click a selected object to deselect it.

✦ Choose Select➪All or use the key command Ctrl+A (Windows) or ⌘+A (Mac).

✦ Use the marquee selection technique and drag outside and over the objects. When you use this technique with the Selection tool, all anchor points in the objects are selected; with the Direct Selection tool, only the points that you drag over are selected.

Saving a selection

Spending way too much time trying to make your selections? Illustrator comes to the rescue with the Save Selection feature. After you have a selection that you may need again, choose Select➪Save Selection and name the selection. It now appears at the bottom of the Select menu. To change the name or delete the saved selection, choose Select➪Edit Selection. This selection is saved with the document.

Grouping and Ungrouping

Keep objects together by grouping them. The Group function is handy in a situation when you're creating something from multiple objects, such as a logo. With the Group function, you can make sure that all the objects that make up the logo stay together when you move, rotate, scale, or copy it. Just follow these steps to create a group:

1. **If you aren't already working with an illustration that contains a whole bunch of objects, create several objects on a new page, anywhere and any size.**

   For example, select the Rectangle tool and click and drag on the page several times to create additional rectangles.

2. **Select the first object with the Selection tool and then hold down the Shift key and click a second object.**

3. **Choose Object➪Group or use the keyboard shortcut Ctrl+G (Windows) or ⌘+G (Mac).**

4. **Choose Select➪Deselect and then click one of the objects with the Selection tool.**

   Both objects become selected.

5. **While the first two objects are still selected, Shift+click a third object.**

6. **With all three objects selected, choose Object⇨Group again.**

   Illustrator remembers the grouping order. To prove that, deselect the group by choosing Select⇨Deselect and switch to the Group Selection tool. (Hold down the mouse button on the Direct Selection tool to access the Group Selection tool.)

7. **Using the Group Selection tool, click the first object, and all anchor points become active. Click again on the first object, and the second object becomes selected. Click yet again on the first object, and the third object becomes selected.**

   This tool activates the objects in the order that you grouped them. After you've grouped the objects together, you can now treat them as a single object.

To Ungroup objects, choose Object⇨Ungroup or use the key command Ctrl+Shift+G (Windows) or ⌘+Shift+G (Mac). In a situation where you group objects twice (because you added an object to the group, for example), you would have to choose Ungroup twice.

Using the Isolation mode

Now in Illustrator you can take advantage of the Isolation mode, which allows you to easily select and edit objects in a group without disturbing other parts of your artwork. Simply double-click a group, and it opens in a separate Isolation mode, where all objects outside of the group are dimmed and inactive. Do the work that you need to on the group and exit out of the Isolation mode by clicking on the arrow to the left of Group in the upper right of the window, as shown in Figure 3-8.

Figure 3-8:
The Isolation mode allows you to edit group contents without disturbing other artwork.

Manipulating Selected Objects

In the following list, you can discover a few other cool things that you can do with selected objects:

+ **Moving selected objects:** When an object is selected, you can drag it to any location on the page, but what if you only want to nudge it a bit? To nudge an item one pixel at a time, select it with the Selection tool and press the left-, right-, up-, or down-arrow key to reposition the object. Hold down the Shift key as you press an arrow key to move an object by ten pixels at a time.

+ **Constraining movement:** Want to move an object over to the other side of the page without changing its alignment? Constrain something by selecting an object with the Selection tool and dragging the item and then hold down the Shift key before you release the mouse button. By pressing the Shift key mid-drag, you constrain the movement to 45-, 90-, or 180-degree angles!

+ **Cloning selected objects:** Use the Selection tool to easily clone (duplicate) an item and move it to a new location. To clone an item, simply select it with the Selection tool and then hold down the Alt key (Windows) or Option key (Mac). Look for the cursor to change to two arrows (see Figure 3-9) and then drag the item to another location on the page. Notice that the original object is left intact and that a copy of the object has been created and moved.

Figure 3-9:
Look for
the double
arrow
before
dragging to
clone the
selected
object.

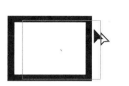

+ **Constraining the clone:** By Alt+dragging (Windows) or Option+dragging (Mac) an item, and then pressing Shift, you can clone the item and keep it aligned with the original. *Remember:* Don't hold down the Shift key until you're in the process of dragging the item; otherwise, pressing Shift will deselect the original object.

After you've cloned an object to a new location, try this neat trick where you create multiple objects equally apart from each other using the

Transform Again command: Choose Object⇨Transform⇨Transform Again, or press Ctrl+D (Windows) or ⌘+D (Mac) to have another object cloned the exact distance as the first cloned object (see Figure 3-10). We discuss transforms in more detail in Chapter 10 of this minibook.

Figure 3-10:
Use the Transform Again command (Ctrl+D Windows or ⌘+D Mac) to repeat transforms and clones.

✦ **Using the Select menu:** Using the Select menu, you can gain additional selection controls, such as Select⇨Inverse, which allows you to select one object and then turn your selection inside out. Also, the Select⇨ Select Same options allow you to select one object and then select additional objects on the page based upon similarities in Color, Fill, Stroke, and other special attributes.

Chapter 4: Creating Basic Shapes

In This Chapter

✔ Introducing rectangles, ellipses, stars, and polygons

✔ Resizing shapes after creation

✔ Creating shapes

Shapes, shapes, shapes . . . they're everywhere in Illustrator. Basic shapes, such as squares, circles, polygons, and stars, are used in all types of illustrations. With the right know-how and the right shape tools, you can easily create these shapes exactly the way you want. In this chapter, we show you how to use these tools to control a shape's outcome, create shapes based on precise measurements, and change the number of points a star has.

The Basic Shape Tools

As a default, the only visible shape tool in the toolbox is the Rectangle tool. Click and hold down that tool, and you have access to the Rounded Rectangle, Ellipse, Polygon, and Star tools, shown in Figure 4-1. (Although you see the Flare tool, it's not a basic shape.)

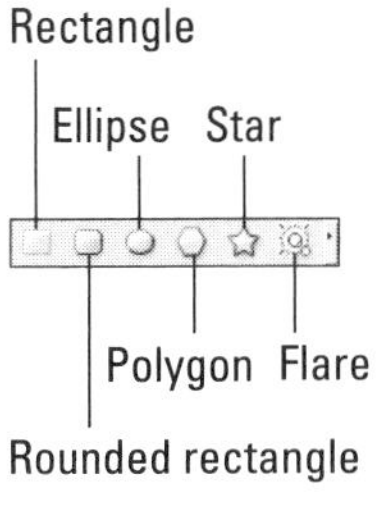

Rectangle

Ellipse Star

Figure 4-1:
The basic
shape tools.

Polygon Flare

Rounded rectangle

You can tear off this tool set so that you don't have to find the hidden shapes in the future. Click and hold on the Rectangle tool and drag to the arrow on the far right. Wait until you see the pop-up hint (Tearoff) and then release the mouse button. These tools are now in a free-floating toolbar that you can drag to another location.

Creating rectangles and ellipses

Rectangles and ellipses are the most fundamental shapes that you can create (see Figure 4-2). To create a rectangle shape freehand, select the Rectangle tool and simply click the page where you want the shape to appear. Then drag diagonally toward the opposite side, drag it the distance that you want the shape to be in size, and release the mouse button. You can drag up or down. You do the same to create an ellipse with the Ellipse tool.

Figure 4-2: Click and drag diagonally to create a rectangle or ellipse.

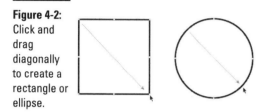

After you create the shape, adjust its size and position by using the Selection tool. Reposition the shape by clicking the selected object and dragging. Resize the object by grabbing a handle and adjusting in or out. To adjust two sides together, grab a corner handle. To resize your shape proportionally, Shift+drag a corner handle.

Using the Rounded Rectangle tool

You can create the rounded rectangle by using one of two methods:

✦ Freehand clicking and dragging to create the rounded rectangle shape.

✦ Clicking once on the artboard to bring up the Rounded Rectangle dialog box, where you can enter values to define the shape.

The difference between these two methods is that when you open the Rounded Rectangle dialog box (see Figure 4-3), you have the option to enter a value in the Corner Radius text field, which determines how much rounding is applied to the corners of the shape. The smaller the value, the less rounded the corners will be; the higher the value, the more rounded. Be careful; you can actually round a rectangle's corners so much that it becomes an ellipse!

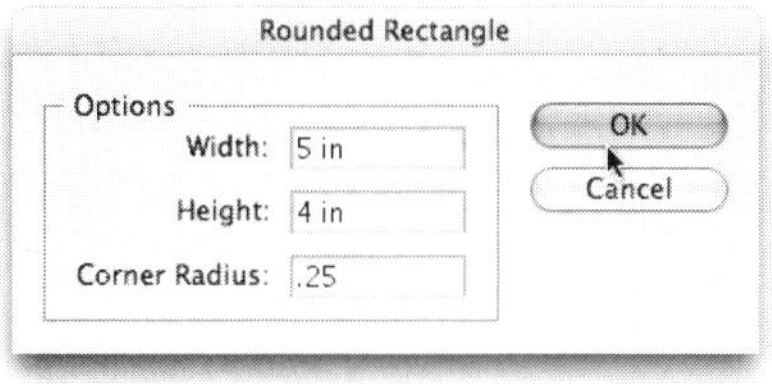

Figure 4-3:
Select the
Rounded
Rectangle
tool and
click once
on the
artboard to
customize
the size.

Using the Polygon tool

You create stars and polygons in much the same way as the rectangles and ellipses. Select the Polygon tool and click and drag from one corner to another to create the default six-sided polygon shape. You can also select the Polygon tool and click once on the artboard to change the Polygon tool options in the Polygon dialog box.

You can change the polygon shape by entering new values in the Radius and Sides text fields, as shown in Figure 4-4. The radius is determined from the center to the edge of the polygon. The value for the number of sides can range from 3 (making triangles a breeze to create) to 1000. Whoa . . . a polygon with 1,000 sides would look like a circle unless it was the size of Texas!

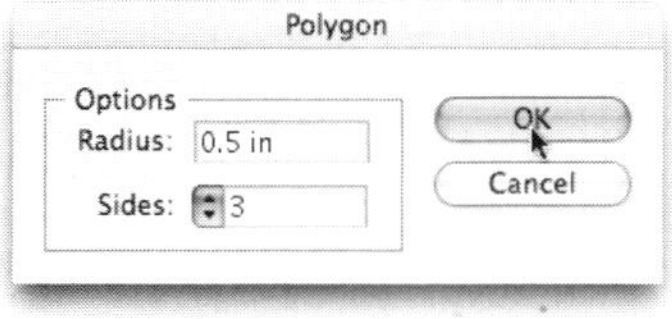

Figure 4-4:
Creating a
polygon
shape.

Using the Star tool

To create a star shape, select the Star tool from the toolbox. (Remember that it may be hiding under other shape tools.) If you click once on the artboard to bring up the Star dialog box, you see three text fields in which you can enter values to customize your star shape:

✦ **Radius 1:** Distance from the outer points to the center of the star.

✦ **Radius 2:** Distance from the inner points to the center of the star.

✦ **Points:** Number of points that make up the star.

The closer together the Radius 1 and Radius 2 values are to each other, the shorter the points on your star. In other words, you can go from a starburst to a seal of approval by entering values that are close in the Radius 1 and Radius 2 text fields, as shown in Figure 4-5.

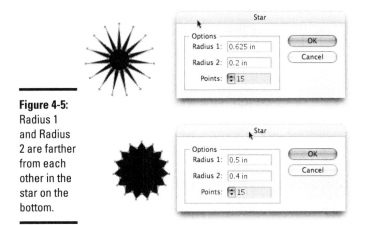

Figure 4-5:
Radius 1 and Radius 2 are farther from each other in the star on the bottom.

Resizing Shapes

You often need a shape to be an exact size (for example, 2 x 3 inches). After you create a shape, the best way to resize it to exact measurements is to use the Transform panel, shown in Figure 4-6. Have your object selected and then choose Window⇨Transform to open the Transform panel. Note that on this panel, you can enter values to place an object in the X and Y fields, as well as enter values in the Width and Height text fields to determine the exact size of an object.

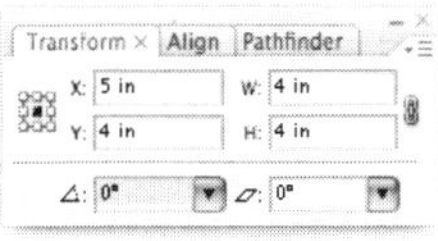

Figure 4-6:
Use the Transform panel to precisely set the size of a shape.

In many of the Adobe Illustrator panels, you may see measurement increments consisting of points, picas, millimeters, centimeters, or inches, which can be confusing and maybe even intimidating. But you can control which measurement increments to use.

Show Rulers by choosing View⇨Show Rulers or press Ctrl+R (Windows) or ⌘+R (Mac). Then right-click (Windows) or Ctrl+click (Mac) on the ruler to change the measurement increment to an increment you're more familiar with. The contextual menu that appears allows you to change the measurement increment right on the document.

Alternatively, you can simply type the number followed by a measurement extension into the Width and Height text fields in the Transform palette (refer to Figure 4-6), and the measurement converts properly for you. Table 4-1 lists the extensions that you can use.

Table 4-1	Measurement Extensions
Extension	*Measurement Unit*
" or in	Inches
pt	Points
mm	Millimeters
cm	Centimeters
p	Picas

If you don't want to bother creating a shape freehand and then changing the size, select the shape tool and click your page. An options dialog box specific to the shape you're creating appears, in which you can type values into the width and height text fields.

If you accidentally click and drag, you end up with a very small shape on your page. If this happens, don't fret. Simply get rid of the small shape by selecting it and pressing the Delete key, and then try again.

Tips for Creating Shapes

The following are simple tips to improve your skills at creating basic shapes in Illustrator:

✦ Press and hold the Shift key while dragging with the Rectangle or Ellipse tool to create a perfect square or circle. This trick is also helpful when you're using the Polygon and Star tools — holding down the Shift key constrains them so that they're straight (see Figure 4-7).

✦ Create a shape from the center out by holding down the Alt (Windows) or Option (Mac) key while dragging (see Figure 4-8). Hold down Alt+Shift (Windows) or Option+Shift (Mac) to pull a constrained shape out from the center.

✦ When creating a star or polygon shape by clicking and dragging, if you keep the mouse button down, you can then press the up- or down-arrow key to interactively add points or sides to your shape.

Figure 4-7:
Use the
Shift key to
constrain
a shape
as you
create it.

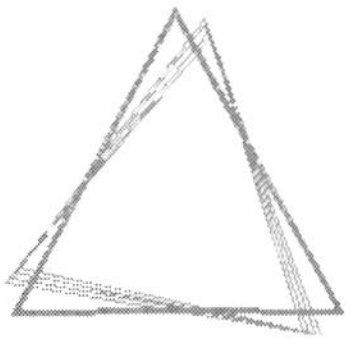

Figure 4-8:
Hold down
the Alt
(Windows)
or Option
(Mac) Key
when
making a
shape to
create it
from a
center point.

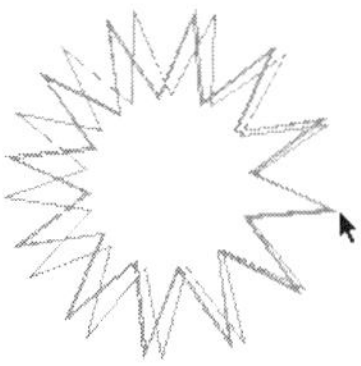

Creating advanced shapes

At times, it may be much easier to use advanced tools in Illustrator to create unique shapes. The Pathfinder panel is an incredible tool that allows you to combine, knock out, and even create shapes from other intersected shapes.

You use the Pathfinder panel, shown in Figure 4-9, to combine objects into new shapes. To use the Pathfinder panel, choose Window➪Pathfinder.

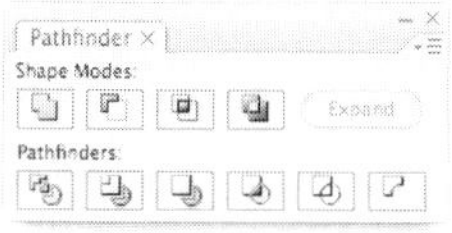

Figure 4-9:
You use the Pathfinder panel to combine objects into new shapes.

Across the top row of the Pathfinder panel are the Shape Modes, which let you control the interaction between selected shapes. You can choose from the shape modes listed in Table 4-2.

Table 4-2		Shape Modes
Button	*Mode*	*What It Does*
	Add To Shape Area	Essentially unites the selected shape into one.
	Subtract from shape area	Cuts out the topmost shape from the underlying shape.
	Intersect shape areas	Uses the area of the topmost shape to clip the underlying shape as a mask would.
	Exclude overlapping shape areas	Uses the area of the shape to invert the underlying shape, turning filled regions into holes and vice versa.

**Book III
Chapter 4**

Creating Basic Shapes

TIP

If you like the Exclude Overlapping Shapes effect, you can also get a similar effect by selecting several shapes and selecting Object➪Compound Path➪Make. This command takes the topmost shapes and "punches" them out of the bottom shape.

TIP

The shapes remain separate so that you can still adjust them, which is great if you like to tweak your artwork (but it drives some people crazy). You can turn the results of the Shape Modes into one shape by either pressing the Expand button after selecting the shape mode or holding down the Alt key (Windows) or Option key (Mac) when selecting a Shape Mode.

Using the Pathfinders

The Pathfinders are the buttons at the bottom of the Pathfinder panel. They also let you create new shapes out of overlapping objects. Table 4-3 offers a summary of what each Pathfinder does.

Table 4-3	The Pathfinders
Button	*What It Does*
	Does exactly that. Create some overlapping shapes, select them, and then press the Divide button on the Pathfinder panel. All the shapes divide into their own shape. This tool is actually very useful tool when you're trying to create custom shapes.
	Removes the part of a filled object that is hidden.
	Removes the part of a filled object that is hidden. Also removes any strokes and merges any adjoining or overlapping objects filled with the same color.
	Deletes all parts of the artwork that fall outside the boundary of the topmost object. It also removes any strokes. If you want your strokes to remain when using this feature, you need to select them and choose Object➪Path➪Outline Stroke.
	Divides an object into its shape's line segments, or edges. Useful for preparing artwork that needs a trap for overprinting objects.

Chapter 5: Using the Pen Tool and Placing Images

In This Chapter

✔ **Familiarizing yourself with the Pen tool**

✔ **Creating paths, closed shapes, and curves**

✔ **Creating template layers**

✔ **Placing images in Illustrator CS3**

*Y*ou've seen illustrations that you know are made from paths, but how do you make your own? In this chapter, we show you how to use the Pen tool to create paths and closed shapes.

The Pen tool requires a little more coordination than other Illustrator tools. Fortunately, Adobe Illustrator CS3 includes new features to help make using the Pen tool a little easier. After you master the Pen tool, the possibilities for creating illustrations are unlimited. Read this chapter to build your skills with the most popular feature in graphic software, the Bézier curve.

Pen Tool Fundamentals

You can use the Pen tool to create all sorts of things, such as straight lines, curves, and closed shapes, which you can then incorporate into illustrations:

✦ **Bézier curve:** Originally developed by Pierre Bézier in the 1970s for CAD/CAM operations, the Bézier curve (shown in Figure 5-1) became the underpinnings of the entire Adobe PostScript drawing model. A *Bézier curve* is one that you can control the depth and size of by using direction lines.

✦ **Anchor points:** You can use anchor points to control the shape of a path or object. Anchor points are automatically created when using shape tools. You can manually create anchor points by clicking from point to point with the Pen tool.

✦ **Direction lines:** These lines are essentially the handles that you use on curved points to adjust the depth and angle of curved paths.

✦ **Closed shape:** When a path is created, it becomes a closed shape when the start point joins the endpoint.

✦ **Simple path:** A *path* consists of one or more straight or curved segments. Anchor points mark the endpoints of the path segments.

Figure 5-1:
The depth and direction of the Bézier curves are controlled by direction lines.

In the next section, we show you how to control the anchor points.

Creating a straight line

A basic function of the Pen tool is to create a simple path. You can create a simple, straight line with the Pen tool by following these steps:

1. **Before you start, press D or click the small black-and-white color swatches at the bottom of the toolbox.**

   You revert back to the default colors of a black stroke and a white fill. With black as a stroke, you can see your path clearly.

2. **Click the Fill swatch, located at the bottom of the toolbox, to make sure that the Fill swatch is in front of the Stroke swatch, and then press the forward slash (/) key to change the fill to None.**

   The trick of pressing D to change the foreground and background colors to the default of black and white also works in Photoshop and InDesign.

3. **Open a new blank page and select the Pen tool.**

   Notice that when you move the mouse over the artboard, the Pen cursor appears with an X beside it, indicating that you're creating the first anchor point of a path.

4. **Click the artboard to create the first anchor point of a line.**

   The X disappears.

   Don't drag the mouse, or you'll end up creating a curve instead of a straight segment.

5. **Click anywhere else on the document to create the ending anchor point of the line.**

Illustrator creates a path between the two anchor points. Essentially, the path looks like a line segment with an anchor point at each end (see Figure 5-2).

Figure 5-2:
A path
connected
by two
anchor
points.

To make a correction to a line you created with the Pen tool (as described in the preceding steps), follow these steps:

1. **Choose Select⇨Deselect to make sure that no objects are currently selected.**

2. **Select the Direct Selection tool from the toolbox.**

Notice that in Illustrator CS3, Adobe has been kind and added a feature that enlarges the anchor point when you pass over it with the Direct Selection tool.

3. **Click to select one anchor point on the line.**

Notice that the selected anchor point is solid and the other is hollow. Solid indicates that the anchor point you clicked is active while the hollow one is inactive.

4. **Click and drag the anchor point with the Direct Selection tool.**

The selected anchor point moves, changing the direction of the path while not affecting the other anchor point. And that's it.

Book III
Chapter 5

Using the Pen Tool
and Placing Images

Use the Direct Selection tool (shortcut to select this tool is A) to make any corrections to paths. Make sure that only the anchor point you want to change is active. If the entire path is selected, all anchor points are solid. If only one anchor point is selected, all but that one point will be hollow.

Creating a constrained straight line

In this section, we show you how to create a real straight line, meaning one that is on multiples of a 45-degree angle. Illustrator makes it easy; just follow these steps:

1. **Select the Pen tool and click anywhere on the artboard to place an anchor point.**

2. **Hold down the Shift key and click another location to place the ending anchor point.**

Notice that when you're holding the Shift key, the line snaps to a multiple of 45 degrees. *Remember:* Release the mouse button before you release the Shift key, or else the line will pop out of alignment.

Creating a curve

In this section, you discover how to use the Bézier path to create a curved segment. We won't guarantee that you'll love it — not at first anyway. But after you know how to use a Bézier path, you'll likely find it useful. To create a Bézier path, just follow these steps:

1. **Starting with a blank artboard, select the Pen tool and click anywhere on the artboard to place the first anchor point.**

2. **Now click someplace else to place your ending anchor point, but don't let go of the mouse button. Drag the cursor until a direction line appears.**

If you look real close, you see that anchor points are square, and the direction lines have circles at the end, as shown in Figure 5-3.

Figure 5-3:
Click and drag with the Pen tool to create a curved path.

3. **Drag the direction line closer to the anchor point to flatten the curve; drag farther away from the anchor point to increase the curve, as shown in Figure 5-4.**

4. **Release the mouse button when you're happy with the curve.**

What you have created is an open path, a path that doesn't form a closed shape. We show you how to reconnect to the starting point of the path to make a closed shape in the next section.

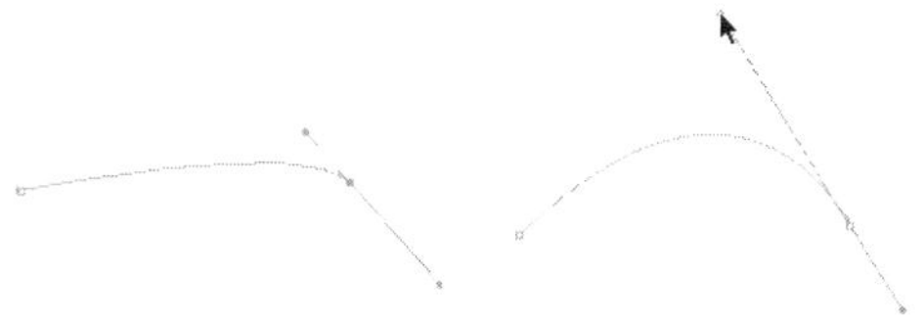

Figure 5-4:
The directional lines determine how the curve appears.

To alter a curved segment after you've created it, follow these steps:

1. **Choose Select➪Deselect to make sure that no objects are currently selected.**

2. **Choose the Direct Selection tool and click the last anchor point created.**

If they're not already visible, the direction lines appear.

If you have a hard time selecting the anchor point, drag a marquee around it using the Direct Selection tool.

3. **Click precisely at the end of one of the direction lines; drag the direction line to change the curve.**

Reconnecting to an existing path

Creating one segment is fine if you just want a line or an arch. But if you want to create a shape, you need to add more anchor points to the original segment. If you want to fill your shape with a color or a gradient, you need to close it, meaning that you need to eventually come back to the starting anchor point.

To add segments to your path and create a closed shape, follow these steps:

1. **Create a segment (straight or curved).**

We show you how in the preceding sections of this chapter.

You can continue from this point, clicking and adding anchor points until you eventually close the shape. For this example, you deselect the path so that you can discover how to continue adding to paths that have already been created. Knowing how to edit existing paths is extremely helpful when you need to make adjustments to artwork.

2. **With the Pen tool selected, move the cursor over an end anchor point on the deselected path.**

3. **To connect your next segment, click when you see the Pen icon with a forward slash.**

   The forward slash indicates that you're connecting to this path.

4. **Click someplace else to create the next anchor point in the path; drag the mouse if you want to create a curved segment.**

5. **Click to place additional anchor points, dragging as needed to curve those segments.**

   Remember that you want to close this shape, so place your anchor points so that you can eventually come back around to the first anchor point.

   Figure 5-5 shows a shape that is a result of several linked anchor points.

6. **When you get back to the first anchor point, move the cursor over it and click when the close icon (a small hollow circle) appears, as shown in Figure 5-6.**

   The shape now has no end points.

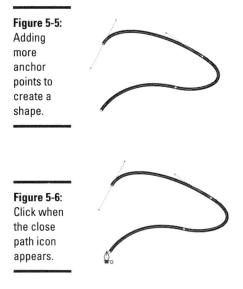

Figure 5-5:
Adding more anchor points to create a shape.

Figure 5-6:
Click when the close path icon appears.

Controlling the curves

After you feel comfortable creating curves and paths, you need to take control of those curves so that you can create them with a greater degree of precision. The following steps walk you through the manual method for changing direction of anchor points, as well as reveal helpful keyboard commands to make controlling paths a little more fluid. At the end of this section, we introduce you to new tools that may also want to take advantage of to help you get control of the Pen tool.

To control a curve, follow these steps:

1. **Create a new document and then choose View⇨Show Grid to show a series of horizontal and vertical rules that act as guides.**

If it helps, use the Zoom tool to zoom in to the document.

2. **Using the Pen tool, click an intersection of any of these lines in the middle area of the page to place your initial anchor point and drag upward.**

Let go, but don't click when the direction line has extended up to the horizontal grid line above it, as shown in Figure 5-7a.

3. **Click to place the second anchor point on the intersection of the grid directly to the right of your initial point; drag the direction line down to the grid line directly below it, as shown in Figure 5-7b.**

If you have a hard time keeping the direction line straight, hold down the Shift key to constrain it.

4. **Choose Select⇨Deselect to deselect your curve.**

Congratulations! You've created a controlled curve. In these steps, we created an arch that is going up, so we first clicked and dragged up. Likewise, to create a downward arch, you must click and drag down. Using the grid, try to create a downward arch like the one shown in Figure 5-7c.

Figure 5-7:
Creating a controlled Bézier Curve.

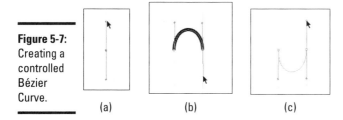

(a)   (b)   (c)

Creating a corner point

To change directions of a path from being a curve to a corner, you have to create a *corner point,* as shown on the right in Figure 5-8. A corner point has no direction lines and allows for a sharp direction change in a path.

You can switch from the Pen tool to the Convert Anchor Point tool to change a smooth anchor point into a corner point, but that process is a bit time consuming. An easier way is to press the Alt (Windows) or Option (Mac) key (the Pen tool temporarily changes into the Convert Anchor Point tool) while clicking the anchor point.

Figure 5-8:
Smooth
versus
corner
points.

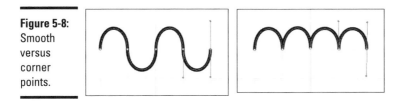

To change a smooth anchor point into a corner point using the shortcut method, follow these steps:

1. **Create an upward arch.**

We show you how in the preceding section, "Controlling the curves" (refer to Figure 5-8b).

2. **Hold down the Alt (Windows) or Option (Mac) key and position the cursor over the last anchor point (the last point that you created with the Pen tool).**

3. **When the cursor changes to a caret (that's the Convert Anchor Point tool), click and drag until the direction line is up to the grid line above, as shown on the left in Figure 5-9.**

Figure 5-9:
Converting a
smooth
anchor point
to a corner
point.

4. **Release the Alt (Windows) or Option (Mac) key and the mouse button, move the cursor to the grid line to the right, and click and drag down.**

The Hidden Pen Tools

Hold down on the Pen tool icon in the toolbox to access additional tools: the Add Anchor Point, Delete Anchor Point, and Convert Anchor Point tools, shown in Table 5-1. In the preceding section, we show you how to create a corner point with the shortcut method, by pressing the Alt (Windows) or Option (Mac) key to access the Convert Anchor Point tool. You may feel more comfortable switching to that tool when you need to convert a point, but switching tools can be more time-consuming.

Table 5-1	The Hidden Pen Tools
Icon	**Tool**
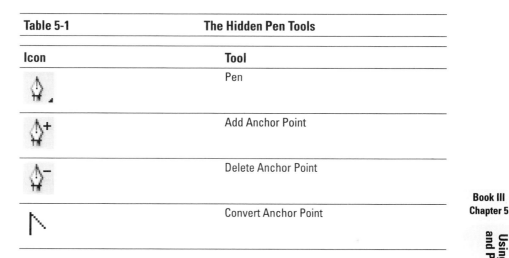	Pen
	Add Anchor Point
	Delete Anchor Point
	Convert Anchor Point

Even though you can use a hidden tool to delete and add anchor points, Illustrator automatically does this as a default when you're using the Pen tool. When you move the cursor over an anchor point with the Pen tool, a minus icon appears. To delete that anchor point, simply click. Likewise, when you move the cursor over a part of the path that doesn't contain anchor points, a plus icon appears. Simply click to add an anchor point.

If you prefer to use the tools dedicated to adding and deleting anchor points, choose Edit (Windows) or Illustrator (Mac)⇨Preferences⇨General; in the Preferences dialog box that appears, select the Disable Auto Add/Delete check box. Then, when you want to add or delete an anchor point, select the appropriate tool and click on the path.

So what's new in CS3?

Some tools have been added to the control panel in Illustrator CS3, and you can take advantage of them to do many of the Pen tool functions you do manually. To tell you the truth, using keyboard modifiers to switch your Pen tool is probably still faster, but some of you who may be resistant to contorting your fingers while trying to create a path may appreciate these new tools.

In order to see the new tools, select the Pen tool and start creating a path. Notice that the control panel has a series of buttons available, as shown in Figure 5-10.

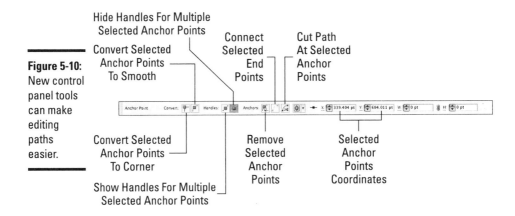

Figure 5-10: New control panel tools can make editing paths easier.

Hide Handles For Multiple
Selected Anchor Points

Convert Selected
Anchor Points
To Smooth

Connect
Selected
End
Points

Cut Path
At Selected
Anchor
Points

Convert Selected
Anchor Points
To Corner

Remove
Selected
Anchor
Points

Selected
Anchor
Points
Coordinates

Show Handles For Multiple
Selected Anchor Points

Using the new Eraser tool

The Eraser tool is a tool both new and old users will love! The Eraser tool allows you to quickly remove areas of artwork as easily as you erase pixels in Photoshop by stroking with your mouse over any shape or set of shapes.

New paths are automatically created along the edges of your erasure, even preserving the smoothness of your erasure as you see in Figure 5-11.

Figure 5-11: Use the new Eraser tool to delete sections of a path.

By double-clicking the Eraser tool, you can define the diameter, angle, and roundness of your eraser and even set Wacom (digitizing) tablet interaction parameters, such as Pressure and Tilt (see Figure 5-12).

If you want to erase more than a single selected object, use Isolation Mode to segregate grouped objects for editing. Remember that to enter Isolation mode, you simply double-click a group of items. You can then use the eraser on all objects in that group at once without disturbing the rest of your design.

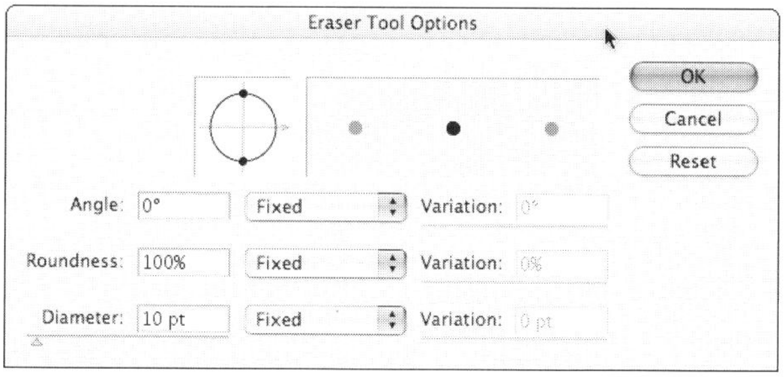

Figure 5-12: Double-click the Eraser tool to set various tool options.

Tracing Artwork

You can use a template layer to trace an image manually. A *template layer* is a locked, dimmed layer that you can use to draw over placed images with the Pen tool, much like you'd do with a piece of onion skin paper over the top of an image.

Just follow these steps to create a template layer:

1. **Take a scanned image or logo and save it in a format that Illustrator can import from your image-editing program, such as Photoshop.**

   Typically, you save the image as an .eps, .tif, or native .psd (Photoshop file).

2. **Choose File⇨Place to open the Place dialog box.**

3. **In the Place dialog box, locate the saved image; then select the Template check box and click Place.**

   Note that the Template check box may be in a different location depending upon your platform, but it's always located at the bottom of the dialog box.

   Selecting the Template check box tells Illustrator to lock down the scanned image on a layer. Essentially, you can't reposition or edit your image.

   After you click Place, a template layer is automatically created for you, and another layer is waiting for you to create your path. The newly created top layer is like a piece of tracing paper that has been placed on top of the scanned image.

**Book III
Chapter 5**

Using the Pen Tool and Placing Images

4. **Re-create the image by tracing over it with the Pen tool.**

5. **When you're done, turn the visibility off the placed image by clicking the Visibility icon to the left of the template layer.**

   You now have a path that you can use in place of the image, which is useful if you're creating an illustration of an image or are digitally re-creating a logo.

For more about layers, check out Chapter 8 of this minibook.

Keep practicing to get yourself more comfortable with clicking and dragging, flowing with the direction line pointing the way that you want the path to be created; everything will fall into place.

Using Live Trace

Use the Live Trace feature, introduced in Illustrator CS2, to automatically trace raster images into vector paths. This does work great in many instances, but is definitely not a "magic pill" for getting your images re-created as vectors. For example, a logo with many precise curves and straight lines isn't a good candidate for this feature, but a hand-drawn illustration, clip art, or other drawing works well.

Here are the steps that you want to take to use Live Trace.

1. **Choose File⇨Place and place a scan or raster illustration that you want to convert to vector paths.**

2. **Immediately after placing, you see that the control panel now has some additional buttons available, as shown in Figure 5-13.**

Figure 5-13:
The Live Trace Control panel features.

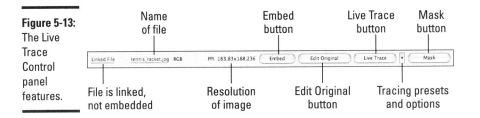

3. **You can either press the Live Trace button to automatically trace based upon default settings or, better yet, click and hold on the Tracing presets and options arrow and choose a more appropriate setting.**

Choose Tracing Options from the very bottom of the Tracing options and presets drop-down menu to customize settings.

4. **After you select the settings you're happy with, you can either use the Live Paint features to color in the work or press the Expand button in the Control panel to expand the trace object to vector paths that can be edited.**

   See Chapter 9 of this minibook for more information on painting fills and strokes.

Other Things You Should Know about Placing Images

In the preceding section, you discover how to place an image as a template. But what if you want to place an image to be utilized in your illustration file? Simply choose File➪Place.

Click once on an image to see the Link check box. If you keep the check box selected, the image is linked to the original file. This is good if you plan on referencing the file several times in the illustration (saves file space) or if you want to edit the original and have it update the placed image in Illustrator. This option is usually checked by those in the prepress industry who want to have access to the original image file. Just remember to send the image with the Illustrator file if it's to be output or used someplace other than on your computer.

If you uncheck the Link check box, the image is embedded into the Illustrator file. This option does keep the filing system cleaner, but doesn't leave much room to edit the original image at a later point. There are certain instances, such as when you want an image to become a Symbol (see Chapter 11 of this minibook), that the image will have to be embedded, but most functions work with linked and unlinked files.

Using Photoshop Layer Comps

Layer Comps are a feature in Photoshop that allow you to set the visibility, appearance, and position of layers. It's a great organizational tool that you can now take advantage of in other Adobe products. Read more about Photoshop in Book IV.

You can place a `.psd` (Photoshop) image that has saved Layer Comps from Photoshop and choose which layer comp set you want visible while placing in Adobe Illustrator CS3.

Book III
Chapter 5

Using the Pen Tool and Placing Images

Chapter 6: Using Type in Illustrator

In This Chapter

✔ Introducing the Type tools

✔ Getting to know text areas

✔ Manipulating text along paths and within shapes

✔ Assigning font styles

✔ Discovering the Character and Paragraph panels

✔ Using the new control panel for text controls

✔ Saving time with text utilities

*O*ne of Illustrator's strongest areas is manipulating text. Whether you're using Illustrator to create logos, business cards, or type to be used on the Web, you have everything you need to create professional text.

In this chapter, you meet the Type tools and discover a few basic (and more advanced) text-editing tricks that you can take advantage of. You then discover other text tools, such as the Character and Paragraph panels. You end the chapter by getting a quick-and-dirty lowdown on the Illustrator text utilities. These utilities can save you loads of time, so don't skip this section.

Working with Type

You can do all sorts of cool things with type, from the simplest tasks of creating a line of text and dealing with text overflow to more complicated tricks, such as placing text along paths and wrapping text around objects.

Figure 6-1 shows the Type tools with an example of what you can do with each one. Click and hold the Type tool to see the hidden tools. The different tools give you the ability to be creative and also accommodate foreign languages.

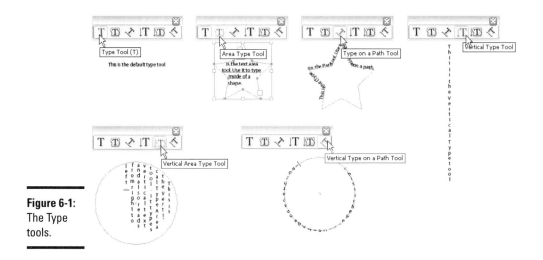

Figure 6-1:
The Type
tools.

Creating text areas

A *text area* is a region that you define. Text, when inserted in this region, is constrained within the shape. To create a text area, click and drag with the Type tool.

As you create and finish typing in a text area, you may want to quickly click and drag a new text area elsewhere on your artboard. Unfortunately, if you're on the Type tool, Illustrator doesn't allow you to do so. You have two options to address this problem:

✦ Choose Select➪Deselect and then create another area.

✦ Hold down the Ctrl (Windows) or ⌘ (Mac) key to temporarily access the Selection tool, and click. When you release the Ctrl (Windows) or ⌘ (Mac) key, you'll still be on the Type tool, and you can then create a new text area.

Creating a line of text

To create a simple line of text, select the Type tool and click the artboard. A blinking insertion point appears. You can now start typing. Using this method, the line of type goes on forever and ever (even beyond the end of the Scratch area) until you press Enter (Windows) or Return (Mac) to start a new line of text. This excess length is fine if you just need short lines of text, say for call-outs or captions, but it doesn't work well if you're creating a label or anything else that has large amounts of copy.

Many new users click and drag an ever-so-small text area that doesn't allow room for even one letter. If you do this, switch to your Selection tool, delete the active type area, and then click to create a new text insertion point.

Flowing text into an area

Select the Type tool and then drag on the artboard to create a text area. The cursor appears in the text area; text you type automatically flows to the next line when it reaches the edge of the text area. You can also switch to the Selection tool and adjust the width and height of the text area using the handles.

Need an exact size for a text area? With the Type tool selected, drag to create a text area of any size. Then choose Window➪Transform to view the Transform panel. Type an exact width in the W text field and exact height in the H text field.

Dealing with text overflow

Watch out for excess text! If you create a text area that's too small to hold all the text you want to put into it, a red plus sign appears in the lower-right corner, as shown in Figure 6-2.

When Illustrator indicates to you that you have too much text for the text area, you have several options:

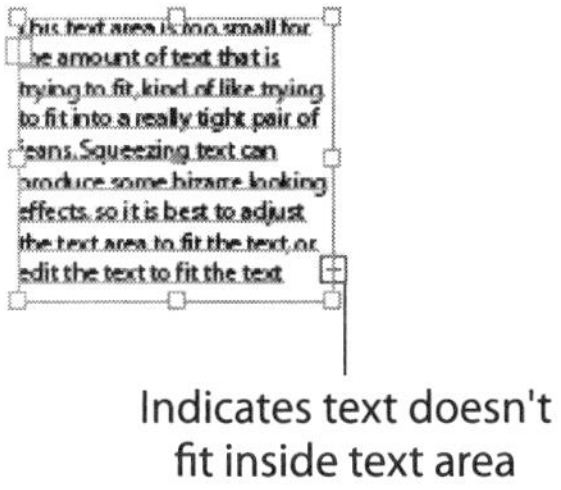

Figure 6-2:
The plus icon notes that text is overflowing.

This text area is too small for the amount of text that is trying to fit, kind of like trying to fit into a really tight pair of jeans. Squeezing text can produce some bizarre looking effects, so it is best to adjust the text area to fit the text, or edit the text to fit the text

Indicates text doesn't
fit inside text area

- ✦ Make the text area larger by switching to the Selection tool and dragging the handles.

- ✦ Make the text smaller until you don't see the overflow indicated.

- ✦ Link this text area to another, which is called *threading* and is covered later in this chapter in the "Threading text into shapes" section.

Creating columns of text with the Area Type tool

The easiest and most practical way to create rows and columns of text is to use the area type options in Adobe Illustrator. This feature lets you create rows and columns from any text area. You can just have rows, or you can just have columns (much like columns of text in a newspaper), or even both.

1. **Select the Type tool and drag to create a text area.**

2. **Choose Type⇨Area Type Options.**

The Area Type Options dialog box appears, as shown in Figure 6-3. At the end of this section, we provide a list explaining all the options in the Area Type Options dialog box.

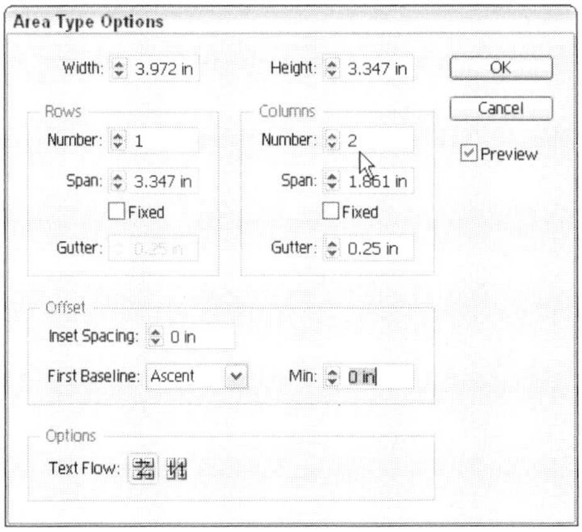

Figure 6-3:
The Area
Type
Options
dialog box
lets you
create
columns of
text.

3. **Enter the desired width and height in the Width and Height text fields.**

The Width and Height text fields contain the height and width of your entire text area. For example, we entered 325 pt in the Width text field and 250 pt in the Height text field.

4. **In the Columns area, enter the number of columns you want to create in the Columns Number text field, the span distance in the Columns Span text field, and the gutter space in the Columns Gutter text field.**

We entered **2** to create two columns in the Columns Number text field.

The *span* specifies the height of individual rows and the width of individual columns. The *gutter* is the space between the columns and is automatically set for you.

5. **Click OK.**

When you create two or more columns of text using the Area Type Options dialog box, text flows to the next column when you reach the end of a column, as shown in Figure 6-4.

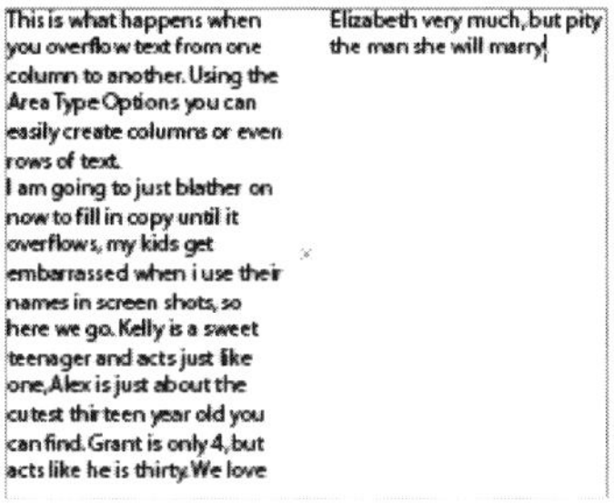

Figure 6-4:
One column
of text flows
into the
next.

This is what happens when you overflow text from one column to another. Using the Area Type Options you can easily create columns or even rows of text.
I am going to just blather on now to fill in copy until it overflows, my kids get embarrassed when i use their names in screen shots, so here we go. Kelly is a sweet teenager and acts just like one, Alex is just about the cutest thirteen year old you can find. Grant is only 4, but acts like he is thirty. We love

Elizabeth very much, but pity the man she will marry!

The following is a breakdown of the other options available in the Area Type Options dialog box (refer to Figure 6-3):

+ **Width and Height:** The present width and height of the entire text area.

+ **Number:** The number of rows and/or columns that you want the text area to contain.

+ **Span:** The height of individual rows and the width of individual columns.

+ **Fixed:** Determines what happens to the span of rows and columns if you resize the type area. When this check box is selected, resizing the area can change the number of rows and columns but not their width. Leave this option deselected if you want to resize the entire text area and have the columns automatically resize with it.

+ **Gutter:** The empty space between rows or columns.

+ **Inset Spacing:** The distance from the edges of the text area.

+ **First Baseline:** Where you want the first line of text to appear. The Ascent option is the default and starts your text normally at the top. If you want to put a fixed size in, such as 50 pts from the top, select Fixed from the drop-down list and enter 50 pt in the Min text field.

+ **Text Flow:** The direction in which you read the text as it flows to another row or column. You can choose to have the text flow horizontally (across rows) or vertically (down columns).

Threading text into shapes

Create custom columns of text that are in different shapes and sizes by threading closed shapes together. This technique works with rectangles, circles, stars, or any closed shape and can lead to some creative text areas.

1. **Create any shape, any size.**

For this example, we've created a circle.

2. **Create another shape (it can be any shape) someplace else on the page.**

3. **Using the Selection tool, select one shape and Shift+click the other to make just those two shapes active.**

4. **Choose Type⇨Threaded Text⇨Create.**

A threading line appears, as shown in Figure 6-5, indicating the direction of the threaded text.

5. **Select the Type tool, click the top of the shape to start the threading, and start typing.**

Continue typing until the text flows over into the other shape.

If you don't want the text to be threaded anymore, choose Type⇨Threaded Text⇨Remove Threading, which eliminates all threading from the text shapes. To remove one or more shapes from the threading but not all the shapes, select the shape you want to remove from the threading and choose Type⇨Threaded Text⇨Release Selection.

Wrapping text

Wrapping text isn't quite the same as wrapping a present — it's easier! A *text wrap* forces text to wrap around a graphic, as shown in Figure 6-6. This feature can add a bit of creativity to any piece.

Follow these steps to wrap text around another object or group of objects:

1. **Select the wrap object.**

This is the object that you want the text to wrap around.

2. **Make sure that the wrap object is on top of the text you want to wrap around it by choosing Object⇨Arrange⇨Bring to Front.**

If you're working in layers (which we discuss in Chapter 8 of this mini-book), make sure that the wrap object is on the top layer.

3. Choose Object➪Text Wrap➪Make.

An outline of the wrap area is visible.

4. Adjust the wrap area by choosing Object➪Text Wrap➪Text Wrap Options.

The Text Wrap Options dialog box appears, as shown in Figure 6-7, giving you the following options:

- **Offset:** Specifies the amount of space between the text and the wrap object. You can enter a positive or negative value.

- **Invert Wrap:** Wraps the text on the inside of the wrap object instead of around it.

5. When you've finished making your selections, click OK.

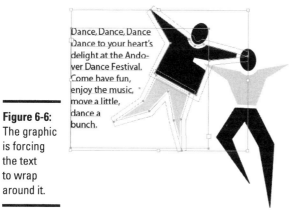

Figure 6-6:
The graphic is forcing the text to wrap around it.

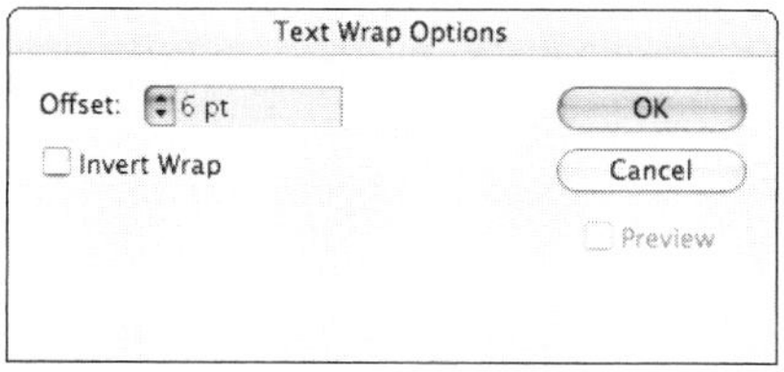

Figure 6-7:
Adjust the distance of the text wrap from the object and where the text starts using Text Wrap Options.

If you want to change the text wrap at a later point, select the object and choose Object⇨Text Wrap⇨Text Wrap Options. Make your changes and click OK.

If you want to unwrap text from an object, select the wrap object and choose Object⇨Text Wrap⇨Release.

Outlining text

Illustrator gives you the opportunity to change text into outlines or artwork. Basically, you change the text into an object, so you can no longer edit that text by typing. The plus side is that it saves you the trouble of sending fonts to everyone who wants to use the file. Turning text into outlines makes it appear as though your text was created with the Pen tool. You want to use this tool when creating logos that will be used frequently by other people or artwork that you may not have control over.

To turn text into an outline, follow these steps:

1. **Type some text on your page.**

   For this example, just type a word (say, your name) and make sure that the font size is at least 36 pts. You want to have it large enough to see the effect of outlining it.

2. **Switch to the Selection tool and choose Type⇨Create Outlines.**

   You can also use the keyboard command Ctrl+Shift+O (Windows) or ⌘+Shift+O (Mac).

   The text is now grouped together in outline form.

3. **If you're being creative, or just particular, and want to move individ-ual letters, use the Group Select tool or choose Object⇨Ungroup to separate the letters, as shown in Figure 6-8.**

Figure 6-8:
Letters become shapes when converted to outlines.

When you convert type to outlines, the type loses its hints. *Hints* are the instructions built into fonts to adjust their shape so that your system displays or prints them in the best way based on the size. Without hints, letters like lowercase *e* or *a* might fill in as the letter forms are reduced in size. Make sure that the text is the approximate size that it might be used at before creating outlines. Because the text loses the hints, try not to create outlines on text smaller than 10 pts.

Putting text on a path, in a closed shape, or on the path of a shape

Wow — that's some heading, huh? You've probably seen text following a swirly path or inside some shape. Maybe you think accomplishing such a task is too intimidating to even attempt. In this section, we show you just how easy these things are! There are Type tools dedicated to putting type on a path or a shape (refer to Figure 6-1), but we think you'll find that the key modifiers we show you in this section are easier to use.

Creating text on a path

Follow these steps to put type on a path:

1. **Create a path using the Pen, Line, or Pencil tool.**

   Don't worry if it has a stroke or fill applied.

2. **Select the Type tool and simply cross over the start of the path.**

3. **Look for an I-bar with a squiggle to appear (it indicates that the text will run along the path) and click.**

   The stroke and fill of the path immediately change to None.

4. **Start typing, and the text runs on the path.**

5. **To reposition where the text falls on the path, choose Window⇨Type⇨ Paragraph and change the alignment in the Paragraph panel.**

   Alternatively, switch to the Selection tool and drag the I-bar that appears, as shown in Figure 6-9, to move the text freehand.

Flip the text to the other side of a path by clicking and dragging the I-bar under or over the path.

Figure 6-9:
Using the
Selection
tool, you
can click
and drag the
I-bar and
adjust the
text.

Creating text in a closed shape

Putting text inside a shape can add spunk to a layout. This feature allows
you to custom-create a closed shape with the shape tools or the Pen tool
and flow text into it. Follow these steps to add text inside a shape:

1. **Create a closed shape — a circle or oval, for example.**

2. **Select the Type tool and cross over the closed shape.**

3. **When you see the I-bar swell or become rounded, click inside the
shape.**

4. **Start typing, and the text is contained inside the shape.**

Text on the path of a closed shape

Perhaps you want text to run around the edge of a shape instead of inside it.
Follow these steps to have text created on the path of a closed shape:

1. **Create a closed shape, such as a circle.**

2. **Select the Type tool and cross over the path of the circle.**

3. **Don't click when you see the I-bar swell up; hold down the Alt
(Windows) or Option (Mac) key instead.**

The icon now changes into the squiggle I-bar that you see when creating
text on a path.

4. **When the squiggle line appears, click.**

5. **Start typing, and the text flows around the path of the shape, as
shown in Figure 6-10.**

Figure 6-10:
By holding down the Alt or Option key, you can flow text around a closed shape.

To change the origin of the text or move it around, use the alignment options in the Paragraph panel or switch to the Selection tool and drag the I-bar to a new location on the path.

You can drag the I-bar in and out of the shape to flip the text so that it appears on the outside or inside of the path.

Assigning Font Styles

After you have text on your page, you'll often want to change it to be more interesting than the typical 12-pt Times font. Formatting text in Illustrator isn't only simple, but you can do it multiple ways. In the following list, we name and define some basic type components (see Figure 6-11):

Figure 6-11:
Components of type.

✦ **Font:** A complete set of characters, letters, and symbols of a particular typeface design.

✦ **X height:** The height of type, based on the height of the small x in that type family.

✦ **Kerning:** The space between two letters. Often used for letters in larger type that need to be pulled closer together, like "W i." Kern a little to get the i to slide in a little closer to the W, maybe even going into the space that the W takes, as shown in Figure 6-12. Kerning doesn't distort the text; it only increases or decreases the space between two letters.

Figure 6-12:
The letters before kerning (left) and after.

Wi Wi

✦ **Tracking:** The space between multiple letters. Designers like to use this technique to spread out words by increasing the space between letters. Adjusting the tracking doesn't distort text; it increases or decreases the space between the letters, as shown in Figure 6-13.

Figure 6-13:
A headline with tracking set at zero (top) and at 300 (bottom).

AGI TRAINING

A G I   T R A I N I N G

Pretty good tracking and kerning has already been determined in most fonts. You don't need to bother with these settings unless you're trying to tweak the text for a more customized look.

✦ **Baseline:** The line that type sits on. The baseline doesn't include descenders, type that extends down, like lowercase *y* and *g*. You adjust the baseline for trademark signs or mathematical formulas, as shown in Figure 6-14.

Figure 6-14:
Adjust the baseline for text characters that need to be above or below the baseline.

The Keyboard shortcuts for type shown in Table 6-1 work with Adobe Illustrator, Photoshop, and InDesign.

Table 6-1	Keyboard Shortcuts for Type	
Command	*Windows*	*Mac*
Align left, right, or center	Shift+Ctrl+L, R, or C	Shift+⌘+L, R, or C
Justify	Shift+Ctrl+J	Shift+⌘+J
Insert soft return	Shift+Enter	Shift+Return
Reset horizontal scale to 100%	Shift+Ctrl+X	Shift+ ⌘+X
Increase/decrease point size	Shift+Ctrl+> or <	Shift+ ⌘+> or <
Increase/decrease leading	Alt+↑ or ↓	Option+↑ or ↓
Set leading to the font size	Double-click the leading icon in the Character panel	Double-click the leading icon in the Character panel
Reset tracking/kerning to 0	Alt+Ctrl+Q	Option+⌘+Q
Add or remove space (kerning) between two characters	Alt+→ or ←	Option+→ or ←
Add or remove space (kerning) between characters by 5 times the increment value	Alt+Ctrl+→ or ←	Option+⌘+→ or ←
Add or remove space (kerning) between selected words	Alt+Ctrl+\ or Backspace	Option+⌘+\ or Backspace
Add or remove space (kerning) between words by 5 times the increment value	Shift+Alt+Ctrl+\ or Backspace	Shift+Option+⌘+\ or Backspace
Increase/decrease baseline shift	Alt+Shift+↑ or ↓	Option+Shift+↑ or ↓

**Book III
Chapter 6**

**Using Type in
Illustrator**

Using the Character Panel

To visualize changes that you're making to text and to see characteristics that are already selected, choose Window➪Type➪Character or press Ctrl+T (Windows) or ⌘+T (Mac), which brings up the Character panel. Click the triangle in the upper-right corner to see a panel menu of additional options. Choose Show Options, and additional type attributes appear, such as baseline shift, underline, and strikethrough.

Pressing Ctrl+T (Windows) or ⌘+T (Mac) is a toggle switch to either show or hide the Character panel. If you don't see the Character panel appear at first, you may have hidden it by pressing the keyboard shortcut. Just try it again.

The following list explains the options in the Character panel (see Figure 6-15):

+ **Font:** Pick the font that you want to use from this drop-down list.

   In this version, you can select the font name in the Character panel or control panel and press the up or down arrow key to automatically switch to the next font above or below on the font list. Do this while you have text selected to see the text change live!

+ **Set Font Style:** Pick the style (for example, bold, italic, or bold italic) from this drop-down list. The choices here are limited by the fonts that you have loaded. In other words, if you have only Times regular loaded in your system, you won't have the choice to bold or italicize it.

+ **Type Size:** Choose the size of the type in this combo box. Average readable type is 12 pt; headlines can vary from 18 pts and up.

+ **Leading:** Select how much space you want between the lines of text in this combo box. Illustrator uses the professional typesetting method of including the type size in the total leading. In other words, if you have 12 pt and want it double-spaced, set the leading at 24 pts.

+ **Kerning:** Use this combo box by placing the cursor between two letters. Increase the amount by clicking the up arrow or by typing in a value to push the letters further apart from each other; decrease the spacing between the letters by typing in a lower value, even negative numbers, or by clicking the down arrow.

+ **Tracking:** Use the Tracking combo box by selecting multiple letters and increasing or decreasing the space between all of them at once by clicking the up or down arrows or by typing in a positive or negative value.

+ **Horizontal Scale:** Distorts the selected text by stretching it horizontally. Enter a positive number to increase the size of the letters; enter a negative number to decrease the size.

+ **Vertical Scale:** Distorts the selected text vertically. Enter a positive number to increase the size of the letters; enter a negative number to decrease the size.

   Using horizontal or vertical scaling to make text look like condensed type often doesn't give good results. When you distort text, the nice thick and thin characteristics of the typeface also become distorted and can produce weird effects.

+ **Baseline Shift:** Use baseline shift for trademark signs and mathematical formulas that require selected letters to be moved above or below the baseline.

✦ **Character Rotation:** Rotate just the selected text by entering an angle in this text field or by clicking the up or down arrows.

✦ **Rotate:** Choose to rotate your selected text on any angle.

✦ **Underline and Strikethrough:** Finally! This simple text attribute was noticeably missing from previous versions, but now a type style you can choose.

✦ **Language:** Choose a language from this drop-down list. *Note:* The language you specify here is used by Illustrator's spell checker and hyphenation feature. We discuss these features in the later section, "Text Utilities: Your Key to Efficiency."

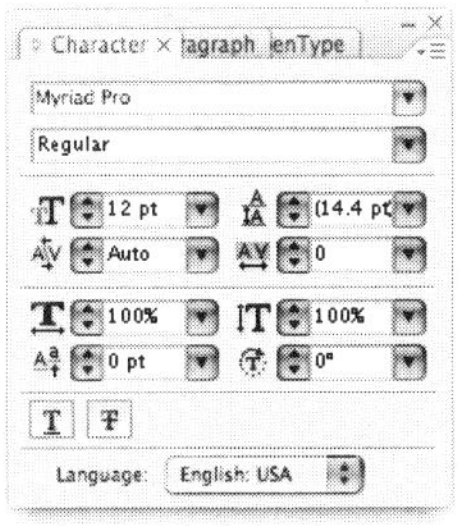

Figure 6-15:
The Character panel with additional options showing.

**Book III
Chapter 6**

**Using Type in
Illustrator**

Using the Control Panel

Try and get used to using the control panel to quickly access your type tools and type panels. Note in Figure 6-16 that, when you have active text, hyperlinked text buttons allow you to quickly access panels, such as the Character and Paragraph panels. You can also use this control panel as a quick and easy way to select fonts, size, alignment, color, and transparency.

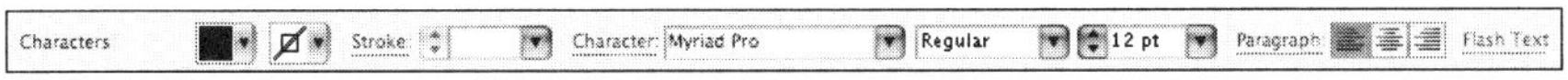

Figure 6-16:
Access type functions quickly using the control panel across the top of your Illustrator document.

Using the Paragraph Panel

Access the Paragraph panel quickly by clicking the Paragraph hyperlink in the control panel or by choosing Window⇨Type⇨Paragraph. In this panel are all the attributes that apply to an entire paragraph, including alignment and indents, which we discuss in this section, and also hyphenation, which we discuss later in this chapter. For example, you can't flush left one word in a paragraph. When you click the Flush Left button, the entire paragraph flushes left. To see additional options in the Paragraph panel, click the triangle in the upper-right of the panel (the panel menu) and choose Show Options.

Alignment

You can choose any of the following alignment methods by choosing the appropriate button on the Paragraph panel:

+ **Flush Left:** All text is flush to the left with a ragged edge on the right. This is the most common way to align text.

+ **Center:** All text is centered.

+ **Flush Right:** All text is flush to the right and ragged on the left.

+ **Justify With The Last Line Aligned Left:** Right and left edges are both straight, with the last line left-aligned.

+ **Justify With The Last Line Aligned Center:** Right and left edges are both straight, with the last line centered.

+ **Justify With The Last Line Aligned Right:** Right and left edges are both straight, with the last line right-aligned.

+ **Justify All Lines:** This method is called *forced justification,* where the last line is stretched the entire column width, no matter how short it is. This alignment is used in many publications, but it can create some awful results.

Indents

You can choose from the following methods of indentation:

+ **First Line Indent:** Indents the first line of every paragraph. In other words, every time you press the Enter (Windows) or Return (Mac) key, this spacing is created.

  To avoid first-line indents and space after from occurring, say if you just want to break a line in a specific place, create a line break or soft return by pressing Shift+Enter (Windows) or Shift+Return (Mac).

+ **Right Indent:** Indents from the right side of the column of text.

+ **Left Indent:** Indents from the left side of the column of text.

Use the Eyedropper tool to copy the character, paragraph, fill, and stroke attributes. Select the text that you want to, select the Eyedropper tool, and click once on the text with the attributes you want to apply to the selected text.

By default, the Eyedropper affects all attributes of a type selection, including appearance attributes. To customize the attributes affected by these tools, double-click the Eyedropper tool to open the Eyedropper dialog box.

Text Utilities: Your Key to Efficiency

After you have text in an Illustrator document, you may need to perform various tasks within that text, such as searching for a word to replace with another word, checking your spelling and grammar, saving and creating your own styles, or changing the case of a block of text. You're in luck, because Illustrator provides various text utilities that enable you to easily and efficiently perform all these otherwise tedious tasks. In this section, we give you a quick tour of these utilities.

Find And Replace

Generally, artwork created in Illustrator isn't text heavy, but the fact that Illustrator has a Find And Replace feature can be a huge help. Use the Find And Replace dialog box (choose Edit➪Find And Replace) to search for words that need to be changed, such as changing Smyth to Smith, or to locate items that may be difficult to find otherwise. This feature works pretty much like all other search and Replace methods.

Spell checker

Can you believe there was a time when Illustrator didn't have a spell checker? Thankfully, it does now — and its simple design makes it easy to use.

To use the spell checker, choose Edit➪Check Spelling, and then click the Start button in the dialog box that appears. The spell checker works much like the spell checker in Microsoft Word or other popular applications: When a misspelled word is found, you're offered a list of Replacements. You can either choose to fix that instance, all instances, ignore the misspelling, or add your word to the dictionary.

If you click the arrow to the left of Options, you can set other specifications, such as whether you want to look for letter case issues or have the spell checker note repeated words.

Note: The spell checker uses whatever language you specify in the Character panel. We discuss this panel in the earlier section, "Using the Character Panel."

If you work in a specialized industry that uses loads of custom words, save yourself time by choosing Edit➪Edit Custom Dictionary and then add your own words. We recommend that you do so before you're ready to spell check a document so that the spell checker doesn't flag the custom words later (which slows you down).

The Hyphenation feature

Nothing is worse than severely hyphenated copy. Most designers either use hyphenation as little as possible or avoid it altogether by turning off the Hyphenation feature.

Here are a few things that you should know about customizing your hyphenation settings if you decide to use this feature:

✦ **Turning the Hyphenation feature on/off:** Activate or deactivate the feature in the Hyphenation dialog box (see Figure 6-17); access this dialog box by choosing Window➪Type➪Paragraph, clicking the arrow in the upper-right of the Paragraph panel to access the panel menu, and then choosing Hyphenation from the list of options that appears. If you're not going to use the Hyphenation feature, turn it off by deselecting the Hyphenation check box at the top of the Hyphenation dialog box.

✦ **Setting specifications in the Hyphenation dialog box:** Set specifications in the dialog box that determine the length of words to hyphenate, how many hyphens should be used in a single document, whether to hyphenate capitalized words, and how words should be hyphenated. The Before Last setting is useful, for example, if you don't want to have a word such as "liquidated" hyphenated as "liquidat-ed." Type 3 in the Before Last text field, and Illustrator won't hyphenate words if it leaves only two letters on the next line.

✦ **Hyphenation Limit and Hyphenation Zone:** They're not diets or worlds in another dimension. The Hyphenation Limit setting enables you to limit the number of hyphens in a row. So, for example, type 2 in the Hyphenation Limit text field so that there are never more than two hyphenated words in a row. The Hyphenation Zone text field enables you to set up an area of hyphenation based upon a measurement. For example, you can specify 1 inch to allow for only one hyphenation every inch. You can also use the slider to determine whether you want better spacing or fewer hyphens. This slider works only with the Single-line composer (the default).

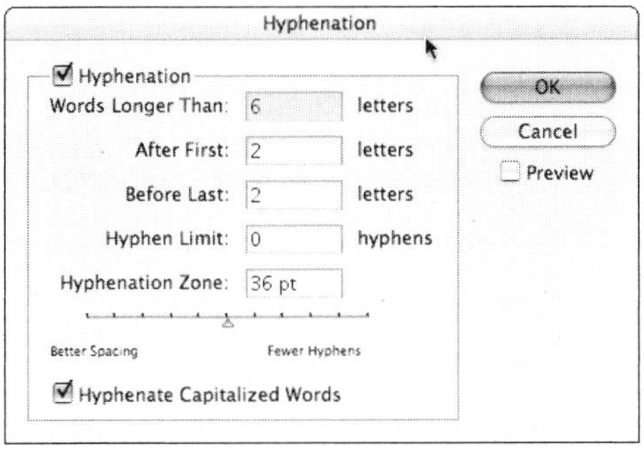

Figure 6-17:
Customizing
hyphenation
settings.

The Find Font feature

If you work in production, you'll love the Find Font feature, which enables you to list all the fonts in a file that contains text and then search for and Replace fonts (including the font's type style) by name. You do so from the Find Font dialog box (see Figure 6-18), accessed by choosing Type⇨Find Font. Select the font that you want to Replace from the Fonts in Document list. Next, select a font from the Replace with Font From list. Note that the font must already appear in the document. Click the Change button to Replace the font (or click the Change All button to Replace all instances of the font) and then click OK. That's it!

This cool feature enables you to Replace fonts with fonts from the current working document or from your entire system. Select System from the Replace with Font From drop-down list to choose from all the fonts loaded in your system.

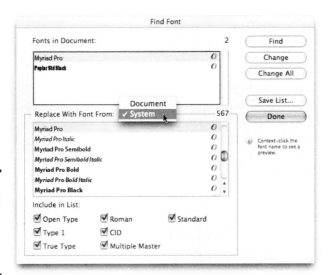

Figure 6-18:
Use the Find
Font dialog
box to find
and replace
typefaces.

The Change Case feature

Doesn't it drive you crazy when you type an entire paragraph before discovering that you somehow pressed the Caps Lock key? Fix it fast by selecting the text, choosing Type⇨Change Case, and then choosing one of the following:

✦ **Uppercase:** Makes the selected text all uppercase.

✦ **Lowercase:** Makes the selected text all lowercase.

✦ **Title Case:** Capitalizes the first letter in each word.

✦ **Sentence Case:** Capitalizes just the first letter in the selected sentence(s).

In Illustrator CS3, you use the same type engine used by InDesign for high-quality text control. As a default, you're working in what is referred to as a single-line composer. Select Single or Every Line composer from the Paragraph panel menu.

The different options include

✦ **Single-Line Composer:** Useful if you prefer to have manual control over how lines break. In fact, this method had been in place in the past. The single-line composer doesn't take the entire paragraph into consideration when expanding letter space and word spacing, so justified text can sometimes look odd in its entire form (see Figure 6-19).

✦ **Every-Line Composer:** The every-line composer is a very professional way of setting text; many factors are taken into account as far as spacing is concerned, and spacing is based on the entire paragraph. Using this method, you see few spacing issues that create strange effects, such as the ones on the left of Figure 6-19.

Figure 6-19:
A paragraph created using the Single-Line Composer (left) and using the Every-Line Composer (right).

AGI was founded as a training provider and maintains a presence as a resource for companies and individuals looking to become more productive with electronic publishing software. AGI maintains a strong relationship with electronic publishing software companies including Adobe Systems and Quark as a member of their authorized training provider network. AGI is also a private, licensed school in the Commonwealth of Pennsylvania.

AGI was founded as a training provider and maintains a presence as a resource for companies and individuals looking to become more productive with electronic publishing software. AGI maintains a strong relationship with electronic publishing software companies including Adobe Systems and Quark as a member of their authorized training provider network. AGI is also a private, licensed school in the Commonwealth of Pennsylvania.

Text styles

A *text style* is a saved set of text attributes, such as font, size, and so on. Creating text styles keeps you consistent and saves you time by enabling you to efficiently implement changes in one step instead of having to select the text attributes for each instance of that style of text (say a heading or caption). So when you're finally happy with the way your headlines appear and the body copy looks or when your boss asks whether the body copy can be a smidgen smaller (okay . . . a smidgen?), you can confidently answer, "Sure!"

If you've created styles, changing a text attribute is simple. What's more, the change is applied at once to all text that uses that style. Otherwise, you'd have to make the attribute change to every occurrence of body text, which could take a long time if your text is spread out.

Illustrator offers two types of text styles:

✦ **Character styles:** Saves attributes for individual selected text. If you want just the word "New" in a line of text to be red 20 pt Arial, you can save it as a character style sheet. Then, when you apply it, the attributes apply only to the selected text (and not the entire line or paragraph).

✦ **Paragraph styles:** Saves attributes for an entire paragraph. A span of text is considered a paragraph until it reaches a hard return or paragraph break. Note that pressing Shift+Enter (Windows) or Shift+Return (Mac) is considered a soft return, and paragraph styles will continue to apply beyond the soft return.

There are many ways to create character and paragraph styles, but we show you the easiest and most direct methods.

Creating character styles

Create a character style when you want individual sections of text to be treated differently from other text in the paragraph. So instead of manually applying a style over and over again, you create and implement a character style. To do so, open a document containing text and follow these steps:

1. **Set up text with the text attributes you want included in the character style in the Character and Paragraph panels and then choose Window⇨Type⇨Character Styles.**

The Character Styles panel opens.

2. **Select the text from Step 1 and Alt+click (Windows) or Option+click (Mac) the New Style button (dog-eared page icon) at the bottom of the Character Styles panel.**

3. **In the Character Styles Options dialog box that appears, name your style and click OK.**

   Illustrator records what attributes have already been applied to the selected text and builds a style for them.

4. **Now create another text area by choosing Select⇨Deselect and using the Type tool to drag out a new text area.**

   We discuss using the Type tool in the earlier section, "Creating text areas."

5. **Change the font and size to something dramatically different from your saved style and type some text.**

6. **Select some (not all) of the new text and then Alt+click (Windows) or Option+click (Mac) the style name in the Character Styles panel.**

   You Alt+click (Windows) or Option+click (Mac) to eliminate any attributes that weren't a part of the saved style. The attributes of the saved character style are applied to the selected text.

When creating a new panel item (any panel) in Adobe Illustrator, InDesign, or Photoshop, we recommend that you get in the habit of Alt+clicking (Windows) or Option+clicking (Mac) the New Style button. This habit allows you to name the item (style, layer, swatch, and so on) while adding it to the panel.

Creating a paragraph style

Paragraph styles include attributes that are applied to an entire paragraph. What constitutes a paragraph is all text that falls before a hard return (you create a hard return when you press Enter [Windows] or Return [Mac]), so this could be one line of text for a headline or ten lines in a body text paragraph.

To create a paragraph style, open a document that contains text or open a new document and add text to it; then follow these steps:

1. **Choose Window⇨Type⇨Paragraph Styles to open the Paragraph Styles panel.**

2. **Find a paragraph of text that has the same text attributes throughout it and put your cursor anywhere in that paragraph.**

   You don't even have to select the whole paragraph!

3. **Alt+click (Windows) or Option+click (Mac) the Create New Style button (the dog-eared icon at the bottom of the Paragraph panel) to create a new paragraph style; give your new style a name.**

   Your new style now appears in the Paragraph Styles panel list of styles.

4. **Create a paragraph of text elsewhere in your document and make its attributes different from the text in Step 2.**

5. **Put your cursor anywhere in the new paragraph and Alt+click (Windows) or Option+click (Mac) your named style in the Paragraph Styles panel.**

The attributes from the style are applied to the entire paragraph.

Updating styles

When you use existing text to build styles, reselect the text and assign the style. In other words, if you put the cursor in the original text whose attributes were saved as a style, it doesn't have a style assigned to it in the Styles panel. Assign the style by selecting the text or paragraph and clicking the appropriate style listed in the Styles panel. By doing so, you ensure that any future updates to that style will apply to that original text, as well as to all other instances.

To update a style, simply select its name in either the Character or Paragraph Styles panel. Choose Options from the panel menu, which you access by clicking the arrow in the upper-right corner of the panel. In the resulting dialog box (see Figure 6-20), make changes by clicking the main attribute on the left and then updating the choices on the right. After you do so, all tagged styles are updated.

Book III Chapter 6

Using Type in Illustrator

Figure 6-20: Updating a paragraph style.

Paragraph Style Options	
Style Name:	Package_side
General	Basic Character Formats
Basic Character Formats	
Advanced Character Formats	Font Family: Book Antiqua
Indents and Spacing	Font Style: Regular
Tabs	
Composition	Size: 12 pt Leading: 16 pt
Hyphenation	Kerning: Optical Tracking: 0
Justification	
Character Color	
OpenType Features	Case: Position:
	Standard Vertical Roman Alignment
☑ Preview	Reset Panel OK Cancel

WARNING! Documents created in older versions of Adobe Illustrator (Version 10 or earlier) contain what is called *legacy text,* which is text using the older text engine. When these files are opened, you see a warning dialog box, such as the one you see in Figure 6-21.

Understand that if you click the Update button, any text on the document will most likely reflow, causing line breaks, leading, and other spacing to change.

Figure 6-21: Legacy text warning. Click OK, not Update!

Click the OK button to update the file after it's opened to lock down the text. If necessary, you can use the Type tool to click a selected text area to update only the contained text. Another Warning dialog box appears that gives you the opportunity to Update the selected text, copy the Text Object, or cancel the text tool selection. This method is the best way to see what changes are occurring so that you can catch any spacing issues right off the bat. See Figure 6-22 for samples of the three options in the warning dialog window.

If you choose to Copy the Text Object, you can use the underlying locked copy to adjust the new text flow to match the old. Throw away the legacy text layer by clicking and dragging it to the trash icon in the Layers panel, or click on the visibility Eye icon to the left of the Legacy Text layer to hide it when you are finished.

Figure 6-22: Original text (left), updated text (middle), and text object copied (right).

tia della minestrone, i ravioli, e la farina-ta.

La città all'ovest della Liguria é San Remo, che é accanto al Monaco. San Remo é famosa per il museo di pas-ta e la festa di musica. La città all'est della Liguria é La Spezia, che é conosciu-ta per una base navale. La Spezia é vicino à Carrara, il posto dové Michelangelo prese la sua marma.

Da Genova si andrà in barca alle Cinque Terre, una zona che non é possibile rag-

noce, e il pesce. E anche la regione nattia della minestrone, i ravioli, e la farinata.

La città all'ovest della Liguria é San Remo, che é accanto al Monaco. San Remo é famosa per il museo di pasta e la festa di musica. La città all'est della Liguria é La Spezia, che é conosciuta per una base navale. La Spezia é vicino à Carrara, il posto dové Michelangelo prese la sua marma.

Da Genova si andrà in barca alle Cinque Terre, una zona che non é possibile raggiungere in machina; si deve andare o in barca o in treno. Le Cinque Terre

noce, e il pesce. E anche la regione nattia della minestrone, i ravioli, e la farinata.

La città all'ovest della Liguria é San Remo, che é accanto al Monaco. San Remo é famosa per il museo di pasta e la festa di musica. La città all'est della Liguria é La Spezia, che é conosciuta per una base navale. La Spezia é vicino à Carrara, il posto dové Michelangelo prese la sua marma. dove

Da Genova si andrà in barca alle Cinque Terre, una zona che non é possibile raggiungere in machina; si deve andare o in barca o in treno. Le Cinque Terre

Chapter 7: Organizing Your Illustrations

In This Chapter

✔ Setting up the ruler

✔ Placing paths and shapes

✔ Rearranging, hiding, and locking objects

✔ Masking objects

*Y*ou can know all the neat special effects in Illustrator, but if you don't have a strong foundation on the organization of your artwork, you can fall flat on your face when it comes to getting some features to work. In this chapter, we focus on a few tricks of the trade.

Setting Ruler Increments

Using rulers to help you accurately place objects in your illustration sounds pretty simple (and it is), but not knowing how to effectively use the rulers in Illustrator can drive you over the edge.

To view rulers in Illustrator, choose View➪Show Rulers or press Ctrl+R (Windows) or ⌘+R (Mac). When the rulers appear, they'll be in the default setting of points (or whatever measurement increment was last set up in the preferences).

You can change the rulers' increments to the measurement system that you prefer in the following ways:

✦ Create a new document and select your preferred measurement units in the New Document dialog box.

✦ Right-click (Windows) or Ctrl+click (Mac) the horizontal or vertical ruler and pick a measurement increment.

✦ Choose Edit➪Preferences➪Units And Display Performance (Windows) or Illustrator➪Preferences➪Units And Display Performance (Mac) to bring up the Preferences dialog box.

Be *very* careful with this dialog box. Change ruler units only by using the General tab of the Preferences dialog box. If you change the units of measurement in the Stroke and Type tabs, you can end up with 12-*inch* type instead of that dainty 12-*point* type you were expecting! ***Remember:*** Setting the General Preferences changes the preferences for all future documents.

✦ Choose File⇨Document Setup to change measurement units only for the document that you're working on.

Using Guides

Guides can make producing accurate illustrations much easier, and they can even go away when you're done with them. You can use two kinds of guides in Illustrator:

✦ **Ruler guides:** Straight-line guides that are created by clicking the ruler and dragging out to the artboard.

✦ **Custom guides:** Guides created from Illustrator objects, such as shapes or paths. Great for copying the exact angle of a path and replicating it, as shown in Figure 7-1.

Figure 7-1:
Turn your
selected
paths and
shapes into
custom
guides.

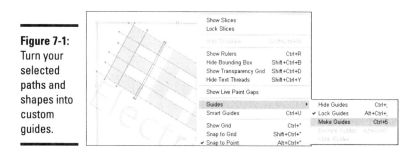

Creating a ruler guide

A ruler guide is the easiest guide to create. Click anywhere on the vertical or horizontal ruler and drag it to the artboard to create a ruler guide, as shown in Figure 7-2. By default, the horizontal ruler creates horizontal guides (no kidding), and the vertical ruler creates vertical guides. You can Alt+drag (Windows) or Option+drag (Mac) to change the orientation of the guide. The vertical ruler then creates a horizontal guide, and the horizontal ruler then creates a vertical guide.

Figure 7-2:
Click
directly on
the ruler
and drag out
a guide.

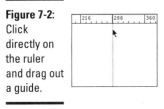

Creating a custom guide

Create a custom guide by selecting a path or shape and choosing View⇨
Guides⇨Make Guides. Whatever is selected turns into a nonprinting guide.
Changing a path into a guide isn't permanent. Choose View⇨Guides⇨Release
Guides to turn guides back into paths.

Using the Transform Panel for Placement

Placing shapes and paths precisely where you want them can be difficult for
those with even the most steady of hands. Save yourself aggravation by
using the Transform panel to perform such tasks as scaling and rotating
objects. On a more practical note, however, the Transform panel also
enables you to type in *x, y* coordinates. This way, you can position your
objects exactly where you want them.

In Adobe Illustrator and InDesign, the *Reference Point Indicator* icon is on
the left side of the Transform panel. Click the handle of the Reference Point
Indicator icon to change the point of reference. If you want to measure from
the upper-left corner, click the indicator on the handle in the upper left.
Want to know exactly where the center of an object is? Click the center point
in the indicator. The point of reference is the spot on the object that falls at
the *x, y* coordinates:

+ **X coordinate:** Sets the placement of the selected object from left to right.

+ **Y coordinate:** Sets the placement of the selected object from top to
  bottom.

Did you ever notice that Adobe Illustrator, which is based on PostScript, considers the lower-left corner the zero point? This can be confusing at first.
You can change the ruler origin if it really drives you crazy by following the
steps in the next section.

**Book III
Chapter 7**

**Organizing Your
Illustrations**

Changing the Ruler Origin

In Adobe Illustrator, InDesign, and Photoshop, you can change your *ruler origin*. This action helps define your measuring starting point and defines the part of the page that will print if you use manual tiling.

To change the ruler origin, follow these steps:

1. **Move the pointer to the upper-left corner of the rulers where the rulers intersect, as shown in Figure 7-3.**

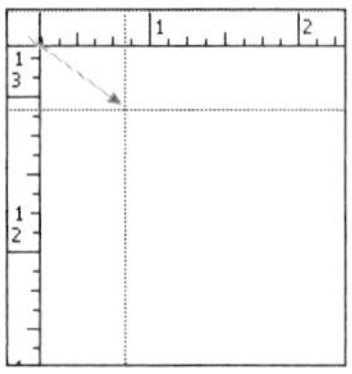

Figure 7-3:
Click and drag where the rulers intersect to change the start origin of your ruler.

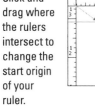

2. **Drag the pointer to where you want the new ruler origin.**

As you drag, a cross hair in the window and in the rulers indicates where the new ruler origin will be placed.

You can put the original ruler origin back in place by double-clicking the ruler intersection.

Thinking about Object Arrangement

Just like stacking paper on your desk, new objects in Illustrator are placed on top of the existing objects. Change this order by using the Object⇨ Arrange choices.

The easiest choices are to bring an object to the front or send it to the back. The results of sending forward or backward can be a little unnerving if you don't know exactly in what order objects were created. Figure 7-4 shows an illustration that we rearranged using four of the available choices. Figure 7-5 shows the result of each choice.

Figure 7-4:
The objects
in their
original
positions.

To change the stacking order, select the object(s) whose placement you want to change and then choose one of the following:

✦ **Object➪Arrange➪Bring To Front:** Brings the selected object(s) to the top of the painting order. In Figure 7-5a, the square is brought in front by using the Bring To Front command.

✦ **Object➪Arrange➪Bring Forward:** Brings the selected object(s) in front of the object created just before it, or one level closer to the front. In Figure 7-5b, the square is pulled up in front of the circle with the Bring Forward command.

✦ **Object➪Arrange➪Send Backward:** Moves the selected object(s) so that it falls under the object created just before it, or one level further to the back. In Figure 6-5c, the triangle is sent backward so that it's just under the circle.

✦ **Object➪Arrange➪Send To Back:** Pushes the selected object(s) to the bottom of the painting order. In Figure 7-5d, the triangle is placed on the bottom using the Send To Back command.

Book III
Chapter 7

Organizing Your
Illustrations

Figure 7-5:
Rearranging
objects.

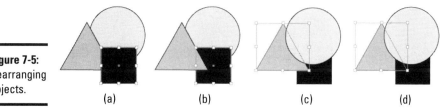

(a)   (b)   (c)   (d)

Hiding Objects

Seasoned Illustrator users love the Hide command. Use it when the object that you want to select is stuck behind something else, or when you need to select one object and another keeps activating instead.

A good opportunity to use the Hide command is when you're creating text inside a shape. In Chapter 6 of this mini-book, we show you that as soon as you turn a shape into a text area, the fill and stroke attributes turn into None. Follow these steps to hide a shape:

1. **Create a shape.**

   For this example, we created a circle.

2. **Click the Fill color box at the bottom of the Illustrator toolbox and then choose Window⇨Swatches.**

   The Swatches panel appears.

3. **In the panel, choose a color for the fill.**

   We've chosen yellow here. The stroke doesn't matter; we've set it to None.

   When changing your shape into a text area, the color you've chosen is going to disappear. To have the colored shape remain, you have to cheat the system.

4. **With your colored shape selected, choose Edit⇨Copy; alternatively, you can press Ctrl+C (Windows) or ⌘+C (Mac).**

   This step makes a copy of your shape.

5. **Choose Edit⇨Paste In Back or press Ctrl+B (Windows) or ⌘+B (Mac).**

   This step puts a copy of your shape exactly in back of the original.

6. **Choose Object⇨Hide or press Ctrl+3 (Windows) or ⌘+3 (Mac).**

   The copy of the shape is now hidden; what you see is your original shape.

7. **Switch to the Type tool by selecting the tool in the toolbox or pressing T.**

8. **With the cursor, cross over the edge of the shape to change it to the Area Type tool.**

   The Area Type tool enables you to type into a shape.

9. **When you see the type insertion cursor swell up (as shown in Figure 7-6), click the edge of the shape.**

   The insertion point is now blinking inside the shape, and the fill and stroke attributes of the shape have been changed to none.

10. **Type some text (see Figure 7-7).**

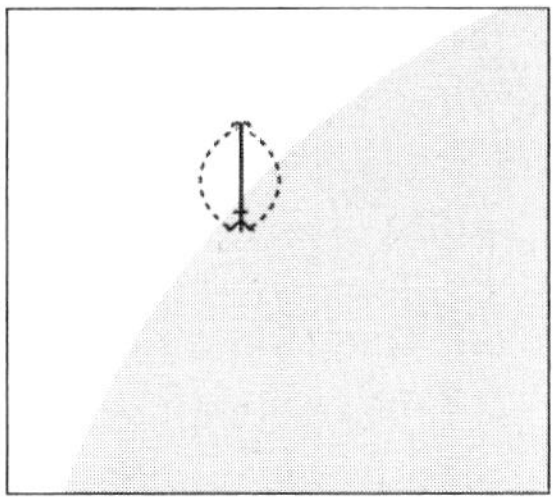

Figure 7-6:
The type insertion tool as it appears when positioned on the edge of a shape.

Figure 7-7:
Type directly into the shape.

Oh
I love a sunny
day!
Camp Jacuzzi 1984|

11. When you're finished entering text, choose Object⇨Show All, or press Ctrl+Alt+3 (Windows) or ⌘+Option+3 (Mac).

Your colored shape reappears with the text in the middle of it (see Figure 7-8).

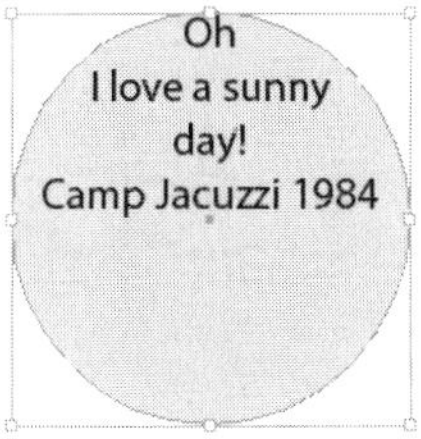

**Book III
Chapter 7**

Figure 7-8:
The hidden shape reappears exactly where it was before the Hide command was used.

Oh
I love a sunny
day!
Camp Jacuzzi 1984

**Organizing Your
Illustrations**

Use the Hide command anytime you want to tuck something away for later use. We promise that anything hidden in Illustrator won't be lost. Just use the Show All command, and any hidden objects are revealed, exactly where you left them. Too bad the Show All command can't reveal where you left your car keys!

Locking Objects

Locking items is handy when you're building an illustration. Not only does the Lock command lock down objects that you don't want to make changes to, but it also drives anyone who tries to edit your files crazy! In fact, we mention locking mainly to help preserve your sanity. There will be many times you need to make simple adjustments to another designer's artwork and you just can't, unless the objects are first unlocked. You can lock and unlock objects as follows:

✦ **Lock an object:** Choose Object➪Lock or press Ctrl+2 (Windows) or ⌘+2 (Mac) to lock an object so that you can't select it, move it, or change its attributes.

✦ **Unlock an object:** Choose Object➪Unlock All or press Ctrl+Alt+2 (Windows) or ⌘+Option+2 (Mac). Then you can make changes to it.

You can also lock and hide objects with layers. See Chapter 8 in this minibook for more information about using layers.

Creating a Clipping Mask

Creating a clipping mask may sound complex, but it's actually easy and brings together some of the items that we talk about in this chapter, such as arranging objects. A *clipping mask* allows a topmost object to define the selected shapes underneath it. It's similar to you cutting a hole in a piece of paper and peering through it to the objects below, except that with a clipping mask, the area around the defining shape is transparent (see Figure 7-9).

Figure 7-9: Examples of items using the clipping mask feature.

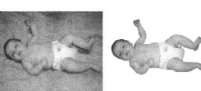

You may remember what a film mask looks like. It's black to block out the picture and clear where you want to view an image, as shown in Figure 7-10.

Figure 7-10:
An illustration of a conventional film mask.

The clipping mask feature uses the same principal as the conventional film mask, but the clipping mask is a whole lot easier to create and modify. To create a clipping mask, follow these steps:

1. **Choose File⇨Place to place an image.**

Masks work with objects created in Illustrator, as well as those placed (scanned or otherwise imported into Illustrator), but an example using a single placed image is less complicated.

2. **Create the item that you want to use as a mask by creating a shape or a closed path with the Pen tool.**

For example, in Figure 7-11, the circle is the mask. (The photo underneath it is the placed image from Step 1.) The circle is placed where the mask will be created. It doesn't matter what the shape's color, fill, and stroke are because these automatically change to None when you create a mask.

Note: When creating a clipping mask, make sure that the object to be used as a mask is a closed shape and is at the top of the stacking order.

**Book III
Chapter 7**

**Organizing Your
Illustrations**

Figure 7-11:
The shape that is to become the mask is positioned over the object, in this case an image.

3. Using the Selection tool, select the placed image and the shape.

Shift+click to add an object to the selection.

4. Choose Object➪Clipping Mask➪Make.

Ta-da! The clipping mask is created. The masked items are grouped together, but you can use the Direct Selection tool to move around the image or the mask individually.

5. To turn off the clipping mask, choose Object➪Clipping Mask➪Release.

You can also use text as a mask. Just type a word, make sure that it is positioned over an image or other Illustrator object(s), select both the text and the object, and then choose Object➪Clipping Mask➪Make.

Chapter 8: Using Layers

In This Chapter

✔ Working with layers

✔ Putting something on a layer

✔ Locking and putting away layers

T his chapter shows you just how simple it is to use layers and how help-ful layers can be when you're producing complex artwork. Layers are similar to clear pages stacked on top of your artwork: You can place content (text, shapes, and so on) on a layer, lift up a layer, remove a layer, hide and show layers, or lock a layer so that you can't edit the content on it. Layers are an incredible feature that can help you:

✦ Organize the painting (stacking) order of objects.

✦ Activate objects that would otherwise be difficult to select with the Selection or Direct Selection tool.

✦ Lock items that you don't want to reposition or change.

✦ Hide items until you need them.

✦ Repurpose objects for artwork variations. For example, business cards use the same logo and company address, but the name and contact information change for each person. In this case, placing the logo and company address on one layer and the person's name and contact infor-mation on another layer makes it easy to create a new business card by just changing the name of the person.

Many Illustrator users don't take advantage of layers. Maybe these users don't understand the basic functions of layers, or maybe they think that layers are much more complicated than they really are. By reading this chapter, you'll be able to take advantage of layers in Illustrator.

Unlike in Photoshop, layers in Illustrator don't add an incredible amount of size to the file.

Creating New Layers

When you create a new Illustrator document, you automatically have one layer to start with. To understand how layers work, create a new file and then follow these steps to create new layers and put objects on them:

1. **If the Layers panel isn't already visible, choose Window⊅Layers.**

The Layers panel appears. In Illustrator CS3, you see new layer color bars to help identify selected objects and the layer they're on, as shown in Figure 8-1.

Active layer   Target radio button

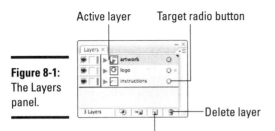

Figure 8-1:
The Layers
panel.

Create New Layer button

Delete layer

2. **Create a shape anywhere on the artboard.**

It doesn't matter what size the shape is, but make sure that it has a colored fill so that you can see it easily. For this example, we created a rectangle.

3. **Click the Fill pop-up menu in the control panel and select any color for the shape, as shown in Figure 8-2.**

The Fill pop-up menu is the swatch with an arrow in the upper left of the control panel.

Figure 8-2:
Select any
color from
the Color
drop-down
panel in the
control
panel.

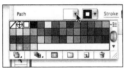

The blue handle color that appears on the active shape matches the blue-color bar you see on the left side of the layer name and the small selection square to the right of the radio button. The small selection square on the right disappears if you choose Select⇨Deselect. You use that square to see what layer a selected object is on.

Also, notice now that you've added a shape to this layer, and an arrow appears to the left of the layer name. This arrow indicates that you now have a *sublayer,* which is essentially a layer within a layer. Click the arrow to expand the layer and show any sublayers nested under it; sublayers are automatically created as you add objects, which helps when you're trying to make difficult selections.

4. **To make a new layer, Alt+click (Windows) or Option+click (Mac) the Create New Layer button at the bottom of the Layers panel.**

    The Layer Options window appears (see Figure 8-3), and you can use it to name a layer and change the selection color. You don't have to hold down the Alt or Option key when making a new layer, but if you don't, you won't have the opportunity to name the layer as you create it.

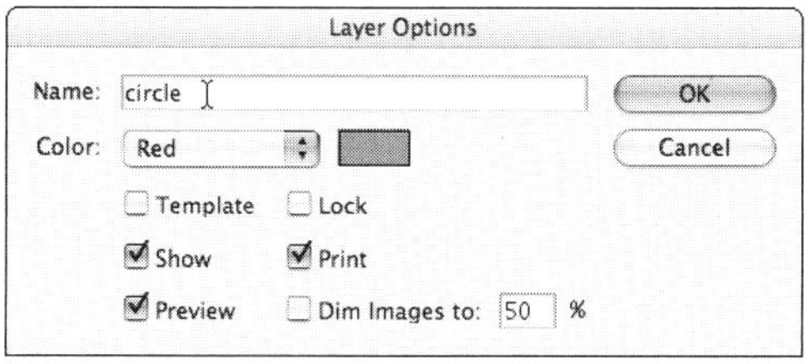

Figure 8-3:
Creating a new layer.

Layer Options
Name: circle
Color: Red
☐ Template ☐ Lock
☑ Show ☑ Print
☑ Preview ☐ Dim Images to: 50 %
OK
Cancel

5. **Enter a name for the new layer in the Name text field and click OK.**

    In this case, we used the name *circle* because it's the shape that we add in the next step.

    A new layer is added to the top of the stack in the Layers panel.

6. **Make a shape on the new layer and overlap the shape you created in Step 2 (see Figure 8-4).**

    For this example, we created a circle.

7. **Change the fill color for your new shape.**

    Check out the selection handles? They change to a different color, indicating that you're on a different layer. The different colors of the handles are for organizational purposes only and don't print.

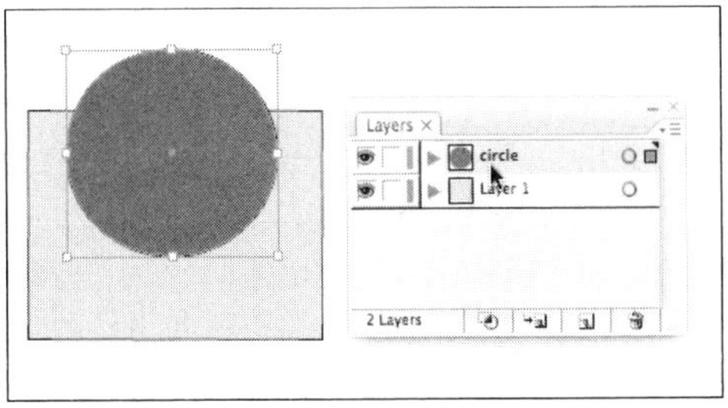

Figure 8-4:
A circle on
the second
layer
overlapping
the square
on the
underlying
layer.

8. **Just to be different, this time choose New Layer from the panel menu.**

The Layer Options dialog box appears.

9. **(Optional) In the Layer Options dialog box, change the color of the selection handles by selecting an option from the Color drop-down list.**

You can also hide or lock the contents of the layer.

10. **Enter a name for this new layer in the Name text field, click OK, and then create a shape on it.**

For this example, we named the layer "star" and used the Star tool to create a star.

11. **Again, change the fill color of your newest shape so that it's different from the other shapes.**

12. **Use the Selection tool to move the new shape (in our case, the star) so that it overlaps the others slightly.**

13. **Rename the original layer (Layer 1) by double-clicking the layer's name in the Layers panel, typing a new name, and then pressing Enter (Windows) or Return (Mac).**

In our case, it would make sense to rename the original layer as "rectangle" (that's nice and descriptive). You can open up the Options dialog box for any existing layer by choosing Options For Layer (Named Layer) from the panel menu in the Layers panel.

Congratulations! You've created new layers and now have a file that you can use to practice working with layers.

Using Layers for Selections

When you have a selected object on a layer, a color selection square appears to the right of the named layer. If you click the radio button directly to the right of the name, all objects are selected on that layer.

Sublayers each have their own radio button as well. If you have sublayers visible, you can use this same technique to select objects that may be buried behind others.

If you think that you'll be selecting sublayers frequently, double-click the default name and type a more descriptive name.

Changing the Layer Stacking Order

In Chapter 7 of this minibook, we tell you about the Object⇨Arrange feature in Illustrator; with layers, this process gets just a little more complicated. Each layer has its own *painting order,* the order in which you see the layers. To move a layer (and thereby change the stacking order of the layers), click and drag that layer until you see the black insertion line where you want the layer to be moved.

As you add shapes to a layer, a sublayer is created, and it has its own little stacking order that is separate from other layers. In other words, if you choose to send an object to the back, and it's on the top layer, it will only go to the back of that layer, and still be in front of any objects on layers beneath.

Understanding how the stacking order affects the illustration is probably the most confusing part about layers. Just remember that for an object to appear behind everything else, it has to be on the bottom layer (and at the bottom of all the objects in that bottom layer); for an object to appear in front of everything else, it has to be on the topmost layer.

Moving and Cloning Objects

To move a selected object from one layer to another, click the small color selection square to the right of the layer's radio button, drag it to the target layer, and release. That's all there is to moving an object from one layer to another.

You can also *clone* items — that is, make a copy of it as you move the copy to another layer. Clone an object by Alt+dragging (Windows) or Option+dragging (Mac) the color selection square to another layer. A plus sign appears as you drag (so you know that you're making a clone of the object). Release when you get to the cloned object's target layer.

**Book III
Chapter 8**

Using Layers

Hiding Layers

On the Layers panel, notice that to the left of each layer is an eye icon. This is a visibility toggle button. Simply clicking this icon hides the layer (the eye disappears, denoting that this layer is hidden). Click the empty square (where the eye icon was) to show the layer again.

Alt+click (Windows) or Option+click (Mac) an eye icon to hide all layers but the one you click; Alt+click (Windows) or Option+click (Mac) again on the eye icon to show all the layers again.

Ctrl+click (Windows) or ⌘+click (Mac) the eye icon to turn just the selected layer into Outline view mode. In Outline view, all you see are the outlines of the artwork with no stroke widths or fill colors. The rest of your artwork remains in Preview mode, with strokes and fills visible. This technique is pretty tricky and helpful when you're looking for stray points or need to close paths. Ctrl+click (Windows) or ⌘+click (Mac) back on the eye icon to return the layer to Preview mode.

Locking Layers

Lock layers by clicking the empty square to the right of the Visibility (eye) icon. A padlock icon appears so that you know the layer is now locked. Locking a layer prevents you from making changes to the objects on that layer. Click the padlock to unlock the layer.

Chapter 9: Livening Up Illustrations with Color

In This Chapter

✔ Using the Swatch and Color panels

✔ Working with strokes and fills

✔ Saving and editing colors

✔ Creating and using color libraries

✔ Using Live Color and the Color Guide

✔ Assigning Pantone colors

✔ Discovering patterns

✔ Employing gradients

✔ Exploring the Live Trace feature

✔ Using the Live Paint feature

*T*his chapter is all about making your brilliant illustrations come alive with color. Here, we show you how to create new and edit existing colors, save custom colors that you create, create and use patterns and gradients, and even apply color attributes to many different shapes.

Choosing a Color Mode

Every time that you create a new file, you choose a profile. This profile determines, among other things, which color mode your document will be created in. Typically, anything related to Web, mobile, and video is in RGB mode, and the print profile is in CMYK. You can also simply choose Basic CMYK or Basic RGB. Here are the differences between the color modes:

✦ **CMYK (Cyan, Magenta, Yellow, and Black):** This mode is used if you're taking your illustration to a professional printer and the files will be separated into cyan, magenta, yellow, and black plates for printing.

✦ **RGB (Red, Green, Blue):** Use this mode if your final destination is the Web, mobile device, video, color copier or desktop printer, or screen presentation.

The decision that you make affects the premade swatches, brushes, styles, and a slew of other choices in Adobe Illustrator. This all helps you to avoid sending an RGB color to a print shop. Ever see how that turns out? If your prepress person doesn't catch that the file isn't CMYK and sends an RGB file as separations (cyan, magenta, yellow, and black) to a printer, you can end up with a black blob instead of your beautiful illustration.

You can change the color mode at any time without losing information by choosing File⇨Document Color Mode.

Using the Swatches Panel

Accessing color from the control panel is probably the easiest way to make color choices, as using the Fill and Stroke drop-down menus allow you to quickly access the Swatches palette, as shown in Figure 9-1, and at the same time make sure that the color is actually applying to either the fill or stroke. How many times have you mixed up colors and assigned the stroke color to the fill or vice versa?

Figure 9-1:
Quickly
access
Swatches
from the
control
panel.

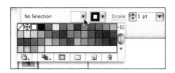

You can also access the Swatches panel, which you open by choosing Window⇨Swatches. Although limited in choice, its basic colors, patterns, and gradients are ready to go. You can use the buttons at the bottom of the Swatches panel (shown in Figure 9-2) to quickly open color libraries, select what kinds of colors to view, access Swatch options, create color Groups, add new swatches, and delete selected swatches.

You may notice some odd color swatches — for example, the cross hair and the diagonal line.

The cross hair represents the Registration color. Only use this swatch when creating custom crop marks or printer marks. It looks black, but it's actually created from 100 percent of all colors. This way, when artwork is separated, the crop mark appears on all color separations.

The diagonal line represents None. Use this option if you want no fill or stroke.

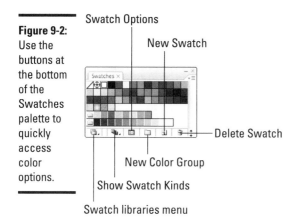

Figure 9-2:
Use the buttons at the bottom of the Swatches palette to quickly access color options.

Swatch Options

New Swatch

Delete Swatch

New Color Group

Show Swatch Kinds

Swatch libraries menu

Applying Color to the Fill and Stroke

Illustrator objects are created from *fills* (the inside) and *strokes* (border or path). Look at the bottom of the toolbox for the Fill and Stroke color boxes. If you're applying color to the fill, the Fill color box must be forward in the toolbox. If you're applying color to the stroke, the Stroke color box must be forward.

Table 9-1 lists keyboard shortcuts that can be a tremendous help to you when applying colors to fills and strokes.

Table 9-1	Color Keyboard Shortcuts
Function	*Keyboard Shortcut*
Switch the Fill or Stroke color box position	X
Inverse the Fill and the Stroke color boxes	Shift+X
Default (black stroke, white fill)	D
None	/
Last color used	<
Last gradient used	>
Color Picker	Double-click the Fill or Stroke color box

Try this trick: Drag a color from the Swatches panel to the Fill or Stroke color box. This action applies the color to the color box that you dragged to. It doesn't matter which is forward!

To apply a fill color to an existing shape, drag the swatch directly to the shape. Select a swatch, hold down Alt+Shift+Ctrl (Windows) or Option+Shift+⌘ (Mac), and drag a color to a shape to apply that color to the stroke.

Changing the Width and Type of a Stroke

Access the Stroke panel by clicking the Stroke Hyperlink in the control panel. In the Stroke panel, you can choose *caps* (the end of a line), *joins* (the end points of a path or dash), and the *miter limit* (the length of a point). The Stroke panel also enables you to turn a path into a dashed line.

As you can see in Figure 9-3, you can choose, in the Stroke panel options, to align the stroke on the center (default) of a path, the inside of a path, and the outside of a path. Figure 9-4 shows the results.

Figure 9-3:
The Align Stroke options in the Stroke panel.

This feature is especially helpful when stroking outlined text. See Figure 9-5 to compare text with the traditional centered stroke, as compared to the new option for aligning the stroke outside of a path.

Figure 9-4:
The Align Stroke options affect the placement of the stroke on a path.

You can't adjust the alignment of a stroke on text unless you change it to outlines first. Select the Selection tool and choose Type➪Create Outlines to enable the Align Stroke options.

Figure 9-5:
The Align Stroke feature is especially important when stroking text.

You can also customize the following aspects of a stroke in the Stroke panel:

✦ **Cap Options:** The endpoints of a path or dash.

- **Butt Cap:** Click this button to make the ends of stroked lines square.

- **Round Cap:** Click this button to make the ends of stroked lines semicircular.

- **Projecting Cap:** Click this button to make the ends of stroked lines square and extend half the line width beyond the end of the line.

✦ **Join Options:** How corner points appear.

- **Miter Join:** Click this button to make stroked lines with pointed corners.

- **Round Join:** Click this button to make stroked lines with rounded corners.

- **Bevel Join:** Click this button to make stroked lines with squared corners.

✦ **Dashed Lines:** Regularly spaced lines, based upon values you set.

To create a dashed line, specify a dash sequence by entering the lengths of dashes and the gaps between them in the Dash Pattern text fields (see Figure 9-6). The numbers entered are repeated in sequence so that after you've set up the pattern, you don't need to fill in all the text fields. In other words, if you want an evenly spaced dashed stroke, just type the same number in the first and second text fields, and all dashes and spaces will be the same length (say, 12 pts). Change that to 12 in the first text field and 24 in the next, and now you have a larger space between the dashes.

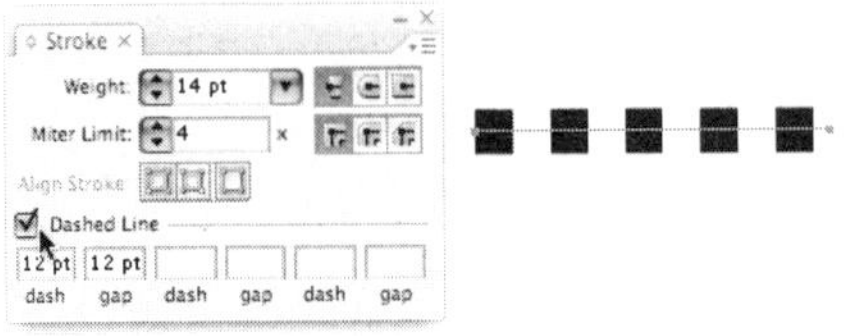

Figure 9-6:
Setting up
a dashed
stroke.

Using the Color Panel

The Color panel (access it by choosing Window➪Color) offers another method for choosing color. It requires you to custom pick a color using values on the color ramp. As a default, you see only the *color ramp* — the large color well spanning the panel. If you don't see all the color options, choose Show Options from the Color panel's panel menu (click the triangle in the upper-right corner to access the panel menu).

Ever want to create tints of a CMYK color but aren't quite sure how to adjust the individual color sliders? Hold down the Shift key while adjusting the color slide of any color and watch how all colors move to a relative position at the same time!

As shown in Figure 9-7, the panel menu offers many other choices. Even though you may be in the RGB or CMYK color mode, you can still choose to build colors in Grayscale, RGB, HSB (Hue Saturation Brightness), CMYK, or Web Safe RGB. Choosing Invert or Complement from the panel menu takes the selected object and inverses the color or changes it to a complementary color. You can also choose the Fill and Stroke color boxes in the upper-left corner of the Color panel.

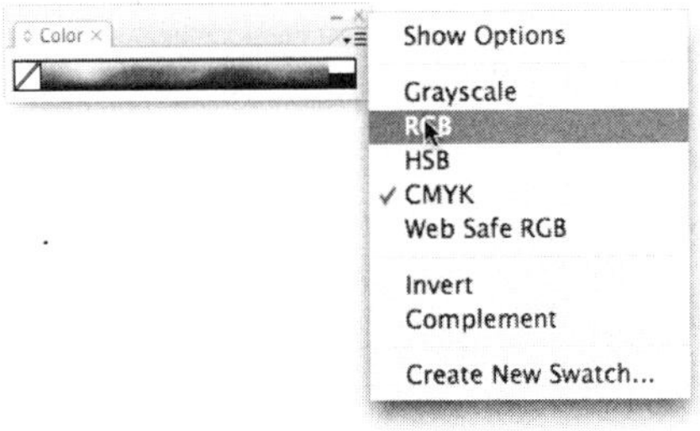

Figure 9-7:
Available
color
models are
available in
the Color
panel.

Show Options

Grayscale
RGB
HSB
✓ CMYK
Web Safe RGB

Invert
Complement

Create New Swatch...

You see the infamous cube and exclamation point in the Color panels in most of Adobe's software. The cube warns you that the color you have selected isn't one of the 216 nondithering, Web-safe colors, and the exclamation point warns you that your color is not within the CMYK print gamut. In other words, if you see the exclamation point in the Color panel, don't expect that really cool electric blue you see on-screen to print correctly — it may print as dark purple!

Click the cube or exclamation point symbols when you see them to select the closet color in the Web safe or CMYK color gamut.

Saving Colors

Saving colors not only keeps you consistent, but it makes edits and changes to colors easier in the future. Any time you build a color, drag it from the Color panel to the Swatches panel to save it as a color swatch for future use. You can also select an object that uses the color and click the New Swatch button at the bottom of the Swatches panel (refer to Figure 9-2 to see this button). To save a color and name it at the same time, Alt+click (Windows) or Option+click (Mac) the New Swatch icon. The New Swatch dialog box opens, where you can name and edit the color if you want. By double-clicking a swatch in the Swatches panel, you can open the options at any time.

A color in the Swatches panel is available only in the document in which it was created. Read the next section on custom libraries to see how to import swatches from saved documents.

Building and using custom libraries

When you save a color in the Swatches panel, you're essentially saving it to your own custom library. You can use Swatches panels from one document to another by using the Libraries feature. Retrieve colors saved in a document's Swatches panel by selecting the Swatch Libraries menu button at the bottom of the Swatches window and dragging down to Other Library. You can also access swatch libraries, including other documents, by choosing Window➪Swatch Libraries➪Other Library. Locate the saved document and choose Open. A panel appears with the document name, as shown in Figure 9-8. You can't edit the colors in this panel. To use the colors in this panel, double-click a swatch or drag a swatch to your current document's Swatches panel.

Figure 9-8:
An imported
custom
swatch
library.

You can also click the Swatch Libraries button to access color libraries for Pantone colors, Web colors, and some neat creative colors, such as jewel tones and metals.

Using the Color Guide and Color Groups

Perhaps you failed at color in art class or just don't feel that you're one of those people who picks colors that look good together. In Illustrator CS3, you can use the Color Guide to find colors and save them to organized color groups in your Swatches panel. You can create color schemes based on 23 classic color-harmony rules, such as Complementary, Analogous, Monochromatic, and Triad, or you can create custom harmony rules.

Sounds complicated, doesn't it? Fortunately, all you have to do is choose a base color and then see what variations you come up with according to rules you choose. Give it a try:

1. **Choose Window⇨Color Guide.**

The Color Guide panel appears, as shown in Figure 9-9.

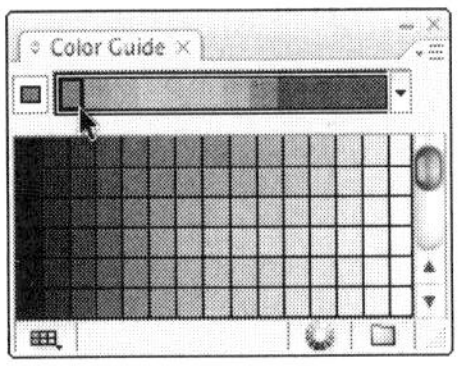

Figure 9-9: The Color Guide helps to identify related colors.

2. **Select a color from your Swatches palette.**

Immediately, the Color Guide kicks in to provide you with colors that are related to your original swatch.

3. **Change the Harmony Rules by selecting the Edit Colors button at the bottom of the Color Guide panel.**

The Live Color panel, shown in Figure 9-10, appears.

You could spend days experimenting in the Live Color window, but for the scope of this book you will delve into changing simple harmony rules. To do this, click on the Harmony Rules arrow to the right of the color bar. A drop-down menu appears with many choices as to how you want colors selected, see Figure 9-11. Choose a Color Harmony.

4. **Save your color selection as a color group by clicking the New Color Group icon.**

If you like, you can rename the color group by double-clicking the group name in the Color Group section of the Live Color window.

5. **Click OK.**

The Color group is added to the Swatches panel.

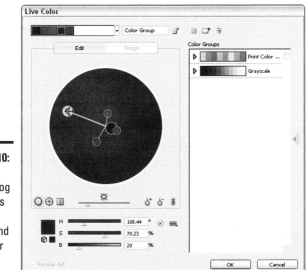

Figure 9-10:
The Live Color dialog box allows you to choose and save color groups.

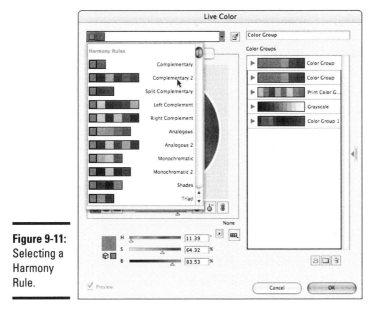

Figure 9-11:
Selecting a Harmony Rule.

You don't have to go through the Live Color window in order to save a group of colors. You can Ctrl+click (windows) or ⌘+Click (Mac) to select multiple colors and then click the New Color Group button at the bottom of the Swatches panel.

Adding Pantone colors

If you're looking for the typical Pantone Matching System-numbered swatches, click the Swatch Libraries menu button at the bottom of the Swatches panel. From the drop-down list, choose Color Books and then Pantone solid coated, or whatever Pantone library you want to access.

Colors for the Pantone numbering system are often referred to as PMS 485, or PMS 201, or whatever number the color has been designated. You can locate the numbered swatch by typing the number into the Find text field of the Pantone panel, as shown in Figure 9-12. When that number's corresponding color is highlighted in the panel, click it to add it to your Swatches panel. Many users find it easier to see colored swatches by using the List View. Choose List View from the panel options menu.

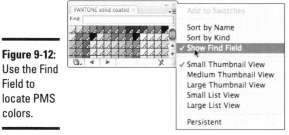

Figure 9-12: Use the Find Field to locate PMS colors.

Editing Colors

Edit colors in the Swatches panel by using the Swatch Options dialog box (shown in Figure 9-13), which you access by double-clicking the color or by choosing Swatch Options from the Swatches panel menu.

Figure 9-13: Edit a color swatch in the Swatch Options window.

Use the Swatch Options dialog box to

✦ **Change the color values:** Change the values in a color by using the sliders or by typing values into the color text fields. Having the ability to enter exact color values is especially helpful if you were given a color build to match. Select the Preview check box to see results as you make the changes.

✦ **Use global colors:** If you plan on using a color frequently, select the Global check box. If the Global check box is selected and you use the swatch throughout the artwork, you only have to change the swatch options one time, and all instances of that color are updated.

One important option to note in the Swatch Options dialog box is the Color Type drop-down list. You have two choices here: Spot Color and Process Color. What's the difference?

✦ **Spot color:** A color that isn't broken down into the CMYK values. Spot colors are used for 1–2 color print runs or when precise color matching is important.

Suppose that you're printing 20,000 catalogs and decide to run only two colors, red and black. If you pick spot colors, the catalogs have to go through the press only two times: once for black and once for red. If the red were a process color, however, it would be created out of a combination of cyan, magenta, yellow, and black inks, and so the catalogs would need to go through the press four times in order to build that color. Plus, if you went to a print service and asked for red, what color would you get? Fire-engine red, maroon, or a light and delicate pinkish-red? But if the red you pick is PMS 485, your printer in Lancaster, Pennsylvania, can now print the same color of red on your brochure as the printer doing your business cards in Woburn, Massachusetts.

✦ **Process color:** A color that is built from four colors (cyan, magenta, yellow, and black). Process colors are used for multicolor jobs.

For example, you'd want to use process colors if you're sending an ad to a four-color magazine. The magazine printers certainly want to use the same inks they're already running, and using a spot color would require another run through the presses in addition to the runs for the cyan, magenta, yellow, and black plates. In this case, you'd take any spot colors created in corporate logos and such and convert them to process colors.

Choose the Spot Colors option from the Swatches panel menu to choose whether you want Spot colors changed to Lab or CMYK values:

✦ Choose Lab to get the best possible CMYK conversion for the actual spot color when using a color-calibrated workflow.

**Book III
Chapter 9**

**Livening Up
Illustrations
with Color**

✦ Choose CMYK (default) to get the manufacturer's standard recommended conversion of spot colors to process. Results can vary depending upon printing conditions.

Building and Editing Patterns

Using patterns can be as simple or complicated as you want. If you become familiar with the basics, you can take off in all sorts of creative directions. To build a simple pattern, start by creating the artwork that you want to use as a pattern on your artboard — polka dots, smiley faces, wavy lines, whatever. Then select all the components of the pattern and drag them to the Swatches panel. That's it, you made a pattern! Use the pattern by selecting it as the fill or stroke of an object.

You can't use patterns in artwork that is then going to be saved as a pattern. If you have a pattern in your artwork and try to drag it into the Swatches panel, Illustrator will kick it back out with no error message. On a good note, you can drag text right into the Swatches panel to become a pattern.

You can update patterns that you created or patterns that already reside in the Swatches panel. To edit an existing pattern, follow these steps:

1. **Click the pattern swatch in the Swatches panel and drag it to the artboard.**

2. **Deselect the pattern and use the Direct Selection tool to change its colors or shapes or whatever.**

   Keep making changes until you're happy with the result.

3. **To update the pattern with your new edited version, use the Selection tool to select all pattern elements and Alt+drag (Windows) or Option+drag (Mac) the new pattern over the existing pattern swatch in the Swatches panel.**

4. **When a black border appears around the existing pattern, release the mouse button.**

   All instances of the pattern in your illustration are updated.

If you want to add some space between tiles, as shown in Figure 9-14, create a bounding box using a rectangle shape with no fill or stroke (representing the repeat that you want to create). Send it behind the other objects in the pattern and drag all objects, including the bounding box, to the Swatches panel.

We cover transformations in detail in Chapter 10 of this minibook, but some specific transform features apply to patterns. To scale a pattern, but not the object that it's filling, double-click the Scale tool. In the Scale dialog box that appears, type the value that you want to scale, but deselect all options except for Patterns, as shown in Figure 9-15. This works for the Rotate tool as well!

Figure 9-14:
A pattern
with a
transparent
bounding
box.

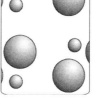

Figure 9-15:
Choose to
scale or
rotate only
the pattern,
not the
object
that the
pattern is
assigned to.

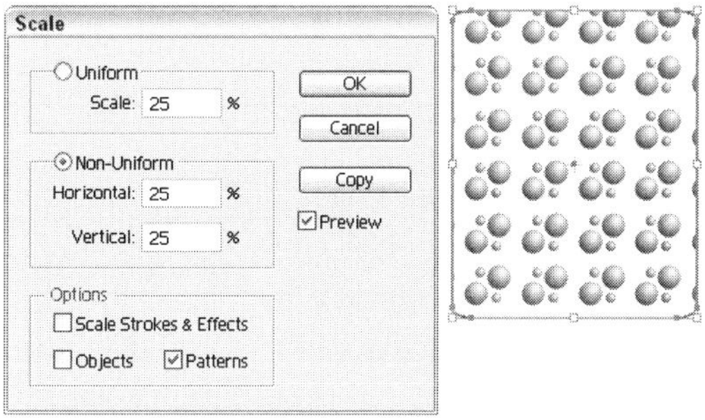

Working with Gradients

Create gradients for nice smooth metallic effects or just to add dimension
to illustrations. If you're not sure which swatches are considered gradients,
choose Gradient from the Show Swatch Kinds button at the bottom of the
Swatches panel.

Once applied, you can access the Gradient panel (shown in Figure 9-16) by
choosing Window⊅Gradient. Choose Show Options from the Gradient panel
menu to see more options.

On the Gradient panel, use the Type drop-down list to choose a Radial gradient (one that radiates from the center point) or a Linear gradient (one that
follows a linear path).

Use the Gradient tool to change the direction and distance of a gradient
blend as follows:

1. **Select an object and apply any existing gradient from the Swatches
panel to its fill.**

2. **Choose the Gradient tool (press G) and drag in the direction that you
want the gradient to go.**

Drag a long path for a smooth, long gradient. Drag a short path for a
short, more defined gradient.

Figure 9-16:
The
Gradient
panel.

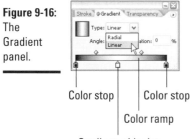

Color stop | Color stop
Color ramp
Gradient midpoint

To create a new gradient, follow these steps:

1. **With the Gradient panel options visible, click the gradient box at the bottom of the panel.**

Two color stops appear, one on each end.

2. **Activate a color stop by clicking it.**

When a color stop is active, the triangle on the top turns solid.

3. **Choose Window⇨Color to access the Color panel and then click the triangle in the upper-right corner to open the panel menu; choose RGB or CMYK colors.**

4. **Click the color ramp (across the bottom) in the Color panel to pick a random color (or enter values in the text fields to select a specific color) for the active color stop in the Gradient panel.**

Repeat this step to select colors for other color stops.

To add additional color stops, click beneath the gradient slider and then choose a color from the Color panel. You can also drag a swatch from the Swatches panel to add a new color to the gradient. To remove a color stop, drag it off the Gradient panel.

Copying Color Attributes

Wouldn't it be great if you had tools that could record all the fill and stroke attributes and apply them to other shapes? You're in luck — the Eyedropper tool can do just that! Copy the fill and stroke of an object and apply it to another object using the Eyedropper tool as follows:

1. **Create several shapes with different fill and stroke attributes, or open an existing file that contains several different objects.**

2. **Select the Eyedropper tool and click a shape that has attributes you want to copy.**

3. **Alt+click (Windows) or Option+click (Mac) another object to apply those attributes.**

Not only is this technique simple, but you can change the attributes that the Eyedropper applies. Do so by double-clicking the Eyedropper tool; in the dialog box that appears, select only the attributes that you want to copy.

The Live Trace feature

If you're looking for good source art to use to experiment with color, look no further than your own sketches and scanned images. You can automatically trace bitmap images using a variety of settings that range from black-and-white line art to vector art with multitudes of color that can be extracted from your image.

To use the Live Trace feature, follow these steps:

1. **Choose File⇨Place and select an image that you want to trace.**

The file you place can be a logo, sketch, or even an image. Notice that after you place the image, the control panel offers additional options.

2. **Click the arrow to the right of the Live Trace button.**

This drop-down list provides Live Trace presets that may help you better trace your image.

3. **Scroll to the bottom and choose Tracing Options.**

The Tracing Options window appears.

4. **Check the Preview check box and experiment with the various settings, as shown in Figure 9-17.**

**Book III
Chapter 9**

Livening Up
Illustrations
with Color

Figure 9-17:
Turn bitmap artwork into vector using the Live Trace feature.

5. **When you find the setting that works best for your image, choose Trace.**

You can return to the Tracing Options window and change settings over and over again, until you find the best one.

The Live Paint Feature

 Painting made easy! Don't worry about filling closed shapes, or letting fills escape out of objects with gaps into unwanted areas. With the Live Paint feature, you can create the image you want and fill in regions with color. The Live Paint bucket automatically detects regions composed of independent intersecting paths and fills them accordingly. The paint within a given region remains live and flows automatically if any of the paths are moved. If you want to give it a try, follow this nifty little exercise to put together an example to experiment with.

1. **Using the Ellipse tool, create a circle on your page.**

   Make it large enough to accommodate two or three inner circles.

2. **Press the letter D (just D, nothing else).**

   As long as you're not on the Type tool, you revert back to the default colors of a black stroke and a white fill.

3. **Double-click the Scale tool and enter 75% in the Uniform Scale text box.**

4. **Press the Copy button and then click OK.**

   You see a smaller circle inside the original.

5. **Press Ctrl+D (Windows) or ⌘+D (Mac) to duplicate the transformation and create another circle inside of the last one.**

6. **Choose Select⇨All or Ctrl+A (Windows) or ⌘+A (Mac) to activate the circles you just created.**

7. **Make sure that the Fill swatch is forward.**

   The Fill swatch is at the bottom of the toolbar.

8. **Use the Swatches or Color panel and choose any fill color.**

9. **Select the Live Paint Bucket tool and move the cursor over the various regions of the circles.**

   See how the different regions become highlighted?

10. **Click when you have the region activated that you want to fill.**

    Now try it with other fill colors in different regions, as shown in Figure 9-18.

Figure 9-18:
Experience
newfound
freedom
when you
paint
objects with
the Live
Paint
feature.

Got Gaps?

A companion feature to the new paint bucket is support for Gap Detection. With this feature, Illustrator is able to automatically and dynamically detect and close small to large gaps that may be part of the artwork. You can determine whether you want paint to flow across region gap boundaries by using the Gap Options dialog box under Object⇨Live Paint⇨Gap Options, as shown in Figure 9-19.

When you save a file with the Live Paint feature back to an older version of Illustrator, it's best to select the occurrences of Live Paint and choose Object⇨Expand. When the Expand window appears, leave the options at their default and click OK. This setting breaks down the Live Paint objects to individual shapes, which older versions can understand.

Figure 9-19:
The Gap
Options
dialog box.

Gap Options

☑ Gap Detection

Paint stops at: ✓ Small Gaps
Medium Gaps
Large Gaps

☐ Custom:

Gap Preview Color: Red

Close gaps with paths

OK
Cancel
Reset
☑ Preview
Gaps Found 1

ⓘ Specifies the largest gap size that paint will stop at.

Chapter 10: Using the Transform and Distortions Tools

In This Chapter

✔ Discovering transformation methods

✔ Putting the Transform tools to work

✔ Becoming familiar with the Liquify tools

✔ Distorting, warping, and otherwise reshaping objects

*T*ransformations that you can give to objects in Illustrator include scaling, rotating, skewing, and distorting. In this chapter, we show you how to use the general transform tools as well as some of the neat Liquify and Envelope Distort features available in Illustrator.

Working with Transformations

With just the Selection tool, you can scale and rotate a selected object. Drag the bounding box handles to resize the object (as shown in Figure 10-1) or get outside a handle, and then, when the cursor changes to a flippy arrow (a curved arrow with arrowheads on both ends), drag to rotate the object.

Figure 10-1:
Use the bounding box to resize or rotate a selected object.

If you want to scale proportionally, hold down the Shift key as you drag to resize. To rotate an object at 45-degree increments, hold down the Shift key while you're rotating.

When you use the bounding box to rotate a selection, the bounding box rotates with the object, but its handles show the object's original orientation, as shown in Figure 10-2. This can help you to keep track of the original placement but can also interfere when you're building additional artwork. To reset the bounding box so that it's straight at the new orientation, choose Object➪Transform➪Reset Bounding Box.

Figure 10-2:
The
bounding
box shows
the original
placement
angle and
can reset to
that angle.

When you scale, rotate, or use any other type of transformation in Illustrator, the final location becomes the *zero point.* In other applications, such as InDesign, you can rotate an object by any number of degrees (45 degrees, for example) and later enter 0 for the rotation angle in the Transform palette or in the Rotate dialog box to return the object to its original position. With Illustrator, if you enter 0 for the rotation angle to return a rotated object to its original position, the object will not change its position. To return the object to the previous position in Illustrator, you have to enter the negative of the number you originally entered to rotate the object, so you would enter –45 for the degree of rotation in this example.

Transforming an object

The Rotate, Reflect, Scale, and Shear tools all use the same basic steps to perform transformations. Read on for those basic steps, and then follow through some individual examples of the most often used transform tools. The following sections show five ways to transform an object: one for an arbitrary transformation and four others for exact transformations based on a numeric amount that you enter.

Arbitrary transformation method

This method is arbitrary, meaning that you're eyeballing the transformation of an object — in other words, you don't have an exact percentage or angle in mind, and you want to freely transform the object until it looks right. Just follow these steps:

1. **Select an object, and then choose a transform tool (the Rotate, Reflect, Scale, or Shear tool).**

2. **Click once on the artboard.**

Be careful where you click because the click determines the point of reference, or *axis point,* for the transformation, as shown in Figure 10-3.

3. **Drag in one smooth movement.**

Just drag until you get the transformation that you want.

Hold down the Alt (Windows) or Option (Mac) key when dragging to clone a newly transformed item while keeping the original object intact. This is especially helpful when you're using the Reflect tool.

Exact transformation methods

In the following methods, we show you how to perform transformations using specific numeric information:

✦ **Exact transformation method 1:** Using the tool's dialog box

1. **Select an object and then choose the Rotate, Reflect, Scale, or Shear tool.**

2. **Double-click the transform tool in the toolbox.**

A dialog box specific to your chosen tool appears. For this example, we selected and then double-clicked the Rotate tool to bring up the Rotate dialog box.

3. **Type an angle, scaled amount, or percentage in the appropriate text field.**

4. **Check preview to see the effect of the transformation before you click OK; click the Copy button instead of OK to keep the original object intact and transform a copy.**

✦ **Exact transformation method 2:** Using the reference point

1. **Select an object, and then choose the Rotate, Reflect, Scale, or Shear tool.**

2. **Alt+click (Windows) or Option+click (Mac) where you want the reference point to be.**

3. **In the appropriate transform tool dialog box that appears, enter your values and click OK or the Copy button to apply your transformation.**

This is the best method to use if you need to rotate an object an exact amount on a defined axis.

✦ **Exact transformation method 3:** Using the Transform menu

1. **Select an object, and then choose a transform option from the Object⇨Transform menu.**

The appropriate transform dialog box appears.

2. **Enter your values and click OK or the Copy button.**

✦ **Exact transformation method 4:** Using the Transform palette

Select an object and choose Window⇨Transform to access the Transform palette, as shown in Figure 10-4.

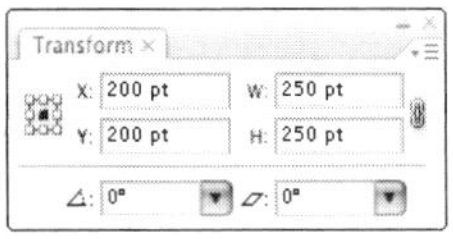

Figure 10-4:
The Transform palette allows you to enter values.

While using this palette is probably the easiest way to go, it doesn't give you the option of specifying where you want your reference point to be or some other options that apply to the individual transform tools.

Using the Transform tools

In this section, we show you how to use some of the most popular transform tools to create transformations.

The Reflect tool

Nothing is symmetrical, right? Maybe not, but objects that are not symmetrically created in Illustrator can look pretty off kilter. Using the Reflect tool, you can reflect an object to create an exact mirrored shape of it; just follow these steps:

1. **Open a new document in Illustrator and type some text or create an object.**

   If you want to reflect text, make sure that you use at least 60-point type so that you can easily see what you're working with.

2. **Select the Reflect tool (hidden under the Rotate tool) and click the object; if you're using text, click in the middle of the text's baseline, as shown on the right in Figure 10-6.**

   This step sets the reference point for the reflection.

3. **Alt+Shift+drag (Windows) or Option+Shift+drag (Mac) and release when the object or text is reflecting itself, as shown on the right in Figure 10-5.**

   This step not only clones the reflected object or text, but also snaps it to 45-degree angles.

Figure 10-5:
Setting the reference point (left); the completed reflection (right).

Reflect Reflect

Book III
Chapter 10

Using the Transform and Distortions Tools

The Scale tool

Using the Scale tool, you can scale an object proportionally or non-uniformly. Most people like to be scaled non-uniformly, maybe a little taller, a little thinner, but on with the topic. Follow these steps to see the Scale tool in action:

1. **Create a shape and give it no fill and a 5-point black stroke.**

   For this example, we created a circle. See Chapter 4 of this minibook if you need a reminder on how to do this.

2. **Select your shape and double-click the Scale tool.**

   The Scale dialog box appears.

3. **Type a number in the Scale text field (in the Uniform section) and click the Copy button.**

   We entered 125 in the Scale text field to increase the size of the object by 125 percent.

4. **Press Ctrl+D (Windows) or ⌘+D (Mac) to repeat the transformation as many times as you want.**

   Each time you press Ctrl+D (Windows) or ⌘+D (Mac), the shape is copied and sized by the percent you entered in the Scale text field. This is especially handy with circles and creates an instant bull's-eye!

To experiment with the Scale tool, create different shapes in Step 1 and enter different values in Step 3. Remember that if you type 50% in the Scale text field, the object is made smaller; go over 100% — say to 150% for example — to make the object larger. Leaving the Scale text field at 100% has no effect on the object.

The Shear tool

The Shear tool enables you to shear an object by selecting an axis and dragging to set a shear angle, as shown in Figure 10-6.

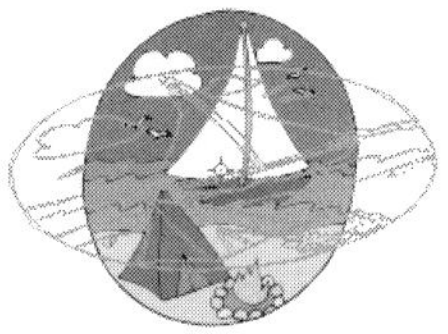

Figure 10-6:
Create perspective using the Shear tool.

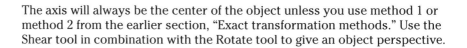

The axis will always be the center of the object unless you use method 1 or method 2 from the earlier section, "Exact transformation methods." Use the Shear tool in combination with the Rotate tool to give an object perspective.

The Reshape tool

The Reshape tool enables you to select anchor points and sections of paths and adjust them in one direction. You determine that direction by dragging an anchor point with the Reshape tool selected.

The Reshape tool works differently from the other transform tools. To use it, follow these steps:

1. **Select just the anchor points on the paths that you want to reshape. Deselect any points that you want to remain in place.**

2. **Select the Reshape tool (hidden under the Scale tool) and position the cursor over the anchor point that you want to modify; click the anchor point.**

   If you click a path segment, a highlighted anchor point with a square around it is added to the path.

3. **Shift+click more anchor points or path segments to act as selection points.**

   You can highlight an unlimited number of anchor points or path segments.

4. **Drag the highlighted anchor points to adjust the path.**

The Free Transform tool

 You use the Free Transform tool pretty much like you use the bounding box. (See the earlier section, "Working with Transformations.") This tool is necessary only if you choose View➪Hide Bounding Box but want free transform capabilities.

Creating Distortions

Bend objects, make them wavy, gooey, or spiky — you can do all of these things by creating simple to complex distortions with the Liquify tools and Envelope Distort features.

The Liquify tools

The Liquify tools can accomplish all sorts of creative or wacky (depending on how you look at it) distortions to your objects. You can choose from seven Liquify tools. Even though we define these for you in Table 10-1, you really need to experiment with these tools to understand their full capabilities. Here are some tips:

✦ A variety of Liquify tools are available by holding down the mouse button on the default selection, the Warp tool. If you use them frequently, drag to the arrow at the end of the tools and release when you see the ToolTip for Tearoff. You can then position the tools anywhere in your work area.

✦ Double-click any of the Liquify tools to bring up a dialog box specific to the selected tool.

✦ When a Liquify tool is selected, the brush size appears. Adjust the diameter and shape of the Liquify tool by holding down the Alt (Windows) or Option (Mac OS) key while dragging the brush shape smaller or larger. Add the Shift key to constrain the shape to a circle.

Table 10-1	The Liquify Tools	
Tool Icon	*Tool Name*	*What It Does*
	Warp tool	Molds objects with the movement of the cursor. Pretend that you're pushing through dough with this tool.
	Twirl tool	Creates swirling distortions within an object.
	Pucker tool	Deflates an object.
	Bloat tool	Inflates an object.
	Scallop tool	Adds curved details to the outline of an object. Think of a seashell with scalloped edges.
	Crystallize tool	Adds many spiked details to the outline of an object, like crystals on a rock.
	Wrinkle tool	Adds wrinkle-like details to the outline of an object.

Using the Envelope Distort command

Use the Envelope Distort command to arch text and apply other creative distortions to an Illustrator object. To use the Envelope Distort command, you can either use a preset warp (the easiest method) or a grid or a top object to determine the amount and type of distortion. In this section, we discuss all three methods.

Using the preset warps

Experimenting is a little more interesting if you have a word or object selected before trying the different warp presets. To warp an object or text to a preset style, follow these steps:

1. **Select the text or object that you want to distort, and then choose Object➪Envelope Distort➪Make With Warp.**

The Warp Options dialog box appears.

2. **Choose a warp style from the Style drop-down list and then specify any other options you want.**

3. **Click OK to apply your distortion.**

Note: If you want to experiment with warping, but also want to revert back to the original at any time, choose Effect⇨Warp. Find out more about exciting Effects that you can apply to objects in Chapter 12 of this minibook.

Reshaping with a mesh grid

You can also assign a grid to the objects to give you the ability to drag different points and create your own custom distortion, as shown in Figure 10-7.

Figure 10-7:
Create your own custom distortion using a mesh grid.

Follow these steps to apply a mesh grid:

1. **Select the text or object that you want to distort, and then choose Object⇨Envelope Distort⇨Make With Mesh.**

The Envelope Mesh dialog box appears.

2. **Specify the number of rows and columns that you want the mesh to contain and then click OK.**

3. **To reshape the object, drag any anchor point on the mesh grid with the Direct Selection tool.**

To delete anchor points on the mesh grid, select an anchor point with the Direct Selection tool and press the Delete key.

You can also use the Mesh tool to edit and delete points when using a mesh grid on objects.

Reshaping an object with a different object

To form letters into the shape of an oval or distort selected objects into another object, use this technique:

1. **Create text that you want to distort.**

2. **Create the object that you want to use as the envelope (the object to be used to define the distortion).**

3. **Choose Object⇨Arrange to make sure that the envelope object is on top, as shown in Figure 10-8.**

Figure 10-8:
Position the
shape over
the text.

4. **Select the text and Shift+click to select the envelope object.**

5. **Choose Object⇨Envelope Distort⇨Make with Top Object.**

The underlying object is distorted to fit the shape of the top (envelope) object.

Chapter 11: Working with Transparency and Special Effects Tools

In This Chapter

✔ Finding out about the Gradient Mesh tool

✔ Getting to know the Blend tool

✔ Using the Symbol Sprayer Brush tools

✔ Discovering transparency, blend modes, and opacity masks

*T*his chapter is full of neat things that you can do using some of the more advanced features in Adobe Illustrator. These special effects tools can help you create art that really makes an impact: Discover how to make your art look like a painting with the Gradient Mesh tool, create morph-like blends with the Blend tool, become a pseudo-graffiti artist by trying out the Symbol Sprayer tool, and see what's underneath objects by using transparency!

The Mesh Tool

If you're creating art in Illustrator that requires solid colors or continuous patterns, you can achieve those results quite easily. But what if you're working on something that requires continuous tones, like a person's face? In that case, you'd turn to the very handy Mesh tool, which enables you to create the impression that you used paint and paintbrushes to create your illustration. Choose to blend one color into another and then use the Mesh tool to adjust where the blends occur and how dramatic the blends should be.

The Mesh tool can be as complex or simple as you want. Create intense illustrations that look like they were created with an airbrush, or just use it to give an object dimension, like the objects shown in Figure 11-1.

We show you how to create a gradient mesh two different ways: First by clicking (which gives you a little more freedom to put mesh points where you want them) and then by manually setting the number of rows and columns in the mesh (which is a more precise method).

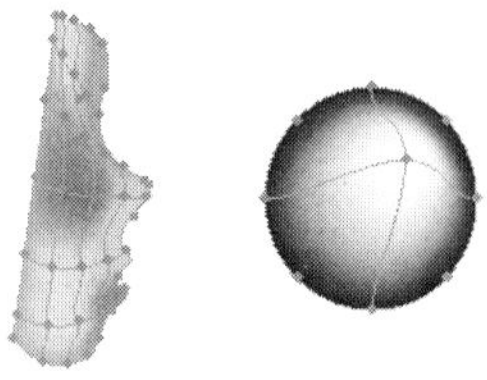

Figure 11-1:
Illustrations can be as complex or simple as you want using the Mesh tool.

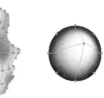

You can change the color in mesh points by choosing the Direct Selection tool and either clicking a mesh point and picking a fill color, or by clicking in the center of a mesh area and choosing a fill. Each gives you a very different result, as shown in Figure 11-2. To add a mesh point without changing to the current fill color, Shift+click anywhere in a filled vector object.

Figure 11-2:
Whether you select the mesh point (left) or area in between the mesh points (right) changes the painting result.

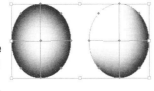

To create a gradient mesh by clicking, follow these steps:

1. **Deselect all objects by choosing Select⇨Deselect.**

2. **Select a fill color that you want to apply as a mesh point to an object.**

For example, if you have a red circle and you want a shaded white spot, choose white for your fill color.

3. **Select the Mesh tool (keyboard shortcut is U) and click anywhere in a filled vector object.**

The object is converted to a mesh object.

4. **Click the object as many times as you want to add additional mesh points.**

To create a gradient mesh by setting the number of rows and columns, follow these steps:

1. **Select a bitmap or filled vector object.**

2. **Choose Object➪Create Gradient Mesh.**

   The Create Gradient Mesh dialog box appears.

3. **Set the number of rows and columns of mesh lines to create on the object by entering numbers in the Rows and Columns text fields.**

4. **Choose the direction of the highlight from the Appearance drop-down list.**

   The direction of the highlight determines in what way the gradient flows (see Figure 11-3); you have the following choices:

   • **Flat:** Applies the object's original color evenly across the surface, resulting in no highlight.

   • **To Center:** Creates a highlight in the center of the object.

   • **To Edge:** Creates a highlight on the edges of the object.

Figure 11-3: Choose a highlight direction for the gradient mesh.

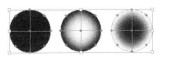

Book III
Chapter 11

Working with
Transparency and
Special Effects
Tools

5. **Enter a percentage of white highlight to apply to the mesh object in the Highlight text field.**

6. **Click OK to apply the gradient mesh to the object.**

The Blend Tool

Use the Blend tool (located in the main Illustrator toolbox) to transform one object to another to create interesting morphed artwork or to create shaded objects. With the Blend tool, you can give illustrations a rendered look by blending from one color to another, or you can create an even amount of shapes from one point to another. Figure 11-4 shows examples of what you can do with this tool.

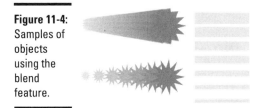

Figure 11-4:
Samples of objects using the blend feature.

Creating a blend isn't difficult, and as you get used to it, you can take it farther and farther, creating incredibly realistic effects with it. Follow these steps to create a simple blend from one sized rectangle to another, creating an algorithmic stripe pattern (a rectangle of one height blended to a rectangle of another height):

1. **Create a shape.**

Size doesn't really matter for this example; you just want to make sure that you can see a difference in shapes when you blend. We're using a rectangle that's roughly 4 x 1 inches.

2. **Give your shape a fill and assign None to the stroke.**

You can use other settings here, but we recommend keeping it simple if you're still new to working with blends.

3. **With the Selection tool, click the rectangle and Alt+drag (Windows) or Option+drag (Mac) toward the bottom of the artboard to clone your shape; press the Shift key before you release the mouse button to make sure that the cloned shape stays perfectly aligned with the original shape.**

4. **Reduce the cloned shape to about half its original height by using the Transform panel (if the Transform panel isn't visible, choose Window⇨Transform).**

Alternatively, you can hold down the Shift key and drag the bottom-middle bounding box handle, as shown in Figure 11-5.

5. **In the Swatches panel (choose Window⇨Swatches), change the cloned shape's fill to a different color, but keep the stroke at None.**

Changing the color just helps you see the blend effect a little better.

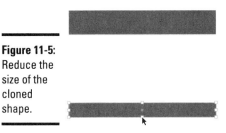

Figure 11-5:
Reduce the size of the cloned shape.

6. **With the Blend tool, click the original shape and then click the cloned shape.**

As a default, the Blend tool creates a smooth blend that transitions from one color to another, as shown in Figure 11-6. To change the blend effect, you need to experiment with the Blend Options dialog box.

Figure 11-6:
A smooth transition is created from one rectangle to the other.

**Book III
Chapter 11**

**Working with
Transparency and
Special Effects
Tools**

You can change the way that a blend appears by using the Blend Options dialog box, which you access by choosing Object➪Blend➪Blend Options. From the Spacing drop-down list, change the blend to one of the following options:

✦ **Smooth Color:** The blend steps are calculated to provide the optimum number of steps for a smooth transition.

✦ **Specified Steps:** You can determine the number of steps in a blend by typing a number in the text field to the right of the drop-down list.

✦ **Specified Distance:** You control the distance between the steps in the blend by typing a number in the text field to the right of the drop-down list.

You can also choose between two orientation options: Align To Page (orients the blend perpendicular to the X-axis of the page) or Align To Path (orients the blend perpendicular to the path). You will probably not see a difference when changing orientation unless you have edited the blend path.

You can easily access the Blend tool options by selecting a Blended object and double-clicking the Blend tool in the toolbox.

If you're feeling adventurous, try changing a smooth blend (such as the one you create in the preceding steps) into a logarithmic blend. In the Blend Options dialog box, choose Specified Steps from the Spacing drop-down list and change the value to 5. This change creates the blend in five steps instead of the 200 plus steps that may have been necessary to create the smooth blend.

Here are a few more tips to help you become more comfortable using blends:

✦ You can blend between an unlimited number of objects, colors, opacities, or gradients.

✦ Blends can be directly edited with tools, such as the Selection tools, the Rotate tool, or the Scale tool.

✦ A straight path is created between blended objects when the blend is first applied. You can switch to the Direct Selection tool and edit the blend path by dragging anchor points.

✦ You can edit blends that you created by moving, resizing, deleting, or adding objects. After you make editing changes, the artwork is automatically reblended.

The Symbol Sprayer Tool

The Symbol Sprayer tool is a super tool that you must experiment with to understand its full potential. In a nutshell, however, what it does is work like a can of spray paint that, instead of spraying paint, sprays *symbols* — objects that, in Illustrator, can be either vector- or pixel-based. Each individual symbol is an *instance.*

Illustrator comes with a library of symbols ready for use in the Symbols panel (if the Symbols panel isn't visible, choose Window➪Symbols Panel). Use this panel as a storage bin or library to save repeatedly used artwork or to create your own symbols to apply as instances in your artwork, like blades of grass or stars in the sky. You can then use the Symbolism tools, described in Table 11-1, to adjust and change the appearance of the symbol instances.

Table 11-1	The Symbolism Tools	
Button	*Tool Name*	*What It Does*
	Symbol Sprayer	Creates a set of symbol instances.
	Symbol Shifter	Moves symbol instances around. It can also change the relative paint order of symbol instances.
	Symbol Scruncher	Pulls symbol instances together or apart.
	Symbol Sizer	Increases or decreases the size of symbol instances.
	Symbol Spinner	Orients the symbol instances in a set. Symbol instances located near the cursor spin in the direction you move the cursor.
	Symbol Stainer	Colorizes symbol instances.
	Symbol Screener	Increases or decreases the transparency of the symbol instances in a set.
	Symbol Styler	Enables you to apply or remove a graphic style from a symbol instance.

Book III
Chapter 11

**Working with
Transparency and
Special Effects
Tools**

Press the Alt (Windows) or Option (Mac) key to reduce the effect of the Symbolism tool. In other words, if you're using the Symbol Sizer tool, you click and hold to make the symbol instances larger; hold down the Alt (Windows) or Option (Mac) key to make the symbol instances smaller.

You can also selectively choose the symbols that you want to effect with the Symbolism tools by activating them in the Symbols panel. Ctrl+click (Windows) or ⌘+click (Mac) multiple symbols to change them at the same time.

Just about anything can be a symbol, including placed objects and objects with patterns and gradients. If you're going to use placed images as symbols, however, choose File⇨Place and deselect the Linked check box in the Place dialog box.

To create a symbol, select the object and drag it into the Symbols panel or click the New Symbol button at the bottom of the Symbols panel. Yes, it's that easy. Then use the Symbol Sprayer tool to apply the Symbol instance on the artboard by following these steps:

1. **Select the symbol instance in the Symbols panel.**

   Either create your own symbol or use one of the default symbols supplied in the panel.

2. **Drag with the Symbol Sprayer tool, spraying the symbol on the artboard (see Figure 11-7).**

   And that's it. You can increase or reduce the area affected by the Symbol sprayer by pressing the bracket keys. Press] repeatedly to enlarge the application area for the symbol or [to make it smaller.

Figure 11-7: Using the Symbol Sprayer tool.

Note that you can access all sorts of Symbol Libraries from the Symbols panel menu. Find 3D, nature, maps, flowers, and even hair and fur symbol collections by selecting Open symbol library.

Want to store artwork that you frequently need to access? Simply drag the selected object(s) into the Symbols panel, or Alt+click (Windows) or Option+click (Mac) the New Symbol button to name and store the artwork. Retrieve the artwork later by dragging it from the Symbols panel to the artboard. In fact, you can drag any symbol out to your artboard to change or use it in your own artwork. To release the symbol back into its basic elements, choose Object⇨Expand. In the Expand dialog box, click OK to restore the defaults.

Transparency

Using transparency can add a new level to your illustrations. The transparency feature does exactly what its name implies: It changes an object to make it transparent so that what's underneath that object is visible to varying degrees.

You can use the Transparency panel for simple applications of transparency to show through to underlying objects, or you can use transparency for more complex artwork using *opacity masks*, masks that can control the visibility of selected objects.

Choosing Window⇨Transparency brings up the Transparency panel where you can apply different levels of transparency to objects. To do so, create an arrangement of objects that intersect, select the topmost object, and then change the transparency level of the object in the Transparency panel, either by moving the Opacity slider or by entering a value of less than 100 in the Opacity text field.

Blend modes

A *blend mode* determines how the resulting transparency will look. So to achieve different blending effects, you choose different blend modes from the Blend Mode drop-down list in the Transparency panel.

Truly, the best way to find out what all these modes do is to create two shapes that are overlapping and start experimenting. Give the shapes differently colored fills (but note that many of the blending modes don't work with black and white fills). Then select the topmost object and change the blending mode by selecting an option from the Blend Mode drop-down list in the Transparency panel. You'll see all sorts of neat effects and probably end up picking a few favorites.

We define each blend mode in the following list (but we'll say it again, the best way to see what each one does is to apply them — so start experimenting!):

+ **Normal:** Creates no interaction with underlying colors.

+ **Darken:** Replaces only the areas that are lighter than the blend color. Areas darker than the blend color don't change.

+ **Multiply:** Creates an effect similar to drawing on the page with magic markers. Also looks like colored film you see on theater lights.

+ **Color Burn:** Darkens the base color to reflect the blend color. If you're using white, no change occurs.

+ **Lighten:** Replaces only the areas darker than the blend color. Areas lighter than the blend color don't change.

+ **Screen:** Multiplies the inverse of the underlying colors. The resulting color is always a lighter color.

+ **Color Dodge:** Brightens the underlying color to reflect the blend color. If you're using black, there is no change.

+ **Overlay:** Multiplies or screens the colors, depending on the base color.

Book III
Chapter 11

Working with Transparency and Special Effects Tools

✦ **Soft Light:** Darkens or lightens the colors, depending on the blend color. The effect is similar to shining a diffused spotlight on the artwork.

✦ **Hard Light:** Multiplies or screens the colors, depending on the blend color. The effect is similar to shining a harsh spotlight on the artwork.

✦ **Difference:** Subtracts either the blend color from the base color or the base color from the blend color, depending on which has the greater brightness value. The effect is similar to a color negative.

✦ **Exclusion:** Creates an effect similar to, but with less contrast than, the Difference mode.

✦ **Hue:** Applies the hue (color) of the blend object onto the underlying objects, but keeps the underlying shading, or luminosity.

✦ **Saturation:** Applies the saturation of the blend color, but uses the luminance and hue of the base color.

✦ **Color:** Applies the blend object's color to the underlying objects but preserves the gray levels in the artwork. This is great for tinting objects or changing their color.

✦ **Luminosity:** Creates a resulting color with the hue and saturation of the base color and the luminance of the blend color. This is essentially the opposite of the Color mode.

Opacity masks

Just like in Photoshop, you can use masks to make more interesting artwork in Illustrator. Create an opacity mask from the topmost object in a selection of objects or by drawing a mask on a single object. The mask uses the grayscale of the object selected to be the opacity mask. Black areas are totally transparent; shades of gray are semi-transparent, depending on the amount of gray; and white areas are totally opaque. Figure 11-8 shows the effect of an opacity mask.

Figure 11-8: An opacity mask takes the topmost object and masks underlying objects.

To create an opacity mask, follow these steps:

1. **Open the Transparency panel menu (click the arrow in the upper-right corner to access this menu) and choose Show Thumbnails.**

Also, be sure that the Blend Mode drop-down list is set to Normal.

2. **Create a shape anywhere on the artboard or open a document that has artwork on it.**

We're using a rectangle, but the shape doesn't matter. Make sure that the artwork has a fill. A solid color will help you see the effect.

3. **Open the Symbols panel (choose Window⇨Symbols Panel) and drag a symbol to the artboard.**

For this example, we're using the butterfly symbol.

4. **With the Selection tool, enlarge your symbol so that it fills your shape (see image on the left in Figure 11-9).**

Figure 11-9:
Creating an
opacity
mask.

Book III
Chapter 11

Working with
Transparency and
Special Effects
Tools

5. **Select both the symbol and the shape and then choose Make Opacity Mask from the Transparency panel menu.**

The symbol turns into a mask, showing varying levels of the underlying box through, depending on the original color value. To delete an Opacity mask, choose Release Opacity Mask from the Transparency panel menu.

Click the right thumbnail (this is the mask) in the Transparency panel, and a black border appears around it, indicating that it's active. You can move the items on the mask, or even create items to be added to the mask. It works just like the regular artboard, except that anything done on the mask side will only be used as an opacity mask. To work on the regular artboard, click the left thumbnail.

Chapter 12: Using Filters and Effects

In This Chapter

✔ Applying filters and effects

✔ Getting to know the Appearance panel

✔ Discovering graphic styles

✔ Making artwork 3D

✔ Playing with additional fills and strokes

*F*ilters and effects give you the opportunity to do jazzy things to your Illustrator objects, such as adding drop shadows and squiggling artwork. You can even use Photoshop filters right in Illustrator. In this chapter, we explain the difference between filters and effects (it's a very big difference); show you how to apply, save, and edit filters and effects; and give you a quick tour of the Appearance panel (your trusty sidekick when performing these tasks).

Working with Filters and Effects

Filters apply permanent changes to artwork. After you use the filter, the only way to remove the change is to undo your actions or choose Object⇨Expand and take it apart. This process can be messy and not near as much fun as using an effect that is dynamically connected to the object. *Effects* are very different in that you can apply, change, and even remove effects at any time with the Appearance panel (Window⇨Appearance).

In Figure 12-1, we applied the drop shadow filter when the shape was a rectangle; then we applied the roughen filter. Notice that the drop shadow has no interaction with the original artwork.

In contrast, in Figure 12-2, we applied the Roughen effect, and the rectangle's drop shadow changed to look like the new shape. In the Appearance panel, you can double-click an effect to change it, or even drag it to the Trash icon in the lower-right corner of the Appearance panel to remove it.

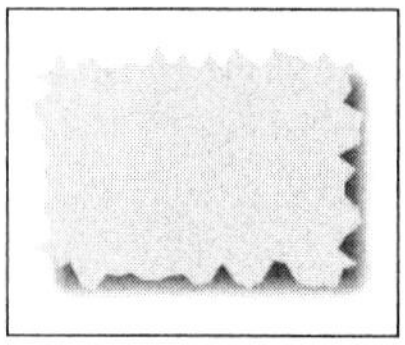

Figure 12-1:
A rectangle with the Drop Shadow and Roughen filter applied.

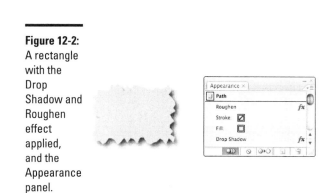

Figure 12-2:
A rectangle with the Drop Shadow and Roughen effect applied, and the Appearance panel.

Understanding the Appearance panel

You can apply multiple effects to one object and even copy the effects to multiple objects. This is when a good working knowledge of the Appearance panel is necessary. If it isn't visible, choose Window⇨Appearance to show the Appearance panel, as shown in Figure 12-3.

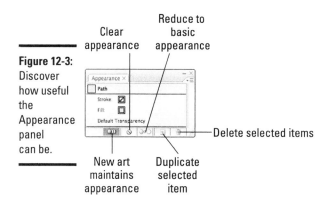

Clear appearance

Reduce to basic appearance

Figure 12-3:
Discover how useful the Appearance panel can be.

Delete selected items

New art maintains appearance

Duplicate selected item

To turn off effects so that they aren't automatically applied to any future objects, use any one of three buttons at the bottom of the Appearance panel:

✦ **New Art Maintains Appearance:** With the New Art Maintains Appearance button selected, your new art maintains the effects that you have applied to the present object.

Click this button to switch to New Art Has Basic Appearance so that when you create the next object, colors are maintained, but just a single fill and stroke are created.

✦ **Clear Appearance:** Click this button if you have a selected object and want the Fill and Stroke color boxes to be set to None.

✦ **Reduce To Basic Appearance:** If you have a selected object and discover that you applied unwanted effects, click this button to reduce it back to a single fill and stroke.

As a default, if you have no effects applied, you see only a fill and a stroke listed in the Appearance panel. As you add effects, they're added to this list. You can even add more strokes and fills to the list. Why would you do that? Because you can do incredible things with additional fills and strokes (which we show you in the upcoming section "Applying an effect."

Applying a filter

If effects are so great, why even use filters? Well, nothing can be all good. If you have lots of RAM (Random Access Memory) and you don't mind running through a few extra steps before printing (see Chapter 13 of this minibook), effects are the way to go. Most people don't mind, but you should see the alternative as well. Plus, some very useful Color filters are available that don't exist as effects — for example, filters that take a full color illustration and change it to grayscale.

If you generally work in the CMYK color mode, you will come across filters and effects that are grayed out. You can apply these filters and effects only in the RGB color mode. Choose File⇨Document Color Mode and change the document to RGB to use them.

Filters aren't dynamically linked to the original object that they were created from.

To apply the Add Arrowhead Filter, follow these steps (which essentially just add arrowheads to a path and are pretty straightforward):

1. **Create a new document, choose any color mode, and draw a path in your document.**

If you haven't mastered the Pen tool yet (see Chapter 5 of this minibook), use the Pencil tool.

2. **To make it clear what is happening with the arrowheads, give the path a 3-pt stroke and make sure that there's no fill.**

   Using a 3-pt stroke enables you to see the stroke a little easier.

3. **Choose Filter⇨Stylize⇨Add Arrowheads.**

   Make sure that you choose the top Stylize menu item.

   The Add Arrowheads dialog box appears (see Figure 12-4).

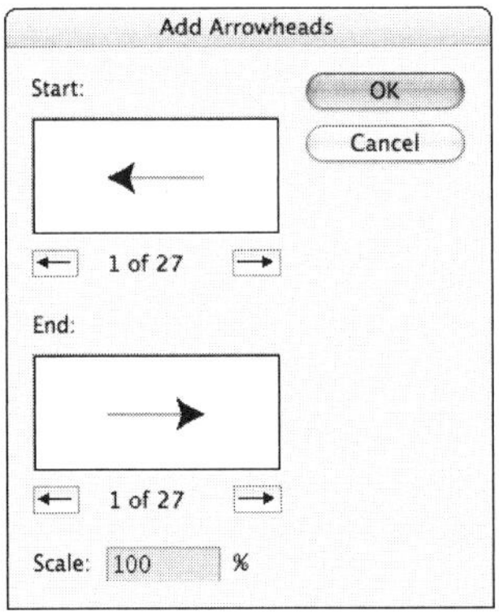

Figure 12-4:
Use the Add Arrowheads Filter to create arrows.

4. **Choose to add an arrowhead to both the start and the end of the path by using the arrow keys to scroll through the selection.**

   Note that the Start arrowhead (top of Add Arrowhead dialog box) will be placed on the first point you created; the End arrowhead (bottom of the dialog box) will be placed on the last point you created.

5. **Choose the size of the arrowhead by typing a number in the Scale text field.**

   You can go anywhere from 1 to 1,000 percent, but typically an arrow is set at 50 percent. There is no preview available, but this scales the arrowhead relative to the selected line stroke weight.

Note that if you used the Arrowhead effect instead of the Filter, the arrowhead would dynamically be linked to the stroke. Scaling and changing direction occur automatically as the stroke weight and direction are updated. See the next section for more information on effects.

Applying an effect

To apply the Add Arrowheads effect, choose Effects⇨Stylize⇨Add Arrowheads. Use the same settings that we describe in the preceding step list and then reposition some of the anchor points on the path by using the Direct Selection tool to see how the arrowhead applied with the effect moves with the direction of the path; the filter keeps the arrowhead in its original position.

Different from filters, the items under the Effect menu are dynamically linked to the object that they were applied to. Effects can be scaled, modified, and even deleted from the original object with no harm done to the original object.

Creating a drop shadow is a quick and easy way of adding dimension and a bit of sophistication to your artwork. The interaction between the object with the drop shadow and the underlying objects can create an interesting look. To add the Drop Shadow effect to an illustration, follow these steps:

1. **Select the object(s) that are to have the drop shadow applied.**

2. **Choose Effect⇨Stylize⇨Drop Shadow.**

3. **In the Drop Shadow dialog box that appears, select the Preview check box in the upper-right corner.**

   You now see the drop shadow applied as you make changes.

4. **Choose from the following options (see Figure 12-5):**

   • **Mode:** Select a blending mode from this drop-down list to choose how you want your selected object to interact with the objects underneath. The default is Multiply, which works well — the effect is similar to coloring with a magic marker.

   • **Opacity:** Enter a value or use the drop-down list to determine how opaque or transparent the drop shadow should be. If it's too strong, choose a lower amount.

   • **Offset:** Enter a value to determine how close the shadow is to the object. If you're working with text or small artwork, smaller values (and shorter shadow) look best. Otherwise, the drop shadow may look like one big indefinable glob.

   The X Offset shifts the shadow from left to right, and the Y Offset shifts it up or down. You can enter negative or positive numbers.

   • **Blur:** Use blur to control how fuzzy the edges of the shadow are. A lower value makes the edge of the shadow more defined.

   • **Color and Darkness:** Select the Color radio button to choose a custom color for the drop shadow. Use Darkness to add more black to the drop shadow. Zero percent is the lowest amount of black, and 100 percent is the highest.

   As a default, the color of the shadow is based upon the color of your object, sort of . . . the Darkness option has a play in this, also. As a default, the shadow is made up of the color in the object if it's solid. Multicolored objects have a gray shadow.

**Book III
Chapter 12**

Using Filters and Effects

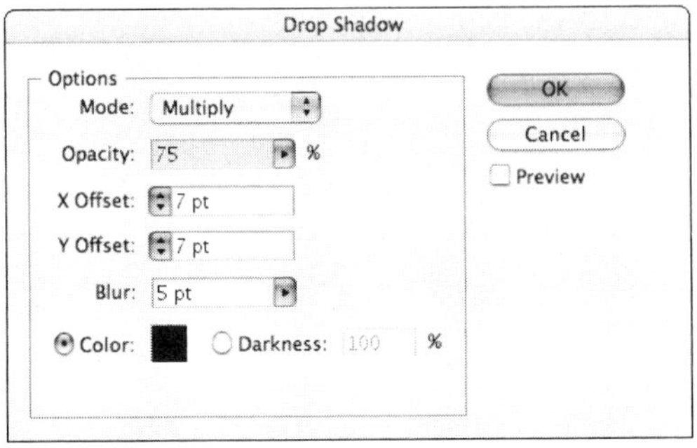

Figure 12-5:
The Drop
Shadow
effect dialog
box gives
the effect's
options and
preview.

Drop Shadow

Options
Mode: Multiply
Opacity: 75 %
X Offset: 7 pt
Y Offset: 7 pt
Blur: 5 pt
Color: ⬛ Darkness: 100 %

OK
Cancel
Preview

Saving Graphic Styles

A *graphic style* is a combination of all the settings you choose for a particular filter or effect in the Appearance panel. By saving this information in a graphic style, you store these attributes so that you can quickly and easily apply them to other objects later.

Choose Window↪Graphics Styles; in the panel that appears are thumbnails of many different styles that Adobe has provided to you as a default. Click any of these graphic styles to apply the style to an active object. Look at the Appearance panel as you click different styles to see that you're applying combinations of attributes, including effects, fills, and strokes (see Figure 12-6).

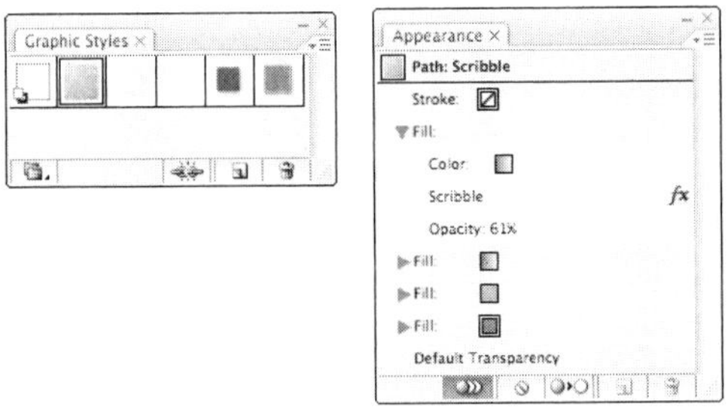

Figure 12-6:
The Graphic
Styles
palette
stores com-
binations
of effects
and other
attributes for
future use.

Graphic Styles

Appearance
Path: Scribble
Stroke:
Fill:
Color:
Scribble *fx*
Opacity: 61%
Fill:
Fill:
Fill:
Default Transparency

Find more styles by choosing the Graphic Styles panel menu (click the arrow in the upper-right corner of the panel) and selecting Open Graphic Style Library.

You can store attributes as a graphic style in several ways; we show you two easy methods. If you have a combination of attributes already applied to an object, store them by doing one of the following:

✦ With the object selected, Alt+click (Windows) or Option+click (Mac) the New Graphic Style button at the bottom of the Graphic Style panel. Alt+clicking (Windows) or Option+clicking (Mac) allows you to name the style as it is added.

✦ Drag the selected object right into the Graphic Style panel. The panel stores its attributes, but you have to double-click the new style to name it.

After you store a graphic style, simply select the object that you want to apply the style to and then click the saved style in the Graphic Styles panel.

Creating 3D Artwork

All the effects in Illustrator are great, but this new feature is really swell. Not only can you add dimension by using the 3D effect, you can also *map artwork* (that is, wrap artwork around a 3D object) and apply lighting to the 3D object. This means that you can design a label for a jelly jar and actually adhere it to the jar to show the client!

Here are the three choices for the 3D effect:

✦ **Extrude & Bevel:** This uses the z-axis to extrude an object. For example, a square becomes a cube.

✦ **Revolve:** Uses the z-axis and revolves a shape around it. You can use this to change an arc into a ball.

✦ **Rotate:** Rotates a 3D object created with the Extrude & Bevel or Revolve effects, or you can rotate a 2D object in 3D space. You can also adjust a 3D or 2D object's perspective.

To apply a 3D effect, you need to create an object appropriate for the 3D effect. Extrude & Bevel works great with shapes and text. If you want to edit an object that already has a 3D effect applied to it, double-click the 3D effect in the Appearance panel.

To apply a 3D effect, follow these steps:

1. **Select the object that you want to apply the 3D effect to.**

For this example, we're choosing Extrude & Bevel.

2. **Choose Effect⇨3D⇨Extrude & Bevel.**

Options for your chosen 3D effect appear. The Extrude & Bevel Options dialog box is shown in Figure 12-7.

3. **Select the Preview check box in the dialog box so that you can see results as you experiment with these settings.**

4. **Click the Preview pane (which shows a cube in Figure 12-7) and drag to rotate your object in space.**

It makes selecting the right angle fun, or you can choose the angle from the Position drop-down list above the preview. This is called positioning the object in space.

You should never rotate a 3D object with the Rotate tool, unless you want some very funky results; use the Preview pane in this dialog box instead.

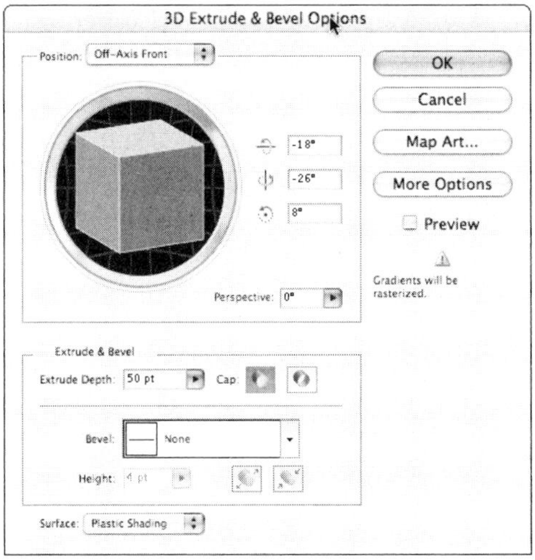

Figure 12-7:
The Extrude
& Bevel
Options
dialog box.

5. **If you want, use the Perspective drop-down list to add additional perspective to your object.**

6. **In the Extrude And Bevel section of the 3D Effects dialog box, choose a depth for your object and a cap.**

The cap determines whether your shape has a solid cap on it or whether it's hollow, as shown in Figure 12-8.

Figure 12-8:
Cap on (left)
and cap off
(right).

7. **Choose a bevel (edge shape) from the Bevel drop-down list and set the height using the Height drop-down list.**

You have a choice of two ways to apply the bevel:

- **Bevel Extent Out:** The bevel is added to the object.
- **Bevel Extent In:** The bevel is subtracted from the object.

8. **Choose a rendering style from the Surface drop-down list or click the More Options button for in-depth lighting options, such as changing the direction or adding additional lighting.**

9. **Click the Map Art button.**

The Map Art dialog box opens. Use this dialog box to apply artwork to a 3D object.

10. **Using the Surface arrow buttons, select which surface you want the artwork applied to and then choose the symbol from the Symbols drop-down list, as shown in Figure 12-9.**

The result is shown on the bottom in Figure 12-9.

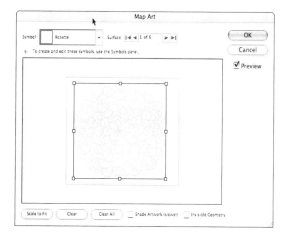

Figure 12-9:
In the Map Art dialog box, you can select a surface and apply a symbol to it.

Keep the following points in mind when mapping artwork:

✦ An object must be a symbol to be used as mapped artwork. You would simply need to select and drag the artwork that you want mapped to the Symbols panel to make it a selectable item in the Map Art dialog box.

✦ The light gray areas in the Preview pane are the visible areas based upon the object's present position. Drag and scale the artwork in this pane to get the artwork where you want it.

✦ Shaded artwork (the check box at the bottom of the dialog box) looks good but can take a long time to render.

Note: All 3D effects are rendered at 72 dpi (low resolution) so as not to slow down processing speed. You can determine the resolution by choosing Effect➪Document Raster Effects Settings, or when you save or export the file. You can also select the object and choose Object➪Rasterize. After the object is rasterized, it can no longer be used as an Illustrator 3D object, so save the original!

Using the panel menu in the Appearance panel, you can add more fills and strokes. With this feature, you can put different colored fills on top of each other and individually apply effects to each one, creating really interesting and creative results.

Just for fun, follow along to see what you can do to a single object with the Appearance panel:

1. **Create a star shape.**

It doesn't matter how many points it has, or how large it is, just make it large enough to work with.

2. **Use the Window➪Swatches panel to fill it with yellow and give it a black stroke.**

3. **Use Window➪Stroke to make the stroke 1 pt or choose 1 from the Stroke drop-down menu in the control panel.**

Notice that in the Appearance panel, the present fill and stroke are listed. Even in the simplest form, the Appearance panel helps track basic attributes. You can easily take advantage of the tracking to apply effects to just a fill or a stroke.

4. **Click Stroke in the Appearance panel.**

5. **Choose Effect➪Path➪Offset Path and in the Offset Panel dialog box that appears, change the Offset to –5pt and select the Preview check box.**

Notice that the stroke moves into the fill instead of on the edge.

6. **Change the offset to something that works with your star shape and click OK.**

Depending on the size of your star, you may want to adjust the amount of offset up or down.

7. **From the panel menu of the Appearance panel, choose to add an additional fill to the star shape.**

This may sound ridiculous, but you can create some super effects with multiple fills.

8. **Click Fill in the Appearance panel (the top one) and choose Effect⇨ Distort and Transform⇨Twist.**

9. **In the Twist dialog box that appears, type 45 into the Angle text field and select the Preview check box.**

Notice how only the second fill is twisted? Pretty neat, right?

10. **Click OK to exit the Twist dialog box.**

11. **Select the top Fill from the Appearance panel again.**

You always have to be sure that they're selected before doing anything that is meant to change just a specific fill or stroke.

12. **Then, using the Transparency panel (choose Window⇨Transparency), choose 50% from the Opacity slider or simply type 50% in the Opacity text field.**

Now you can see your original shape through the new fill!

13. **With that top fill still selected, change the color or choose a pattern in the Swatches palette for a really different appearance.**

You could go on for hours playing around with combinations of fills and strokes. Hopefully, this clicks, and you can take it further on your own.

Chapter 13: Using Your Illustrator Images

In This Chapter

✔ Saving Illustrator files

✔ Exporting files to other programs

✔ Preparing art for the Web

✔ Flattening transparency

✔ Printing from Illustrator

So you have beautiful artwork, but you aren't sure how to get it off your screen. You could have a party and invite all interested clients to stand around your monitor and ooh and ah, or you could actually share or sell your artwork by putting it on the Internet or printing it.

In this chapter, we show you how to use your illustrations in a variety of work-flows, from using Illustrator files in page layout programs, to exporting files for Photoshop (and other programs) and the Web. Hopefully, this chapter can help you really use your artwork and understand the saving and flattening choices available in Adobe Illustrator.

Saving and Exporting Illustrator Files

In this section, we show you how the general choices in the Save As dialog box (choose File➪Save As) differ and the benefits of each.

If you need a particular file format that is not listed in the regular Save As dialog box, choose File➪Export for additional choices. Using the File Export command, you can choose to save your files in any of the formats in Table 13-1.

Table 13-1	Available File Formats
File Format	**Extension**
BMP	.bmp
Targa	.tga
PNG	.png

(continued)

Table 13-1 *(continued)*

File Format	Extension
AutoCAD Drawing	.dwg
AutoCAD Interchange File	.dxf
Enhanced Metafile	.emf
Flash	.swf
JPEG	.jpg
Macintosh PICT	.pct
Photoshop	.psd
TIFF	.tif
Text Format	.txt
Windows Metafile	.wmf

Many of these formats *rasterize* your artwork, meaning that they'll no longer maintain vector paths and the benefits of being vector. Scalability is not limited, for example. If you think that you may want to edit your image again later, be sure to save a copy of the file and keep the original in the .ai format.

The native Adobe Illustrator file format

If your workflow can handle it, the best way to save your file is as a native Illustrator .ai file. By workflow, we mean that you're working with Adobe applications such as Adobe InDesign for page layout, Adobe Dreamweaver for Web page creation, Adobe Photoshop for photo-retouching, and Adobe Acrobat for cross-platform documents.

Understanding when it's best to use the .ai format is important. Saving your illustration as an .ai file ensures that your file is editable; it also ensures that any transparency is retained, even if you use the file in another application.

To save and use a file in the native Illustrator format, follow these steps:

1. **Make an illustration with transparency (50 percent transparent, for example) in Adobe Illustrator and choose File⇨Save As.**

2. **Select Adobe Illustrator Document (.ai) from the Save As Type drop-down list, give the file a name, and click Save.**

3. **Leave the Illustrator Native Options at the defaults and click OK.**

After you follow the preceding steps to prepare your Illustrator file, you can use the illustration in other Adobe applications:

✦ **Adobe Acrobat:** Open the Acrobat application and choose File➪Open. Locate the .ai file. Native Illustrator files open in Acrobat when you open them from within the Acrobat application.

✦ **Adobe InDesign:** Choose File➪Place. This method supports transparency created in Adobe Illustrator. (However, copying and pasting from Illustrator to InDesign does *not* support transparency.) See Figure 13-1.

Figure 13-1: Choose to place an Illustrator file into InDesign to support transparency, even over InDesign text.

✦ **Adobe Photoshop:** Choose File➪Place. By placing an Illustrator file into Adobe Photoshop, you automatically create a Photoshop Smart Object. You can scale, rotate, and even apply effects to the Illustrator file and return to the original illustration at any time. Read more about Smart Objects in Photoshop in Chapter 9 of the Photoshop CS3 minibook.

If you really want to go crazy with an Illustrator file in Photoshop, when you save the file in Illustrator, choose File➪Export and select the Photoshop (.psd) format from the Save As Type drop-down list. Choose a resolution from the options window. If you used layers, leave the Write Layers option selected.

In Photoshop, choose File➪Open, select the file that you just saved in Illustrator as a .psd, and click Open. The file opens in Photoshop with the layers intact.

✦ **Adobe Flash:** New integration features built into Adobe Illustrator CS3 allow you to cut and paste directly into Adobe Flash CS3. If you Choose Edit➪Copy from Adobe Illustrator, you can then switch to Adobe Flash CS3 and choose Edit➪Paste. The Paste dialog box appears.

✦ **Adobe Dreamweaver:** By choosing File➪Save for Web & Devices, you can choose to save your Illustrator document in the .gif, .jpg, .png, .swf, .svg, or WBMP format. You can then insert these formats into Dreamweaver by choosing Insert➪Image in Adobe Dreamweaver.

Select the Image button from the Insert panel in Dreamweaver. When the Select Image Source dialog box appears, navigate to the location which you saved your optimized file. Select it and click Choose. If your file is located out of the root folder for the site you're working on, an alert window appears, offering the opportunity to save the file with your other site assets. See Book VI, Chapter 3 for more information about importing images in Dreamweaver.

Saving Illustrator files back to previous versions

When saving an .ai or .eps file, you can choose a version from the Version drop-down menu. Keep in mind that any features specific to newer versions of Illustrator will not be supported in older file formats, so make sure that you save a copy and keep the original file intact. Adobe helps you understand the risk of saving back to older versions by putting a warning sign next to the version drop-down menu and showing you specific issues with the version you have selected in the Warnings window.

The EPS file format

EPS is the file format that most text editing and page layout applications accept; EPS supports vector data and is completely scalable. The Illustrator .eps format is based on PostScript, which means that you can reopen an EPS file and edit it in Illustrator at any time.

To save a file in Illustrator as an EPS, follow these steps:

1. **Choose File⇨Save As and select EPS (Encapsulated PostScript File) from the Save As Type drop-down list.**

2. **From the Version menu, choose the Illustrator version you're saving to.**

3. **In the EPS Options dialog box that appears (shown in Figure 13-2), choose the preview from the Format drop-down list:**

   - **TIFF (8-bit Color):** A color preview for either Mac or PC.

   - **TIFF (Black & White):** A low-resolution black-and-white preview.

4. **Select either the Transparent or Opaque option, depending on whether you want the non-image areas in your artwork to be transparent or opaque.**

5. **Set your Transparency Flattening settings.**

   These settings are grayed out if you haven't used transparency in the file. (See the "Flattening Transparency" section, later in this chapter, for more about this setting.)

6. **Leave the Embed Fonts (For Other Applications) check box selected to leave fonts you used embedded in the EPS file format.**

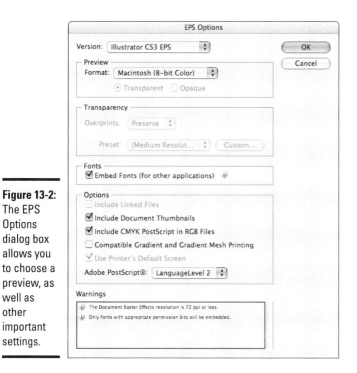

Figure 13-2:
The EPS
Options
dialog box
allows you
to choose a
preview, as
well as
other
important
settings.

7. In the Options section, leave the Include CMYK PostScript In RGB Files check box selected.

If you don't know which Adobe Postscript level you want to save to, leave it at the default.

8. Click OK to save your file as an EPS.

The PDF file format

If you want to save your file in a format that supports over a dozen platforms and requires only the Acrobat Reader, available as a free download at www. adobe.com, choose to save in the PDF format.

If you can open an Illustrator file in Acrobat, why would you need to save a file in the PDF format? Well, for one thing, you can compress a PDF down to a smaller size; also, the receiver can double-click the file, and Acrobat or Acrobat Reader launches automatically.

Depending on how you save the PDF, you can allow some level of editability in Adobe Illustrator. To save a file in the PDF format, follow these steps:

1. Choose File➪Save As; select Illustrator PDF (.pdf) from the Save As Type drop-down list and then click Save.

2. **In the Adobe PDF Options dialog box that appears, select one of the following options from the Preset drop-down list:**

- **Illustrator Default:** Creates a PDF file in which all Illustrator data is preserved. PDF files created with this preset can be reopened in Illustrator without any loss of data.

- **High Quality Print:** Creates PDFs for desktop printers and proofers.

- **PDF/X-1a:2001:** This method is the least flexible delivery of PDF content data, but it can be very powerful. It requires that the color of all objects be in CMYK or spot colors. Elements in RGB or Lab color spaces or tagged with ICC profiles are prohibited. It also requires that all fonts used in the job be embedded in the supplied PDF file.

- **PDF/X-3:2002:** This method of creating a PDF has slightly more flexibility than the X-1a:2001 method in that color managed workflows are supported elements in Lab, and attached ICC source profiles may also be used.

- **PDF/X-4:2007:** This preset is based on PDF 1.4, which includes support for live transparency. PDF/X-4 has the same color management and *International Color Consortium* (ICC) color specifications as PDF/X-3. You can open PDF files created with PDF/X-4 compliance in Acrobat 7.0 and Reader 7.0 and later.

- **Press Quality:** Creates a PDF file that can be printed to a high-resolution output device. The file will be large, but it will maintain all the information that a commercial printer or service provider needs to print your file correctly. This option automatically converts the color mode to CMYK, embeds all fonts used in the file, prints at a higher resolution, and uses other settings to preserve the maximum amount of information contained in the original document.

- **Smallest File Size:** Creates a low-resolution PDF suitable for posting on the internet or sending via e-mail.

Before creating an Adobe PDF file using the Press preset, check with your commercial printer to find out what the output resolution and other settings should be.

- **Standard:** Don't pick a PDF/X standard unless you have a specific need or have been requested to. Through the Standard drop-down menu, you can select the type of PDF/X file you want to create.

- **Compatibility:** Different features are available for different versions, such as the ability to support layers in Version 6 or higher. If you want the most compatible file type choose Acrobat 5 (PDF 1.4). But if you want to take advantage of layers or need to preserve spot colors, you must choose Acrobat 6 or higher.

3. Click Save PDF to save your file as a PDF.

If you want to be able to reopen the PDF file and edit it in Illustrator, make sure that you leave the Preserve Illustrator Editing Capabilities check box selected in the Adobe PDF Options dialog box.

In the Adobe PDF Options dialog box, to the left of the preset choices are options that you can change to customize your settings. Scan through them to see how you can change resolution settings and even add printer's marks. Take a look at Book V on Acrobat to find out more about the additional PDF options.

Want a Press Quality PDF, but don't want to convert all your colors to CMYK? Choose the Press setting and then click the Output options. In the Color section, select No Conversion from the Color Conversion drop-down list.

Saving Your Artwork for the Web

If you need to save artwork for the Web, there is no better feature than Save For Web. The Save For Web dialog box gives you a preview pane where you can test different file formats before you actually save the file.

To save an Illustrator file that you intend to use in a Web page, just follow these steps:

1. Choose File➪Save For Web & Devices.

The Save For Web & Devices dialog box appears, showing your artwork on the Optimized tab.

2. Choose a tabbed view: Original, Optimized, 2-Up, or 4-Up.

As a default, you see the artwork in the Optimized view, which previews the artwork as it will appear based upon the settings on the right. The 2-Up view is probably the best choice because it shows your original image versus the optimized version.

3. Choose a setting for your file from the options on the right.

If you want to make it easy on yourself, choose a preset from the Preset drop-down list. Keep in mind these points:

- GIF is generally used for artwork with spans of solid color. GIF is not a lossy format. You can make your artwork smaller by reducing the number of colors in the image — hence the choices, such as GIF 64 No Dither (64 colors). The lower the amount of colors, the smaller the file size. You can also increase or decrease the number of colors in the file by changing the preset values in the Color text field or by using the arrows to the left of the Color text field.

Book III
Chapter 13

Using Your
Illustrator Images

- Dithering tries to make your artwork look like it has more colors by creating a pattern in the colors. It looks like a checkerboard pattern up close and even far away, as shown in Figure 13-3. It also makes a larger file size, so why use it? Most designers don't like the effect and choose the No Dither option.

- JPEG is used for artwork that has subtle gradations from one shade to another. Photographs are often saved in this format. If you have drop shadows or blends in your artwork, you should select this format. JPEG is a lossy file format, meaning that it will reduce your image to a lesser quality and can create odd artifacts in your artwork. You have choices such as High, Medium, and Low in the Settings drop-down list. Make sure that you choose wisely. You can also use the Quality slider to tweak the compression.

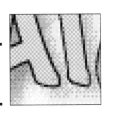

Figure 13-3:
An example
of dithering.

- PNG-8 is very similar to a GIF file format. Unless you have a certain reason for saving as PNG-8, stick with the GIF file format.

- PNG-24 supports the best of two formats. Not only does the PNG format support the nice gradients from one tonal value to another (like JPEG), but it also supports Transparency (like GIFs). Not just any old transparency, if you make an object 50% transparent in Adobe Illustrator, then choose to save it, using Save For Web & Devices, as a PNG-24 file with the Transparency check box checked, the image will show through to any other objects underneath it on its destination page.

- The SWF graphic file format is a version of the Adobe Flash Player vector-based graphics format. Because a SWF file is vector-based, its graphics are scalable and play back smoothly on any screen size and across multiple platforms. Using the Save For Web & Devices dialog box, you can save your image directly to SWF from Adobe Illustrator. With the SWF choice, you can preview and make decisions as to how you want to export to the file, as well as make decisions about how layers should be exported.

- Scalable Vector Graphics (SVG) is an emerging Web standard for two-dimensional graphics. SVG is written in plain text and rendered by the browser, except that in this case, it's not just text that is rendered but also shapes and images, which can be animated and made interactive. SVG is written in XML (Extensible Markup Language). You can choose to save Scalable Vector Graphics out of Adobe Illustrator using the Save For Web & Devices dialog box.

- Use the Wireless Application Protocol Bitmap Format (WBMP) format for bitmap images for mobile devices.

4. When you're satisfied with your chosen settings, save your file by clicking Save.

When saving illustrations for the Web, you should keep the following points in mind, which will make the whole process much easier for you and anyone who uses your illustrations:

✦ **Keep it small.** Don't forget that if you're saving illustrations for a Web page, many other elements will be on that page. Try to conserve on file size to make downloading the page quicker for viewers using dial-up connections. Most visitors won't wait more than 10 seconds for a page to download before giving up and moving on to another Web site.

As you make your choices, keep an eye on the file size and the optimized artwork in the lower-left corner of the preview window. On average, a GIF should be around 10K and a JPEG around 15K. These rules aren't written in stone, but please don't try to put a 100K JPEG on a Web page!

You can change the download time by selecting the panel menu in the upper-right corner of the Save For Web & Devices dialog box and choosing Optimize to File Size to input a final file size and have Illustrator create your settings in the Save For Web & Devices dialog box.

✦ **Preview the file before saving it.** If you want to see the artwork in a Web browser before saving it, click the Preview In Default Browser button at the bottom of the Save For Web & Devices dialog box. The browser of choice appears with your artwork in the quality and size in which it will appear. If you have no browser selected, click and hold down the Preview In Default Browser button to choose Other and then browse to locate a browser that you want to use for previewing. Close the browser to return to the Save for Web & Devices dialog box.

✦ **Change the size.** Many misconceptions abound about size when it comes to Web artwork. Generally, most people view their browser windows in an area approximately 700 x 500 pixels. Depending on the screen resolution, this may cover the entire screen on a 14-inch monitor, but even viewers with 21-inch monitors with a high resolution often don't want to have their entire screen covered with a browser's window, so they still have a browser window area of around 700 x 500 pixels. When choosing a size for your artwork, use proportions of this amount to help you. For example, if you want an illustration to take up about a quarter of the browser window's width, you should make your image about 175 pixels wide (700÷4 = 175). If you notice that the height of your image is over 500 pixels, you should whittle the height down in size as well, or your viewers will have to scroll to see the whole image (and it will probably take too long to download!).

Use the Image Size tab to input new sizes. As long as the Constrain Proportions check box is selected, both the height and width of the image will be changed proportionally. Click the Apply button to change the size but do not close the Save For Web & Devices dialog box.

✦ **Finish the save.** If you aren't finished with the artwork, but you want to save the settings, hold down the Alt (Windows) or Option (Mac) key and click the Remember button. (When you're not holding down the Alt or Option key, the Remember button is the Done button.) If you're finished, click the Save button and save your file in the appropriate location.

Flattening Transparency

You may find that all those cool effects that you put into your illustration don't print correctly. When you print a file that has effects such as drop shadows, cool gradient blends, and feathering, Illustrator turns transparent areas that overlap other objects into pixels and leaves what it can as vectors — this process is called *flattening*.

So what actually is flattening? Look at Figure 13-4 to see the difference between the original artwork (on the left) and the flattened artwork (on the right). Notice that in Figure 13-4, when the artwork was flattened, some of the areas turned into pixels. But at what resolution? This is why you want to know about flattening, so that you can determine the quality of art yourself — before getting an unpleasant surprise at the outcome.

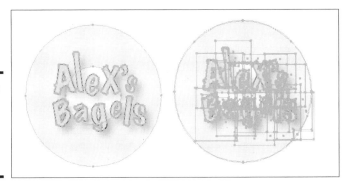

Figure 13-4: Artwork before and after flattening applied.

Flattening a file

If you've taken advantage of transparency or effects using transparency (which we discuss in Chapter 11 of this minibook), follow these steps to get the highest quality artwork from your file:

1. **Make sure that you've created the artwork in the CMYK mode.**

   You can change the document's color mode by choosing File⇨Document Color Mode.

2. **Choose Effects⇨Document Raster Effects Settings.**

   The Document Raster Effects Settings dialog box appears, as shown in Figure 13-5.

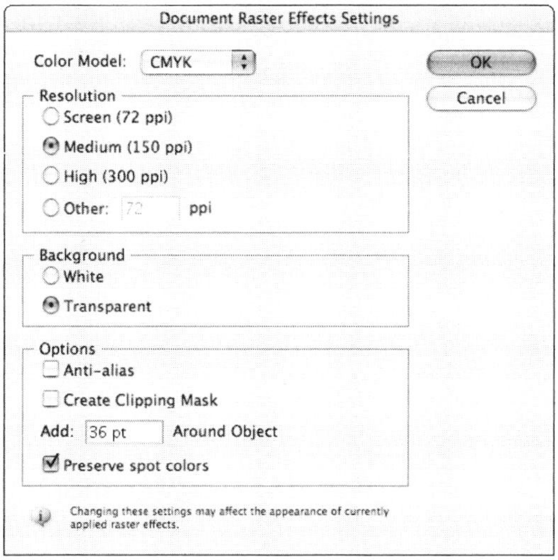

Figure 13-5: Choosing the quality of your rasterized artwork.

3. **Choose the resolution that you want to use by selecting an option in the Resolution area.**

   As a default, the rasterization setting is the Screen (72 ppi) option, which is fine for the screen. Select the Medium (150 ppi) option for printers and copiers and select the High (300 ppi) option for press.

4. **Choose whether you want a white or transparent background.**

   If you select the Transparent option, you create an alpha channel. The alpha channel is retained if the artwork is exported into Photoshop.

5. **You can generally leave the items in the Options section deselected:**

   • The Anti-Alias check box applies anti-aliasing to reduce the appearance of jagged edges in the rasterized image. Deselect this option to maintain the crispness of fine lines and small text.

- The Create Clipping Mask check box creates a mask that makes the background of the rasterized image appear transparent. You don't need to create a clipping mask if you select the Transparent option for your background.

- The Add Around Object text field adds the specified number of pixels around the rasterized image.

6. Click OK.

The next step is to set the transparency options in the Document Setup dialog box.

7. Choose File⇨Document Setup⇨Transparency.

The Export And Clipboard Transparency Flattener Settings options appear. From the Preset drop-down list, select the Low, Medium, High, or Custom option. Select the Low option for on-screen viewing, the Medium option for printers and copiers, or the High option for press. Choose the Other option if you want to control more of the settings yourself.

8. Click OK.

If you find yourself customizing the settings on a regular basis, choose Edit⇨Transparency Flattener Presets to create and store your own presets.

You can apply the flattening in several ways. Here are three simple methods.

✦ Select the object(s) that require flattening and choose Object⇨Flatten Transparency. Choose one of the default settings or a custom preset that you created from the Preset drop-down list and click OK.

✦ Choose File⇨Print and select Advanced from the list of print options on the left. Choose a preset from the Overprint and Transparency Flattener options. If you used the Attributes panels to create overprints (for trapping used in high-end printing), make sure that you preserve the overprints.

Note: Overprints will not be preserved in areas that use transparency.

✦ Choose File⇨Save As and choose Illustrator EPS. In the Transparency section of the EPS Options dialog box, choose a flattening setting from the Preset drop-down list. If your Transparency options are grayed out, you have no transparency in your file.

Using the Flattener Preview panel

Want to preview your flattening? Use the Flattener Preview panel by choosing Window⇨Flattener Preview.

The Flattener Preview panel doesn't apply the flattening, but it gives you a preview based upon your settings. Click the Refresh button and choose Show Options from the panel menu. Test various settings without actually flattening the file. Experiment with different settings, and then save your presets by selecting Save Transparency Flattener Preset from the panel menu. The saved settings can be accessed in the Preset drop-down list in the Options dialog boxes that appear when you save a file as an EPS or in the Document Setup dialog box.

Click the Refresh button after making changes to update the preview.

Zoom in on the artwork by clicking in the preview pane. Scroll the artwork in the preview pane by holding down the spacebar and dragging. Zoom out by Alt+clicking (Windows) or Option+clicking (Mac).

Printing from Illustrator

Printing from Illustrator gives you lots of capabilities, such as printing composites to separations and adding printer's marks.

To print your illustration, follow these steps:

1. **Choose File⇨Print.**

2. **In the Print dialog box that appears, select a printer if one isn't already selected.**

3. **If the PPD isn't selected, choose one from the PPD drop-down list.**

   A *PPD* is a printer description file. Illustrator needs this to determine the specifics of the PostScript printer you're sending your file to. This setting lets Illustrator know whether the printer can print in color, the size paper it can handle, and the resolution, as well as many other important details.

4. **Choose from other options as follows:**

   Use the General options area to pick what pages to print. In the Media area, select the size of media that you're printing to. In the Options area, choose whether you want layers to print and any options specific to printing layers.

5. **Click the Print button to print your illustration.**

And that's it. Printing your illustration can be really simple, but the following list highlights some basic things to keep in mind as you prepare your illustration for printing:

+ **Printing a composite:** A *composite* is the full-color image, where all the inks are applied to the page (and not separated out onto individual pages, one for cyan, one for magenta, one for yellow, and one for black). To make sure that your settings are correct, click Output in the print options pane on the left side of the Print dialog box and select Composite from the Mode drop-down list.

**Book III
Chapter 13**

**Using Your
Illustrator Images**

✦ **Printing separations:** To separate colors, click Output in the print options pane on the left side of the Print dialog box; from the Mode drop-down list, choose the Separations (Host-Based) option. Select the In-RIP Separations option only if your service provider or printer asks you to. Other options to select from are as follows:

- The resolution is determined by your PPD, based upon the dpi in the printer description. You may have only one option available in the Printer Resolution drop-down list.

- Select the Convert Spot Colors to Process check box to make your file 4-color.

- Click the printer icons to the left of the listed colors to turn off or on the colors that you want to print.

✦ **Printer's marks and bleeds:** Click Marks And Bleeds in the print options pane on the left side of the Print dialog box to turn on all printer's marks, or just select the ones that you want to appear.

Specify a bleed area if you're extending images beyond the trim area of a page. If you don't specify a bleed, the artwork will stop at the edge of the page and not leave a trim area for the printer.

After you've created a good set of options specific to your needs, click the Save Preset button at the bottom of the Print dialog box. Name your preset appropriately; when you want to use that preset, select it from the Print Preset drop-down list at the top of the Print dialog box for future print jobs.

Book IV

Photoshop CS3

The 5th Wave   By Rich Tennant

"I'm going to assume that most of you — but not all of you — understand that this session on 'masking' has to do with Photoshop."

Contents at a Glance

Chapter 1: Exploring New Features in Photoshop CS3

In This Chapter

✔ Working with the new interface

✔ Getting smart with filters

✔ Improving curve corrections

*P*hotoshop CS3 includes significant improvements to the workspace, filters, and selection tools. In this chapter, you take a quick tour of some of most exciting new capabilities. The features you see depend on the Photoshop that you have (Standard or Extended).

This quick rundown of what is new and exciting in Photoshop CS3 is hopefully a help to you as you start experimenting with the new tools and features.

If you really want to dive into the new features, choose Window⇨Workspace⇨ What's New In CS3. Instantly all new features are highlighted in the menus!

A New Efficient Workspace

As soon as you launch Photoshop CS3, the more efficient workspace — meaning more space is available for you to work on your images — is apparent (see Figure 1-1).

The toolbar is now single column. If you don't like the change in the toolbar, you can return to the old two-column display by clicking the gray bar at the top of the toolbar.

Additionally, palettes are collapsed to a compact view and represented by icons, saving even more space. The new workspace makes focusing on the images easier, and the tools become a natural extension of your work.

Figure 1-1:
The new
space-
saving
Photoshop
CS3
workspace.

Photoshop continues to make extensive use of palettes. To activate a palette in this new version, simply click the appropriate palette icon. If you select another palette icon, its pane is brought to the front of the display. You can return them to icons by clicking the Collapse To Icons bar at the top of the palette drawer. When an icon is dragged out to the work area, it automatically expands and then returns to an icon when dragged back into dock.

Showing and hiding all your tools and palettes is easier as well. Press the Tab key to hide all your tools and palettes. To cause them to reappear, move your cursor over the left or right side of your screen and pause at the vertical gray bar.

Do you have Standard or Extended?

How can you tell whether you have Photoshop Standard or Extended? If you purchase the master, Design Premium, or Web Premium Suite, you have Photoshop Extended.

Do you need Extended? Most likely not. The typical designer, whether Web or print, will most likely never need the advanced tools that separate Standard from Extended.

But if you're into 3D, life sciences, manufacturing, or the medical field, you may want to take advantage of the 3D, counting, and analysis tools now available in Photoshop.

Super Selection Tools and Features

If you want the ability to paint your selections, you'll love the new Quick Selection tool. With this tool, you can easily brush over the image area that you want to select. By default, additional strokes with the Quick Selection tool add to the selection. You can delete by holding down Alt (Windows) or Option (Mac OS) as you stroke. The toolbar provides more options, including New Selection, Add To Selection, and Subtract From Selection buttons.

The new Refine Edge button, available from any of the selection tool's options, is quite helpful in cleaning up selections or adding feathering to create a vignette of a selection. All of these options are available in a preview window that includes choices for five different ways to preview the selection, as shown in Figure 1-2. (Read more detail about selections in Chapter 4 of this minibook.)

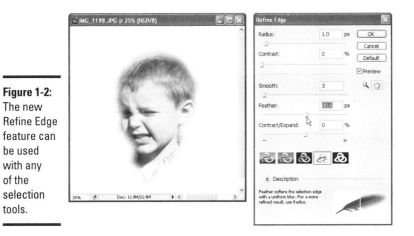

Figure 1-2: The new Refine Edge feature can be used with any of the selection tools.

Smart Filters

Photoshop CS3 has taken nondestructive imaging editing to the max with Smart filters. Don't worry about destroying your image with filters because you can now edit filters after they're applied. When you use a Smart Filter, a Filter effects mask thumbnail appears in the Layer's palette. You can select the mask thumbnail and then, using your paint tools, paint black (or shades of) to change where and how the filter is applied, or paint white to bring back the filter.

You can turn off the Smart Filters by selecting the visibility icon in the Layers palette or adjust filter settings by double-clicking the icon to the right of the listed filter. It's worth experimenting with this feature because you can apply multiple filters. Read more about applying filters in Chapter 8 of this minibook.

Black-and-White Conversion like a Pro

Photoshop CS3 makes creating great-looking black-and-white images easier. With an image open, you can click the Create New Fill or Adjustment Layer button in the Layers palette and then select Black & White. The Black and White dialog box appears, as shown in Figure 1-3. Choose a preset, or customize the color conversion by using the Channel mixer adjustments. If you're converting multiple images, you can save your settings by selecting the Preset options button to the right of the Presets drop-down menu. If you want to experiment with more creative options, use the Tint box and add a color tint to your image as it's converted.

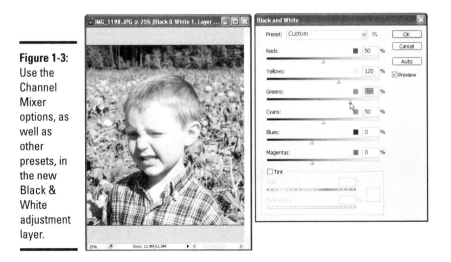

Figure 1-3:
Use the Channel Mixer options, as well as other presets, in the new Black & White adjustment layer.

Multiple Planes in Vanishing Point Filter

In Photoshop CS3, you can create images wrapped around multiple perspective planes, which is great if you're creating package design or needing spatial illustrations. To experiment with this incredible feature:

1. **Copy an image and choose Filter⇨Vanishing Point.**

The Vanishing Point dialog box appears.

2. **Using the Create Plane tool, click four corners to make a perspective plane.**

   Note that the plane is accurate if the grid is blue.

3. **If the grid isn't blue, use the Edit Plane tool to adjust the corners.**

4. **Hold down the Ctrl key (Windows) or ⌘ (Mac OS) and drag one of the middle nodes.**

   An additional perspective plane, generated from the original, appears.

5. **Paste your image and drag it into your plane.**

   The image wraps the planes (see Figure 1-4).

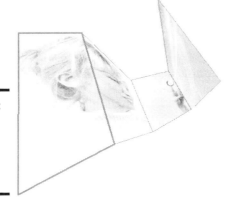

Figure 1-4:
An image
wrapped
around
multiple
planes.

Even better, Vanishing Point adjusts brush strokes, healing, and cloning as you paint over the planes. Note that in Photoshop CS3, you're no longer restricted to adding planes at 90-degree angles.

Help with Aligning

Ever take several versions of a picture and wish that you could easily combine and align the images to pick the best of each? With the new Align feature, you can do just that:

1. **Drag similar images into a file to create layers.**

   These images may be several versions of a group picture, for example.

2. **Select the Move tool and Shift+click to select the multiple layers.**

3. **Click the Auto-Align Layers button in the options bar.**

The Auto-Align Layers dialog box appears.

4. **Choose your alignment method and click OK.**

Improved Curve Controls

Check out Image➪Adjustment➪Curves for a look at the new improved curves palette. Wow! It's like a perfect combination of Levels and Curves. If you know that you should use Curves, but like the interface of the Level controls, the improved curve controls are a dream come true. Read about using the Curves palette in Chapter 7 of this minibook.

Performance Improvements on Intel Macintosh

If you're a Macintosh user, you'll appreciate that Adobe has done a great job at porting the software to the Intel-based processors. As a Universal application, the software can run in a native mode on both Intel and PowerPC Macintosh systems. As part of our testing, we've been using both PC and Macintosh systems, both using Intel Core2 Duo processors. The performance is strong on both platforms. Most noticeable is the huge speed improvement between Photoshop CS3 running on an Intel-based Macintosh and Photoshop CS2 running on the same system.

Before Photoshop CS3, the Intel-based Macintosh computers had to interpret the software so that it could be used because the earlier versions of software weren't made for the Intel processors but for the PowerPC processors in the last generation of Macintosh systems. This release of Photoshop CS3 has been developed to run efficiently on either legacy or new Macintosh computers, regardless of the processor.

Compared to earlier versions of Photoshop running on the Intel-based Macintosh systems, Photoshop CS3 is blazing fast. And if you still have an older Macintosh system with a PowerPC processor, Photoshop CS3 still runs on these computers as well.

Additional Features in Photoshop Extended

If you have Photoshop CS3 Extended, it's probably because you purchased the Master or one of the Premium Suites, or because you're in the medical, architecture, manufacturing, or construction business. Photoshop CS3 Extended isn't necessarily a better version of Photoshop, but it does contain additional tools to help those users in certain industries get the counting, viewing, and analysis tools that they need to do their job. As a designer, you may never need the Counting tool, but it can be invaluable to someone in manufacturing.

Some features are in Photoshop Standard, but are enhanced in Photoshop Extended. For example, although you have animation in the Standard version, you see a timeline in the Extended version that has a higher level of functionality. The following sections are by no means a complete list of Extended features, but a quick look at some incredibly different features that have been included in Photoshop CS3 Extended.

3D Layers

For those involved in 3D graphics, Photoshop Extended is a great tool. You don't build 3D elements in Photoshop, but you can take advantage of 3D model visualization and texture editing and export of 3D models from 2D images. Support for common 3D interchange formats lets you import 3D models, edit their textures, and easily composite designs with images, such as site photographs.

You can freely rotate and manipulate these models in 3D space in a Photoshop document. Access the textures applied to the model surfaces and edit them with the full range of tools in Photoshop CS3 Extended. You can even create 3D models from 2D images, by defining perspective planes in an image with Vanishing Point and then exporting the model to a 3D format.

Due to the scope of this book, we don't discuss 3D features in detail, but you can get step-by-step information by choosing Help➪Photoshop Help.

New Video Layers and Movie Paint

Now with the new video layers and the Animation (Timeline) palette, Photoshop CS3 Extended offers a great new feature for video professionals, Movie Paint. Movie Paint brings the power of Photoshop painting, retouching, and pixel level editing to every frame of a movie file. Using the Animation palette to navigate, you can quickly find and edit any frame of the movie file. Due to the advanced level of this feature, we don't cover the Animation (Timeline) palette in this book.

Comprehensive Image Analysis

Physicians, radiologists, and technicians using Photoshop? Absolutely, thanks to the new selection, measurement, and analysis tools that let them quickly extract and export a wide array of quantitative data from microscopic and radiological images (see Figure 1-5).

**Book IV
Chapter 1**

Photoshop CS3

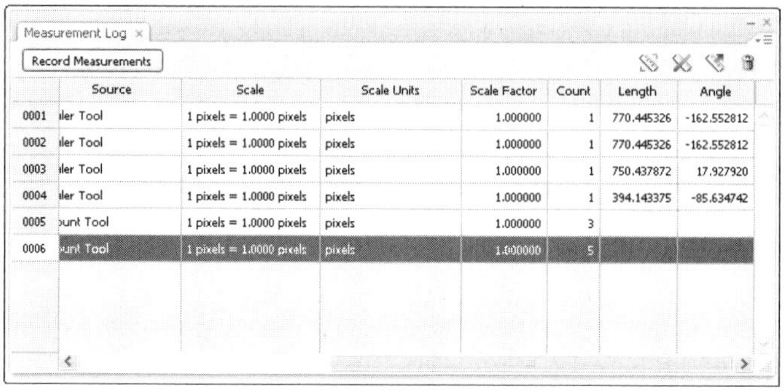

Figure 1-5:
Photoshop
Extended
includes
new
analysis
tools.

Photoshop Extended provides users with tools to count, rulers that can be recorded in a measurement log, and other high-end analysis tools.

Chapter 2: Getting into Photoshop CS3 Basics

*N*avigating the work area in Photoshop can be slightly cumbersome at first, especially if you've never worked in a program that relies so heavily on palettes. In this chapter, we introduce you to Photoshop CS3 and show you how to do basic tasks, such as opening and saving an image. We also introduce you to the work area, show you what the Photoshop CS3 tools are all about, and reveal how to neatly organize and hide palettes.

Getting Started with Photoshop CS3

Unless you use Photoshop as a blank canvas for painting, you may rarely create a new file in Photoshop because you usually have a source image that you start with. This image may have been generated by a scanner, digital camera, or stock image library. You can open existing Photoshop images by choosing File➪Open, selecting the file in the Open dialog box, and then clicking the Open button.

Photoshop can open a multitude of file formats, even if the image was created in another application, such as Illustrator or another image-editing program, but you have to open the image in Photoshop by choosing File➪Open. If you just double-click an image file in a directory (one that wasn't originally created in Photoshop, or from different versions), the image may open only in a preview application.

If you're opening a folder of images that you want to investigate first, choose File➪Browse to open Adobe Bridge, the control center for Adobe Creative Suite. You can use Adobe Bridge to organize, browse, and locate the assets you need to create your content. Adobe Bridge keeps native PSD, AI, INDD, and Adobe PDF files, as well as other Adobe and non-Adobe application files, available for easy access.

Discover Camera RAW

If you haven't discovered the Camera RAW capabilities in Adobe Photoshop, you'll want to give them a try. Camera RAW is a format available for image capture in many cameras. Simply choose the format in your camera's settings as RAW instead of JPEG or TIFF. These raw files are a bit larger than the standard JPEG files, but you capture an enormous amount of data with the image that you can retrieve upon opening. (See www.adobe.com for a complete list of cameras supporting Camera RAW.)

A Camera RAW file contains unprocessed picture data from a digital camera's image sensor, along with information about how the image was captured, such as the camera and lens used, the exposure settings, and white balance setting. When you open the file in Adobe Photoshop CS3, the built-in Camera RAW plug-in interprets the raw file on your computer, making adjustments for image color and tonal scale.

When you shoot JPEG images with your camera, you're locked into the processing done by your camera, but working with Camera RAW files gives you maximum control over your image, such as controlling the white balance, tonal range, contrast, and color saturation, as well as image sharpening. Cameras that can shoot in RAW format have a setting on the camera that changes its capture mode to RAW. Instead of writing a final JPEG, a RAW data file is written, which consists of black-and-white brightness levels from each of the several million pixel sites on the imaging sensor. The actual image hasn't yet been produced, and unless you have specific software, such as the plug-in built into Adobe Photoshop, opening the file can be very difficult, if not impossible.

To open a Camera RAW file, simply choose File⇨Browse. Adobe Bridge opens, and you see several panels, including the Folders, Content, Preview, and Metadata panels. Using the Folders panel, navigate to the location on your computer where you have saved your Camera RAW images; thumbnail previews appear in the Content panel. Think of camera RAW files as your photo negative. You can reprocess the file at any time to achieve the results you want.

If Adobe Photoshop CS3 doesn't open your RAW file, you may need to update your RAW plug-in. (See www.adobe.com for the latest plug-in.) The plug-in should be downloaded and placed in this location in Windows: C:\Program Files\Common Files\Adobe\Plug-Ins\CS3\File Formats, and this location on the Macintosh: Library\Application Support\Adobe\Plug-Ins\CS3\File Formats.

Adobe Bridge is a standalone application that you can access from all applications in the Creative Suite by choosing File⇨Browse or by clicking the Go To Bridge icon in the upper-right corner of the application window. Use the Bridge interface to view your images as thumbnails and look for Metadata information.

Creating a new file

If you're creating a new file, you may be doing so to create a composite of existing files or to start with a blank canvas because you're super creative.

For whatever reason, note that when you choose File➪New, you have a multitude of basic format choices that you can select from the Preset menu. They range from basic sizes and resolutions, such as U.S. Paper or Photo, to other final output such as the Web, Mobile Devices, or Film.

Keep in mind that you're determining not only size but resolution in your new file. If your new file is to contain images from other files, make sure the new file is the same resolution. Otherwise, you may get unexpected size results when cutting and pasting or dragging images into your new file. Choose Image➪Image Size to see the document dimensions.

Saving documents

Save an image file by choosing File➪Save. If you're saving the file for the first time, the Save As dialog box appears. Notice in the Format drop-down list that you have plenty of choices for file formats. The different file formats are discussed in more detail in Chapter 10 of this minibook. You can always play it safe by choosing the Photoshop (PSD) file format. The native Photoshop format supports all features in Photoshop. Choosing some of the other formats may eliminate layers, channels, and other special features.

Many users choose to save a native Photoshop file as a backup to any other file formats. It's especially important to have a backup or original file saved as a native Photoshop file (PSD) as you increase in capabilities and start taking advantage of layers and the other great capabilities of Photoshop.

Getting to Know the Tools

Tools are used to create, select, and manipulate objects in Photoshop CS3. When you open Photoshop, the toolbox appears along the left edge of the workspace (see Figure 2-1). We discuss palettes and the palette well in the upcoming section, "Navigating the Work Area."

In the toolbox, look for the name of the tool to appear in a ToolTip when you hover the cursor over the tool. Following the tool name is a letter in parentheses, which is the keyboard shortcut command that you can use to access that tool. Simply press the Shift key along with the key command you see to access any hidden tools. In other words, pressing P activates the Pen tool, and pressing Shift+P activates the hidden tools under the Pen tool in the order that they appear. When you see a small triangle at the lower-right corner of the tool icon, you know that this tool contains hidden tools.

Figure 2-1:
Photoshop
CS3
workspace
includes the
toolbox,
palettes,
and palette
well.

Table 2-1 lists the Photoshop tools, what each is used for, and in what chapter you can find more about each.

Table 2-1		Photoshop CS Tools	
Button	*Tool*	*What It Does*	*Chapter It's Covered in This Minibook*
	Move (V)	Moves selections or layers	4
	Marquee (M)	Selects image area	4
	Lasso (L)	Makes freehand selections	4
	Quick Selection Tool (New) (W)	Selects similar pixels	4

Button	Tool	What It Does	Chapter It's Covered in This Minibook
	Crop (C)	Crops an image	2
	Slice (K)	Creates HTML slices	n/a
	Spot Healing Brush (J)	Retouches flaws	8
	Brush (B)	Paints foreground color	8
	Clone Stamp (S)	Copies pixel data	8
	History Brush (Y)	Paints from selected state	8
	Eraser (E)	Erases pixels	8
	Gradient (G)	Creates a gradient	8
	Blur (R)	Blurs pixels	8
	Toning (O)	Dodges, burns, saturates	8
	Pen (P)	Creates paths	5
	Type (T)	Creates text	9
	Path Selection (A)	Selects paths	5
	Vector Shape (U)	Creates vector shapes	9

**Book IV
Chapter 2**

Getting into
Photoshop CS3
Basics

(continued)

Table 2-1 *(continued)*

Button	Tool	What It Does	Chapter It's Covered in This Minibook
	Notes (N)	Makes annotations	n/a
	Eyedropper (I)	Samples pixels	8
	Hand (H)	Navigates page	9
	Zoom (Z)	Increases, decreases view	2

Looking for the Magic Wand tool? Click and hold on the Quick Selection tool in the toolbar to access it.

Navigating the Work Area

Getting around in Photoshop isn't much different from getting around in other Adobe applications. All Adobe applications make extensive use of palettes, for example. In the following sections, we cover the highlights on navigating in Photoshop.

Docking and saving palettes

Palettes, palettes everywhere . . . do you really need them all? Maybe not just yet, but as you increase your skill level, you'll take advantage of most (if not all) of the Photoshop palettes. The palettes give you easy access to important functions. Book I, Chapter 3 provides a lot of basic information about using palettes in the Adobe Creative Suite, so check out that chapter if you need a refresher on using palettes. We add only a few things here that are specific to using the palettes in Photoshop.

As you work in Photoshop, keep in mind these two key commands:

✦ Press Tab to switch between hiding and showing the tools and palettes.

✦ Press Shift+Tab to hide the palettes, leaving only the toolbox visible.

On the far right of the Options bar (a toolbar that contains the options for each tool and appears across the top of the work area) is the *palette well,* which helps you organize and manage palettes. The palette well stores, or *docks,* palettes so that you can access them easily. (See Figure 2-1, earlier in this chapter.)

The palette well is available only when using a screen resolution greater than 800 x 600 pixels (a setting of at least 1024 x 768 is recommended). Dock palettes in the palette well by dragging the palette's tab into the palette well; release when the palette well is highlighted.

If you find that you're always using the same palettes, hide the palettes that you don't need and arrange your other palettes on-screen where you want them. Then follow these steps to save that palette configuration:

1. **Choose Window⇨Workspace⇨Save Workspace.**

2. **In the Save Workspace dialog box that appears, name the Workspace and click Save.**

3. **Any time you want the palettes to return to your saved locations, choose Window⇨Workspace⇨*Name of Your Workspace* (where *Name of Your Workspace* is the name you supplied in Step 2).**

Choose Window⇨Workspace⇨Reset Palette Locations to put the palettes back in the same order they were upon the initial installation.

Taking advantage of new workspace features

Photoshop CS3 now has included many saved workspaces that you can take advantage of to streamline workspaces and open the palettes you need for specific tasks. These new features include workspaces for Web Design, Painting and Retouching, and Color and Tonal Correction to name a few.

Increase your work area by turning your palettes into icons, as shown in Figure 2-2. Do so by either right-clicking the tab of a palette and selecting Collapse To Icons or clicking the Auto Collapse gray bar at the top of the palette drawer. Yes, you heard it correctly — the area where the palettes are located is actually a drawer that can be adjusted in or out by clicking and dragging on the vertical pane to the left of the palettes.

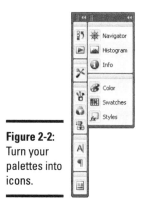

Figure 2-2:
Turn your palettes into icons.

Zooming in to get a better look

What looks fine at one zoom level may actually look very bad at another. You'll find yourself zooming in and out quite often as you work on an image in Photoshop. You can find menu choices for zooming in the View menu; a quicker way to zoom is to use the keyboard commands listed in Table 2-2.

Table 2-2	Zooming and Navigation Keyboard Shortcuts	
Command	*Windows Shortcut*	*Mac Shortcut*
Actual size	Alt+Ctrl+0	⌘+1
Fit in window	Ctrl+0 (zero)	⌘ +0 (zero)
Zoom in	Ctrl++ (plus sign) or Ctrl+Spacebar	⌘ ++ (plus sign) or ⌘ +Spacebar
Zoom out	Ctrl+– (minus) or Alt+Spacebar	⌘ +– (minus) or Option+Spacebar
Hand tool	Spacebar	Spacebar

Here are a few things to keep in mind as you work with the Zoom tool to get a better look at your work:

✦ **100-percent view:** Double-clicking the Zoom tool in the toolbox puts you at 100 percent view. Do this before using filters to see a more realistic result of your changes.

✦ **Zoom marquee:** Drag from the upper left to the lower right of the area you want to zoom to. While dragging, a marquee appears; When you release the mouse button, the marqueed area zooms up to fill the image window. The Zoom marquee gives you much more control than just clicking on the image with the Zoom tool. Zoom back out to see the entire image by pressing Ctrl+0 (Windows) or ⌘ +0 (Mac). It fits the entire image in the viewing area.

✦ **Zoom using the keyboard shortcuts:** If you have a dialog box open and you need to reposition or zoom to a new location on your image, you can use the keyboard commands without exiting the dialog box.

✦ **A new window for a different look:** Choose Window⇨Arrange⇨New Window to create an additional window for your front-most image. This technique is helpful when you want to see the entire image (say, at actual size)or to see the results as a whole, yet zoom in to focus on a small area of the image to do some fine-tuning. The new window is dynamically linked to the original window so that as you make changes, the original and any other new windows created from the original are immediately updated.

✦ **Cycle through images:** Press Ctrl+Tab (Windows) or ⌘ +Tab (Mac) to cycle through open images.

Choosing Your Screen Mode

You have a choice of three screen modes in which to work. Most users start and stay in the default (standard screen mode) until they accidentally end up in another. The four modes are

✦ **Maximized Screen mode** displays a maximized document window that fills all available space between docks and that resizes when dock widths change.

✦ **Standard mode** is the typical view, where you have an image window open but can see your desktop and other images open behind.

✦ **Full-screen mode with menu** view surrounds the image out to the edge of the work area with a neutral gray. This mode not only prevents you from accidentally clicking out of an image and leaving Photoshop, but also from seeing other images behind your working image.

✦ **Full screen mode, no menu** is a favorite with multimedia types. It shows your image surrounded by black and also eliminates the menu items from the top of the window. Press Tab to hide all tools, and you have a very clean work environment.

Cropping an Image

A simple but essential task is to crop your image. *Cropping* means to elimi-nate all that is not important to the composition of your image. Cropping is especially important in Photoshop. Each pixel, no matter what color, takes up the same amount of information, so cropping eliminates unneeded pixels and saves on file size and processing time, so you want to crop your image before you start working on it.

Book IV
Chapter 2

Getting into
Photoshop CS3
Basics

You can crop an image in Photoshop CS3 in two ways:

✦ Use the Crop tool.

✦ Select an area with the Marquee tool and choose Image⇨ Crop.

To crop an image by using the Crop tool, follow these steps:

1. **Press C to access the Crop tool and drag around the area of the image that you want to crop to.**

2. **If you need to adjust the crop area, drag the handles in the crop-bounding area.**

3. **When you're satisfied with the crop bounding area, double-click in the center of the crop area or press the Return or Enter key to crop the image.**

4. **If you want to cancel the crop, press the Esc key.**

Ever scan in an image crooked? When using the Crop tool, if you position the cursor outside any of the handles, a rotate symbol appears. Drag the crop's bounding area to rotate it and line it up as you want it cropped. When you press Return or Enter, the image is straightened out.

Chapter 3: Messing with Mode Matters

In this Chapter
- ✔ Working in black and white
- ✔ Understanding Photoshop image modes

*B*efore diving into Photoshop, you must know what image mode you should be working in and how important color settings are. So no matter whether you're doing a one-color newsletter, a full-color logo, or something in between, this chapter can help you create much better imagery for both Web and print.

Working with Bitmap Images

You may have already discovered that Photoshop works a little differently than most other applications. In order to create those smooth gradations from one color to the next, Photoshop takes advantage of pixels. *Bitmap images* (sometimes called *raster images*) are based on a grid of pixels. The grid is smaller or larger depending on the resolution that you're working in. The number of pixels along the height and width of a bitmap image are called the pixel dimensions of an image, which are measured in pixels per inch (ppi). The more pixels per inch, the more detail in the image.

Unlike *vector graphics* (mathematically created paths), bitmap images can't be scaled without losing detail. (See Figure 3-1 for an example of a bitmap image and a vector graphic.) Generally, it's best to use bitmap images at or close to the size that you need. If you resize a bitmap image, it can become jagged on the edges of sharp objects. On the other hand, you can scale vector graphics and edit them without degrading the sharp edges.

Bitmap   Vector

Figure 3-1:
Bitmap
versus
vector.

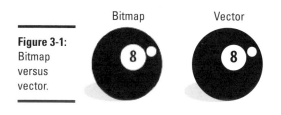

Photoshop has the capability to work on both bitmap and vector art. (See the path line around the vector shape layer and notice that the path isn't pixilated.) It gives you, as a designer, incredible opportunities when combining the two technologies.

For information on changing and adjusting image resolution, see Chapter 6 of this minibook.

Choosing the Correct Photoshop Mode

Choose Image⇨Mode to view the image mode choices you can choose from. Selecting the right one for an image is important because each mode offers different capabilities and results. For example, if you choose the Bitmap mode, you can work only in black and white . . . that's it. No shades of color, not even a gray. Most features are disabled in this Bitmap mode. This is fine if you're working on art for a black-and-white logo, but not for most images. If, instead, you work in the RGB mode, you have full access to Photoshop's capabilities. So read on to see what image mode is best for your needs. When you're ready to make your mode selection, have a file open and choose a selection from Image⇨Mode. You can read descriptions of each image mode in the following sections.

Along with a description of each image mode, we include a figure showing the Channels palette set to that mode. A *channel* is simply the information about color elements in the image. The number of default color channels in an image depends on its color mode. For example, a CMYK image has at least four channels, one each for cyan, magenta, yellow, and black information. Grayscale has one channel. If you understand the printing process, think of each channel representing a plate (color) that, when combined, creates the final image.

Bitmap

Bitmap mode offers little more than the ability to work in black and white. Many tools are unusable, and most menu options are grayed out in this mode. If you're converting an image to bitmap, you must convert it to Grayscale first.

Grayscale

Use Grayscale mode, shown in Figure 3-2, if you're creating black-and-white images with tonal values, specifically for printing to one color. Grayscale mode supports 256 shades of gray in the 8-bit color mode. Photoshop can work with Grayscale in 16-bit mode, which provides more information, but may limit your capabilities when working in Photoshop.

When you convert to Grayscale mode, you get a warning message confirming that you want to discard all color information. If you don't want to see this warning every time you convert an image to grayscale, select the option to not show the dialog box again before you click Discard.

Figure 3-2:
Grayscale supports 256 shades of gray.

Duotone

Use Duotone mode when you're creating a one- to four-color image created from spot colors (solid ink, such as Pantone colors). You can also use the Duotone mode to create Monotones, Tritones, and Quadtones. If you're producing a two-color job, duotones create a beautiful solution to not having full color.

The Pantone Matching color system helps to keep printing inks consistent from one job to the next. By assigning a numbered Pantone color, such as 485 for red, you don't risk one vendor (printer) using fire-engine red, and the next using orange-red for your company logo.

To create a Duotone, follow these steps:

1. **Choose Image➪Mode➪Grayscale.**

2. **Choose Image➪Mode➪Duotone.**

3. **In the Duotone dialog box, choose Duotone from the Type drop-down list.**

Your choices range from Monotone (one-color) up to Quadtone (four-color). Black is automatically assigned as the first ink. But you can change that if you like.

4. **To assign a second ink color, click the white swatch immediately under the black swatch to open the Color Libraries dialog box, as shown in Figure 3-3.**

5. **Now comes the fun part: Type (quickly!) the Pantone or PMS number that you want to access and then click OK.**

   There is no text field for you to enter the number in, so don't look for one. Just type the number while the Color Libraries dialog box is open.

   Try entering **300** for an easy one. That selects PMS 300.

6. **You can already see that you have created a tone curve, but click the Curve button to the left of the ink color to further tweak the colors.**

7. **Click and drag the curve to adjust the black in the shadow areas, perhaps to bring down the color overall; experiment with the results.**

Figure 3-3:
Click the white swatch to open the Color Libraries dialog box.

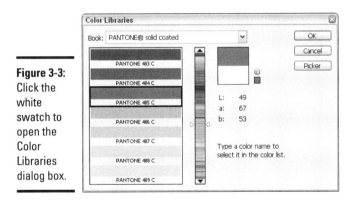

8. **(Optional) If you like your Duotone settings, store them by clicking the Save button.**

   Click the Load button to find your customized presets and to find preset Duotones, Tritones, and Quadtones supplied to you by Adobe.

   Duotone images must be saved in the Photoshop EPS format in order to support the spot colors. If you chose another format, you risk the possibility of converting your colors into a build of CMYK (Cyan, Magenta, Yellow, and Black.)

9. **Click OK when you're finished.**

Index color

You may not work in Index color, but you probably have saved a file in this mode. Index color mode (see Figure 3-4) uses a color look-up table (CLUT) in order to create the image.

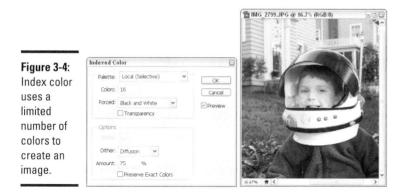

Figure 3-4:
Index color uses a limited number of colors to create an image.

A *color look-up table* contains all the colors that make up your image, like a box of crayons used to create artwork. If you have a box of eight crayons and only those crayons are used to color an image, you have a color look-up table of only eight colors. Of course, your image would look much better if you used the 64-count box of crayons with the sharpener on the back, but those additional colors increase the size of the color look-up table, as well as the file size.

The most colors that can be in index mode are 256. When saving Web images, you often have to define a color table. We discuss the Save For Web feature (which helps you to more accurately save an index color image) in Chapter 10 of this minibook.

Choose Image➪Mode➪Color Table to see the color table making up an image.

RGB

RGB (Red, Green, Blue), shown in Figure 3-5, is the standard format that you work in if you import images from a digital camera or you scan images on a scanner in RGB mode. For complete access to features, RGB is probably the best color mode to work in. If you're working on images for use on the Web, color copiers, desktop color printers, and on-screen presentations, you want to stay in the RGB mode.

If you're having your image printed on a press (for example, if you're having the image professionally printed), it must be separated. Don't convert images to CMYK mode until you're finished with the color correction and you know that your color settings are accurate. A good print service may want the RGB file so that it can do an accurate conversion.

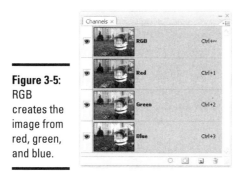

Figure 3-5:
RGB
creates the
image from
red, green,
and blue.

CMYK

CMYK (Cyan, Magenta, Yellow, Black) is the mode used for final separations for the press. Use a good magnifying glass to look closely at anything that has been printed in color, and you may see the CMYK colors that created it. A typical four-color printing press has a plate for each color and runs the colors in the order of cyan, magenta, yellow, and then black.

Don't take converting an image into this mode lightly. You need to make decisions when you convert an image to CMYK, such as where the file is going to be printed and on what paper stock, so that the resulting image is the best it can be. Talk to your print provider for specifications that are important when converting to CMYK mode.

Lab color

Lab (Lightness, A channel, and B channel) is a color mode that many high-end color professionals use because of its wide color range. Using Lab, you can make adjustments to *luminosity* (lightness) without affecting the color. In this mode, you can select and change an L (Lightness or Luminosity) channel without affecting the A channel (green and red) and the B channel (blue and yellow).

Lab mode is also a good mode to use if you're in a color-managed environment and want to easily move from one color system to another with no loss of color.

Some professionals prefer to sharpen their images in LAB mode because they can select just the Lightness channel and choose Filter➪Sharpen➪ Unsharp Mask to sharpen only the gray matter of the image, leaving the color noise-free.

Multichannel

Multichannel is used for many things; sometimes you end up in this mode, and you're not quite sure how. Deleting a channel from an RGB, CMYK, or Lab image automatically converts the image to Multichannel mode. This mode supports multiple spot colors.

Bit depth

You have more functionality in 16-bit and even 32-bit mode. Depending upon your needs, you may spend most of your time in 8-bit mode, which is more than likely all that you need.

Bit depth, also called *pixel depth* or *color depth,* measures how much color information is available to display or print each pixel in an image. Greater bit depth means more available colors and more accurate color representation in the digital image. In Photoshop, this increase in accuracy does also limit some of the features available, so don't use it unless you have a specific request or need for it.

To use 16-bit or 32-bit color mode, you also must have a source to provide you with that information, such as a scanner or camera that offers a choice to scan at 16-bit or 32-bit.

Chapter 4: Creating a Selection

In This Chapter

✓ Discovering the selection tools

✓ Painting selections the easy way

✓ Giving transformed selections a try

✓ Feathering away

✓ Keeping selections for later use

✓ Using the new Vanishing Point feature

*I*t's common to use Photoshop to create compositions that may not actually exist and to retouch images to improve them. What you don't want is obvious retouching or a composition that looks contrived. (The exception is if you intend an image to be humorous, such as putting baby Joey's head on Daddy's body.)

That's where the selection tools come in. In this chapter, you discover several selection methods and how to use the selection tools to make your images look as though you *haven't* retouched or edited them. Even if you're an experienced Photoshop user, this chapter provides a plethora of tips and tricks that can save you time and help make your images look absolutely convincing.

Getting to Know the Selection Tools

You create selections with the selection tools. Think of *selections* as windows in which you can make changes to the pixels. Areas that aren't selected are *masked,* which means that these unselected areas are unaffected by changes, much like when you tape around windows and doors before you paint the walls. In this section, we briefly describe the selection tools and show you how to use them. You must be familiar with these tools in order to do *anything* in Photoshop.

As with all the Photoshop tools, the Options bar across the top of the Photoshop window changes with each selection tool. The keyboard commands you read about in this section exist on the Options bar as buttons.

If you move a selection with the Move tool, pixels move as you drag, leaving a blank spot in the image. To *clone* a selection (that is, to copy and move the selection at the same time), Alt+drag (Windows) or Option+drag (Mac) the selection with the Move tool.

The Marquee tool

The Marquee tool is the main selection tool; by that, we mean that you'll use it most often for creating selections. The exception, of course, is when you have a special situation that calls for a special tool, either the Lasso, Magic Wand tool, or the new Quick Selection tool. Throughout this section, we describe creating (and then deselecting) an active selection area; we also provide you with tips for working with selections.

The Marquee tool includes the Rectangular Marquee (for creating rectangular selections), Elliptical Marquee (for creating round or elliptical selections), and Single Row Marquee or Single Column Marquee tools (for creating a selection of a single row or column of pixels). You can access these other Marquee tools by holding down on the default, Rectangle Marquee tool.

To create a selection, select one of the Marquee tools (remember you can press M) and then drag anywhere on your image. When you release the mouse button, you create an active selection area. When you're working on an active selection area, whatever effects you choose are applied to the whole selection. To deselect an area, you have three choices:

✦ Choose Select➪Deselect.

✦ Press Ctrl+D (Windows) or ⌘+D (Mac).

✦ While using a selection tool, click outside the selection area.

How you make a selection is important because it determines how realistic your edits appear on the image. You can use the following tips and tricks when creating both rectangular and elliptical selections:

✦ Add to a selection by holding down the Shift key; drag to create a second selection that intersects the original selection (see the left image in Figure 4-1). The two selections become one big selection.

✦ Delete from an existing selection by holding the Alt (Windows) or Option (Mac) key and then drag to create a second selection that intersects the original selection where you want to take away from the original selection (on the right in Figure 4-1).

✦ Constrain a rectangle or ellipse to a square or circle by Shift+dragging; make sure that you release the mouse button before you release the

Shift key. Holding down the Shift key makes a square or circle only when there are no other selections. (Otherwise, it adds to the selection.)

✦ Make the selection from the center by Alt+dragging (Windows) or Option+dragging (Mac); make sure that you release the mouse button before the Alt (Windows) or Option (Mac) key.

✦ Create a square or circle from the center out by Alt+Shift+dragging (Windows) or Option+Shift+dragging (Mac). Again, make sure that you always release the mouse button before the modifier keys.

✦ When making a selection, hold down the spacebar before releasing the mouse button to drag the selection to another location.

Figure 4-1:
You can add and delete from selections.

Fixed size

If you've created an effect that you particularly like — say, changing a block of color in your image — and you'd like to apply it multiple times throughout an image, you can do so. To make the exact same selection multiple times, follow these steps:

1. **With the Marquee tool selected, select Fixed Size from the Style drop-down list on the Options bar.**

You can also select Fixed Ratio from the Style drop-down list to create a proportionally correct selection, but not fixed to an exact size.

2. On the Options bar, type the Width and Height values into the appropriate text fields.

You can change ruler increments by choosing Edit⇨Preferences⇨Units And Rulers (Windows) or Photoshop⇨Preferences⇨Units And Rulers (Mac).

3. Click the image.

A selection sized to your values appears.

4. With the selection tool, drag the selection to the location that you want selected.

Shift+drag a selection to keep it aligned to a straight, 45-degree, or 90-degree angle.

Floating and nonfloating selections

As a default, when you're using a selection tool, such as the Marquee tool, your selections are *floating,* which means that you can drag them to another location without affecting the underlying pixels. You know that your selection is floating by the little rectangle that appears on your cursor (see the left image in Figure 4-2).

If you want to, however, you can move the underlying pixels. With the selection tool of your choice, just hold down the Ctrl (Windows) or ⌘ (Mac) key to temporarily access the Move tool; the cursor changes to a pointer with scissors, denoting that your selection is nonfloating. Now, when you drag, the pixel data comes with the selection (as shown on the right in Figure 4-2).

Hold down Alt+Ctrl (Windows) or Option+⌘ (Mac) while using a selection tool and drag to clone (copy) pixels from one location to another. Add the Shift key, and the cloned copy is constrained to a straight, 45-degree, or 90-degree angle.

Figure 4-2:
The Float icon is used on the left, and the Move icon is used on the right.

The Lasso tool

Use the Lasso tool for *freeform selections* (selections of an irregular shape). To use the Lasso tool, just drag and create a path surrounding the area to be selected. If you don't return to your start point to close the selection before you release the mouse button, Photoshop completes the path by finding the most direct route back to your starting point.

Just like with the Marquee tool, you can press the Shift key to add to a lasso selection and press the Alt (Windows) or Option (Mac) to delete from a lasso selection.

Hold down on the Lasso tool to show the hidden Lasso tools, the Polygonal Lasso and the Magnetic Lasso tool. Use the Polygonal Lasso tool by clicking on a start point and then clicking and releasing from point to point until you come back to close the selection. Use the Magnetic Lasso tool by clicking to create a starting point and then hovering the cursor near an edge in your image. The Magnetic Lasso tool is magnetically attracted to edges; as you move your cursor near an edge, the Magnetic Lasso tool creates a selection along that edge. Click to manually set points in the selection; when you get back to the starting point, click to close the selection.

You may find that the Polygonal Lasso and the Magnetic Lasso tools don't make as nice of a selection as you'd like. Take a look at the upcoming section, "Painting with the Quick Mask tool," for tips on making finer selections.

The new Quick Selection tool

The Quick Selection tool lets you quickly "paint" a selection using a round brush tip of adjustable size. Click and drag and watch as the selection expands outward and automatically follows defined edges in the image. A Refine Edge command lets you improve the quality of the selection edges and visualize the selection in different ways for easy editing.

Follow these steps to find out how you can take advantage of this new tool:

1. **Start by choosing File⇨Open and opening a file named Sunflower.psd that already exists in your Photoshop CS3 Samples folder.**

You can find the file in the following location on the Windows OS: C:\Program Files\Adobe\Adobe Photoshop CS3\Samples and on the Mac OS at: Applications\Adobe\Adobe Photoshop CS3\Samples.

2. **Select the Quick Selection tool.**

3. **Position the cursor over the yellow petals of the sunflower and notice the brush size displayed with the cursor; click and drag to start painting the selection.**

   You can adjust the size of the painting selection by pressing [to make the brush size smaller or] to make the brush size larger.

4. **Using the Add To Selection or Subtract From Selection buttons in the toolbar options, you can paint more of the selection or deselect active areas (see Figure 4-3).**

Figure 4-3: The Quick Selection tool allows you to paint your selection.

The Magic Wand tool

The Magic Wand tool is particularly helpful when you're working on an image of high contrast or with a limited number of colors. This tool selects individual pixels of similar shades and colors. Select the Magic Wand tool, click anywhere on an image, and hope for the best — the Magic Wand tool isn't magic at all. You decide how successful this tool is. What we mean by that is that you control how closely matched each pixel must be in order for the Magic Wand tool to include it in the selection. You do so by setting the tolerance on the Options bar.

When you have the Magic Wand tool selected, a Tolerance text field appears on the Options bar. As a default, the tolerance is set to 32. When you click with a setting of 32, the Magic Wand tool selects all pixels within 32 shades (steps) of the color that you clicked. If it didn't select as much as you want, increase the value in the Tolerance text field (all the way up to 255). The amount that you enter really varies with each individual selection. If you're selecting white napkins on an off-white tablecloth, you can set as low as 5 so that the selection doesn't leak into other areas. For colored fabric with lots of tonal values, you might increase the tolerance to 150.

Don't fret if you miss the entire selection when using the Magic Wand tool. Hold down the Shift key and click in the missed areas. If it selects too much, choose Edit⇨Undo (Step Backwards) or press Ctrl+Z (Windows) or ⌘+Z (Mac), reduce the value in the Tolerance text field, and try again.

Manipulating Selections

After you master creating selections, you'll find that working with the selections — painting, transforming, and feathering them — can be easy and fun.

Painting with the Quick Mask tool

If you have fuzzy selections (fur, hair, or leaves, for example) or you're having difficulty using the selection tools, the Quick Mask tool can be a huge help because it allows you to paint your selection uniformly in one fell swoop.

To enter into Quick Mask mode, create a selection and then press Q. (Pressing Q again exits you from Quick Mask mode.) You can also click the Quick Mask button at the bottom of the toolbox. If you have a printing background, you'll notice that the Quick Mask mode, set at its default color (red), resembles something that you may want to forget: rubylith and amberlith. (Remember slicing up those lovely films with Exacto blades before computer masking came along?) In Quick Mask mode, Photoshop shows your image as it appears through the mask. The clear part is selected; what's covered in the mask isn't selected.

To create and implement a quick mask, follow these steps:

1. **Press Q to enter Quick Mask mode.**

2. **Press D to change the foreground and background color boxes the default colors of black and white.**

3. **Select the Brush tool and start painting with black in the clear area of the image in Quick Mask mode.**

   It doesn't have to be pretty; just get a stroke or two in there.

4. **Press Q to return to the Selection mode.**

   You're now out of Quick Mask mode. Notice that where you painted with black (it turned red in the Quick Mask mode), the pixels are no longer selected.

5. **Press Q again to re-enter the Quick Mask mode and then press X.**

   This step switches the foreground and background colors (giving you white in the foreground, black in the background).

6. **Using the Brush tool, paint several white strokes in the red mask area.**

   The white strokes turn clear in the Quick Mask mode.

7. **Press Q to return to the Selection mode.**

   Where you painted white in the Quick Mask mode is now selected.

When in Quick Mask mode, you can paint white over areas you want selected and black over areas that you don't want selected. When painting in the Quick Mask mode, increase the brush size by pressing the] key. Decrease the brush size by pressing the [key.

In the Selection mode, your selection seems to have a hard edge; you can soften those hard edges by using a softer brush in the Quick Mask mode. To make a brush softer, press Shift+[and press Shift+] to make a brush harder.

Because the Quick Mask mode makes selections based on the mask's values, you can create a mask by selecting the Gradient tool and dragging it across the image in Quick Mask mode. When you exit Quick Mask mode, it looks as though there is a straight-line selection, but actually the selection transitions as your gradient did. Choose any filter from the Filters menu and notice how the filter transitions into the untouched part of the image to which we applied the new and improved Graphic Pen filter.

If you're working in Quick Mask mode, choose Window➪Channels to see that what you're working on is a temporary alpha channel. See the later section, "Saving Selections," for more about alpha channels.

Transforming selections

Don't deselect and start over again if you can just nudge or resize your selection a bit. You can scale, rotate, and even distort an existing selection. Follow these steps to transform a selection:

1. **Create a selection and then choose Select↩Transform Selection.**

You can use the bounding box to resize and rotate your selection.

- Drag the handles to make the selection larger or smaller. Drag a corner handle to adjust width and height simultaneously. Shift+drag a corner handle to size proportionally.

- Position the cursor outside of the bounding box to see the Rotate icon; drag when it appears to rotate the selection. Shift+drag to constrain to straight, 45-degree, or 90-degree angles.

- Ctrl+drag (Windows) or ⌘+drag (Mac) a corner point to distort the selection, as shown in Figure 4-4.

2. **Press Return or Enter or double-click in the center of the selection area to confirm the transformation; press Esc to release the transformation and return to the original selection.**

Figure 4-4:
Distort,
resize, and
rotate a
selection
using the
Transform
Selection
feature.

Feathering

Knowing how to retouch an image means little if you don't know how to make it discreet. If you boost up the color using curves to the CEO's face, do you want it to appear like a pancake has been attached to his cheek? Of course not — that isn't discreet at all (or very wise). That's where feathering comes in. *Feathering* a selection blurs its edges, so as to create a natural-looking transition between the selection and the background of the image.

To feather an image, follow these steps:

1. **Create a selection.**

   For the nonfeathered image shown on top in Figure 4-6, we used the Elliptical Marquee tool to make a selection. We then copied the selection, created a new, blank image, and pasted the selection into the new image.

To create the feathered image on the bottom in Figure 4-6, we used the Elliptical Marquee tool to select the same area on the original image and went on to Step 2.

2. **Choose Select⇨Modify⇨Feather.**

3. **In the Feather dialog box that appears, type a value in the Feather Radius text field and then click OK.**

   For example, we entered **20** in the Feather Radius text field. (We then copied the selection, created a new image, and pasted the feathered selection into the new image to create the image on the bottom of Figure 4-5.) Voilà! The edges of the image are softened over a 20-pixel area, as shown on the bottom of Figure 4-5. This technique is also referred to as a *vignette* in the printing industry.

The results of the feathering depend upon the resolution of the image. A feather of 20 pixels in a 72-ppi (pixels per inch) image will be a much larger area than a feather of 20 pixels in a 300-ppi image. Typical amounts for a nice vignette on an edge of an image would be 20 to 50 pixels. Experiment with your images to find what works best for you.

This feathering effect created a nice soft edge to your image, but it's also useful when retouching images:

1. **Using any selection method, create a selection around a part of an image that you want to lighten.**

2. **Choose Select⇨Modify⇨Feather; in the Feather dialog box that appears, enter 25 in the Feather Radius text field and click OK.**

   If you get an error message stating, No Pixels are more than 50% selected, click OK and create a larger selection.

3. **Choose Image⇨Adjustments⇨Curves.**

4. **Click in the center of the curve to add an anchor point and drag up to lighten the image.**

   This step lightens the midtones of the image.

Notice how the lightening fades out so that there is no definite edge to the correction. You can have more fun like this in Chapter 7 of this minibook, where we cover color correction.

Figure 4-5:
The top
image
doesn't
have
feathering,
while the
second has
feathering
applied.

Saving Selections

The term *alpha channel* sounds pretty complicated, but it's simply a saved selection. Depending upon the mode you're in, you already have several channels to contend with. A selection is just an extra channel that you can call on at any time.

To create an alpha channel, follow these steps:

1. **Create a selection that you want to save.**

2. **Choose Select⇨Save Selection.**

3. **Name the Selection and click OK.**

In the Channels palette is an additional named channel that contains your selection.

To load a saved selection, follow these steps:

1. **Choose Select⇨Load Selection.**

The Load Selection dialog box appears.

2. **Select your named channel from the Channel drop-down list.**

If you have an active selection and then choose to load a selection, you have additional options. You can do the following with an active selection when loading a channel by selecting one of the following options:

• **New Selection:** Eliminate the existing selection and create a new selection based upon the channel you select.

• **Add To Selection:** Add the channel to the existing selection.

• **Subtract From Selection:** Subtract the channel from the existing selection.

• **Intersect With Selection:** Intersect the channel with the existing selection.

3. **Click OK.**

Other Adobe applications, such as InDesign, Illustrator, Premiere, and After Effects, can also recognize alpha channels.

Using the New Vanishing Point Feature

This incredible new feature lets you preserve correct perspective in edits of images that contain perspective planes, such as the sides of a building. You

can do so much with this feature, and we provide you with a simple intro-
duction. Try experimenting with multiple planes and copying and pasting
items into the Vanishing Point window for even more effects. Follow these
steps:

1. Open a file that you want to apply a perspective filter to.

For this example, we used the file named Vanishing Point.psd. You can
find the file in Windows OS at C:\Program Files\Adobe\Adobe Photoshop
CS3\Samples and on the Mac OS at Applications\Adobe\Adobe
Photoshop CS3\Samples.

**2. Create a new blank layer by clicking the Create A New Layer button at
the bottom of the Layers palette.**

If you create a new layer each time you use Vanishing Point, the results
appear on a separate, editable layer. You can then use layer features,
such as opacity, layer styles, and blending modes. Putting the Vanishing
Point results in a separate layer also preserves your original image.

3. Choose Filter⇨Vanishing Point.

A separate Vanishing Point window appears. If you receive an error message about an existing plane, click OK.

If you're using a sample file from Photoshop, it may or may not have the
plane at release time. To help you understand this feature better, you
should delete the existing plane by pressing the Delete or Backspace key.

**4. Select the Create Plane tool and define the four corners nodes of the
plane surface.**

Try to use objects in the image to help create the plane.

After the four corner nodes of the plane are created, the tool automatically is switched to the Edit Plane tool.

5. Select and drag the corner nodes to make an accurate plane.

The plane grid should appear blue, not yellow or red, if it's accurate.

After creating the plane, you can move, scale, or reshape the plane. Keep
in mind that your results depend on how accurately the plane lines up
with perspective of the image.

You can use your first Vanishing Point session to simply creating perspective planes and then click OK. The planes appear in subsequent
Vanishing Point sessions when you choose Filter⇨Vanishing Point.
Saving perspective planes is especially useful if you plan to copy and
paste an image into Vanishing Point and need to have a ready-made
plane to target.

6. **Choose the Stamp tool in the Vanishing Point window and then choose On from the Heal drop-down menu in the options bar.**

   You're going to love where this is going. In the example, we simply clone the blue broom, but it should get your brains working about all the ways that you can apply this greatly improved feature.

7. **With the Stamp tool still selected, cross over the middle part of the broom and Alt+click (Windows) or Option+Click (Mac) to define it as the source that is to be cloned.**

8. **Without clicking, move toward the back of the perspective plane and click and drag to reproduce the cloned part of the image, in this case the broom.**

   Notice that it's cloned as a smaller version, in the correct perspective for its new location.

9. **Start from Step 7 and clone the broom in front of the dog or clone any region of an image up closer to the front of the perspective pane.**

   The cloned region is now cloned as a larger version of itself.

   You can use the Marquee tool options (Feather, Opacity, Heal, and Move Mode) at any time, either before or after making the selection. When you move the Marquee tool, the Stamp tool, or the Brush tool into a plane, the bounding box is highlighted, indicating that the plane is active.

10. **Click OK.**

    To preserve the perspective plane information in an image, save your document in PSD, TIFF, or JPEG format.

Chapter 5: Using the Photoshop Pen Tool

In this Chapter

✔ **Putting shape layers to work**

✔ **Using a path as a selection**

✔ **Creating clipping paths**

The Pen tool is the ultimate method to make precise selections. You can also use it to create vector shapes and clipping paths (silhouettes). In this chapter, you discover how to take advantage of this super multitasking tool. This chapter also shows you how to apply paths made with the Pen tool as shapes, selections, and clipping paths. If you're interested in the fundamentals of creating paths with the Pen tool in Illustrator, check out Book III, Chapter 5, where we cover the Pen tool in more detail.

We recommend that you use the Pen tool as much as you can to truly master its capabilities. If you don't use it on a regular basis, it will seem awkward, but it does get easier! Knowing how to effectively use the Pen tool puts you a grade above the average Photoshop user, and the quality of your selections will show it. Read Chapter 9 of this minibook to find out how to use the Pen tool to create layer masks and adjustment layers.

Using Shape Layers

As a default, when you start creating with the Pen tool, Photoshop automatically creates a *shape layer,* which is useful for adding additional elements, but is frustrating if you're attempting to create just a path with the Pen tool. Select the Pen tool and note the default setting on the left side of the Options bar. You can choose from the following options:

✦ **Shape layers:** Creates a new shape layer, a filled layer that contains your vector path.

✦ **Paths:** Creates a path only; no layer is created.

✦ **Fill Pixels:** Creates pixels directly on the image. No editable path or layer is created. This option may not be useful to new users, but some existing users prefer to use this method because it's the only way to access the Line tool from previous versions.

Shape layers can be very useful when the goal of your design is to seam-lessly integrate vector shapes and pixel data. A shape layer can contain vector shapes that you can then modify with the same features of any other layer. You can adjust the opacity of the shape layer, change the blending mode, and even apply layer effects to add drop shadows and dimension. Find out how to do this in Chapter 9 of this minibook.

Create a shape layer using any of these methods:

✦ **Create a shape with the Pen tool.** With the Pen tool, you can create interesting custom shapes and even store them for future use. We show you how in the following section.

✦ **Use one of the Vector Shape tools shown in Figure 5-1.** Vector shapes are premade shapes (you can even create your own!) that you can create by dragging on your image area with a shape tool.

✦ **Import a shape from Illustrator.** Choose File⇨Place to import an Illustrator file as a shape layer or path into Photoshop.

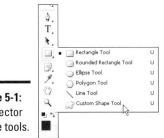

Figure 5-1:
The Vector Shape tools.

Creating and using a custom shape

Perhaps you like the wave kind of shape (see Figure 5-2) that has been crop-ping up in design pieces all over the place.

Figure 5-2:
A custom wave shape integrated with an image in Photoshop.

Copy and paste shapes right from Illustrator CS3 to Photoshop CS3. Simply select your shape in Adobe Illustrator and choose Edit➪Copy, then switch to the Photoshop application, and with a document open, choose Edit➪Paste.

You can create a wavy shape like that, too. With an image or blank document open, just follow these steps:

1. **Click and drag with the Pen tool to create a wavy shape.**

Don't worry about the size of the shape. The shape is vector, so you can scale it up or down to whatever size you need without worrying about making jagged edges. Just make sure that you close the shape (return back to the original point with the end point).

As you create the shape, it fills in with your foreground color. Try to ignore it if you can; the next section shows you how to change the fill color, and Chapter 8 of this minibook covers how to change it to a transparent fill.

2. **With the shape still selected, choose Edit➪Define Custom Shape, name the shape, and click OK.**

After you have saved your custom shape, you can recreate it at any time. If you don't like the shape, choose Windows➪ Layers to open the Layers palette and then drag the shape layer you just created to the Trash icon in the lower-right corner of the palette. If you'd like to experiment with your custom shape now, continue with these steps.

3. **Click and hold on the Rectangle tool to access the other hidden vector tools; select the last tool, the Custom Shape Tool.**

When the Custom Shape tool is selected, a Shape drop-down menu appears on the Options bar at the top of the screen, as shown in Figure 5-3.

You have lots of custom shapes to choose from, including the one you've just created. If you just saved a shape, yours is in the last square; you have to scroll down to select it.

4. **Select your custom shape; click and drag in the image area to create your shape.**

You can make it any size that you want.

5. **To change the shape's size, choose Edit➪Free Transform Path, press Ctrl+T (Windows) or ⌘+T (Mac), or grab a bounding box handle and drag.**

Shift+drag a corner handle to keep the shape proportional as you resize it.

Figure 5-3:
A Shape drop-down menu appears in the Vector Shape options toolbar when the Custom Shape tool is active.

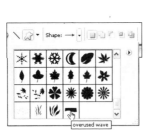

 Because a shape is created on its own layer, you can experiment with different levels of transparency and blending modes in the Layers palette. Figure 5-4 shows shapes that are partially transparent. Discover lots of other features you can use with shape layers in Chapter 9 of this minibook.

Figure 5-4:
Experiment with blending modes and opacity changes on shape layers.

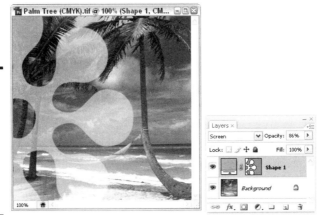

Changing the color of the shape

When you create a shape with a shape tool, the shape takes the color of your present foreground color. To change the color of an existing shape, open the Layers palette by choosing Window⇨Layers; notice that the Vector Shape tool creates a new layer for every shape you make. Creating a new layer is a benefit when it comes to creating special effects because the shape layer is independent of the rest of your image. (Read more about using layers in Chapter 9 of this minibook.)

To change a shape's color, double-click the color thumbnail, on the left in the shape layer. The Color Picker appears, as shown in Figure 5-5. To select a new color, drag the Hue slider up or down or click in the large color pane to select a color with the saturation and lightness that you want to use. Click OK when you're done.

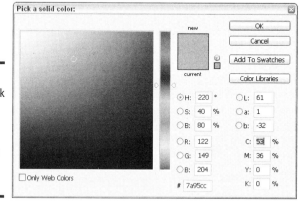

Figure 5-5: Double-click the color Thumbnail on the shape layer to select a new color.

Editing a shape

Like Adobe Illustrator, Photoshop provides both a Path Selection tool and a Direct Selection tool. The Direct Selection tool is hidden under the Path Selection tool. To move an entire shape on a layer, choose the Path Selection tool and drag the shape.

To edit the shape, deselect the shape (while using the Path Selection or Direct Selection tool, click outside the shape). Then select the Direct Selection tool. With the Direct Selection tool, click individual anchor points and handles to edit and fine-tune the shape, as shown in Figure 5-6.

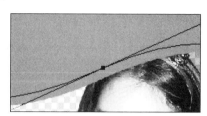

Figure 5-6: Edit individual anchor points with the Direct Selection tool.

Removing a shape layer

Because the Pen tool now has multiple options, you may find yourself unexpectedly creating a shape layer. Delete a shape layer by dragging the layer thumbnail to the Trash icon in the lower-right corner of the Layers palette.

If you want to keep your path but throw away the shape layer, choose Window➪Paths. Then drag the shape vector mask to the New Path icon, as shown in Figure 5-7, which creates a saved path. Now you can throw away the shape layer.

Figure 5-7:
Save your path by dragging the shape path to the Create New Path icon before throwing away the shape layer.

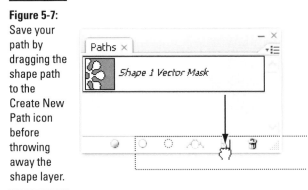

Using a Path as a Selection

You can use the Pen tool to create precise selections that would be difficult to create with other selection methods. The Pen tool produces clean edges that print well and can be edited using the Direct Selection tool. Before using the Pen tool, make sure that you click the Paths button on the Options bar.

To use a path as a selection (which is extremely helpful when you're trying to make a precise selection), follow these steps:

1. **Open any file, or create a new blank file.**

2. **Using the Pen tool (make sure that the Paths button is selected on the Options bar or else you will create a Shape layer!), click to place anchor points; drag to create a curved path around the image area that you want selected; and completely close the path by returning to the start point (see Figure 5-8).**

   Use the techniques that we discuss in Book III, Chapter 4 to perform this step. A circle will appear before you click to close the path.

Figure 5-8:
Make sure
that you
select the
Paths
button to
create only
the pen
path, not a
shape layer.

3. Choose Window⇨Paths.

In the Paths palette, you can create new and activate existing paths,
apply a stroke, or turn paths into selections by clicking the icons at the
bottom of the palette (see Figure 5-9).

Figure 5-9:
The Paths
palette and
its options.

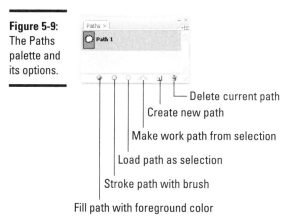

—— Delete current path

Create new path

Make work path from selection

Load path as selection

Stroke path with brush

Fill path with foreground color

4. Click the Load Path As Selection icon.

The path is converted into a selection.

Use this quick and easy method for turning an existing path into a selection:
Ctrl+click (Windows) or ⌘+click (Mac) the path thumbnail in the Paths
palette.

Clipping Paths

If you want to create a beautiful silhouette that transfers well to other applications for text wrapping (see Figure 5-10), create a clipping path.

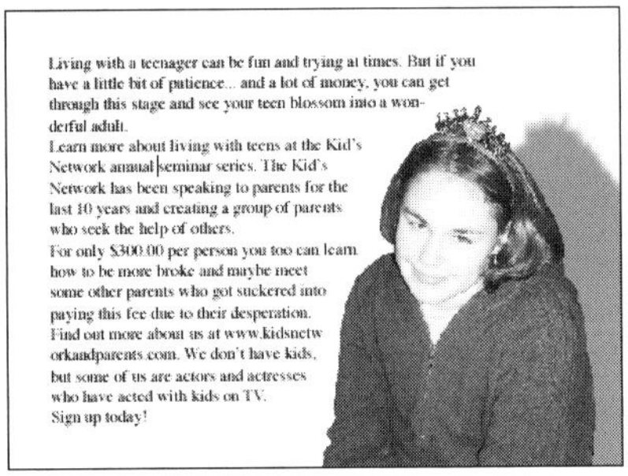

Living with a teenager can be fun and trying at times. But if you have a little bit of patience... and a lot of money, you can get through this stage and see your teen blossom into a wonderful adult.
Learn more about living with teens at the Kid's Network annual seminar series. The Kid's Network has been speaking to parents for the last 10 years and creating a group of parents who seek the help of others.
For only $300.00 per person you too can learn how to be more broke and maybe meet some other parents who got suckered into paying this fee due to their desperation.
Find out more about us at www.kidsnetworkandparents.com. We don't have kids, but some of us are actors and actresses who have acted with kids on TV.
Sign up today!

Creating a clipping path is easy when you have a good path! Just follow these steps:

1. **Use the Pen tool to create a path around the image area that is to be the silhouette.**

2. **In the Paths palette, choose Save Path from the palette menu (click the triangle in the upper-right corner of the palette to access this menu), as shown in Figure 5-11, and then name the path.**

(If Save Path isn't an option, your path has already been saved; skip to Step 3.)

3. **From the same palette menu, choose Clipping Path.**

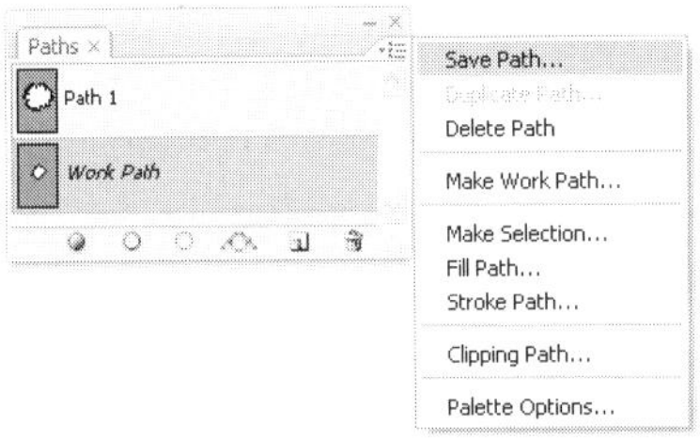

Figure 5-11:
Convert
your work
path to a
saved path.

Paths ×
Path 1
Work Path

Save Path...
Duplicate Path...
Delete Path

Make Work Path...

Make Selection...
Fill Path...
Stroke Path...

Clipping Path...

Palette Options...

4. **In the Clipping Paths dialog box, choose your path from the drop-down list if it's not already selected; click OK.**

Leave the Flatness Device Pixels text field blank unless you have a need to change it. The flatness value determines how many device pixels are used to create your silhouette. The higher the amount, the less points are created, thereby allowing for faster processing time. This speed does come at a cost, though; set the flatness value too high, and you may see (you'd have to look really close) straight edges instead of curved edges.

5. **Choose File➪Save As and in the Format drop-down list, select Photoshop EPS; in the EPS Options dialog box that appears, accept the defaults and click OK.**

   If you get PostScript errors when printing, choose Clipping Path from the palette menu and up the value to 2 pixels in the Flatness Device Pixels text field. Keep returning to this text field and upping the value until the file prints, or give up and try printing your document with another printer.

   If you're placing this file in other Adobe applications, such as InDesign, you don't need to save the file as EPS; you can leave it as a Photoshop (.psd) file.

Chapter 6: Thinking about Resolution Basics

In This Chapter

✔ Understanding resolution basics

✔ Adjusting file size

✔ Applying the Unsharp Mask filter to an image

Something as important as getting the right resolution for your images deserves its own chapter, but fortunately, the topic isn't all that complex. In this chapter, you discover the necessary resolution for various uses of Photoshop imagery (from printing a high-resolution graphic to e-mailing a picture of your kids to Mom), how to properly increase the resolution, and how to adjust image size.

Having the proper resolution is important to the final outcome of your image, especially if you plan to print that image. Combine the information here with using the correction tools that we show you in the next chapter, and you should be ready to roll with great imagery.

Creating Images for Print

To see and make changes to the present size and resolution of an image in Photoshop, choose Image⇨Image Size. The Image Size dialog box appears.

The Width and Height text fields in the Pixel Dimensions area of the Image Size dialog box are used for on-screen resizing, such as for the Web and e-mail. The Width and Height text fields in the Document Size area show the size at which the image will print. The Resolution text field determines the resolution of the printed image; a higher value means a smaller, more finely detailed printed image.

Before you decide upon a resolution, you should understand what some of the resolution jargon means:

✦ **dpi (dots per inch):** The resolution of an image when printed.

✦ **lpi (lines per inch):** The varying dot pattern that printers and presses use to create images (see Figure 6-1). This dot pattern is referred to as the lpi, even though it represents rows of dots. The higher the lpi, the finer the detail, and the less of the dot pattern or line screen you see.

✦ **Dot gain:** The spread of ink as it's applied to paper. Certain types of paper will wick a dot of ink farther than others. For example, newsprint has a high dot gain and typically prints at 85 lpi; a coated stock paper has a lower dot gain and can be printed at 133–150 lpi and even higher.

Human eyes typically can't detect a dot pattern in a printed image at 133 dpi or higher.

Figure 6-1:
The dot pattern used to print images is referred to as lpi (lines per inch).

Deciding the resolution or dpi of an image requires backward planning. If you want to create the best possible image, you should know where it will print *before* deciding the resolution. Communicate with your printer service if the image is going to press. If you're sending your image to a high-speed copier, you can estimate that it will handle 100 lpi; a desktop printer will handle 85 lpi to 100 lpi.

The resolution formula

When creating an image for print, keep this formula in mind:

2 x lpi = dpi (dots per inch)

This formula means that if your image is going to press using 150 lpi, have your image at 300 dpi. To save space, many designers use 1.5 x lpi and get pretty much the same results; you can decide which works best for you.

Changing the resolution

Using the Image Size dialog box is only one way that you can control the resolution in Photoshop. Even though you can increase the resolution, do so sparingly and avoid it if you can. The exception is when you have an image that is large in dimension size but low in resolution, like those that you typically get from a digital camera. You may have a top-of-the-line digital camera that produces 72 dpi images, but at that resolution, the pictures are 28 x 21 inches (or larger)!

To increase the resolution of an image without sacrificing quality:

1. Choose Image⇨Image Size.

The Image Size dialog box appears.

2. Deselect the Resample Image check box.

This way, Photoshop doesn't add additional pixels.

3. Enter the desired resolution in the Resolution text field.

Photoshop keeps the pixel size (the size of the image on screen) the same, but the document size (the size of the image when printed) decreases when you enter a higher resolution.

4. If the image isn't the size that you need it to be, select the Resample Image check box and type the size in the Width and Height text fields in the Document Size section.

Note that it's best to reduce the size of a bitmap image, such as a digital photo, rather than increase it.

You can also deselect the Resample Image check box and essentially play a game of give and take to see what the resolution will be when you enter the size you want your image printed at in the Width and Height text fields in the Document Size area.

Images can typically be scaled from 50 to 120 percent before looking jagged (to scale by a percentage, select Percent from the drop-down lists beside the Width and Height text fields). Keep this in mind when placing and resizing your images in a page layout application, such as InDesign.

5. Click OK when you're finished; double-click the Zoom tool in the toolbox to see the image at actual size on-screen.

To increase the resolution *without* changing the image size, follow these steps. (This situation isn't perfect because pixels that don't presently exist are created by Photoshop and may not be totally accurate. Photoshop tries to give you the best image, but you may have some loss of detail.)

1. Choose Image⇨Image Size.

2. When the Image Size dialog box appears, make sure that the Resample Image check box is selected.

Note that Bicubic is selected in the method drop-down list. This method is the best, but slowest, way to reinterpret pixels when you resize an image. Using this method, Photoshop essentially looks at all the pixels and takes a good guess as to how the newly created pixels should look, based upon surrounding pixels.

3. **Enter the resolution that you need in the Resolution text field, click OK, and then double-click the Zoom tool to see the image at actual size.**

Determining the Resolution for Web Images

Did you ever have somebody e-mail you an image, and, after spending 10 minutes downloading it, you discover that the image is so huge that all you can see on the monitor is your nephew's left eye? Many people are under the misconception that if an image is 72 dpi, it's ready for the Web. Actually, pixel dimension is all that matters for Web viewing of images; this section helps you make sense of this.

Most people view Web pages in their browser windows in an area of about 640 x 480 pixels. You can use this figure as a basis for any images you create for the Web, whether the viewer is using a 14-inch or a 21-inch monitor. (Remember, those people who have large monitors set to high screen resolutions don't necessarily want a Web page taking up the whole screen!) If you're creating images for a Web page or to attach to an e-mail message, you may want to pick a standard size to design by, such as 600 x 400 pixels at 72 dpi.

To use the Image Size dialog box to determine the resolution and size for on-screen images, follow these steps:

1. **Have an image open and choose Image⇨Image Size.**

   The Image Size dialog box appears.

2. **To make the image take up half the width of a typical browser window, type 300 (half of 600) in the top Width text field.**

   If a little chain link is visible to the right, the Constrain Proportions check box is selected, and Photoshop automatically determines the height from the width that you entered.

3. **Click OK and double-click the Zoom tool to see the image at actual size on-screen.**

   That's it! It doesn't matter whether your image is 3,000 or 30 pixels wide, as long as you enter the correct dimensions in the Pixel Dimension area, the image works beautifully.

Applying the Unsharp Mask Filter to an Image

When you resample an image in Photoshop, it can become blurry. A good practice is to apply the Unsharp Mask filter. This feature sharpens the image based upon levels of contrast, while keeping the areas that don't have contrasting pixels smooth. You do have to set up this feature correctly to get good results. Here is the down-and-dirty method of using the Unsharp Mask filter:

1. **Choose View⇨Actual Pixels or double-click the Zoom tool.**

   When you're using a filter, you want to view your image at actual size to best see the effect.

2. **Choose Filter⇨Sharpen⇨Unsharp Mask.**

   In the Unsharp Mask dialog box that appears, set these three options:

   - **Amount:** The Amount value ranges from 0 to 500. The amount that you choose has a lot to do with the subject matter. Sharpening a car or appliance at 300 to 400 is fine, but do this to the CEO's 75-year-old wife, and you may suffer an untimely death because every wrinkle, mole, or hair will magically become more defined. If you're not sure what to use, start with 150 and play around until you find an Amount value that looks good.

   - **Radius:** The Unsharp Mask filter creates a halo around the areas that have enough contrast to be considered an edge. Typically, leaving the amount between 1 to 2 is fine for print, but if you're creating a billboard or poster, increase the size.

   - **Threshold:** This option is the most important one in the Unsharp Mask dialog box. The Threshold setting is what determines what should be sharpened. If left at zero, you'll see noise throughout the image, much like the grain that you see in high-speed film. Bring it up to 10, and this triggers the Unsharp Mask filter to apply only the sharpening when the pixels are ten shades or more away from each other. The amount of tolerance ranges from 1 to 255. Apply too much, and no sharpening appears; apply too little, and the image becomes grainy. A good number to start with is 10.

To compare the original state of the image with the preview of the Unsharp Mask filter's effect in the preview pane of the Unsharp Mask dialog box, click and hold on the image in the Preview pane; this shows the original state of the image. When you release the mouse button, the unsharp mask is previewed again.

3. When you've made your choice, click OK.

The image appears to have more detail.

Once in a while, stray colored pixels may appear after you apply the Unsharp Mask filter. Get in the habit of choosing Edit⇨Fade Unsharp Mask immediately after applying the Unsharp Mask filter. In the Fade dialog box, select the Luminosity blend mode from the Mode drop-down list and then click OK. This step applies the Unsharp Mask filter to the grays in the image only, thereby eliminating sharpening of colored pixels.

New in Photoshop CS3 you can use smart filters. Smart filters allow you to undo, all or some of any filter, including sharpening filters, that you apply to a layer. Find out how by reading Chapter 8 in this minibook.

Chapter 7: Creating a Good Image

*W*ith all the incredible things you can do in Photoshop, you can easily forget the basics. Yes, you can create incredible compositions with special effects, but if the people look greenish, it detracts from the image. Get in the habit of building good clean images before heading into the artsy filters and fun things. Color correction isn't complicated, and if done properly, it will produce magical results in your images. In this chapter, you discover how to use the values you read in the Info palette and use the Curves dialog box to produce quality image corrections.

Reading a Histogram

Before making adjustments, look at the image's *histogram,* which displays an image's tonal values, to evaluate whether the image has sufficient detail to produce a high-quality image. In Photoshop CS3, choose Window➪Histogram to display the Histogram palette.

The greater the range of values in the histogram, the greater the detail. Poor images without much information can be difficult, if not impossible, to correct. The Histogram palette also displays the overall distribution of shadows, midtones, and highlights to help you determine which tonal corrections are needed.

Figure 7-1 shows a good full histogram that indicates a smooth transition from one shade to another in the image. Figure 7-2 shows that when a histogram is spread out and has gaps in it, the image is jumping too quickly from one shade to another, producing a posterized effect. *Posterization* is an effect that reduces tonal values to a limited amount, creating a more defined range of values from one shade to another. Great if you want it, yucky if you want a smooth tonal change from one shadow to another.

Figure 7-1:
A histogram shows lots of information, and this one shows an image that has smooth transitions from one color to another.

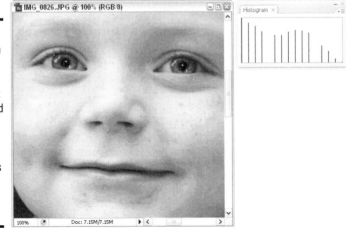

Figure 7-2:
A histogram showing little information; the enlarged image shows the lack of smoothness in the gradation of color.

So how do you get a good histogram? If you're scanning, make sure that your scanner is set for the maximum amount of colors. Scanning at 16 shades of gray gives you 16 lines in your histogram . . . not good!

If you have a bad histogram, we recommend that you rescan or reshoot the image. If you have a good histogram to start with, keep the histogram good by not messing around with multiple tone correction tools. Most professionals use the Curves feature . . . and that's it. Curves (choose Image⇨Adjustments⇨Curves), if used properly, do all the adjusting of levels (brightness and contrast) and color balance, all in one step. You can read more about curves in the section "Creating a Good Tone Curve," later in this chapter.

Figure 7-3 shows what happens to a perfectly good histogram when someone gets a little too zealous and uses the entire plethora of color correction controls in Photoshop. Just because the controls are there doesn't mean that you have to use them.

Figure 7-3:
Tonal information is broken up as more and more adjustments are made to an image.

If you see a Warning icon appear while you're making adjustments, double-click anywhere on the histogram to refresh the display.

Breaking into key types

Don't panic if your histogram is smashed all the way to the left or right. The bars of the histogram represent tonal values. You can break down the types of images, based upon their values, into three key types:

✦ **High key:** A very light-colored image, such as the image shown in Figure 7-4. Information is pushed toward the right in the histogram. Color correction has to be handled a little differently for these images to keep the light appearance to them.

✦ **Low key:** A very dark image, such as the image shown in Figure 7-5. Information is pushed to the left in the histogram. This type of image is difficult to scan on low-end scanners because the dark areas tend to blend together with little definition.

✦ **Mid key:** A typical image with a full range of shades would be considered mid key, such as the image shown in Figure 7-6. These images are the most common and easiest to work with. In this chapter, we deal with images that are considered mid key.

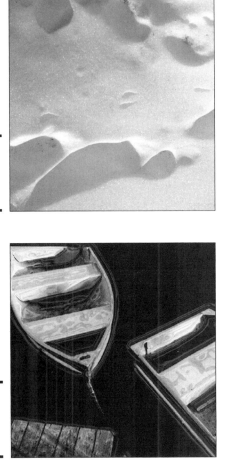

Figure 7-4:
A high key image is a light image.

Figure 7-5:
A low key image is a dark image.

Figure 7-6:
A typical image with a full range of values is a mid key image.

Setting up the correction

To produce the best possible image, try to avoid correcting in CMYK mode. If your images are typically in RGB or LAB mode, keep them in that mode throughout the process. Convert them to CMYK only when you're finished manipulating the image.

Don't forget! Press Ctrl+Y (Windows) or ⌘+Y (Mac) to toggle on and off the CMYK preview so that you can see what your image will look like in CMYK mode without converting it!

Set up these items before starting any color correction:

1. **Select the Eyedropper tool; on the Options bar, change the sample size from Point Sample to 3 By 3 Average in the Sample Size drop-down list.**

   The Eyedropper tool is hidden in the Count Tool if you have Photoshop Extended.

   This setting gives you more accurate readings.

2. **If the Histogram palette isn't already visible, choose Window⇨Histogram.**

3. **If the Info palette isn't already visible, choose Window⇨Info to show the Info palette so that you can check values.**

4. **Make sure that your color settings are correct.**

   If you're not sure how to check or set up color settings, see Chapter 3 of this minibook.

Creating a Good Tone Curve

A *tone curve* represents the density of an image. To get the best image, you must first find the highlight and shadow points in the image. An image created in less-than-perfect lighting conditions may be washed out or have odd color casts. See Figure 7-7 for an example of an image with no set highlight and shadow. Check out Figure 7-8 to see an image that went through the process of setting a highlight and shadow.

To make the process of creating a good tone curve more manageable, we've broken the process into four parts:

✦ Finding the highlight and shadow

✦ Setting the highlight and shadow

✦ Adjusting the midtone

✦ Finding a neutral

Figure 7-7:
The image is murky before defining a highlight and shadow.

Even though each part has its own set of steps, you must go through all four parts to accomplish the task of creating a good tone curve (unless you're working with grayscale images, in which case you can skip the neutral part). In this example, an Adjustment layer is used for the curve adjustments. The benefit is that you can turn off the visibility of the adjustment at a later point or double-click the adjustment layer thumbnail to make ongoing edits without destroying your image.

Figure 7-8:
The tonal values are opened up after highlight and shadow have been set.

Finding and setting the highlight and shadow

In the noncomputer world, you'd spend a fair amount of time trying to locate the lightest and darkest part of an image. Fortunately, you can cheat in Photoshop by using some of the new features in the Curves palette. Here's how you access the palette:

1. **With an image worthy of adjustment — meaning one that isn't perfect already — choose Window⇨Layer (if the Layers palette isn't already open).**

2. **Click and hold on the Create New Fill Or Adjustment Layer button at the bottom of the Layers palette and select Curves.**

The Curves palette, shown in Figure 7-9, appears.

Notice the grayed-out histogram behind the image Curve window. The histogram aids you in determining where you need to adjust the image's curve.

If you're correcting in RGB (as you should be!), the tone curve may be opposite of what you think it should be. Instead of light to dark displaying as you'd expect, RGB displays dark to light. Now think about it: RGB is generated with light, and no RGB means that there is no light and you therefore have black. Turn all RGB on full force, and you create white. Try pointing three filtered lights, one red, one green, and one blue. The three lights pointed in one direction really do create white.

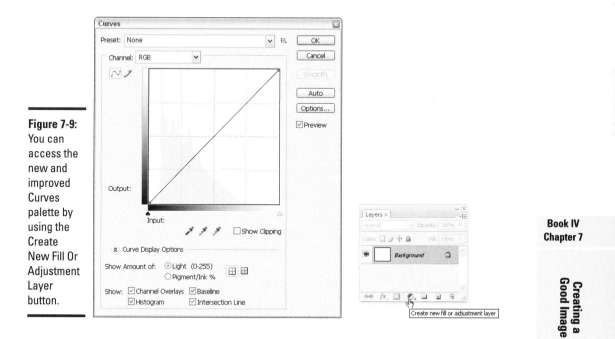

Figure 7-9:
You can access the new and improved Curves palette by using the Create New Fill Or Adjustment Layer button.

If working with RGB confuses you, simply click on the Pigment/Ink% check box, shown in Figure 7-10. The sample in this example uses the curve based upon pigment.

Note that in the new Curves palette, you see a Preset drop-down menu that offers quick fixes using standard curves for certain corrections. These settings are great for quick fixes, but for the best image, you should create a custom curve.

The first thing you need to do in the Curves palette is determine the lightest and darkest part of the image, which is referred to as locating the highlight and shadow:

1. **To help you see where the highlight and shadow are in the image, check the Show Clipping check box.**

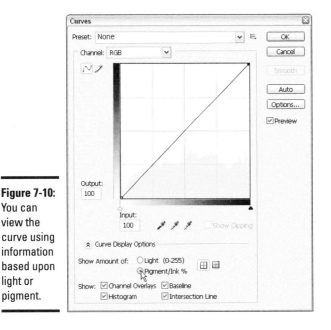

Figure 7-10:
You can view the curve using information based upon light or pigment.

2. **Grab the right modify curve slider, shown in Figure 7-11, and slide it until you start to see white appear.**

Coincidently, the white should appear where you see your histogram (grayed out in the curves palette) begin.

3. **Now grab the left modify curve slider and drag it until you see the darker part of the image peak in, as shown in Figure 7-12, and then uncheck the Show Clipping check box.**

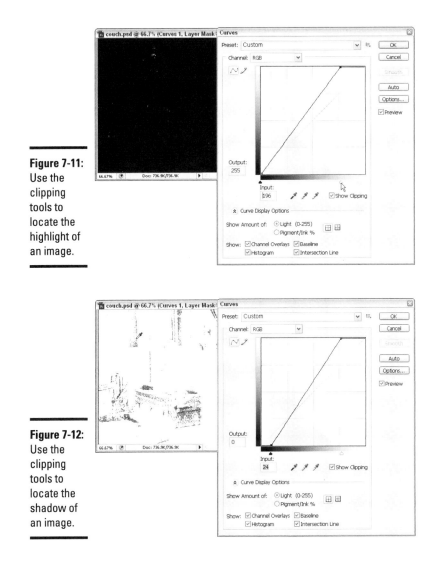

Figure 7-11: Use the clipping tools to locate the highlight of an image.

Figure 7-12: Use the clipping tools to locate the shadow of an image.

Adjusting the midtone

You may have heard the statement, "Open up the midtones." This phrase essentially means that you're lightening the midtonal values of an image. In many cases, opening up the midtones is necessary to add contrast and bring out detail in your image.

To adjust the midtones, follow these steps:

1. **In the Curves dialog box, click the middle of the curve ramp to create an anchor point; drag up slightly.**

The image lightens. (If you're in Pigment/Ink % mode, drag down to lighten the image.) Don't move a dramatic amount and be very careful to observe what is happening in your Histogram palette (which you should always have open when making color corrections).

Because you set highlight and shadow (see preceding section) and are now making a midtone correction, you see the bars in the histogram spreading out. The spreading of the information is necessary to a point, and it's the reason why you don't click OK until *all steps* have been taken in the Curves dialog box.

2. **To adjust the three-quarter tones (the shades around 75 percent), click halfway between the bottom of the curve ramp and the midpoint to set an anchor point.**

Use the grid in the Curves dialog box to find it easily. (In Pigment/Ink %, the three-quarter point is in the upper section of the color ramp.) Adjust the three-quarter area of the tone curve up or down slightly to create contrast in the image. Again, keep an eye on your histogram!

3. **If you're working on a grayscale image, your tonal correction is done, and you can click OK.**

If you're working on a color image, don't click OK; keep the Curves dialog box open for the final step, which is outlined in the next section.

Finding a neutral

The last step in creating a tone curve only applies if you're working on a color image. The key to understanding color is knowing that equal amounts of color create gray. By positioning the mouse cursor over gray areas in an image and reading the values in the Info palette, you can determine what colors you need to adjust.

1. **With your Curves dialog box open, position it so that you can see the Info palette.**

If the Info palette is buried under another palette or a dialog box, choose Window⇨Info to bring it to the front.

2. **Position your cursor over your image and, in the Info palette, look for the RGB values in the upper-left section.**

You see color values and then forward slashes and more color values. The numbers before the slash indicate the values in the image before you opened the Curves dialog box; the numbers after the slash show the values now that you have made changes in the Curves dialog box. Pay attention to the values after the slashes.

3. **Position the cursor over something gray in your image.**

   It can be a shadow on a white shirt, a counter top, a road — anything that is a shade of gray. Look at the Info palette. If your image is perfectly color balanced, the RGB values following the forward slashes should all be the same.

4. **If your color isn't balanced, click the Set Gray Point Eyedropper in the Curves dialog box and click the neutral or gray area of the image.**

   The middle eyedropper (Set Gray Point) is a handy way of bringing the location that you click on closer together in RGB values, thereby balancing the colors.

5. **Now you can click OK; if you're asked whether you want to save your color target values, click Yes.**

Curves can be as complex or simple as you make them. As you gain more confidence using them, you can check neutrals throughout an image to ensure that all unwanted color casts are eliminated. You can even individually adjust each color's curve by selecting them from the Channel drop-down list in the Curves dialog box.

When you're finished with color correction, using the Unsharp Mask filter on your image is a good idea. Chapter 5 of this minibook shows you how to use this filter.

Using an Adjustment Layer

You may go through a curve adjustment only to discover that some areas of the image are still too dark or too light. If this is the case, you're better off using an *adjustment layer,* which is a layer that adjusts a selected area of your image, based upon a correction applied on the layer. By using an adjustment layer, you can turn off the correction or change it over and over again with no degradation to the quality of the image. You can apply an adjustment layer by following these steps:

1. **Select the area of the image that needs adjustments.**

   See Chapter 4 of this minibook if you need a refresher on how to make selections in Photoshop.

2. **Choose Select⇨Modify⇨Feather to soften the selection.**

   The Feather dialog box appears.

3. Enter a value into the Feather dialog box.

If you're not sure what value will work best, enter 15 in the Feather Radius text field and click OK.

4. If the Layers palette isn't visible, choose Windows⇨Layers; click and hold on the Create New Fill Or Adjustment Layer icon and select Curves from the menu that appears.

5. In the Curves dialog box, click the middle of the curve ramp to create an anchor point; drag up or down to lighten or darken your selected area and click OK.

Notice in the Layers palette (see Figure 7-13) that your adjustment layer, named Curves 2, has a mask to the right of it. The selected area is white; unselected areas are black.

Figure 7-13:
You can paint on the Adjustment Layer mask to apply correction to different parts of the image.

6. With your adjustment layer selected in the Layers palette, use the Brush tool to paint white to apply the correction to other areas of the image; paint with black to exclude areas from the correction.

You can even change the opacity using the Brush tool Options bar at the top to apply only some of the correction!

Testing a Printer

If you go through all the work of making color corrections to your images and you still get printed images that look hot pink, it may not be you! Test your printer by following these steps:

1. **Create a neutral gray out of equal RGB values (double-click the Fill Color swatch in the toolbar).**

2. **Create a shape, using your neutral gray as the fill color.**

   For example, you can use the Ellipse tool to create a circle or oval.

3. **Choose File⇨Print and click OK to print the image from your color printer.**

If you're seeing heavy color casts, you need to adjust your printer; cleaning or replacing the ink cartridge may fix the problem. Check out Chapter 10 of this minibook for more about printing your Photoshop files.

Chapter 8: Working with Painting and Retouching Tools

In This Chapter

✓ Using the Swatches palette

✓ Getting to know foreground and background colors

✓ Introducing painting and retouching tools

✓ Discovering blending modes

This chapter shows you how to use the painting and retouching tools in Photoshop. If you're unsure about how good the painting you're about to do will look, create a new layer and paint on that. (See Chapter 9 of this minibook to find out how to create and use layers.) That way, you can delete the layer by dragging it to the Trash icon (at the bottom of the Layers palette) if you decide that you don't like what you have done. Don't forget to make the Eraser tool your friend! You can also repair painting or retouching mistakes by Alt+dragging (Windows) or Option+dragging (Mac) with the Eraser tool selected to erase the last version saved or present history state.

Have fun and be creative! Because Photoshop is pixel-based, you can create incredible imagery with the painting tools. Smooth gradations from one color to the next, integrated with blending modes and transparency, can lead from super-artsy to super-realistic effects. In this chapter, you discover painting fundamentals, and we show you how to use retouching tools to eliminate wrinkles, blemishes, and scratches. Don't you wish you could do that in real life?

Using the Swatches Palette

Use the Swatches palette to store and retrieve frequently used colors. The Swatches palette allows you to quickly select colors.

The Swatches palette also gives you access to many other color options. By using the palette menu, you can select from a multitude of different color schemes, such as Pantone or Web-safe color sets. These color systems are converted to whatever color mode in which you're working.

To sample and then store a color for later use, follow these steps:

1. **To sample a color from an image, select the Eyedropper tool in the toolbox and click a color on the image.**

   Alternatively, you can use any of the paint tools (the Brush tool for example) and Alt+click (Windows) or Option+click (Mac).

   The color you click becomes the foreground color.

2. **Store the color in the Swatches palette by clicking the New Swatch button at the bottom of the Swatches palette.**

Anytime you want to use that color again, simply click it in the Swatches palette to make it the foreground color.

Choosing Foreground and Background Colors

At the bottom of the toolbox reside the foreground and background color swatches. The *foreground color* is the color that you apply when using any of the painting tools. The *background color* is the color that you see if you erase or delete pixels from the image.

Choose a foreground or background color by clicking the swatch, which opens the Color Picker dialog box. To use the color picker, you can either enter values in the text fields on the right, or you can slide the hue slider.

Pick the hue (color) that you want to start with and then click in the color pane to the left to choose the amount of light and saturation (grayness or brightness) you want in the color. Select the Only Web Colors check box to choose one of the 216 colors in the Web safe color palette. The hexadecimal value used in HTML documents appears in the text field in the lower right of the color picker.

Add To Swatches   New in Photoshop CS3, you can click the Add To Swatches button right in the Color Picker to save a color for future use.

The Painting and Retouching Tools

Grouped together in the toolbox are the tools used for painting and retouching. The arrow in the lower right of a tool indicates that the tool has more related hidden tools; simply click and hold on the tool to see additional painting and retouching tools. In this chapter, we show you how the Spot Healing Brush, Healing Brush, Patch, Red Eye, Brush, Clone Stamp, History

Brush, Eraser, and Gradient tools work. You also discover ways to fill shapes with colors and patterns.

Changing the brush

As you click to select different painting tools, note the Brush menu, second from the left, on the Options bar, as shown in Figure 8-1. Click the arrow to open the Brush Picker. You can use the Master Diameter slider to make the brush size larger or smaller, as well as change the hardness of the brush.

The hardness refers to how "fuzzy" the edges are; a softer brush is more feathered and soft around the edges, while a harder edge would be more definite with a harder edge (see Figure 8-2).

Don't feel like accessing the Brushes palette every time you want to make a change? Press the right bracket] several times to make your brush diameter larger or press the left bracket [to make the brush diameter smaller. Press Shift+] to make the brush harder or Shift+[to make the brush softer.

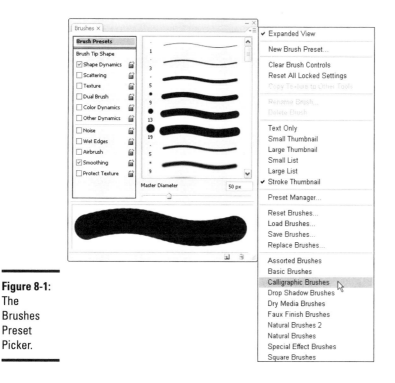

Figure 8-1:
The
Brushes
Preset
Picker.

Choose Window⟶Brushes to see a list of Brush presets, plus many more brush options that you can use to create custom brushes. You can also choose other brush libraries using the palette menu (click the triangle in the upper-right corner of the Brushes Preset Picker). When you select an additional library, a dialog box appears, asking whether you want to replace the current brushes with the brushes in the selected library. Click the Append button to keep existing brushes and add the library to the list, or click OK to replace the existing brushes.

Figure 8-2:
A soft edge (left) as compared to a hard edge (right) brush stroke.

Access the Brushes Preset Picker as you're painting by right-clicking (Windows) or Ctrl+clicking (Mac) anywhere in the image area. Double-click a brush to select it; press Esc to hide the Brushes palette.

The Spot Healing Brush Tool

The Spot Healing Brush tool is destined to become everyone's favorite. Who wouldn't love a tool that can remove years from your face and any blemishes, too?

The Spot Healing Brush tool quickly removes blemishes and other imperfections in your images. Click a blemish and watch it paint matching texture, lighting, transparency, and shading to the pixels being healed. The Spot Healing Brush doesn't require you to specify a sample spot. The Spot Healing Brush automatically samples from around the retouched area.

The Healing Brush Tool

You can use the Healing Brush tool for repairs, such as eliminating scratches and dust from scanned images. The difference between the Spot Healing

Brush tool (see preceding section) and the Healing Brush tool is that a sample spot is required before applying the Healing Brush. Follow these steps to use this tool:

1. **Select the Healing Brush tool in the toolbox (it's a hidden tool of the Spot Healing Brush tool).**

2. **Find an area in the image that looks good and then Alt+click (Windows) or Option+click (Mac) to sample that area.**

   For example, if you're going to eliminate wrinkles on a face, choose a wrinkle-free area of skin near the wrinkle. (Try to keep it relatively close in skin tone.)

3. **Position the mouse cursor over the area to be repaired and start painting.**

   The Healing Brush tool goes into action, blending and softening to create a realistic repair of the area.

4. **Repeat Steps 2 and 3 as necessary to repair the blemish, wrinkles, or scratches.**

The Patch Tool

Hidden behind the Healing Brush tool in the toolbox is the Patch tool. Use the Patch tool to repair larger areas, such as a big scratch or a large area of skin, by following these steps:

1. **Click and hold the Healing Brush tool to select the Patch tool; on the Options bar, select the Destination radio button.**

   You can either patch the source area or the destination. The preference is really up to you. We recommend taking a good source and dragging it over the location of the image that needs to be repaired.

2. **With the Patch tool still selected, drag to create a marquee around the source that you want to use as the patch.**

   The source would be an unscratched or wrinkle-free area.

3. **After you create the marquee, drag the selected source area to the destination that is to be repaired.**

   The Patch tool clones the selected source area as you drag it to the destination (the scratched area); when you release the mouse button, the tool blends in the source selection and repairs the scratched area!

Make the patch look even better by choosing Edit⇨Fade Patch Selection immediately after you apply the patch. Adjust the opacity until there are no tell-tale signs that you made a change.

The Red Eye Tool

So you finally got the group together and shot the perfect image, but red eye took over! *Red eye* is caused by a reflection of the camera's flash in the retina of your photo's subject(s). You see it more often when taking pictures in a dark room because the subject's iris is wide open. If you can, use your camera's red-eye reduction feature. Or, better yet, use a separate flash unit that you can mount on the camera farther away from the camera's lens.

You will love the fact that red eye is extremely easy to fix in Photoshop CS3. Just follow these steps:

1. **Select the Red Eye tool (hidden behind the Spot Healing Brush tool).**

2. **Click a red eye.**

   You should see a change immediately, but if you need to make adjustments to the size or the darkness amount, you can change options in the tool options bar at the top of your work area.

The Brush Tool

Painting with the Brush tool in Photoshop is much like painting in the real world. What you should know are all the nifty keyboard commands that you can use to be much more productive when painting. These shortcuts are really great, so make sure that you try them as you read about them. By the way, the keyboard commands you see in Table 8-1 work on all the painting tools.

Table 8-1	Brush Keyboard Shortcuts	
Function	*Windows*	*Mac*
Choose the Brush tool	B	B
Increase brush size	]	]
Decrease brush size	[	[
Harden brush	Shift+]	Shift+]
Soften brush	Shift+[	Shift+[
Sample color	Alt+click	Option+click
Switch foreground and background color	X	X
Change opacity by a given percentage	Type a number between 1 and 100	Type a number between 1 and 100

If you're really into the brushes, you have lots of great options available in the Brushes palette (choose Window⇨Brushes to open the palette).

You have several choices of attributes, most of which have dynamic controls in the menu options that allow you to vary brush characteristics by tilting or applying more pressure to a stylus pen (if you're using a pressure-sensitive drawing tablet), among other things.

Note: A warning sign indicates that you don't have the appropriate device attached to use the selected feature, such as a pressure-sensitive drawing tablet.

The following options are available in the Brushes palette:

✦ **Brush Tip Shape:** Select from these standard controls for determining brush dimensions and spacing.

✦ **Shape Dynamics:** Change the size of the brush as you paint.

✦ **Scattering:** Scatter the brush strokes and control brush tip count.

✦ **Texture:** Choose a texture from pre-existing patterns or your own.

Create a pattern by selecting an image area with the Rectangular Marquee tool. Choose Edit⇨Define Pattern, name the pattern, and then click OK. The pattern is now available in the Brush palettes Texture choices.

✦ **Dual Brush:** Use two brushes at the same time.

✦ **Color Dynamics:** Change the color as you paint.

✦ **Other Dynamics:** Change the opacity and flow.

If you've been using Photoshop for several versions, you may notice that with Photoshop CS3, the attributes at the bottom of the Brushes palette aren't necessarily new, but have been moved from their old positions on the Options bar. Here is what these attributes do:

✦ **Noise:** Adds a grainy texture to the brush stroke.

✦ **Wet Edges:** Makes the brush stroke appear to be wet by creating a heavier amount of color on the edges of the brush strokes.

✦ **Airbrush:** Gives airbrush features to the Brush tools (CS3 no longer has a standalone Airbrush tool as in previous versions of Photoshop). You can also turn on the Airbrush feature by clicking the Airbrush button and adjusting the pressure and flow on the Options bar.

**Book IV
Chapter 8**

If you click and hold with the Brush tool out on the image area, the paint stops spreading. Turn on the Airbrush feature and notice that when you click and hold, the paint keeps spreading, just like with a can of spray paint. You can use the Flow slider on the Options bar to control the pressure.

✦ **Smoothing:** Smoothes the path that you create with the mouse.

✦ **Protect Texture:** Preserves the texture pattern when applying brush presets.

In addition to the preceding options, you can also adjust the jitter of the brush. The *jitter* specifies the randomness of the brush attribute. At 0 percent, an element doesn't change over the course of a stroke; at 100 percent, a stroke will totally vary from one attribute to another. For example, if you select Other Dynamics in the Brushes palette and then change the Opacity Jitter to 100 percent, the opacity will vary from 0 to 100 percent while you're painting.

After going through all the available brush options, you may want to start thinking about how you'll apply the same attributes later. Saving the Brush tool attributes is important as you increase in skill level.

The Clone Stamp Tool

The Clone Stamp tool is used for pixel-to-pixel cloning. It's different from the Healing Brush tool in that it does no automatic blending into the target area. You can use the Clone Stamp tool for removing a product name from an image, replacing a telephone wire that is crossing in front of a building, or duplicating an item.

Here's how you use the Clone Stamp tool:

1. **With the Clone Stamp tool selected, position the cursor over the area that you want to clone and then Alt+click (Windows) or Option+click (Mac) to define the clone source.**

2. **Position the cursor over the area where you want to paint the cloned pixels and start painting.**

   Note the cross hair at the original sampled area, as shown in Figure 8-3. As you're painting, the cross hair follows the pixels that you're cloning.

When using the Clone Stamp tool for touching up images, it's best to resample many times so as to not leave a seam where you replaced pixels. A good clone stamper Alt+clicks (Windows) or Option+clicks (Mac) and paints many times over until the retouching is complete.

Figure 8-3:
A cross hair over the source shows what you are cloning.

The History Brush Tool

Choose Window⇨History to see the History palette. You could work for weeks playing around in the History palette, but this section gives you the basics.

At the top of the History palette is a snapshot of the last saved version of the image. Beside the snapshot is an icon noting that it's the present History state.

By default, when you paint with the History Brush tool, it will paint back to the way the image looked at the last saved version, but you can click the empty square to the left of any state in the History palette to make it the target for the History Brush tool.

Use the History Brush tool to fix errors and add spunk to your images.

The Eraser Tool

You may not think of the Eraser tool as a painting tool, but it can be! When you drag on the image with the Eraser tool, it rubs out pixels to the background color. (Basically, it paints with the background color.) If you're dragging with the Eraser tool on a layer, it rubs out pixels to reveal the layer's transparent background. (You can also think of the Eraser tool as painting with transparency.)

The Eraser tool uses all the same commands as the Brush tools. You can make an eraser larger, softer, and more or less opaque. But even better, follow these steps to use the Eraser tool creatively:

1. **Open any color image and apply a filter.**

For example, we chose Filter⇨Blur⇨Gaussian Blur. In the Gaussian Blur dialog box that appeared, we changed the blur to 5 and then clicked OK to apply the Gaussian Blur filter.

2. **Select the Eraser tool and press 5 to change it to 50 percent opacity.**

   You can also use the Opacity slider on the Options bar.

3. **Hold down the Alt (Windows) or Option (Mac) key to paint back 50 percent of the original image's state before applying the filter; continue painting in the same area to bring the image back to its original state!**

   The original sharpness of the image returns where you painted.

Holding down the Alt (Windows) or Option (Mac) key is the key command to erase to the last saved version (or history state) of the image. This tool is incredible for fixing little mistakes, or when you applied cool filters and you want to bring back some of the original image.

The Gradient Tool

Choose the Gradient tool and click and drag across an image area to create a gradient in the direction and length of the mouse motion. A short drag creates a short gradient; a long drag produces a smoother, longer gradient.

Using the Options bar, you can also choose the type of gradient that you want: Linear, Radial, Angle, Reflected, or Diamond.

As a default, gradients are created using the current foreground and background colors. Click the arrow on the gradient button on the Options bar to assign a different preset gradient.

To create a gradient, follow these steps:

1. **Choose the Gradient tool and click the Gradient Editor button on the Options bar.**

   The Gradient Editor dialog box appears. At the bottom of the gradient preview, you see two or more stops. The stops are where new colors are inserted into the gradient. They look like little house icons. Use the stops on the top of the gradient slider to determine the opacity.

2. **Click a stop and click the color swatch to the right of the word Color to open the color picker and assign a different color to the stop.**

3. **Click anywhere below the gradient preview to add more color stops.**

4. **Drag a color stop off the Gradient Editor dialog box to delete it.**

5. **Click on the top of the gradient preview to assign different stops with varying amounts of opacity, as shown in Figure 8-4.**

6. **When you're finished editing the gradient, name it and then click the New button.**

The new gradient is added to the preset gradient choices.

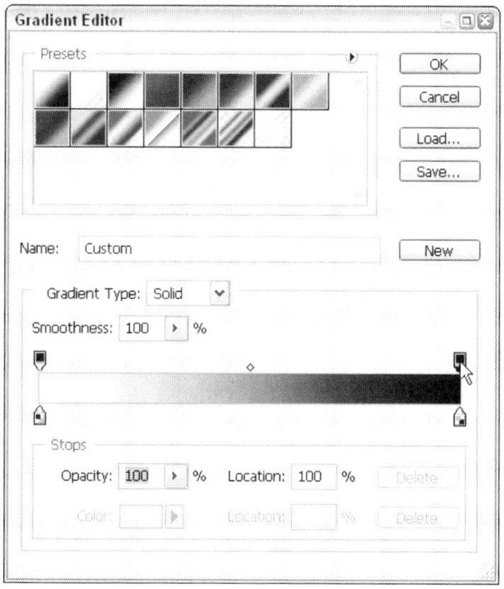

Figure 8-4:
Assigning
varying
amounts of
opacity
using the
stops on
top of the
gradient
slider.

7. **To apply your gradient, drag across a selection or image using the Gradient tool.**

Blending Modes

You can use blending modes to add flair to the traditional opaque paint. Use blending modes to paint highlights or shadows that allow details to show through from the underlying image or to colorize a desaturated image. You access the blending modes for paint tools from the Options bar.

You really can't get a good idea of how the blending mode will work with the paint color and the underlying color until you experiment. (That's what multiple undos are for!) Alternatively, you can copy the image you want to experiment with onto a new layer and hide the original layer; see Chapter 9 of this minibook for more about layers.

**Book IV
Chapter 8**

Working with
Painting and
Retouching Tools

The following list describes the available blending modes:

+ **Normal:** Paints normally, with no interaction with underlying colors.

+ **Dissolve:** Gives a random replacement of the pixels, depending on the opacity at any pixel location.

+ **Behind:** Edits or paints only on the transparent part of a layer.

+ **Darken:** Replaces only the areas that are lighter than the blend color. Areas darker than the blend color don't change.

+ **Multiply:** Creates an effect similar to drawing on the page with magic markers. Also looks like colored film that you see on theatre lights.

+ **Color Burn:** Darkens the base color to reflect the blend color. If you're using white, no change occurs.

+ **Linear Burn:** Looks at the color information in each channel and darkens the base color to reflect the blending color by decreasing the brightness.

+ **Lighten:** Replaces only the areas darker than the blend color. Areas lighter than the blend color don't change.

+ **Screen:** Multiplies the inverse of the underlying colors. The resulting color is always a lighter color.

+ **Color Dodge:** Brightens the underlying color to reflect the blend color. If you're using black, there is no change.

+ **Linear Dodge:** Looks at the color information in each channel and brightens the base color to reflect the blending color by increasing the brightness.

+ **Overlay:** Multiplies or screens the colors, depending on the base color.

+ **Soft Light:** Darkens or lightens the colors, depending on the blend color. The effect is similar to shining a diffused spotlight on the artwork.

+ **Hard Light:** Multiplies or screens the colors, depending on the blend color. The effect is similar to shining a harsh spotlight on the artwork.

+ **Vivid Light:** Burns or dodges the colors by increasing or decreasing the contrast.

+ **Linear Light:** Burns or dodges the colors by decreasing or increasing the brightness.

+ **Pin Light:** Replaces the colors, depending on the blend color.

+ **Hard Mix:** Paints strokes that have no effect with other Hard Mix paint strokes. Use this mode when you want no interaction between the colors.

✦ **Difference:** Subtracts either the blend color from the base color or the base color from the blend color, depending on which has the greater brightness value. The effect is similar to a color negative.

✦ **Exclusion:** Creates an effect similar to, but with less contrast than, the Difference mode.

✦ **Hue:** Applies the hue (color) of the blend object onto the underlying objects but keeps the underlying shading or luminosity intact.

✦ **Saturation:** Applies the saturation of the blend color but uses the luminance and hue of the base color.

✦ **Color:** Applies the blend object's color to the underlying objects but preserves the gray levels in the artwork. This mode is great for tinting objects or changing their colors.

✦ **Luminosity:** Creates a resulting color with the hue and saturation of the base color and the luminance of the blend color. This mode is essentially the opposite of the Color mode.

✦ **Lighter Color:** Compares the total of all channel values for the blend and base color and displays the higher value color.

✦ **Darker Color:** Compares the total of all channel values for the blend and base color and displays the lower value color.

Painting with color

This section provides an example of using the blending modes to change and add color to an image. A great example of using a blending mode is tinting a black-and-white (grayscale) image with color. You can't paint color in Grayscale mode, so follow these steps to add color to a black-and-white image:

1. **Open an image in any color mode and choose Image⇨Mode⇨RGB.**

2. **If the image isn't already a grayscale image, choose Image⇨ Adjustments⇨Desaturate.**

This feature makes it appear as though the image is black and white, but you're still in a color mode with which you can apply color.

3. **Choose a painting tool (the Brush tool, for example) and, using the Swatches palette, choose the first color that you want to paint with.**

4. **On the Options bar, select Color from the Mode drop-down list and then use the Opacity slider to change the opacity to 50 percent.**

You could also just type 5.

5. **Start painting!**

The Color blending mode is used to change the color of the pixels, while keeping the underlying grayscale (shading) intact.

Another way to bring attention to a certain item in an RGB image (like those cute greeting cards that have the single rose in color and everything else in black and white) is to select the item you want to bring attention to. Choose Select⟶Modify⟶Feather to soften the selection a bit (5 pixels is a good number to enter in the Feather Radius text field). Then choose Select⟶Inverse. Now with everything else selected, choose Image⟶Adjustments⟶Desaturate. Everything else in the image looks black and white, except for the original item that you selected.

Filling selections

If you have a definite shape that doesn't lend itself to being painted, you can fill it with color instead. Make a selection and choose Edit⟶Fill to access the Fill dialog box. From the Use drop-down list, you can choose from the following options to fill the selection: Foreground Color, Background Color, Color (to open the color picker while in the Fill dialog box) Pattern, History, Black, 50% Gray, or White.

If you want to use an existing or saved pattern from the Brushes palette, you can retrieve a pattern by selecting Pattern in the Fill dialog box as well. Select History from the Use drop-down list to fill with the last version saved or the history state.

If you would rather use the Paint Bucket tool, which fills based upon the tolerance set on the Options bar, it's hidden in the Gradient tool.

To use the Paint Bucket tool to fill with the foreground color, simply click the item that you want to fill. This technique isn't as exact as using the Fill dialog box, but it's good for filling solid areas quickly.

Saving Presets

All the Photoshop tools allow you to save presets so that you can retrieve them from a list of presets. The following steps show you an example of saving a Brush tool preset, but the same method can be used for all other tools as well:

1. **Choose a brush size, color, softness, or anything!**

2. **Click the Tool Preset Picker button on the left side of the Options bar.**

The preset menu for that tool appears.

3. **Click the triangle in the upper-right corner to access the fly-out menu and then choose New Tool Preset.**

The New Tool Preset dialog box appears.

4. **Type a descriptive name in the Name text field (leave the Include Color check box selected if you want the preset to also remember the present color) and then click OK.**

Your preset is created and saved.

5. **Access the preset by clicking the tool's Preset Picker button and choosing it from the tool's Preset Picker list.**

Each preset that you create is specific to the tool that it was created in, so you can have a crop preset, an eraser preset, and so on. After you get in the habit of saving presets, you'll wonder how you ever got along without them!

Chapter 9: Using Layers

In This Chapter

✓ Discovering layers

✓ Using type as a layer

✓ Implementing layer masks

✓ Organizing your layers

✓ Using Smart Objects

✓ Playing with layer effects

*L*ayers are incredibly helpful in production. By using layers, you can make realistic additions to an image that you can remove, edit, and control with blending modes and transparency. Unfortunately, to show you all the features of layers goes beyond what we can cover in this chapter. This chapter covers layer basics to get you started working with layers in Photoshop. We show you how to create composite images using easy layer features — just enough knowledge to get yourself into a pretty complex mess of layers! Even if you're an experienced Photoshop user, read this chapter to discover all sorts of neat key commands that can help you in your workflow.

If you're a video professional, open some videos in Photoshop Extended CS3. Photoshop Extended automatically creates a Movie layer, and using the timeline, you can do pixel editing frame by frame!

Have fun with layers and don't worry if you mess up; you can always press F12 to revert the image to the state it was in at the last time you saved it.

Creating and Working with Layers

Layers make creating *composite images* (images pieced together from many other individual images) easy because you can separate individual elements of the composite onto their own layers. Much like creating collages by cutting pictures from magazines, you can mask out selections on one image and place them on a layer in another image. When pixel information is on its own layer, you can move it, transform it, correct its color, or apply filters just to that layer, without disturbing pixel information on other layers.

The best way to understand how to create and use layers is to, well, create and use layers. The following steps show you how to create a new, layered image:

1. **Create a new document by choosing File⇨New.**

The New dialog box appears.

2. **Select Default Photoshop Size from the Preset Sizes drop-down list, select the Transparent option from the Background Contents area, and then click OK.**

Because you selected the Transparent option, your image opens with an empty layer instead of a white background layer. The image appears as a checkerboard pattern, which signifies that it's transparent.

If you don't like to see the default checkerboard pattern where there is transparency, choose Edit⇨Preferences⇨Transparency And Gamut (Windows) or Photoshop⇨Preferences⇨Transparency And Gamut (Mac). In the Preferences dialog box that appears, you can change the Grid Size drop-down list to None to remove the checkerboard pattern entirely. If you don't want to totally remove the transparency grid, you can change the size of the checkerboard pattern or change the color of the checkerboard.

When you open an existing document (say a photograph), this image will be your background layer.

3. **Create a shape on the new image.**

For example, create a red square by using the Rectangular Marquee tool to create a square selection; we then filled the selection with red by double-clicking the Foreground color swatch, selecting a red from the color picker, and clicking in the selection with the Paint Bucket tool (hidden under the Gradient tool).

After you've selected the color, you can also use the key command Alt+Delete (Windows) or Option+Delete (Mac) to fill the selected area with color.

4. **To rename the layer, double-click the layer name (Layer 1) in the Layers palette and type a short, descriptive name.**

A good practice is to name your layers based on what they contain; for this example, the layer was named the catchy name of "square."

5. **Create a new layer by Alt+clicking (Windows) or Option+clicking (Mac) the New Layer button at the bottom of the Layers palette.**

The New Layer dialog box appears.

6. **Give your new layer a descriptive name and then click OK.**

7. **Create a shape on the new layer.**

We created a circle by using the Elliptical Marquee tool and filling the selection with yellow.

The new shape can overlap the shape on the other layer, as shown in Figure 9-1.

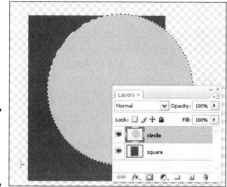

Figure 9-1:
The circle overlaps the square.

Duplicating a layer

Perhaps you want to create a duplicate of a layer for your composite. This technique can be helpful for do-it-yourself drop shadows, as well as adding elements to an image, such as more apples in a bowl of fruit.

 Alt+drag (Windows) or Option+drag (Mac) the square layer to the New Layer button at the bottom of the Layers palette to duplicate it. Again, by holding down Alt (Windows) or Option (Mac), you can name the layer as you create it.

Selecting a layer

When you start working with layers, you may find yourself moving or adjusting pixels, only to discover that you accidentally edited pixels on the wrong layer. Select the layer that you plan to work on by clicking the layer name in the Layers palette.

 Unlike previous versions of Photoshop, Photoshop CS3 represents a selected layer by simply highlighting the layer in the Layer's palette. Don't bother looking for an indicator paintbrush icon in this version.

Here are some tips to help you select the correct layer:

✦ Select the Move tool and then right-click (Windows) or Ctrl+click (Mac) to see a contextual menu listing all layers that have pixel data at the point you clicked and to choose the layer that you want to work with.

✦ Get in the habit of holding down the Ctrl (Windows) or ⌘ (Mac) key while using the Move tool and when selecting layers. This technique temporarily turns on the Auto Select feature, which automatically selects the topmost visible layer that contains the pixel data that you clicked.

✦ Press Alt+[(Windows) or Option+[(Mac) to select the next layer down from the selected layer in the stacking order.

✦ Press Alt+] (Windows) or Option+] (Mac) to select the next layer up from the selected layer in the stacking order.

Controlling the visibility of a layer

Hide layers that you don't immediately need by clicking the eye icon in the Layers palette. To see only one layer, Alt+click (Windows) or Option+click (Mac) the eye icon of the layer you want to keep visible. Alt+click (Windows) or Option+click (Mac) the eye icon again to show all layers.

Rearranging the stacking order

Layers are like clear pieces of film lying on top of each other. Change the stacking order of the layers in the Layers palette by dragging a layer until you see a black separator line appear, indicating that you're dragging the layer to that location. You can also use these great commands to help you move a layer:

Command	Windows Shortcut	Mac Shortcut
Move selected layer up	Ctrl+]	⌘+]
Move selected layer down	Ctrl+[	⌘+[

Creating a Text Layer

When you create text in Photoshop, the text is created on its own layer. By having the text separate from the rest of your image, applying different styles and blending modes to customize the type, as well as repositioning the text, are simplified.

To create a text layer, choose the Type tool and click the image area. You can also click and drag to create a text area. The Options bar, shown in Figure 9-2, gives you the controls to change font, size, blending mode, and color of the text.

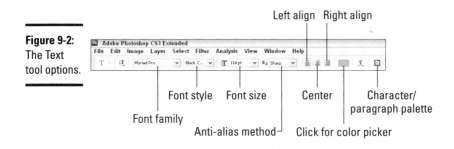

Figure 9-2:
The Text
tool options.

Left align   Right align

Font style   Font size   Center   Character/
paragraph palette

Font family

Anti-alias method   Click for color picker

Warping text

When you click the Create Warped Text button on the Options bar, the Warp Text dialog box appears. This dialog box enables you to apply different types of distortion to your text.

You can still edit text that has been warped. To remove a warp, click the Create Warp Text button again and select None from the Style drop-down list.

Fine-tuning text

For controls such as leading, baseline shift, and paragraph controls, click the Toggle The Character And Paragraph Palettes icon near the right end of the Options bar.

Use the keyboard commands in Table 9-1 to build text in Photoshop. Make sure that you have text selected when you use these shortcuts.

Table 9-1	Helpful Typesetting Key Commands	
Function	*Windows*	*Mac*
Increase font size	Shift+Ctrl+>	Shift+⌘+>
Decrease font size	Shift+Ctrl+<	Shift++⌘ +<
Increase kerning (cursor must be between two letters)	Alt+→	Option+→
Decrease kerning (cursor must be between two letters)	Alt+←	Option+←
Increase tracking (several letters selected)	Alt+→	Option+→
Decrease tracking (several letters selected)	Alt+←	Option+←
Increase or decrease leading (several lines selected)	Alt+↑ or Alt+↓	Option+↑ or Option+↓

**Book IV
Chapter 9**

Using Layers

To change the font, drag over the font family name on the Options bar and then press the up-arrow key (↑) to go up in the font list or the down-arrow key (↓) to go down in the font list.

After you're finished editing text, confirm or delete the changes by clicking the buttons on the right of the Options bar.

If you'd rather use key commands to confirm or delete your changes, press the Esc key to cancel text changes; press Ctrl+Enter (Windows) or ⌘+Return (Mac) to commit text changes (or use the Enter key on the numeric keypad).

Using Layer Masks

In this section, we show you how to create a layer mask from a selection or a pen path. A *layer mask* covers up areas of the image that you want to make transparent and exposes pixels that you want visible. Masks can be based upon a selection that you've created with the selection tools, by painting on the mask itself, or by using the Pen tool to create a path around the object you want to keep visible.

Creating a layer mask from a selection

You need to have two images open to follow these steps where we show you how to create layer masks from a selection:

1. **When combining images, choose Image⇨Image Size to make sure that the images are approximately the same resolution.**

   Otherwise, you may create some interesting, but disproportional, effects.

2. **Using the Move tool, click one image and drag it to the other image window.**

   A black border appears around the image area when dropping an image into another image window. By dragging and dropping an image, you automatically create a new layer on top of the active layer.

   Hold down the Shift key when dragging one image to another to perfectly center the new image layer in the document window.

3. **Using any selection method, select a part of the image that you want to keep on the newly placed layer. Choose Select⇨ Modify⇨Feather to soften the selection (5 pixels should be enough).**

4. **Click the Layer Mask button at the bottom of the Layers palette.**

   A mask is created off to the right of your layer, leaving only your selection visible, as shown in Figure 9-3.

5. **If you click the Layer thumbnail in the Layers palette, the mask thumbnail shows corner edges, indicating that it is activated.**

While the layer mask is active, you can paint on the mask.

6. **Press** D **to return to the default black-and-white swatch colors in the toolbox.**

Figure 9-3:
A custom
mask is
created
automatic-
ally from
an active
selection
on a layer
when the
Layer Mask
button is
clicked.

7. **Select the Brush tool and paint black while the mask thumbnail is selected to cover up areas of the image that you don't want to see; press** X **to switch to white and paint to expose areas on the image that you do want to see.**

You can even change the opacity as you paint to blend images in with each other.

To create a smooth transition from one image to another, drag the Gradient tool across the image while the layer mask is selected in the Layers palette.

Creating a vector mask from a pen path

A *vector mask* masks a selection, but it does so with the precision that you can get only from using a path. The following steps show you another, slightly more precise, way to create a layer mask by using a pen path:

1. **Use the Pen tool and click from point to point to make a closed pen path.**

If you already have a path, choose Windows⇨Paths and click a path to select it.

See Chapter 4 of this minibook for more about working with the Pen tool.

2. **On the Layers palette, click the Layer Mask button and then click it again.**

   Wow! A mask from your pen path! Anything that wasn't contained within the path is now masked out. Use the Direct Selection tool to edit the path, if necessary.

If you no longer want vector mask, drag the thumbnail to the Trash icon in the Layers palette. An alert dialog box appears, asking if you'd like to discard the mask or apply it. Click the Discard button to revert your image back to the way it appeared before applying the mask or click the Apply button to apply the masked area.

Organizing Your Layers

As you advance in layer skills, you'll want to keep layers named, neat, and in order. In this section, we show you some tips to help you organize multiple layers.

Activating multiple layers simultaneously

Select multiple layers simultaneously by selecting one layer and then Shift+clicking to select additional layers. The selected layers are highlighted. Selected layers will move and transform together, making repositioning and resizing easier than activating each layer independently.

Select multiple layers to keep their relative positions to each other and take advantage of alignment features. When you select two or more layers and choose the Move tool, you can take advantage of alignment features on the Options bar (see Figure 9-4). Select three or more layers for distribution options.

New Auto-Align Layers tool

Ever have multiple shots of a group, one with the guy's eyes shut, and the girl looking the other way? Or maybe you like the smile in one better than in another. Using the new auto-alignment feature, you can pull the best parts of multiple images into one "best" image.

To use the new tool, simply have the Move tool active, select multiple layers, and then click the Auto-Align Layers button to the right of the alignment tools. The window you see in Figure 9-5 appears; make your selection and click OK.

Align horizontal centers

Align bottom

Distribute bottom edges

Distribute top edges

Distribute horizontal centers

Align top

Figure 9-4:
Align layers
using the
Move tool's
align
options.

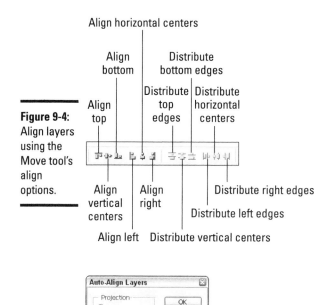

Align vertical centers

Align right

Distribute right edges

Distribute left edges

Align left   Distribute vertical centers

Figure 9-5:
The new
Auto-Align
Layers
feature can
help create
a better
composite.

Layer groups

After you start using layers, you'll likely use lots of them, and your Layers palette will become huge. If you find yourself scrolling to navigate from one layer to another, take advantage of *layer groups,* which essentially act as folders that hold layers that you choose. Just like a folder you use for paper, you can add, remove, and shuffle around the layers within a layer set. Use layer sets to organize your layers and make the job of duplicating multiple layers easier.

To create a layer group, follow these steps:

1. **After creating several layers, Shift+click to select the layers that you want to group together in a set.**

Book IV
Chapter 9

Using Layers

2. **Choose New Group From Layers from the Layers palette menu, name the group, and then click OK.**

   That's it. You've created a layer group from your selected layers.

Pass through in the blending mode indicates that no individual blending modes are changed. Using the Blending Mode drop-down list in the Layers palette, you can change all the layers within a group to a specific blending mode, or you can use the Opacity slider to change the opacity of all layers in a group at once.

After you create a layer group, you can still reorganize layers within the group or even drag in or out additional layers. You can open and close a layer group with the arrow to the left of the set name.

Duplicating a layer group

After you've created a layer group, you may want to copy it. For example, you may want to copy an image, such as a button created from several layers topped off with a text layer. The most efficient way to make a copy of that button is to create a layer group and copy the entire group. To copy an image made up of several layers that aren't in a layer group would require you to individually duplicate each layer — how time-consuming!

To duplicate a layer group, follow these steps:

1. **Select a group from the Layers palette.**

2. **From the palette menu, choose Duplicate Group.**

   The Duplicate Group dialog box appears.

3. **For the destination, choose the present document or any open document or create a new document.**

   Be sure to give the duplicated set a distinctive name!

4. **Click OK.**

Using Layer Styles

Layer styles are wonderful little extras that you can apply to layers to create drop shadows, bevel and emboss effects, apply color overlays, gradients, patterns and strokes, and more.

Applying a style

To apply a layer style (for example, the drop shadow style, one of the most popular effects) to an image, just follow these steps:

1. **Create a layer on any image.**

For example, you could create a text layer to see the effects of the layer styles.

2. **With the layer selected, click and hold the Layer Style button at the bottom of the Layers palette; from the menu options, choose Drop Shadow.**

In the Layer Style dialog box that appears, you can choose to change the blending mode, color, distance spread, and size of a drop shadow. You should see it has already applied to your text. Position the cursor on the image area and drag to visually adjust the position of the drop shadow.

3. **When you're happy with the drop shadow, click OK to apply it.**

To apply another effect and change its options, click and hold the Layer Style button in the Layers palette and choose the name of the layer style from the menu that appears — Bevel And Emboss, for example. In the dialog box that appears, change the settings to customize the layer style and click OK to apply it to your image. For example, if you choose Bevel And Emboss from the Layer Styles menu, you can choose from several emboss styles and adjust the depth, size, and softness.

Here are some consistent items that you see in the Layer Style dialog box, no matter what effect you choose:

✦ **Contour:** Use contours to control the shape and appearance of an effect. Click the arrow to open the Contour fly-out menu to choose a contour preset or click the contour preview to open the Contour Editor and create your own edge.

✦ **Angle:** Drag the cross hair in the angle circle or enter a value in the Angle text field to control where the light source comes from.

✦ **Global light:** If you aren't smart about lighting effects on multiple objects, global light will make it seem as though you are. Select the Use Global Light check box to keep the angle consistent from one layer style to another.

✦ **Color:** Whenever you see a color box, you can click it to select a color. This color can be for the drop shadow, highlight, or shadow of an emboss, or for a color overlay.

Creating and saving a style

If you come up with a combination of attributes that you like, click the New Style button in the upper right of the Layer Style dialog box. Name the style, and it's now stored in the Styles palette. After you click OK, you can retrieve the style at any time by choosing Window⇨Styles. If it helps, click the palette menu button and choose either Small or Large List to change the Styles palette to show only the name of the styles.

After you've applied a layer style to a layer, the style is listed in the Layers palette. You can turn off the visibility of the style by turning off the eye icon or even throw away the layer style by dragging it to the Layers palette's Trash icon.

Thinking about opacity versus fill

In the Layers palette, you have two transparency options, one for opacity and one for fill. Opacity affects the opacity of the entire layer, including effects. Fill, on the other hand, affects only the layer itself, but not layer styles. Figure 9-6 shows what happens when the Bevel And Emboss style is applied to text and the fill is reduced to 0 percent. It looks like the text was embossed onto the image. You can do lots of neat stuff with the Layer Fill feature!

Figure 9-6:
A text layer with styles applied and the fill reduced to 0 percent.

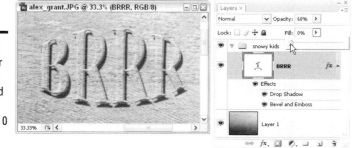

Smart, Really Smart! Smart Objects

Choose File⇨Place and place an image, illustration, or even a movie into a Photoshop document and discover that, as always, a new layer is created, but even better than that, a Smart Object is created. The icon in the lower right of the layer thumbnail indicates that this layer is a Smart Object.

What does being a Smart Object mean? It means that you have much more flexibility with the placement of your images. Have you ever placed a logo, to find out later you need it to be three times the size? Resizing is no longer an issue, as the Photoshop Smart Object is linked to an embedded original. If the original is vector, you can freely resize the image over and over again without worrying about poor resolution. Want to change the spelling of your placed Illustrator logo? Just double-click the Smart Object, the embedded original is opened right in Adobe Illustrator, make your changes and save the file, and viola . . . it's automatically updated in the Photoshop file.

What could be better than this? Smart filters, of course. You can apply Smart filters to any Smart Object layer, or even convert a layer to use Smart Filters, by choosing Filters⇨Convert For Smart Filters. Once a layer has been converted to a Smart Object, you can choose filters, any filters, and apply them to the layer. If you want to paint out the effects of the filter on the layer, simply paint with black on the Filter effects thumbnail. Paint with different opacities of black and white to give an artistic feel to the Filter effect, as shown in Figure 9-7. You can even turn off the filters by turning off the visibility on the Filter Effects thumbnail by clicking the eye icon to the left of the Filter Effects Thumbnail.

Figure 9-7:
Cover the filter effects by painting on the filter effects thumbnail.

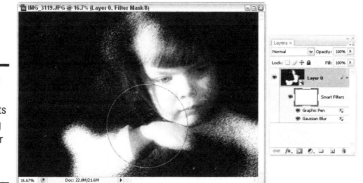

Merging and Flattening the Image

Merging layers combines several selected layers into one layer. *Flattening* is when you reduce all layers to one background layer. Layers can increase your file in size, thereby also tying up valuable processing resources. To keep file size down, you may choose to merge some layers or even flatten the entire image down to one background layer.

Merging

Merging layers is helpful when you no longer need every layer to be independent, like when you have a separate shadow layer aligned to another layer and don't plan on moving it again, or when you combine many layers to create a composite and want to consolidate it to one layer.

To merge layers (in a visual and easy way), follow these steps:

1. **Turn on the visibility of only the layers that you want merged.**

2. **Choose Merge Visible from the Layers palette menu.**

   That's it. The entire image isn't flattened, but the visible layers are now reduced to one layer.

To merge visible layers onto a target (selected) layer that you create while keeping the visible layers independent, do the following: Create a blank layer and select it. Hold down Alt (Windows) or Option (Mac) when choosing Merge Visible from the palette menu.

Flattening

If you don't have to flatten your image, don't! Flattening your image reduces all layers down to one background layer, which is necessary for certain file formats, but after you flatten an image, you can't take advantage of blending options or reposition the layered items. (Read more about saving files in Chapter 10 of this minibook.)

If you absolutely must flatten layers, keep a copy of the original, unflattened document for additional edits in the future.

To flatten all layers in an image, choose Layer⇨Flatten Image or choose Flatten Image from the palette menu on the Layers palette.

Chapter 10: Saving Photoshop Images for Print and the Web

In This Chapter

✔ Determining the correct file formats for saving

✔ Preparing your images for the Web

✔ Discovering the color table

A productive workflow depends on you choosing the proper format in which to save your Photoshop files. Without the correct settings, your file may not be visible to other applications, or you may delete valuable components, such as layers or channels. This chapter provides you with the necessary information to save the file correctly for both print and Web. We cover the file format choices before moving on to the proper use of the Save For Web & Devices feature (for saving in the GIF, JPEG, PNG, and WBMP file formats).

 Saving files in the correct file format is important not only for file size, but in support of different Photoshop features, as well. If you're unsure about saving in the right format, save a copy of the file, keeping the original in the PSD format (the native Photoshop format). Photoshop alerts you automatically when you choose a format in the Save As or the Save For Web & Devices dialog box that doesn't support Photoshop features. When you choose a format that doesn't support some of the features you've used, such as channels or layers, a yield sign appears when a copy is being made. It's a good idea to save an original backup just in case you need to return to the original file.

Choosing a File Format for Saving

When you choose File⇨Save for the first time (or you choose File⇨Save As to save a different version of a file), you see at least 18 different file formats that you can choose from in the Save As Type drop-down list. We don't cover each format in this chapter (some are specific to proprietary work-flows), but we do show you which formats are best for the typical workflow that you may face.

Creating a PDF presentation

You can create a multipage PDF file or presentation by using Adobe Bridge (choose File⇨Browse). While in Adobe Bridge, choose Tools⇨Photoshop⇨PDF Presentation. In the PDF Presentation dialog box, use the Browse button to choose the files that you want to add to the Source list. You can Ctrl+click (Windows) or ⌘+click (Mac) to select multiple files and add them to the Source list.

In the output options section, choose Multi-Page or Presentation PDF. If you choose

Presentation, you're given the opportunity to set up slide show options, such as timing and transition effects.

Click Save, name the file, and click Save again. The Save Adobe PDF dialog box appears. If you want to see the PDF immediately, make sure that you select the View PDF After Saving check box, choose any other specific options that you want for the PDF (see Book V for more specifics on PDF settings), and click OK.

Wonderful and easy Photoshop PSD

If you're in an Adobe workflow (you're using any Adobe products), you can keep the image in the native Photoshop PSD format. By choosing this format, transparency, layers, channels, and paths are all maintained and left intact when placed in the other applications.

To maximize compatibility with previous versions of Photoshop and with other applications, choose Edit⇨Preferences⇨File Handling (Windows) or Photoshop⇨Preferences⇨File Handling (Mac). Choose Always from the Maximize PSD File Compatibility drop-down list. This choice saves a composite (flattened) image along with the layers of your document.

Leaving the Maximize PSD File Compatibility drop-down list set to Always creates a larger file. If file size is an issue, leave the drop-down list set to Ask, and only use the feature when you need to open the Photoshop file in older versions of Photoshop.

Photoshop EPS

Virtually every desktop application accepts the EPS (Encapsulated PostScript) file format. The EPS format is used to transfer PostScript-language artwork between various applications. It supports vector data, duotones, and clipping paths.

When you choose to save in the EPS format, an EPS Options dialog box appears. Leave the defaults and click OK.

Alter the settings in the EPS Options dialog box *only* if you're familiar with custom printer calibration, or you need to save your image to a specific screen ruling. Screen rulings (lpi) are usually set in a page layout application, such as Adobe InDesign or QuarkXPress.

Photoshop PDF

If compatibility is an issue, save your file in the Photoshop PDF (Portable Document Format) format. PDF files are supported by more than a dozen platforms when viewers use Acrobat or Adobe Reader. (Adobe Reader is available for free at www.adobe.com.) What a perfect way to send pictures to friends and family! Saving your file in the Photoshop PDF format supports your ability to edit the image when you open the file by choosing File⇨Open in Photoshop.

TIFF

TIFF (Tagged Image File Format) is a flexible bitmap image format that is supported by most image-editing and page-layout applications widely supported by all printers. TIFF supports layers and channels, but it has a maximum size of 4GB. We hope your files aren't that large!

DCS

The Photoshop DCS (Desktop Color Separation) 1.0 and 2.0 formats are versions of EPS that enable you to save color separations of CMYK or multichannel files. Some workflows require this format, but if you have implemented spot color channels in your image, using the DCS file format is required to maintain them.

Choose the DCS 2.0 format unless you received specific instructions to use the DCS 1.0 format — for example, for reasons of incompatibility in certain workflows.

Saving for the Web and Devices

To access the maximum number of options for the GIF, JPEG, PNG, and WBMP file formats, save your image by choosing File⇨Save For Web & Devices. The Save For Web & Devices dialog box appears, which allows you to optimize the image as you save it. This procedure may sound big, but it's just the process of making the image as small as possible while keeping it visually pleasing.

Saving images for the Web is a give-and-take experience. You may find yourself sacrificing perfect imagery to make the image small enough in size that it can be downloaded and viewed quickly by users. Read the upcoming sections on GIF and JPG formats to see how you can best handle creating Web images.

The following sections describe the differences between GIF, JPEG, PNG, and WBMP. Choose the appropriate format based upon the type of image you're saving.

Having the image size correct before you save the file for the Web is a good practice. If you need to read up on resizing images, see Chapter 6 of this minibook. But generally speaking, you want to resize the image to the right pixel dimensions. Choose Filter➪Sharpen➪Unsharp Mask to gain back some of the detail lost when resizing the image and then save the image for the Web.

GIF

Supposedly, the way you pronounce GIF (Graphics Interchange Format) is based on the type of peanut butter you eat. Is it pronounced like the peanut butter brand (Jiff), or with a hard G, like gift? Most people seem to pronounce it like gift (minus the T).

Use the GIF format if you have lots of solid color, such as a logo like the one shown in Figure 10-1.

Figure 10-1:
An image with large amounts of solid color is a good candidate for the GIF file format.

The GIF format is not *lossy* (it doesn't lose data when the file is compressed in this format), but it does reduce the file size by using a limited number of colors in a color table. The lower the number of colors, the smaller the file size. If you've ever worked in the Index color mode, you're familiar with this process.

Transparency is supported by the GIF file. But generally, GIFs don't do a good job with anything that needs smooth transitions from one color to another because of its poor support of anti-aliasing. *Anti-aliasing* is the method that Photoshop uses to smooth jagged edges. When pixels transition from one color to another, Photoshop produces multiple color pixels to evenly blend from one pixel to another.

Because anti-aliasing needs to create multiple colors for this effect, GIF files are generally not recommended. In fact, when you reduce a GIF in size, you're more apt to see *banding* because the anti-aliasing can't take place with the limited number of colors available in the GIF format.

You can, of course, dramatically increase the number of colors to create a smoother transition, but then you risk creating monster files that take forever to download.

Saving a GIF

When you choose File⇨Save for Web, you first see the available GIF format options. The GIF options may be more clear to you if you have an image (with lots of solid color) open.

To save a file for the Web as a GIF, follow these steps:

1. **Choose File⇨Save For Web & Devices.**

The Save For Web & Devices dialog box appears.

2. **At the top, click the 2-Up tab.**

You see the original image on the left and the optimized image on the right (or top and bottom, depending upon the proportions of your image).

In the lower portion of the display, you see the original file size compared to the optimized file size, as well as the approximate download time. This time is important! Nobody wants to wait around for a Web page to load; most people won't wait more than ten seconds for the entire Web page to appear, so try to keep an individual image's download time down to five seconds or less. Remember, all the images on a page can add up to one monstrous wait time for the viewer!

Change the download speed by choosing from the Preview menu (it's the arrow on the upper-right side of the Save For Web & Devices dialog box). The Preview menu isn't labeled, so look for the ToolTip to appear when you hover your cursor over the arrow icon.

3. **Choose GIF 32 No Dither from the Preset drop-down list.**

You may see a change already. Photoshop supplies you with presets that you can choose from, or you can customize and save your own.

4. **Choose whether you want dithering applied to the image by selecting an option from the Specify The Dither Algorithm drop-down list.**

   This choice is purely personal. Because you may be limiting colors, Photoshop can use dithering to mix the pixels of the available colors to simulate the missing colors. Many designers choose the No Dither option.

Using the color table

When you save an image as a GIF using the Save For Web & Devices dialog box, you see the color table for the image on the right side of the dialog box. The color table is important because it not only allows you to see the colors used in the image, but also enables you to customize the color table by using the options at the bottom of the color table.

You may want to customize your color table by selecting some of your colors to be Web safe and locking colors so that they're not bumped off as you reduce the amount of colors.

To customize a color table, follow these steps:

1. **If your image has only a few colors that you'd like to convert to Web-safe colors, choose the Eyedropper tool from the left of the Save For Web & Devices dialog box and click the color, in the Optimized view.**

   The sampled color is highlighted in the color table.

2. **Click the Web Safe button at the bottom of the color table.**

   A ToolTip appears when you cross over this button with the text; Shifts/Unshift selected colors to web palette.

   A diamond appears, indicating that the color is now Web safe.

3. **Lock colors that you don't want to delete as you reduce the number of colors in the color table.**

   Select a color with the Eyedropper tool or choose it in the color table and then click the Lock Color button. A white square appears in the lower-right corner, indicating that the color is locked.

   If you lock 32 colors and then reduce the color table to 24, some of your locked colors will be deleted. If you choose to add colors, those locked colors will be the first to return.

How is the color table created? Based upon a color reduction algorithm method that you choose, the Save For The Web feature samples the number of colors that you indicate. If keeping colors Web safe is important, select the Restrictive (Web) option for the method; if you want your image to look better on most monitors, but not necessarily be Web safe, choose the Adaptive option.

4. **Use the arrows to the right of the Colors combo box or enter a number to add or delete colors from the color table.**

5. **If your image uses transparency, select the Transparency check box.**

Remember that transparency is counted as one of your colors in the color table.

6. **Select the Interlaced check box only if your GIF image is large in size (25K or larger).**

Selecting this option causes the image to build in several scans on the Web page, a low-resolution image that pops up quickly to be refreshed with the higher resolution image when it's finished downloading. Interlacing gives the illusion of the download going faster but makes the file size larger, so use it only if necessary.

7. **Click Save.**

Now the image is ready to be attached to an e-mail message or used in a Web page.

JPEG

JPEG (Joint Photographic Experts Group) is the best format for continuous tone images (those with smooth transitions from one color to another, as in photographs), like the image shown in Figure 10-2.

The JPEG format is lossy, so you should not save a JPEG, open it, edit it, and save it again as a JPEG. Because the JPEG compression causes data to be lost, your image will eventually look like it was printed on a paper towel. Save a copy of the file as a JPEG, keeping the original image in the PSD format if you need to later edit the image, open the original PSD, make your changes, save the PSD, and then save a copy of the edited file as a JPEG.

The JPEG format does *not* support transparency, but you can cheat the system a little by using matting.

A good image to save in the JPEG format is a typical photograph or illustration with lots of smooth transitions from one color to the next. To save an image as a JPEG, follow these steps:

1. **Choose File⇨Save For Web & Devices and then click the 2-Up tab to view the original image (left) at the same time as the optimized image (right).**

2. **Choose one of the JPEG preset settings from the Settings drop-down list.**

You can choose Low, Medium, High, or customize a level in between the presets by using the Quality slider.

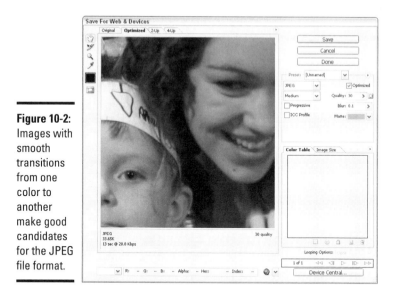

Figure 10-2: Images with smooth transitions from one color to another make good candidates for the JPEG file format.

3. **Leave the Optimized check box selected to build the best JPEG at the smallest size.**

   The only issue with leaving this check box selected is that some very old browsers won't read the JPEG correctly. (This is probably not an issue for most of your viewers.)

4. **Deselect the ICC Profile check box unless you're in a color-managed workflow and color accuracy is essential.**

   Deselecting the ICC Profile check box dramatically increases the file size, and most people aren't looking for *exact* color matches from an image on the monitor . . . and it's scary if they are!

5. **Use the Blur slider to bring down some detail.**

   It's funny, but one JPEG that's the exact same pixel dimensions as another may vary in file size because the more detailed an image, the more information is needed. So an image of lots of apples will be larger than an image the same size that has a lot of clear blue sky in it. The blur feature does blur the image (surprise!), so you may want to use this for only a Low Source image in Dreamweaver.

6. **(Optional) Choose a matte color from the Matte drop-down list.**

   Because JPEG doesn't support transparency, you can flood the transparent area with a color that you choose from the Matte drop-down list.

Choose the color that you're using for the background of your Web page by choosing Other and entering the hexadecimal color in the lower portion of the color picker.

7. **Click Save.**

PNG

PNG (Portable Network Graphics) is almost the perfect combination of JPEG and GIF. Unfortunately, PNG isn't yet widely supported . . . note, as well, that PNG-24 images have file sizes that can be too large to use on the Web.

PNG supports varying levels of transparency and anti-aliasing. This variation means that you can specify an image as being 50 percent transparent, and it will actually show through to the underlying Web page! You have a choice of PNG-8 and PNG-24 in the Save For Web & Devices dialog box. As a file format for optimizing images, PNG-8 doesn't give you any advantage over a regular GIF file.

PNG files are *not* supported by all browsers. In older browsers, a plug-in may be required to view your page. Ouch . . . by choosing PNG, you could shoot yourself in the foot because not all your viewers will be able to view the PNG.

If you're saving a PNG file, you have a choice of PNG-8 or PNG-24. The PNG-8 options are essentially the same as the GIF options; see the "Saving a GIF" section, earlier in this chapter, for details.

PNG-24 saves 24-bit images that support anti-aliasing (the smooth transition from one color to another). They work beautifully for continuous-tone images, but are much larger than a JPEG file. The truly awesome feature of a PNG file is that it supports 256 levels of transparency. In other words, you can apply varying amounts of transparency in an image, as shown in Figure 10-3, where the image shows through to the background.

Figure 10-3:
A PNG-24 file with varying amounts of transparency.

La Kelly
The magazine for the rest of us...

Book IV
Chapter 10

Saving Photoshop
Images for Print and
the Web

WBMP

WBMP is short for Wireless BitMap, a format optimized for mobile computing, has no compression, is one-bit color (just black and white, no shades!), and is one bit deep. WBMP images aren't necessary pretty, but functional (see Figure 10-4). You do have dithering controls to show some level of tone value.

If you're creating images for mobile devices, you should know that WBMP is part of the Wireless Application Protocol, Wireless Application Environment Specification Version 1.1.

Select the Preview In Default Browser check box at the bottom of the Save For Web & Devices dialog box to launch your chosen Web browser and display the image as it will appear with the present settings. If you haven't set up a browser, click the down arrow and choose Other from the drop-down menu. Browse to locate a browser that you want to preview your image in.

Want to see how your mobile content is going to look on specific devices? Then click the Device Central button in the lower right of the Save For Web & Devices dialog box.

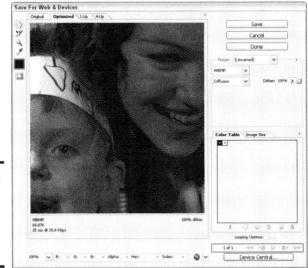

Figure 10-4:
The WBMP
format
supports
black and
white only.

Matte

Matting appears as a choice in the JPEG, GIF, and PNG format options. Matting is useful if you don't want ragged edges appearing around your image. Matting looks for pixels that are greater than 50 percent transparent and makes them fully transparent; any pixels that are 50 percent or less transparent become fully opaque.

Even though your image might be on a transparent layer, there will be some iffy pixels, the ones that aren't sure what they want to be . . . to be transparent or not to be transparent. Choose a matte color to blend in with the transparent iffy pixels by selecting Eyedropper, White, Black, or Other (to open the color picker) from the Matte drop-down list in the Save For Web & Devices dialog box.

Saving Settings

Whether you're saving a GIF, JPG, or PNG file, you probably spent some time experimenting with settings to find what works best for your needs. Save your selected options to reload at a later time by saving the settings. Do so by clicking the arrow to the right of the Preset drop-down list. Choose Save Settings from the menu that appears and give your settings a name. Your named, customized settings then appear in the Settings drop-down list.

Book V

Acrobat 8

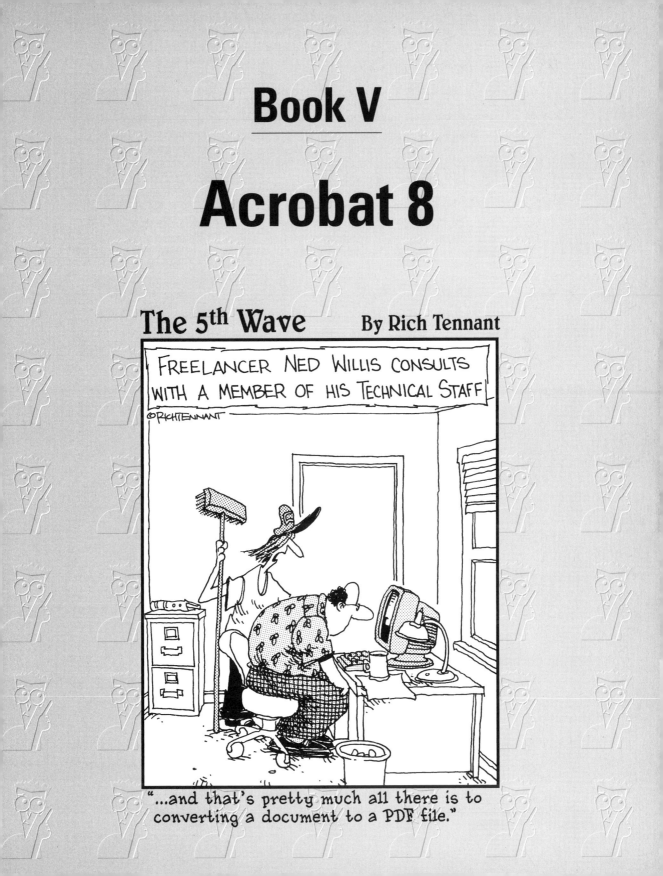

The 5th Wave · By Rich Tennant

FREELANCER NED WILLIS CONSULTS WITH A MEMBER OF HIS TECHNICAL STAFF

©RICHTENNANT

"...and that's pretty much all there is to converting a document to a PDF file."

Contents at a Glance

Chapter 1: Discovering Essential Acrobat Information

In This Chapter

✔ Discovering Acrobat and PDF files

✔ Knowing when to use PDF files

✔ Becoming familiar with the Acrobat workspace and tools

*A*dobe Acrobat 8 provides a variety of tools for sharing and reviewing documents. Although the Adobe Creative Suite applications can create Portable Document Format (PDF) files without Acrobat, you can use Acrobat to create PDF files from programs that aren't part of the Creative Suite. You can also use Adobe Acrobat to enhance PDF files, regardless of how they were created. You can add security to restrict features such as printing or editing, change the page order, merge documents together, add comments and annotations, and even create PDF forms.

In this chapter, you find out why you may want to create PDF files and acquaint yourself with the Adobe Acrobat tools and workspace. You'll see how easy it is to navigate through PDF files using the navigational tools, tabs, and viewing options in Acrobat. In the following chapters of this minibook, you explore how to use Acrobat to create Adobe PDF files from documents produced in a variety of programs and discover ways to enhance your Adobe PDF files.

Working with PDF Files

Adobe Acrobat is used to create Adobe PDF files, review existing PDF files, and modify existing PDF files. When you work with programs in the Adobe Creative Suite, such as Adobe InDesign, and you want to share your work with colleagues or clients, you need to find a way to deliver the documents to them. Of course, you can always print your documents and send them via courier, the mail, or even fax. But all these methods take time and don't provide for easy collaboration. This area is where PDF files are helpful.

Many people prefer to receive documents electronically, but there's a small problem: All the people with whom you need to share files probably don't have the same software you use. They may not all have InDesign — or whatever part of the Adobe Creative Suite you're using. PDF provides a common file format that everyone can open to review your documents. PDF provides an application independent method for viewing your files, regardless of what computer program was used to create them. The PDF file format also lets Mac users share their files with Windows users, and vice versa. Additionally, Acrobat provides extensive tools for review, commenting, and marking up so that you can easily collaborate on a project without modifying the original document.

You can view PDF files on many different computer types, including Macintosh computers, Windows computers, Unix computers, and even some cell phones and handheld PDAs. Because the software to view Adobe PDF files is free, you can be assured that those receiving your files don't need to purchase any special software. In fact, the odds are quite good that most users already have this free software, called Adobe Reader, as more than 500 million copies have been distributed. Adobe has actually released the underpinnings of PDF to all computer software makers, allowing them to freely create different programs to read and create PDF files.

What makes PDF so useful is that it provides a true reproduction of original documents. The fidelity of PDF files is so good that the Internal Revenue Service uses this format to distribute tax forms online. Likewise, many banks, insurance agencies, and financial services firms use PDF as a method for distributing documents. We even use PDF files to send books like the one you're reading now to the printing plant.

Although PDF files provide a high-quality representation of an original file, they're more than just a picture of the document from which they were created. PDF files retain the high-quality appearance of text so that they print clearly and are searchable. Logos and illustrations created using Adobe Illustrator retain the same high-quality appearance within a PDF file. PDF files also may contain the intricate details that are captured in bitmap images, such as those edited using Adobe Photoshop — but PDF files are able to keep both bitmap and vector information together in the same file, making them a great choice for distributing documents electronically. You don't have to sacrifice quality to distribute a file electronically. You do need to know a few things about Acrobat to create the right type of PDF files for your needs, though. The PDF file you'd send to a printer may be too big for anyone to post on a Web site or send as an e-mail attachment, for example.

One new feature in Acrobat 8 lets you create PDF packages. A PDF package contains multiple PDF files and can also contain other file types that aren't PDF files. A PDF package may contain a few pages from a PowerPoint presentation, part of a spreadsheet, a CAD drawing, some text documents, perhaps an e-mail or two, and so on. This great flexibility is a powerful enhancement to Adobe Acrobat.

Adobe Acrobat is a tool for distributing documents; it's *not* a design tool. You generally don't use Acrobat to build new documents, although Acrobat 8 does let you create a blank page and put text and objects on that page. However, Acrobat is meant to be a medium for sharing files, not for creating them. Simply put, you don't use Acrobat to create new documents. But Acrobat is still incredibly useful. Using Acrobat, you can

✦ Share documents with users who don't have the same software or fonts that you use.

✦ Review and mark up PDF files that others send you. You can also enable a PDF file to be reviewed by users with the free Adobe Reader software.

✦ Combine documents created in other programs. You can use Acrobat to merge PDF files that may have been originally created in different programs.

✦ Create a PDF Package. You can combine various file formats into a single PDF Package and yet retain the files in their original file formats.

✦ Edit Adobe PDF files.

✦ Apply security to PDF files when you don't want them changed.

✦ Add interactivity to PDF files by infusing them with sounds, movies, and buttons.

✦ Create interactive forms, where you can collect information without requiring a user to print, write, and then fax or mail information back to you.

We cover these capabilities throughout the rest of this minibook.

Knowing When to Use Adobe PDF Files

So when does it make sense to use Adobe PDF files? Here are some examples:

✦ **When you've created a spreadsheet that includes numbers, formulas, and tables that you don't want others to edit:** Your recipients may have the same software you used to build the document, but you can keep them from editing the original spreadsheet file by distributing it as a PDF file.

✦ **When you've created a presentation that you want others to deliver, but you work on a PC and some of them use Macintosh systems:** By converting the document to PDF, you don't have to worry about issues that can arise when sharing files between different computer types. For example, fonts are typically included within PDF documents and can be used on any computer systems with the free Adobe Reader or the complete Adobe Acrobat software.

In addition, by sending the presentation in PDF format rather than in the original presentation file format, you don't have to be concerned that the recipients may edit the file.

✦ **When you have a sensitive document that will be shared only with certain authorized colleagues:** If you have a document containing information that you don't want unauthorized persons viewing, you can add security to a PDF file by using Adobe Acrobat's security tools. Using these options, you can require users to enter a password to view the file, and you can limit other features, such as the ability to print or edit the document.

✦ **When you want to review a document quickly and efficiently:** When documents need to be reviewed or approved, Acrobat really shines. You can use commenting, markup, and annotation tools to add suggestions and edits to a file, regardless of where it was created. You can even combine comments from multiple reviewers into a single document.

Introducing the Adobe Acrobat Workspace and Tools

To take advantage of all that Adobe Acrobat has to offer, you'll want to discover the workspace and tools Acrobat uses. Adobe has significantly revised the Acrobat 8 interface. Unlike previous versions of Acrobat, which opened with a blank workspace, Acrobat 8 opens with a Getting Started screen. It provides eight possible tasks: Create PDF, Combine Files, Export, Start Meeting, Secure, Sign, Forms, and Review & Comment. These tasks are also incorporated in Acrobat's toolbar once you begin working with your document. You can click a task in the Getting Started window, or if you just want to review a file, you can close the Start Up window like you would any other document window by clicking the Close Window button in the corner.

The Getting Started window appears each time you open Acrobat unless you click the Do Not Show At Startup check box.

Once you open a document, you see the Acrobat workspace, which is divided into three areas: the document window, the toolbar well, and the navigation panes. When you open a PDF document using Acrobat, you can use the toolbars, buttons, and navigation panes to work with and manipulate the PDF file. For example, a PDF file may contain multiple pages. You can use the navigational buttons or the Pages navigation panel to move between pages and then use commenting tools to mark up the file.

The toolbar provides useful information for navigating through your document, including:

✦ **Current page and total pages:** Click in the area showing the current page, type a different page number, and press Enter (Windows) or Return (Mac) to view a specific page.

✦ **Previous Page/Next Page:** Use these navigational buttons to skip forward or backward by one page.

The Zoom tools

If things are a bit too small for you to see clearly, increase the magnification used for viewing pages with the Zoom drop-down menu in the toolbar. Using the toolbar, select from a preset magnification by choosing the drop-down list showing magnification percentages. The preset magnification choices are available to the right of the current magnification level, which is displayed in the menu bar. You can use the minus (–) and plus (+) symbols to the left of the current magnification level to zoom out or in from the current magnification.

The Marquee Zoom tool is the magnifying glass icon, and you can use it to identify specific portions of a page that you want to magnify. Select this tool and then click and drag around a portion of the page to increase the magnification. You can also click multiple times on an area to increase its magnification, but clicking and dragging a box with the Zoom In tool is generally a much faster way to focus on a portion of a page you want to view. You can change the Zoom In tool to the Zoom Out tool (magnifying glass with a minus sign) by selecting the Marquee Zoom tool and Alt-click (PC) or Option-click (Mac) in the document window. The magnifier's plus (+) sign changes to a minus (-) to indicate that you're decreasing the document's magnification. But it's usually faster to choose a preset zoom percentage.

To the right of the magnification percentage box are page icons that you can use to change the page magnification:

✦ **Scrolling Pages:** Use this button to avoid scrolling from left to right when reading a document. The view is changed to fit the document's width in the available space on your display, making it necessary to only scroll up and down on a page. This also sets the page view to display the top or bottom of adjacent pages. When you scroll and reach the bottom of one page, the top of the next page becomes visible.

✦ **One Full Page:** Use this button to fit the current page within the available screen space on your monitor. For smaller documents, such as a business card, the magnification is increased. For larger documents, the magnification is generally decreased unless you have a large monitor. When viewing pages in the Fit Page mode, only one page is displayed at a time. This mode is good for viewing the entire display of a page layout.

Toolbars

The toolbars in Acrobat 8 are now customizable, so you can combine functions from different toolbars to meet your needs.

For example, Acrobat also includes several additional tools for navigation, which are accessible by choosing View➪Toolbars➪More Tools. In the More Tools window that appears, select the navigation tools you'd like to have displayed in the toolbar. The Selecting and Zoom Toolbar section displays the navigation tool choices that can be displayed.

Less than half of the toolbars are visible in the default Acrobat display. You can add to the tools that are displayed or limit them by clicking the check box next to those you want to display or hide in the More Tools window. Toolbars that have a check mark next to their names are visible, while those without a check mark aren't visible.

Customizing the location of toolbars on your screen can make it easier for you to work with PDF files using Acrobat. For example, you may want all the tools for navigating through your documents in one section of the toolbar well. To achieve this, you can rearrange the location of specific toolbars.

Along the left edge of every group of tools is a dotted double line. By clicking and holding onto this edge with your mouse, you can drag any toolbar to a new location on your screen. This new location can be within the same area holding the other toolbars, or anywhere in the Acrobat work area. If you pull a toolbar out of the docking area, it becomes an independent, floating toolbar. You can reposition or drag floating toolbars back into the docking area when you're finished working with them. You can also close a floating toolbar by clicking its Close Window button. You can place toolbars along the left or right of the Acrobat work area — turning either side of the Acrobat workspace into a docking area for toolbars.

Although the flexibility of placing toolbars anywhere you like is useful, it may lead to a chaotic work environment. Instead of leaving toolbars all over your screen, you can have Acrobat clean up the workspace by choosing View⇨Toolbars⇨Reset Toolbars.

Toolbars contain both tools and buttons. For example, you choose the Marquee Zoom tool to change the magnification by clicking or selecting an area of the page. Buttons perform an immediate task, such as printing, saving, or applying security to a PDF document. In general, most of the task buttons are on the top row of the docking area, immediately below the menu bar, and most of the tools are on the bottom row — but you can move these toolbars.

Some tools and task buttons also include additional options that you can access through drop-down lists within the toolbars. Tools and buttons that contain additional choices are noted by the small triangle immediately to the right of the icon. Click this small triangle, and you see a menu listing the additional choices for that tool or button.

Viewing modes

Acrobat provides several viewing modes that control how the entire document is displayed. You can choose which viewing mode is used by choosing View⇨ Page Display and selecting the viewing option you want.

The viewing modes are

✦ **Single Page:** This mode displays only the current document page on-screen and does not show any adjoining pages. When you scroll to the top or bottom of the current page, other pages aren't visible at the same time as the current page.

✦ **Single Page Continuous:** With this mode, you can see the current document page, and if you scroll to the top (or bottom) of the current page, the adjoining page is also visible. If you reduce your page viewing magnification, many document pages are visible.

✦ **Two-Up (previously known as Facing):** Use this mode to see pages as a *spread,* where you can view both the left and right side of adjoining pages at the same time. When you have documents with pictures or text that spans a pair of pages, use this option to see the pages presented side-by-side in Acrobat. As with the Single Page mode, other pages that go before or fall after the spread aren't visible — only the one pair of pages is visible on-screen, regardless of the magnification or scrolling.

✦ **Two-Up Continuous (previously known as Continuous-Facing):** If you have a document with many pages containing text or pictures on their adjoining pages, you can use this mode to scroll from one pair of visible pages to the next. When the Continuous-Facing view is selected, you can see adjoining page spreads. This option is identical to the Facing option, but it also shows pages above or below the spread you are presently viewing.

If you have pages where images or text go across pages, the Two-Up choice is useful. By default, the pages generally display incorrectly. For example, a magazine will display the cover (page 1) and page 2 together, instead of pages 2 and 3. To correct this, you need to choose View⇨Page Display⇨Show Cover Page During Two-Up.

You can add viewing modes as menu buttons using the More Tools window, described earlier in the Tools section.

Additional viewing options

Acrobat has two options for changing your document display.

✦ **Full Screen Mode (View⇨Full Screen Mode):** You can use the Full Screen View option to hide all menus, toolbars, and other parts of the Acrobat interface. This option is useful if you want to focus on the document being displayed, not the program being used to view it. Use this mode, for example, when you've a converted PowerPoint file to a PDF document and want to deliver the presentation using Acrobat. If you're viewing a document in the Full Screen Mode, press the Esc key to return to the regular viewing mode.

You can set a document to automatically open in Full Screen Mode by choosing File⇨Properties and choosing this option from the Initial View panel of the Document Properties window. Additionally, you can choose Edit⇨Preferences and select the Full Screen option along the top left side of the Preferences window to control various aspects of the Full Screen Mode. Some choices include the transition between pages and whether pages advance automatically, allowing you to create a self-running PDF presentation.

✦ **Reading Mode (View⇨Reading Mode):** With so many toolbars, they sometimes get in the way. Reading Mode temporarily hides all your toolbars.

Navigation panels

Acrobat offers a variety of panels that are helpful when navigating through PDF documents. The term *panel* may be a bit misleading because similar options are called *palettes* or *panes* in the other Adobe Creative Suite programs. Regardless of the name, however, you use them to get around PDF files more easily.

The navigation panels are visible along the left side of your document window as small icons (refer to Figure 1-2). Click an icon to make its panel visible. For example, click the Pages icon to display thumbnail-size representations of each page, as shown in Figure 1-5. You can click a thumbnail page to have that page displayed in the document window. You can also choose View⇨Navigation Panels to access the panels. There are 14 panels: Articles, Attachments, Bookmarks, Comments, Content, Destination, How To, Info, Layers, Model Tree, Order, Pages, Signatures, and Tags.

Many panels have more advanced uses that are covered in later chapters of this minibook. In this chapter, we provide you with a brief understanding of how you can use the Pages tab to more easily navigate through a PDF document. Just do this:

1. **Make sure that the Pages panel is visible by clicking its panel icon.**

2. **In the Pages panel, click any page thumbnail to navigate directly to that page.**

   A dark border appears around the selected page. In the lower-right corner of the page is a very small red box.

3. **Drag the small red box up and toward the left, in a diagonal movement, to focus the magnification on a smaller portion of the page.**

Chapter 2: Creating PDF Files

In This Chapter

✓ Creating PDF files from Microsoft Word, Excel, and PowerPoint documents

✓ Creating PDF files from Adobe Creative Suite applications

✓ Creating PDF files from all other electronic formats

✓ Creating PDF files from paper documents and the Web

*Y*ou don't need Adobe Acrobat to create Portable Document Format (PDF) files from Adobe Creative Suite documents — this capability is built right into the Creative Suite application — but you do need Acrobat for creating PDF files from many other programs. Converting documents to the PDF format is a great way to share information. In this chapter, you find out how to create Adobe PDF files from a variety of programs.

Creating PDF Files from Microsoft Office

Adobe Acrobat includes tools that make it easy to convert Microsoft Word, Excel, and PowerPoint files to PDF. These capabilities are much more robust for the Windows versions of these programs, so Macintosh users may find that not all these options are available.

When you install Acrobat on your computer, it looks for Microsoft Office programs. If it locates Word, Excel, PowerPoint, or Outlook, it installs a utility called PDF Maker 8 that helps convert Microsoft Office documents to PDF. This utility installs a PDF Maker 8 toolbar that appears in these programs, allowing for one-click PDF creation.

You can tell whether Adobe Acrobat PDF Maker 8 has been installed for these Microsoft Office programs by looking for the Adobe PDF menu to the right of the Help menu, and the PDF Maker 8 toolbar. If the Adobe PDF menu is not there, check View➪Toolbars to see whether Adobe Acrobat PDF Maker 8 is available to select in the Toolbars submenu. If it still isn't available, it's possible that Acrobat did not install Adobe PDF Maker 8. To gain access to the Adobe PDF Maker 8 utility, you can reinstall Adobe Acrobat.

When you convert documents to Adobe PDF, the original file remains unchanged, so you'll have both the original file and a separate PDF document. The original document and the PDF aren't linked, so changes to the original source file aren't reflected in the PDF file.

PDF conversion options

Adobe PDF Maker 8 provides a variety of controls over how PDF files are created. For example, you can have Acrobat create the file without asking you to confirm the location and name of the file each time you click the Convert To Adobe PDF button, and it will simply save the file in the same location as the original document. Similarly, you can choose to create PDF files that balance your need for quality and file size.

PDF Maker 8 provides controls over the type of PDF file you create. This is because some PDF files may need to be of a higher quality for printing, and others may need to be smaller to allow for fast electronic distribution. For example, you may want to post a PDF document to a Web site, where you want to make the file small so that it can be quickly downloaded.

When working in Microsoft Word, Excel, or PowerPoint, you can access the PDF Maker 8 controls by choosing Adobe PDF⇨Change Conversion Settings. In the Acrobat PDF Maker 8 dialog box that appears, you can then choose from a variety of settings that control how the PDF file is created. In this section, we focus on the most useful options for Microsoft Office users.

From the Conversion Settings drop-down list in the Acrobat PDF Maker 8 dialog box, you can find these useful options that control how the PDF file is generated:

✦ **Standard:** Choose this option to create PDF files that will be printed on an office laser printer or distributed via e-mail. This setting meets the needs of most users — it provides some compression of graphics, but they remain clear on-screen and look reasonably good when printed. In addition, this setting builds the fonts into the PDF file to maintain an exact representation of the document, regardless of where the file is viewed.

✦ **Smallest File Size:** With this setting, you can control the file size of the PDF documents you create. This setting provides significant compression of images and also reduces resolution, which causes graphics within the files to lose some clarity and perhaps appear jagged.

In addition, fonts aren't embedded in PDF files created with this setting. If the fonts used in the document aren't available on a computer where a PDF created with the Smallest File Size setting is viewed, Acrobat uses a font substitution technology to replicate the size and shape of the fonts used in the document. This feature typically provides a similar appearance to the original document, but it's not always an exact match of the original file.

Because this setting is so lossy you would only want to use it if you needed to compress a large file to a small enough size to send as an email attachment. Make certain the recipient has the fonts used in the document installed on their computer. Otherwise, Adobe uses font substitution.

✦ **Press Quality:** If you need to provide PDF files to your commercial printer or copy shop, use this setting to create a PDF file that is designed for high-quality print reproduction. Along with including fonts in the PDF file, the graphics aren't significantly compressed, and they maintain a much higher resolution. Overall, these files tend to be larger than similar PDF files created using different settings, but the quality of the PDF file is more important than the file size when you're having the PDF professionally printed.

PDF conversion options from Microsoft Word and Excel

Although Microsoft Word and Excel are widespread standards on many corporate computers, they aren't always the best choice for distributing documents. Formatting of Microsoft Word documents and Excel spreadsheets changes depending on the fonts available on users' computers or even the printer they choose to print with. In addition, Microsoft Word and Excel files can be easily edited, and users can also copy and extract information from these files with very few limitations.

Converting a Word or Excel file to PDF overcomes these limitations and is quite straightforward. Choose from two methods:

✦ From inside Microsoft Word or Excel (make sure that the document you want to convert to an Adobe PDF file is open), simply click the Convert To PDF button in the main toolbar to convert the document.

✦ Alternatively, choose Adobe PDF⇨Convert To Adobe PDF.

No matter which method you choose, you must specify the location of the PDF file that is created and name the file.

Choose Adobe PDF⇨Change Conversion Settings and deselect the Prompt For PDF Filename option so that PDF files are generated in one step, without having to input the name of the PDF file.

Not only can you create PDF files from Microsoft Office applications, but you can add other functionality into PDF documents. Choose Adobe PDF⇨Change Conversion Settings and in the dialog box that appears, use the following settings:

✦ **Add Links:** Automatically converts Word links, such as Web addresses, into PDF links that you can use when viewing the file in Acrobat or the Adobe Reader. Click the Word tab to access additional link options that can be built into PDF files created from Word.

✦ **Add Bookmarks:** Adds interactive bookmarks that make navigating the PDF file easy. Bookmarks are added based on Microsoft Word styles, such as text that is styled as Heading 1. The bookmarks appear in the Bookmarks palette when viewing the PDF.

Converting PowerPoint files to PDF

You can convert your PowerPoint presentations to Adobe PDF documents using PDF Maker 8. PDFs make it easy to distribute electronic versions of presentations, without worrying that the file may be edited, or that the recipient may not have the same fonts that you used.

From PowerPoint, click the Convert To Adobe PDF button to save the file as an Adobe PDF file. (Make sure that the presentation you're converting is open before you click the button!).You can also choose Adobe PDF⇨Convert To Adobe PDF from PowerPoint's main menu. If you're working with a new file, you must save it before Adobe PDF Maker 8 will convert it.

As with Word and Excel, you can choose Adobe PDF⇨Change Conversion Settings within PowerPoint to select options relating to the conversion. Along with the conversion settings that impact the quality of the resulting PDF file, you should select two additional options:

✦ **Save Slide Transitions In Adobe PDF:** With this option, you can have the slide transitions that were created in PowerPoint converted into PDF transitions that will be used when the presentation is delivered using Adobe Acrobat's Full Screen View option.

✦ **Convert Multimedia To PDF Multimedia:** Because Adobe PDF files are able to contain integrated sound and movie files, you can choose this option to have sounds and movies used in a PowerPoint file converted into the PDF document.

You can even use PDF as the method for delivering presentations that have been created using PowerPoint by choosing Window⇨Full Screen View after you've converted the file to PDF. You can also click the Full Screen option in the lower left corner of the document window. Press the Esc key to stop viewing the document in the Full Screen mode.

Creating PDF Files from Adobe Creative Suite Applications

Throughout this book, we discuss how to integrate the applications within the Adobe Creative Suite. You won't be surprised to know that you can easily convert a Photoshop file, an Illustrator file, or an InDesign document to the PDF format. In this section, we show you how.

Converting Photoshop and Illustrator files to PDF

Both Adobe Photoshop CS3 and Adobe Illustrator CS3 can save documents directly in the Adobe PDF file format. To do so, simply choose File➪Save or File➪Save As. Then, from the File Type drop-down list, choose Adobe PDF (Illustrator) or Photoshop PDF (Photoshop). In these programs, you can create PDF files without Adobe Acrobat or Acrobat Distiller.

You can view PDF files created from Photoshop or Illustrator using Adobe Acrobat or Adobe Reader. But you can also open and edit these PDF files using the same program in which they were created. For example, you can open and modify a logo created using Adobe Illustrator and saved as a PDF file from Illustrator at a later time with Illustrator. You can also view the same file using either Adobe Reader or Adobe Acrobat software.

Converting InDesign documents to PDF

Like in Photoshop and Illustrator, the ability to convert InDesign documents to PDF is integrated into the application. Using Adobe InDesign CS3, you can choose File➪Export and select Adobe PDF from the File Type drop-down list. InDesign provides a significant number of options for controlling the size and quality of the resulting PDF file. Many of these options are similar to those available for PDF Maker 8 for Microsoft Office.

In the Adobe InDesign Export PDF dialog box, you can choose from the Preset drop-down list at the top of the dialog box. The choices are many, but we list and describe here the most commonly used settings:

✦ **Smallest File Size:** Creates compact Adobe PDF files that are intended for display on the Internet or to be distributed via e-mail. Use this setting to create PDF files that will be viewed primarily on-screen.

✦ **High Quality Print:** Creates Adobe PDF files that are intended for desktop printers and digital copiers.

✦ **Press Quality:** Use this setting to create PDF files that will be delivered to a commercial printer, for high-quality, offset print reproduction.

When creating PDF files to be used for high-resolution printing, be certain to select Marks And Bleeds in the list on the left in the Export PDF dialog box, as shown in Figure 2-1, and specify the amount of space items need to extend off the page (*bleed*). If you're delivering the file to a printing firm, they can provide you with guidance as to the value you should use for bleed and marks offset. A good rule to follow is to use at least .125 inches if you have items extending all the way to the edge of your document pages. Specify the value you want by entering the value in the Bleed And Slug section of the Marks And Bleeds tab. If the amount of bleed is to be the same on all four sides, type the value in the Top text field and then click the link icon to the right of the Top and Bottom Bleed text fields.

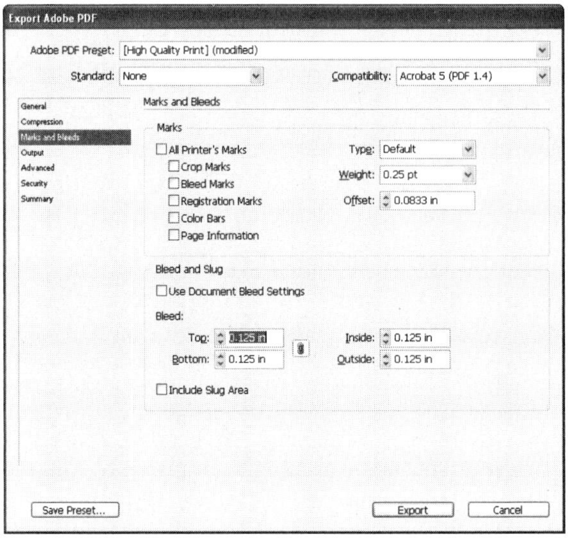

Figure 2-1:
Setting the bleed values in the InDesign Export Adobe PDF dialog box.

Converting Other Electronic Documents to PDF

Adobe has made it quite easy to create PDF files from other Adobe Creative Suite applications and Microsoft Office programs, but you can also create PDF files from many other programs. When you installed the Adobe Creative Suite on your computer, you also installed a new printer, called the Adobe PDF 8 printer, which is used to convert documents to Adobe PDF files. This printer captures all the same information that is normally sent to your printer, and, instead of creating a piece of paper, the information is converted into an Adobe PDF file.

To create a PDF file from any program, choose File⇨Print. In the Print dialog box, select Adobe PDF 8 as the printer and click OK (Windows) or Print (Mac).

To change the type of PDF file that is created, such as a smaller file for Internet Web posting, or a higher quality file for delivery to a commercial printer, do this:

✦ **Windows:** Click the Properties button in the Print dialog box to open the Adobe PDF Document Properties dialog box, shown in Figure 2-2. Here, you can choose the PDF settings you want to use to control the quality and size of the resulting PDF file.

✦ **Mac OS:** Choose PDF Options from the Copies And Pages menu and then choose the PDF settings.

We discuss the settings earlier in this chapter, in the "PDF conversion options" section.

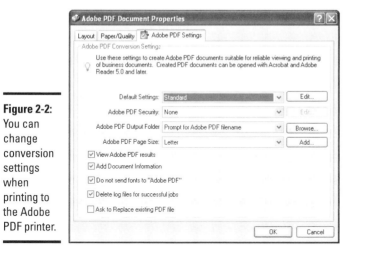

Figure 2-2:
You can
change
conversion
settings
when
printing to
the Adobe
PDF printer.

This process of navigating through the Print menu may appear strange, but it is probably the easiest way for Adobe to capture all the same information that you'd expect to see when you print your files. This provides an easy and standard method for generating PDF files from any program. In fact, you can even use this method for creating PDF files from Microsoft Office programs or other programs in the Adobe Creative Suite if you want.

Bookmarks and links aren't exported if a PDF is generated using the Print menu option.

Creating PDF Files from Paper Documents and the Web

PDF files don't need to start as electronic publishing files. Adobe Acrobat provides options for converting both paper documents and Internet Web pages into PDF format.

Converting paper documents to PDF

To convert paper documents into PDF, you need a scanner to digitize the information. If you expect to scan a large number of pages into PDF, consider purchasing a scanner with an automatic document feeder. Some scanners can scan both the front and backside of a document at the same time.

Unfortunately, we can't fully describe all the ins and outs of choosing a scanner to fit your needs, but Mark L. Chambers does a swell job of it in his book, *Scanners For Dummies* (Wiley Publishing, Inc.).

If a scanner is already hooked to the computer on which you use Acrobat, follow these steps to scan in a paper document and then convert it to PDF format:

1. **From the Acrobat main menu, choose File➪Create PDF➪From Scanner.**

   The Create PDF From Scanner dialog box appears.

2. **Make sure that your scanner is turned on, put the document to be scanned into the scanner, and then click the Scan button.**

   If necessary, continue to scan multiple pages into a single document. When you're done scanning, the scanned page appears in Acrobat.

3. **Choose File➪Save to save the PDF.**

   If you have a PDF open and choose Create PDF From Scanner, a window appears, giving you the opportunity to *append* the file (add to the existing file) or create a new PDF file.

   The document opens in Acrobat.

If the pages need to be rotated, you can choose Document➪Rotate Pages. Some scanners now automatically convert scanned documents to Adobe PDF files and automatically rotate them.

Use the Zoom In tool to increase the magnification of what you've just scanned. You can see that the text is jagged because it's a picture of the text. If you need the text to be searchable, use Document➪OCR Text Recognition➪Recognize Text Using OCR. This command makes the text you have just scanned searchable. Otherwise, you have only a picture of the text.

Scanned text is unlike text from electronic documents that you create using either PDF Maker 8 or the Adobe PDF Printer. Both of these options create text that looks very clear, even when enlarged.

Converting Web pages to PDFs

By converting online content to Adobe PDF, you can capture contents from an Internet Web site. Because Web content can change rapidly, you can capture something that may not remain online for a long period of time. You can convert things such as news stories or competitive information ca from a Web site into PDF in a single click. And because PDF files can easily be combined with other PDF documents, you can merge information from a variety of sources, such as spreadsheets, word-processing documents, and brochures.

If you want to convert only a single page and are using Internet Explorer, click the Convert Web Page To PDF button. This step converts the current web page to a PDF. If you want to convert more than a single page, follow these steps from within Acrobat (not your Web browser):

1. **From the Acrobat main menu, choose File⊅Create PDF⊅From Web Page.**

The Create PDF From Web Page dialog box opens.

2. **In the URL text field, enter the URL for the Web site you're converting to PDF.**

3. **To capture additional pages that are linked from the main page you're capturing, select the Get Only radio button (selected by default), enter the number of levels to be captured in the Levels text field, and then select one of the following:**

- Select the Stay On Same Path check box if you want only URLs (pages) subordinate from the entered URL converted to PDF.

- Select the Stay On Same Server check box to download only pages that are on the same server as the entered URL.

Be cautious about selecting the Get Entire Site radio button instead of the Get Only radio button. The Get Entire Site option may take an enormous amount of time and not have any relevance to what you need.

4. **Click the Settings button to open the Web Page Conversion Settings dialog box and see accepted File types and change PDF settings (on the General tab), as shown in Figure 2-3.**

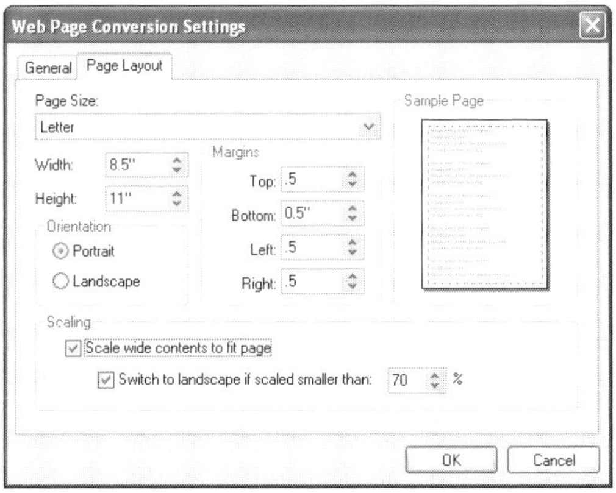

Figure 2-3:
Changing
file type and
PDF
settings.

5. **On the Page layout tab of the Web Page Conversion Settings dialog box, make changes to page size, orientation, and margins.**

6. **When you're done making changes in the Web Page Conversion Settings dialog box, click OK.**

7. **Back in the Create PDF From Web Page dialog box, click the Create button.**

   The Downloading Status window opens, showing the rate of download.

When the download is complete, the Web page (for the entered URL) selected appears as a PDF with existing hyperlinks (links to other pages within the site) left intact. When links on the converted Web page are selected, the viewer can open the page either in Acrobat or the Web browser.

Chapter 3: Adding Interactivity to PDF Files

*B*ecause many Adobe PDF documents are viewed online, you need to make the documents easy for readers to navigate. Using Acrobat, you can design documents that are easier to navigate than their printed counterparts and that include rich interactive features that simply aren't available with paper documents.

Rather than making readers scroll through a document to find what they want, you can add links within an index or table of contents, or you can add links to Web sites and e-mail addresses. Acrobat also includes features (known as *bookmarks*) to build your own online table of contents, and you can add buttons that link to specific pages within a PDF document or that cause an action to occur when clicked, such as closing the document. We discuss all these features in this chapter.

Adding Bookmarks to Ease PDF Navigation

One reason for distributing PDF documents is that it's convenient and cost-effective. But if users can't easily find the information they need, or they're unable to effectively understand how the contents of a file are structured, they may become frustrated, or they may need to print the document, which defeats the purpose of electronic distribution.

A table of contents in a traditional, printed book doesn't work well with electronic PDF files. It requires you to constantly return to the page containing the contents and then navigate to the page containing the data you need. But you can make your documents more user-friendly by adding bookmarks, which are the equivalent of a table of contents that is always available, no matter what page is being viewed in the document window.

Bookmarks provide a listing of contents that reside within a PDF file, or links to relevant external content. Bookmarks sit within a panel, and when you click one, you're taken to a specific destination in the PDF document (or possibly to an external file), much like a hyperlink. Acrobat technically calls the panel a panel, but all other Adobe Creative Suite programs call them panels — so that's what we call them here. You can create bookmarks from existing text, or you can use your own text to describe the content, such as a chart or graphic.

By default, the Bookmarks icon resides along the left side of the Acrobat document window in what is called the *navigation pane.* Click the Bookmarks icon to make the panel appear; click the Bookmarks icon a second time to hide it. If the icon isn't visible, choose View➪Navigation Panels➪Bookmarks to make it appear.

Creating bookmarks that link to a page

By navigating to a page, and to a specific view on a page, you can establish the destination of a bookmark link. With a PDF document open, follow these steps:

1. **If the Bookmark icon isn't visible, choose View➪Navigation Panels➪ Bookmarks.**

The Bookmarks panel appears on the left of the document window.

2. **In the document window, navigate to the page that you want as the bookmark's destination.**

3. **Set the magnification of the view that you want by using the Marquee Zoom tool to either zoom in or zoom out.**

The zoom level that you are at when you create the bookmark is the view that viewers see when they click the bookmark.

4. **In the Bookmarks panel, choose Options➪New Bookmark.**

The new bookmark appears in the Bookmarks panel as Untitled.

5. **Change the name by typing something more descriptive.**

If you leave the bookmark as Untitled but want to rename it later, you must click the bookmark and then choose Options➪Rename Bookmark from the menu in the Bookmark panel.

6. **Test your bookmark by scrolling to another page and view in the document window; then click your saved bookmark in the Bookmark panel.**

The document window shows the exact location and zoom that you selected when you created the bookmark.

If you use the Selection tool to highlight text, such as a headline or a caption, that is a part of the bookmark destination and then choose Options⇨New Bookmark, the selected text becomes the title of the new bookmark. You can use this shortcut to avoid entering a new name for new bookmark titles. You can also press Ctrl+B (PC) or ⌘+B (Mac) to quickly create a bookmark.

Creating bookmarks that link to external files

Although bookmarks are most commonly used to link to content within a PDF file, you can also use bookmarks to create links to other documents. To create a link to an external file, follow these steps:

1. **Choose Options⇨New Bookmark in the Bookmarks panel.**

2. **Replace the Untitled bookmark entry that appears in the Bookmarks panel with an appropriate title for the bookmark.**

3. **Choose Options⇨Properties from the Bookmarks panel.**

   The Bookmark Properties dialog box appears. Using this dialog box, you can change a bookmark so that it links to any type of file. In this example, we use a PDF document, but the bookmark could be a link to another PDF file, a Photoshop file, or even a Microsoft Excel file. Just remember that this bookmark creates a relative link. The linked file must travel with the PDF document in order for the link to work.

4. **In the Bookmark Properties dialog box, click the Actions tab and choose Open A File from the Select Action drop-down list and then click the Add button.**

   The Select File To Open dialog box appears.

5. **Click the Browse button, choose a file to which the bookmark will navigate, and then click the Select button.**

6. **In the Specify Open Preference window, choose whether you want the linked file to open in a new document, new window, or existing window and then click OK.**

Note that the other file isn't attached to the current document. If you distribute a PDF file containing the bookmarks to external files, you must distribute any external files that are referenced along with the source file; otherwise, the links will not work. In addition, the linked files need to be in the same relative location as the original documents — so don't change the name of the linked file or the folder in which it is located.

You can create links to non-PDF files. Instead of choosing Go To A Page In Another Document, choose Open A File to open a non-PDF file or choose Open A Web Link to access an Internet Web address.

Using bookmarks

Bookmarks are intuitive to use, which makes them an attractive option to add to PDF files. After you click a bookmark, the action associated with it is performed, which typically navigates you to a certain page within the PDF file.

Unfortunately, the Bookmarks panel doesn't open automatically with a document, even when bookmarks are present within a file. To display the Bookmarks panel when a file is opened, follow these steps:

1. **Choose File⇨Properties.**

2. **In the Document Properties dialog box that opens, select the Initial View tab, as shown in Figure 3-1.**

3. **From the Navigation drop-down list, choose Bookmarks Panel And Page and then click OK.**

After the file is saved and then reopened, the Bookmarks panel is displayed whenever the document is opened.

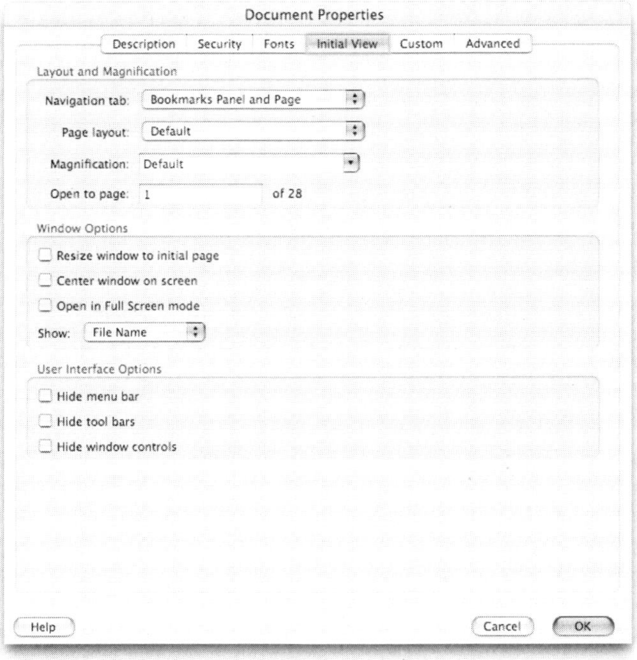

Figure 3-1:
The
Documents
Properties
window in
Adobe
Acrobat.

Editing bookmarks

You can change the attributes of bookmarks so that they link to other locations by clicking to select a bookmark and then choosing Options⇨ Properties in the Bookmarks panel. In the Bookmark Properties dialog box, choose the color and font type of the bookmark on the Appearance tab: To change the bookmark's font style, choose a style from the Style drop-down list; to change the bookmark's color, click the Color box and choose a color from the color picker.

On the Actions tab of the Bookmark Properties dialog box, you can delete existing actions (in the Actions section of the Actions tab) by clicking to select an action and then clicking the Delete button. Also, you can add actions by choosing another action from the Add Action section and then clicking the Add button. You can add more than one action to a bookmark.

Adding Interactive Links

When viewing a PDF file electronically, you can add links for e-mail addresses, Web addresses, and references to other pages. Links are attached to a region of a page, which you identify with the Link tool.

To add an interactive link to your PDF document, follow these steps:

1. **Choose Options⇨New Bookmark in the Bookmarks panel.**

2. **After locating an area of a page where you want to add a link, Choose View⇨Toolbars⇨Advanced Editing to display the Advanced Editing toolbar.**

3. **Select the Link tool and then click and drag to select the region that you want to link to.**

The Create Link dialog box appears.

4. **Choose a Link Action:**

- **Go To A Page View:** This option is the default, where you can scroll to the page that is the destination of the link.

- **Open A File:** Alternatively, you can choose to link to another file; click the Browse button to locate the file.

- **Open A Web Page:** If you choose this option, you're choosing to link to a Web address. In the Address text field, enter the complete address of the Web site to which the link should direct viewers. To create a link to an e-mail address, type **mailto:** followed by an e-mail address. Note that mailto: is all one word with no spaces.

- **Custom Link:** Use this option to choose from other types of links in the Link Properties dialog box.

5. **Click Next, and follow the instructions in the next dialog box before clicking OK.**

The Link tool is relatively simple to use, but you may prefer to create links from text in another way: Using the Selection tool, select the text, right-click (Windows) or Ctrl+click (Mac) the selected text, and then choose Create Link from the contextual menu that appears.

Remember that you can also have links automatically transferred from your original Microsoft Office documents when using PDF Maker.

You can edit links by choosing the Link tool and double-clicking the link to open the Link Properties dialog box. While editing a link, you can change how it's presented in the Appearance tab. Make a link invisible or add a border to the link, such as a blue border that commonly is used to define hyperlinks. On the Actions tab of the Link Properties dialog box, you can add, edit, or delete actions, just as you can with bookmarks (see the preceding section).

Adding Buttons to Simplify Your PDF Files

Along with links and bookmarks, buttons provide another way to make your files more useful when they're viewed online. You can create interactive buttons entirely within Acrobat — designing their appearance and adding text to them. Or you can import buttons created in other Adobe Creative Suite applications, such as Photoshop and Illustrator. For example, you can create buttons that advance the viewer to the next page in a document.

Buttons are added by using the Button tool located on the Forms toolbar. Choose View⇨Toolbars⇨Forms to open the Forms menu.

To add a button to your PDF document, follow these steps:

1. **Click the OK Button tool and click and drag to create the region where the button will appear.**

The Button Properties dialog box appears.

2. **In the General tab, you can enter a name for the button in the Name text field and provide a Tooltip in the Tooltip text field.**

    A *ToolTip* is the text that appears whenever the mouse cursor is positioned over the button.

3. **In the Appearance tab, establish how your button will look:**

    - **Border Color/Fill Color:** Click the square to the right of the appropriate attribute in the Borders And Colors section of the Appearance tab and then choose a color from the color picker.

    - **Line Thickness and Style:** These options don't appear unless you change the border color from none (red diagonal line) to another selection.

    - **Font Size/Font:** Change the size and font of the button text by making a selection from the Font Size and the Font drop-down lists.

    - **Text Color:** Change the color of the text by clicking the color square and choosing a color from the color picker.

4. **In the Options tab, make these selections:**

    - **Layout:** Use the Layout drop-down list to specify whether you want to use a *label* (text that you enter in Acrobat that appears on the face of the button) or whether you want an *icon* (an imported button graphic that you may have designed using Photoshop or Illustrator).

    - **Behavior:** Choose Push from the Behavior drop-down list to create different appearances for a button so that it changes based upon whether the mouse cursor is positioned over the button. The button appearance can also change when clicked.

    - **State:** To specify the different appearances (see Behavior, discussed in the preceding paragraph), click the State on the left side of the Options tab and then choose the Label or Icon status for each state.

    - **Label:** If you choose to use a label, enter the text for it in the Label text field.

    - **Icon:** If you choose to use an icon, specify the location of the graphic file by clicking the Choose Icon button. You can create button icons in either Photoshop or Illustrator.

5. **In the Actions tab, you can choose an action from the Select Action drop-down list and then click the Add button.**

    Actions are applied to buttons similar to the way in which they're applied to links and bookmarks.

    - To choose actions that are a part of the menu commands, such as printing a document, closing a file, or navigating to the next or preceding page, choose the Execute Menu Item action and then specify the command to be accessed.

- You can also choose the activity that causes the action to occur, known as the *trigger*. The default trigger is Mouse Up, which causes the action to occur when the mouse button is depressed and then released. You can choose other actions, such as the mouse cursor merely rolling over the button without the need to click it.

6. After you make all your changes in the Button Properties dialog box, click Close and you're done.

Chapter 4: Editing and Extracting Text and Graphics

In This Chapter

✔ Manipulating text with the TouchUp tools

✔ Modifying graphics with the TouchUp tools

✔ Pulling text and graphics out of PDFs for use in other documents

*Y*ou may assume that PDF files are mere pictures of your documents and can't be edited, but nothing is further from the truth. Adobe Acrobat includes a variety of tools for editing both text and graphics. You can use these tools as long as the file has not been secured to prohibit editing. We introduce you to these great tools in this chapter. (We discuss security, which allows you to limit access to these tools, in Chapter 6 of this minibook.)

Editing Text

The tools for editing text and graphics are located on the Advanced Editing toolbar (see Figure 4-1). You can add several TouchUp tools to the Advanced Editing tool bar by choosing View⇨Toolbars⇨More tools and checking the tools you want to add. You have three choices:

✦ **TouchUp Text Tool:** Used to manipulate text.

✦ **TouchUp Object Tool:** Used to manipulate objects.

✦ **TouchUp Reading Order Tool:** Used to correct the reading order or structure of the document.

The TouchUp Reading Order tool isn't used for changing the appearance of the document, so we don't discuss it in this chapter.

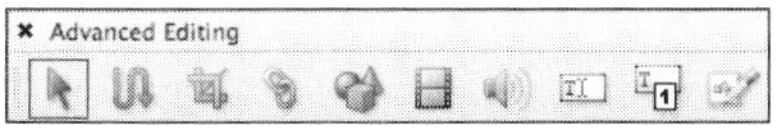

Figure 4-1:
The Advanced Editing toolbar.

Using the TouchUp Text tool to manipulate text

The TouchUp Text tool is used for *touching up,* or manipulating, text. This touchup can include changing actual text characters or the appearance of text. You can change the word "cat" to read "dog," or you can change black text to make it blue, or you can even change the Helvetica font to the Times font.

When you change a PDF file, the original source document isn't modified.

You have a few ways to accomplish text edits:

✦ Choose the TouchUp Text tool, click within the text that you want to change to obtain an insertion point, and then start typing the new text.

✦ Insert the TouchUp tool into your text and press the Backspace or Delete key to delete text.

✦ Drag, using the TouchUp tool, to highlight text and enter new text to replace the highlighted text.

When changing text — whether you're adding or deleting — Acrobat tries to use the font that was specified in the original document. Sometimes, this font is built into the PDF file, which means that it's *embedded* in the file. Other times, the font may not be available either because it hasn't been embedded or it's been embedded as a *subset* where only some of the characters from the font are included in the PDF file. In these cases, Acrobat may provide the following warning message:

```
All or part of the selection has no available system font. You cannot add or
    delete text using the currently selected font.
```

Fortunately, you can change the font if you need to edit the text. However, when you change the font, the text may not retain the same appearance as the original document. In some instances, you may not have the exact same font on your computer as the font used in the PDF document, but you may have a similar font you can use without causing a noticeable change — most people won't notice the difference between Helvetica and Arial or between Times and Times New Roman. Fonts with the same name but from different font designers often look very similar. For example, Adobe Garamond looks similar to ITC Garamond, even though they're two different fonts.

To change the font that is used for a word or range of words, follow these steps:

Typewriter tool

You can use the Typewriter tool to type anywhere on the document. This tool resembles the Text Box tool, though its default properties are different. Access the Typewriter tool by choosing Tools⇨Typewriter⇨Show Typewriter Toolbar. Then, select the Typewriter icon, position your cursor where you want to begin typing and type, pressing the Enter key whenever you want to add a line. The Increase and Decrease size buttons will enlarge or diminish your type size.

Likewise, to change the leading, you select the text and choose the Increase or Decrease Line Spacing buttons. You can move or resize the Typewriter block by selecting it with the Select tool and either moving or resizing the text box. Your text remains editable. So, if you've made a mistake and want to correct it, or want to add or delete text, you select the Typewriter tool again and double-click in the type box.

1. **Select the text with the TouchUp Text tool by dragging across it.**

You will probably get a message that reads `Loading System Fonts` followed by another message that reads `Loading Document Fonts`. Depending on the number of fonts installed on your system, it may take a while for this message to appear.

2. **Right-click (Windows) or Ctrl+click (Mac) the highlighted text and then choose Properties from the contextual menu.**

The TouchUp Properties dialog box appears, as shown in Figure 4-2.

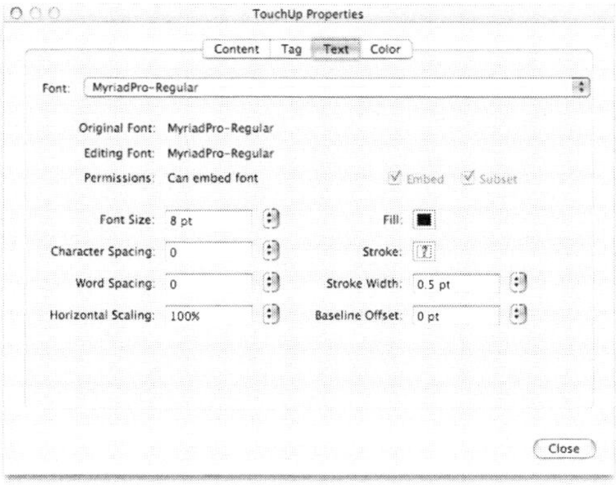

Figure 4-2:
The
TouchUp
Properties
dialog box.

3. **In the Text tab, choose the typeface you want to use from the Font drop-down list and make any other changes you want.**

In this dialog box, you can also change the size by selecting or typing a number into the Font Size drop-down list. In addition, you can modify the color by clicking the Fill color swatch.

4. **When you're satisfied with your changes, click the Close button to apply your changes to the selected text.**

Using the TouchUp Object tool to edit graphics

You can use the TouchUp Object tool to access editing software for modifying graphics. For example, you can use the TouchUp Object tool to select a graphic, bring the graphic into Photoshop, and then save the modified version back into the PDF file. In other words, you can edit the graphics used in PDF documents, even if you don't have access to the original graphic files.

To edit a photographic file from Acrobat in Photoshop, follow these steps:

1. **Select the image using the TouchUp Object tool, right-click (Windows) or Ctrl+click (Mac) on a photographic image with the TouchUp Object tool, and then choose Edit Image from the contextual menu.**

   The image file opens in Adobe Photoshop.

2. **Using the many tools of Photoshop, make the necessary changes to the graphic and then choose File⇨Save.**

   When you return to the PDF file in Acrobat, the graphic is automatically updated in the PDF document.

If you have the original graphic file, it remains untouched — only the version used within the PDF file is modified. It isn't necessary to have the original graphic file to perform these steps.

You can also use Acrobat to edit vector objects from within PDF files, such as those created using Adobe Illustrator. Just follow these steps:

1. **Select a piece of vector artwork using the TouchUp Object tool, right-click (Windows) or Ctrl+click (Mac) on the vector artwork, and then choose Edit Object from the contextual menu.**

   Note that Acrobat displays Edit Object in the contextual menu if it detects a vector object, and it displays Edit Image if it detects a bitmap image. Acrobat also displays Edit Objects (note the plural) if you have more than one object selected.

   If you're editing a complex illustration, be sure to select all its components by holding down the Ctrl (PC) or ⌘ (Mac) while clicking them with the TouchUp Object tool.

After choosing Edit Object, the object opens for editing in Adobe Illustrator.

2. **Make the necessary changes in Illustrator, choose File⇨Save.**

   The graphic is updated in the PDF document.

If Acrobat doesn't start Photoshop or Illustrator after choosing the Edit Image or Edit Object command, you may need to access preferences by choosing Edit⇨Preferences⇨Touch Up and then specify which programs should be used for editing images or objects.

You can also use the TouchUp Object tool to edit the position of text or graphic objects on a page, which includes the ability to relocate individual lines of text or to change the position of a graphic on a page. After you've selected an object with the TouchUp Object tool, you can simply drag it to a new location on the page.

Exporting Text and Graphics

Although editing text and graphics is helpful, you may need to take text or images from a PDF document and use them in another file. Fortunately, Acrobat also includes tools to make this a breeze. Of course, you should always make certain that you have the permission of the owner of a document before reusing content that is not your original work.

You need the Select & Zoom toolbar for extracting text and graphics, so make sure that it's visible. If it isn't, choose View⇨Toolbars⇨Select & Zoom.

You can export text, images, or charts from Acrobat in three ways:

+ Select/Copy/Paste.

+ Save As To Word Document, JPEG, TIFF, HTML Web Page, XML 1.0, Encapsulated PostScript, HTML 3.2, JPEG 2000, PNG, PostScript, Rich Text Format, Text Accessible, Text (Plain).

+ Use the Snapshot tool to send selected areas to the Clipboard where they will be available to use in other applications or save the selected area as a TIFF file.

Exporting text using Select, Copy, and Paste

Make sure that the Select & Zoom toolbar is visible and then follow these steps to select, copy, and paste text from a PDF file:

1. **Using the Select tool, highlight the text you want to export.**

The Select tool is the I-Bar/Black Arrow in the toolbar. When you hold the arrow over a section of your document, it will turn into an I-Bar cursor, which you can drag to select the text you want to copy.

If the Cut, Copy, and Paste commands are unavailable after you've selected some text, the author of the document may have set the security settings to disallow copying. If you can't select the text, you may be trying to copy text that is part of an image.

2. **Right-click (Windows) or Ctrl+click (Mac) the selected text and choose Copy from the contextual menu.**

Being able to extract the text out of a PDF document by selecting and copying it is useful if you don't have access to the original source document, but you need to use the text from a PDF file.

3. **Open another text-editing program, such as Adobe InDesign or Microsoft Word.**

You can paste the copied text into a new document or a preexisting file.

4. **Insert your cursor in the document at the appropriate spot and choose File⇨Paste.**

The text is pasted into the document, ready for you to use.

Exporting text using Save As

The File⇨Save As command exports all the text in your PDF file. A drop-down menu gives you various format options. After choosing an option and any settings, click the OK button to select the settings and the Save button to save the text. The File⇨Export command gives you the same options.

Here are the formats you can use to export text:

✦ **Microsoft Word Document:** Use the Settings button to choose whether or not to save the comments or images with your document. If you choose to save the comments or images, you can select additional formatting options.

✦ **Rich Text Format:** Use the Settings button to choose whether or not to save the comments or images with your document. If you choose to save the comments or images, you can select additional formatting options.

✦ **Text (Accessible):** Use this format to create a file that can be printed to a Braille printer.

Extracting graphics

You can also extract graphics from DF files, but extracting graphics is very different from editing them. We discuss editing graphics and vector objects earlier in this chapter. When editing graphics, you open the original graphic file at its highest possible quality. Extracting graphics is different because they're removed at the quality of the screen display resolution, which may be of much lower quality than the original, embedded graphics.

With the Select tool, right-click (Windows) or Ctrl+click (Mac) an image, or drag with the Select tool to select a part of the image. Then you can either drag and drop the selection into an open document or choose Copy Image from the contextual menu. The image is now available to be pasted into other applications. The other option in the contextual menu is to Save Image As and save the selected area as a TIFF file.

✦ **Text (Plain) (secondary Settings):** This format creates a plain vanilla file with no formatting. You can save some secondary options in various file encodings. Also, you can select to save the images in your PDF in a separate images folder.

✦ **Adobe PDF, Encapsulated PostScript, PostScript.**

✦ **Various Adobe PDF Options.**

✦ **Various graphics formats (JPEG, JPEG2000, PNG, TIFF), but your text will no longer be editable.**

Text that is copied from a PDF file is no longer linked to the original document. Edits made to the extracted text aren't reflected within the PDF file, and it is extremely difficult to have the extracted text reinserted into the PDF document. Think of the extraction process as a one-way trip for the text, which can be extracted but not reinserted.

You can also copy text within a table to the Clipboard or open it directly in a spreadsheet program, such as Microsoft Excel. And you maintain the table's formatting after it is extracted. Just follow these steps:

1. **Click the Select tool and click and drag to select the text in the table.**

You can also position your cursor just outside the edge of the table and then draw a box around a table.

A border appears around the selected table.

2. **Right-click (Windows) or Ctrl+click (Mac) and choose Open Table In Spreadsheet from the contextual menu or save the table directly to a file or save a copy to the Clipboard to be later pasted.**

The table opens in Excel or whatever spreadsheet program you have installed on your computer.

To save the table directly to a file, choose Save Table As from the contextual menu.

To copy the table to the Clipboard so that you can paste it into other documents, choose Copy As Table from the contextual menu.

And that's it. You can now use that table in another program.

Snapshot tool

You can use the Snapshot tool to select both text and images and create a picture of a certain area within a PDF file. The result is commonly referred to as a *screen grab* of a section within a PDF file. The result is an image, and your text is no longer editable.

To use the Snapshot tool, choose Tools⇨Select & Zoom⇨Snapshot Tool. You then have two options.

+ After you select the Snapshot tool, click anywhere in the page. The snapshot tool automatically captures everything displayed on the screen.

+ After you select the Snapshot tool, click and drag a rectangle around an area of the page.

You can include text and images. The area you've selected will be saved to the Clipboard so that you can paste it into another document. The Snapshot tool remains active so that you can keep selecting areas and saving them to the Clipboard. However, the previous selection in your Clipboard is deleted when you make a new selection. So, make certain you've pasted a selection into your other document before you make a new selection.

You have to select another tool to deactivate the Snapshot tool.

Chapter 5: Using Commenting and Annotation Tools

In This Chapter

✔ Adding comments to PDF files

✔ Working with comments

*O*ne of the fantastic features of Acrobat is the capability to mark up documents electronically using virtual sticky notes called *comments*. You can mark up text to indicate changes and add annotations and drawing comments to a PDF file. The Acrobat commenting tools do not change the original file, and you can remove the comments at any time, which means you can disable comments for printing or viewing at any time. In this chapter, we describe these great features and show you how to put them to work for you.

Creating Comments

You can easily add annotations to PDF files, including stamps, text highlights, callouts, and electronic sticky notes, by using the Comment & Markup Toolbar, which you can access by clicking the Review & Comment option in the Tasks toolbar. You can then choose to display the Comment & Markup Tools.

You can also access the Comment & Markup toolbar by choosing View⇨Toolbars⇨Comment & Markup.

The Comment & Markup toolbar

The Comment & Markup toolbar, shown in Figure 5-1, provides several tools for adding comments to PDF documents. It also includes a Show menu to help manage comments and the process of adding comments. We discuss these tools in the following sections.

Figure 5-1:
Use the
Comment &
Markup
toolbar
to add
comments
to your
document.

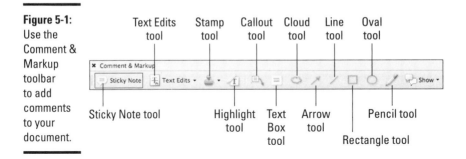

The Sticky Note tool

Use the Sticky Note tool to add electronic sticky notes to your files. You can click the location where you want the note to appear within a PDF document. An icon, representing the note, appears, along with a window where you can enter text. After entering text in the sticky note, close the window so that the document isn't hidden beneath it. You can change the icon and color used to represent the note by right-clicking (Windows) or Ctrl+clicking (Mac) the note and choosing Properties from the contextual menu. In the Properties dialog box that appears, make the changes to the note icon or color and then click Close.

The Text Edits tool

The Text Edits tool is actually six separate text commenting tools. Use these tools to replace selected text, highlight selected text, add a note to selected text, insert text at cursor, underline selected text, and cross out text for deletion.

To use the Text Edits tool, follow these steps:

1. **Choose the Text Edits tool and drag to select text that requires a change or comment.**

2. **Click the arrow to the right of the Text Edits tool to access the drop-down list containing your six choices.**

3. **Choose an option from the list of available editing choices:**

   • **Replace Selected Text:** Replaces the selected text.

   • **Highlight Selected Text:** Highlights the selected text.

   • **Add A Note To Selected Text:** Allows you to add a note to the selected text.

   • **Insert Text At Cursor:** Places a cursor at the end of the selected text.

- **Underline Selected Text:** Underlines the selected text.

- **Cross Out Text For Deletion:** Crosses out the selected text.

Your selected text changes, depending on what you choose from the list.

After selecting the text that requires a comment, you can press the Delete or Backspace key to indicate a text edit to remove the text. Similarly, you can start to type, and Acrobat will create an insertion point. Also, if you right-click (Windows) or Ctrl-click (Mac OS) after selecting the text, you can select the type of edit or comment you want to insert from the contextual menu.

The Stamp tool

You can use stamps to identify documents or to highlight a certain part of a document. Common stamps include Confidential, Draft, Sign Here, and Approved.

The stamps are grouped into sections. Some stamps automatically add your default user name along with the date and time you applied them to the document; these stamps are available under the Dynamic category in the Stamps menu. The more traditional business stamps, such as Confidential, appear under the Standard Business category. You can access each of the different categories by clicking the arrow to the right of the Stamp tool in the Comment & Markup toolbar, as shown in Figure 5-2.

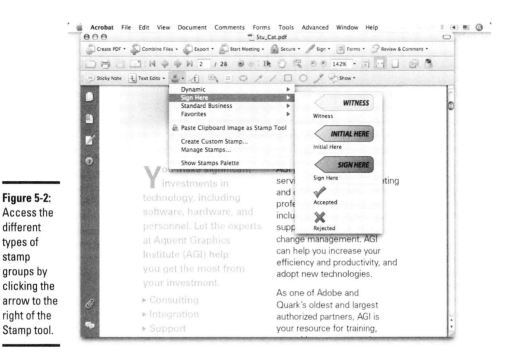

Figure 5-2:
Access the different types of stamp groups by clicking the arrow to the right of the Stamp tool.

To apply a stamp to your document, follow these steps:

1. **Select the Stamp tool from the Comment & Markup toolbar.**

2. **Click the arrow to the right of the stamp tool and, from the menu, choose the stamp you want to apply to the document.**

3. **Drag within your document at the location where you want the stamp to appear.**

The Highlight, Underline Text, and Cross-Out, Callout, and Textbox tools

The Highlight, Cross-Out, and Underline text tools provide the same functionality and options that are available with the Text Edits tool, but with easier access. If you want to delete the highlighted, crossed-out, or underlined formatting to your text, just click the formatted area and hit the Delete key. Your text will remain, but the formatting will disappear.

You can also call attention to areas in your document by using the Callout and Textbox tools. If you want to delete a Callout or Text box after you've added them, just highlight them and hit the Delete key.

To highlight text, follow these steps:

1. **Select the Highlight Text tool from the Comment & Markup toolbar.**

2. **Drag over the text that you want highlighted.**

   The text is now highlighted.

To underline text, follow these steps:

1. **Select the Underline Text tool by selecting in the Task tools Review & Comment➪Comment & Markup Tools➪Underline Text tool.**

2. **Drag over the text that you want underlined.**

   The text is now underlined.

To cross out text, follow these steps:

1. **Select the Cross-Out Text tool by selecting in the Task tools Review & Comment➪Comment & Markup Tools➪Cross-Out Text Tool.**

2. **Drag over the text that you want crossed out.**

   The text is now crossed out.

The Attach File tools

Using the Attach File tools, you can attach an existing text file, sound file, or any file copied to the Clipboard from your computer (or computer network) and attach it to the PDF.

Follow these steps for file and sound attachments:

1. **In the Task tools, choose Review & Comment⇨Comment & Markup Tools⇨Attach A File As A Comment.**

   A pushpin icon appears.

2. **Click where you want the attachment noted.**

   The Add Attachment dialog box appears.

3. **In the Add Attachment dialog box, browse to the file that you want to attach and click the Select button.**

   You can attach text, graphic, or sound files.

4. **Select the type of icon to represent the attached file and then click OK.**

   There are several types of icons to represent the attached file. You can select a paperclip, graph, pushpin, or tag. Whatever icon you select appears on your document to denote that another file is attached. When you roll over the icon, a little annotation appears telling you the filename.

   With the Record Audio Comment tool, you can share a verbal comment by using a microphone and recording a message directly into the PDF. The sound is added as a comment.

The file(s) that you attach with the Attach File tools becomes embedded within the PDF file. The attached file remains in its original file format, even if the attached file is not a PDF file. For example, you can attach an Excel spreadsheet to a PDF document.

The Drawing tools

There are three shape tools, two line tools, and a pencil in the Comment & Markup toolbar. Use the drawing tools to add lines, ovals, rectangles, and other shapes to your PDF file. These shapes can call attention to specific portions of a document.

To use the Cloud Shape tool:

1. **Select the Cloud Shape from the Comment & Markup toolbar.**

2. **Click in your document to begin the shape.**

3. Click again in another position to set the length of the first part of the cloud and then click again to begin shaping your cloud.

Click as often as you like to create your shape.

4. When you're finished with your shape, double-click to close the Cloud Shape.

5. While the Drawing tool is selected, click the shape you created and drag the corner points to resize, if necessary.

6. After creating the cloud shape, right-click (Windows) or Ctrl+click (Mac) the shape and choose Properties from the contextual menu to change the color and thickness of the line values; when you're finished, click OK.

You can also use the Properties toolbar to change the appearance of a selected comment. Instead of the cloud edges, you can change them to dotted lines, dashed lines, and so on.

To use the Rectangle and Oval Shapes:

1. Select either the Rectangle or Oval Shape from the Comment & Markup toolbar.

2. Click and drag in your document to draw the shape.

3. While the Drawing tool is selected, click the shape you created and drag the corner points to resize, if necessary.

4. After creating the shape, right-click (Windows) or Ctrl+click (Mac) the shape and choose Properties from the contextual menu to change the color and thickness of the line values; when you're finished, click OK.

You can also use the Properties toolbar to change the appearance of the shape.

The Text Box tool

When creating notes that you want to prominently display on a document, you can use the Text Box tool.

Follow these steps to add a text box to hold your comments:

1. Select the Text Box tool from the Comment & Markup toolbar.

A text field is placed directly on the document.

2. Drag to add the comment.

3. Right-click (Windows) or Ctrl+click (Mac) and choose Properties from the contextual menu to set the color of the text box that contains the note.

You can also use the Properties toolbar to modify the selected text box.

4. Make your choices to modify the appearance of the text box and then click OK.

You can select the text box and move it to another position any time you want. You can resize the text box by dragging an anchor point.

The Callout Box tool

The Callout Tool creates a callout text box that points to a section of your document with an arrow. The Callout text box is made up of three parts: the text box, the knee line, and the end point line. You can resize each part individually to customize the callout area of your document. To use the Callout tool, follow these steps:

1. Select the Callout Tool from the Comment & Markup toolbar.

2. Click where you want the arrowhead point to be.

3. Drag down or to the side to position the text box and begin typing.

You can click anchor points on the knee line, end point line, or text box to resize them. You can change the size, color, and font characteristics of the text in the Callout text box.

4. Right-click (Windows) or Ctrl+click (Mac) and choose Properties from the contextual menu to set the color of the Callout text box.

5. Make your choices to modify the appearance of the Callout text box and then click OK.

You can select the Callout text box and move it to another position any time you want. You can resize the text box by dragging an anchor point.

The Pencil tool

With the Pencil tool, you can create freeform lines on your documents. These lines can be useful when you're trying to attract attention to a specific portion of a page. Just follow these steps:

1. Select the Pencil tool from the Comment & Markup toolbar.

2. Click and drag to draw on your document.

3. **Edit the color and thickness of lines created with the Pencil by right-clicking (Windows) or Ctrl+clicking (Mac) on the line and choosing Properties from the contextual menu or press Ctrl+E (Windows) or ⌘+E (Mac) to access the Properties toolbar.**

4. **Make your choices and click OK.**

By right-clicking (Windows) or Ctrl+clicking (Mac) on the Pencil tool, you can choose the Pencil Eraser tool. Use the Pencil Eraser tool to remove portions of lines that had previously been created with the Pencil tool.

Managing Comments

One of the most powerful features of PDF commenting is the ability to easily manage and share comments and annotations among reviewers. For example, you can determine which comments are displayed at any time, and you can filter the comments by author or by the type of commenting tool used to create the comment. In addition, you can indicate a response to a comment and track the changes that may have been made to a document based upon a comment. Also, you can consolidate comments from multiple reviewers into a single document.

Viewing comments

You can use any of several methods to see a document's list of comments:

✦ Click the Comments tab along the left side of the document window in the Navigation pane.

✦ Choose Review & Comment➪Show Comments List.

✦ Choose View➪Navigation Panels➪Comments.

No matter which method you use, the Comments List window that shows all the comments in the document appears along the bottom of the document window. You can see the author of each comment and any notes entered by reviewers. By clicking the plus sign to the left of a comment, you can view more information about it, such as what type of comment it is and the date and time it was created.

If you've clicked the plus sign to the left of the comment to expand the view, it changes to a minus sign, which you can then click to return to the consolidated view showing only the author and the initial portions of any text from the note.

To the right of the plus sign is a check box that you can use to indicate that the comment has been reviewed or to indicate that a certain comment needs further attention. Use these check boxes for your own purposes; their status doesn't export with the document if you send the file to others, so they're for your own personal use only.

Changing a comment's review status

Acrobat makes it easy to indicate whether a comment has been reviewed, accepted, or has additional comments attached to it. To change the status of a comment, follow these steps:

1. **Choose Comments⇨Show Comments List to see the entire list of comments and the status of each one.**

   You can also click the Comments tab located on the bottom left side of the screen to display the comments.

2. **In the Comments List, Right-click (Windows) or Ctrl+click (Mac) on a comment and choose Set Status⇨Review from the contextual menu.**

3. **Select Accepted, Rejected, Cancelled, or Completed, depending on what's appropriate to your situation.**

   The comment you modified appears in the list, showing the new status you assigned to it.

Replying to a comment

You can right-click (Windows) or Ctrl+click (Mac) on a comment in the Comments List and choose Reply from the contextual menu to add a follow-up note to the comment. This way, new comments can be tied to existing comments. If your documents go through multiple rounds of review, adding a reply allows a secondary or final reviewer to expand on the comments from an initial reviewer. This also allows an author or designer to clearly respond to the suggestions from an editor.

Collapsing or hiding comments

Because the Comments List can become rather large, you can choose to collapse all comments so that only the page number on which comments appear is displayed in the list. To do so, click the Collapse All button in the upper-left of the Comments List window; it has a minus sign next to it. To view all comments, click the Expand All button in the same location; this button has a plus sign next to it.

To hide all the comments within a document, click and hold the Show button on the Commenting toolbar and choose Hide All Comments. You can then click the Show button in the Comments toolbar and choose to show comments based upon:

+ Type of comment, such as note, line, or cross out

+ Reviewer, such as Bob or Jane

+ Status, such as accepted or rejected

+ Checked State, which can be checked or unchecked

Use these filtering options to view only those comments that are relevant to you.

Sharing comments

You can share your comments with other reviewers who have access to the same PDF document by following these steps:

1. **Make sure that the Comments List is visible by clicking the Comments tab on the left side of the document window.**

2. **Select the comment that you want to export by clicking it (Shift+click for multiple selections).**

3. **Choose Options⇨Export Selected Comments from the Comments List window.**

The Export Comments dialog box appears.

4. **Browse to the location where you want the comments to be saved and give the saved file a new name.**

You now have a file that includes only the comments' information, and not the entire PDF file.

You can share your file with reviewers who have the same PDF file, and they can choose Options⇨Import Comments in the Comments List window to add the comments into their document. You can use this method to avoid sending entire PDF files to those who already have the document.

Summarizing comments

You can compile a list of all the comments from a PDF file into a new, separate document. To summarize comments, follow these steps:

1. **Choose Options⇨Summarize Comments in the Comments List window.**

The Summarize Options dialog box appears.

2. **Create a listing of the comments with lines connecting them to their locations on the page by selecting the second radio button from the top of the list.**

   In the Include section, you can choose which comments should be summarized.

3. **Click Create PDF Comment Summary.**

   This step creates a new PDF document that simply lists all the comments, as shown in Figure 5-3.

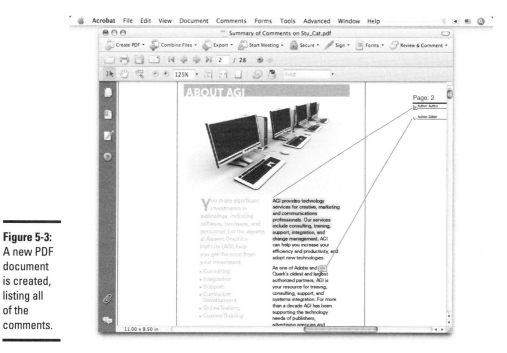

Figure 5-3:
A new PDF document is created, listing all of the comments.

Enabling commenting in Adobe Reader

Acrobat 8.0 Professional makes it easy to include users of the free Adobe Reader in a review process. To include Adobe Reader users in a review, choose Comments⇨Enable For Commenting in Adobe Reader. After saving the file, you can share it with users of Adobe Reader, who can then use commenting and markup tools and save their comments into the file. A user of Adobe Acrobat 8.0 Professional must enable commenting in a PDF file before users of Adobe Reader can add comments to a file.

Chapter 6: Securing Your PDF Files

You may think that because you've converted your documents to PDF that they're secure. This is not quite true, because Adobe Acrobat includes tools for changing text and images, as well as extracting them. For example, you can use the Select tool (see Chapter 4 of this minibook) to select and copy a passage of text or graphics.

Applying security provides you with control over who is able to view, edit, or print the PDF documents you distribute. You can restrict access to certain features, which deters most users from manipulating your files. All Adobe applications recognize and honor security settings applied in Acrobat, but some software ignores Adobe's security settings or can bypass them all together. For this reason, we recommend that you share your most sensitive documents only when you've applied password security protection. This way the only users who can open a file are those who know the password.

In this chapter, we discuss using password protection to limit access to PDF files and show you how to limit what users can do within your PDF documents.

Understanding Password Security

By requiring users to enter a password to open and view your PDF files, you limit access to those files so that only certain users can view them. You can also apply security to limit access to certain Acrobat and Adobe Reader features, such as copying text or graphics, editing the file, and printing. Adobe calls this type of security *password security* because it requires a password to either open the document or to change the security that has been applied to the document.

Apply security options that limit the opening and editing of your PDF document to those who supply the proper password by using the Secure button on the Tasks toolbar. If the Secure button isn't visible, choose View➪ Toolbars➪Tasks.

Click and hold down the Secure button in the Tasks toolbar and choose 2 Password Encrypt to bring up the Password Security – Settings dialog box.

In the Password Security – Settings dialog box, you choose an Acrobat version from the Compatibility drop-down list. The higher the version of Acrobat, the greater the level of security.

Your choice here is based on your needs for security and also the version of Acrobat or Adobe Reader that your audience will be using. In the following list, we explain the compatibility choices before showing you how to enable security in the following sections:

✦ **Acrobat 3 And Later:** If the users who receive your PDF files may have older versions of the software, you can choose Acrobat 3 And Later from the Compatibility drop-down list to ensure that they can work with the files you provide. This option provides compatibility for users who may not have updated their software in many years, but the level of security is limited to 40-bit encryption. While this amount will keep the average user from gaining access to your files, it won't deter a determined hacker from accessing them.

✦ **Acrobat 5 And Later:** When sharing files with users who have access to Adobe Reader or Adobe Acrobat Version 5 or 6, this option provides expanded security, increasing the security level to 128-bit, which makes the resulting PDF files more difficult to access. Along with the enhanced security, you can also secure the files while still allowing access to the file for visually impaired users. Earlier versions of security don't provide this option, but it's included when you choose either Acrobat 5- or 6-compatible security.

✦ **Acrobat 6 And Later:** Along with the enhanced security offered with Acrobat 5 compatibility, this setting adds the ability to maintain plain text metadata. In short, this option allows for information about the file, such as its author, title, or creation date, to remain visible while the remainder of the file remains secure.

✦ **Acrobat 7 And Later:** This choice includes all security options of Acrobat 6 compatibility and also allows you to encrypt file attachments that are a part of a PDF file. It uses the Advanced Encryption Standard, which is a very high level of encryption, making it unlikely that an unauthorized user can decrypt the file without the password.

Applying password security to your PDF documents

Selecting the Require A Password To Open The Document check box in the Password Security – Settings dialog box limits access to the PDF file to only those who know the password. The only practical way to open password-protected files, especially those secured with the most recent versions of Acrobat, is by entering the password. This safeguard provides a good incentive to use passwords that you can easily remember but are difficult for others to guess.

To apply password security to a file, follow these steps:

1. **With a PDF file open, click and hold the Secure button on the Security taskbar and choose Manage Security Policies.**

The Managing Security Policies window appears, as shown in Figure 6-1.

Figure 6-1:
The Managing Security Policies window.

If there is no Password Encrypt policy showing in the Name/Description/ Last Edited section, then you have to create one following the directions in Step 2. If there is a Password Encrypt policy, you can skip Step 2 and go to Step 3.

2. **Close the Managing Security Policies window; hold the Secure button on the Security taskbar and select 2 Password Encryption and create your encryption policy.**

After you have created your Password Encrypt policy, click and hold the Secure Button on the Security taskbar and choose Manage Security Policies. The Password Security – Settings window opens.

3. **Click the Require A Password to open the document check box.**

Enter a logical password that will be required to open the file in the Document Open Password text field.

You can also add additional security settings, which we outline in the next section. Or you can use this setting as the only security to be applied to the document.

If password protection is the only security measure you apply to the document, authorized users are able to access the document by entering a password. Users with the password are also able to edit or print the document.

4. **Click the OK button.**

5. **Confirm the password, click OK again, and the dialog box closes.**

6. **Save, close, and then reopen the PDF file.**

A password dialog box appears asking for the proper password to be entered for access to this file. Now, every time a user accesses the file, this dialog box appears.

Limiting editing and printing

In addition to restricting viewing of a PDF file, you can also apply restrictions to editing and printing PDF files. In doing so, you restrict users from making changes to your document. Users are only able to view the file.

To limit editing and printing of your PDF document, follow these steps:

1. **With a PDF file open, click and hold the Secure button on the Security taskbar and choose 2 Password Encrypt.**

The Password Security — Settings window opens.

2. **In the Permissions area, select the check box labeled Restrict Editing And Printing Of The Document.**

Whew! This check box may win the prize for the longest name ever placed in a software program, but it allows you to require a password to edit the file or change the security settings.

With this option selected, you can apply a password for access to features such as printing or editing. This password can be different than the password used to open the document — in fact, you don't even need to use a document open password if you don't want to, but it is a good idea to use both of these passwords for sensitive data.

3. **In the Change Permissions Password text field, enter a password.**

4. **Choose whether users are able to print the document by selecting from the Printing Allowed drop-down list.**

   The choices include low resolution or high resolution.

5. **To restrict editing, choose from the Changes Allowed drop-down list (see Figure 6-2).**

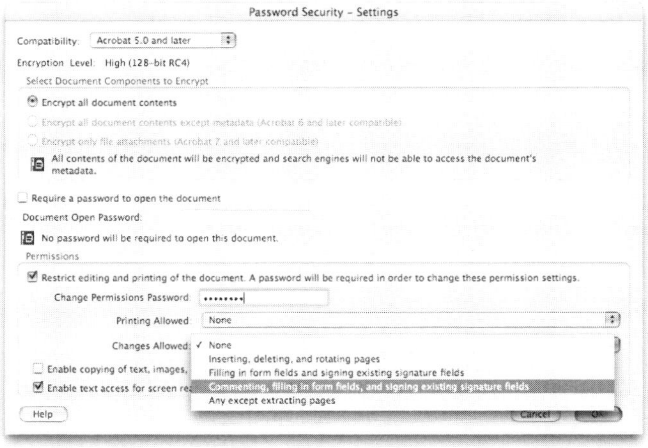

Figure 6-2:
The
Password
Security –
Settings
window.

6. **If you want, enable the last two check boxes:**

   • **Enable Copying Of Text, Images, and Other Content:** Restrict the ability to copy and paste text and graphics into other documents by deselecting this check box.

   • **Enable Text Access For Screen Reader Devices For The Visually Impaired:** When you choose Acrobat 5 or later compatibility, you can also select this check box to allow visually impaired users to have the PDF file read aloud to them.

7. **After you're satisfied with the settings, click OK.**

By choosing Acrobat 6 and later or Acrobat 7 and later from the Compatibility drop-down list, you can choose to Encrypt All Document Contents Except Metadata. If you choose Acrobat 7 and later from the Compatibility drop-down list the additional option to Encrypt Only File Attachments (Acrobat 7 and later compatible).

Book VI

Dreamweaver CS3

The 5th Wave   By Rich Tennant

"I love the way this program justifies the text in my resume. Now if I can just get it to justify my asking salary."

Contents at a Glance

Chapter 1: Getting Familiar with New Features in Dreamweaver

In This Chapter

✔ Integrating Dreamweaver with Photoshop and Fireworks

✔ Checking browser compatibility

✔ Understanding the Spry Framework

✔ Finding out about the improved CSS capabilities

Dreamweaver CS3 lets you create and manage single pages, such as e-mail newsletters, or groups of pages that are linked to each other, referred to as a *site*. Users can create basic Web sites with simple links from one page to another or advanced Web sites that include custom coding and interaction with those viewing the pages.

Now part of the Adobe Creative Suite, Dreamweaver CS3 works better than ever with other Adobe applications, such as Photoshop CS3, Illustrator CS3, Bridge, and Device Central. Even if you've never used Dreamweaver, you'll be interested in its new features because they put Dreamweaver ahead of the curve. If you're a GoLive user, moving to Dreamweaver is actually a smooth transition. Dreamweaver CS3 is a great product, especially if you plan to do advanced coding or create data-driven Web sites.

Improved Streamlined Interface

If you've used past versions of Dreamweaver, you may notice a little difference in the interface. If you're a new user, Dreamweaver's interface (see Figure 1-1) looks similar to your other Creative Suite applications. (Remember that Dreamweaver was a Macromedia product not too long ago, so you have to give them time to add the cool iconic collapsible panels available in the other applications.)

The panels are tabbed, and you can separate them by dragging the tab to another location, just as in other Adobe applications. If you choose View⟹ Toolbars⟹Standard, you can even use the Go To Bridge button to navigate and use Adobe Bridge. Using Adobe Bridge with Dreamweaver CS3 is a big improvement, as you can search and navigate your assets, such as text, flash, and other images files. You can then drag and drop them right on to your page. (Read more about adding imagery to your Web page in Chapter 4 of this minibook.)

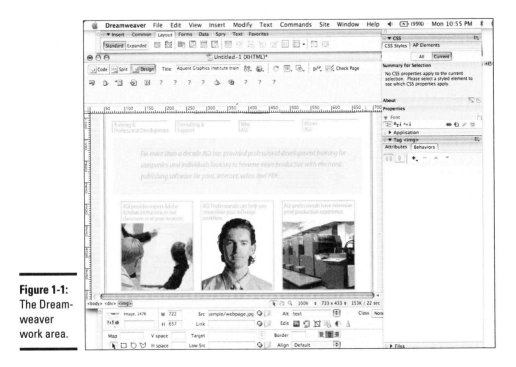

Figure 1-1: The Dream-weaver work area.

Better Integration with Photoshop and Fireworks

You'd expect better integration with Photoshop and Fireworks, as Dreamweaver and Photoshop are part of the same family. This improvement is great for Dreamweaver users, as you can now drag and drop native PSD and Fireworks files from Adobe Bridge right onto a Dreamweaver page. The Optimize window opens immediately, allowing you to choose the best format for your image and then save it. Want to return to the original to make additional edits? Dreamweaver maintains the link to the original, as you can see in Figure 1-2. Unfortunately, it's not a dynamic link like GoLive users are used to. If you edit the original, you need to save and overwrite your optimized image in order for it to update on your Web page.

Fireworks, formerly a Macromedia product that wasn't included with Creative Suite, is an image-editing program that you can use to build and comp pages, as it supports links and other help features.

Figure 1-2: New integration features include the ability to edit the original `.psd` file.

Optimize — — Crop

Browser Compatibility Check

This browser compatibility check is like no other. Sure, in GoLive, you could check the view to see what your page would look like in various browsers and versions, but Dreamweaver is different, as it checks cross-platform browsers no matter what computer you're using and provides a report explaining the problem. Browser compatibility doesn't stop there, though. Dreamweaver gives you a link to a Web site where you can discover how to fix the problems it finds. Because the site is updated regularly, it provides you with the most up-to-date information available anywhere.

To use this feature, select the Check Page button on the Document toolbar (see Figure 1-3). (If you don't see your Document toolbar, choose View➪ Toolbars➪ Document.) From the Check Page drop-down list, choose Check Browser Compatibility.

After Dreamweaver runs through the process of checking your file, a Reference panel appears, providing you with information about errors, if you have any. Note that in Figure 1-3, there is a compatibility issue, which is defined, and that a Web site link takes you to the solution. The solution may involve hand-coding some code, but using the Code tab in Dreamweaver shouldn't be too difficult. (Read about basics of coding and HTML in Chapter 3 of this minibook.)

Figure 1-3:
Feel
confident
that your
page will
work in
most
browsers
after using
the Browser
Compatibility
Check.

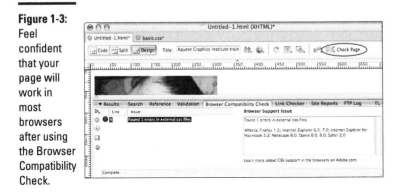

Spry Framework

The Spry Framework s really too advanced for this book, but you should at least be familiar with what it allows you to create. The Spry Framework helps users, beginner to advanced, take advantage of AJAX. AJAX stands for Asynchronous JavaScript and XML, and it's a Web development technique for creating interactive Web applications. The intent is to make Web pages feel more responsive by exchanging small amounts of data with the server behind the scenes, so that the entire Web page doesn't have to be reloaded each time the user requests a change. By not reloading the entire page, you can increase the Web page's interactivity, speed, and usability. Still confused? Check out the samples on Adobe Labs at `http://labs.adobe.com/technologies/spry`.

Basically, AJAX is a technique that required a lot of hand-coding in the past. Using Dreamweaver, you don't need to know complicated scripting languages, such as JavaScript and XML, to create interactive Web sites.

Dreamweaver CS3 includes a collection of objects (a *library*) that contains ready-to-use spry elements. When one of these elements is placed on a page, it creates an area that can change without the entire page reloading. For example, a user can create a photo gallery (see Figure 1-4) in which a person can click a smaller image and see a larger image using a Spry Framework Library item.

This feature is really worth investigating, especially if you're leaning toward the more advanced coding side of Web page creation. Included in this Spry framework are also *Spry widgets,* which are commonly used objects that you can easily add to pages without complex code. Widgets include form elements, database tables, and menu bars.

Figure 1-4:
A photo gallery created using the new Spry Framework feature in Dream-weaver CS3.

You can also use Spry *effects* to apply fun transition effects, such as grow and shrink, appear and fade, and shake, to objects on the page. Because these effects are based on the Spry framework, when the transition is applied, only the object is affected.

Improved CSS Capabilities

Cascading Style Sheets (CSS) is a language that gives Web site developers and users more control over how pages are displayed. With CSS, designers and users can create style sheets that define how different elements, such as headers and links, appear, and then apply these style sheets to any Web page. If you're familiar with Paragraph and Character Styles in InDesign and Illustrator, you'll understand the concept of CSS.

Using Cascading Styles, you not only have a wealth of additional attributes that you can apply to a page's format and text, but also the ability to make changes across an entire Web site quickly. You could always create Cascading Styles in previous versions. However, Dreamweaver CS3 now includes a number of starter pages that you can choose from to instantly create a page based upon CSS, giving them a professional look right from the beginning. You can also now manage your Cascading Style Sheets (CSS) so that you can copy and move styles more freely from one page to another.

Last, but not least, a CSS Advisor feature has been added. Adobe provides a link to the Adobe CSS Advisor Web site. On this site, you can get all the latest information about designing with the most up-to-date technologies. You find tips for creating, as well as places where users can go to ask questions of other Dreamweaver users. (You can find out more about creating pages in Dreamweaver using the CSS technology in Chapter 5 of this minibook.)

Chapter 2: Introducing Dreamweaver CS3

In This Chapter

✔ Setting up the workspace

✔ Finding out about panels

✔ Understanding Dreamweaver preferences

✔ Previewing your page in a Browser

Dreamweaver CS3 gives you the ability to create and manage Web pages and sites. In this chapter, you find out how to start a Web site and build pages within it. Basically, a Web site is simply a group of linked pages and images.

Getting to Know the Workspace Setup

As a default, most workspace options are available to you in the form of either panels, toolbars, or inspectors. This workspace can take some getting used to because it isn't totally consistent with the other Adobe applications in the suite.

When Dreamweaver is first launched, you see a Welcome screen. This screen provides the option to open any recent items (if you've already created pages), but also allows you to create new HTML, CSS, XML, sites, and many other files. You can also choose a selection from the Create From Samples column.

Dreamweaver provides you with all the tools you need in the initial workspace (see Figure 2-1).

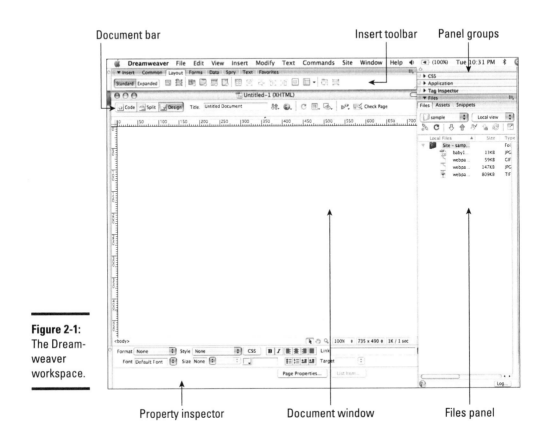

Document bar Insert toolbar Panel groups

Figure 2-1:
The Dream-
weaver
workspace.

Property inspector Document window Files panel

The Insert toolbar

The Insert toolbar provides you with tools to insert hyperlinks, e-mail links, tables, and images to your page, as well as more advanced coding related to CSS (Cascading Style Sheets and AJAX (Spry elements).

The Insert toolbar contains eight tabs, which provide you with different elements to add to your page:

✦ **Common:** Contains the most commonly used objects, such as images and tables.

✦ **Layout:** Contains elements, such as tables and CSS elements like the DIV tag, that help you create a Web page layout.

✦ **Forms:** Contains the elements necessary to create a form in your Dreamweaver page.

✦ **Data:** Contains elements related to dynamic content and some spry data objects.

✦ **Spry:** Contains the new spry framework objects, used to create pages, and widgets, such as spry tables and accordion menus.

✦ **Text:** Provides you with text formatting tags.

✦ **Favorites:** Allows you to group and organize the Insert toolbar buttons you use the most in one common location.

To bring up the Customize window, simply right-click (Windows) or Ctrl+click (Mac OS) in the Insert toolbar and choose Customize Favorites from the contextual menu. The Customize Favorite Objects dialog box, shown in Figure 2-2, appears. Click an object in the Available objects window and then click the double-arrow to add the object to your Favorite tab.

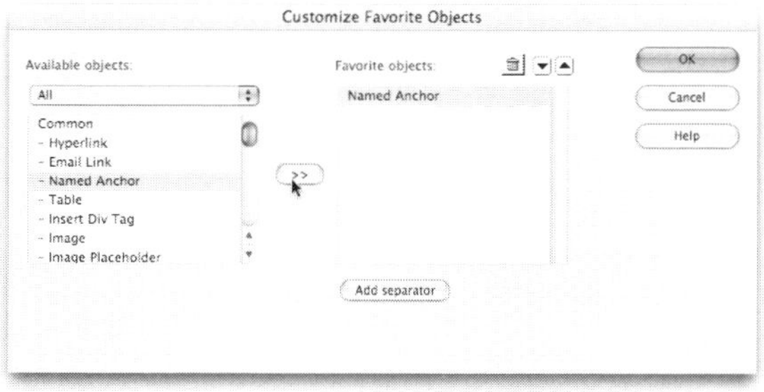

Figure 2-2:
Customizing
your
Favorites
tab in the
Insert
toolbar.

The Document toolbar

The Document toolbar, shown in Figure 2-3, contains helpful tools to help you view your document in different modes, such as code and design views, as well as address such items as the document title and browser compatibility.

✦ **Show Code View:** Show the code and only the code using this view. Dreamweaver helps you to decipher code by color coding tags, attributes, CSS and other elements.

✦ **Show Code and Design Views:** Selecting this option splits the Document window between the Code and Design views. If you understand a little about code, this view can be extremely helpful because you see both the design and code simultaneously.

✦ **Show Design View:** This option displays only the Design view in the Document window.

Note: If you're working with XML, JavaScript, CSS, or other code-based file types, you can't view the files in Design view, and the Design and Split buttons are dimmed out.

Figure 2-3:
The Document toolbar helps you address issues relating to your page.

A B C   D   E F G H I   J K

A. *Show Code View* **B**. *Show Code and Design Views* **C**. *Show Design View* **D**. Document Title **E**. File Management **F**. Preview/Debug In Browser **G**. Refresh Design View **H**. View Options **I**. Visual Aids **J**. Validate Markup **K**. Check Browser Compatibility

✦ **Document Title:** Enter the name of your document in this field.

✦ **File Management:** Click this button to display the File Management pop_up menu. Use this menu to check in and out of your document.

✦ **Preview/Debug In Browser:** Selecting this button allows you to preview or debug your document in a browser that you select from a drop-down list.

✦ **Refresh Design View:** Click this button to refresh the document's Design view after you make changes in Code view. Changes you make in Code view don't automatically appear in Design view until you perform certain actions, such as saving the file or clicking this button.

Note: Refreshing also updates code features that are Document Object Model (DOM) dependent, such as the ability to select a code block's opening or closing tags.

✦ **View Options** Click and select options from the View Options drop-down list. This button allows you to set options for Code view and Design view, including which view should appear above the other. Options in the menu are for the current view: Design view, Code view, or both.

✦ **Visual Aids:** Click this button to select different visual aids to help you see various elements and make designing your pages easier.

✦ **Validate Markup:** Click this button to validate the current document or a selected tag.

✦ **Check Browser Compatibility:** This option lets you check whether your CSS is compatible across different browsers.

Using the Panel Groups

Dreamweaver provides you with a panel docking area off to the right of your workspace. The panels in Dreamweaver are collapsible, organized, and neat. You can easily access the appropriate panel for the job by either clicking the title bar of the panel or by selecting the named panel from the Window menu.

Close a panel group by either selecting the name of the panel from the Window menu or by choosing Close Panel Group from the panel menu on the right side of the titlebar.

Saving your workspace

Just like the other Creative Suite 3 Applications, you can organize your workspace by turning on the visibility of the panels and toolbars that you use on a regular basis and closing the others. You can also save your workspace:

**Book VI
Chapter 2**

**Introducing
Dreamweaver CS3**

1. **Choose Window➪Workspace Layout➪Save Current.**

The Save Workspace Layout dialog box appears.

2. **Type an appropriate name in the name textbox.**

Creating a Site

Sites are very important to maintain links, consistency, and general organization of your Web pages. (See Chapter 3 of this minibook for more on sites.)

To create a site:

1. **Choose Site➪New Site.**

The Site Definition wizard appears. This series of dialog boxes takes you through the steps to create a site. In this chapter, you breeze through the dialog boxes, but you can find more details about them in Chapter 3 of this minibook.

2. **Name the site and click Next.**

For this example, we named the site chap2.

3. **Leave the radio button on the server technology page set to No and click Next.**

4. **Leave the radio button on the files page set to Edit Local Copies On My Machine.**

5. **Type a location where you want the site to be stored or use the Browse button to the right of the site location textbox to locate a folder to put site assets into and click Next.**

6. **Choose None from the How Do You Want To Connect To Your Remote Server drop-down menu and click Next.**

7. **Click Done in the Summary page.**

    The site appears in the files panel.

Checking out the Property Inspector

After you have a site created, you can put some assets, such as pages with images, into that site. The Property inspector becomes one of your most used toolbars, because it provides you with information about any element that you've selected. This contextual toolbar, shown in Figure 2-4, displays text attributes when text is selected, or image attributes when images are selected, and so on.

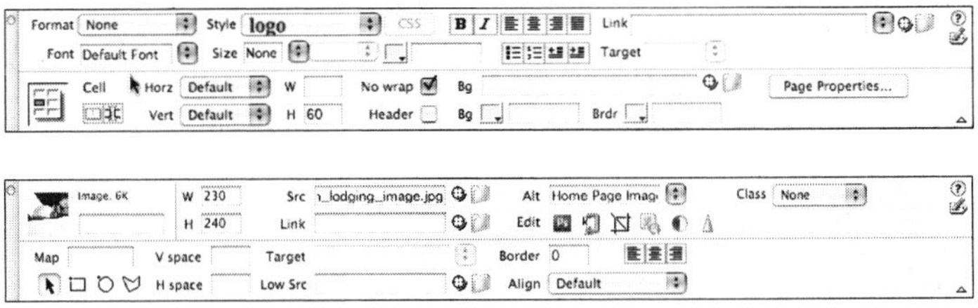

Figure 2-4:
The Property inspector as it appears with text selected (top) and with an image selected (bottom).

To see this toolbar in action, place a page with various elements on it. For this example a sample page is opened in Dreamweaver. The sample pages are loaded with your Dreamweaver CS3 installation, so you can follow along if you like.

1. **Open a sample page in Dreamweaver by choosing File➪New.**

    The New Document dialog box appears.

2. **Click the Page From Sample icon on the left side of the New Document dialog box and then choose Starter Page (Theme) from the Sample Folder column, Lodging — Home from the Starter page column, or any page that you think looks interesting and click Create.**

   Just make sure that the page you select has text and images on it.

   The Save As dialog box appears. Dreamweaver wants to make sure that the page is saved immediately.

3. **Type a name in the Save As textbox.**

   The location is automatically routed to the site folder that you created. Refer to the "Creating a Site" section in this chapter to see how to create a site.

4. **Click Save.**

   The Copy Dependent Files dialog box appears. Dreamweaver even provides you with the image files.

5. **Click Copy.**

   Dreamweaver places the image files into your site folder, and the sample page appears.

After you have a document with text and images, click to select various elements, such as an image, text, table, or hyperlink (linked text). With each selection, your Property inspector provides you with specific information about that element.

If you're a former GoLive user, the concept of using the Inspector is very familiar to you because this same feature existed in that application as well.

Previewing Your Page

Perhaps you've completed your page and want to investigate how it looks on a browser. You can quickly preview your file by simply clicking the Preview/Debug In Browser button on the Document toolbar and selecting the browser you'd like to preview your page in.

Adobe Device Central CS3 is a new application included with Creative Suite 3. Device Central CS3 helps people who design for mobile phones and other handheld devices, such as PDAs. Because screen sizes and types of these mobile devices are constantly changing, Device Central CS3 has a library of profiles that is regularly updated. Designers and developers can easily test their information through Device Central from any number of different programs within the Creative Suite.

Understanding Dreamweaver Preferences

You can change many preferences in Dreamweaver CS3 (see Figure 2-5). You see categories, such as General, Accessibility, and AP Elements, in the pane on the left, along with subcategories that appear in the pane to the right when selected.

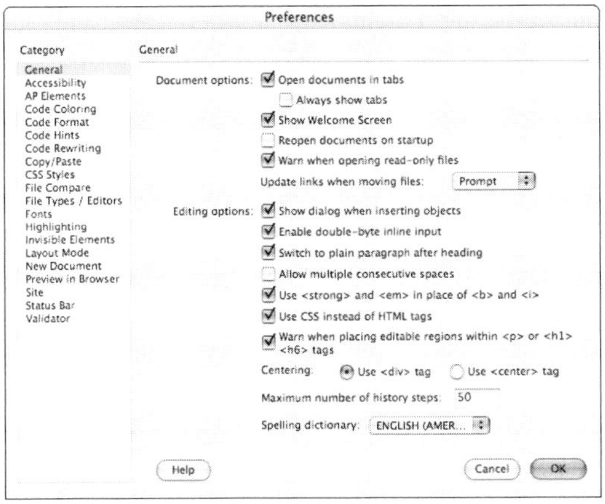

Figure 2-5:
You can change numerous preferences to help you work better in Dream-weaver CS3.

To access general preferences, choose Edit⇨Preferences (Windows) or Dreamweaver⇨Preferences (Mac OS). The general rule is, if you don't know what it means, don't touch it. But if you want to tweak certain things, this is the place to go.

Preferences are especially helpful to those who hand-code and want to enter their own code hints, highlight colors, or change the font that appears in the Code view and Code Inspector.

Chapter 3: Creating a Web Site

*I*n this chapter, you discover the basics of putting a Web site together, from creating that first new, blank site, to adding files to Web sites, to playing (just a little bit) with HTML.

Web Site Basics

A *Web site* is a collection of related pages linked to one another, preferably in an organized manner. With the proper planning and an end goal in sight, you can easily accomplish the task of creating a great Web site. Figure 3-1 shows the general structure of a Web site. Web sites start with a main page (also called the *home page*), the central link to other pages in the site. The main page is also the page viewers see first when they type your URL in a browser. The main page is typically named index.html, but, depending on your Internet service provider, it may be called index.html or even home.html. Check with your provider to find the correct name.

Pages are linked together with *hyperlinks,* references that take viewers from one point in an HTML document to another or from one document to another. (You can read more about hyperlinks and how to create them in Chapter 6 of this minibook.)

The following are terms that you should understand as you forge through the steps to create a Web site:

✦ **TCP/IP (Transmission Control Protocol/Internet Protocol):** Underlying protocols that make communication between computers on the Internet possible. TCP/IP ensures that information being exchanged goes to the right place, in a form that can be used, and gets there intact.

✦ **URL (Universal Resource Locator):** A standard for specifying the location of an object on the Internet, such as a file. The URL is what you type into a Web browser to visit a Web page, such as www.dummies.com. URLs are also used in HTML documents (Web pages) to specify the target of a link, which is often another Web page.

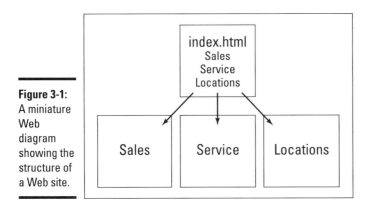

Figure 3-1:
A miniature
Web
diagram
showing the
structure of
a Web site.

✦ **FTP (File Transfer Protocol):** Allows a user on one computer to transfer files to and from another computer over a TCP/IP network. FTP is also the client program the user executes to transfer files. You may use FTP to transfer Web pages, images, and other files to a host Web server when you publish your site.

✦ **HTTP (Hypertext Transfer Protocol):** The client-server TCP/IP protocol used on the World Wide Web for the exchange of HTML documents.

How Web sites are organized is important. Typically, the purpose of a Web site is to sell something — a product, service, or just a thought, such as "Vote for me!" Without sound organization, a Web site may fail to sell to its visitors. Read these words slowly: *Plan your site.* Seriously, you'll save an extraordinary amount of time if you just think ahead and plan your site's organization. Think about the topics you want to cover and then organize your site as you would a high school essay project, planning the topic sentence, subtopics, and so on. This plan can be a tremendous aid when you start mapping out which pages should be linked to others.

Starting a New Site

Even if you're creating only one page, it's best to create a site. A site gives you an organized method for keeping images and other assets together and offers additional options for management of those files.

To create a new site, follow these steps:

1. **In Dreamweaver CS3 choose Site⇨New Site.**

   You could also choose Dreamweaver Site from the Create New Column of the Welcome Screen. The Site Definition dialog box appears.

2. **In the site name text box, name the site and click Next.**

   In this example, the site was named biking, as this site's focus will be on bikes. Because this example is being created, but not immediately uploaded, the HTTP address has been left blank.

3. **Choose the No, I Do Not Want To Use Server Technology radio button and click Next.**

   This step allows you to design a Web site on your computer and test it in various browsers without setting up complicated server information. If you're actually using ASP, ColdFusion, and JSP, you can choose your server technology, but that path isn't covered in this example.

4. **Because you haven't yet defined a server (where your pages will be accessible on the World Wide Web), leave the development radio button set to Edit Local Copies.**

   It's best to leave this option selected, even if you do have a server set up, because you can keep originals intact on your computer until you're sure that they're ready to be uploaded.

5. **Click the Browse folder icon to the right of the file path text box and browse to the location where you want to create the site folder that you'll use to store all the site's assets; click Next.**

   The site's assets include images, scripts, and finished pages. The Sharing Files Site Definition dialog box appears.

6. **Choose None from remote server drop-down list.**

   You can set up the server information later.

7. **Click Next.**

   The Summary window appears.

8. **Review the information and, if you want to make changes, click the Back button; otherwise, click Done.**

   You've created a local folder on your computer.

As soon as you create a site, your site folder is waiting and waiting in the Files panel. Think of the Files panel as the central control center for all your files, folders, and other assets that you'll use to create your Web site.

The Finals panel allows you to view files and folders, whether they're related to your Dreamweaver site or not. You can use the Files panel to do typical file operations, such as opening and moving your files.

Creating a New Page for Your Site

After create a site, you typically create your main page, called the `index .html` or `index.htm` page. Check with your Web service provider because in some instances, your server may require a different name.

The following steps walk you through creating a new page and placing an image on it.

1. **Choose File➪New.**

You can create many types of new files, from blank pages to more advanced pages that include layouts already created in CSS.

2. **To create a blank page, choose Blank Page➪HTML➪<none> and then click Create.**

A blank untitled HTML page appears.

3. **Choose File➪Save.**

The Save As dialog box appears.

4. **Name the file** index.html.

Note that the file is already mapped to your site file. If you're not mapped to the site root folder (your main file where all of the pages and assets are stored), you can click the Site Root button in the Save As dialog box.

5. **Click Save.**

Note that when you save a file, it appears in your Files panel.

Adding an Image to Your Page

After you have a blank page, you can add an image, including native PSD and Fireworks images, to it. You can find out more about images in Chapter 4 of this minibook, but take a look how placing images affects your Files panel.

To place an image on a page, follow these steps:

1. **Choose Insert⇨Image.**

Or click the Common tab of the Insert toolbar and click the Images button.

The Select Image Source dialog box appears.

2. **Navigate to the location of your image and click Choose.**

If you choose a native PSD or Fireworks file, an Image Preview dialog box appears, allowing you to optimize your image right in Dreamweaver.

If you choose an image already in an optimized format, such as JPG, GIF, PNG, but outside your site folder, you see a warning window. Dreamweaver is basically alerting you to the fact that your image is outside the root folder and verifying that you'd like it copied into your site root folder. Click Yes. A Copy File As dialog box appears. Change the name here or just click Save to keep it the same name and copy the image file into your site folder.

The Image Tag Accessibility Attributes dialog box appears.

All images should have Alt text — the text that appears before the image has downloaded or that appears if the viewer has turned off the option to see images.

3. **Add an appropriate description of the image.**

If the image were a logo, the description should include the company name as the Alt text or, if it's an image, describe the image in a few words. This description is helpful for the visually impaired who use software that reads Alt tags.

4. **Click OK.**

The image is added to the page and to the Files panel.

You can edit your image by double-clicking it in the Files panel.

When you create a larger site with multiple pages linked to each other, you may want to change the view of the Files panel. By clicking the drop-down menu (on the left side of the Files panel) where your site is located, you can locate folders and other sites that you've recently used. By clicking the View drop-down menu to the right, you can change the appearance of the Files panel. See Figure 3-2 for an example of how a site can appear in Map view.

Open your files directly from the files panel by double-clicking them.

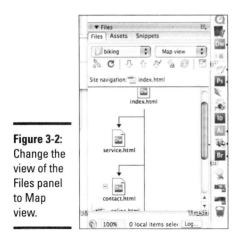

Figure 3-2:
Change the
view of the
Files panel
to Map
view.

Naming Files

Get in the habit right away of naming your files and folders correctly.
Follow these rules to make sure that links and pages appear when they
are supposed to:

✦ **Use lowercase for all filenames.** Some functions are case-sensitive,
meaning that they won't work if you don't get the capitalization right.
Using all lowercase letters in filenames is an easy way to ensure that you
don't have broken links because you couldn't remember whether you
initial-capped a filename. Some Web servers require filenames to be in
lowercase, as well.

✦ **Don't use spaces in filenames.** If you need to separate words in a filename,
use the underscore character instead of a space. For example, instead of
`file new.html`, use `file_new.html` or even `filenew.html`.

✦ **Use only one dot, followed by the extension.** Macintosh users are used
to having no naming restrictions, so this rule can be the toughest to
adhere to. Don't name your files something like `finally.done.feb.9.`
`jpg`. That is B-A-D for the Internet. Examples of dot-extensions are as
follows: `.jpg`, `.gif`, `.png`, `.htm`, `.html`, `.cgi`, `.swf`, and so on.

✦ **Avoid odd characters.** Characters to avoid include dashes (-) or forward
slashes (/) at the beginning of the filename. These characters mean
other things to the Web server and will create errors on the site.

Managing Your Web Site Files

You can find out more about uploading your site in Chapter 8 of this mini-book, but for now, understand that you can go back into your Site Definition dialog box at any time by choosing Site⇨Manage Sites. The Manage Sites dialog box that appears offers options for editing, duplicating, removing, exporting, and importing sites. Click Edit to add an FTP server or change the name of your site, as well as change any of your original site definition settings.

Delving into HTML Basics

The Web page itself is a collection of text, images, links, and possibly media and script. It can be as complex or simple as you want, both being equally effective if created properly. In this section, we show you how to create a page in Dreamweaver and then investigate the HTML that creates it.

To create a blank page, select Blank Page⇨HTML⇨<none> and then click OK. A blank untitled HTML page appears. It has no formatting until you add tables or layers (see Chapter 6 of this minibook). When you type on the page in the document, text appears on the Web page. But there is much more to it than that; type some text (say, your name) on the page and click the Code button on the Document toolbar.

Dreamweaver is working in the background to make sure that your page works in Web browsers. Lots of code is created to help the Web browser recognize that this is HTML and which version of HTML it uses.

Return to the Design view by clicking the Design button on the Document toolbar and then select the text that you want to be bold and click the Text tab in the Insert toolbar. Select B (for bold), and the text turns bold. Click the Code button to switch back to the Code view, and you see that the <strong> tag was added before the text and the </strong> tag was added after the text.

HTML code, though easy, is just like any other language in that you must learn the *syntax* (the proper sequence and formation of the code) and vocabulary (memorize lots of tags). You don't have to have gobs of tape on your glasses to build good, clean Web pages, but you should review the following HTML basics.

If you're an experienced user, you know that by copying and pasting code, you can figure out a lot about HTML code. If you're a new user, copying and pasting code can help you understand what others have implemented on their pages and perhaps give you some ideas.

In general, HTML tags have three parts to them:

✦ **Tag:** The main part of the HTML information — for example, `<strong>` for strong or bold, `<font>` for the font tag, `<table>` for an HTML table, and so on. Most tags come in pairs, meaning that you must enter an opening tag (like `<p>`) and a closing tag (like `</p>`).

For example, if you make text bold by adding the tag `<b>`, you need to tell it where to stop being bold by inserting a closing tag `</b>`. Otherwise, the text will continue to bold throughout the remainder of the page.

✦ **Attribute:** The part of the tag that can be changed. You can specify attributes for color, size, the destination of a link, and so on. For example, `bgcolor` is an attribute of the `<body>` tag that specifies what color the background of the Web page should be.

✦ **Value:** The actual color, size, destination of a link, and so on, in an attribute. For example, you can specify a hexadecimal number as the value for a color attribute.

One last thing: *Nesting* is the order in which your tags appear. If a `<b>` tag is applied, it looks like this: `<b>This text is bold</b>`. Add an italic tag, and you have `<b><i>This text is bold and italic.</i></b>`. Notice the in-to-out placement of the tags; you work your way from the inside to the outside when closing tags.

Chapter 4: Working with Images

In This Chapter

- ✓ **Making images work for the Web**
- ✓ **Creating backgrounds from images**
- ✓ **Making a rollover**
- ✓ **Putting a Flash file on your page**

*P*lacing images that are interesting and informative is one of the most exciting parts of building a Web page. In this chapter, you discover how to optimize native PSD or Fireworks files directly in Dreamweaver, as well take care of basic needs, such as resizing, cropping, and positioning the image. You also find out how to create interesting backgrounds and create easy rollovers.

If you plan on following along with some of the steps in this chapter, create a site or have a practice site open. Images are much-needed linked assets on your page. You don't want to lose track of them in your filing system. If you don't know how to create a site, read Chapter 3 of this minibook.

Creating Images for the Web

Placing images isn't difficult, but you must consider which format images are saved in and how large the files are. (See Book IV, Chapter 10 for details on selecting the correct format and using the Save For Web & Devices feature in Photoshop.)

Putting images on a Web page requires planning to make sure that sizes are exactly what you want them to be. You also need to make sure that you don't have too many images to keep the page loading quickly.

If you look in the lower-right of your document window, you see the page file size and its approximate download time. In Figure 4-1, the page file size is 23K, and the download time is 3 seconds. This download time is based upon the preference of 56K per second. You can change the download speed by choosing Edit⇨Preferences (Windows) or Dreamweaver⇨Preferences (Mac OS), selecting the Status Bar category, and clicking the Connection Speed drop-down list.

Figure 4-1:
Check your
document
window for
file size and
download
time.

The jury is always out as to how fast a page should download, but less than 15 seconds is a good target. Unless you have some really compelling content, you'll probably lose viewers after that.

Putting Images on a Page

Putting your images on a Web page in Dreamweaver is easier than ever, mostly because of the integration with other Adobe products. You can use menu items, copy and paste, and even drag and drop images on to your Dreamweaver page. In this section, you not only find out how to place your images, but you also discover some general helpful tips that relate to putting graphics on the Web.

Inserting an image

If you're preparing images ahead of time, save to or move the optimized images into your site folder. It's not that you can't select an image from anywhere in your directory; it just adds another step, copying the image into your site folder.

After you have a page open, you can insert an image:

1. **Click to put your insertion point on the page where you'd like the image placed.**

2. **Locate the Common tab on the Insert panel and click the Insert Image button or choose Insert⊃Image.**

The image is placed.

Gotta have that Alt text

You've probably seen *Alt text* a gazillion times; it's the text that appears before an image when a Web page is loading. It also appears as a ToolTip when you hover your mouse cursor over an image in a Web page.

Alt text is helpful because it tells viewers something about the image before the image appears, but Alt text also is necessary for viewers who turn off their preference for viewing graphics, or for folks using a Web-reading

program, like those for the visually impaired. U.S. Federal regulations also require Alt tags for any work completed for federal agencies. These tags are also helpful for people with slow Internet connections.

To assign or change Alt text to an image that has already been placed, type your descriptive copy in the Alt text box located in the Properties panel.

If image isn't the default for your Insert Image button, click and hold the arrow to the right of the button and choose Image from the drop-down list.

Next, the Select Image Source dialog box appears. Simply navigate to where your image is located and click OK (Windows) or Choose (Mac). You're now taken through several additional dialog boxes. It may seem overwhelming, but in the long run, it's better for your site and page organization.

If your images are located in your site folder, you can click the Site Root button to navigate there quickly. If your image isn't in your site folder. You see an alert dialog box, asking whether you want to copy the file there now. Click Yes. In the Copy File As dialog box that appears, verify that the name is correct in the File Name text box and click Save.

An Image Tag Accessibility Attributes dialog box appears, requesting that you enter Alt text. (For more on Alt text, see the sidebar "Gotta have that Alt text.") Type a descriptive word or two in here and click OK. The image is placed.

Dragging and dropping an image

If you're taking advantage of the Adobe Bridge workflow, you can leave Bridge running and drag images as you need them right from the Bridge window into your Dreamweaver page. You can access Bridge by choosing File⇨Browse In Bridge.

If the image is a native PSD or Fireworks file, the Image Preview dialog box appears, giving you the opportunity to optimize the image before placing it.

You can also drag and drop an optimized image from your desktop of other folders right into a Dreamweaver page. If they're not in your site folder, you get the opportunity to copy it.

Getting to Know the Properties Panel

Many of the tools you use when working with images are located on the Properties panels (see Figure 4-2).

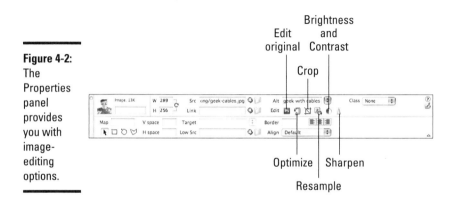

Figure 4-2:
The Properties panel provides you with image-editing options.

You can choose from these properties when an image is selected:

+ **Editing the original:** If you want to make a quick change, it shouldn't have to involve a lot of navigating through your directory. To edit your original image file, select it and click the Edit button in the Properties panel. The image is launched in its original application, where you can make changes and re-save the image.

+ **Optimizing an image:** You do have the opportunity to optimize images right off your Dreamweaver page, but this method doesn't provide quite the same capabilities that you have when placing a native PSD or Fireworks file because the image you're selecting is already optimized. It may already be a JPEG or GIF — and yes, you can reduce the number of colors in the GIF or change a JPEG to a GIF, but you really can't increase color levels or quality on these images, as they're not linked to the original image file. (This is something that GoLive users will sorely miss, as this is possible with Smart Objects in GoLive.)

✦ **Cropping an image:** This feature is sure to become a favorite as you can now make cropping decisions right on your Dreamweaver page. Simply click the Crop tool, acknowledge the warning message telling you that you're editing the image, and then click and drag the handles to the desired size. Press the Enter key, and you're done!

✦ **Resampling an image:** You may have heard that you shouldn't resize an image placed on a Dreamweaver page because, if you were making the image larger, it would become pixilated and if you were making the image smaller, you were wasting lots of bandwidth downloading the file. Fortunately, you can now use the Resample button on the Properties panel after you have resized the image. Just keep in mind that making the image larger still causes some quality issues, so it's best to reduce the file size before choosing the Resample button. If you need to make an image considerably larger, find the original and optimize it to the proper size.

To resize an image, you can either click and drag out the lower-right corner handle of the image or type a pixel value in the W (Width) and H (Height) text boxes in the Properties panel.

✦ **Brightness and Contrast:** If high quality is important to you, open your original image in Photoshop and make tonal corrections using professional digital imaging tools. If volume and quickly getting lots of images and pages posted is important, take advantage of the Brightness and Contrast controls built right into Adobe Dreamweaver. Simply click the Brightness And Contrast button, in the Properties panel, acknowledge the Dreamweaver dialog box, and adjust the sliders to create the best image.

✦ **Sharpen:** Add crispness to your image by applying the Sharpness controls available in Dreamweaver. Just like some of the other image-editing features in Dreamweaver, you'd be better off using the Unsharp mask filter in Photoshop, but in a pinch, this feature is a great quick tool to take advantage of. To use the Sharpening feature, click the Sharpen button, acknowledge the warning that you're changing the image, and use the slider to sharpen the image. Click OK.

Book VI
Chapter 4

Working with Images

Aligning an Image

As a default, images only allow text to run in one line off to the right of the image. To control the runaround of the text, change the alignment of the image by selecting the image and then an option from the Alignment drop-down list in the Properties panel.

The Align drop-down list provides the following options:

✦ **Default:** One line of text on the right side of the image.

✦ **Baseline:** Aligns the bottom of the image with the baseline of the current line of text.

✦ **Top:** Image aligns itself with the top of the tallest item in the line of text.

✦ **Middle:** Image aligns the baseline of the current line of text with the middle of the image.

✦ **Bottom:** Baseline aligns the bottom of the image with the baseline of the current line of text.

✦ **Text Top:** Image aligns itself with the top of the tallest text in the line. This is usually (but not always) the same as `ALIGN=top`.

✦ **Absolute Middle:** Aligns the middle of the current line with the middle of the image.

✦ **Absoluter Bottom:** Aligns the bottom of the image with the bottom of the current line of text.

✦ **Left:** Aligns the image to the left, text flushes to the right of the image.

✦ **Right:** Aligns image to the right, text flushes to the left of the image.

Adding Space around the Image

You may want some space around the image to keep the text from butting right up to the image. To create a space around the image, enter values into the H space and V space text fields in the Properties panel.

If you want space added only to one side of the image, open the image in Photoshop and choose Image⇨Canvas Size. In the Canvas Size dialog box that appears, click the middle left square in the Anchor section and add a value in pixels to your total image size. Click the right middle square to add the size to the left side of the image.

Using an Image as a Background

Creating backgrounds for Web pages is fun and can be pursued in more ways than most people think. You don't have to settle for an image repeating over and over again in the background; this feature offers many creative solutions. As a default, HTML backgrounds repeat the selected image until the entire screen is filled. If you're filling your background with a pattern, make sure that you create a pattern that has no discernable edges. (In Photoshop, choose Filter⇨Texture⇨Texturizer to see some good choices in the Texturizer dialog box.) Patterns that repeat are typically 100 x 100 pixels in size.

To utilize the default, repeated tiling for a background image to your advantage, follow these steps:

1. **In Photoshop, choose File⇨New to create a new image.**

2. **In the New dialog box that appears, create an image that's much wider than it is high, choose RGB, choose 72 dpi, and then click OK.**

For example, enter 2000 in the Width text field and 20 in the Height text field.

3. **Select a foreground and background color to create a blend; then with the Gradient tool, Shift+drag across the image area.**

4. **Choose File⇨Save For Web and save the image as a JPEG into your site's Web content folder and then close the image.**

See Book IV, Chapter 10 for more about the Save For Web feature.

5. **In Dreamweaver, place the image as a background image in your Web page by choosing Page Properties in the Properties panel.**

If the Page Properties button isn't visible, click the page, making sure that you don't select another element, such as an image.

6. **When the Page Properties dialog box appears, click the Browse button to the right of Background image, navigate to the location of your saved background image, and then click Choose; click OK in the Page Properties dialog box.**

The image appears in the background.

Because browser windows are rarely opened more than 2,000 pixels wide, your image is forced to repeat stacked on top of itself (rather than tiled across and down, as with a square image), producing an effect similar to what's shown in Figure 4-3. Use this technique to create the look of ruled paper, corrugated steel, and so on.

You may not see your background until you click the Preview/Debug In Browser button and view the page in your default browser.

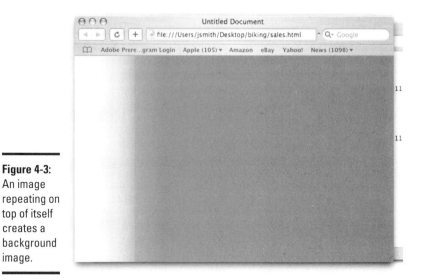

Figure 4-3:
An image repeating on top of itself creates a background image.

Creating Rollovers

Using Dreamweaver, you can insert image objects. These image objects include image placeholders, *rollover images* (images that change when a viewer crosses over the image), navigation bars, and Fireworks HTML. Access these image objects by choosing Image➪Image Objects.

To create a rollover image:

1. **Create the images that will be used as the rollover.**

You can generate these images from Illustrator, Photoshop, Fireworks, or any application capable of saving images optimized for the Web.

2. **Put your cursor on the page where you want the rollover to appear and choose Image➪Image Objects➪ Rollover Image.**

The Insert Rollover Image dialog box, shown in Figure 4-4, appears.

3. **Type an image name without spaces.**

This name is used in the script creating the rollover.

4. **Click the Browse buttons to the right of Original Image and Rollover Image text boxes to locate the image that you want to appear as a default on the page and the image that will appear only when someone crosses over the image.**

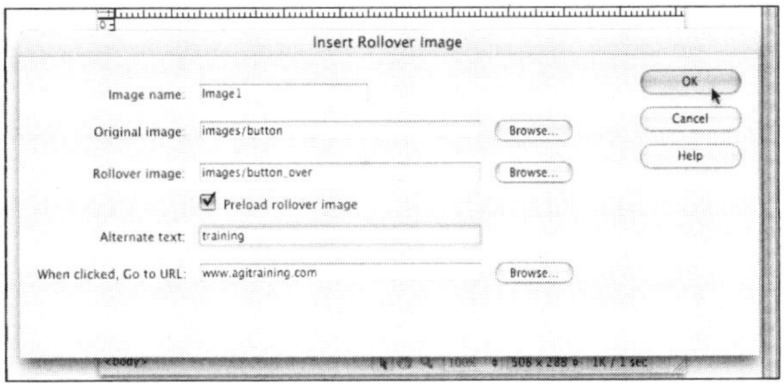

Figure 4-4:
Rollovers
are made
easy in
Dream-
weaver.

5. **Leave the Preload Rollover Image check box checked.**

   This option downloads the rollover image when the page is downloaded to avoid delays in rollovers.

6. **Type the appropriate descriptive Alt text in the Alternate Text text box.**

7. **In the When Clicked, Go To URL text box, instruct Dreamweaver as to where the viewer should be directed when they click your rollover image.**

   You can either use the Browse to locate another page in your site or enter an URL.

8. **Click OK.**

   The rollover is created on your page.

**Book VI
Chapter 4**

Working with
Images

Inserting Media Content

Make your pages more interactive and interesting by adding Flash and Shockwave content. Dreamweaver makes it simple by providing you with the tools that you need to add Flash animation, FlashPaper, Flash Text, Flash Button, and Flash Videos.

To place a Flash file on to your Dreamweaver page:

1. **Put the cursor on your page where you'd like to insert the Flash file.**

2. **Choose Insert➪Media➪Flash.**

   The Select File dialog box appears.

3. **Navigate to the** `.swf` **file that you want to place and click OK (Windows) or Choose (Mac).**

4. **In the Object Tag Accessibility Attributes dialog box, type the appropriate Alternative text (Alt text) and click OK.**

   The Flash file is placed on the page.

Preview in the browser to see it in action or click the Play button in the Properties panel.

Chapter 5: Putting Text on the Page

In This Chapter

✔ **Adding text to your page**

✔ **Choosing and editing a font family**

✔ **Understanding Cascading Style Sheets**

✔ **Creating an external style sheet**

*A*dding text to your Web page requires more than just typing on a page. You must carefully plan your Web pages so that search engines (and therefore viewers) can easily find relevant content on your Web site. In this chapter, you discover fundamentals of text formatting for your Web pages, from the basics of font size and font family, to spell-checking your text, to implementing Cascading Style Sheets (CSS).

Because you can assign type properties quickly and update all instances in a few easy steps with CSS, using CSS is viewed as the most efficient method of applying text attributes on a Web page. As you create text for the body of your page, you'll want to include keywords that provide descriptions of your site's content. This makes your page more relevant to the search engine and the viewer.

CSS and Dreamweaver: The Good and the Bad

As a default, Dreamweaver converts your HTML tags to CSS, whether you want it to or not. Normally, this conversion would be a good thing, but if you were to investigate your text in Code view (by clicking the Show Code View button), you'd see that a new span tag is created for each and every attribute change that you make. This feature is actually intelligent for users who don't know how to use CSS, but rather cumbersome for those who want to control the text totally on their own.

To disable the CSS instead of HTML preference, choose Edit➪Preferences (Windows) or Dreamweaver➪Preferences (Mac OS). The Preferences dialog box appears. Select the General category and uncheck Use CSS Instead Of HTML tags under the Editing Options section. Click OK.

Adding Text

To add text to your Web page, simply click the page wherever you want the text to appear; an insertion point appears where you can start typing. You can add text right to the page, in a CSS layer, or in the cell of a table. (In Chapter 6 of this minibook, you see how to integrate text with layers, tables, and frames.)

Formatting text

Formatting text in Dreamweaver can be as simple as formatting text in any other application, such as InDesign or Illustrator. By clicking the Text tab of the Insert toolbar, you can select from a variety of different HTML text tags to apply to your selected text (see Figure 5-1).

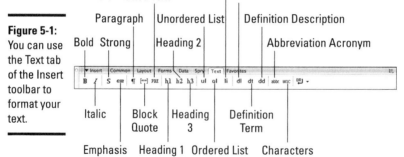

Figure 5-1:
You can use the Text tab of the Insert toolbar to format your text.

Most of the options in the Text tab are apparent, but here's a breakdown of some text tags that may be unfamiliar to you. To use these tags, simply select the text that you want the tag to be applied to and then click the tag on the Insert panel:

✦ **Bold:** Bolds text

✦ **Italic:** Italicizes text

✦ **Strong:** Bolds text

✦ **Emphasis:** Indicates emphasis, looks like italic

See Figure 5-2 for samples of how these tags look when applied to your selected text.

Figure 5-2:
Sample of text with the bold, italic, strong, and emphasis.

When you press the Enter or Return key, a `<p>` tag is automatically created in the HTML source code. This tag may create more space than you like between lines and create new list items. Pressing Shift+Enter (Windows) or Shift+Return (Mac) creates a `<br>` tag, which is essentially a line break or soft return.

Using the Properties panel for text

Use the Properties panel, shown in Figure 5-3, to apply HTML tags and additional attributes to your text, such as font selection, size, and alignment.

Here's what all those buttons on the Properties panel mean:

✦ **Format:** Use the Format drop-down list to apply heading tags that affect an entire paragraph. These heading tags are generally added to headings and titles, and they can help you process and organize copy in order of importance. You can easily change heading tags attributes (size, font-family, and so on) by using Cascading styles.

   Note that Heading1 is the largest format size, and Heading 6 is the smallest. This makes sense if you think about how these tags were originally used to create technical documents and outlines on the internet, where Heading 1 is more important than Heading 2 or 3.

   The last format selection is preformatted. Sometimes, you'll want the browser to display text exactly the way you composed it — with indents, line breaks, and extra spaces. You can line up text this way if you choose preformatted; it's not pretty, but for down and dirty lists and columns, it can work well.

Assigning a font

You should be wary of assigning a font in the Properties panel because (with the Use CSS Instead Of HTML preference deselected) it creates a `<font>` tag that overrides any font family attributes in Cascading Style Sheets.

When a viewer opens a page referencing a font set, the text is displayed using the first available font in the font family. If the first font face on the list isn't available, the next font face is referenced, continuing down the list in the font family until a font in the font set is found on the viewer's computer. If you choose Edit Font List from the Font drop-down list, the Edit Font List dialog box appears (see figure).

Click the existing font lists to see which fonts are included in each of them. You can add new fonts to the sets by clicking the double arrow pointing from the Available fonts Pane into the Chosen Fonts pane. Delete a font from an existing font list by clicking the font in the Chosen Font pane and clicking the double arrow pointing toward the Available Fonts pane. You can even create an entirely new list yourself. To create a new font list, click the + (plus sign) in the upper-left of the Edit Font List dialog box.

Edit Font List
Font list:
Times New Roman, Times, serif
Courier New, Courier, monospace
Georgia, Times New Roman, Times, serif, Garamond
Verdana, Arial, Helvetica, sans-serif
Geneva, Arial, Helvetica, sans-serif
(Add fonts in list below)

Chosen fonts:
Georgia
Times New Roman
Times
serif
Garamond

Available fonts:
Footlight MT Light
Futura
Futura Condensed
Garamond
Garamond Premr Pro

Garamond

OK · Cancel · Help

+ **Font:** Use this drop-down list to select a font family. The font is the typeface that you choose to display your text in. The lack of typeface selection isn't a restriction in Dreamweaver. Keep in mind that what font the viewer sees on your Web page is based upon the availability of the fonts on his computer.

The viewer may not have fonts that you load in your font sets, so try to stick to common typefaces, like the ones already included in Dreamweaver's existing font sets.

+ **Styles:** Apply an existing class style sheet or create a new style by clicking the Apply CSS Style button and choosing a class style from the list that appears. We show you how to create and apply style sheets in the "Understanding Cascading Style Sheets" section of this chapter.

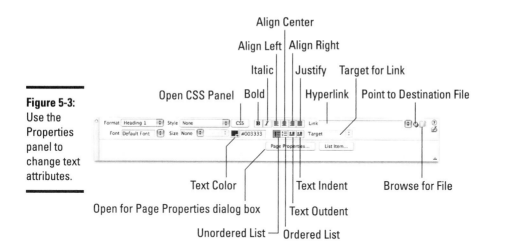

Figure 5-3:
Use the
Properties
panel to
change text
attributes.

Align Center

Align Left | Align Right

Italic | Justify | Target for Link

Open CSS Panel | Bold | Hyperlink | Point to Destination File

Text Color | Text Indent | Browse for File

Open for Page Properties dialog box | Text Outdent

Unordered List — Ordered List

+ **Size:** Using the Font Size drop-down list, you can apply a fixed font size from 1–7 (seven being the largest). Or you can use the relative sizes indicated with the plus or minus signs, which resize the font larger or smaller according to the user's browser preferences for font size. If you leave the font size at None, it defaults to 3. Keep in mind that the browser preference of the viewer may be changed to a different default font size.

  If you're planning to use Cascading Style Sheets, don't use the Font Size drop-down list as font size attribute overrides any text size changes set with CSS.

+ **Open CSS Panel:** Opens the CSS panel where you can see what CSS styles have been applied to your selected text.

+ **Color:** Assign a color to your text by selecting the text you want to change. Then click the bottom-right corner of the Set Text Color button on the Properties panel. Choose a swatch from the Swatches drop-down list that appears.

+ **Bold:** Bold your selected text.

+ **Italic:** Italicizes your text.

+ **Alignment:** You can click the alignment buttons on the toolbar to apply left, center, and right alignment. To revert to the default of left alignment, click the currently selected alignment button again.

+ **Unordered List:** Automatically puts bullets in front of the listed items. As you advance in the use of Cascading Style Sheets, you can apply many more attributes to lists, including customizing the bullets.

✦ **Ordered List:** Automatically numbers each additional line of text every time you press the Enter (Windows) or Return (Mac) key. To force the text to another line without adding the automatic numbering, press Shift+Enter (Windows) or Shift+Return (Mac).

✦ **Text Outdent:** Undo an Indent using the Text Outdent button. This removes the <blockquote> tag that the Text Indent button creates.

✦ **Text Indent:** Use to indent your text. Simply put your cursor in the paragraph of text that you want to indent and press the Text Indent button. A <blockquote> tag is applied. You can apply this tag multiple times to a paragraph to indent it further and further.

✦ **Link:** Type an address in this text box to turn your selected text into a hyperlink.

✦ **Target:** Choose where the linked target will appear. (Read about targets in Chapter 7 of this minibook.)

Spell-checking your text

Choose to spell-check just the file that you have open or multiple files by choosing Text⇨Check Spelling. Using the Check Spelling dialog box, shown in Figure 5-4, you can choose to add words to your personal dictionary, ignore words, or change the spelling of words.

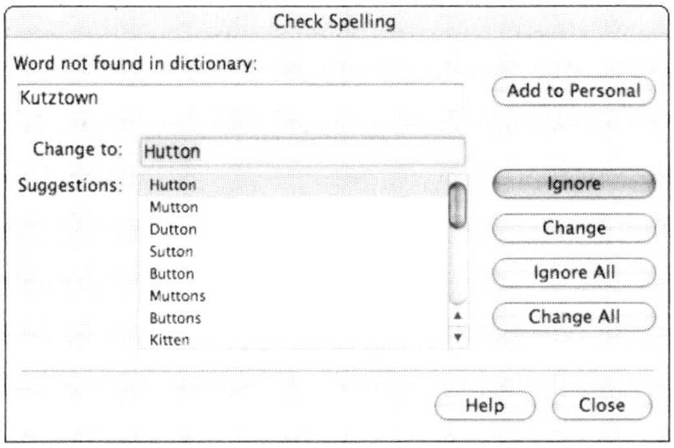

Figure 5-4: Make sure that your spelling is correct.

Check Spelling
Word not found in dictionary:
Kutztown — Add to Personal
Change to: Hutton
Suggestions: Hutton / Mutton / Dutton / Sutton / Button / Muttons / Buttons / Kitten
Ignore / Change / Ignore All / Change All
Help / Close

Understanding Cascading Style Sheets

Using Cascading Style Sheets (CSS) is definitely the cleanest and most efficient method for stylizing text on your Web pages. Style sheets are a powerful design tool that allows you to assign type properties quickly and offer the opportunity to update all instances in a few easy steps. The reason for the name Cascading Style Sheets is because certain *cascading rules* apply when styles are used.

If you apply many different styles to a page, whether they're internally built on the page or linked to external style sheets, you may have conflicts. Conflicts occur when two (or more) styles assign different properties to the same element. For example, if you specify in an internal style sheet that anything bolded is blue but an external style sheet instructs the browser to display anything bolded as red, which style wins? The blue instruction from the internal style sheet wins. If conflicts occur in external style sheets, you can set the order of importance by using the up and down arrow. By default, the Web page's style sheet overrides the browser's default values.

Keep in mind that style sheets are compatible with most, but not all, browsers. Generally, the Internet Explorer and Netscape Navigator browsers (Version 4x or higher) can display style sheets properly, as well as Opera and Safari. But even with the latest and greatest browser, some attributes may work in one browser but not in another. Always preview your pages in multiple browsers. As you're creating pages using CSS, take advantage of the Check Page button in your document panel because it will make sure that your page is compatible with most browsers and provide a solution if it is not.

We definitely offer the quick-and-dirty course on CSS here. If you're interested in finding out more about this topic, check out *Cascading Style Sheets For Dummies* by Damon Dean (published by Wiley Publishing, Inc.).

Dreamweaver's default is to use Cascading Styles Sheets (CSS) to format text. Dreamweaver offers CSS starter pages that have CSS layouts available and that include CSS hints visible only in the Code view (see Figure 5-5). Find the CSS Starter pages by choosing File⇨New⇨Blank Page⇨HTML Template.

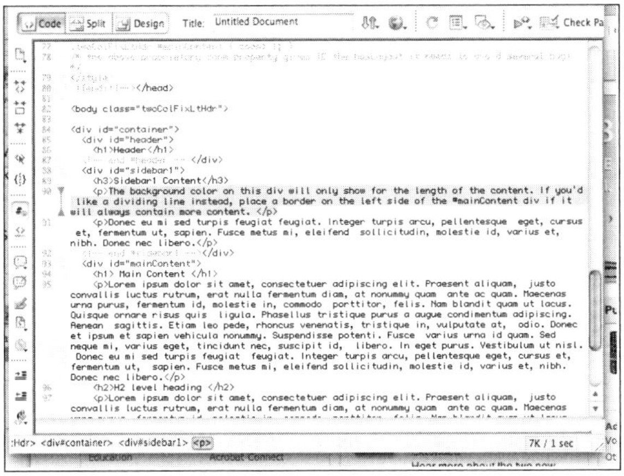

Book VI
Chapter 5

Putting Text on the Page

Figure 5-5:
CSS tips are built into the CSS Starter pages.

Using CSS for text

Using Cascading sheets in Dreamweaver isn't that difficult. Simply create a blank HTML page, put text on it, and then check out what you can do with styles.

With CSS, it doesn't matter if you have text selected for Dreamweaver to start applying styles to the text. Dreamweaver looks for selectors. These selectors may be an existing tag, such as B (for bold) or P (for paragraph), or an assigned name, such as `.coolfunkytext`.

Several types of selectors determine what style properties should be applied and where. When Dreamweaver finds a selector, it applies the declaration. The style properties that you set up when you create a selector put these both together, and you have a CSS rule. For example, every time you see the <strong> tag (selector), make it italic, 20px, and bold (declaration). (You can find out how to take advantage of advanced tags for layout in Chapter 8 of this minibook.)

Creating a new Tag style

Creating styles isn't difficult, and if you haven't discovered them already, you'll wonder why you haven't used them in the past. Using the tag selector is the simplest and safest route for new users to CSS because a page using tag styles still has tags that older browsers understand, such as H1, H2, and so on. Using existing element tags on your page, you can choose to make all your text tagged with <H1> blue or a certain size, or any number of additional character changes, many of which aren't available through straight HTML.

Using existing code to create a Tag style:

1. **Open a blank HTML page containing text.**

2. **Select some text and assign the <strong> tag by clicking the B button in the Properties panel.**

3. **Locate your CSS panel, off to the right.**

   If you've been re-arranging your panels, you may want to choose Window➪Workspace Layout➪Designer to put the panels back in the order that they were in when you first launched Dreamweaver. You can also choose Text➪CSS Styles➪New.

 4. **Click the new CSS Rule button at the bottom of the expanded CSS panel.**

   The new CSS Rule dialog box, shown in Figure 5-6, appears.

Figure 5-6:
Define
the CSS
selector in
the New
CSS Rule
dialog box.

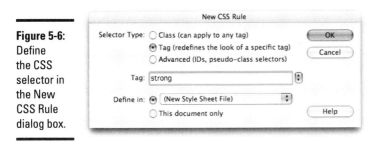

5. **Select Tag as the Selector Type and replace the text in the tag text box
with *strong* if is not already present.**

This step defines strong as the selector. Next, you tell CSS what to do
every time it sees the <strong> tag in your HTML page.

At the bottom of the New CSS Rule dialog box, you see choices as to
where you can define the style you're creating. The intelligent choice
here, if you're planning on implementing your style site-wide, is to define
your style in a New Style Sheet File.

6. **Choose New Style Sheet File from the Define In drop-down list.**

This step creates an external style (a .css file), which multiple pages
can be linked to. Essentially, an external style sheet allows you to define
the <strong> tag once, and it reflects the style changes on all your
pages linked to that external style. Change the color of the <strong> tag
one time, and the change is reflected throughout the site. How easy is
that? And it helps you be more consistent with your type styles, too.

If you choose to define the style in the document only, it inserts the CSS
rule in the head section of this page only. The <strong> tag would be
adjusted to your definition only on this page. This can be beneficial if
you have one page in your site that is black, for example, and you want
the <strong> tag to be white for that one page only.

7. **Click OK to open the Save Style Sheet File As dialog box.**

This is when you would locate your site folder or, if you haven't defined
a site, a folder where you'll keep all relevant information, such as links
and pages for your site.

8. **Name your style sheet.**

Choose something appropriate, such as "main" or "basic" if it's the main
set of styles you're creating for your Web site.

9. **Leave the URL and the Relative To drop-down list set to Document.**

10. **If you want to store your CSS rules in a separate document, you can
use the New Folder; otherwise, click Save.**

You've now created a `.css` file. The CSS Rule Definition dialog box appears.

Now you set up the definition for the Selector you defined. In the CSS Rule Definition dialog box, you are by default in the Type category shown in Figure 5-7.

11. Apply a font, size, style, leading (line height), and any other attributes that you couldn't apply to text using straight HTML coding.

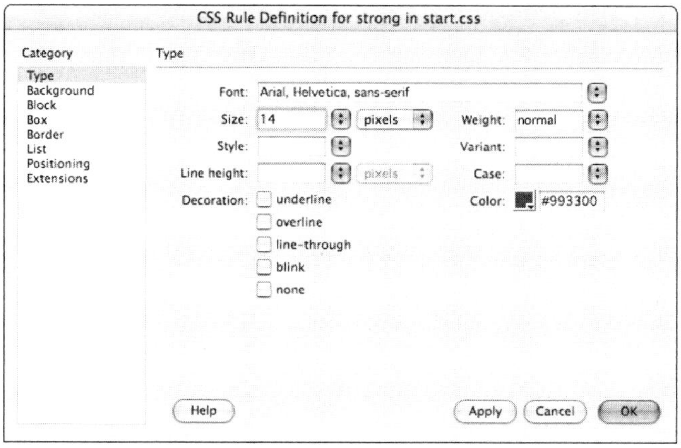

Figure 5-7:
Choose the attributes that you want assigned to the CSS selector.

Here are a few things to keep in mind as you choose your attributes:

- **Font:** Notice that you can apply a Font family using the Font drop-down menu. This is the preferred method of assigning a font family.

- **Size:** Enter a text size and then, using the unit drop-down list to the right of the size, entered it as pixels, points, in, cm and other sizes. By specifying a size here — 12 px, for example — you can be assured that the text appears as relatively the same size on both the Windows and Macintosh platform.

- **Line height:** By assigning a size in any unit, you can define the space between lines of text. For example, if the type size is 12, the line height of 24 px is essentially the same as double-spacing. If you come from the typesetting or design world, it works much like leading.

- **Decoration:** Hmm, if you want it, get it here! Blinking is not a good idea, as it is just plain B-A-D and also not compatible on all browsers.

    Don't like underlines under your links? Create a tag style called *a* (this is the HTML tag for a link) and select None in the Decoration section.

Block level versus inline

You may find that when you assign certain properties, you see varying results because some properties that you select affect only block level elements as compared to inline elements. *Block level elements* apply to an entire paragraph, like the `<H1>` and `<p>` tags. Applying a style to these types of tags changes an entire paragraph of text. If you create an element style named `H1` and change the line spacing, the space takes effect within the block-level element.

An *inline element* is one that doesn't apply to an entire paragraph but is used to apply formatting, such as the `<b>` tag to selected text only. If you choose to apply line spacing to the b element, the leading in paragraphs that contain the `<b>` tag will not be affected.

You'll eventually figure out which properties work with which tags. Just keep this point in mind so that you're not dumbfounded when some properties don't work as expected!

- **Weight:** Make your text lighter or heavier using this drop-down list. Just so you know, a value of 700 is the typical boldness of bold text; any heavier will be bolder than bold.

- **Variant:** Use this drop-down list to choose small caps.

   You may be wondering why normal is a choice in the Style drop-down list. It's because you may have defined small caps, for example, as the Variant for all instances of the `<strong>` tag, but then decided that on one page you wanted to override that attribute. By creating a style defined in the document only with Normal selected in Variant, you can override the style (small-caps) definition on the external style sheet.

- **Case:** Choose from Capitalize, uppercase, lowercase, or none.

- **Color:** Assign a color to your selector by clicking the arrow in the lower-right corner of the Color definition swatch or type a number in the Color text box.

12. **Click Apply.**

Creating a new Class style

Giving your HTML page some Class style doesn't have to involve a huge makeover. By creating class selectors, you can create named styles for body, text, headlines, subheads, and so on. Essentially, it's like creating your own paragraph styles, if you're familiar with that feature from page-layout applications.

Unlike Tag styles (see preceding section), class styles won't apply to text until you assign it. So first you create a style, perhaps for headline text, and then you apply it to the text on your page:

1. Locate your CSS panel, off to the right, and click the New CSS Rule button at the bottom or choose Text⇨CSS Styles⇨New.

The New CSS Rule dialog box appears.

2. Select Class and create an appropriate name for your class style.

You can name your style (or selector) anything that you want, but make sure that it has no spaces, and that it's descriptive of how you'll use it. `Reallycoolstyle` would be a bad choice; `headlinestyle` would be a better choice. Dreamweaver inserts the period at the front of the style name as is necessary for a class style to function.

You may have the same external style sheet already appearing in the Define drop-down list. If not, you can choose to create a new External Style here or check this document only to put the CSS rule right in the header of this document.

3. Click OK.

The CSS Rule Definition dialog box opens. In this dialog box, you can create the set of attributes that you want included in the CSS definition for the style you're creating. As you might notice, this dialog box is the same definition that you work with when you create a Tag style. The difference with the Tag and Class style is really only in the application of the style.

4. Once you have selected attributes for your Class style, click OK.

Now you can apply the CSS class style to some text. When applying a class style, you can choose to apply it to only some text or to an entire paragraph of text. Follow these steps to apply a class style to an entire paragraph:

1. Place your cursor into a paragraph of text.

2. If the Properties inspector isn't visible, choose Window⇨Properties.

3. From the Style drop-down list in the Properties Inspector, choose your style.

Here's how to apply a class style to selected text:

1. Select a word in a paragraph or line of text that doesn't have any styles applied to it.

2. Select your class style from the Style drop-down list in the Properties Inspector.

The selected text has the class applied. If you were to look at the Code view, you would see that a <span> tag has been created surrounding the selected word, as shown in Figure 5-8. This tag acts very much like a character style would in a page layout application like InDesign.

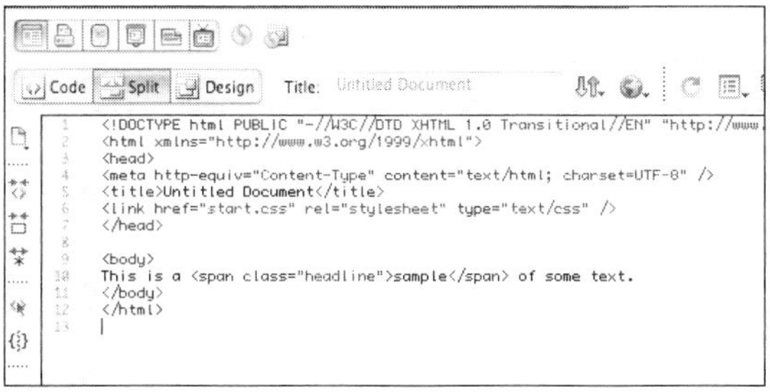

Figure 5-8:
Note the
<span>
tag
surrounding
the word
sample.

**Putting Text
on the Page**

Chapter 6: Linking It Together

*L*inks are a major component of any Web site. You must incorporate links on your Web site; otherwise, your viewers aren't able to navigate your site — not good! In this chapter, we show you how to add links easily and effectively with Dreamweaver.

The Basics of Linking

Links (short for *hyperlinks*) are navigational aids; viewers click links to go to other Web pages, a downloadable resource file, an e-mail address, or a specific spot on a Web page (known as an *anchor*). As you create the first link from one of your Web pages to another, you have essentially created a Web site — it may be a small site, but it's a start. While you're still in the small site stage, here are a few things we recommend that you keep in mind as you add more pages and create more links, making your site ever bigger:

✦ Essentially, there are two kinds of links: internal and external. *Internal links* connect viewers to other parts of your Web site; *external links* connect viewers to other pages or content outside your site. We show you how to create each kind of link in this chapter.

✦ Before you start working with any pages that are to be linked, make sure that you've created a Dreamweaver site; otherwise, you won't have options available that make saving files to your site folder easier.

Implementing Internal Links

Internal links, an essential part of any user-friendly site, help your viewers easily and quickly navigate to other parts of your Web site.

Just a note of caution: If you need to change names of files after they've been linked anywhere, do so *only* within the Files panel in Dreamweaver. Otherwise, you'll end up with broken links. Take a look at the "Resolving Link Errors" section, later in this chapter, to find out how to change the names of linked files without breaking the links.

Linking to pages in your own site

You can create a link out of text or an image (like a button image). The following sections outline several methods that you can use for creating links.

Using the Hyperlink command

To create a hyperlink using text as the link, you can use the Hyperlink command:

1. **Select some text, make sure that the common tab of the Insert toolbar is forward, and click the Hyperlink button.**

The Hyperlink dialog box appears with your selected text already entered in the Text text box, as shown in Figure 6-1. (You can also choose Insert⇨Hyperlink.)

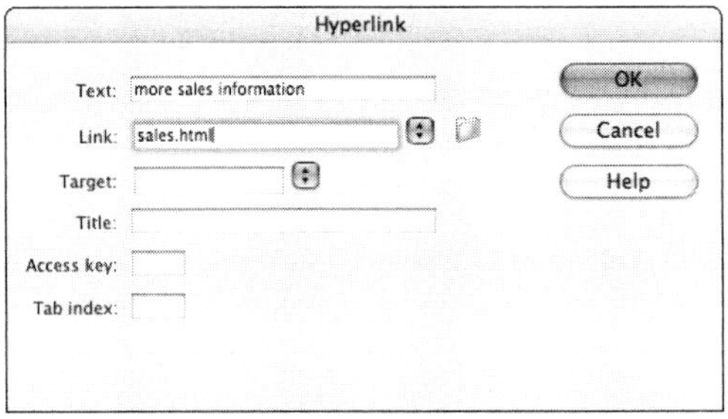

Figure 6-1:
Create a link from selected text using the Hyperlink button.

	Hyperlink	
Text:	more sales information	OK
Link:	sales.html	Cancel
Target:		Help
Title:		
Access key:		
Tab index:		

2. **You can either enter a URL, or location of a file, or click the Browse (folder) icon to the right of the Link drop-down list and browse to the file you want to link to.**

You can also enter an external link here; see how to link to external locations a little later in the "Linking to Pages and Files Outside Your Web Site" section in this chapter.

3. **If you want the page to appear in the same document window, essentially replacing the existing page, leave Target blank. If you want to force the link to create its own document window choose _blank.**

4. **Click OK.**

Using the Link Command

You can link text and images using the Link command in Dreamweaver.

1. Select the element that you want to link from and press Ctrl+L (Windows) or ⌘+L (Mac OS).

The Select File dialog box appears, like the one you see in Figure 6-2.

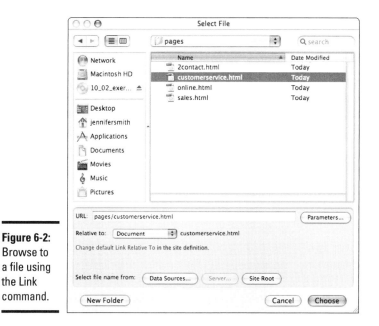

Figure 6-2:
Browse to
a file using
the Link
command.

Link is also available in the Property Inspector.

2. With your text or image selected, type the link location into the Link text box or click the cool little Point To File button and drag the cursor over to the Files panel and release on the page that you want to link to.

3. If you want to browse to locate the destination file, click the Browse button to the right of the Point to file button.

The Select File dialog box opens.

4. Navigate to the folder containing the file you want to link to, select it, and click OK (Windows) or Choose (Mac OS).

Creating Anchors

Anchors are a link to a specific section of a page, either on the same page as the link or on another page entirely. Anchors are especially handy for long pages that have a lot of text. You have probably seen and used anchors, for example, when clicking a Back To Top button. Anchors are extremely helpful to the viewer and should be implemented whenever possible.

To create an anchor in Dreamweaver, follow these steps:

1. **Insert your cursor where you want the destination to be for your link.**

This destination may be before a line of text, or on its own line.

2. **Click the Named Anchor button in the Common tab of the Insert toolbar.**

The Named Anchor dialog box, shown in Figure 6-3, appears.

You can avoid clicking the Anchor button by using the keyboard shortcut Ctrl+Alt+A (Windows) or ⌘+Option+A (Mac OS).

3. **Type a short name that is relevant to what the link is connected to.**

In Figure 6-3, you see that esp was used for Esteson State Park. Keep the name all lowercase, as anchors are case sensitive.

4. **Click OK.**

Figure 6-3:
Create a simple, easy-to-remember anchor name.

You've now created the anchor, but have no links being directed to it yet. You can define an anchor as a link manually or by using the Point To File tool.

Linking to an anchor manually

Here's one reason why a short appropriate name is useful; you may end up having to type it! By manually linking to an anchor, you can link within the page you're working on or direct the link to an anchor on a completely different page.

You can manually define an anchor as a link by following these steps:

1. **Select the text that is to be the link.**
2. **If the Properties Inspector isn't open, choose Window⇨Properties.**
3. **Type the # sign and then the anchor name in the Link text box.**

   In the example in Figure 6-4, #esp is used. The link has now been defined. When someone clicks the linked word, he'll be directed to the anchor.

**Book VI
Chapter 6**

Linking It Together

Figure 6-4:
Type the anchor name in the Link text box.

You can also link to a page and add an anchor reference to it. For example, if you wanted to link to this spot from another page, you'd select an element on that page and in the Link text box, type birds.html#esp. This directs the browser to the birds page and then to the link within that page.

Frequently, you see anchors separated by the pipe sign (|). You can create this type character by pressing Shift+\. The backslash key is directly above the Enter (Windows) or the Return (Mac) key.

Using the Point To File for button anchors

In a hurry and not very good at typing? You'll love this quick method for creating linked anchors:

1. **Position the cursor where you want the destination or anchor to be placed.**
2. **Press Ctrl+Alt+A (Windows) or ⌘+Option+A (Mac OS) to open the Named Anchor dialog box.**
3. **Type an appropriate anchor name.**

   Remember, short and sweet!

4. Select the element that is to link to the anchor and then click and drag the Point To File button to the anchor, as shown in Figure 6-5.

Voilá! The connection is made, and no typing is necessary.

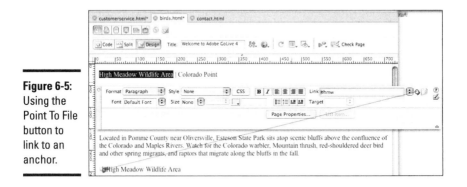

Figure 6-5: Using the Point To File button to link to an anchor.

Linking to Pages and Files Outside Your Web Site

You can link to pages anywhere, in your site or out. An internal link is one within your site. The link to another page in your site may appear as contact.html in your Link text box in the Properties Inspector. But if you're directing people to a contact page posted on another site, you'd have a link that looks more like http://www.aquent.com/contact/. By typing the http:// and the address of the external link in the Properties Inspector, you're essentially directing the browser to a site out on the World Wide Web and away from your site.

Linking to E-Mail

Linking to an e-mail address opens a new mail message addressed to the address you specify as a link on the viewer's computer. This, of course, depends that the viewer has set up an e-mail program on his machine.

Linking to an e-mail address is easy and extremely helpful if you're just starting to make your pages interactive. To create an e-mail link, follow these steps:

1. Select the element that will be the link to an e-mail.

It can be text or an image.

2. **In the Properties Inspector, locate the Link textbox and type mailto: (address).**

For example, type mailto:info@agitraining.com and press the Return key.

Linking to a PDF File

To link to a PDF file instead of a Web page, you link to the name and location of the PDF file. If you link to a PDF file and the Acrobat PDF plug-in is loaded in the viewer's browser, the PDF is opened in the browser window. If the viewer doesn't have the Acrobat plug-in (free from www.adobe.com), the Save dialog box appears, and you can browse to save the file to open with Acrobat Reader at another time.

Resolving Link Errors

Page names can change and pages can be deleted (intentionally or not), so checking for broken links is a good idea. You can check to make sure that links are working correctly in several ways. The most cumbersome is previewing your page and clicking each and every link. This method would take you a long time and wouldn't be much fun. To check your local links, try the following.

1. **Choose Window➪Results.**

The Results panel appears.

2. **Click the Link Checker tab.**

3. **Click the green arrow on the left side of the Link Checker tab and choose whether you want to check just this one page, all pages in your site, or just selected pages in your site.**

Your links, including page, scripts, images, and so on, appear, as you see in Figure 6-6.

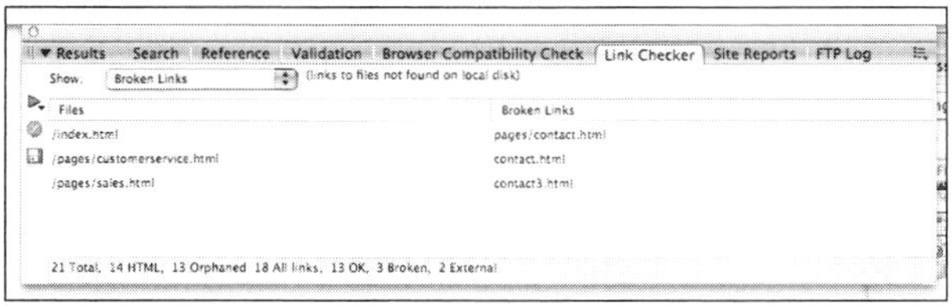

Figure 6-6:
Check to
make sure
that your
links aren't
broken.

If you don't have broken links . . . congratulations! If you do, you can fix them right in the Results panel. The page that has the broken link is listed in the Files column on the left. The Broken link appears under the Broken Link column on the right.

4. Click the name of the broken link and correct the filename, if it's a problem, or click the Browse folder icon to locate the correct location or file.

5. Click OK (Windows) or Choose (Mac OS).

The broken link is repaired.

Chapter 7: Setting Your Table

In This Chapter

✔ Creating tables

✔ Selecting a table and cell

✔ Manipulating rows, columns, and cells

✔ Changing the color of a table or cells

✔ Adjusting borders, spacing, and padding

✔ Adding and importing content

*T*ables are great for presenting data, such as schedules and pricing, and can be helpful in instances where you're trying to arrange elements in a tabular format. In this chapter, you find out how to create a table and make changes that alter the look of the table. (In Chapter 8 of this minibook, you discover how to use layers, the Cascading Style Sheet (CSS) alternative that enables you to position elements exactly where you want them on a page.)

Working with Tables

When you think of a *table,* think of a grid that has multiple cells in it. Tables are used in HTML pages so that elements can be held in specific cells. You can change the colors of cells in tables, *span* or expand the cells (that is, combine them with other cells), and apply borders to them.

In many cases, you don't actually see the table because tables enable you to put content into row and column form without showing the table itself; in this case, the table is just a formatting tool. When you create a table, you can determine how many rows and columns it contains. You can also choose to span rows and columns to create unique tables, such as the one shown in Figure 7-1.

To create a table in Dreamweaver, follow these steps:

1. **Put your cursor where you want the table to appear and make sure that the Common tab of the Insert toolbar is visible; then click the Table button.**

   Or choose Insert⇨Table. The Table dialog box appears, as shown in Figure 7-2.

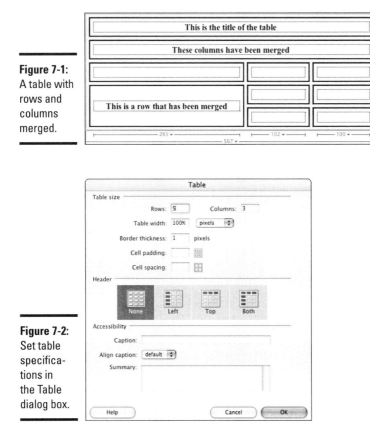

Figure 7-1:
A table with rows and columns merged.

Figure 7-2:
Set table specifications in the Table dialog box.

2. **Enter the attributes of the table that you want to create:**

   • **Row:** How many rows you want in your table. These stack vertically and can be added or deleted after you've created the table.

   • **Column:** How many columns you want in your table. These are created horizontally across your table and can be added or deleted after you've created the table.

   • **Table Width:** An important attribute as it sets the default size for the table. By leaving this set to 100 percent, the table will take up 100 percent of your Web page, dynamically expanding and reducing in size as the page is resized. You can change this to a different percentage, such as 50 percent, to have it take up half the width of your Web page, or enter a pixel value to assure that it always stays the same size. Switch from percentage to pixels using the drop-down list to the right of Table width.

- **Border Thickness:** The pixel width of the border surrounding the cells and outside of the table. If you don't want to see the table formatting, type **0** in this text box.

- **Cell Padding:** Use padding to give you a margin around all sides of the cell.

- **Cell Spacing:** Change spacing to change the size of cell walls.

- **Header:** It is important to include headers, especially if you're creating a table containing data, as it helps viewers clearly associate the header with the data and also because screen readers rely on them to help visually impaired users navigate through the table without getting lost.

- **Accessibility:** You can provide some additional information to help visually impaired users understand the contents of your table. Add a caption that is relevant to your table. In the Align Caption drop-down list, position your caption either on the top, bottom, left, or right. Last, in the Summary area, include several lines of text to provide more information about the purpose of the table.

3. Click OK.

Your table is created.

When working with tables, it may help to take advantage of the expanded table feature in Dreamweaver. (Find the Expanded button on the Layout tab of the Insert toolbar.) The Expanded view adds cell padding and spacing in a table, as well as increases the size of the border. It's important to return to the Standard view (click the Standard button in the Layout tab of the Insert toolbar) after you're finished editing for the most accurate preview.

Editing your table's attributes

Even if you've already created your table, you can go back and edit the table's attributes by selecting the table and entering changes in the Property inspector, as shown in Figure 7-3.

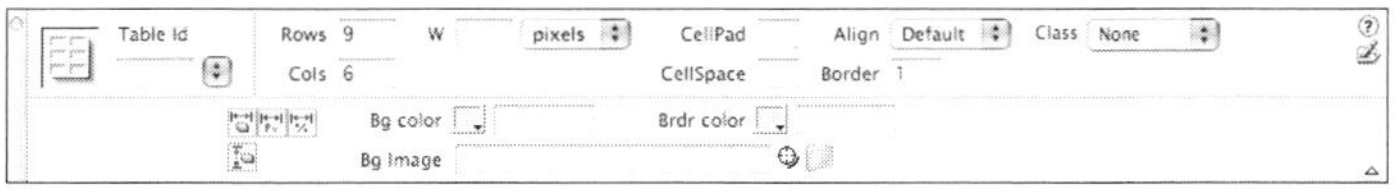

Figure 7-3:
Make changes to your table using the Property inspector.

Table Id	Rows 9	W	pixels	CellPad	Align Default	Class None
	Cols 6			CellSpace	Border 1	
	Bg color		Brdr color		
	Bg Image				

If your Property inspector isn't expanded, as you see in Figure 7-3, click the arrow in the lower right of the Inspector. The Inspector then becomes expanded, offering you additional options.

Adding and deleting rows and columns

You can add rows and columns, as well as delete them, as fast as your client's (or Boss's) needs require using the Property inspector, but using the Modify menu gives you a little more control as to which rows and columns are deleted, and where new ones are added.

To add a row:

1. **Insert your cursor in the cell in a row that you want a new cell added above or below.**

2. **Choose Insert⇨Table Objects⇨Insert Row Above or Insert Row Below.**

The new row appears.

To delete a row:

1. **Insert your cursor in a cell of the row you want to delete.**

2. **Choose Modify⇨Table⇨Delete Row.**

The row is deleted.

Or you can use Shift+Ctrl+M (Windows) or Shift+⌘+M (Mac).

To add a column:

1. **Insert your cursor in a cell.**

It should be the cell in a column that you want a new column added to the left or right of.

2. **Choose Insert⇨Table Objects⇨Insert Column To The Left or Insert Column To The Right.**

The new column appears.

To delete a column:

1. **Insert your cursor in a cell of the column you want to delete.**

2. **Choose Modify⇨Table⇨Delete Column.**

The column is deleted.

Or you can use Shift+Ctrl+- (minus) (Windows) or Shift+⌘+- (minus) (Mac).

Spanning or merging cells

Often, you need to span or merge cells together. You can combine cells with other cells horizontally or vertically. By merging cells, you can create more interesting and useful tables. Figure 7-4 contains a table with one large merged cell across the top that has a picture inserted into it.

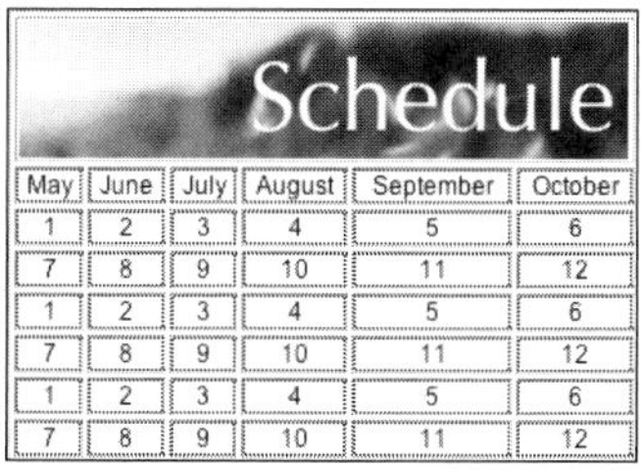

Figure 7-4:
The top
row's
columns
have been
merged.

To merge cells in a row or columns:

1. **Double-click a cell to select it and drag across to select contiguous cells in the row, or down to select contiguous cells in the column.**

2. **Choose Modify⇨Table⇨Merge Cells.**

   The cells are merged.

To split the cells:

1. **Put your cursor in the merged cell or column.**

2. **Choose Modify⇨Table⇨Split Cell.**

   The Split Cell dialog box appears, as shown in Figure 7-5.

3. **Choose whether you want to split into Rows or Columns and how many.**

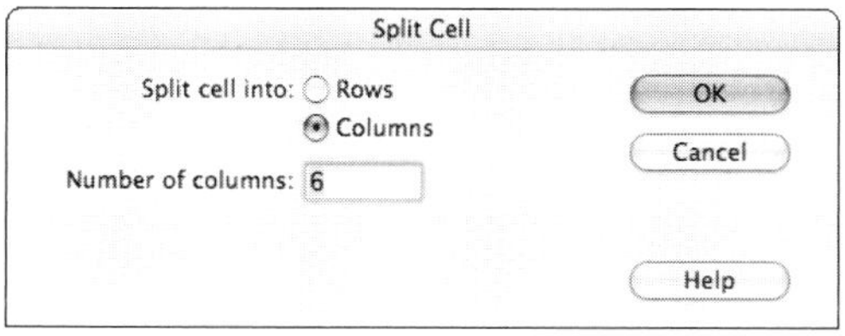

Figure 7-5:
You can split
cells as
easily as
you can
merge them.

4. Click OK.

The merged cells are now split.

Selecting a Table and Cell

You can use several methods to select a cell or the table. Once a cell or table is selected, you can change all sorts of attributes, including color, size, and format of its contents.

To select a table or cell:

1. In Design view, select the Layout tab from the Insert toolbar and select Expanded to put your table in the Expanded view.

It's easier to select and make changes in this view. (Just remember to return to Standard view by clicking the Standard button to get a more realistic preview of what your table will look like.)

2. Select a cell by Ctrl+clicking (Windows) or ⌘+clicking (Mac) on it.

Another option is to use the tag selector in the lower-left corner of your Document window, shown in Figure 7-6. The tag selector is an incredible tool to use to select any tag element, but it's especially helpful when selecting individual components of a table. To use the tag selector, just put your cursor inside a cell. The tag selector shows the tags that apply to where the insertion point is. Then select <td> to select the cell that you're in, <tr> to select the entire row, or <table> to select the entire table.

The tag for table is <table> (a difficult one to remember, right?), and each row is in a <tr> tag, which stands for *Table Row.* Each cell is in a <td> tag, which stands for *Table Data.* 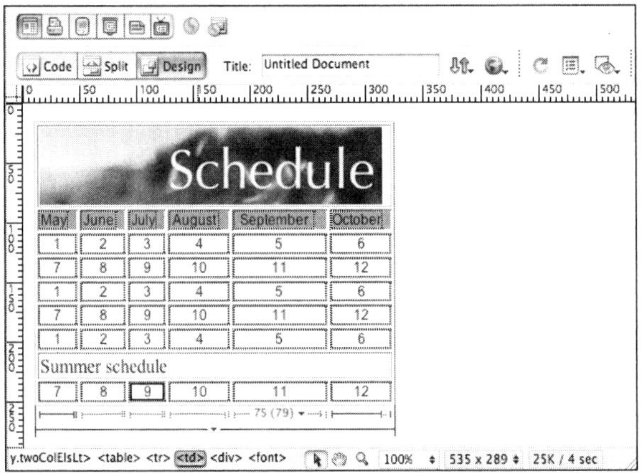

Figure 7-6:
Use the tag selector to select cells and tables.

Changing the Color of a Table or Cells

You can change colors of multiple cells at once, just one cell, the entire table, and even the border of a table in Dreamweaver.

To change the color of an entire table, click `<table>` in the tag selector. The Properties table reflects that you have a table selected. Then assign a color to a table using one of the following methods:

✦ Click the color fill box to the right of Bg color and select a color from the color picker that appears. You can choose from additional color models by clicking the palette menu in the upper right of the color picker, as you see in Figure 7-7.

✦ If you know the hexadecimal number for your color, you can type it in the Bg color text box. A hexadecimal (Hex) color is a six-digit alphanumeric representation for colors on the Web. Hex colors are browser-safe colors that ensure cross-browser/cross-platform compatibility and consistency.

**Book VI
Chapter 7**

Setting Your Table

Figure 7-7:
Select a color from the color picker or click the palette menu to access additional color models.

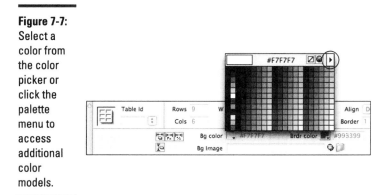

✦ Selecting a color for your table from an image is probably one of the most fun ways to select a color. Simply click the Bg color fill box and when the color picker appears, move your cursor over an image — or really any element in or out of your Dreamweaver page, whether it be a folder icon on your desktop or an image on your page. When you find the color you want (the color is previewed in the color picker), release the mouse and it's applied to the background of the table.

If you change the color of a table and then apply a cell color, the cell color overrides the table color.

You can also change the border of your table:

1. Change the color of the border by selecting the table.

To select the table, insert the cursor anywhere inside the table and click `<table>` in the tag selector at the bottom left of your document window.

2. Click and hold the color fill box to the right of Brdr color in the Property inspector and select a color from the color picker.

Or you can enter a hexadecimal color in the Brdr color text box in the Property inspector.

To change the color of a cell, or multiple selected cells:

1. Insert your cursor in the cell and then click `<td>` in the tag selector in the lower left of your document or Ctrl+click (Windows) or ⌘+click (Mac).

2. Add cells to the selection by Ctrl +clicking (Windows) or ⌘+clicking (Mac) on additional cells.

The Properties table reflects that a cell(s) is selected.

3. Assign color to a cell(s) using one of the following methods.

- Click the color fill box to the right of Bg and select a color from the color picker that appears. Remember that you can choose from additional color models by clicking the palette menu in the upper right of the color picker.

- If you know the hexadecimal number for your color, you can type it in the Bg textbox.

- Select a color from any element that you can see on the screen by clicking and holding the color fill box to the right of Bg and then moving over the color on your screen that you want the cell color to be. Click when the color appears in the color picker preview window.

Adding and Importing Content

Adding content to a table is easy — you just insert your cursor in to the cell and type directly into a cell for text or click Image in the Common tab of the Insert toolbar to insert an image in a cell.

As a default, all elements center vertically inside a cell and are flush left. Change this on a cell-by-cell basis by selecting the cell(s) and then changing the Alignment in the Property inspector.

If you select every cell in a row, you also have the opportunity to change the alignment of an entire row. To the right of Row (the Property inspector palette must be expanded to see the row) is a Horizontal alignment drop-down list that changes the alignment Default to Left, Center, or Right. Note that any changes you make in the individual cell alignment override the row alignment.

You can also change the Vertical alignment (up and down) in the Property inspector when you have a row selected. Click the Vert drop-down list and choose Default, Top, Middle Bottom, or Baseline.

To select an entire row at once, position your cursor on the left side of the row you want to select. When the arrow appears, simply click. You can also use this method for selecting an entire column by positioning your cursor on the top of the column you want to select.

If you already have data in text form, from other text-editing software, don't bother retyping it into a Dreamweaver table. Dreamweaver has an incredibly easy feature that you can use to bring in tabular data as a formatted table. Note that as a default, tabs on the imported data become columns, and any returns become rows.

To import table data:

1. **Put your cursor on the page where you want the table created.**

2. **Choose File⇨Import⇨Tabular Data.**

   The Import Tabular Data dialog box appears.

3. **Browse to the location of the data using the Browse button.**

4. **Select the Delimiter.**

   Typically, the delimiter (where a new column will be created) is left at Tab, but you can also instruct Dreamweaver to create a new column when it reads a Comma, Semicolon, Colon, or Other.

5. **Determine the table width.**

   You can choose to let it automatically fit the data, by leaving Fit To Data selected, or you can change the Set To to a percent or pixel value.

6. **At the bottom of the dialog box, set the padding, spacing, formatting, and border for the table you're about to create.**

7. **When you're finished with these settings, click OK, and your table is created!**

You can export table data from Dreamweaver just as easily by selecting a table and choosing File➪Export➪Table. When the Export Table dialog box appears, choose what you want the Delimiter to be, as well as the type of line break. Click Export, determine a location where you want to save the file, and click Save.

Chapter 8: Creating CSS Layouts

In This Chapter

✔ **Getting started with CSS pages**

✔ **Positioning content with the new AP Div tool**

✔ **Using behaviors with layers**

Creating a page layout sometimes requires more precision than what tables or standard HTML tags are capable of. More designers are moving to the flexible and preferred method of CSS positioning to create innovative layouts without boundaries. Dreamweaver provides you with an extensive gallery of CSS-based layouts to get started, or you can build your own using the Insert bar's Layout tools, including the new AP Div object.

Using CSS Starter Pages

Dreamweaver provides you with a library of sample pages with CSS-based layouts as an alternative to starting from scratch. These CSS sample pages feature useful and common layout ideas, and because they're created with CSS positioning, they're highly flexible. You can modify them directly from the CSS panel. Just add your content and go!

To create a new document from a CSS sample page:

1. **Choose File⇨New.**

   The New Document panel appears.

2. **Choose Blank Page from the left, select a layout from the Layout column on the right and click Create.**

   A new untitled page opens based on the layout you chose.

3. **Choose File⇨Save to name and save the document.**

4. **Replace the placeholder text in each column with your own content.**

Modifying a New Layout

As the name indicates, CSS layouts are controlled completely by style sheet rules, so you can modify the look and feel of the page directly from the CSS Styles panel and Property inspector. Each column, box, and space on your new page is positioned and sized using CSS rules and properties, all of which you can adjust from either the Property inspector (on the CSS Styles panel) or the CSS Rule Definition panel.

To modify the layout:

1. **If necessary, choose Window➪CSS Styles to open the CSS Styles panel.**

2. **Select the All tab to display the style sheet and its rules.**

   The internal style sheet is shown as `<style>` at the top. Click the arrow to its left to expand it and show all the rules it contains.

3. **Select the rule that reads *body*.**

   This tag-based style controls the general formatting of the entire page (everything inside the `<body>` tag).

4. **Click the field next to the background rule to edit it; instead of #666666, type #CC0000 to change your page's background color to red.**

5. **Click the swatch next to the color rule to open the swatches panel; pick a new default type color for the text on your page.**

6. **Back at the top of the CSS styles panel, select the** `.twoColHybLtHdr #container` **style to view its properties.**

   This ID style controls the size and appearance of the main layout container on your page.

7. **Under the Properties pane, click the field next to the width rule and edit it to read 95%.**

   This change makes the entire layout wider.

Each column and section that composes your layout is controlled by one of the ID styles listed in the CSS Styles panel. Most every ID style will feature a width property that you can use to change the size of different areas on the page.

Continue to modify different styles listed in the CSS Styles panel and see how they affect different elements on your page. Try changing type color, font family, and other properties, such as padding and background color.

To figure out exactly which ID controls which column or section, click within the area and look at the Tag Chooser at the bottom of the document window. The last <div> tag at the end of the chain shows you which container you're currently in and its corresponding ID in the CSS Styles panel.

Creating AP Divs

Dreamweaver uses CSS-positioned virtual containers, or "boxes," created by the DIV tag to freely position content on a page. You can create DIV tags from several places in Dreamweaver, including the Layout insert bar. Each DIV tag can have a unique ID style assigned to it to control its position, appearance, and size. The process of placing content often requires two steps: creating the DIV and its corresponding style.

Dreamweaver makes this task easy with the AP Div tool, which enables you to draw boxes freely on the page and place your content inside.

For those of you who have used earlier versions of Dreamweaver, you may remember Dreamweaver layers. The AP Div object replaces the Layer object, and the AP Elements panel now replaces the Layers panel.

CSS thinks of every element on a page as a "box" that holds content; this approach is referred to as the CSS Box model. While CSS can consider most any containing element on a page (such as a table or a list) a box, DIV tags are most commonly used to create virtual boxes that you can use to position text, images, and even other boxes.

Each box can have its own width, height, position (via the top and left properties), border, margins, and padding; each one is set using CSS rules.

AP Div is short for *Absolute-Positioned* DIV; an item with an *absolute* position means that it's fixed at a specific location on the page. When you draw an AP Div, its position is set using the *top* and *left* CSS properties, with the top left corner of the page as its reference.

To create AP Divs:

1. **On the Insert bar, select the Layout category.**

2. **Click the AP Div object.**

Your cursor appears as a crosshair when you move it back on the page.

3. **Click anywhere on the page and drag to draw a new AP Div; release the mouse button.**

4. **Move the mouse pointer over the edge of the box until it changes to a hand; click once, and handles appear on all sides.**

5. **Click and drag any of these handles to resize the box vertically or horizontally.**

6. **To move the box, click and drag it by the tab that sits on its top left edge and place the box at the top of the page.**

Take a look at the Property inspector, and you see the name as well as many of the properties listed.

7. **If it's not open, choose Window⇨CSS Styles to open the CSS Styles panel; under the All pane, click to the left of the style sheet (<style>) to expand it.**

You see a new ID style named #apDiv1 that's attached to the new AP Div you created.

8. **Click inside of the new box to type, paste, or insert new content.**

When you draw an AP Div on the page, two things occur: Dreamweaver inserts a tag to create the box and creates an ID style that stores the DIVs position, width, height, and other properties. After you create an AP Div, you can type, paste, or insert content directly inside of it.

Each AP Div that you draw is automatically listed in the AP Elements panel (choose Window⇨AP Elements to display it). The AP Elements panel can help you select, hide, and show any AP Divs on the page. This panel is handy when you've got lots of AP Divs on the page and want to navigate between them accurately. Most of all, because you can modify the properties for any AP Div from its corresponding ID style, the panel helps you figure out which ID style belongs to an AP Div.

The AP Elements panel is often grouped with the CSS Styles panel, just in case you're looking for it!

To modify a box (AP Div):

1. **Choose Window⇨AP Elements to open the AP Elements panel.**

2. **In the panel, locate and select apDiv1 to highlight it on the page.**

The Property inspector displays its size and position in addition to other properties.

3. **Using the type-in fields on the Property inspector, set the box's width to 500 pixels by typing into the W field and its height to 250 pixels in the H field below it.**

4. **Click the swatch next to Bg Color and choose a color from the pop-up swatches panel to set a background color for the box.**

For additional properties, such as border or padding, you'll need to add them in the CSS styles panel.

5. **If the CSS styles panel isn't already visible, open it now by choosing Window⇨CSS Styles.**

6. **Double-click the** `#apDiv1 ID` **style that controls the box.**

The CSS Rule Definition dialog box appears.

7. **Select the Border category from the left.**

8. **Under Style, select solid for the Top side (it will apply it to all sides), select Medium for Width, and set the color to black.**

9. **In the Box category on the left, under Padding, set the padding for all four sides to 10px.**

You only need to enter the size once in the Top field, when Same For All is selected.

10. **Click OK to exit the panel and apply the changes.**

You see how the CSS properties you applied affect the apDiv1 box on the page.

To hide a box shown under the AP Elements panel, click the column to the left of its name (under the eye) until a closed eye appears. To make it re-appear, click the eye until it opens again.

Using Behaviors with Boxes

To add cool effects and serious interactivity, you can use Dreamweaver's built-in *behaviors,* a collection of ready-to-use scripts that you can apply to boxes, form elements, text, and images on your page. When used with boxes (AP Divs), behaviors can enhance them with special effects or mouse interaction (such as clicks and rollovers) to make your page more exciting.

The Behaviors panel features a whole new set of effects, such as Fade/Appear, Shrink, Highlight, Slide, and more — all of which you can apply to the AP Divs that you create.

To add behaviors:

1. **Choose Window⇨Behaviors to open the Behaviors panel.**

2. **Choose a box on the stage using the AP Elements panel or select it directly on the stage.**

3. **On the Behaviors panel, locate and click the plus sign.**

The list of available behaviors appears.

4. **From the list, choose Effects⇨Appear/Fade.**

The Appear/Fade dialog box appears.

5. **Make sure the effect is set to Fade and click the Toggle Effect check box to make sure that the box reappears when it's clicked a second time.**

The behavior is added to the list. The phrase onClick to its left indicates this action occurs when the box is clicked.

6. **Choose File⇨Save to save the page.**

To see the effect in action, you'll need to preview the page in a browser.

7. **Choose File⇨Preview In Browser and pick a browser to launch the page in.**

When you test the page, clicking the box makes it disappear or reappear — lots of fun for you, and highly interactive for your user!

When Spry effects are used, Dreamweaver copies several essential files to the same directory where your page is saved. These files are necessary to produce the effects you're using, so make sure to upload them with your page when you publish your site to a Web server.

Dreamweaver's new Spry effects

The new effects shown under the Behaviors panel are part of the new assortment of Spry objects added to the Dreamweaver CS3. The Spry Framework is a popular and versatile JavaScript library for developers that features everything from data-display objects to cool effects, all of which can be customized and integrated within your sites.

The new Spry category on your insert bar features many of these new objects that can help build truly interactive pages that work with real-time data and flexible display items.

When effects behaviors are used, Dreamweaver will need to copy several files to your local site that make the effects possible.

Chapter 9: Publishing Your Web Site

In This Chapter

✔ Checking for broken links and missing files

✔ Checking browser compatibility

✔ Publishing to a web server

*W*hen you're ready to launch your Web site, you can take lots of steps to take to ensure that your site looks and works great. Dreamweaver's tools and reports streamline the process of testing and fixing any problems so that you can present your visitors with a great first impression.

Clean Up After Yourself!

The first step toward getting your Web site ready for the world is making sure everything works and all your files are in order. Dreamweaver is packed full of tools that let you know exactly what's broken, what can be done better, and how your site will perform across a spectrum of different browsers.

One of the key benefits of a Dreamweaver site is its ability to see relationships between your various pages and files and detect any broken links or missing images before you copy the site up for public viewing. Choose Files➪Check Links Sitewide to comb your entire site to find broken links, missing, or *orphaned* (unlinked) files.

To use the Check Links Sitewide feature:

1. **Choose Window➪Files to open the Files panel.**

You can also use the F8 shortcut key (Windows or Mac).

2. **Choose Files➪Site➪Check Links Sitewide.**

The Link Checker panel appears and displays the results (if any). Each listing shows the broken link and the name of the page that contains it to the left, as shown in Figure 9-1.

3. **To open and edit the page to correct the link, double-click the filename shown.**

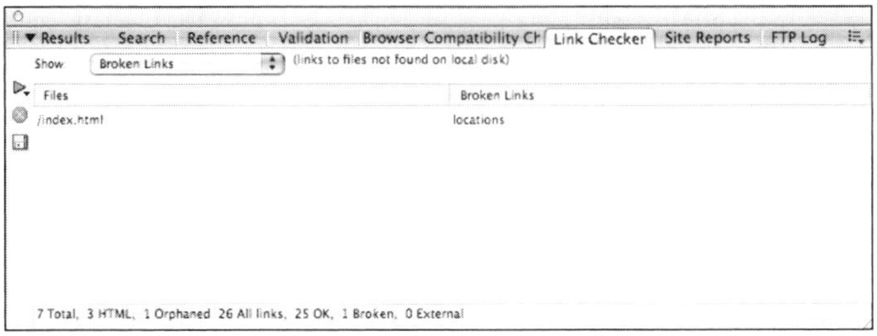

Figure 9-1:
If any
broken links
are found,
the Link
Checker
results
panel lists
the filename
and link
to be
corrected.

| Results | Search | Reference | Validation | Browser Compatibility CF | Link Checker | Site Reports | FTP Log |

Show Broken Links (links to files not found on local disk)

Files   Broken Links
/index.html   locations

7 Total, 3 HTML, 1 Orphaned 26 All links, 25 OK, 1 Broken, 0 External

You can then edit the broken link directly from the Link Checker panel without opening the file. Click the broken link displayed, and a folder icon appears next to it on the right.

4. **Double-click the folder to open the Select File dialog box and choose an available file to correct the link or relink it to a different file.**

5. **Click OK (Windows) or Choose (Mac OS).**

If you want to change a link that appears across several pages, you can choose Files⇨Site⇨Change Links Sitewide. When the panel appears, you're what file the original link points to and you can specify a new file to link to instead. Be careful: This answer changes all links to that file sitewide, so don't use it if you want to change that link only on certain pages.

Running Site Reports

Dreamweaver's site reports provide a detailed look at potential issues lurking within your site, as well as assistance in cleaning out redundant or empty tags from your pages.

Reports are broken down into two categories:

✦ **Workflow reports** show you where your files have been and when and are useful if you're using functions such as the Check In/Check Out feature to share your work with others.

✦ **HTML reports** point out design and accessibility issues, such as missing
ALT tags for images, improperly nested tags, or empty tags that you can
clean up.

To run site reports:

1. **Choose Window⇨Files to open the Files panel.**

2. **Choose File⇨Site⇨Reports.**

The Reports panel, shown in Figure 9-2, appears.

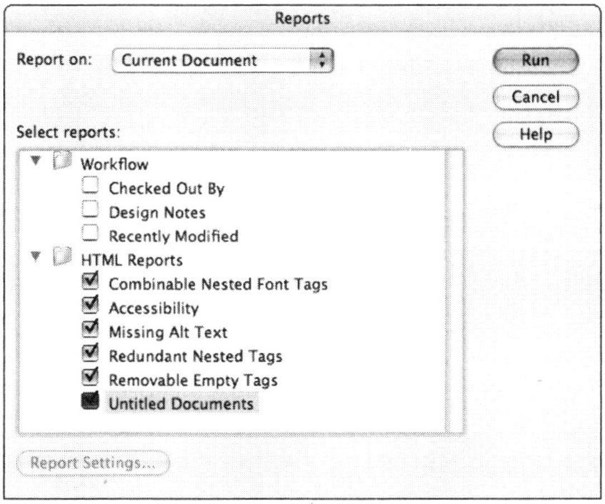

Figure 9-2:
Use the
Reports
panel to
choose
reports
you'd like
to run.

```
Reports

Report on:   Current Document  ⬦          Run

                                          Cancel

Select reports:                           Help

▼ 🗁 Workflow
    ☐ Checked Out By
    ☐ Design Notes
    ☐ Recently Modified
▼ 🗁 HTML Reports
    ☑ Combinable Nested Font Tags
    ☑ Accessibility
    ☑ Missing Alt Text
    ☑ Redundant Nested Tags
    ☑ Removable Empty Tags
    ▉ Untitled Documents

  Report Settings...
```

3. **Choose each report that you'd like to see.**

For this example, we chose all the reports under the HTML Reports
category.

4. **Click Run to run the selected reports.**

The Results panel appears to display the results of each report.

Each report result displays the file, line number, and a description of the
problem.

5. **To address a problem shown, double-click the filename to open the
page.**

The page opens for editing, and the section in which the problem occurs
appears highlighted in Split view.

Checking CSS Compatibility

If you're using CSS for formatting and layout throughout your site, you'll want to make sure that your page appears properly across all popular browsers, such as Internet Explorer, Firefox, Netscape, and Safari. Over the years, different browsers adopted CSS at different levels and paces, requiring designers to test pages in a variety of browsers and versions.

To eliminate this time-consuming task, Dreamweaver introduces the new Browser Compatibility Check, which works hand-in-hand with the CSS Advisor to discover and report any CSS-related display issues that may occur in selected browsers and versions. By default, the Browser Compatibility Check checks CSS compatibility in the following browsers: Firefox 1.5; Internet Explorer (Windows) 6.0 and 7.0; Internet Explorer (Macintosh) 5.2; Netscape Navigator 8.0; Opera 8.0 and 9.0; and Safari 2.0.

For any problem that the Browser Compatibility Check discovers, the results panel displays a description of the problem along with a direct link to Adobe CSS Advisor Web site. The CSS Advisor reports on known browser display issues and possible solutions for fixing them.

To test a page using the Browser Compatibility Check:

1. **Open a page for editing by choosing File⇨Open or by selecting it from the Files panel.**

2. **Choose Window⇨Results to open the Results panel; at the top of the Results panel, choose the Browser Compatibility Check tab.**

3. **On the left side of the panel, click the green arrow and choose Check Browser Compatibility.**

4. **To view details and possible solutions for any results that may appear, select the result.**

   The description, as well as a link to the Adobe CSS Advisor, appears on the right side of the panel.

   Possible compatibility issues are listed along with the file name, line number, and a description of the problem.

5. **Click the link below the detail panel to jump to Adobe's CSS Advisor Web site for solutions (see Figure 9-3).**

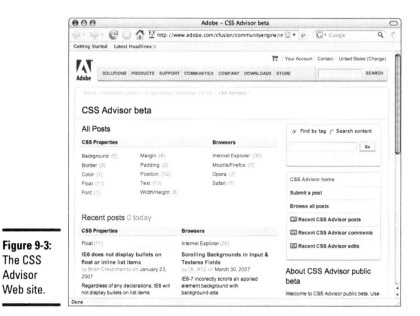

Figure 9-3:
The CSS
Advisor
Web site.

Getting Connected

Once you're ready to publish your site for the world to see, you need to set up a remote server in your site definition so that you can connect and copy files to your Web-hosting account or dedicated server.

Typical remote server information consists of an id and password, an FTP or network address, and the name of the specific directory where your files need to go. This information should be available from the company whom your hosting service was purchased from or from your network administrator.

To set up your remote connection:

1. **Choose Site➪Manage Sites.**

The Manage Sites panel appears.

2. **Select your site from the list and click Edit.**

3. **When the Site Definition dialog box appears, select Advanced from the top and choose the Remote Info category on the left.**

4. **Choose your Access type.**

For most hosting accounts, choose FTP. If you're unsure of how to connect to your remote server, contact your hosting company or network administrator.

5. **For FTP host, enter the address.**

   The address is typically a numerical IP or FTP address, such as 192.1.1.1 or `ftp.mywebsite.com`.

6. **If necessary, enter the Host Directory.**

   This is the path to the specific folder where your site files are kept on the server. Some FTP addresses bring you directly to the right directory.

7. **Enter the Login and Password for your account; to avoid being prompted for your password in the future, click the Save check box next to the Password field.**

8. **To make sure that all your information is correct and the connection is set up properly, click the Test button.**

   A dialog box lets you know that Dreamweaver connected to your site successfully. If it doesn't, double-check the information you entered and try again.

9. **Click OK to update the site definition.**

If you experience difficulty connecting to your remote server or the connection is taking unusually long, try checking the Use Passive FTP option found by choosing Site⇨Manage Sites⇨[Your Site]⇨Advanced⇨Remote Info. Passive FTP can be a workaround if you're trying to connect from behind a firewall.

Your Web site — live!

After your connection is up and running, you're ready to upload your files and present your Web site to the world. Files can be transferred to and from your remote Web server using the built-in FTP functionality of the Files panel. The Files panel displays files in your local directory and the remote server, and between them, you can *put, get,* or *synchronize* site files.

To upload your Web site to a remote web server:

1. **Choose Window⇨Files to open the Files panel.**

2. **Click the Expand To Show Local And Remote Sites icon.**

   The panel expands so that you see both local site and the remote site in which you want to copy (upload) the files to.

3. **Make sure that the correct site definition is selected in the Show menu at the top-left corner of the panel.**

   Your local files appear on the right.

4. **To connect to and display files on the remote Web server, click the Connect button at the top of the panel.**

   When the connection is made, all the files (if any) are displayed on the left side of the panel.

5. **To copy files, select and drag them from the local files on the right to the remote files on the left, or select the files you want to copy on the right and click the Put button at the top of the Files panel.**

   You can put an entire site at once by selecting the root folder at the top of your local files panel and clicking the Put button.

6. **After you've copied all the files to the remote web server, test your site by opening a browser and typing the Web site's URL.**

   The URL will be a full address, such as `www.mywebsite.com`, or an IP address, such as `http://192.1.1.1`.

   If you notice broken images or files, return to Dreamweaver and double-check that all files were copied to the server and run the Link Checker located at Site⇨Check Links Sitewide.

To retrieve files from a remote Web server:

1. **Select the file(s) you want to retrieve from the remote files on the left side of the Files panel.**

2. **Click the Get button at the top of the panel or drag the files to the local root folder on the right.**

Synchronizing your site

Dreamweaver's handy site synchronization feature compares files between your local and remote sites to ensure that both are using the same and the most recent versions of your site files. This check is essential if there's a chance that files on the remote server may be more up-to-date or if you're unsure which files have been updated since the last time you worked on a Web site.

To synchronize your local and remote directories:

1. **If the Files panel isn't already visible, choose Window⇨Files to open the Files panel.**

2. **Select the site you want to synchronize in the Show menu at the top-left corner of the panel.**

   Your local files appear on the right.

3. **Click the Connect button at the top of the panel to connect to the remote server and display your remote files.**

**Book VI
Chapter 9**

**Publishing
Your Web Site**

4. **Click the Synchronize button at the top of the Files panel.**

The Synchronize Files dialog box appears.

5. **From the Synchronize drop-down list, choose whether you want to synchronize the whole local site or only files selected in the Files panel (if any).**

6. **From the Direction list, choose whether you want newer files put to the remote server, retrieved from the remote sever, or both.**

7. **To clean up unused or old files on your remote server, check the Delete Remote Files Not On Local Drive option.**

8. **Click Preview to begin the process.**

This step may take a while depending on the number of files in your site.

The Synchronize panel appears and displays all changes that will be made between the local and remote folders as shown in Figure 9-4.

9. **Select, change, or delete any actions as necessary.**

10. **Click OK to have Dreamweaver complete the synchronization process.**

Be careful when using the Delete Remote Files Not On Local Drive option; some files on the remote server are installed by the web-hosting company and are necessary for the operation of your site.

Figure 9-4:
The Synchronize panel displays a preview of the actions that will take place; take a moment to review them and remove any unwanted actions before running the Synchroni- zation process.

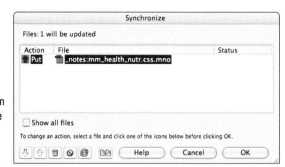

Improving Your Site

Remember that a site is like a living organism; it continues to grow and will need aftercare once it's live. As you add to your site, find new and innovative ways to present information to site visitors; after all, it's all about giving your visitors what they came looking for.

To improve your site and keep visitors coming back, try the following tips:

✦ **Solicit feedback from focus groups or colleagues in different fields on best and worst features of the site.** Use this feedback to assist in design, layout, and content decisions.

✦ **Use Web statistics (often provided free by web-hosting companies) to see where your users are spending the most time and where they exit the site.**

✦ **Provide a feedback form to allow site visitors to comment on service and information they received, with the opportunity to provide comments and suggestions.**

✦ **Always keep your content fresh.** Stale information and features can deter return visits and ruin first impressions.

✦ **Don't ignore problems that surface.** Address broken links, images, or misspellings right away.

Book VII

Flash CS3

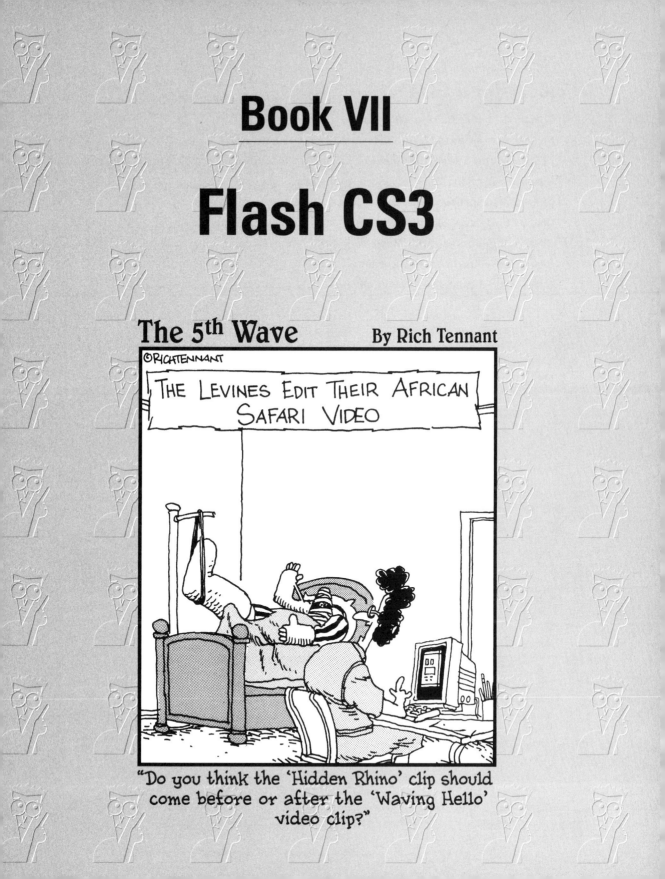

The 5th Wave   By Rich Tennant

THE LEVINES EDIT THEIR AFRICAN SAFARI VIDEO

"Do you think the 'Hidden Rhino' clip should come before or after the 'Waving Hello' video clip?"

Contents at a Glance

Chapter 1: Getting Started with Flash 9

In This Chapter

✔ Creating and saving new documents

✔ Getting familiar with the workspace and tools

✔ Managing your workspace and panels

✔ Thinking about FLA and SWF file formats

✔ Introducing Flash Player 9

✔ Understanding the publishing process

*W*elcome to the world of Flash, one of today's hottest applications for creating eye-catching motion graphics featuring sound, video, and visual effects. In this chapter, you explore the whole process, from basic graphics creation and animation to complex effects and user interaction.

Creating Your First Flash Document

To get started, you're going to create a new blank Flash document and set up your workspace. You can create a new document in two ways:

✦ From the Start page, choose Flash File (ActionScript 3.0) under the Create New column.

✦ Choose File⇨New Flash File⇨(ActionScript 3.0).

Your new document is created, and the workspace appears. Before you get to work, you need to specify some important settings, such as width and height, for your file by using the Document Properties dialog box.

To open the Document Property inspector dialog box, choose Modify⇨ Document and set the following options:

✦ **Title:** This is simply the title of your new Flash file. Although you can leave this blank, it's typically a good idea to name it from the beginning using a short but intuitive name, such as Home Page.

✦ **Description:** This is optional and can contain descriptive text about your file, including a summary, last revision date, or any info you feel may be helpful later. This information is only visible when viewing Document Property in the authoring environment and has no impact on the final movie.

✦ **Frames Per Second:** Because Flash files behave like movies, the frame rate is an important setting that impacts the performance of your movie. The default setting of 12fps should do fine.

✦ **Dimensions:** The width and height set here determine the size of your stage and in turn, the visible area of your final movie. For now, leave the default setting of 550 pixels wide by 400 pixels in height.

✦ **Background Color:** Click the swatch to pick a background color for your stage from the Web-safe color panel. This also sets the background color of any Web pages created by Flash if and when you publish your movie to the Web.

When you're done fine-tuning your document Property, choose OK.

Getting Familiar with the Workspace

The most prominent item you'll notice is dead center on the screen: the stage. The *stage* is where the action happens — where you draw, build, or import graphics, create text, and construct layouts.

The grey area surrounding the stage is your work area. Items placed here aren't visible in your final movie because they're outside the bounds of the stage. However, it helps to think of this area as *backstage* — where text, artwork, and images can make their entrance or exit or be placed until they're ready to appear in your movie.

The Tools panel

What CS application would be complete without a fancy toolbar? Flash has a comprehensive set of tools for just about any drawing task you'll need to wrap your hands around. Table 1-1 gives you a rundown and description of the tools you'll find. The Tools panel, shown in Figure 1-1, has been redesigned to make your work area flow better. A double arrow at the top lets you toggle between a single column and double column to maximize your work area.

Table 1-1	The Tools Panel
Tool	*Description*
Selection tool	Selects and moves objects on the stage and work area
Subselection tool	Selects and moves specific points on a path or shape
Free Transform tool	Changes the dimensions, rotation, or proportions of an object
Gradient Transform tool	Changes the size, intensity, and direction of a gradient fill
Lasso tool	Creates freehand selections around one or more points
Pen tool	Creates accurate , point-by-point straight and curved paths
Add Anchor Point	Adds anchor points along an existing path
Delete Anchor Point	Removes anchor points from an existing path
Convert Anchor Point	Changes the curve orientation of an existing point
Text tool	Creates text on the stage
Line tool	Draws straight lines
Shape tools	Creates rectangular, oval, or multisided shapes on the stage
Pencil tool	Draws freehand paths
Brush tool	Draws broad, freehand fill areas
Ink Bottle	Applies or modifies the stroke color and style of a shape or path
Paint Bucket	Applies or modifies the fill color of an area
Eyedropper	Samples the color Property from an object
Eraser	Erases parts of a fill or path
Hand	Repositions the stage and work area within the workspace
Zoom	Zooms in or out of a selected area of the stage

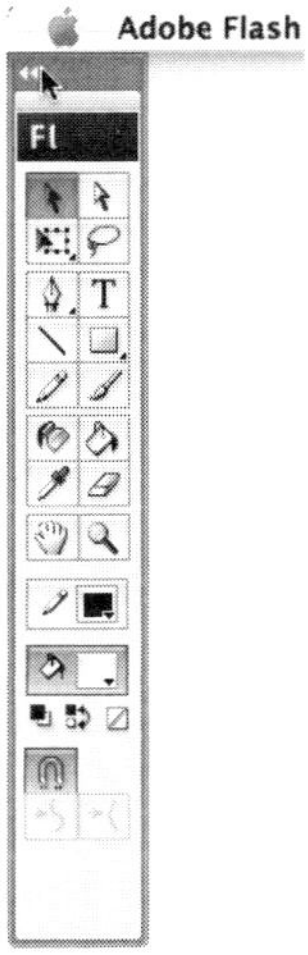

**Book VII
Chapter 1**

**Getting Started
with Flash 9**

Figure 1-1:
Use the double arrows on top of the new Flash CS3 Tools panel to switch between double and single column views.

The timeline

Above your stage sits the timeline, where you bring your artwork to life through animation. The timeline is broken out into *layers;* new documents automatically contain one new layer labeled *Layer 1*. Each layer on the timeline is composed of frames that span horizontally from left to right, each one representing a point in time, just like frames in a movie reel (see Figure 1-2).

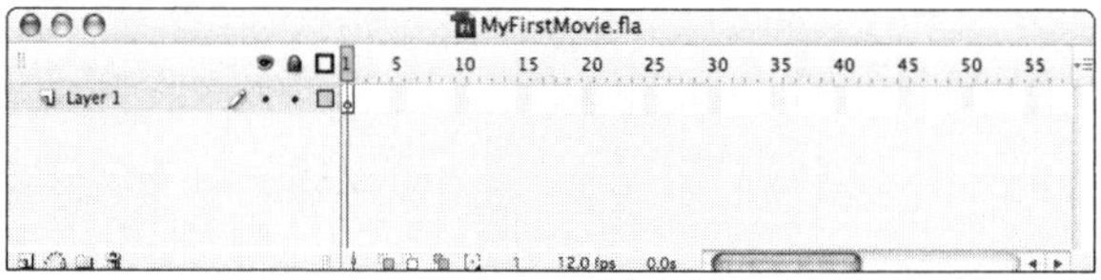

Figure 1-2:
The timeline is composed of frames, each one representing a point in time moving left to right.

(Figure shows the Flash timeline window for MyFirstMovie.fla, with Layer 1, frame numbers 5, 10, 15, 20, 25, 30, 35, 40, 45, 50, 55, and a status bar showing 12.0 fps 0.0s)

The Property inspector

Sitting at the bottom of your workspace, the Property inspector allows you to get (and set) attributes (such as height and width) for a selected item on the stage or work area. When nothing is selected, the Property inspector, shown in Figure 1-3, shows your document properties.

TIP

You can modify your document Property at any time from the Property inspector when no items on the stage are selected or by choosing Modify⇨ Document.

Panels (right side)

The many panels included in Flash give you total control over most aspects of your movie, from creating and managing colors to exploring the structure of your project.

The default workspace launches with three panels: the Color, Swatches, and Library panels.

You'll want to get familiar with panel behaviors and features so that you can manage their appearance and make organizing your workspace a snap.

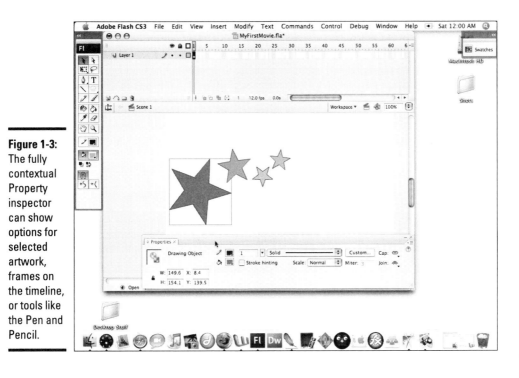

Figure 1-3:
The fully contextual Property inspector can show options for selected artwork, frames on the timeline, or tools like the Pen and Pencil.

The panel group

The panel group sits on the right of the workspace and features multiple panels *docked,* or grouped, together. In the default workspace, the Color and Swatches panels are docked together.

The panel group can't be freely repositioned in the workspace. However, it can be resized or collapsed down to icon view using the double arrows found in its upper-right corner).

You can undock panels from the panel group. Simply click and drag a panel away from the group by its title tab. To dock a panel into the group, drag it into the panel group.

Managing individual panels

You can position each panel individually anywhere in the workspace by dragging it from its top bar or title tab. You can find additional appearance options under the panel's *flyout* menu, accessible from the icon in its upper-right (see Figure 1-4). The flyout menu also provides another way of getting to the panel's primary tasks.

Resize the pane group.

The double arrows toggle the group into icon mode (right).

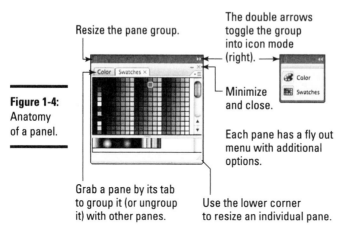

Minimize and close.

Each pane has a fly out menu with additional options.

Figure 1-4:
Anatomy of a panel.

Grab a pane by its tab to group it (or ungroup it) with other panes.

Use the lower corner to resize an individual pane.

To dock panels together, simply drag one on top of the other; once docked together, you can move, minimize, or close several panels as one unit. This is handy for keeping commonly used or related panels together.

You can save panel and panel positions and groups as part of custom workspaces. (See the section "Creating and Saving Workspaces," later in this chapter.)

Panels can always be toggled on or off from the Window menu. If you don't see a panel or have accidentally closed one, look for it in the Window menu. Many panels have shortcut keys; if you use a panel often, use its shortcut key combination for easy access.

Creating and Saving Workspaces

One of the most useful additions in recent versions of Flash is the ability to save your workspaces, or the appearance and layout of workspace items such as the Toolbar, Timeline, Property inspector, and panels.

Saving workspaces is essential if you're sharing a computer workstation with others and want to recall your favorite panels and setup instantly. However, it can be useful for maintaining different workspaces for different projects, even if you're the only person working on your computer.

To create and save your workspace layout:

1. **Open and position any panels or panels you want available, including the Toolbar, Timeline, and Property inspector.**

   You can toggle panels and panels on or off from the Window menu.

2. **Choose Window⮕Workspace⮕Save Current.**

3. **Assign your workspace a new name and click OK.**

   Your workspace is now available by name under the Workspaces menu.

To recall a workspace, choose Window⮕Workspace⮕[*Your workspace name*]. The current workspace rebuilds and appears exactly as you saved it.

You can view all your saved workspaces at any point by choosing Window⮕ Workspace⮕Manage. From this panel, you can choose to delete or rename existing workspaces at any point.

The default workspace can't be modified, deleted, or renamed.

Saving and Opening Documents

It's always recommended that you save your document after you make any significant changes or additions, and although not necessary, it's also a good idea to save a new document immediately after creating it. To save a document, choose File⮕Save. Enter a name for your file and choose a location on your hard drive to save it to.

To open an existing document, choose File⮕Open and locate the FLA file on your hard drive.

You may need at some point to save a copy of your document under a new name, either to create an alternate version or perhaps to make it compatible with an older version of Flash.

To save a copy of your document under a new name, choose File⮕Save As. Choose a location on your hard drive and enter a new filename. The drop-down menu at the bottom of the Save As dialog box lets you choose what version of Flash you want to save the file in. From Flash CS3, you can save files into Flash 8 format as well.

Saving a document in an older version of Flash may make some newer features unavailable. Avoid saving your file in an older file format unless you absolutely need to make it available to an older version of Flash.

Getting to Know Flash Player 9

The Flash Player is at the heart of Flash technology. The player, which you can find as a plug-in to Web browsers or as a standalone application, runs and plays completed Flash movies, known as SWF (ShockWave Flash) files.

**Book VII
Chapter 1**

**Getting Started
with Flash 9**

The Flash Player: New and improved for CS3!

If you've used previous versions of Flash and the Flash Player, it's worth mentioning some significant improvements in Flash Player 9.

✔ **For the speed demons out there:** Flash Player 9 can achieve up to 10 times faster performance than its predecessor, thanks to improvements and revisions in Action Script 3.0, as well as the new ActionScript Virtual Machine 2 (VM2).

✔ **Behind the times?** Don't worry — Flash Player 9 features a second ActionScript Virtual Machine (VM1) side by side with

VM2, dedicated strictly to handling the golden oldies (ActionScript Versions 1.0 and 2.0).

✔ **Don't let the debugs bite:** Improved debugging and error reporting means troubleshooting is easier and more intuitive. If something doesn't go quite right during playback of your movie, error reports appear. Previously, the Flash Player handled runtime errors gracefully, but silently — very considerate, but not very useful.

Beyond simple playback, the Flash Player is also responsible for deciphering and carrying out instructions written in ActionScript, Flash's powerful built-in scripting language. ActionScript, which is introduced in Chapter 7, gives your Flash movies many more abilities, including playback control, real-time user interaction, and complex effects.

Your end user needs the Flash Player in order to view your movies. Fortunately, at the time of this writing, the Flash Player is in use by 96 percent of Internet-enabled PCs worldwide. If a user doesn't have the Flash Player installed, it's available as a free download from the Adobe Web site at www.adobe.com.

Talking about Layers

If you've worked with other programs that utilize Layers (such as Photoshop or Illustrator), the concept is very much the same. If you're new to *layers,* it's best to think of them as clear pieces of film stacked on top of each other. Each layer can contain its own artwork and animations.

In Flash, you use layers to stack artwork and animations on the stage, allowing them to exist together visually but to be edited or moved independently from one another. You can reorder layers to position artwork in front of or behind artwork on other layers.

To create a new layer, click the New Layer icon at the bottom of the timeline. The layer is automatically assigned a name; you can rename any layer by double-clicking its name and typing a new name.

To delete a layer:

1. **In the Timeline window above the stage, select the layer you want to delete.**

   Hold down the Shift key to select multiple layers. You can then click the Trash icon to delete all the selected layers at once.

2. **Click the Delete Layer icon below the timeline.**

The beauty of working with layers is that you can easily change the stacking order and appearance of artwork and animations distributed across those layers. To reorder layers, simply select a layer by clicking its label on the timeline and then click and drag the layer up or down in the stacking order and release it to its new position (see Figure 1-5). Layers at the top of the list will appear in front of other objects in lower layers; in contrast, layers at the bottom of the list will appear below or behind items on higher layers.

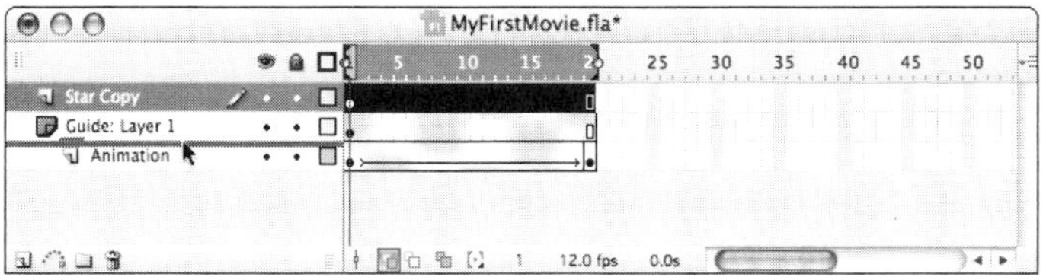

Figure 1-5:
It's easy to shuffle layers — just click and drag to reorder any layer.

Book VII Chapter 1

Getting Started with Flash 9

Two additional aspects of managing layers include toggling a layer and its contents visible or invisible, and locking layers to prevent their contents from being accidentally moved or modified.

 To toggle a layer's visibility on or off, click any layer in the column below the Visibility icon. To toggle all layers on or off, click the Eye icon at the top of the column.

To prevent layer contents from being modified, click any layer in the column below the Padlock. To unlock it, click the Padlock again. To lock or unlock all layers, click the Padlock icon at the top of the column.

Locking layers ensures that you won't accidentally move or delete the artwork it contains. Make a habit of locking layers whenever you're not working with them.

 Layer visibility only affects what you see inside of the authoring environment and has no effect on the finished SWF file. Layers whose visibility is toggled off in your document will still appear when published.

Importing Files

There will be times when you need to bring resources — such as artwork or photo files created in Adobe Photoshop or Illustrator, .MP3 sound files, and even video files — that were not created in Flash. You can import the following file formats into Flash:

+ JPEG, GIF and PNG, TIFF, EPS

+ Flash SWF Files

+ Adobe Illustrator (.ai) and Photoshop (.psd)

+ AIFF, WAV, and MP3 audio files

+ MPEG, MOV, QuickTime, and FLV video formats (Import Video only)

You can import these files directly to the stage for immediate use or to your document's Library (see Chapter 2 of this minibook) for storage until you're ready to place them on the stage.

To import files to the stage:

1. **Choose File➪Import➪Import To Stage.**

2. **Select the file(s) from your hard drive that you want to import.**

   Imported items are placed on the stage on the currently selected layer and frame.

To import files directly to the Library:

1. **Choose File➪Import➪Import To Library.**

2. **Select the files from your hard drive that you want to import and click the Open button.**

   Imported files don't appear on the stage, but are available in the Library panel for use later on.

To select multiple files for import, hold down the Shift key when prompted to select files from your hard drive. You'll be able to bring several files to the Stage or Library in one step.

Exporting Files from Flash

In contrast to the Import menu, the Export menu is used to generate files from your current document *out* of Flash, most often to create a compressed SWF file for final publishing. Additionally, it can be used to generate static images (such as a JPEGs or GIFs) from specific frames in your movie.

FLA and SWF files

The life of a Flash project involves at least two different types of files: your authoring file (FLA) in which all your work is created, and the final product: your compressed movie or SWF file.

FLA files work only within the Flash CS3 application (the authoring environment). When you're ready to distribute your finished movie, you'll need to publish an SWF file that can be played back by the Flash Player.

These SWF files can be created from the Publish or Export menu options and are compressed movie files (typically smaller than their .FLA counterparts) that contain all the graphics and information necessary to display your movie.

The Flash Player can't read FLA files, and SWF files can't be deconstructed into usable FLA files. Changes to your Flash movie are always done in the original FLA file and must be re-exported to a new SWF file if you want to view them in the Flash Player.

Publishing Your Final Movie

The final step in getting your movie ready to be posted on the Web, distributed on a CD-ROM, or sent through e-mail is the *publishing* process. The publishing process handles two important tasks: Exporting the final SWF file playable by the Flash Player, and creating any additional files (such as Web pages) necessary to display your movie. The File menu's Publish Settings and Publish options handle the setup and publishing of your movie so that you can show the world your new creation.

Flash can create any and all of the following file types at Publish time:

+ SWF files

+ JPG, GIF, or PNG bitmap files

+ Projector files

    If you want to distribute your movie as a standalone file, you can create a Mac or PC compatible *projector* that includes the Flash player.

+ HTML files

    To display your movies on the Web, you'll need to contain it within a Web page, or HTML file. Flash takes care of creating this page for you.

+ QuickTime movies

Chapter 2 of this minibook explores publishing in more detail.

Book VII
Chapter 1

Getting Started
with Flash 9

Chapter 2: Drawing in Flash

In This Chapter

✔ Creating and selecting shapes

✔ Using the Pen and Pencil tools

✔ Transforming shapes and artwork

✔ Working with colors and gradients

Many great creations start with the most basic of shapes and go from there. In this chapter, you discover the secrets of drawing shapes and lines and working with colors.

Drawing Shapes

To get your creation started, you'll want to become familiar with the Shape tools on the Tools panel and use them as the starting point for anything from basic buttons to complex illustrations.

On the Tools panel, locate the Rectangle tool; you'll also notice a small arrow at the lower right corner of the icon, which means that more tools are hidden underneath. Click and hold the Rectangle tool to reveal the Oval and Polystar tools; select the Oval tool.

Before you get started, set some colors for your shape using the two swatches located at the bottom of the Tools panel. The Fill color swatch (indicated by the paint bucket icon) lets you set what color your shape will be filled with. The Stroke Color swatch (indicated by the ink bottle icon) controls the outline color.

Flash lets you choose colors from the Swatches panel. You can add your own colors to this panel, but for now, choose one of the available colors for your shape's fill and stroke.

Click and drag on the stage to create an oval. Notice that by default, shapes are drawn from the left corner outward. You can draw shapes from the center (which is sometimes easier) by holding down the Option (Mac), or Alt (Windows) key while drawing the shape.

To constrain a shape proportionally, hold down the Shift key while drawing or resizing.

Creating Perfect Lines

The Line tool makes constructing perfect straight lines quick and easy. To create a straight line, choose the Line tool from the Tools panel, click and drag on your stage where you want the line to start, and release the mouse button where you want the line to end.

To modify your line's color or appearance, select it with the Selection tool, and use the Property inspector to change its stroke color and size. You will also find a stroke style menu, which lets you choose between straight, dotted, dashed, and artistic stroke styles.

To create perfectly vertical or horizontal lines, hold down the Shift key while using the Line tool. You can also create diagonal lines in 45-degree increments with this same method.

Selecting, Moving, and Resizing Shapes

Once you've created a shape, you can select and move it by using the Selection tool at the top of the Tools panel. Flash shapes are easy to edit, as you can select the stroke and fill independently to separate one from the other.

To select and move the stroke or fill only:

1. **Choose the Selection tool from the Tools panel.**

2. **Click once on either your shape's stroke or fill to activate it.**

   To select the entire shape, double-click the fill of your shape or use the Selection tool to click, drag, and draw a selection around it on the stage (see Figure 2-1).

3. **Click and drag the selected stroke or fill or use the arrow keys to separate it.**

Figure 2-1:
Select the
stroke or fill
of a shape
individually
to separate
them.
Double-click
the fill to
select the
entire
shape.

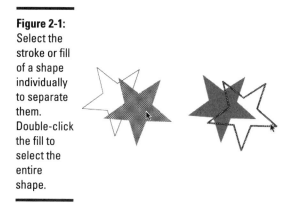

Merging Shapes

If you overlap two or more shapes in Flash, they automatically *merge,* or
become one complete shape. You can take advantage of this behavior by
using an overlapping shape to knock out another, or you can make more
complex shapes by combining simpler ones.

You may also find that overlapping strokes will result in divided fill areas,
which can be a desirable effect. Experiment by drawing and overlapping
shapes and using the Selection tool to select parts of the resulting object.

Modifying Fill and Stroke Colors

You can choose your Fill and Stroke colors ahead of time before you start
drawing, but if you change your mind, modifying colors is easy to do.

You can modify either the Fill or Stroke colors of a pre-existing shape in the
three ways:

✦ Select the entire shape and change your Fill and/or Stroke colors from
the swatches on the Property inspector (see Figure 2-2).

✦ Select the entire shape and change your Fill and/or Stroke colors using
the Fill/Stroke swatches on the Tools panel.

✦ Set your colors on the Tools panel and use the Ink Bottle tool by clicking
on the stroke, or Paint Bucket tool by clicking on the fill.

To apply a fill and a stroke color to your shape, select it on the stage and choose a color from the Fill swatch on the Tools panel. Grab the Ink Bottle tool and choose a different color from the Stroke swatch. Click once on the stroke of your oval to set the color.

 To remove a fill or stroke completely, select either the Fill or Stroke swatch and choose the None icon.

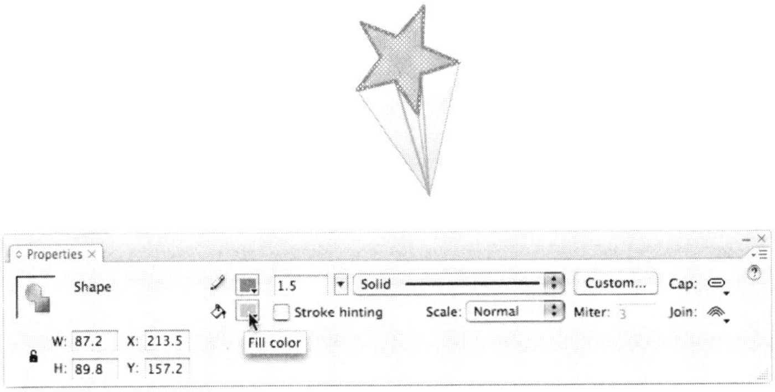

Figure 2-2:
Use the Property inspector on a selected shape on your stage to change fill or stroke color, stroke width and style.

Standard verseus Object Drawing Mode

The ability to freely tear apart shapes can be very flexible and useful, but some prefer to work with shapes as single objects (similar to how Illustrator CS3 does). For this reason, *Object Drawing* mode was created; this optional mode automatically combines the stroke and fill of a shape into a single object, which you can move and resize as a whole.

 You can enable Object Drawing mode, shown in Figure 2-3, for any active Shape tool by using the Object Drawing mode button at the bottom of the Tools panel. Try drawing a shape on the stage with this enabled; you'll notice that it has a blue bounding box around it, and the stroke and fill can no longer be separated.

To convert a shape drawn with Object Drawing mode to its raw form, select the shape and choose Modify➪Break Apart, or double-click the shape to edit it within the drawing object itself.

 Unlike shapes drawn in standard mode, Drawing Objects can't be merged together; you'll need to break any Drawing Objects apart first.

Figure 2-3:
Shapes
drawn in
Object
Drawing
mode have
a bounding
box around
them. The
stroke and
fill are
moved
together as
one object.

Splicing and Tweaking Shapes and Lines

You can easily dissect raw shapes (not Drawing Objects) by selecting only certain portions using the Selection or Lasso tools, as shown in Figure 2-4. Try drawing a marquee around only half the shape using the Selection or Subselection arrows; you'll notice that only half of the shape or line becomes selected, and you can then separate it.

Figure 2-4:
Grab edges
or corners
with the
Selection
tool to
reshape
your
artwork.

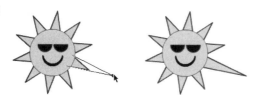

If you need to tweak the shape beyond it's original form, you can use Selection or Subselection tools to tweak, distort, and reshape. To tweak or reshape using the Selection tool, move it outside and close to an edge or corner of your shape; you'll notice a small curved or angled line icon appears next to your pointer. Click and drag to bend, reshape, and distort the outline of your shape, as shown in Figure 2-5.

Figure 2-5:
You can modify curves using the Selection tool; just click and drag an edge.

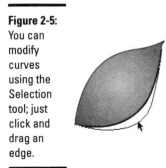

To tweak or reshape using the Subselection tool, click the outside edge or stroke of a shape, to activate its path. You'll see each point represented by a hollow box. Click any point to activate it; click and drag it or move it using the arrow keys to reshape (see Figure 2-6).

Figure 2-6:
Use the Sub-selection tool to modify specific points that make up your shape.

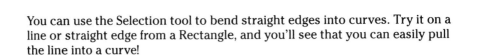

You can use the Selection tool to bend straight edges into curves. Try it on a line or straight edge from a Rectangle, and you'll see that you can easily pull the line into a curve!

The Lasso tool

When you need to create a selection with more precision than the Selection tool allows (for example, around an odd shape or tricky area), use the Lasso tool. This selection tool draws freehand selections around specific areas of your artwork. To draw a selection with the Lasso tool, select it from the Tools panel and click and drag to draw a selection around the target area, as shown in Figure 2-7. Make sure to close the selection by overlapping the starting and ending points.

You can perform partial selections only with raw (broken apart) shapes and lines. Artwork drawn in Object Drawing mode needs to be broken apart first (choose Modify➪Break Apart) or modified in edit mode. To enter a Drawing Object's edit mode, double-click it with the Selection tool.

Figure 2-7:
Create meticulous selection areas with the Lasso. Remember to close the path for best results.

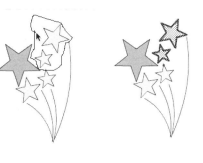

When you're ready to create more complex artwork beyond what the Shape and Line tools offer, the Pen and Pencil tools are standing by. These tools work very differently, and for that reason, should be chosen based on the kind of artwork you want to create.

The Pen tool

Using the Pen tool may be a bit different than you're used to, unless of course, you've used the Pen tool in applications such as Illustrator or Photoshop. The Pen tool isn't a freehand drawing tool; rather, it allows you to create *paths,* or outlines, composed by connecting anchor points. As you click and create new points, lines are automatically drawn connecting those points together. You can then either bend those lines into precise curves or leave them straight.

The best way to understand the Pen tool is to practice working with it. Visualize a shape you want to draw (for example, a leaf), and try to create it using the Pen tool.

To get started:

1. **Select the Pen tool from the Tools panel.**

2. **Use the Stroke Color swatch on the bottom of the Tools panel to set a stroke color.**

3. **Click to set the first point on the stage and then construct a line by clicking again to set a second point where you want the line to end.**

4. **To create a curve, click to set a new point and, before releasing the mouse button, drag to the left or right to bend the new line into a curve.**

The more you drag in a particular direction, the more extreme the curve will be.

5. **Continue creating new points and experimenting with different curves.**

6. **To close the path and complete the shape, move your mouse pointer over the first point you created (a loop appears above the icon) and click.**

The Pen tool will attempt to continue a curve in the same direction even after a new point is set. To reset the last point drawn back to a straight line, hold down the Option (Mac) or Alt (Windows) key and click the last point created before setting a new one.

The Pencil tool

The precise nature of the Pen tool is great for certain situations, but if you prefer the intuitive feel of freehand drawing or want to create more natural or rough artwork, consider using the Pencil tool.

An attractive feature of the Pencil tool is that it has three different modes to choose from. Each mode provides a different level of *smoothing,* so even if your hand isn't the steadiest, it will compensate by automatically smoothing out lines or curves as you create them.

Select the Pencil tool and choose the appropriate smoothing mode using the selector at the bottom right corner of the Tools panel:

+ **Straighten:** Forces lines to the nearest straight line; perfect for drawing or tracing straight edges or boxy outlines.

+ **Smooth:** Smoothes out lines or curves to the next closest perfect curve.

+ **Ink:** Provides less smoothing and keeps lines and curves as natural as possible.

The mode you select depends completely on what type of shapes and lines you're trying to draw. If your shape is more diverse than one mode can handle, you can switch modes from line to line as needed.

Modifying Artwork Created with the Pen and Pencil Tools

Interestingly enough, while the Pen and Pencil tools behave in completely different ways, both ultimately create the same thing: paths. These paths can be filled (if closed) or modified on a point-by-point basis, or you can apply a stroke to them.

To fine-tune a path, choose the Subselection tool (white arrow) from the Tools panel. Click the path, and it becomes highlighted, and the points show up as hollow boxes. You can now select any individual point and selectively drag it or move it using the arrow keys to reshape the path.

To adjust a curve, using the Direct Selection tool, highlight the point adjacent to the curve you want to modify. You should see a handle appear; you can grab and move this handle to adjust the curve.

To add or subtract points, click and hold down on the Pen tool to select the Add Anchor Point or Subtract Anchor Point tools. Click exactly on the path where you'd like to add an anchor point or click directly on a point to remove it.

Transforming Artwork and Shapes

Once you've gotten some drawing done, you may want to adjust the width, height, or rotation of your artwork. Depending on the level of precision you're looking for, you can do this in two ways: manually using the Transform tool or by dialing in exact values on the Transform panel.

Using the Transform tool

Select a shape or artwork on your stage and then choose the Transform tool from the Tools panel. A bounding box with handles at all four sides and corners appears, as shown in Figure 2-8. You can drag any of the side handles to resize the width and height.

To rotate your artwork, hover over any corner handle until you see the rotation icon (a circular arrow) and then click and drag to rotate your artwork freely.

To resize your art proportionally, hold down the Shift key while dragging a handle. If you hold down the Shift key while in rotation mode, it limits your movements to precise 45-degree increments.

Figure 2-8:
Use the
Transform
tool on a
drawing to
rotate and
resize.

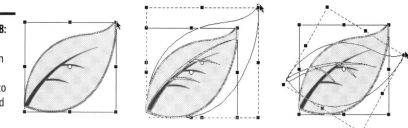

Using the Transform panel

For those times when you need to dial in exact transformation values, you can use the Transform panel, which you can open by choosing Window⊃ Transform (see Figure 2-9). The Transform panel uses type in areas where you can punch in exact transformation values for width and height or a specific rotation angle in degrees.

To transform artwork using the Transform panel:

1. **Select the object you want to transform on the stage and open the Transform panel by choosing Window⊃Transform.**

2. **To increase the size of the artwork, dial in width and height percentage values above 100%; to decrease it, dial in values below 100%. To keep the sizes proportional, check the Constrain Values check box.**

3. **To rotate your artwork, type a value above 0 degrees and press Enter.**

   Rotation is performed clockwise; to rotate counter-clockwise, enter a negative number.

Figure 2-9:
The Transform panel lets you dial in precise amounts of scaling, rotation, and skewing options.

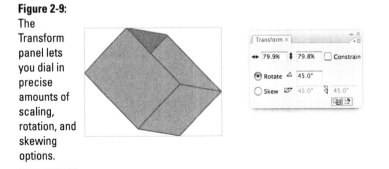

Skewing your artwork

Skewing transforms your artwork on a 3D plane and can add interesting perspective to your shape. You can perform skewing by using the Transform panel by selecting the Skew option and dialing in values for horizontal and vertical skew amount.

Give it a try: select your shape, type in some Skew values, and hit Enter to see the transformation applied (see Figure 2-10). If you're not happy, don't fret; simply click the Reset button in the lower-right corner of the Transform panel to set everything back to normal.

Figure 2-10:
Skewing can create interesting perspectives; use the Transform panel to dial in exact skew values.

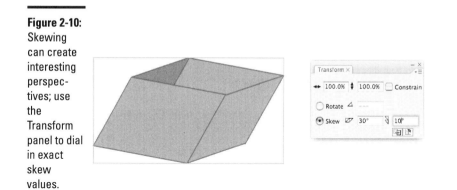

Working with Type

If you're looking to display important information in your Flash movie or simply want to add creative text elements to your design, Flash's flexible Type tool can create attractive type for design elements, buttons, titles, and informational text areas.

To create a line of type, select the Text tool from the Tools panel, click a location on the stage, and begin typing. Using the Property inspector, fine-tune your type's size, typeface, alignment, and color, as shown in Figure 2-11.

To edit type, choose the Text tool and click the text you want to edit. When the blinking cursor appears, you can select, add, or modify the text. While the text is selected, you can also change colors, typeface, and size using the Property inspector.

Transforming type

You can transform type just like shapes and artwork by using either the Transform tool or the Transform panel. Regardless of any transformations you put your type through, it remains editable.

To transform a line of type, make sure that it's active by first selecting it with the Selection or Type tools. To transform, choose the Transform tool or open the Transform panel.

**Book VII
Chapter 2**

Drawing in Flash

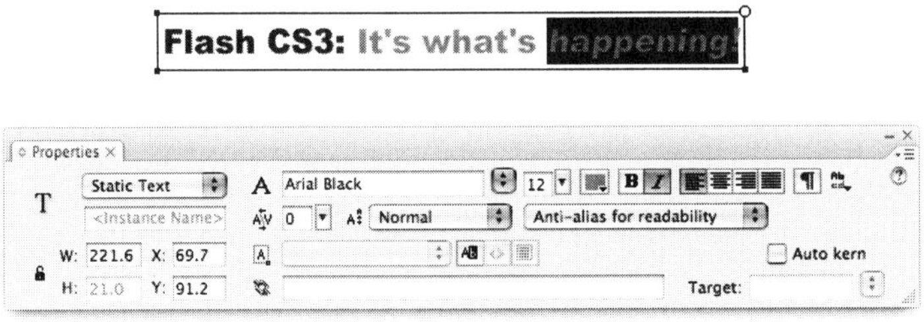

Figure 2-11:
Use the
Property
inspector to
modify
typeface,
style, size,
and colors.
Additional
options,
such as
paragraph
formatting,
can help
with larger
blocks of
text.

Flash CS3: It's what's happening

Distorting and modifying character shapes

You can distort and modify type outlines just like any other shape or path.
However, type is created on a special type path so that it can be edited at
any point. You need to break it off this path first in order to tweak any of its
outlines.

To modify or distort type outlines:

1. **Select the type you want to modify and choose Modify⇨Break Apart.**

2. **Repeat Step 1.**

3. **Use the Selection or Subselection arrows to modify the outlines
   (as demonstrated with shapes earlier in the chapter).**

4. **(Optional) Use the Ink Bottle tool to apply a stroke to your type.**

Creating Colors and Gradients

You've undoubtedly seen and made use of the built-in color swatches in
Flash, but suppose that you'd like to use colors that are *not* included in the
Swatches panel? Here's where the Color panel comes into play. From this
panel, you can mix and create your own color swatches, make gradients, and
even apply transparency effects to existing colors on the stage.

You've already seen the Swatches panel in action — you used it to select Fill and Stroke colors from the Tools panel and Property inspector. The Swatches panel exists on its own free-floating panel as well, which you can open by choosing Window⇨Swatches.

The 256 colors on this panel represent the Web-safe color spectrum, which is optimized to make sure that any user, even those with monitors using lower color depth settings, can enjoy your creations.

You can add colors to the Swatches panel from the Color panel, which means that you have access to your own custom colors from anywhere the Swatches panel appears.

Creating and adding colors from the Color panel

The Color panel (see Figure 2-12) features two ways to dial in a precise color: the color wheel on the right or the sliders on the left. You can combine the two methods to hone in on just the right shade. After you've chosen the color you want, you can easily add it as a swatch to the Swatches panel.

Figure 2-12: Dial in a custom color for either the stroke or fill using the sliders, color wheel, and slider. Save colors into your Color panel by choosing Add Swatch from the flyout menu.

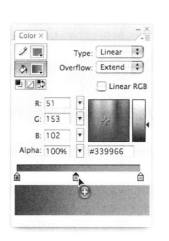

To apply a color choice automatically to the stroke or fill swatches, click to the left of either the Fill or Stroke swatch on the top left corner of the Color Mixer panel. Any changes made using the color wheel or sliders are automatically applied to the selected swatch.

To select a color using the color wheel, click and drag the cross hair inside the color wheel until you find the right hue (for example, greens). Use the slider to the right to dial in the exact shade of that color.

To select a color using the sliders, first select either the RGB (Red-Green-Blue) or HSB (Hue-Saturation-Brightness) sliders from the Color Mixer's flyout menu. Move the sliders to dial in the exact color you want. You can fine-tune this color further with the color wheel and slider.

To save your new color as a swatch, dial in your desired color and choose Add Swatch from the Color Mixer's flyout menu. Your new color appears as a new swatch on the Swatches panel, and you can select it anywhere the Swatches panel appears.

Creating gradients

Gradients are blends between two or more colors that you can use to fill any area or shape, just like a solid color. If you look at the Swatches panel, you see some gradient presets that you can use right away. You can use the Color panel to create your own gradients and add them to the Swatches panel.

To create a gradient:

1. **Open the Color Mixer by choosing Window⇨Color Mixer and use the drop-down menu labeled Type to switch your color mode from Solid to Linear.**

   This is one of two gradient types that you can create.

2. **Double-click each of the horizontal sliders that appears above the color ramp at the bottom to pop-up the Swatches panel; pick a color to apply to each slider.**

3. **Adjust the intensity of the gradient by moving the sliders closer together or further apart.**

4. **To save your new gradient, choose Add Swatch from the Color Mixer's flyout menu.**

   The gradient swatch is added to your Swatches panel alongside the existing gradients.

To add more colors to your gradient, click anywhere on the color ramp to add a slider. You can then double-click this slider to set a color to it.

To remove colors or sliders, click and drag the slider you want to remove off of the panel to the left or right.

Radial gradients are a special type of gradient shape where colors blend from the center outward in a circular motion. To set a gradient as a Radial gradient, choose Radial from the Type drop-down menu on the Color panel.

Linear gradients blend evenly in a straight line. To set a gradient as a Linear gradient, choose Linear from the Type drop-down menu on the Color panel.

Both gradient types are created and added to the Swatches panel in the exact same manner, as described earlier.

Applying and transforming gradients

After you've created a gradient, you can use it to fill a shape the same way you'd set a solid Fill color. After you've applied a gradient to a shape on the stage, you can use the Gradient tool to modify the gradient's direction, size, and intensity.

To modify a gradient fill:

1. **Click and hold down your mouse pointer on the Free Transform tool to locate and choose the Gradient Transform tool. Click the fill of the shape you want to modify.**

2. **Use the center point to move the transition point of the Gradient.**

3. **Use the handle on the right side to modify the intensity of the gradient.**

4. **Change the direction of the gradient by using the rotating arrow icon at the upper-right corner of the selection area.**

If you're working with a radial gradient, you'll notice the Gradient Transform tool behaves slightly differently. An extra round handle appears to let you scale the gradient, and the rotating arrow icon (which rotates the gradient area) is located on the bottom right. Experiment with both Linear and Radial gradients to see the differences.

Working with the Paintbrush Tool

Tools such as the Pen and Pencil tools offer you different ways of creating strokes or paths. In contrast, the Paintbrush tool paints with fills. A lot like a good old-fashioned paintbrush, this tool can create thick, broad strokes with fill colors (or gradients) for excellent artistic effects.

The Paintbrush features several different brush sizes and tips, as well as five modes for controlling how (and where) the Paintbrush does its magic. Similar to the Pencil tool, the Paintbrush provides a level of smoothing that you can dial in from the Property inspector.

To use the Paintbrush:

1. **With the Paintbrush tool selected, choose a brush size and tip shape from the very bottom of the Tools panel.**

**Book VII
Chapter 2**

Drawing in Flash

2. **Choose a fill color from Fill swatch on either the Tools panel, Property inspector, or Color panel.**

3. **Freely paint on the stage to see it in action.**

The different Paintbrush modes change where and how the tool works against different objects on the stage. A good way to see these modes in action is to draw a shape on the stage and make sure that the shape has both a stroke and fill set. Experiment by changing between the different modes and trying to paint over the shape (see Figure 2-13).

Figure 2-13: Paint a selected object with the paintbrush in Paint Selection mode; it affects only the fill area of the shape. Experiment with different Paintbrush modes for different effects.

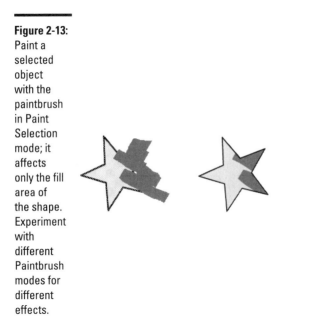

Because the strokes left behind by the Paintbrush are simply filled shapes, you can apply a stroke to it, change its fill color, or use it to create interesting shapes that you can tweak by using the same methods demonstrated in the "Transforming Artwork and Shapes" section.

To apply an outline to a painted area, set a color by using the Stroke swatch on the Tools panel, select the Ink Bottle tool, and click the outer edge of the fill. You can now use the Property inspector to change the width, color, and style of the stroke as well.

Chapter 3: Now You're in Motion . . .

In This Chapter

✔ Understanding symbols and the Library

✔ Working with frames and the timeline

✔ Creating animations with tweens

After you're familiar with Flash's drawing tools, you'll want to explore what Flash is best known for: animation. In this chapter, you bring your creations to life with movement, interactivity, and sounds.

Visiting the Library

Each Flash document contains a *Library,* a repository of reusable graphics, animations, buttons, sounds, and even fonts. As you build your Flash movie, you can add any piece of artwork you've created on the stage to your Library, where it's stored as a *symbol* (shown in Figure 3-1).

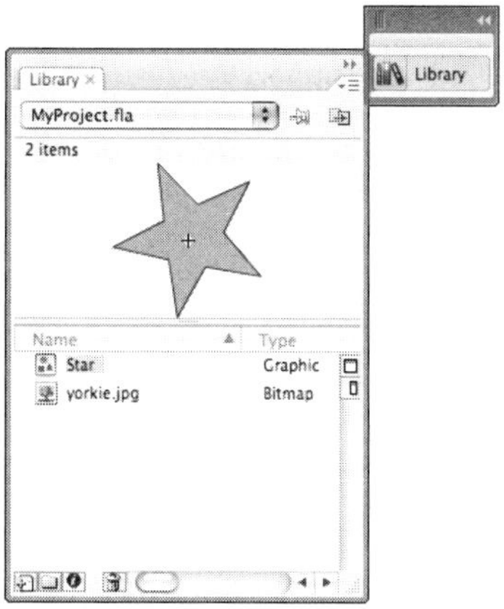

Figure 3-1:
Your Library panel stores symbols that you create from graphics and animations, as well as sounds, images, and fonts.

What makes symbols so powerful is that you can reuse them as many times as necessary. Simply drag and drop a copy (referred to as an *instance*) from the Library panel onto the stage anywhere in your movie. Most importantly, each instance remains linked to the original in your Library. Any changes made to the original (or "master") automatically updates any instances of that same symbol used throughout the movie.

Symbols are broken down into three main categories: graphics, buttons, and movie clips. You can find out more about button and movie clip symbols in Chapters 6 and 7 of this minibook.

Creating and Modifying Graphic Symbols

Certain types of animation in Flash require the use of symbols, so it's a good time to become familiar with the most basic of symbol types: *graphics*. You can convert any object on the stage into a graphic symbol, allowing you to take advantage of additional features allowed only to symbols. You can also create empty graphic symbols from the Library panel or by choosing Insert⇨ New Symbol and add content to them afterward.

To create a graphic symbol:

1. **Choose Insert⇨New Symbol or choose New Symbol from the fly-out menu located on the top-right corner of the Library pane.**

2. **Assign a name to the symbol, set the Type as Graphic from the radio buttons shown, and click OK.**

   You see a blank slate on the stage where you can add to your symbol.

3. **Choose *Scene 1* from the navigation bar above the stage to exit the symbol and return to the main timeline,**

   You should now see your new symbol listed in the Library pane.

To create a graphic symbol from existing artwork on the stage:

1. **Using the Selection tool, select the object(s) on the stage that you want to convert to a symbol.**

2. **Choose Modify⇨Convert To Symbol.**

3. **Assign a name to the symbol, set the Type as Graphic from the radio buttons shown, and click OK.**

   Your new symbol is now listed in the Library pane.

Whenever you convert existing artwork to a symbol, it remains on the stage, enclosed inside of a blue bounding box (see Figure 3-2). Your Property inspector confirms that the selection is now a Graphic symbol (indicated by the icon).

Figure 3-2:
A symbol on the stage will be enclosed in a bounding box. The Property inspector shows the graphic symbol icon followed by the symbol's name in the Library.

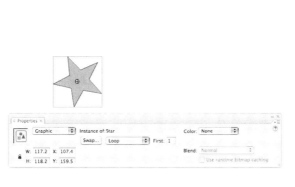

 Don't confuse symbols with Drawing Objects — both display artwork inside of a blue bounding box, but Drawing Objects don't have the same abilities that symbols have, nor are they stored automatically in your Library. Use the Property inspector to determine whether an object is a symbol or Drawing Object if you're unsure.

Adding symbols to the stage

After you've added graphic symbols to your Library, if you need to reuse one, you can simply drag a copy from the Library panel and drop it on to your stage (see Figure 3-3). Each copy of a symbol is referred to in Flash as an instance. While all of these instances remain linked to the original, you have the flexibility to scale, transform, and rotate each instance individually.

Try this exercise to become familiar with adding symbols to the stage:

1. **Locate a symbol in your library that you'd like to add to the stage.**

2. **Drag a copy from the Library panel to the stage; repeat this a few times so that you have several instances on the stage at once.**

3. **Select each instance individually and experiment with different scaling, transformation, and rotation for each one.**

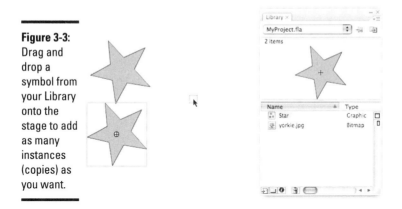

Figure 3-3:
Drag and drop a symbol from your Library onto the stage to add as many instances (copies) as you want.

Modifying symbols

After symbols are created, you can modify them from within the Library or directly on the stage. Changes made to a symbol are applied to all instances of that symbol throughout the movie.

To edit a symbol from within the library:

1. **Select a symbol in your Library panel and choose Edit from the fly-out menu, or double-click any symbol in the Library pane.**

To really see the effect of editing the master symbol, use the same symbol you dragged to the stage in the last exercise.

The symbol appears on the stage in edit mode.

2. **Make some changes in color, shape, or size.**

3. **Exit the symbol by selecting Scene 1 from the navigation bar above the stage to return to the main timeline.**

Instances of this symbol on the stage reflect the changes you've made.

Editing a symbol in place on the stage can be more intuitive, as you may want to modify it to work better with other artwork on the stage. You can directly edit a symbol from any of its instances on the stage (as shown in Figure 3-4), but keep in mind that regardless of which instance you edit, all instances will be affected.

To edit a symbol in place:

1. **Select and double-click any symbol instance on the stage.**

You'll be in the symbol's edit mode and will still see the other objects on the stage in the background.

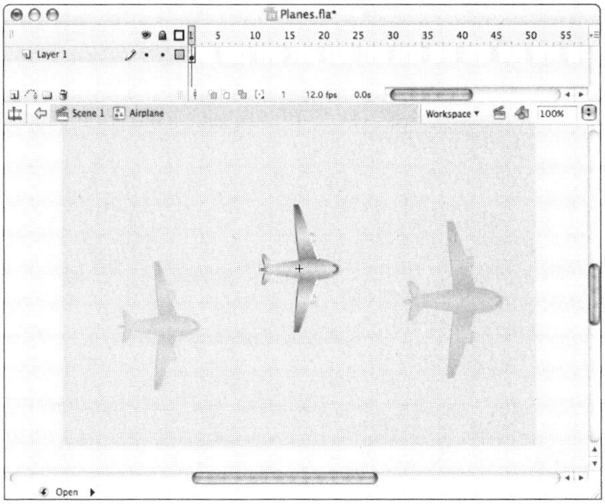

Figure 3-4:
You can double-click a symbol instance to edit the symbol in place on the stage. Other artwork is visible, but dimmed out, in the background so that you can see your changes in context.

2. **Make your changes and exit the symbol's edit mode by selecting Scene 1 on the navigation bar above the stage.**

Sorting symbols

Symbols in your Library can be sorted using any of the column headers at the top of the symbol list. You may only be able to see Name and Type at first glance, but if you use the horizontal scroll bar at the bottom of the pane, you can see additional columns for Use Count, Linkage, and Date Modified.

To sort by any column, click the column name. If the arrow next to the column name is pointing up, the sort is descending, with the highest value up; if the arrow is pointing down, the sort is ascending, with the lowest value up top.

To see as many columns and rows as possible, resize the Library panel by clicking and dragging its lower-right corner.

Duplicating symbols

You may want to create a variation of one of your symbols that goes beyond what you can do on an instance-by-instance basis. A good example is two birds that are similar in appearance, but one has different shaped wings or a different base color. This instance would be a good case for duplicating an existing symbol so that any changes can be made to the copy and treated as a new symbol.

**Book VII
Chapter 3**

Now You're in
Motion . . . .

A closer look at the Library panel

Your Library panel is the main storage location for all your symbols, and very much like any library, it has essential organizational tools that make managing your symbols easy.

The most basic and common functions are made easy through several icons found along the bottom of the panel (see figure):

New Symbol: Create a new symbol, identical to the command found by choosing Insert↔New Symbol.

New Folder: Create folders that you can sort your symbols into for easy categorization. You can create folders within folders for even finer sorting capabilities.

Properties: If a symbol is highlighted in your Library, this icon opens your Symbol Properties window. From here, you can redefine the symbol's name, type, or registration point.

Fly-out menu: All panes have fly-out menus, which offer additional options or modify the view of the panel itself. The Library pane's fly-out menu carries out additional symbol and library-related tasks.

Pin Library: Selecting this icon makes sure that the current Library stays active even when you switch between other open documents. Normal behavior (unpinned) is for Library views to switch automatically when moving between open documents.

New Library: Creates a duplicate Library panel in case you want multiple, distinctive views of your current Library. You can also open a new Library panel to view libraries from other currently open documents.

Trash Can: Yes, you guessed it — this symbol deletes (trashes) the currently highlighted symbol in the Library. *Be careful with this:* No warning is given before the deed is done. However, you can choose Edit↔Undo to reverse this action, if necessary.

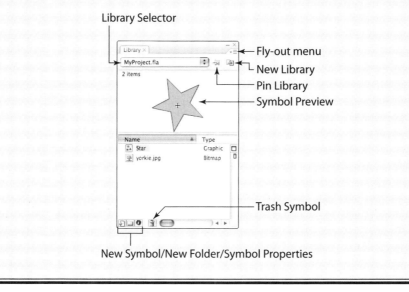

Library Selector

Fly-out menu

New Library

Pin Library

Symbol Preview

Trash Symbol

New Symbol/New Folder/Symbol Properties

To duplicate a symbol, select the symbol in the library you want to copy and choose Duplicate from the fly-out menu on the top-right corner of the pane. You're given a chance to rename the symbol when the Duplicate Symbol dialog box appears.

TIP

You can rename any symbol directly from the Library pane. Select the symbol and choose Rename from the Library pane's fly-out menu.

Understanding Frames and Keyframes

The timeline, located above your stage, is where your animation is created. It's important to take a detailed look at the components that make the timeline tick: frames, keyframes, and the play head.

The timeline is composed of a series of consecutive frames (see Figure 3-5), each of which represents a point in time (much like a historical timeline). When the Flash player plays your movie, the play head moves from left to right across the timeline. The play head is represented by a red vertical line in your timeline window. The numbers above the timeline represent specific frame numbers.

Think of historical milestones represented at specific points on a timeline with prominent markers. On a Flash timeline, significant events (such as the beginning and end of an animation sequence) are represented as *keyframes*.

**Book VII
Chapter 3**

**Now You're in
Motion....**

Figure 3-5:
The timeline is composed of frames, which the play head passes as your movie plays back. To add graphics or animation at specific points along the timeline, you need to create keyframes.

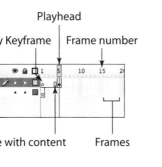

Playhead

Empty Keyframe | Frame number

Frame with content   Frames

Every time you want to place a graphic or animation, you need to first create a keyframe at the specific point on the timeline where you want it to occur. When you create a new document, a single keyframe is automatically created on Frame 1. Keyframes look like standard frames, except with a hollow or black circle inside.

You'll be adding more keyframes as necessary to create animations or have graphics appear and disappear at specific points along the timeline.

Your First Motion Tween

After you understand the timeline (see preceding section), you're ready to create your first animation. The good news is that Flash does a lot of the hard work for you!

Flash can automatically create animation sequences from nothing more than a starting point and ending point, figuring out everything in between. This type of animation is known as a *tween*. There are two types of tweens: *motion* and *shape*.

Motion tween

A motion tween is a type of Flash-generated animation that requires the use of symbols and is best for creating movement, size, and rotation changes, fades, and color effects. All you need to do is tell Flash where to start and end, and it fills in the blanks in between to complete your animation sequence.

It's important to note that only one object can be tweened on one layer at a time. If you want to tween several objects simultaneously, each object needs to occupy its own layer and have its own tween applied.

To create a motion tween:

1. **Drag a symbol from your library to the stage.**

   The symbol is added to Frame 1. Position the symbol on the left edge of the stage, which is where the motion will begin.

2. **Click and select frame 30 on the timeline.**

   Note the numbers above the timeline. Frame 30 is the point in time where your animation will end.

3. **Create a keyframe on frame 30 by choosing Insert⇔Timeline⇔ Keyframe.**

A new keyframe is created at frame 30, accompanied by a copy of the symbol you placed on frame 1. This is default behavior; Flash automatically copies the contents of the last keyframe to any new ones created after it.

4. **Position the symbol on frame 30 on the right edge of the stage.**

   This position is where you want the symbol to end up at the end of the animation.

5. **Select frame 1 and choose Insert⇨Timeline⇨Create Motion Tween.**

   An arrow and blue shaded area appear between the two keyframes to let you know you've successfully created a motion tween (see Figure 3-6).

6. **Hit the Return key to play back your animation.**

   The symbol glides across the stage from the left edge to the right.

To see all frames of your animation at once, select the Onion Skin option underneath the timeline. This option lets you select and show several frames at once so that you see the frames that the Flash tween has created for you.

**Book VII
Chapter 3**

Now You're in Motion . . .

Figure 3-6:
A 30-frame motion tween shown with onion skinning turned on. The position of the airplane on frames 1 and 30 creates the distance that it travels, while the number of frames in between determines how long the animation plays.

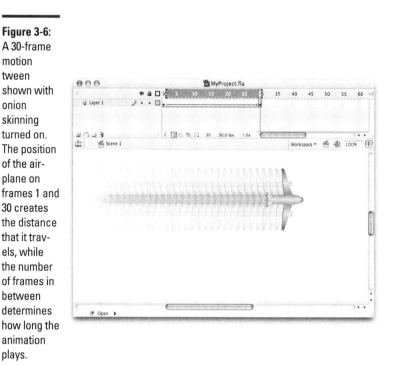

You're just scratching the surface of what Flash can do, and you should feel free to experiment further using different symbols and positions, and alter the length of your animations by placing starting and ending keyframes closer together or further apart.

Shape tween

It's easy to see how Flash can open up new worlds for creating quick, sleek animation without too much effort. After experimenting with motion tweens (see preceding section), you may find the need to work with symbols a bit limiting, especially if your goal is to modify the shape of an object from start to finish, such as morphing a star into a circle. In this case, you'd want to take advantage of *shape tweens.*

For the most part, shape tweens are created in a very similar manner to motion tweens. However, unlike motion tweens, shape tweens must use raw shapes instead of symbols.

In addition to morphing between distinctively different shapes, shape tweens can morph color. Like motion tweens, you can tween only one shape at a time on a single layer. If you want to create multiple shape tweens simultaneously, you need to isolate each one on its own layer.

To create a shape tween:

1. **Draw a shape (for example, a star or polygon using the Polystar tool) on frame 1.**

   You can include a stroke and fill, as the shape tween can handle both.

2. **Create a blank keyframe on frame 30 by choosing Insert⇨Timeline⇨ Blank Keyframe.**

   As opposed to the motion tween, we choose a blank keyframe here because we don't want a copy of the shape drawn on frame 1 to be carried over to the new keyframe.

3. **Draw a distinctively different shape on the new blank keyframe on frame 30.**

4. **Select frame 1 and choose Insert⇨Timeline⇨Create Shape Tween.**

   You should see an arrow and green shaded area appear between the starting and ending keyframes, indicating that you've successfully created a shape tween.

5. **To see the frames that Flash has created for you, turn on the Onion Skin Outlines option below the Timeline (see Figure 3-7).**

Figure 3-7:
A shape tween with Onion Skin Outlines turned on. Place different artwork on the starting and ending frames to create a shape morph between the two. Just like motion tweens, the distance between the starting and ending keyframes determines the length of the animation.

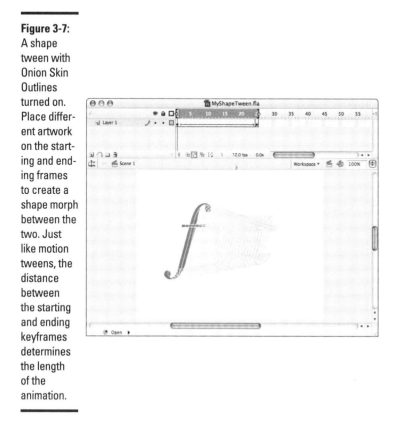

6. **Hit the Return key to play back your animation.**

You now see the original shape transform into the final shape.

Try creating a tween between two type characters, as shown in the preceding steps. Create the letters using the Type tool. You will need to break the characters into their raw forms before creating a shape tween by choosing Modify⇨Break Apart.

Fine-Tuning Tweened Animation

After you've gotten your hands into tweens, you can further fine-tune your animations in a variety of ways. As you work more with tweens, it will be easier for you to create exactly what you want to see.

You can fine-tune two important aspects of tweened animation:

✦ **Duration:** The length of a tweened animation is set by the distance between its starting and ending keyframes. Try creating tweens with fewer or greater frames in between the starting and ending keyframes to see the differences.

✦ **Distance:** Experiment having your objects travel different distances across the stage. Longer distances mean more work for Flash when creating tweens; consider balancing distance and duration to create the smoothest animation possible.

Tweened versus Frame-by-Frame Animation

If you come from a traditional animation background, you may want to create animation the old-fashioned way: frame-by-frame. Flash easily supports this method, but it's best to decide which method you want to use based on what type of animation you want to create.

There are advantages to both methods: While motion and shape tweens give you the power to create sleek animations quickly and easily, you may find they're limited. Frame-by-frame animation, shown in Figure 3-8, is significantly more time consuming and complex to create, but can afford some detail and flexibility that you can't otherwise achieve.

Figure 3-8:
A frame-by-frame animation with Onion Skin Outlines turned on. Each frame contains a different piece of artwork, similar to traditional animation or old-time flip books.

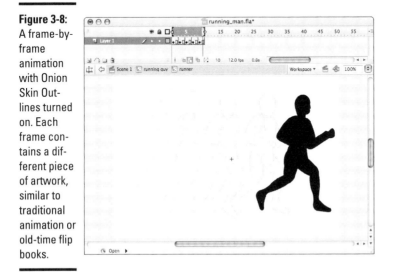

To create a frame-by-frame animation:

1. **Create a blank keyframe for each frame you want to include in your animation.**

   Frames don't have to be consecutive; you can leave space between keyframes to control the time that elapses between each.

2. **Draw (or insert) a graphic for each state of your animation on the appropriate keyframes.**

3. **Play back your animation using the Return key.**

If your goal is to simply move an object from one location to another, create fades, or transform size and rotation, it makes sense to use motion tweens and let Flash do the thinking for you. If you're trying to create highly complex animations that tweens aren't able to handle (for example, a person running), you may want to try the more traditional frame-by-frame approach.

In some cases, you can break your artwork into individual moving parts (like wheels on a bicycle) across several layers to achieve similar affects to frame-by-frame by using motion tweens. You can explore these further in the next chapter.

Understanding Frame Rate

Frame rate plays an important part in the performance and appearance of your Flash movie. It dictates how many frames are played back per second by the Flash player, in turn affecting the speed and smoothness of your animations.

You can modify frame rate in three ways:

✦ Choose Modify⇨Document.

✦ With nothing on the stage selected, use the Property inspector. (You'll see your document properties.)

✦ By clicking the frame rate displayed on the divider below the timeline panel and above the stage.

Frame rate is completely based upon the result you're trying to achieve. While the default frame rate in Flash is 12 fps (frames per second), you may want to consider something around 30fps, which is closer to digital video frame rates and should provide a good starting point for smooth, consistent animation. To keep things in perspective, keep in mind that a film projector (like the one at your local movie theater) runs at 24 fps.

If you want to increase the overall speed and smoothness of your animation, you can try increasing the frame rate gradually until you find the one that's right for you. Flash can support frame rates of up to 100fps.

Changing frame rate affects the playback of your entire movie. If you're trying to adjust the speed of one specific animation, consider removing or adding frames to that particular animation instead.

Chapter 4: Applying More Advanced Animation

In This Chapter

✔ Animating zoom and fade effects

✔ Using the Copy and Paste motion feature

✔ Animating on a path

✔ Masking artwork and animation

*W*ith motion and shape tweens, creative animation possibilities are limited only by your imagination. You'll no doubt want to explore what's possible, and there's no better place to start than some popular animation effects, such as fades and transformations. In addition, new features such as Copy and Paste motion make it easier than ever to re-use complex animations across multiple objects on the stage.

Creating Transformations

Some of the most common effects, such as zooms, flips, leans, and spins, are all different types of *transformations,* or changes to a symbol's dimensions, rotation, or skew. You can perform transformations on a symbol from the Tool pane, Transform panel, or Modify menu, and combine transformations for many animation possibilities.

To create a zoom-in effect:

1. **On the first frame of a new layer, create an interesting shape on the stage using one of the Shape tools.**

2. **With the shape selected, choose Modify⇨Convert To Symbol.**

   The Convert To Symbol dialog box appears.

3. **Name the symbol Zoom Shape, choose the type as Graphic, and click OK.**

   The symbol is added to your Library and is ready to be used as part of a motion tween.

4. **On the same layer, create a keyframe at Frame 25 by choosing Insert⇨ Timeline⇨Keyframe.**

A keyframe is created, and a new instance of the symbol is placed on it, as shown in Figure 4-1.

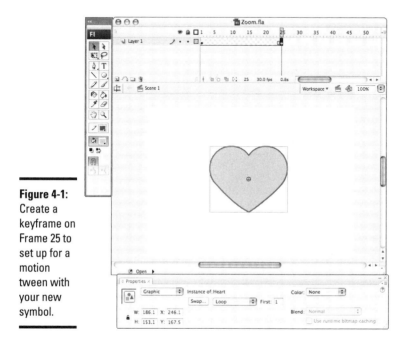

Figure 4-1: Create a keyframe on Frame 25 to set up for a motion tween with your new symbol.

5. **Select the new instance of the symbol using the Selection tool and then choose Window⇨Transform.**

The Transform panel opens.

6. **Using the Transform panel, set the horizontal and vertical scaling to 300%.**

When the animation is added, the smaller instance transforms into the current one, giving the impression of a zoom-in effect.

7. **Set the tween by choosing Motion from the Tween drop-down list.**

An arrow and blue shaded area appears to confirm that the tween has been created.

8. **Click Return to play your movie.**

The smaller instance slowly tweens into the larger one, creating the illusion that you're zooming in closer to the object.

The zoom-out effect is identical to the animation you just created, but in reverse. Rather than starting with the smaller symbol instance, you start with the larger one and gradually pull away by tweening into the smaller one. Instead of creating a new animation, you can copy and reverse the existing one using a few handy shortcuts from the Timeline menu, which appears when you right-click (Windows) or Ctrl+click (Mac) on a frame.

To duplicate and reverse the existing tween:

1. **While holding down the Shift key, select Frame 1 and Frame 25 of your new tween.**

   All frames are now highlighted in black.

2. **Right-click (Windows) or Ctrl+click (Mac) anywhere on the selected frames.**

   The Timeline menu appears.

3. **Choose Copy Frames from the menu to copy the tween to the Clipboard.**

4. **On Frame 26 of the same layer, use the F7 keyboard shortcut key to insert a new Blank Keyframe.**

5. **Select the new keyframe and once again launch the Timeline menu by right-clicking (Windows) or Ctrl+clicking anywhere on the keyframe.**

6. **Choose Paste Frames.**

   The tween you copied is pasted starting on Frame 26.

7. **Select the entire newly pasted tween while holding down the Shift key, starting at Frame 26.**

8. **Using the Timeline menu, select Reverse Frames to reverse the sequence of the newly pasted tween.**

9. **Press Enter to play back the new animation.**

   The animation now appears to zoom in on the symbol and then zoom out!

While the preceding tween is a somewhat simple, the effect can be very much larger than the sum of its parts. Try this on some other symbols and use it to add a dramatic feel to important text.

Creating Fade Ins and Fade Outs

Fade effects are very popular because they can add a cinematic feel to images, text, and graphics. You can see fades used in familiar mediums, such as film, where scenes fade from one to another.

In Flash, fades are a type of basic color transformation that you can apply to any symbol by modifying its transparency, or *alpha*.

To create a fade in:

1. **Create some text on a new layer on the stage using the Type tool.**

   Use no more than two words with a font size of 24 points. You can set the type size and style from the Property inspector when the Type tool is active, so make sure that the panel is visible by choosing Window➪ Properties➪Properties.

2. **Select the type using the Selection tool and convert it to a Graphic symbol by choosing Modify➪Convert To Symbol.**

   This step adds type to the library as a symbol and makes it available for tweening.

3. **On the same layer, select and insert a keyframe at Frame 25 using the F6 keyboard shortcut to create another instance of the symbol at the new keyframe.**

4. **Select the instance of the text on Frame 1 using the Selection tool, locate the Color drop-down list on the right side of the Property inspector, and choose Alpha.**

   Alpha sets the transparency of the symbol from 0 to 100 percent (default is 100 percent, or fully opaque).

5. **Using the slider or type-in box next to the color menu, set the Alpha of the symbol instance to 0 percent.**

   The symbol becomes fully transparent and seems to disappear. (Don't worry; it's still there!)

6. **Select Frame 1 of the layer and set the Motion tween by choosing Motion from the Tween drop-down list on the Property inspector .**

7. **Press Enter to play the movie.**

   The text appears to fade in from nowhere onto the stage (see Figure 4-2)!

Very much like your zoom-out effect, the fade out is simply a reverse of a fade in. You can use the Timeline menu's Reverse Frames command to turn your fade in into a fade out. However, this time you aren't duplicating the tween, just simply reversing it.

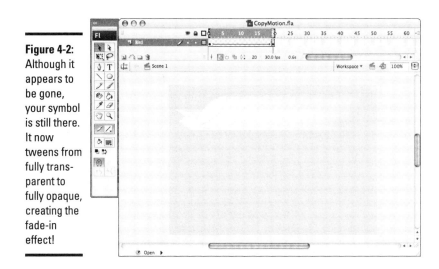

Figure 4-2:
Although it appears to be gone, your symbol is still there. It now tweens from fully trans-parent to fully opaque, creating the fade-in effect!

1. **While holding down the Shift key, select the first and last keyframes of your fade-in tween.**

This step highlights all the frames in the animation.

2. **Right-click (Windows) or Ctrl+click (Mac) anywhere on the selected frames to open the Timeline menu and choose Reverse Frames.**

The action reverses so that the starting symbol instance is fully opaque.

3. **Press Enter to play the movie.**

The text you created now fades out on the stage.

Try duplicating and then reversing the fade-in tween to have the text fade in and then out.

Copying and Pasting Motion

One of the most welcome new additions to Flash is the ability to copy the behavior of a motion tween and then paste it to a completely different symbol instance. This technique is handy if you need to have multiple objects follow the same exact animation behavior, such as birds of different colors and sizes all following the same flight pattern.

Book VII
Chapter 4

Applying More
Advanced
Animation

To copy and paste motion, you need an existing tween to copy from and then a symbol instance on a different layer to copy *to*. The following steps create a basic motion tween that you can then copy and apply to a different symbol later.

1. **Draw a basic shape on a new layer using one of the Shape tools and position the shape on the left side of the stage using the Selection tool.**

2. **Select the shape and choose Modify⇨Convert to Symbol.**

3. **When the dialog box appears, enter a name for your symbol, set the type as Graphic, and click OK.**

   The symbol is added to the Library and is ready to be tweened.

4. **On the same layer, select and create a keyframe on the timeline where you'd like the tween to complete using the F6 keyboard shortcut.**

5. **Select the new instance of your symbol on the ending keyframe and position it on the opposite side of the stage.**

6. **Create a motion tween on the starting keyframe using the Tween menu on the Property inspector .**

   The symbol now moves from left to right across the stage.

7. **While holding down the Shift key, select the first and last keyframes of the new tween and right-click (Windows) or Ctrl+click (Mac) to open the Timeline menu; choose *Copy Motion* to copy the tween behavior.**

8. **Create a new layer and drag an instance of the new symbol you created from the Library onto the stage on Frame 1.**

9. **Select Frame 1 of the new layer and right-click (Windows) or Ctrl+ click (Mac) to open the Timeline menu; choose Paste Motion.**

   This step applies the tween behavior you copied earlier to the new symbol instance, and a tween that follows the same pattern appears.

10. **Press Enter to play your movie.**

    Both symbol instances should now have the identical tween in play.

In the preceding example, you worked with two instances of the same symbol, but the beauty of this new feature is that you can copy and paste tweens between completely nonrelated symbol instances. You can also paste motion between symbol instances that have drastically different size, color, and rotation properties.

Animating Along a Path with Motion Guides

The motion tweens described earlier in the chapter have involved simple animation from one location to another, always following a straight path of movement. For some tweens, you'll want to have your symbol follow a more elaborate path of motion, such as a racecar following a track. For these cases, you can give your tween a specific path to follow using a *motion guide*. A motion guide is a special layer that contains a single path that a tween can follow. On the motion guide layer, you draw the path using tools, such as the Pen, Pencil, or Line Tools.

A motion guide layer can control several tweens at once, but a tween can follow only one motion guide at a time. Before adding a motion guide, you first need a layer that contains a tween. Then you can create and guide the tween along the new motion guide path.

Before you begin, make sure that you enable snapping by choosing View➪ Snapping➪Snap To Objects. (Snap To Objects should be checked.) Snapping makes connecting your tween to the new motion easier.

Motion guides are even better when you work with a shape that has an obvious orientation (or direction, such as the nose of a car or airplane). For this reason, you'll be creating a triangle as your tweened object in the following steps.

1. **Select the PolyStar tool on the Tools panel and choose both a fill and stroke color from the bottom of the panel or Property inspector .**

2. **On the Property inspector , select the Options button and use the dialog box that appears to set the number of sides for your Polygon to 3.**

Choosing this option enables you to easily create a triangle on the stage.

3. **Draw a triangle on the bottom-left corner of the stage and, while it's still selected, use the F8 shortcut key to convert it to a symbol.**

4. **When the Convert To Symbol dialog box appears, set the Type as Graphic and assign it a name.**

5. **Create a motion tween from Frame 1 to Frame 20; have the triangle move from the bottom-left to the bottom-right corner, as shown in Figure 4-3.**

**Book VII
Chapter 4**

**Applying More
Advanced
Animation**

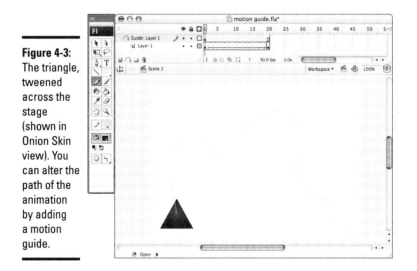

Figure 4-3:
The triangle, tweened across the stage (shown in Onion Skin view). You can alter the path of the animation by adding a motion guide.

(If you're not sure how to create a motion tween, see Chapter 3 of this minibook.) When your tween is complete, you add the motion guide layer where you create a new path for the tween to follow.

6. **Select the layer you're working on and click the Add Motion Guide icon below the timeline.**

   A new layer appears above the one you're working on; this new motion guide layer is now attached to your tween layer.

   You now need to create a path on the motion guide layer for your tween to follow.

7. **Select the Motion Guide layer and then, using your Pencil tool from the Tools panel, draw a freehand path that starts on the lower-left corner and works its way around the stage and down to the lower-right corner where your motion tween currently ends.**

8. **After completing your path, create a keyframe on the motion guide layer at Frame 20 using the F6 shortcut key.**

   This keyframe ensures that the path will be visible (and available) from the beginning to the end of the tween.

9. **Return to your tween layer and select the instance of the triangle symbol on Frame 1.**

   You need to snap the symbol to the beginning of the path you've created on the motion guide layer so that it 'finds' the path and knows where to begin.

Snap to it: The importance of snapping

Snapping is an essential part of your workflow and can very often make positioning items on the stage much easier and more accurate. Snapping is like turning on a magnet; when you drag an object, it jumps to the closest guide, path, or object that it finds on the stage, depending on what type of snapping you've enabled. Snapping is great for lining up objects with each other, positioning artwork on a ruler guide, and especially when positioning a symbol on the beginning or end of a motion guide path.

By default, snapping is enabled for alignment, guides, and objects. Additionally, you can enable *Snap To Grid* (when working with a grid) or *Snap To Pixels*, which makes sure that objects are positioned on the stage to the nearest whole pixel.

You can find snapping options by choosing View⇨Snapping, where you can also fine-tune snapping behavior by choosing the Edit Snapping menu.

10. **Grab the symbol by its registration point (the circle in the center) and drag it until it 'snaps' to the beginning of the path.**

11. **Select the instance of the triangle symbol on Frame 20 and drag the symbol by its registration point until it 'snaps' to the end of the path you created.**

12. **Press Enter to play your movie.**

    The symbol follows the path you created.

You can create motion guide paths using any tool that creates paths, even the Shape tools. The Brush tool, however, can't be used to create a motion guide path because it creates fills, not paths. While it's easier to use paths that have an obvious beginning and end, closed paths work fine most of the time.

Be cautious of paths that overlap themselves; the results may not be what you expect!

Fine-Tuning Motion Guides

After you set up a motion guide, you can use the Property inspector to fine-tune how your tween follows and moves along the new path. One of the most common options is Orient To Path, a check box found on the Property inspector when you select the first frame of the tween. This option makes sure that the symbol maintains its orientation as it follows the path by facing itself in the direction that the path is going. Orientation is especially important for something like a car or airplane, which needs to always face the direction in which it's traveling.

To use Orient To Path:

1. **Select the first frame of a tween layer.**

2. **On the Property inspector, locate and check the box that reads Orient To Path.**

3. **Press Enter to play your movie.**

The symbol rotates and faces the direction it's traveling as the tween plays.

If your symbol needs to face down at the end of the tween, rotate it on the last frame using the Transform tool so that it's pointing downward. Otherwise, the symbol tries to position itself upright on the last frame, even if the path is pointing downward and Orient To Path is selected.

Creating Inertia and Gravity with Easing

When objects take motion in real life, several factors affect their speed as they move. You can reproduce the two most recognizable forces, inertia and gravity, by using a special tween option known as *Ease*. Ease is available as a tween option on the Property inspector and controls the variation in the speed of an object from the beginning of a tween to the end.

Take the example of a ball bouncing up and down on a sidewalk: When the ball hits the ground and bounces, it loses speed as it moves upward because gravity pulls it back toward the ground. When the ball changes direction and moves back downward, increased gravity makes it pick up speed as it nears the ground again.

To use the Ease option:

1. **Select the Oval tool, and on a new layer, create a perfect circle at the bottom of the stage.**

Hold down the Shift key to constrain the circle as you draw it.

2. **With the new circle selected, use the F8 keyboard shortcut to convert it to a Graphic symbol and name the circle.**

In this example, we named the circle Ball.

3. **Create a second keyframe on the same layer using the F6 keyboard shortcut.**

A new instance of the Ball symbol appears.

4. **Position this symbol at the top of the stage while leaving its horizontal position the same (see Figure 4-4).**

Hold down the Shift key while dragging upward to keep the symbol from shifting left or right.

5. **Create a motion tween from the first keyframe.**

If you want to preview the tween, press Enter. The ball should move from the bottom of the stage to the top.

6. **To add some gravitational pull, select the starting keyframe of the tween and locate the Ease slider on the Property inspector.**

By default, Ease is set a 0. Setting it to a positive number sets the Ease to Out, decreasing the speed as the tween approaches the end.

7. **Because your ball needs to fight gravity going up, set the value of the slider to 100.**

8. **Preview the animation by pressing Enter.**

The ball slows down as the tween comes to a close, as if it's fighting gravity on the way up.

Figure 4-4:
Move the
Ball
instance on
Frame 25
straight up
while
holding the
Shift key.
The result-
ing tween
moves the
ball from the
bottom to
the top of
the stage
in a straight
line.

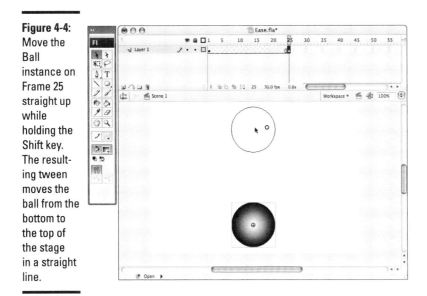

You can see how Ease affects the speed of the tween as it progresses, and now a simple animation becomes much more lifelike. However, what goes up must come down, so the following steps walk you through making the ball return to the ground.

1. **While holding down the Shift key, select the starting and ending keyframes of your tween to highlight the entire motion tween.**

2. **Right-click (windows) or Ctrl+click (Mac) any of the selected frames to open the Timeline menu and choose Copy Frames.**

3. **Select the frame] right after the last keyframe and create a Blank Keyframe using the F7 keyboard shortcut.**

   You'll be pasting the frames you copied on this new keyframe.

4. **With the new keyframe selected, launch the Timeline menu and choose Paste Frames to paste the tween you copied in Step 2.**

5. **Select the entire newly pasted tween and launch the Timeline menu; choose Reverse Frames to flip the tween backward.**

6. **Preview your animation by pressing Enter.**

   The ball now goes up and then down, and conveniently the animation is not only reversed, but so is the Ease.

Animating Across Layers

You can tween only one object on a layer at a time. If you want to create more complex animations, however, all you need to do is use layers to stack tweens that need to play simultaneously.

For example, for a bouncing ball animation, you can add an animated shadow on a new layer that occurs at the same time as your bouncing ball. (To find out how to create a bouncing ball, see the preceding section.)

Before you get started, create a new layer using the Insert Layer icon on the left below the timeline. Name the layer Shadow and drag it below the layer that contains your Ball tween. Then follow these steps:

1. **Select the Oval tool and, using the Tools panel, choose a Fill color and set the Stroke to None.**

   For this example, we chose a light grey Fill color.

2. **On the new shadow layer, draw an oval below the ball.**

The oval should be about the same width as the ball, but with a shorter height setting.

3. **Convert the new oval to a Graphic symbol using the F8 keyboard shortcut.**

   Your symbol is now ready to be tweened.

4. **Create a keyframe on a later frame on the same layer, and create a motion tween starting at the first frame of the layer.**

   In the next step, you manipulate the shadow on the last keyframe to appear as it should when the object moves further away from the ground.

5. **Select the instance of the oval on the last keyframe and use the Transform tool to reduce its size by about 50 percent.**

6. **With the oval still selected, locate the Color drop-down list on the Property inspector and set it to Alpha; reduce the transparency of the oval to 50 percent using the slider.**

7. **Select Frame 1 of the layer and locate the Ease slider on the Property inspector.**

8. **You need to ease the animation of the shadow to match that of the ball, so set the Ease to 100 for an ease out.**

9. **Press Enter to preview your animation.**

   The shadow animates simultaneously to the ball and appears to become smaller and lighter as the ball leaves the ground.

Fine-Tuning Shape Tweens with Shape Hinting

Chapter 3 of this minibook explores the possibilities of morphing shape and color with Shape tweens. Flash does a great job of recalculating shapes during a tween, but sometimes you need to give it a little help, especially when you have two shapes that have common features. Flash may overthink things and perform more shape morphing than it has to. For these cases, you can use shape hints — sets of matched markers that can tell Flash that two points on two different shapes are related. You can attach shape hints to the outlines of shapes on starting and ending frames of a shape tween to let Flash know what common points exist between the two.

A good example of related shapes are the letters F and T. The two letters have many common angles. A shape tween between the two is a great way to make use of shape hints.

Before you get started, create a new document. Select the Type tool and, using the Property inspector, set the font style to Arial Black (or equivalent) and the font size to 200.

1. **On the first frame of a new layer, type the letter F in the middle of the stage.**

2. **Select the letter using the Selection tool and choose Modify⇨ Break Apart to break the type down to its raw outlines.**

3. **On a later frame on the same layer, create a new blank keyframe using the F7 keyboard shortcut.**

4. **Type the letter T on the new keyframe and position it in the same place as the F on first frame.**

   You can use the Property inspector to match the X and Y positions, if necessary.

5. **Break the T apart by choosing Modify⇨Break Apart.**

6. **Create a shape tween on from the first frame by choosing Shape from the Tween menu on the Property inspector.**

   An arrow and green shaded area appears, indicating that the tween was created successfully.

7. **Press Enter to preview your movie.**

   The F morphs into the T.

Even though the shape tween was successful, the outcome may not have been what you expected. Chances are the F seems to get mashed up (instead of a smooth transition) before being completely reconstructed into the T because Flash can't see the common angles between the two shapes (even though you can). That's where shape hints come in. You can add shape hints to suggest common points to Flash and smooth out the tween.

Before you get started, make sure that Snap To Objects is enabled by choosing View⇨Snapping⇨Snap To Objects.

1. **Select Frame 1 of your shape tween and choose View⇨Show Shape Hints to turn on shape hinting.**

2. **Choose Modify⇨Shape⇨Add Shape Hint to create a new shape hint on the stage.**

   A red button, labeled with the letter *a*, appears.

3. **Repeat Step 2 to add another shape hint.**

This time, the shape hint appears labeled with the letter b.

Sometimes shape hints stack on top of each other; move one to reveal the others underneath if only one is visible.

4. **Position the two shape hints on the outline of the F.**

To do so, move shape hint (b) over just a bit so that you can see shape hint (a). Then move (a) and snap it to the upper left corner of the F. Position the second shape hint (b) in the lower left corner of the F.

5. **Select Frame 20.**

You see the companions to the shape hints you created, waiting to be positioned.

6. **Position (a) and (b).**

This step matches the left top and bottom corners of the T to the ones in F, and the buttons turn green to indicate a successful match.

7. **Press Enter to preview your animation.**

If you watch carefully, you see that the shape hints are keeping those two corners anchored while the rest of the shape transforms, creating a smoother transition.

Note: Like motion guides, shape hints don't appear in your final, published movie.

Add Shape Hints using the shortcut key combination: Shift+Ctrl+H (Windows) or Shift+⌘+H (Mac).

You can also add some remaining hints to finalize your tween.

1. **Select Frame 1 of your shape tween and make sure that shape hints are still visible by choosing View⫐Show Shape Hints.**

If they're already enabled, you see a check mark.

2. **Create three new shape hints using the keyboard shortcut Shift+Ctrl+H (Windows) or Shift+⌘+H (Mac).**

3. **Position the shape hints on the F (see Figure 4-5) on the top right, bottom right, and middle.**

4. **Select Frame 20, and you see the companions to the three new shape hints waiting to be placed.**

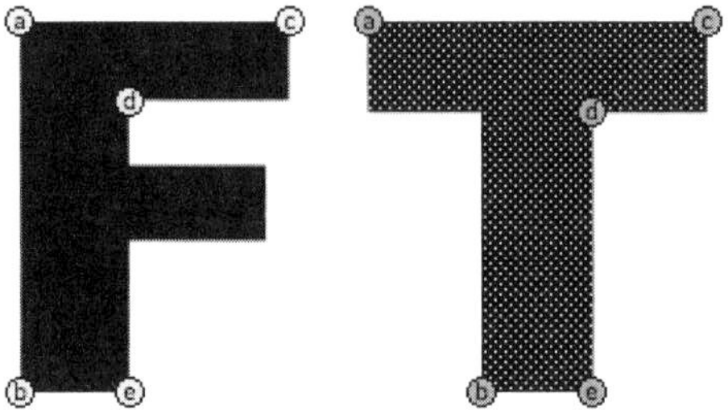

Figure 4-5:
Position the
three new
shape hints
as shown
on both the
F and T.

5. **Position them on the T to match the angles you marked on the F.**

6. **Press Enter to play your animation.**

> You see that the shape hints have provided a much smoother transition from what you initially started with.

Shape hints have their own contextual menu that appears when you right-click (Windows) or Ctrl+click (Mac) on any shape hint on the first frame of a shape tween. To clear a selected shape hint, choose Remove Shape Hint or choose Remove All Hints to clear all hints on the stage and start over.

Using Mask Layers

The concept of masking involves using a shape (or shapes) to hide or reveal portions of a piece of artwork — working very much like a small window in your house. You can see only what the window allows you to see when you're inside. Flash features a special type of layer, known as a *mask,* and its contents are used to selectively reveal (or hide) artwork or animation on another layer.

You can convert any layer into a mask by using the Layer contextual menu, which is launched with a right-click (Windows) or Ctrl+click (Mac) on the layer's name area. Artwork on a mask layer isn't visible; the content of a mask layer always represents the *visible* area of the layer underneath.

Animated text is a great candidate for masking. The following steps take you through creating a tween to which you add a mask layer for added effect. Before you get started, create a new document and select the Type tool. Choose a stroke and fill color and use your Property inspector to set the type face to Arial Black (or similar) and font size to 40.

1. **Select your Text tool and type** FLASH ROCKS **in capital letters.**

   You animate this text via a motion tween.

2. **Select the text using the Selection tool, and convert it to a new graphic symbol by choosing Modify⇨Convert To Symbol or by using the F8 keyboard shortcut.**

3. **Place the text off of the stage to the left so that it's sitting in the work area.**

   You'll be animating the text and bringing it across the stage entering from one side and exiting on the other (see Figure 4-6).

4. **Create a keyframe on Frame 40 of the same layer.**

   An instance of the text is created there as well.

5. **Move this text off the stage all the way to the right.**

6. **Create a motion tween between Frames 1 and 40.**

   This tween animates the text across the stage left to right. Now you're ready to create a mask layer.

7. **Insert a new layer above the tween layer and name it Mask; use the Polystar tool to create a star in the center of the stage.**

   The Star option for the Polystar tool is available on the Property inspector under Options. Make sure that the star is at least as tall as the text symbol you created.

8. **Right-click (Windows) or Ctrl+click (Mac) the new layer name and choose Mask from the Layer menu that appears.**

   The new layer is converted to a mask layer, and the tween layer appears indented underneath. Both layers are automatically locked.

9. **Press Enter to play your movie.**

   The text animates, appearing through the shape of the star, much like viewing the animation through a window.

For the masking layer to take effect, both the mask layer and the layer being masked must be locked. However, to edit the contents of either layer, just unlock them.

Mask layers can contain just about anything a standard layer can, including tweens. Try to create a motion tween on your mask layer and see what happens!

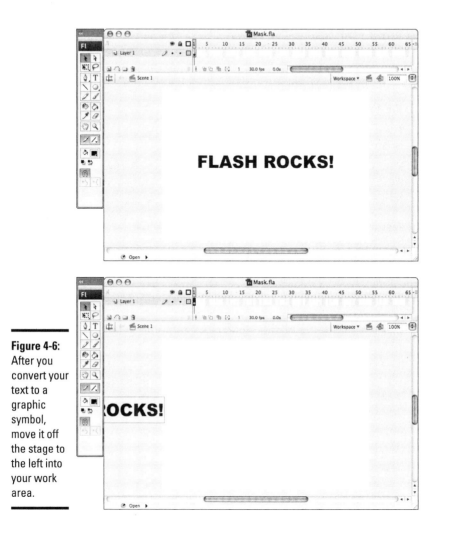

Figure 4-6:
After you convert your text to a graphic symbol, move it off the stage to the left into your work area.

Previewing Your Movie

Previewing your movie in the Flash player to check its speed and size is a good idea. To view your movie in Preview mode, choose File⇨Publish Preview⇨Flash or use the keyboard shortcut Ctrl+Enter (Windows) or ⌘+Return (Mac).

This step creates an `.swf` file from your current authoring file and displays it immediately in the Flash player. Previewing is a great way to see how your movie will actually appear to your users and can highlight any potential snags.

Ultimately, the final viewing environment for most Flash movies is on the Web in a browser, such as Internet Explorer, Safari, or Firefox. Part of what Flash creates for you at publish time isn't only a finished `.swf`, but also an HTML page to contain your movie. To see how your movie looks as viewed in a browser, choose File⇨Publish Preview⇨Default (HTML). Your default system browser launches and presents your movie in a Web page, just as your user will see it.

Chapter 5: Importing Graphics and Sounds

In This Chapter

✔ Importing photos and vector artwork

✔ Using the new Photoshop & Illustrator Import panel

✔ Adding sounds to your movie

✔ Getting ready to publish

*Y*ou may decide to enhance your Flash movies with the addition of photos or graphics created in other applications, such as Photoshop CS3 and Illustrator CS3. Flash natively supports Photoshop and Illustrator file format imports, as well as many popular image formats. Combine this feature with the ability to import and utilize `.mp v3` and other popular sound formats, and you can truly make your Flash movies a multimedia experience.

Bitmap versus Vector Artwork

In computer-based design, you need to be aware of two graphic types: bitmap and vector. The drawing environment in Flash natively creates vector graphics, but you can use both bitmap and vector graphics in a Flash movie.

Vector graphics refers to scaleable artwork consisting of points, paths, and fills that the computer creates based on mathematical formulas. While you may see a plain red rectangle, Flash sees an equation that creates the points, paths, and fill color necessary to recreate the graphic. Changing the rectangle's size, position, or color is a matter of simply recalculating the formula and redrawing the shape. As a result, vector graphics maintain crisp quality even when scaled far beyond their original size. Flash (like its cousin Illustrator CS3) can natively create detailed vector illustrations and typography that you can easily scale or modify.

Bitmap graphics are created very much like the picture on your TV set. If you've ever looked closely at a tube television, you'll see the picture is created from lots of multicolored, tightly arranged dots. The same is true of bitmap graphics, which are created from many pixels of varying colors on your computer screen. The detail of the image can vary based on how many *pixels,* or dots, are used per inch to create the image. This amount is referred to as *dpi.* Due to the immense range of colors and detail that bitmap images can recreate, they're the format of choice for digital photographs and photo art. Flash does not natively create bitmap graphics, but easily imports a variety of popular image formats and natively supports Photoshop (.psd) files.

Bitmap images are created with a certain amount of pixel data; rescaling the image means either eliminating that data or trying to create information where it didn't exist before. For this reason, bitmaps are far more limited than vectors in terms of scalability, and can lose quality quickly if scaled too far beyond their original size, as shown in Figure 5-1.

Figure 5-1:
Left: A star created with vector graphics uses points, lines, and fills. Right: The same star created as a bitmap. Both are 40 x 40 pixels, zoomed at 400 percent. The bitmap image begins to pixelate as you zoom in, revealing the pixels that create it.

Importing Other File Formats

Your choice of file formats is going to be based on what applications you commonly work with. Flash supports many popular file formats, as well as industry-standard Photoshop and Illustrator file formats, giving you lots of flexibility. Flash doesn't generate bitmap artwork, though, so you may ask yourself what format you should use to save photos, graphics, and type created in other applications before you import them into Flash.

Flash supports and imports the following file formats:

✦ Illustrator CS3 (.ai)

✦ Photoshop CS3 (.psd)

✦ Encapsulated PostScript (.eps)

✦ Flash SWF (.swf)

✦ JPEG

✦ GIF

✦ PNG

Flash, like many Web-centric applications, works at screen resolution: 72 dpi. Images at higher (or lower) resolutions are conformed to screen resolution upon import, and their sizes on the Flash stage may be different than what you expect.

Vector graphics, such as illustrations and typography, can be created in applications like Adobe Illustrator CS3. Artwork that contains layers should be saved natively as Illustrator (.ai) format because Flash can import and re-create those layers exactly as they were in the original document without loss of quality. You work with the Adobe Illustrator Import panel to view and distribute imported layers in the "Importing Photoshop and Illustrator Files" section in this chapter.

Bitmap graphics, such as photos, can be saved and imported in a variety of formats. If you're working with a layered Photoshop document, you can import the document (.psd) directly into Flash using the new Photoshop Import panel. Like the Illustrator Import panel, you can view and choose how to distribute layers into Flash. Layer effects, such as drop shadows, are maintained, and where possible, they're converted into their Flash equivalents.

Other popular formats include JPEG, GIF, and PNG:

✦ **JPEG** (Joint Photographic Experts Group) can reproduce the wide range of color and detail necessary to reproduce photographs while keeping file size reasonable, and as such, are the best choice for photo-centric documents (see Figure 5-2).

Figure 5-2:
JPEGs have the color depth necessary to reproduce rich and detailed photos, as shown here.

+ **GIF** (see Figure 5-3) is a lightweight format with a limited color gamut (range) of 256 colors and is a good choice for reproducing crisp type, logos, and titling. GIF also supports transparency, so it's a good choice when the graphics you need to import need to be placed discretely against varying backgrounds.

Figure 5-3:
GIFs have a limited color range, but they are great for generating lightweight, clean bitmap graphics such as logos and type.

★ Stellar Graphics

+ **PNG** format has capabilities that cross over between those of JPEGs and GIFs. PNG also supports transparency and, based on the PNG type (PNG-8 or PNG-24), can reproduce both simple graphics and photos with depth and accuracy.

Ultimately, your choice of format depends on what type of graphics you're working with and how they work in context with the rest of your Flash movie.

Importing Bitmap Images

When you need to make use of a photo or graphic file, such as a JPEG, GIF, or PNG, you need to import it into Flash by choosing File⇨Import.

Imported bitmaps are added to your Library as *assets*. Assets aren't to be mistaken for symbols, which you can duplicate and manage from the Library. Assets are simply non-Flash items that you import, store, and use throughout your movie. While bitmap assets can be converted to symbols, they're not automatically converted upon import; you still need to add them as symbols (see Chapter 3 of this minibook).

To import a bitmap image:

1. **In a new Flash document, choose File⇨Import⇨Import To Stage.**

The Import dialog box appears, asking you to find a file on your local computer.

To import an image (or images) to the Library for later use, such as a series of photos that will be used in a photo gallery, choose File⇨Import⇨Import To Library. This command places the chosen images directly in the Library so that you can use them when you're ready.

2. **Locate a photo file (such as a JPEG or GIF) from your hard drive, select it, and click Open (Windows) or Import (Mac).**

The file will be imported and placed on your stage on the currently active layer.

3. **Locate and open your Library panel (Window⇨Library), and you see that the photo has also been placed in your Library.**

If you try to import an image to the stage and the currently active layer is locked, the Import To Stage option will be unavailable (grayed out). In that case, choose a different, unlocked layer or unlock the currently active layer.

Converting Bitmap Images to Symbols

Once on the stage or in the Library, a bitmap image can be converted to a symbol just like any other graphic on your stage. The process is the same, and the image inherits the same abilities that graphic symbols do, including tween ability, tint, transparency, and management from a master symbol in the Library.

To convert a bitmap image to a symbol:

1. Choose an imported bitmap from the Library and drag it to the stage.

If you already have a bitmap on the stage, select it with the Selection tool.

2. Choose Modify⇨Convert To Symbol.

The Convert To Symbol dialog box will appear.

3. Select the Type as Graphic, assign the bitmap a name, and set the registration point using the grid.

You can also convert bitmaps to button and Movie Clip types as well. Just change the symbol type when you define the symbol.

4. Click OK to complete the conversion.

Your bitmap image appears as a new Graphic symbol in your Library. You can now drag several instances to the stage, tween, and transform it.

Symbols created from imported bitmaps create dependencies and continue to reference the original raw bitmaps in the Library. Deleting raw bitmap assets from the Library causes them to disappear from any symbols that use them.

Modifying tint and transparency

After you convert a bitmap image to a symbol, you can apply the same transparency and color effects available to graphic symbols. To create these effects, you'll use the Color drop-down list on the Property inspector , so make sure that your Property inspector is visible (choose Window⇨ Properties⇨Properties) before you get started.

To apply a color tint:

1. Drag a symbol from your Library panel onto the stage that uses an imported image.

2. Locate the Color drop-down list on the right side of your Property inspector and select Tint.

A percentage slider and color swatch appear.

3. Click the swatch and choose a color from the swatches panel and then adjust the amount of color applied using the percentage slider (see Figure 5-4).

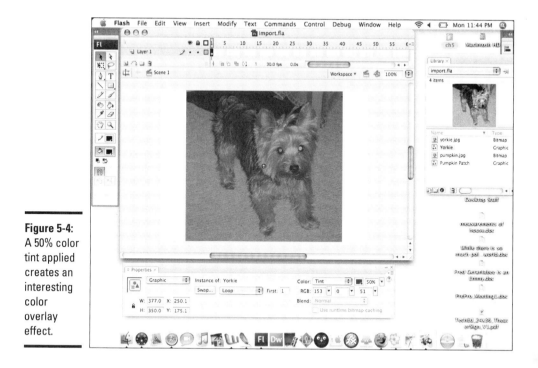

Figure 5-4:
A 50% color tint applied creates an interesting color overlay effect.

Note: Flash remembers Color settings, such as Tint and Alpha percentages between uses (see Figure 5-5). If you set an object to 50 percent alpha, the next time you select Alpha for a symbol, Flash automatically applies the same 50 percent setting again (which you can easily change using the slider).

Applying motion tweens

Any bitmap that has been converted to a symbol can have motion tweens applied in the exact same way as you would with any other symbol.

When you're working with symbols created from images, you open up creative options, such as cinematic fades, moving slideshows, and unique presentation ideas.

To create a motion tween with a bitmap image:

1. **Drag an instance of a bitmap-based symbol to your stage from the Library panel onto a new, empty layer.**

The instance should be on Frame 1 of the new layer.

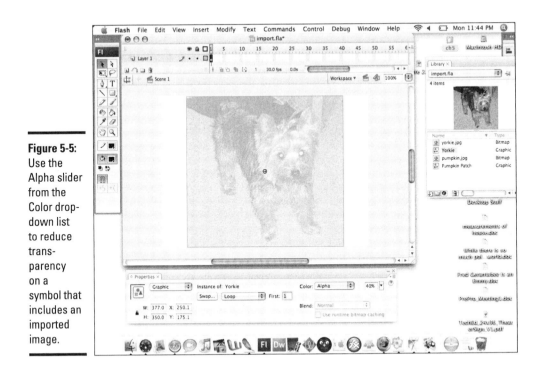

Figure 5-5:
Use the
Alpha slider
from the
Color drop-
down list
to reduce
trans-
parency
on a
symbol that
includes an
imported
image.

2. **Create a keyframe on Frame 20 of the same layer (F6 key).**

An instance of the symbol is created on this frame as well.

3. **Select the instance of the symbol on Frame 1; position it off the stage to the left.**

4. **While Frame 1 is still selected, launch the Property inspector and choose alpha from the Color drop-down list; set the Alpha percentage to 0%.**

5. **Select Frame 1 and use the Tween menu on the Property inspector to create a motion tween between Frames 1 and 20.**

6. **Press Enter to play the animation.**

The image (symbol) appears to slide and fade in from the left side of the stage, as shown in Figure 5-6.

Figure 5-6:
The
completed
tween has
your image
fading and
flying in
from the left
(shown here
in Onion
Skin view).

Creating Bitmap Fills

As an alternative to solid colors or gradients, bitmap images can be used as fills for shapes, illustrations, and even type. Bitmap fills can create very cool effects and let you add interesting photographic textures to enhance your artwork.

You can create bitmap fills from existing bitmaps already been imported into your Library, or you can use the Color panel to import a bitmap whenever you need to create a new bitmap fill.

To create a bitmap fill:

1. **Create a shape on the stage, as shown in Figure 5-7; set a fill and stroke color using the swatches at the bottom of the Tools panel.**

2. **Select the shape using the Selection arrow and launch the Color panel by choosing Window⇨Color.**

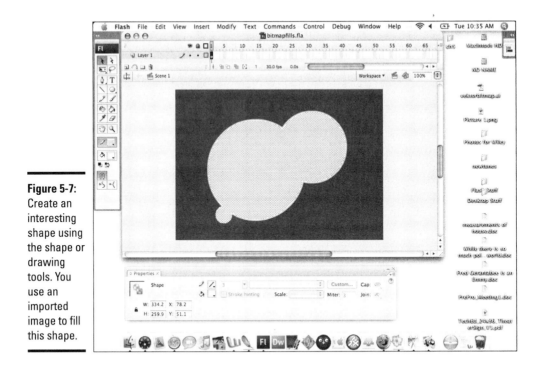

Figure 5-7:
Create an
interesting
shape using
the shape or
drawing
tools. You
use an
imported
image to fill
this shape.

3. **Make the fill color active by clicking the Paint Bucket icon.**

4. **Locate the Type menu and choose Bitmap from the list.**

If you have no bitmaps in your Library, choose a bitmap file from the Import To Library dialog box that appears.

Or, if you have bitmaps already in your Library, a thumbnail preview of each appears at the bottom of the Color panel. Choose the one you want to fill the shape with.

The shape is now filled with the bitmap you chose (see Figure 5-8).

To use a bitmap fill on type, you first have to break the type apart by choosing Modify⇨Break Apart. Type is created and edited on a type path, so you need to break it off the path and down to its raw form (points and paths).

After you apply a bitmap fill, you may want to adjust the positioning and size of the bitmap within the fill area. Use the Gradient Transform tool (located underneath the Transform tool). Gradients and Bitmap fills, while very different, both have a visible orientation point that you can adjust.

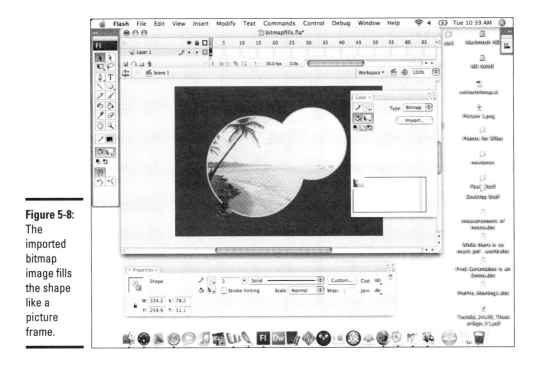

Figure 5-8:
The imported bitmap image fills the shape like a picture frame.

To position a bitmap fill, select the Gradient Transform tool and select a shape that uses a bitmap fill. Drag the center point of the circular bounding box that appears to reposition the bitmap, or use the outside handles to rotate, scale, and skew the bitmap.

Importing Photoshop and Illustrator Files

Flash now offers seamless import of Photoshop and Illustrator files with the all-new Illustrator and Photoshop Import panels. Graphics created in these applications can now be imported with ease and the highest quality possible, which is great news if Photoshop and Illustrator are already an essential part of your creative workflow.

With the new Import panels, you can view, select, and convert Photoshop layers to symbols or keyframes or distribute them to Flash layers while maintaining common layer effects, such as drop shadows and blurs. The ability to select individual layers means that you can use specific elements from .psd and .ai files without the need to bring in lots of unnecessary art from complex files.

Importing Photoshop (.psd) files

Whether you need simple photography or complex compiled artwork, the new Photoshop Import options make it easy to import any level of .psd file while keeping individual layers editable, even with Type layers and effects. You can distribute Photoshop layers to Flash layers, sequence them as keyframes, or individually convert layer contents to symbols that are added to your Library.

Flash even supports Photoshop Layer Comps, so you can choose from and import any Layer Comp in your .psd file.

Before you begin, locate a Photoshop file that you'd like to import into Flash. A great example would be a file that combines layers, type, and basic use of Photoshop Layer styles (such as drop shadows).

To import a Photoshop file:

1. **Choose File⇨Import⇨Import To Stage.**

2. **When the Import dialog box appears, choose a Photoshop file from your hard drive and click Open (Windows) or Choose (Mac).**

   The Import To Stage dialog box appears with full Photoshop file import options and a full view of all layers in your file.

3. **Using the check boxes next to each layer, select the layers you want to import into Flash.**

   Now, you can set options for how to import the contents of each layer.

4. **Highlight one of the layers you've chosen to Import.**

   You can choose from several options appear on the right side of the panel. (See the sidebar on the Photoshop Import options panel for a detailed explanation of each option.)

5. **Set options and check the box next to each layer you want to import.**

6. **Click OK to import the file.**

   The artwork you selected appears on your stage (see Figure 5-9.)

Because you can selectively import layers, as well as merge layers together directly from the Import panel, consider using .psd files instead of importing flattened artwork (such as JPEGs or GIFs). This new panel allows you to extract specific elements and maintain transparency from Photoshop layers.

The new Photoshop Import Options panel

The new Photoshop Import Options panel gives you a detailed choice of what and how it gets imported from `.psd` files. You can send bitmap artwork directly to the Library as assets or movie clips; type and vector layers can be converted or kept as editable paths or type layers.

Here's a detailed look at what you see in this new panel:

Select Photoshop Layer Comp: If your document contains Layer Comps, you can select one from this menu. The layers and positioning that makes up the selected comp become active in the Layers view.

Layers View: All layers in your `.psd` appear in this panel, and you can choose which layers to import by selecting the check boxes to the left. Highlighting a layer displays its Import Options on the right.

Merge Layers button: When more than one layer is highlighted, you can choose to merge the layers on import into a single layer, which has no effect on the original `.psd`.

Convert Layers To [Flash Layers | Keyframes]: The Flash Layers option keeps layer structure (as well as layer groups) and distributes layer contents exactly as they are in your `.psd` file. The Keyframes option distributes layer contents across a sequence of keyframes on the timeline.

Place Layers At Original Position: This option (checked by default) positions layer contents exactly as they are in the original `.psd`.

Set Stage To Same Size As Photoshop Canvas: This option resizes your movie to match the original size of the `.psd` file.

Import This Image As: This option converts the layer contents to either a bitmap image with editable Flash filter effects (converted from Photoshop layer styles or a Flattened Bitmap image which merges any applied Layer styles along with the bitmap image).

Editable Paths And Layer Styles (Shape Layers Only): You can keep shape layers and vector artwork editable in Flash with this option, which places artwork on the stage as drawing objects.

Editable Text (Type Layers Only): This option keeps imported text layers editable, recreating Photoshop type layers as Flash type layers.

Vector Outlines (Type Layers Only): This option converts type layers into raw vector graphics (drawing objects). Type is no longer editable, but its outline can be manipulated using tools such as the Subselection arrow and Pen tool.

Create Movie Clip For This Layer: This option converts the layer contents to a new Movie clip symbol that is also added to your Library. You have the option of setting a registration point as well as an instance name. (See Chapter 6 of this minibook for more on instance names.)

Publish Settings: For each layer, you can set individual compression and quality settings or choose to use the document's Publish Settings instead. A handy Calculate Bitmap Size button lets you see how your selected compression and quality settings affect the resulting file size of the imported content.

**Book VII
Chapter 5**

Importing Graphics and Sounds

Figure 5-9:
The Photoshop file has been successfully imported, and the layers are ordered exactly as they were in the original file.

Importing Illustrator (.ai) files

Because Illustrator and Flash both natively create vector artwork, you can import graphics created in Illustrator into Flash for placement or editing using tools such as the Pen tool and Subselection arrows.

Importing .ai files is nearly identical to importing .psd files, with a full layer view and lots of options for converting and distributing artwork and type from Illustrator layers. In addition to the new import options, the quality of imported Illustrator artwork is superior to past versions of Flash.

Before you begin, select an Illustrator file that you'd like to use. The flexibility of the Illustrator Import panel can best be explored with files that make use of type and graphics.

To import an Illustrator file:

1. **In a new Flash document, choose File➪Import➪Import To Stage; choose an Illustrator file from your hard drive and choose Open (Windows) or Import (Mac).**

The Import To Stage panel appears with a full view of all layers in your Illustrator document.

2. **Using the check boxes, select the layers you want to import into your document.**

3. **Highlight each layer you've chosen for import to set options for each one, as shown in Figure 5-10.**

   You can import each layer and individual path as either a bitmap or editable path. You can import groups as bitmaps or movie clips.

4. **Click OK to import the artwork to the Flash stage.**

   Check out the stage and the Library panel to see how your artwork was placed in Flash (see Figure 5-11).

Look for the Incompatibility Report button at the bottom of the layer view in your Import panel. This button can indicate potential problems that can prevent the artwork from importing properly into Flash. If you see the Incompatibility Report button, click it and read the warnings to address any pending issues before import.

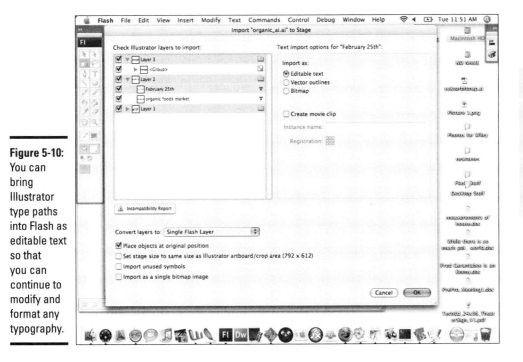

Figure 5-10:
You can bring Illustrator type paths into Flash as editable text so that you can continue to modify and format any typography.

Book VII
Chapter 5

Importing Graphics
and Sounds

A view of the new Illustrator Import Options panel

The new Illustrator Import Options panel gives you a detailed choice of what gets imported from .ai files. You can convert grouped artwork, compound paths, and type layers to movie clips or bitmaps or keep them as editable paths or type layers.

Layers View: All layers in your .ai appear in this panel, and you can choose which layers to import by selecting the check boxes to the left. Highlighting a layer displays its Import Options on the right.

Incompatibility Report button: When this button is active, it means potential issues exist in your Illustrator file that may need to be resolved for a clean, successful import. Click this button and review the report to resolve any problems before completing the import.

Convert Layers To [Flash Layers | Keyframes]: The Flash Layers option keeps layer structure (as well as layer groups) and distributes layer contents exactly as they are in your .ai file. The Keyframes option will distribute layer contents across a sequence of keyframes on the timeline.

Place Layers At Original Position: This option (checked by default) positions layer contents exactly as they appear in the original Illustrator file.

Set Stage To Same Size As Illustrator Canvas: This option resizes your movie dimensions to match the original size of the .ai file.

Import As:

✔ **Bitmap Image:** This option rasterizes (converts vector to bitmap) the selected artwork and imports it to the stage and Library as a bitmap. Any vector artwork or type loses its editability.

✔ **Editable Path (Individual Paths Only):** You can place vector paths in Illustrator as drawing objects that you can further modify on the Flash stage.

✔ **Editable Text (Type Layers Only):** This option keeps imported text layers editable, recreating Illustrator type paths as Flash type layers.

Create Movie Clip For This Layer: This option converts the layer contents to a new Movie clip symbol, which is also added to your Library. You have the option of setting a registration point as well as an instance name. (See Chapter 5 of this minibook for more on instance names.) This option and Convert To Bitmap are the only available options for entire Illustrator layers and grouped artwork.

Import Unused Symbols: Illustrator CS3 files can contain their own symbol libraries, which work in a similar manner to Flash symbols. Symbols that exist in an imported .ai file but that aren't being used on the canvas are added to the Flash library with this option checked.

Note: You can choose to import an Illustrator document's entire symbol library without importing any visible artwork from its canvas.

Import As A Single Bitmap Image: This option flattens and rasterizes the entire Illustrator document and places it as a bitmap image on the stage, as well as a bitmap asset in your Flash document's Library.

Figure 5-11:
A finished import, with all the Illustrator layers converted to Flash layers. The quality of Illustrator artwork stays top-notch through the import, so you know that what you created in Illustrator is what you'll get in Flash.

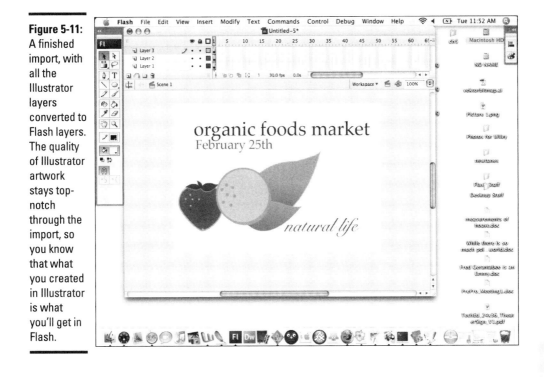

Importing Sounds

The best multimedia creations not only use visuals and motion, but sound and music, so your Flash movies should, too! Flash fully supports the import, placement, and control of sounds in lots of different formats, so you can easily bring in loops, sound effect files, and even music from your .mp3 library.

You can enhance your movie with background music or narrative, and sound effects can make using buttons and menus more intuitive. Flash can stream longer sounds (such as soundtracks or long form narration) to minimize loading time so that your user gets right to the good stuff.

Flash imports the following audio file formats:

✦ .mp3

✦ Windows WAV

✦ AIFF

Note: Additional file formats are available with optional QuickTime installed.

To import a sound into your Library:

1. **Create a new Flash document and choose File⇨Import⇨Import To Library.**

2. **Browse and choose an `.mp3`, `.wav`, or `.aiff` file from your hard drive and click Open (Windows) or Choose (Mac).**

3. **Choose Window⇨Library to launch your Library panel.**

   The sound appears in the Library with a speaker icon, as shown in Figure 5-12.

4. **Select the sound and check out the Preview window.**

   A waveform preview of your sound appears, and you can listen to your sound using the Stop and Play buttons in the upper corner of the panel.

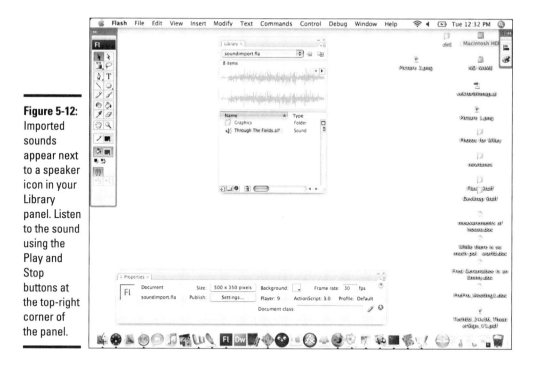

Figure 5-12: Imported sounds appear next to a speaker icon in your Library panel. Listen to the sound using the Play and Stop buttons at the top-right corner of the panel.

If you need audio files to work with, many Web sites, such as Flashkit, Flashsound, and ShockwaveSound.com, provide low-cost or free sound effects and loops in Flash-friendly formats. Adobe also has a listing of sound effects sites at `www.adobe.com/cfusion/knowledgebase/ index.cfm?id=tn_14274`.

Placing sounds on the timeline

After you have your favorite sounds into your Flash document, you can place them on keyframes along the timeline to have them play at specific points in your movie.

You can assign sounds using the Property inspector, which displays a set of Sound options when a keyframe is selected. Sounds can be combined across different layers and utilized inside of buttons to create sound effects for controls and navigation menus.

To place a sound on the timeline:

1. **On a new layer, create a blank keyframe in the timeline and launch the Property inspector (if it's not already visible).**

2. **On the right side of the Property inspector, locate the Sound menu and select a sound from the menu.**

    This menu lists all the sounds currently in your Library (see Figure 5-13).

    The sound is now on your timeline.

3. **Press Enter to play your movie.**

    The sound plays when the play head reaches the keyframe.

After you've placed a sound on your timeline, you can use additional options on the Property inspector to control looping, repeats, and playback performance. The most common options to experiment with are the Repeat and Loop options, which control the number of times (if any) a sound should repeat when it's played:

1. **Select the keyframe where you already have a sound placed and locate the Sound options on the Property inspector.**

2. **On the far right, locate the menu, which reads Repeat, and enter 2 in the box to the right.**

    By default, the sound repeats at least once, but this step makes your sound Repeat twice.

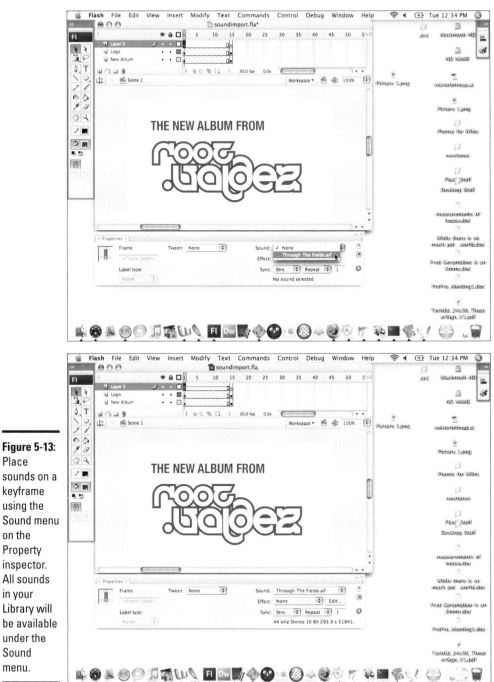

Figure 5-13:
Place sounds on a keyframe using the Sound menu on the Property inspector. All sounds in your Library will be available under the Sound menu.

3. **Press Enter to play your movie.**

The sound you placed plays and then repeats again.

4. **Select the keyframe again and, using the Sound options, change Repeat to Loop using the drop-down list.**

The sound is now set to loop continuously until the movie is shut down or another action turns it off.

5. **Choose File⇨Publish Preview⇨Flash to preview your movie.**

The sound plays and then continues to repeat until you close the preview.

Editing sounds

One of Flash's hidden treasures is the Sound editing panel, which performs trims and volume effects and lets you dial in volume and pan settings for each sound placed in your movie. While nothing quite replaces well-recorded and edited source files, you can do last-minute, nondestructive edits so that your sounds complement the rest of your movie.

To edit a sound, select a keyframe that has a sound placed on it or add a sound to a new keyframe:

1. **Select the keyframe on which the sound is placed.**

2. **Locate and click the Edit button underneath the Sound menu on the right.**

The Edit Sound panel appears with a waveform preview. The center time ruler has two sliders on the far left and far right.

3. **Move these sliders to edit the in and out points of the sound or to trim unnecessary silence, as shown in Figure 5-14.**

The lines above each waveform represent the volume envelope.

4. **Click the lines above each waveform and drag them up or down to adjust the overall volume of the sound or to add handles and vary the volume at different points during the sound.**

The higher the line or handle, the louder the sound.

5. **Use the Effect menu in the top-left corner to choose from several preset volume and pan effects to enhance your sound.**

6. **When you're done, click OK and press Enter to play your movie and hear the changes made to your sound.**

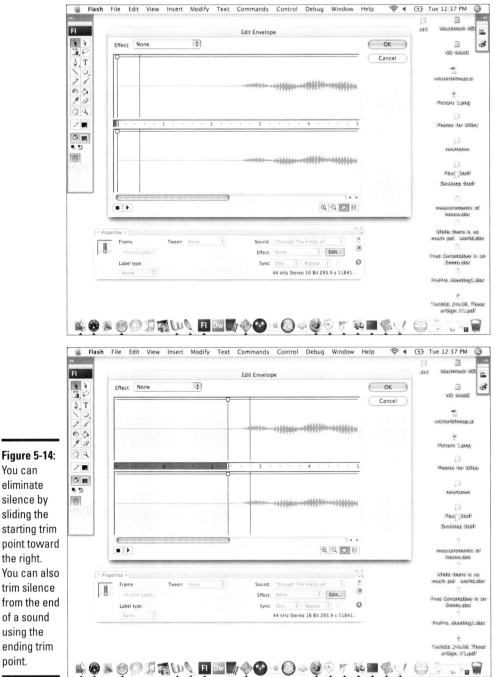

Figure 5-14:
You can eliminate silence by sliding the starting trim point toward the right. You can also trim silence from the end of a sound using the ending trim point.

Playing it right with Sync options

Below the Sound menu, you see the Sync Options menu, which controls how individual sounds load and play in your movie. Because a sound can serve different purposes (background music, narrative, sound effect), the Sync options can tell sounds to stream, stop, start, or fully load before playback so that they keep in step with animation and events in your movie.

Here are four sync types, each of which is tailored for a specific sound situation:

✔ **Start** sets a sound in motion, but also keeps more than one instance of that sound from playing at a time, preventing overlap. You can use this option for sounds that can potentially be triggered multiple times (such as an introductory narrative on the first frame). A Start sound plays until the end and can be interrupted only by a Stop sound.

✔ **Stop** doesn't actually play a chosen sound, but stops that sound if it's already playing.

A stop sound can be used to terminate a Start or Event sound of the same name.

✔ **Stream** sounds are the best choice for long form sounds, such as a soundtrack or narrative that needs to remain in sync with animation on the timeline. When a sound is set to stream, it starts immediately, even as the remainder of the sound continues to load in the background. Flash ensures that the sound keeps playing in sync with the timeline, even if it has to drop frames from the animation.

✔ **Event** sounds need to fully load in your movie before they can play and are a good choice for short sounds and effects used on the timeline, buttons, or navigation elements. Like their namesake, these sounds are best suited for responding to nonsynchronized events, such as a button being clicked or the play head hitting a specific frame.

**Book VII
Chapter 5**

**Importing Graphics
and Sounds**

Chapter 6: Lights, Camera, Movie Clips!

In This Chapter

✔ Exploring movie clip uses and advantages

✔ Creating and updating movie clips

✔ Transforming and tweening movie clip instances

✔ Previewing movie clip animation

Complicated machines, such as an automobile, are made from many smaller machines and moving parts. To build an automobile any other way is just not possible. Along those lines, you may find that some animations are too elaborate to create on the main timeline alone. You'll want to break them down into smaller animations that can be brought together as part of a larger animation.

You'll also find that your movie needs to reuse several, identical animations. (Think about the four spinning wheels on a car.) For these cases, you have movie clips.

What Are Movie Clips?

The *movie clip* is a powerful and versatile symbol type that can include entire, independent animations, yet be placed and maintained in your movie just as easily as graphic symbols. It's one of three symbol types in Flash, and just like graphic symbols (see Chapter 3 of this minibook), they can be easily duplicated and maintained from a single master symbol in the Library.

Movie clips are unique in that each one contains its very own timeline that looks and works just like the main timeline. This timeline is completely self-contained, so animations in movie clips don't depend on or rely on the length of an animation contained within the main timeline. Movie clips can almost be thought of as movies within your movie. Movie clips behave just like other symbols, so several instances of the same movie clip can be dragged to the main stage to easily duplicate animations. If you need to change an animation that appears several times throughout your movie, you need to modify only the original movie clip in the library that contains it.

Movie clips have all the same features as graphic symbols: You can easily drag multiple instances to the stage, and each instance can have its own scaling, tint, alpha, and rotation applied.

Because movie clips are capable of containing entire animations, they're a great way to break down complex animations into smaller, more manageable pieces. Trying to coordinate too many animations across the main timeline may not only be very difficult, but in some cases impossible, depending on what you're trying to create. (Imagine taking your whole car apart and rebuilding it just to replace a battery!) Each movie clip, and the animation contained within, can be treated as an independent little machine of its own. Of course, when the project demands it, you can put them all together to create a bigger, more complex machine with the flexibility to tweak and manage each part individually. Movie clips can also be nested inside of other movie clips, giving you virtually unlimited levels of depth and complexity!

While movie clip timelines are independent of the main timeline, they share the same *frame rate* as your main movie. This is because frame rate is a global setting for your movie, not for any specific timeline. The frame rate you set in Document Properties (choose Modify➪Document) affects the main timeline as well as all movie clips throughout your project.

To speed up or slow down individual movie clip animations, consider modifying the length of any included tweens before adjusting the overall frame rate.

Creating and Placing Movie Clips

Movie clips are created as new, empty symbols as well as from existing content on the stage. If you create a movie clip from scratch, you can add animation and graphics later on by editing the symbol.

To create a movie clip from existing graphics:

1. **Create some interesting graphics on the stage using the drawing tools.**

2. **Select the new artwork and choose Modify➪Convert To Symbol.**

   The Convert To Symbol dialog box appears (see Figure 6-1).

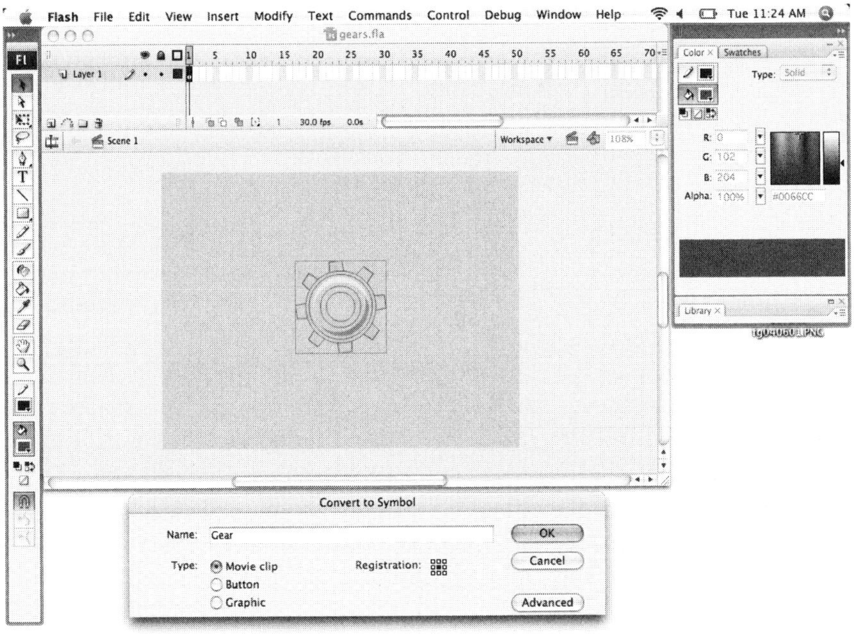

**Book VII
Chapter 6**

**Lights, Camera,
Movie Clips!**

Figure 6-1:
Choose
Modify⇨
Convert To
Symbol to
add artwork
to your
Library as a
movie clip
symbol.

3. Assign a name for your new movie clip, select the type as Movie Clip, and click OK.

The graphic now appears as a movie clip on the stage.

4. Choose Window⇨Library to check out your new symbol in the Library with a special Movie Clip icon next to it.

Nonanimated graphics converted to movie clips behave the same as graphic symbols, so you can place, tween, and modify instances on the stage. The difference, however, is that you can always add animated content later to the movie clip by editing it and creating tweens on its own timeline.

In most cases, you'll want to take full advantage of movie clips by adding animation in a new movie clip symbol. To do so, you can start with a new empty movie clip symbol and add the animated content afterward.

To create a new movie clip symbol and add animation:

1. **Choose Insert⇨New Symbol.**

The Create New Symbol dialog box, shown in Figure 6-2, appears.

2. **Assign your movie clip a new name, set the type as Movie Clip, and click OK to create the new symbol.**

You see a new timeline, and you see the symbol's Edit mode, ready to add animation. This timeline works just like the main timeline: You can add and reorder layers and create tweens. You still need to convert any artwork to graphic symbols before creating motion tweens.

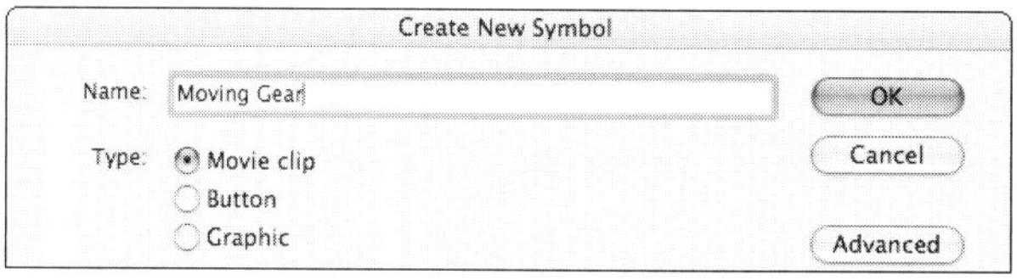

Figure 6-2:
Choose
Insert⇨
New
Symbol to
create a
new movie
clip symbol.

3. **Create a new graphic on Frame 1 of the existing Layer 1 and convert it to a Graphic symbol by choosing Modify⇨Convert To Symbol.**

4. **Select Frame 20 on the same layer and insert a new keyframe using the F6 shortcut key.**

You see a new instance of your graphic symbol, which you can move, transform, or apply a color effect to.

5. **Set a motion tween on Frame 1 by using the Tween menu on the Properties inspector; exit the symbol by clicking the *Scene 1* icon above the timeline.**

6. **Locate your new movie clip symbol in the Library panel and drag an instance of it to the stage, as shown in Figure 6-3.**

If you hit the Return key to watch your movie clip play on the stage, you'll probably be a little disappointed. Don't worry; to see your movie clip in action, you just need to preview your movie in the Flash player.

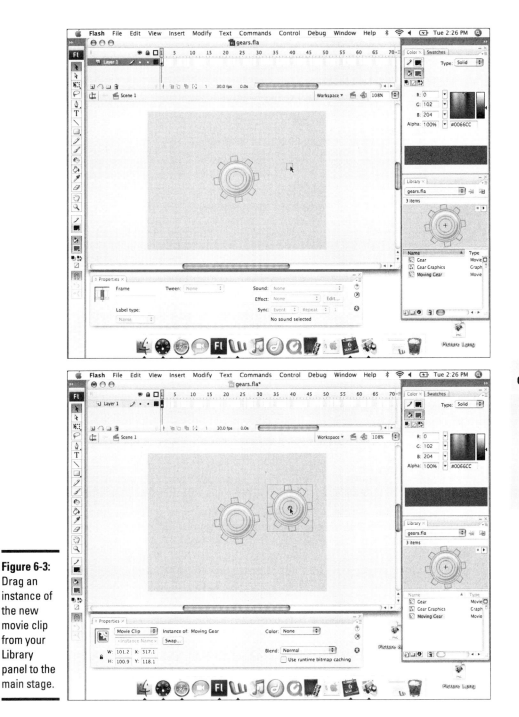

Figure 6-3:
Drag an
instance of
the new
movie clip
from your
Library
panel to the
main stage.

Previewing Movie Clip Animation

Movie clips contain their own timelines, and pressing Enter doesn't start the movie clip play head, but rather the main timeline play head. To view movie clip animation, you need to preview your movie in the Flash player using one of two methods:

+ **Test Movie** mode exports a compressed (.swf) Flash movie and immediately launches it in the Flash player. Test Movie is used to give you a quick look at how the finished movie will appear to your end user as you build. Test the new movie clip by choosing Control⇨Test Movie.

  You can preview your movie in Test Movie mode using the shortcut key combination Ctrl+Enter (Windows) or ⌘+Return (Mac).

+ **Publish Preview** works similar to Test Movie, but exports the .swf (compressed Flash movie) using the final delivery settings you've already created under File⇨Publish Settings. Publish Preview can also display your movie in an HTML (Web) page in your system's default browser. To preview your movie in Publish Preview, choose File⇨ Publish Preview⇨HTML or File⇨Publish Preview⇨Flash.

Chapter 9 of this minibook covers publish settings for your movie, but it's important to know how these seemingly identical methods differ. Both methods let you accurately preview movie clip animation as you create it in your movie.

Modifying Movie Clip Instances

You can modify each movie clip instance with its own size, transformation, and color settings. This type of flexibility lets you get lots of mileage from a single movie clip symbol before having to create a new version or variation of your symbol in the Library panel. Just like graphic symbols, these transformations do not affect the master symbol or other instances on the stage.

While all instances of a movie clip share a timeline with its master symbol in the library, each individual instance can be stopped, started, and controlled individually using ActionScript. For more on how to control movie clip instances using ActionScript, see Chapter 9 of this minibook.

To transform any instance of a movie clip, you can use the Transform tool, the Transform panel, or the Transform submenu located at Modify⇨ Transform. Try dragging two more instances of your new movie clip on the stage and applying different transformations to each.

To apply a transformation to a movie clip instance, choose the Transform tool from the Tools panel and select an instance on the stage. Use the handles to resize, distort, and skew the instance or select an instance on the stage with the Selection tool and use the Transform panel located at Window⇨Transform to type exact amounts for horizontal and vertical scale, rotation, and skew.

Use the Color drop-down list on the right side of the Properties inspector with any selected movie clip instance to apply unique tints and alpha (transparency) effects and change brightness. To apply a color effect to a movie clip instance, select an instance on the stage and choose an effect from the Color drop-down list. Use the option controls to dial in the exact amount and type of color effect you need.

Combining Movie Clips

To create a new animation from several smaller ones, you can create a new movie clip from other movie clip instances on the stage. This technique allows you to group together several movie clips and drag them as one instance to the stage. Unlike a group, however, you gain all the advantages of working with symbols, including the ability to duplicate, maintain, and tween the combined movie clips as one unit.

The practice of including one movie clip inside of another is sometimes referred to as *nesting*. While movie clips can include other movie clips, graphic symbols, and buttons, graphic symbols shouldn't include movie clip instances. Movie clips should always be included in other movie clips so that their animation functions properly.

To create a new movie clip from other movie clips on the stage:

1. **Select two or more movie clip instances on the stage.**

These can be instances of different movie clips symbols in your Library or of the same symbol.

2. **Choose Modify⇨Convert To Symbol.**

The Convert To Symbol dialog box appears.

3. **Assign a name to your new symbol, set the type as movie clip, and set the registration point; click OK to create the new symbol.**

The symbol instances now appear on the stage as a single movie clip, and a new movie clip appears in your Library.

Convert the selected instances to a new movie clip symbol as you would with a single graphic.

You can now drag and drop several instances of the new movie clip to the stage. Experiment by adding a few instances to the stage and applying different transformations or color effects to each. Preview your movie by choosing Control⇨Test Movie, and you see that the movie clips now are treated as one item, but still animate and behave as they did when they were separate instances on the stage.

When you nest movie clips inside of each other, you're creating *dependencies* between those symbols in your library. Movie clips that include other movie clip symbols do so by *reference;* the included movie clip symbols aren't duplicated but are *connected* to the movie clip that includes them.

Movie clips become dependent on any other symbols they're created from. The smaller symbols remain in the Library and are referenced by the movie clip that includes them. This means that you can't remove included movie clips without destroying the symbols that they're part of. For this reason, make sure that you don't trash any symbols in your Library panel until you're sure that they're not being used in your movie *or* by another movie clip symbol.

A great way to check what symbols are in use is to choose Show Unused Items from the menu in the upper-right corner of your Library panel. This highlights symbols in your Library panel that aren't being used anywhere on the stage or by other symbols in the library. If a movie clip isn't used on the stage but is included in another symbol, it will not be highlighted, indicating that it's "in use."

Chapter 7: Controlling Your Movie with ActionScript

In This Chapter

✔ **Introducing ActionScript**

✔ **Working with the Actions panel**

✔ **Adding actions to the timeline**

✔ **Creating button controls**

*W*hether you're creating a Web site, presentation, or game, a truly interactive experience is one in which your users can control the action. If you want to take your movies to the next level, ActionScript can help. Flash's built-in scripting language has come a long way and can do anything from controlling movie playback to creating complex games.

Getting to Know ActionScript

ActionScript is a powerful scripting language that you can incorporate into your movies to control playback, navigation, and imported media, such as images, video, and audio. ActionScript is written as a series of commands (or *actions*) that are placed on the timeline, buttons, movie clip, and external files using the Actions panel. Think of ActionScript as a set of instructions that you can give your movie to tell it how to behave and add abilities.

ActionScript is often used for timeline control so that your animations can be told when and where to stop, loop, play, or jump to other points on the timeline. You can also make truly interactive movies by adding ActionScript to buttons on the stage so that your user can control the animation, too!

The Actions panel

All ActionScript throughout your movie is placed using the Actions panel (see Figure 7-1), which acts as a wizard, reference book, and script editor all in one. You can add actions from the Actions Toolbox using a categorized tray or drop-down menu, or you can type them directly into the script editor. A handy Script Assist mode (see the next section) is available for novice users so that you can add and modify actions without typing the code in by hand (using the Script Assist is highly recommended for new users).

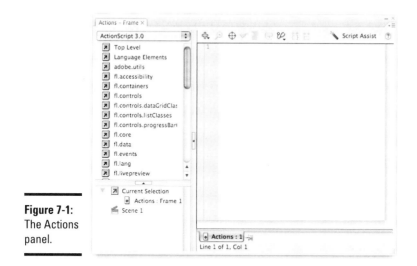

Figure 7-1:
The Actions
panel.

To launch the Actions panel, choose Window➪Actions or use the F9 (Windows) or Option+F9 (Mac) shortcut key combination.

To place an action on a frame, select the frame on the timeline and launch the Actions panel. To place an action on a button or movie clip (ActionScript 2.0 only), select the button or movie clip instance on the stage and launch the Actions panel.

Script Assist mode

For users who are new to ActionScript, the Script Assist mode is a wizard that lets you choose from a series of menus, buttons, and type-in boxes to build your scripts without getting into the nuts and bolts of the code itself. Using Script Assist mode helps prevent time-consuming errors so that you spend more time being creative and less time troubleshooting.

Throughout this chapter, you use Script Assist mode while you become more familiar with ActionScript and how it works.

To enable Script Assist mode, select the Script Assist button in the upper-right corner of the Actions panel.

ActionScript is understood and processed by the Flash player, so some scripted movies need to be tested by choosing Control➪Test Movie. However, you can also enable simple actions in the authoring environment so that you can see your work in progress while still working on the timeline.

ActionScript 3.0 versus ActionScript 2.0

ActionScript Version 3.0 brings many new major changes and improvements to the way ActionScript performs, as well as how it's created within your movies. ActionScript 3.0 requires the placement of actions on the timeline or within external files (you can no longer place actions directly on movie clips or buttons) to make the code as modular as possible.

For first-time coders or users who aren't familiar with the principles of OOP (Object Oriented Programming) languages, these concepts may present a significant learning curve.

ActionScript 2.0 doesn't take advantage of the new methods, abilities, and speed improvements of ActionScript 3.0, but it does allow for more flexibility by allowing scripts to be added directly on buttons and movie clips. In addition to a smaller learning curve, ActionScript 2.0 is still utilized in movies created in earlier versions of Flash.

For this reason, this chapter illustrates both methods wherever possible to give you the ability to work with movies created in either version.

Specifying the correct Publish Settings

Depending on whether you choose to do the lessons in ActionScript 2.0 or 3.0, you'll need to adjust the ActionScript version in your Publish Settings to match the version you choose to work in. In most cases, you can't publish newer 3.0 scripts in a Version 2.0 movie, and vice versa. To choose the appropriate ActionScript version, choose File➪Publish Settings and use the ActionScript Version menu located under the Flash pane.

You can also open your Publish Settings from the Property inspector. A Publish Settings button appears when no object or frame is selected.

Adding Scripts to the Timeline

To add actions to a specific point on the timeline, you create a keyframe that you can put your ActionScript in. You can add ActionScript to keyframes with existing content, but it's always a good practice to separate your scripts from visual elements on the stage by creating a dedicated layer for your ActionScript. This layer prevents accidentally selecting the wrong thing when you try to add ActionScript to a keyframe or symbol.

The following sections use basic ActionScript to control a new tween on your timeline. Before getting started, you need to create a new graphic symbol from artwork or typography on your stage.

Using stop ( )

The stop action does exactly what it sounds like: stops the timeline at whatever frames it's placed on. A common use of stop is to keep a movie from looping, which is default behavior for the Flash player.

1. **On a new layer, create a motion or shape tween from frames 1–30 and press Enter to play back and preview the animation.**

   For more information on creating tweens, see Chapter 3 of this minibook.

2. **Create a new layer and name it** Actions.

   This dedicated layer is where you add ActionScript to control your new motion tween.

3. **Add a keyframe on Frame 30 of the new Actions layer using the F6 shortcut key.**

4. **Select the keyframe and choose Window⇨Actions to launch the Actions panel.**

5. **In the Actions panel, locate the Script Assist button and select it.**

   The top panel expands, and you're now working in Script Assist mode.

6. **Add a stop method, which stops the timeline of a movie clip (including the main timeline).**

   Here's how:

   • **In ActionScript 3.0:** Click the plus sign at the top of the Actions panel and choose flash.display⇨MovieClip⇨Methods⇨Stop. Specify the name of the object you want to control in the Object field up top. Because you're stopping the current (main) timeline, have it refer to itself by entering this in the Object field. The actions panel should read:

   ```
   import flash.display.MovieClip;
   this.stop();
   ```

   • **In ActionScript 2.0:** Click the plus sign at the top of the Actions panel and choose Global Functions⇨Timeline Control⇨Stop. The actions panel should read stop();.

   Take a look at your timeline and you'll notice that a lower case *a* now appears inside of the keyframe, which indicates that ActionScript on the keyframe. These scripts will run when the play head passes that keyframe.

7. **Preview your movie by choosing Control⇨Test Movie.**

   The animation plays up until Frame 30 and then stops.

Using goto: gotoAndPlay ( ) and gotoAndStop ( )

To loop a movie or to send the play head to a different point on the timeline, you can tell your movie to jump forward or backward to a specific frame using one of two variations of *goto* action: gotoAndPlay() and gotoAndStop(). Each of these two actions requires a frame name or number so that it knows where to send the play head. When placed on a frame, these actions send the play head forward or backward to the specified frame and stop, or they resume playback from that point. To use gotoAndStop:

1. **On a new layer, select and create a new keyframe at Frame 29.**

2. **Open the Actions panel by choosing Window⟿Actions.**

3. **Apply a gotoAndStop action on this frame to send the play head to a specific frame and have it stop.**

   Here's how:

   - **In ActionScript 3.0:** Use the plus sign to choose flash.display⟿MovieClip⟿Methods⟿gotoAndStop. In the Object field, have the timeline refer back to itself by entering `this`. Set the Frame number to 1 and clear out the Scene field. The actions should now read:

     ```
     import flash.display.MovieClip;
     this.gotoAndStop(1);
     ```

   - **In ActionScript 2.0:** Use the plus sign to choose Global Functions⟿Timeline Control⟿Goto. The action defaults to gotoAndPlay() - click the radio button to select gotoAndStop() instead. Leave the frame number at 1. The actions should now read

     ```
     gotoAndStop(1);
     ```

4. **Choose Control⟿Test Movie to preview your movie.**

   The tween plays and jumps to the first frame, where it stops.

To use gotoAndPlay():

1. **Select and create a new keyframe at Frame 28 on your Actions layer and launch your Actions panel.**

2. **Apply a gotoAndPlay action at Frame 28 to create a loop between this frame and Frame 15 of your movie.**

   Here's how:

   - **In ActionScript 3.0:** Use the plus sign to choose flash.display⟿MovieClip⟿Methods⟿gotoAndPlay. In the Object field, have the timeline refer back to itself by typing `this`. Set the Frame number to 15 and clear out the Scene field (see Figure 7-2). The actions should now read:

```
import flash.display.MovieClip;
this.gotoAndPlay(15);
```

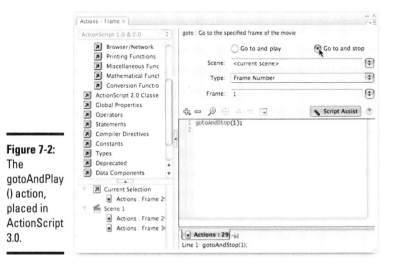

Figure 7-2:
The
gotoAndPlay
() action,
placed in
ActionScript
3.0.

• **In ActionScript 2.0:** Use the plus sign to choose Global Functions⇨Timeline Control⇨Goto. The action defaults to gotoAndPlay(), so you don't need to change it. Change the frame number to 15. The actions should now read:

```
gotoAndPlay(15);
```

3. **Choose Control⇨Test Movie to preview your movie.**

The animation will now play until Frame 28 and begin to loop between Frames 15 and 28.

Creating Button Symbols

In everyday life, buttons give you control over your world, whether it's switching on a light or TV at home or navigating through Web pages and e-mail messages online. To make your movies better, you can use buttons to give your users control over the action with timeline control and navigation.

In Flash, buttons are special symbol types built to respond to mouse or keyboard interaction, such as clicks, rollovers, and specific key presses. When paired up with ActionScript, buttons can be used for just about any navigation or control task. Buttons are created in the same way as other symbol types, and you can easily drag instances to the stage from your Library to create more buttons.

Creating a new button

Like graphic symbols, you can create buttons from existing content on the stage or as new empty symbols to which you can add content later.

To create a new button symbol from existing content:

1. **On a new layer in your document, create a new, solid shape on the stage that you'd like to use as a button and select the shape with the Selection tool.**

2. **Choose Modify⇨Convert To Symbol.**

The Convert To Symbol dialog box appears.

3. **Assign your new button a name and select the Type as Button.**

4. **Choose OK to create the button.**

Choose Window⇨Library to launch the Library panel, and you see the new symbol with the special button icon next to it.

Button states

Take a look inside your button by double-clicking it on the stage or in the Library panel; it contains four specially marked frames: Up, Over, Down, and Hit. Each frame represents a button *state,* or the appearance of a button, as it interacts with a mouse in different ways.

Each frame, or state, can contain unique artwork so that your button can change appearance as its clicked, pressed, or released. You can even add layers inside of your button to stack artwork for more creative flexibility. Here are the states and what they represent:

✦ **Up:** The appearance of your button when it's not being pressed or rolled over. This is the state you see most of the time as the button sits on the stage.

✦ **Over:** The appearance of the button when the mouse pointer rolls over it. Adding unique content to this frame creates the rollover effect many people know and love from web buttons.

✦ **Down:** The appearance of the button when it's clicked and the mouse button is held down.

✦ **Hit:** This state isn't actually visible, but sets the hot spot, or clickable area, of your button. If the Hit frame is empty, it uses the shape on the last available state by default. You can create a more specific Hit area if you want to give the user more or less area to work with or simplify the clickable area for odd-shaped buttons.

Use a filled shape in this state so that the end user has no problem interacting with your button.

Adding content to button states

You can add content to each frame in your button to make it complete:

1. **If it's not already open, edit your new button by double-clicking it on the stage or in the Library panel.**

   You should have some content on the Up state from when you created the button. Now you can define content for remaining states as well.

2. **Select the Over frame on the button's timeline and add a new blank keyframe using the F7 shortcut key.**

3. **Use the drawing tools to add artwork to the Over frame (see Figure 7-3).**

4. **Select the Down frame and insert a new blank keyframe using the F7 shortcut key.**

5. **Create content on your new frame.**

   This content appears when the user clicks and holds down the mouse button.

6. **Select the Hit frame and create a new blank keyframe.**

7. **Use one of the shape tools with a fill to create a large, defined hit area.**

8. **Exit the button by clicking Scene 1 above the timeline.**

9. **Choose Control➪Test Movie to preview your movie.**

   Rollover and click your new button to see the different states in action.

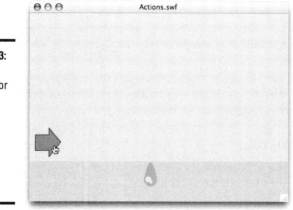

Figure 7-3:
Modified content for the Over frame appears when the user rolls over the button.

Enable simple buttons

While it's always a good idea to choose Control⇨Test Movie to preview your work, you may want to see how certain elements of your movie behave in real time on the stage. To see buttons in action on the stage as you build your movie, you can choose Control⇨Enable Simple Buttons. You then see buttons as they'd appear and respond to your user in the Flash player.

Keep in mind that buttons can't be selected or modified on the stage in this mode; you need to disable it to apply actions or transformations or edit in place.

Modifying Button Instances

Individual button instances can each have unique transformations and color effects applied, just like graphic symbol instances. In addition, each button can have unique ActionScript applied to it, so you can use several instances of a single button symbol to create an entire menu or control bar.

Here's how you add and modify additional instances of your button on the stage. Before you get started, make sure that your Library panel is visible by choosing Window⇨Library.

1. **Drag two more instances of your button symbol onto the same layer as your existing button instance.**

   If necessary, position the buttons so that they're spread apart from each other.

2. **Select one of the button instances and choose Window⇨Properties⇨Properties.**

   The Property inspector opens.

3. **Locate and choose Color⇨Tint.**

4. **Select a color and set the tint percentage to 100%.**

   The button becomes tinted with the chosen color.

5. **Select a different button instance, choose the Transform tool from the Tool panel, and use the Transform tool to resize or rotate the selected button.**

Preview your buttons by choosing Control⇨Test Movie or by choosing Control⇨Enable Simple Buttons.

Using Buttons with ActionScript

The real power of buttons is realized when you combine them with ActionScript. In ActionScript 2.0, you can apply actions directly to button instances; in ActionScript 3.0, you define button actions and the events that trigger them on the timeline or in external ActionScript files.

The tasks described in the following sections take place in ActionScript 2.0. Before you get started, make sure to switch your Publish Settings to ActionScript Version 2.0. Choose File⇨Publish Settings⇨Flash, and choose ActionScript 2.0 from the ActionScript Version menu.

Understanding event handlers

In the following steps, you get a chance to define actions for your button, as well as the *event handlers* that trigger them. An *event handler* tells your button when to run actions by reacting to a number of possible events including clicks, rollovers, and key presses.

Unlike frame-based actions, which always occur at the same time and only respond to the play head, you can use buttons at any time (or not at all) and respond to several different types of user interaction. For this reason, as you place actions on buttons in Script Assist mode, event handlers are automatically added.

Creating stop and play buttons

To get rolling (or clicking), you can use the button instances you've already placed as controls for the tween on your timeline. You can add unique scripts to each of these buttons to tell the timeline to stop, play, or jump to specific points on the timeline.

Before you get started, make sure that you remove the Actions layer if you created one; the actions on this layer will conflict with your button actions.

To create a stop button:

1. **Select one of the button instances on the stage and launch the Actions panel by choosing Window⇨Actions.**

2. **Make sure that the Script Assist is enabled by selecting Script Assist at the top-right corner of the Actions panel.**

3. **Click the plus sign and choose Global Functions⇨Timeline Control⇨ Stop.**

   The stop action appears in the script window, surrounded by an event handler:

   ```
   on(release) {
   stop();
   }
   ```

Using Buttons with ActionScript **727**

Book VII
Chapter 7

Controlling
Your Movie with
ActionScript

By default, the event handler is set to release, which is the action of the user clicking and releasing the button (what most people know as a click with normal Web buttons).

4. Choose Control⇨Test Movie to see your button in action.

The tween you created should play, but comes to a stop at whatever point you click the new button.

To create a play button:

1. Select a different button instance and launch the Actions panel

2. Click the plus sign and choose Global Functions⇨Timeline Control⇨ Play.

The play action appears in the script window, surrounded by an event handler:

```
on(release) {
play();
}
```

3. Choose Control⇨Test Movie to see your buttons in action.

You can now stop the timeline with the stop button, but resume the action with the new play button.

Using goto

Unlike stop or play, which park or resume playback at the current frame, you can use goto to jump forward or backward on the timeline. You can use one of two variations: gotoAndPlay() or gotoAndStop() to resume or stop playback from the selected frame, respectively.

1. Select the third button instance and launch the Actions panel.

2. Click the plus sign and choose Global Functions⇨Timeline Control⇨ Goto.

By default, gotoAndPlay is selected, with Frame 1 as the target frame. The script window should read:

```
on(release) {
gotoAndPlay(1);
}
```

3. Choose Control⇨Test Movie.

When you click the new button, the play head jumps to Frame 1 and resumes playback.

Now you try to switch the goto action to use gotoAndStop() instead.

4. **Close your preview window and reselect the button; launch the Actions panel if it's not open already.**

5. **Highlight the line that reads** gotoAndPlay(1).

   You see the option to switch to gotoAndStop as well as set a different frame number up top.

6. **Click the radio button next to** gotoAndStop **and enter 15 in the Frame field.**

   The script window should now read:

   ```
   on(release) {
   gotoAndStop(15);
   }
   ```

7. **Choose Control⊏⊃Test Movie.**

   Clicking the button now forces the play head to Frame 15 and playback stops.

Specifying event handlers

Event handlers specify what type of mouse interaction a button should respond to. You can choose from several different event handlers, including key presses.

To modify an event handler:

1. **Select the first (stop) button on the stage and launch the Actions panel.**

   The script window should read:

   ```
   on(release) {
   stop();
   }
   ```

2. **Select the line that reads** on(release), **and the panel on top reveals a series of check boxes next to different event handlers.**

3. **Uncheck the Release check box and instead check the Rollover check box.**

   The event handler responds to a mouse rollover instead of a click. The script window should read:

   ```
   on(rollOver) {
   stop();
   }
   ```

4. **Choose Control⊏⊃Test Movie to preview your modified button.**

   The button should now stop the timeline when the mouse pointer rolls over it.

5. **Close your preview window and return to the timeline. Reselect the button and launch the Actions panel.**

6. **Select the line that reads** on(rollOver.

Once again, the event handler check boxes appear on top of the Actions panel.

7. **Check the box next to Key Press.**

8. **In the type-in field that appears, type the letter** s.

The script window should now read:

```
on (rollOver, keyPress "s") {
    stop();
}
```

9. **Choose Control⇨Test Movie to preview your modified button.**

The button now stops the timeline when the mouse pointer rolls over it, and when the letter *s* is pressed on the keyboard.

Using Frame labels

The goto actions often reference exact frame numbers to move backward and forward on the timeline. If you happen to change a significant event on your timeline, however (such as the start or end of an animation), frame numbers may become inaccurate. For cases like these, you assign names directly to keyframes on the timeline that you can call directly from ActionScript.

Frame labels are familiar names that you can assign to any keyframe (such as "start", "end" or "big_finale"). You can then tell ActionScript to jump to these frames by name as an alternative to using a frame number. If the location of the named frame changes, scripts still function as long as the label name is the same.

Here's how you can modify a button to use a frame label instead of a frame number:

1. **On a new layer, create a keyframe at Frame 15.**

2. **Select the new keyframe and open the Property inspector.**

3. **Locate the type-in field on the Property inspector that reads** <Frame Label>.

You can type directly into this field to assign the keyframe a name.

4. **Enter the name** my_label.

5. **Select the button you added the** gotoAndStop() **action to and launch the Actions panel.**

   The script window should currently read:

   ```
   on(release) {
   gotoAndStop(15);
   }
   ```

6. **Select the line that reads** gotoAndStop(15).

7. **Choose Type⇨Frame Label.**

   The value of the Frame field is interpreted as a frame label, not a number.

8. **Type my_frame in place of 15 in the Frame field.**

   The script now references the labeled keyframe you created. The script window should now read:

   ```
   on(release) {
   gotoAndStop("my_label");
   }
   ```

9. **Choose Control⇨Test Movie to preview your changes.**

   The gotoAndStop button now jumps to the my_label keyframe when clicked.

Now, no matter where you move the keyframe, the script automatically follows as long as the frame label remains the same.

Frame labels: What you can and can't do

Because ActionScript uses frame labels as locators, you're limited to using certain naming conventions:

✔ Frame labels can't contain empty spaces, such as "my label." You can, however, use underscores if you want to mate several words together, as inmy_label.

✔ Frame labels can contain numbers but not in the first characters, such as 2ndframe.

✔ Frame labels can't contain punctuation of any type, such as My_label!!!!

✔ You can use both upper- and lowercase letters, but make sure that you reference the frame using the exact case you named it with; ActionScript interprets myLabel and mylabel as completely different frames.

Chapter 8: Getting into the (Work) flow

In This Chapter

✔ Creating and managing workspace layouts

✔ Setting up grids and guides

✔ Using snap options and the Align palette

✔ Creating custom keyboard shortcuts

Sometimes the difference between a good project and a great project is having a seamless workflow. Visual aids such as guides and grids and alignment aids, as well as proper placement of tools and palettes, are an essential part of creating better movies in less time. The Flash workspace is highly customizable so that you can work in the most efficient way possible and spend more time being creative.

Using Workspace Layouts

Your Flash workspace consists of all the palettes and tools you rely on, so why not take some time to customize it? You can save the position and appearance of these essential components by creating custom workspace layouts.

Workspace layouts take a snapshot of the appearance and position of panels you're using so that you can recall that same configuration at any time. You can save as many workspace layouts as you want for different projects or different designers who may share the same computer with you.

Choose Window➪Workspace to recall, save, or manage your workspace layouts.

Flash CS3 comes with three default layouts: Default, Icons Only, and Icons and Text Only. You can select and use these layouts as a starting point for a new workspace layout or to reset the workspace. The default layouts *can't* be deleted or overwritten (even by a layout saved by the same name).

Creating new layouts

Before creating a new workspace layout, open any palettes you need, close any palettes you don't use often, and position and size them exactly where you think is best. All palettes can be toggled on or off using the Window menu. Grouping options for each palette are available under their respective fly-out menus, or you can drag and drop palettes on top of one another to group them together.

To create a new workspace layout:

1. **Position all palettes and toolbars as you'd like to see them.**

2. **Group any palettes together or resize individual palettes and groups.**

You can also collapse any palettes or groups down to Icon mode to maximize screen area.

3. **Choose Window⇨Workspace⇨Save Current.**

A dialog box appears, prompting you to name the new layout.

4. **Name the new layout and click OK.**

The new workspace is created.

5. **Choose Window⇨Workspace.**

You see the new workspace as an available selection.

Managing layouts

After you've created workspace layouts, you can rename, delete, or update them as needed. Deleting layouts you no longer use is a good practice so that you can keep the list manageable. You should also rename layouts to indicate when it was created (for example, MyLayoutFeb2007). You can manage layouts by the Manage panel (choose Window⇨Workspace⇨Manage).

To delete a layout, choose Window⇨Workspace⇨Manage. Select the layout you want to delete and choose Delete. Click OK to exit the Manage panel. *Note:* You can't undo this action, but a dialog box gives you the same warning and a chance to change your mind.

To rename a layout, choose Window⇨Workspace⇨Manage. Select the layout you want to rename and choose Rename. Enter the new name, click OK, and then click OK again to exit the panel.

To update (overwrite) an existing layout, recall the layout by choosing it under the Workspace menu. Make any adjustments to your workspace and choose Window⇨Workspace⇨Save Current. When prompted, assign it the name of the layout you're trying to update. A warning alerts you that you're about to replace an existing layout by the same name; click OK to overwrite the layout with the new changes.

To condense right-side palettes down to Icon view, collapse the entire panel group using the double arrows at the top-right corner of the screen. To hide the labels and just view the icons alone, use the ridged handle at the top-left corner of the panel group to resize it as narrow as it will go.

Fine-Tuning with Grids and Guides

Having lots of visual aides right at your fingertips is indispensable when you need to line up, arrange, or measure objects on your stage with absolute accuracy. You'll want some designs to take advantage of the "place it anywhere" flexibility that Flash provides, but other designs demand more precise control over placement and sizing. For these cases, you can take advantage of Flash's large array of visual aides and helpers, many of which you can enable and set under the View menu.

These visual aides don't appear in any way in your final movie; they're strictly for your benefit during the design and building process.

Enabling rulers and guides

Flash's built-in rulers appear on the top and left edges of your stage and are used to position and measure objects on the stage. You also use the rulers to create vertical and horizontal guides from the rulers, by dragging them off the ruler bar. Ruler units are in pixels by default, but you can choose Modify➪Document Properties to change to other measurement units, such as inches, centimeters, or millimeters.

The top ruler represents the X, or horizontal axis, and the left ruler represents the Y, or vertical axis. The top-left corner of the stage represents absolute 0 for both X and Y, with X increasing as you move right, and Y increasing as you move down.

To set up and use rulers and guides:

1. **In a new document, choose View➪Rulers.**

The rulers appear on the top and left edges of your stage.

2. **Click and drag anywhere on the stage.**

Markers on both rulers follow to indicate your X and Y position and the width of your selection area. Now you can create guides that you can use to position artwork on the stage.

3. **Click the top ruler bar and drag down.**

You're carrying a guide with you.

4. **Watch the ruler on the left and drop the guide at 200 pixels (see Figure 8-1).**

5. **Click the ruler on the left and drag toward the right to place another guide.**

Position this one at 250 pixels using the top ruler for reference.

6. **Grab your Type tool and create a single line of type on the stage, as shown in Figure 8-2.**

Use a large enough font so that you can easily see and drag the new text.

7. **Select the text with the Selection tool and drag it by the center until it 'snaps' in place where the new guides intersect.**

Your text snaps easily to the new guides because of a built-in mechanism called *snapping*. Think of snapping as turning on a magnetic force that allows objects to adhere to each other or to visual helpers (such as guides) to make positioning easier. By default, Snap Align, Snap To Guides, and Snap To Objects are enabled (choose View➪Snapping). You can also enable Snap To Pixels and Snap To Grid.

Figure 8-1:
To create a new horizontal guide, click and drag from the top ruler and release a guide on your stage. Use the left ruler for reference so that you know exactly how far down you're placing the new guide.

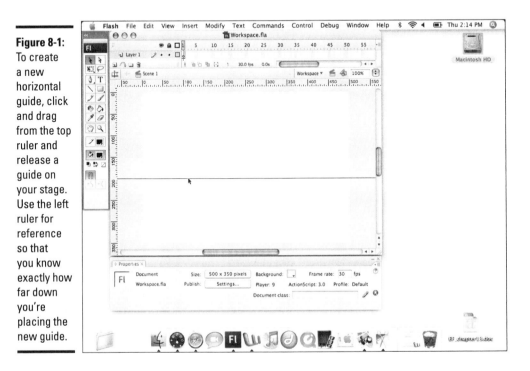

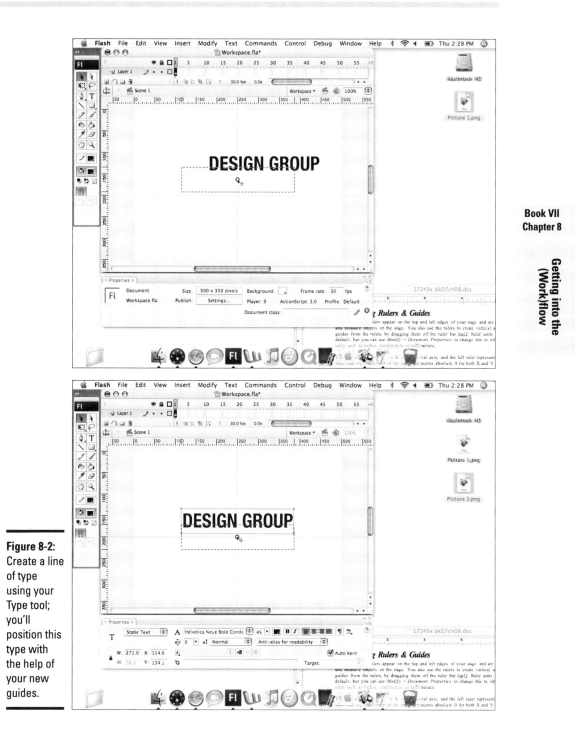

Figure 8-2:
Create a line
of type
using your
Type tool;
you'll
position this
type with
the help of
your new
guides.

Enabling the grid

If you've ever drawn on graph paper, you know how fun it can be to 'follow the lines' and create perfect shapes and drawings. Like good old graph paper, you can enable and use the Flash grid to draw and position objects and create precise layouts by just following the lines. Like guides, you can snap type, drawing objects, and symbols to gridlines. You can also draw along gridlines to easily measure and match shapes.

To enable the grid, choose View➪Grid➪Show Grid (see Figure 8-3). To take full advantage of the grid, choose View➪Snapping➪Snap To Grid to make it 'magnetic'.

To draw and position objects using the grid:

1. **Make sure the Grid is enabled by choosing View➪Grid➪Show Grid and that snapping for the grid is turned on by choosing View➪Snapping➪ Snap To Grid.**

2. **Grab your Rectangle tool, choose a stroke color, and set the fill color to none.**

3. **Draw a rectangle using the gridlines as a guide.**

   The square snaps to the nearest gridline as you draw (see Figure 8-4).

Figure 8-3: The grid now appears in the background of your document, like a sheet of graph paper that you can position and draw on top of.

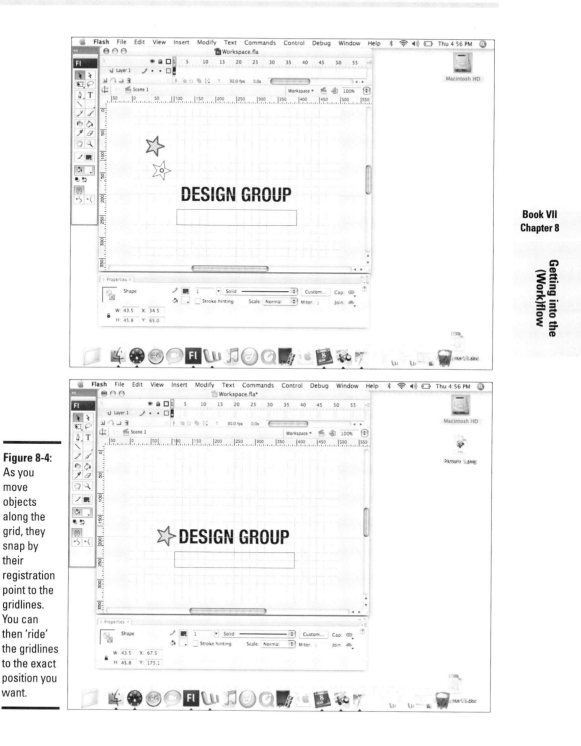

Figure 8-4:
As you move objects along the grid, they snap by their registration point to the gridlines. You can then 'ride' the gridlines to the exact position you want.

4. Create a new shape.

For this example, select the Polystar tool (located under the Shape tools) to draw a star shape. *Note:* Use the Options button on the Properties panel to make the Polystar tool draw star shapes.

5. Use the selection tool to click and drag the new shape and snap it into place.

To customize the appearance of your Grid, choose View⇨Grid⇨Edit Grid. From this panel, you can specify grid size, color, and Snap Accuracy.

Aligning Artwork

If you need to line up or space out several graphics on the stage, you can use the handy Align palette to assist you. The Align palette lets you line up, distribute, or space two or more objects relative to each other or the stage.

Create a new layer, draw a shape on the stage, and place it on the bottom below any graphics you already have on the stage.

To align and distribute two or more graphics:

1. Select a graphic on the stage and duplicate it two to three times by choosing Edit⇨Copy And Edit⇨Paste.

2. Loosely position the graphics across the stage from left to right.

3. Select all the new copies you created with the Selection arrow and launch the Align panel by choosing Window⇨Align.

The first row contains all your Align buttons, broken down into two groups: vertical and horizontal.

4. Click the Align Vertical Center button to align the selected graphics horizontally by their top edge.

The graphics reposition themselves so that they're all flush by the top edge. Align the selected graphics horizontally with each other using the buttons under the Align row. The second row contains buttons that evenly distribute graphics vertically or horizontally by their center, top, or bottom edges.

5. Click the middle button of the second group to distribute your graphics evenly based on their center points, as shown in Figure 8-5.

Distributing to the stage

The stage button (located on the bottom-right corner of the Align panel) can be enabled so that any distribution uses the stage as a point of reference. The distribute options are useful if you want to distribute objects across the full width of the stage regardless of their distance from each other.

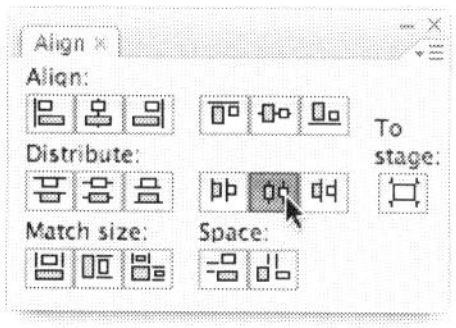

Figure 8-5:
Distribute
the graphics
evenly
across
the stage
using the
horizontal
Distribute
buttons.

To distribute objects across the stage:

1. **Select two or more graphics on the stage.**

2. **Locate the Stage button on the Align panel and select it.**

3. **Click any of the horizontal distribution buttons under the Distribute row.**

The graphics redistribute and spread across the full width of the stage.

Using match size

If you need to resize two or more objects on the stage so that they're all the same width and height, you can take advantage of the Match Size option on the Align panel. Match size can conform two objects to the same width, height, or both.

To match two objects using match size:

1. **Select two different-sized graphics, symbols, or drawing objects on the stage, as shown in Figure 8-6.**

2. **Choose Window⇨Align to launch the Align panel (if it's not already open).**

3. **Locate Match Size button group on the bottom of the panel and click the last button of the three.**

The objects resize to the same width and height.

Note: You can also match only width or height using either the first or second buttons of the group, respectively.

With the Stage button pressed, match size resizes any selected object(s) to the full width and height of your stage. This is an easy way to create a full-sized background or to stretch a graphic to fit the entire stage.

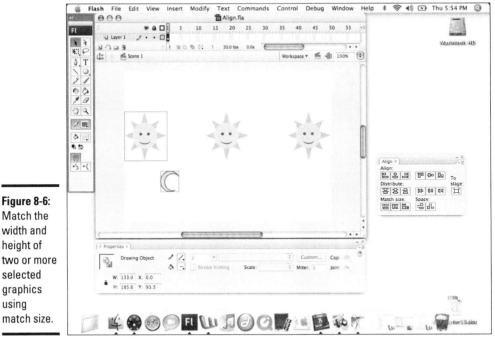

Figure 8-6:
Match the width and height of two or more selected graphics using match size.

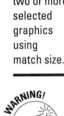

When using match size, the largest of the selected objects always dictates the resize. All other objects are resized to match the largest selected object.

Experimenting with Animation Helpers

Sitting discretely below the timeline are some highly useful icons that can be a big help while developing and fine-tuning your animations. The Onion Skin, Onion Skin Outlines, and Edit Multiple Frames options let you view, move, and manipulate entire animations at once to save time and guarantee better results.

When creating animation, you can enable onion skinning to view several frames at a time. With tweened animation, onion skinning can reveal all frames created in between the starting and ending keyframes to help you make adjustments and see them in action. You can choose between two types of onion skinning depending on whether you want to view frames as outlines or full-color previews.

Before you get started, create a new motion tween or open a document with an existing tween that you can use for this example.

To enable onion skinning:

1. **Select the Onion Skin icon underneath the timeline.**

A set of brackets appears above the timeline.

2. **Adjust the brackets so that all the frames in your tween are selected.**

You see a full preview of all the frames generated by your tween.

You can't select the frames shown in between, but you can move the instances on the starting and ending keyframe. Select the symbol instance on the starting keyframe of your tween and move it. The onion skin reveals how the frames in between change as you shift your starting or ending instances.

As an alternative to seeing frames in your tween in full color, you can preview them as outlines by using the Onion Skin Outlines option (see Figure 8-7). This option works exactly like the Onion Skin option, but shows selected frames using a wire frame-style outline view. The Onion Skin Outlines option can be a better choice if the full-color preview looks too cluttered.

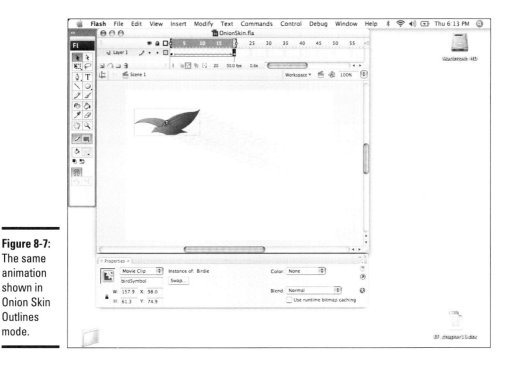

Figure 8-7:
The same animation shown in Onion Skin Outlines mode.

Using Keyboard Shortcuts

Part of creating a smooth and fast work environment is having your favorite commands, palettes, and tools right at your fingertips. Most Flash menu items and palettes are equipped with shortcut key combinations that provide easy access without the need to comb through several menus. If you need to create your own custom keyboard shortcuts, Flash lets you create and save keyboard shortcut sets that you can fully customized to speed up your workflow.

To view the default keyboard shortcuts and create your own, choose Edit⇨Keyboard Shortcuts (Windows) or Flash⇨Keyboard Shortcuts (Mac).

You can map almost any available tool, command, or palette to a keyboard shortcut. You can choose to memorize existing keyboard shortcuts for commonly used items or create custom keyboard shortcuts that are more intuitive for you.

To create a new keyboard shortcut:

1. **Choose Edit⇨Keyboard Shortcuts (Windows) or Flash⇨Keyboard Shortcuts (Mac).**

   The Keyboard Shortcuts panel launches (see Figure 8-8).

2. **Scroll down and click the triangle (Mac) or plus sign (PC) to the left of where it reads View.**

   You see all menu items under the View menu and any keyboard shortcuts assigned to them.

3. **Locate and select the menu command you want to create a shortcut for.**

   For this example, we selected Magnification⇨50%.

   The default set can't be modified, so you'll need to duplicate the default set and make changes to the new copy.

4. **Click the Duplicate Set icon at the top of the panel and rename the new set "My Shortcuts" when prompted; click OK to create the new set.**

5. **With the current menu item selected locate and click the plus sign below to add a new shortcut for the menu item.**

   The word <empty> appears, ready for you to enter a keyboard shortcut.

6. **Hold down Shift+Ctrl (Windows) or Shift+⌘ (Mac).**

   The type-in field fills in the keyboard shortcut as you hold it.

7. **To confirm the shortcut, click Change.**

8. **Click OK to exit the panel and save the shortcut to your new set.**

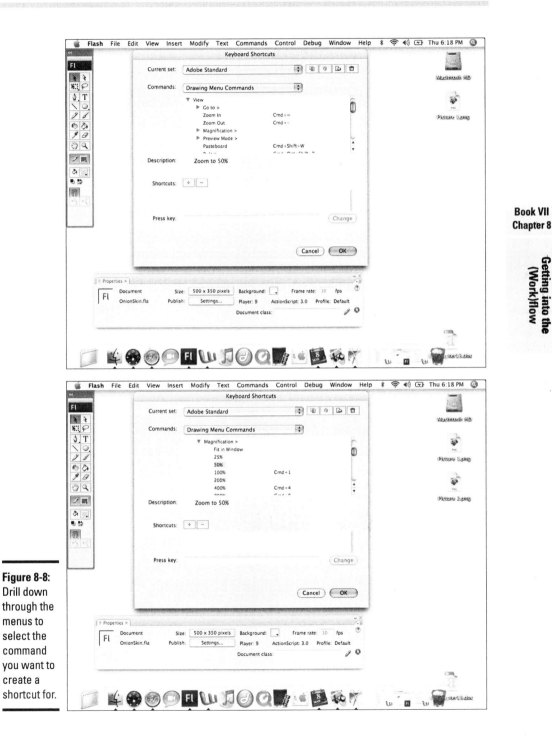

Figure 8-8:
Drill down
through the
menus to
select the
command
you want to
create a
shortcut for.

At any time, you can return to your custom set in the Keyboard Shortcuts panel to add new shortcuts or modify existing ones. If at any point you want to switch sets, return to the Keyboard Shortcuts panel and select a different set from the Current Set menu.

Working with the Movie Explorer

As a Flash project grows and becomes more complex, getting around your document can be a bit of a guessing game. As you add movie clips, ActionScript, media files, and more, the inner workings can overwhelm even the most organized of designers.

For these cases, the Movie Explorer panel (see Figure 8-9) offers an at-a-glance view of your movie. From this panel, you see exactly what's being used and where and can navigate directly to any item on the list. You can sort the panel to show only the types of items you want, whether it's ActionScript, movie clips, sounds, or type. To launch the Movie Explorer, choose Window⇨Movie Explorer.

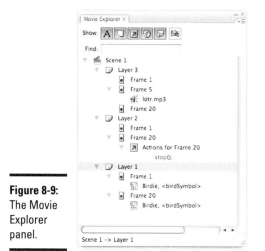

Figure 8-9:
The Movie
Explorer
panel.

Chapter 9: Publishing and Final Delivery

In This Chapter

✔ **Getting ready to publish**

✔ **Previewing your work**

✔ **Publishing your final movie**

✔ **Publishing for the Web and CD-ROM**

To show your creations to the world, you need to publish the final movie using the Publish command. Before publishing, you can use the Publish Settings option to specify important settings for your final movie, including quality and version settings as well as your choice of file formats. Different options let you publish for the Web, CD-ROM, and even mobile phones.

Getting Familiar with the Publish Process

The `.fla` file you build your movie in is intended for the Flash authoring environment only. When you're ready to deliver a final product, you need create a final `.swf` (compressed movie) file that the Flash Player can play. The Flash Player is responsible for displaying your movie in Web pages, mobile phones, and on CD-ROM (when packaged as a projector).

The Publish command, located at File⇨Publish creates your final `.swf` (or 'swiff'), as well as additional files, such as `.html` (Web) pages that you need to display your movie in different environments. When the Publish process is complete, you can then upload the completed files to the Web, copy them to CD-ROM, or package them for mobile phone delivery.

Before publishing your final movie, you use the Publish Settings panel to tell Flash exactly what files you want to generate and what settings to use for each file type. You can specify settings for every file format you choose, as well as quality settings for sounds and images used in your movie. The file types you choose depends on your movie's final destination, whether it be Web, CD-ROM, mobile devices, or standalone, kiosk-style presentation.

Selecting Your Formats

Depending on where and how you plan to distribute your movie, you can have Flash create a variety of different formats at publish time. While the most common deployment for Flash is an .swf and companion HTML file for the Web, it's capable of generating files that can be used for CD-ROMs and mobile phones as well.

To choose your file formats, choose File⇨Publish Settings and open the Publish Settings panel (see Figure 9-1). In the Formats panel, .swf check the box next to each format you want to create. Use the type-in box and folder icon to set a name and destination (optional) for each file you create. By default, all files use the same name and are published to the same location as the original .fla file.

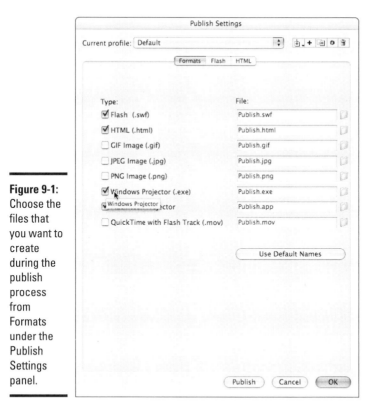

Figure 9-1:
Choose the files that you want to create during the publish process from Formats under the Publish Settings panel.

Take a look at the different file formats you can publish and where they're used:

✦ **.swf:** The .swf is the most common file type you'll publish; it's what the Flash Player and plug-in use. Think about the Flash Player as a movie projector, and the .swf file as a movie reel that you load onto it. When publishing for the Web, this is the file type you will choose, most often accompanied by an HTML (Web) page that contains it.

✦ **HTML:** An HTML file, or Web page, is used as a container for your Flash movie when the target venue is the Web. HTML files also can provide an extra level of abilities, such as checking for the Flash plug-in or enabling additional run-time parameters, such as Looping.

✦ **Projector (Mac/Win):** A *projector* is a package that includes your movie and the Flash Player all in one. Projectors are commonly used for delivery on non-Web formats, such as CD-ROM, but you can use them for any situation where you want standalone distribution, such as through e-mail. Because the projector contains the Flash Player, your user doesn't need anything (even the Flash Player installed) to view your movie. Projectors are created as .exe files for the PC or .app files for the Mac. If you're delivering to users on both platforms, you need to publish a projector for each.

Projectors can't be viewed in a Web browser, so they're not a viable choice if you're trying to work around requiring your user to have the Flash Player or plug-in.

✦ **JPEG, GIF, and PNG:** This selection creates static images from your movie in the Web-friendly JPEG, GIF, and PNG formats. You can use these images as placeholders (in the event that the user doesn't have the Flash Player or plug-in) or as elements that you can use if you're creating a non-Flash version of your site. Keep in mind, however, that images are generated only from the first frame of your movie, so exporting an image from your movie may not yield too much if your movie starts out blank or with minimal content.

✦ **QuickTime with Flash Track:** In earlier (prevideo) versions of Flash, you could publish a flash movie as a *Flash Track,* a companion file used by a QuickTime Movie to include Flash animation. Now, with Flash's full support for video, you can publish video and Flash together as an .swf file just as you'd normally do. Because QuickTime doesn't support Flash tracks beyond Flash Version 5, you need to set your Flash Player version to 5 (by choosing Publish Settings⇨Flash) to create a compatible Flash track. The resulting file is in .mov (QuickTime movie) format.

**Book VII
Chapter 9**

**Publishing and
Final Delivery**

Previewing Your Setting

Before you publish, it's always a good idea to use publish Preview to test the settings you created under the Publish Settings panel. Like Test Movie, Publish Preview can immediately create and display an .swf file in the Flash Player for immediate viewing, but that's where the similarity ends.

Publish Preview creates a preview for any of the file formats you choose under Publish Settings, including Web pages, images, and projectors. The preview lets you see how these files will look before you do your final publish and gives you a chance to adjust your publish settings for the best results possible.

To preview any of your selected publish formats, choose File⟿Publish Preview and select the format you want to preview. The default is an .swf file with an accompanying HTML page.

A publish preview shows how the final movie will look in an HTML page. To preview an HTML and an embedded .swf file, choose File⟿Publish Preview⟿HTML.

Use the Publish Preview shortcut key combination ⌘+F12 (Mac) or Ctrl+F12 (Windows) to create a preview from the default selection (HTML page + .swf file) at any time.

If HTML or .swf aren't among your selected publish formats, the Publish Preview defaults to the next chosen format.

When previewing your movie in either Test Movie or Publish Preview (Flash option only), you can use the Bandwidth Profiler. This graph, shown in Figure 9-2, at the top of your preview window shows the total file size of your movie, as well as where and how data is loaded as the movie plays. This step can be important in gauging whether the file size may be too much to download for the end user or whether you should distribute data-intensive items (such as sound files or images) more effectively across the timeline.

The bars across the graph appear at frames where data is loaded, and the height of the bar indicates how much data was loaded when the play head reached that frame.

To view your movie with the Bandwidth Profiler, choose Publish Preview⟿Flash. When the movie appears in the Flash Player, choose View⟿Bandwidth Profiler.

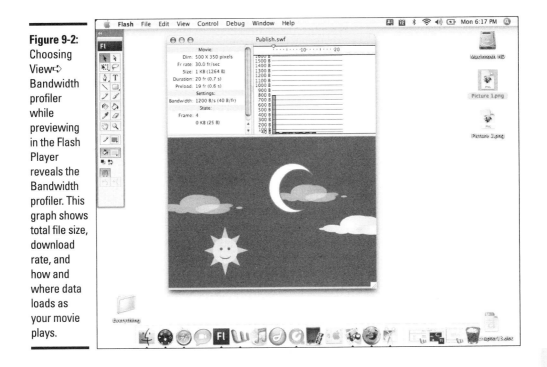

Figure 9-2:
Choosing
View⇨
Bandwidth
profiler
while
previewing
in the Flash
Player
reveals the
Bandwidth
profiler. This
graph shows
total file size,
download
rate, and
how and
where data
loads as
your movie
plays.

Publishing for the Web

If your final destination is the Web, you'll be selecting two necessary file formats in the Publish Settings panel: HTML and Flash (.swf). The HTML file (or Web page) acts as a container for your .swf file, displaying it in the browser and placing it against a matching background. This HTML file also contains code that sets additional options in your movie at run time (such as instructions to automatically Loop).

Playback of the actual .swf file is handled by the Flash Player, which works as a plug-in for all major Web browsers.

When you publish your final movie and HTML file, you'll upload both files to your Web hosting account, company server, or wherever your movie needs to go to make it available for public viewing.

To publish the necessary files for the Web viewing, choose Publish Settings and check off HTML and Flash (.swf) under the Formats panel. Choose Publish to create the final files that you'll upload to your Web server of choice.

Uploading your files to the Web using FTP

File Transfer Protocol (FTP) is the method used to connect and transfer files between your local computer and a remote Web server and is the most common way of posting your finished files onto the Web for the public to see.

FTP connections occur between a client running FTP software (your computer) and a server that opens the connection to receive the files. Servers often are maintained by a hosting company that provides you an account and space for your Web site files. You may also be posting your work to a network machine or dedicated server maintained by your company. Flash itself doesn't have FTP capabilities, but many programs are out there that vary in price and feature set that have FTP capabilities.

Adobe's own Dreamweaver CS3 includes full FTP functionality and can create and store connections to several different servers or hosting accounts. If you want a more basic (and free) option, you can FTP directly from Windows Explorer or choose Go⇨Connect To Server option in the Finder on Macintosh OS X. In most applications, copying files to and from the server is as simple as drag and drop from one window to another.

Note: In order to connect to a server, you need to purchase or have access to a web-hosting account, network computer, or dedicated server. Most FTP connections require a user ID and password; check with your server administrator or hosting company to get information for your specific account.

Publishing for CD-ROM

Flash's ability to include full-featured video, audio, and graphics have made it a very popular choice for creating CD-ROM based presentations, e-brochures, learning materials, and interactive application installers. When packaging for CD-ROM, you need to consider that an `.swf` file alone may not be enough, especially because it's possible that the user will not have a standalone version of the Flash Player installed on his computer.

For this reason, you'll package movies for CD-ROM as projectors. (See the section "Selecting Your Formats," earlier in this chapter, for more on projectors.)

To create standalone projectors for Mac and/or Windows, check off the Windows Projector and/or Macintosh Projector formats under Publish Settings⇨Formats. The projector(s) are created when you publish, along with other formats you've chosen. These projectors can then be copied to and distributed on a CD or DVD.

Choosing the Right Settings

After you've picked the file types you want to publish, you can specify settings for each selected format in the Publish Settings panel. Make sure that you take time to familiarize yourself with the available options and experiment with different settings until you get a finished movie that's just right.

Flash stores Publish Settings as part of your document, so you need to set these settings only once for each Flash movie. Make sure to save your movie after you've set your Publish Settings so that your settings are available the next time you open the document.

For Flash (.swf)

.swf files are compressed movies used by the Flash Player for display on the Web or directly on a user's computer. When you choose to publish an .swf, you have the opportunity to specify settings that determine version, security, and quality.

The Flash (.swf) settings are available under the Publish Settings panel (see Figure 9-3) when you check Flash (.swf) under Publish Settings⇨Formats. The following list takes a look at some of the settings you'll work with and how each one affects the performance and quality of your Flash movie:

+ **Version:** This setting controls which version of the Flash Player your movie is created for. In most cases, you'll select the latest version, Flash Player 9, so that you can take advantage of the latest features. In some cases, you may need to publish your movie to be compatible with a previous version of the Flash Player; here, you can specify versions going as far back as Flash Player 1.

+ **Load Order:** As your movie loads into the Flash Player, information across several layers can load either from the bottom layer up or the top layer down. Generally, the default option works fine, but if the bottom layers depend on data from the layers above it (for example, ActionScript variables or symbols), you can switch the order to load from the top down to ensure your movie performs properly.

+ **ActionScript Version:** What you choose here is completely dependent on which version of ActionScript (if any) you're working with. Because each version contains differences in both features and structure (particularly between ActionScript 3.0 and previous versions), you need to publish in the version you've used throughout your movie. If your movie doesn't use any ActionScript, leave the default setting ActionScript 3.0.

Chapter 7 of this minibook discusses ActionScript and the differences between Versions 2.0 and 3.0.

Book VII
Chapter 9

Publishing and Final Delivery

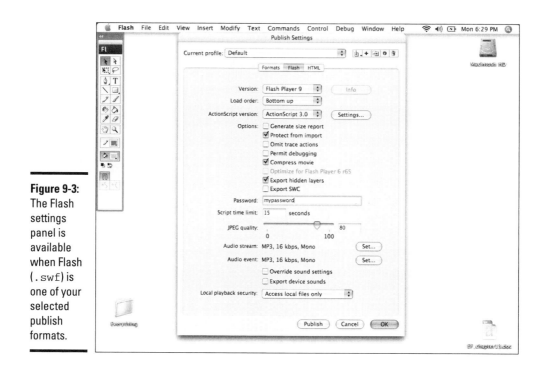

Figure 9-3:
The Flash settings panel is available when Flash (.swf) is one of your selected publish formats.

✦ **Protect From Import:** The Flash authoring software can't open or decompile .swf files for editing, but it can import them as frame-by-frame movies into a .fla document. This opens up the door for artwork and graphic resources to be extracted, perhaps against your will. The Protect From Import option prevents .swf files from being imported into the Flash authoring environment. The Password field below the check boxes becomes active when this option is selected so that you can assign a password to allow only certain parties (such as a colleague or client, for example) to import the .swf if they need to.

✦ **Compress Movie (Flash Player 6 or later):** This option, which is selected by default, compresses your swf file to reduce the file size and, in turn, download time. You should leave this option selected, especially if your file is ActionScript or text intensive.

✦ **JPEG Quality:** Flash performs a certain amount of compression on bitmap graphics in your movie (such as imported photos) to reduce file size and increase performance. Use this slider to determine the amount of compression applied and, in turn, the resulting file size and quality of your movie. The higher the quality, the less compression applied, and the larger the resulting file size.

✦ **Audio Stream and Audio Event:** If your movie includes sound, you can set the quality of the sound in your final `.swf` using the Set button for either Audio Streams or Audio Events. By default, sound is converted to 16khz, mono `.mp3` format, but you can change both compression and quality settings as needed. Keep in mind that, like the JPEG quality settings, higher quality settings for sound will likely increase the overall file size of your movie.

Chapter 5 of this minibook discusses stream and event sounds.

For HTML

For presentation on the Web, you need to publish an HTML file that will contain your `.swf` file. This HTML file not only displays your movie, but also includes all the code necessary to control dimensions, appearance, and run-time options (such as telling your movie to Loop). Your HTML file features the same background color as your movie so that it matches seamlessly when viewed in a browser.

You can set the following options for your published HTML file:

✦ **Template:** This setting generates your HTML file based on different possible environments, such as standard browsers, Pocket PCs, or additional options for full-screen support.

For any template selected, a file named AC_RunActiveContent.js is created. You need to copy this file to your Web server with any other files generated. This file compensates for recent updates to the way Microsoft Internet Explorer handles active content.

✦ **Detect Flash Player Version check box:** This option adds code in your HTML file to display alternate content if the end user doesn't have the Flash Player installed. You can customize this content in any HTML editor. The default content provides a link for the user to download and install the latest version of Flash Player.

✦ **Dimensions:** The code in your HTML file specifies a size for your Flash movie, which, by default, matches your movie's actual dimensions. You can override this setting and force your movie to a different size in either pixels or percent.

✦ **Playback:** Check boxes in this category set some run-time options for your Flash movie. By default, the Flash Player is directed to loop movies and to make the contextual (right-click) menu available to the user. You can disable either of these features, as well as force the movie to pause at the start, or use *device fonts* (fonts from the end user's machine instead of embedded fonts).

✦ **Quality:** Controls the overall appearance and quality of your movie.

+ **Window Mode:** This option controls how Flash appears in context of your Web page. You can set Flash movies to be opaque or transparent to reveal the background of the page.

+ **HTML Alignment:** Controls the alignment of your movie as determined by the HTML code.

+ **Scale:** You set the HTML page to scale the Flash movie to a size other than its default size.

+ **Flash alignment:** This option controls the positioning of your Flash movie within the page.

Creating Publish Profiles

If you'd like to use the same publish settings across multiple movies, you can capture your settings as a profile that you can recall and use in other documents.

To create a new publish profile:

1. **Choose File➪Publish Settings to open the Publish Settings panel, shown in Figure 9-4.**

2. **Select your formats and choose your settings.**

3. **Locate the Create New Profile icon in the upper-right corner of the panel and click it.**

The Create New Profile dialog box appears, prompting you to assign the new profile a name.

4. **Assign the profile a name and click OK.**

The profile is created and is an available option under the Current Profile menu at the top of the Publish Settings panel.

To make your profile available to other documents, you need to export it:

1. **Choose File➪Publish Settings to open the Publish Settings panel.**

2. **Choose Export from the Import/Export icon at the top of the Publish Settings panel.**

You're prompted to name and save your profile (stored as a separate .xml file). While you can save the file anywhere, it's best to keep it in the Flash application's Publish Profiles folder, which is the default location.

3. **Assign the .xml file a name and click Save.**

To import a profile from another document:

1. **Choose File⇨Publish Settings to open the Publish Settings panel, shown in Figure 9-4.**

2. **Choose Import from the Import/Export icon at the top of the panel.**

3. **Locate the .xml file you created when you exported the profile and click Open.**

The profile is now available under the Current Profiles menu at the top of the Publish Settings panel.

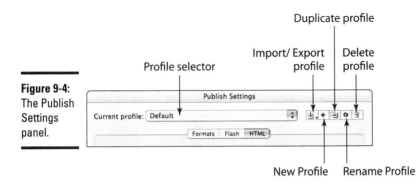

Figure 9-4:
The Publish
Settings
panel.

Additional resources

One of the great things about working with Flash is the community that supports it. Countless Web sites are dedicated to Flash tutorials, training videos, example files, free resources (such as fonts and sounds), and forums to discuss and assist developers of all levels with a variety of Flash help topics.

There are too many to list, but here's a short list of established and highly visited sites that can you get you started. (***Note:*** This is not a complete list, nor is it an indication of endorsement of any specific Web site. These Web sites have been shown to be reputable and highly useful resources for Flash developers. You're encouraged to be a part of the Flash community by utilizing and contributing to these and other online resources to further your own knowledge.)

Adobe's FLASH Exchange and Support Center:
`www.adobe.com/cfusion/exchange/index.cfm`

Colin Moock: `www.moock.org`

FFiles.com: `www.ffiles.com`

Kirupa.com: `www.kirupa.com`

ActionScript.org:
`www.actionscript.org`

FlashKit: `www.flashkit.com`

Moluv.com: `www.moluv.com`

Flash Magazine:
`www.flashmagazine.com`

Fonts for Flash:
`www.fontsforflash.com`

Index